AVEBURY WITHOUT THE STONES

Sir Richard Holford

Avebury Without the Stones

A Social History
*c.*1550–1800

STUART A. RAYMOND

THE HOBNOB PRESS

First published in the United Kingdom in 2024

by The Hobnob Press,
8 Lock Warehouse, Severn Road, Gloucester GL1 2GA
www.hobnobpress.co.uk

© Stuart A Raymond 2024

The Author hereby asserts his moral rights to be identified as the Author of the Work.

All rights reserved. No part of this publication may be reproduced, stored in a retrieval system, or transmitted in any form or by any means, electronic, mechanical, photocopying, recording or otherwise, without the prior permission of the publisher and copyright holder.

British Library Cataloguing in Publication Data
A catalogue record for this book is available from the British Library

ISBN
978-1-914407-77-2 paperback
978-1-914407-78-9 casebound

Typeset in Adobe Garamond Pro, 11/14 pt
Typesetting and origination by John Chandler

Front cover illustration is a detail from an engraving in William Stukeley's Abury, a temple of the British Druids *(1743), photographed from a copy belonging to Wiltshire Museum, Devizes (DZSWS:Book.144 / 13), by kind permission of the Wiltshire Archaeological and Natural History Society.*

CONTENTS

Abbreviations	vi
List of Illustrations	vi
Map	vii
Pedigrees	viii
Introduction	1
1. Introducing Avebury	3
Illustrations	43
2. The Demography of Avebury: People and Population	51
3. Avebury Families	55
4. Avebury's Local Government	168
5. Landowners, Tenants, and Wealth	208
6. Sheep, Dung, and Wheat: Avebury's Agriculture	250
7. Earning a Living: Occupations, Trades, and Professions	276
8. Living Conditions in Avebury: Housing, Food and Possessions	329
9. Religion in Avebury: Church and Dissent	384
Subject Index	439
Place Index	448
Name Index	454

ABBREVIATIONS

GA	Gloucestershire Archives
LMA	London Metropolitan Archives
TNA	The National Archives
WANHS	Wiltshire Archaeological & Natural History Society
WSHC	Wiltshire & Swindon History Centre

LIST OF ILLUSTRATIONS

Sir Richard Holford	ii
John Aubrey, from Britton's Memoir of John Aubrey	43
William Stukeley (courtesy Wikimedia)	44
Reuben Horsell, parish clerk	45
Thomas Robinson, stone destroyer	45
Stukeley's view of Avebury	46
Stukeley's view from the Church Tower	46
Avebury Manor	47
The Bear (now the Waggon and Horses)	47
The Dovecote at Avebury Manor	48
Green Street	48
Sheep at Avebury: the mainstay of the economy	49
The 15th century rood screen	49
The Dissenters' Chapel	50

MAP OF AVEBURY PARISH

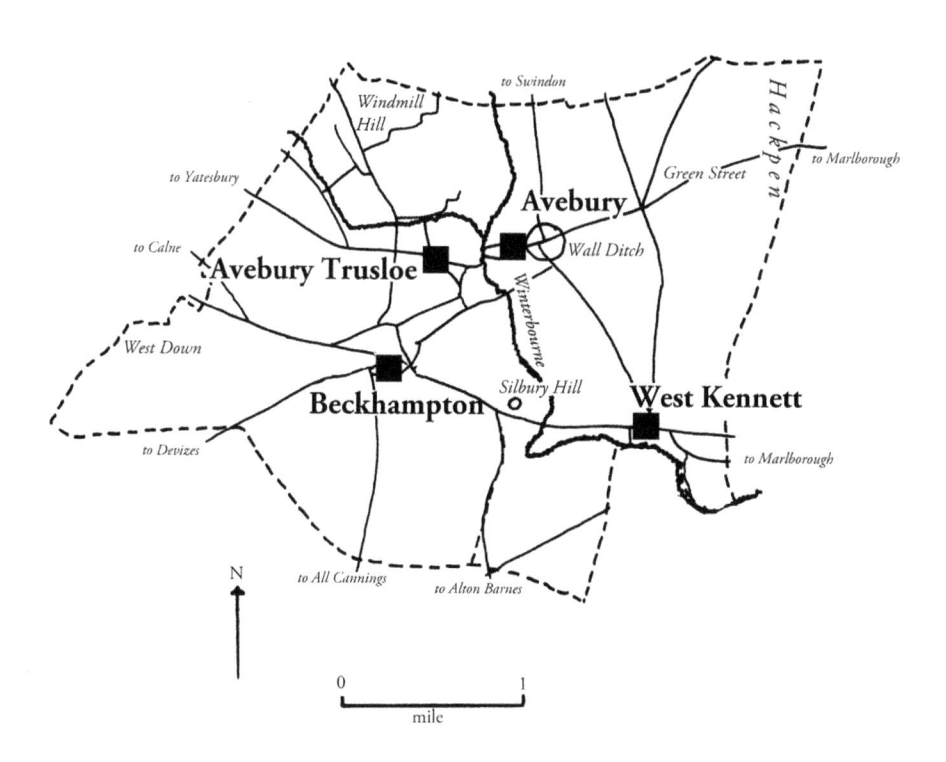

The parish of Avebury (derived from map in Victoria History of Wiltshire, vol. XII)

PEDIGREES

CASWELL

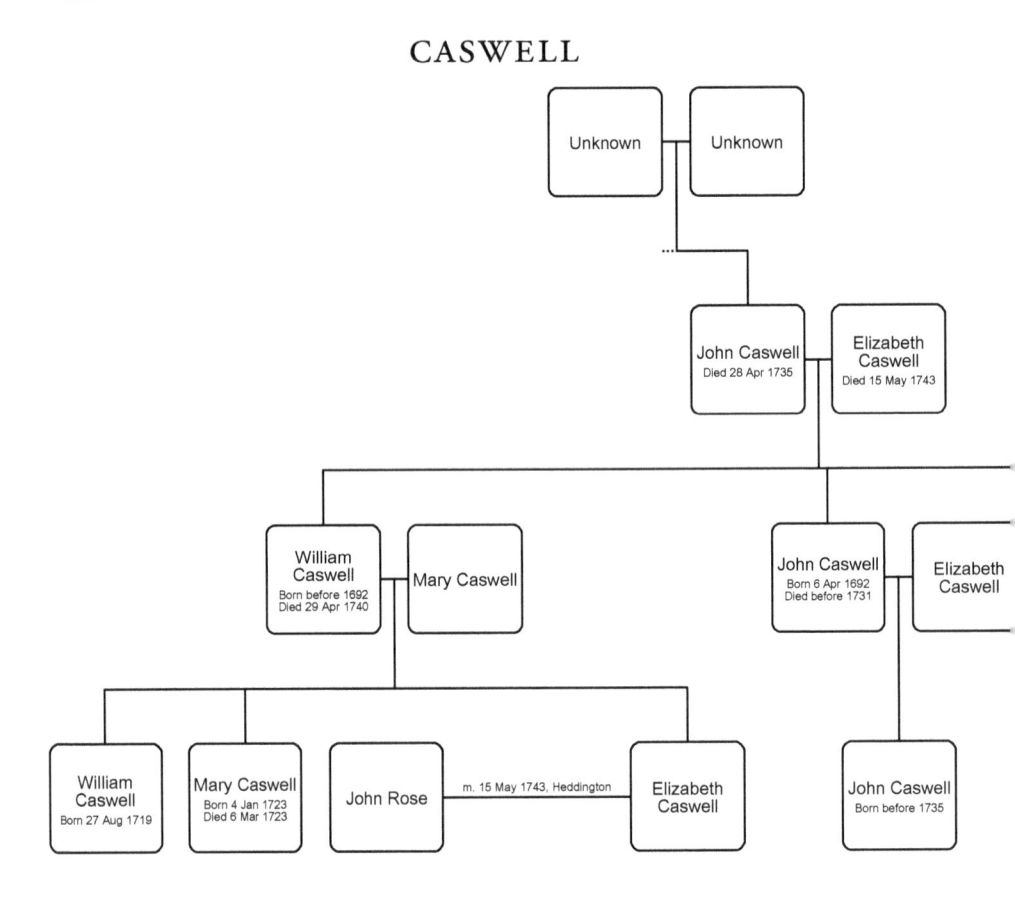

- Unknown — Unknown
  - John Caswell (Died 28 Apr 1735) — Elizabeth Caswell (Died 15 May 1743)
    - William Caswell (Born before 1692, Died 29 Apr 1740) — Mary Caswell
      - William Caswell (Born 27 Aug 1719)
      - Mary Caswell (Born 4 Jan 1723, Died 6 Mar 1723)
      - John Rose — m. 15 May 1743, Heddington — Elizabeth Caswell
    - John Caswell (Born 6 Apr 1692, Died before 1731) — Elizabeth Caswell
      - John Caswell (Born before 1735)

CLEMENTS

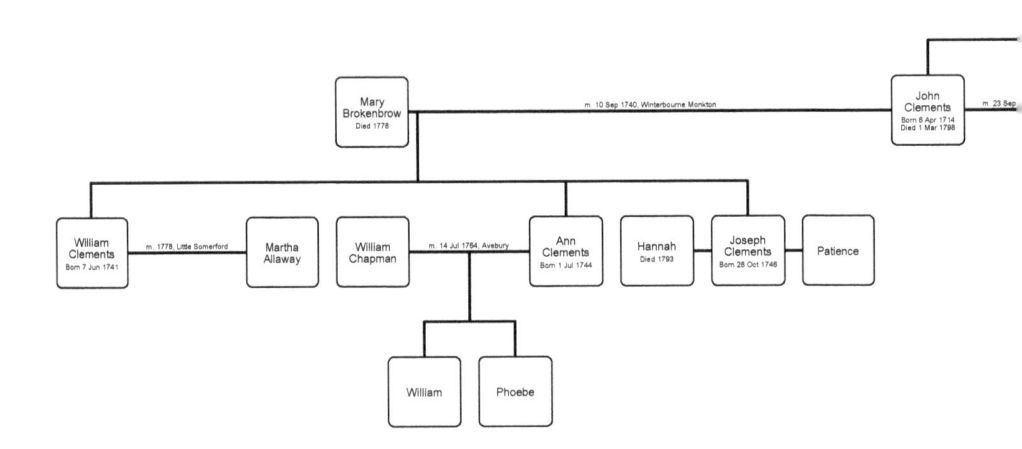

- Mary Brokenbrow (Died 1778) — m. 10 Sep 1740, Winterbourne Monkton — John Clements (Born 6 Apr 1714, Died 1 Mar 1798) — m. 23 Sep
  - William Clements (Born 7 Jun 1741) — m. 1778, Little Somerford — Martha Allaway
  - William Chapman — m. 14 Jul 1764, Avebury — Ann Clements (Born 1 Jul 1744)
    - William
    - Phoebe
  - Hannah (Died 1793)
  - Joseph Clements (Born 28 Oct 1746) — Patience

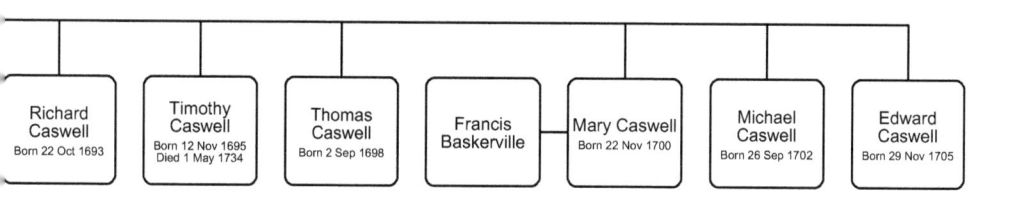

PEDIGREES

- Richard Caswell — Born 22 Oct 1693
- Timothy Caswell — Born 12 Nov 1695, Died 1 May 1734
- Thomas Caswell — Born 2 Sep 1698
- Francis Baskerville — Mary Caswell — Born 22 Nov 1700
- Michael Caswell — Born 26 Sep 1702
- Edward Caswell — Born 29 Nov 1705

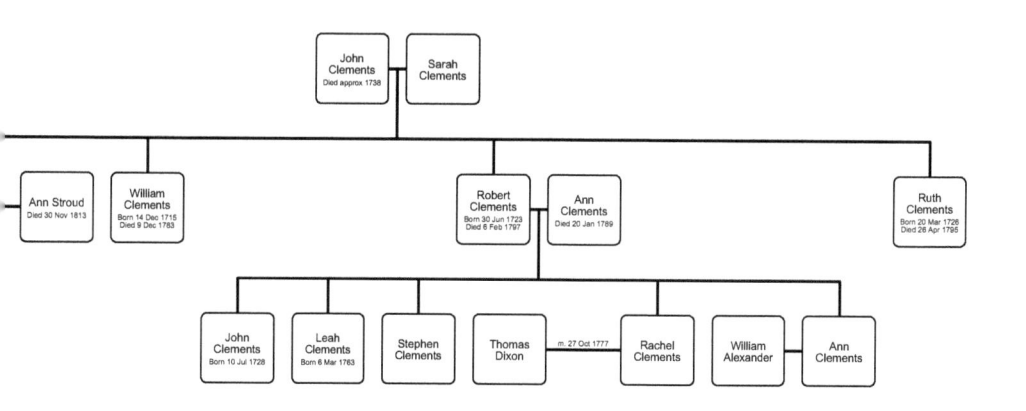

John Clements (Died approx 1738) — Sarah Clements

- Ann Stroud — Died 30 Nov 1813
- William Clements — Born 14 Dec 1715, Died 9 Dec 1783
- Robert Clements — Born 30 Jun 1723, Died 6 Feb 1797 — Ann Clements — Died 20 Jan 1789
- Ruth Clements — Born 20 Mar 1726, Died 26 Apr 1795

Children:
- John Clements — Born 10 Jul 1728
- Leah Clements — Born 6 Mar 1763
- Stephen Clements
- Thomas Dixon — m. 27 Oct 1777 — Rachel Clements
- William Alexander
- Ann Clements

HOLFORD: DESCENDANTS OF SIR RICHARD'S SECOND MARRIAGE

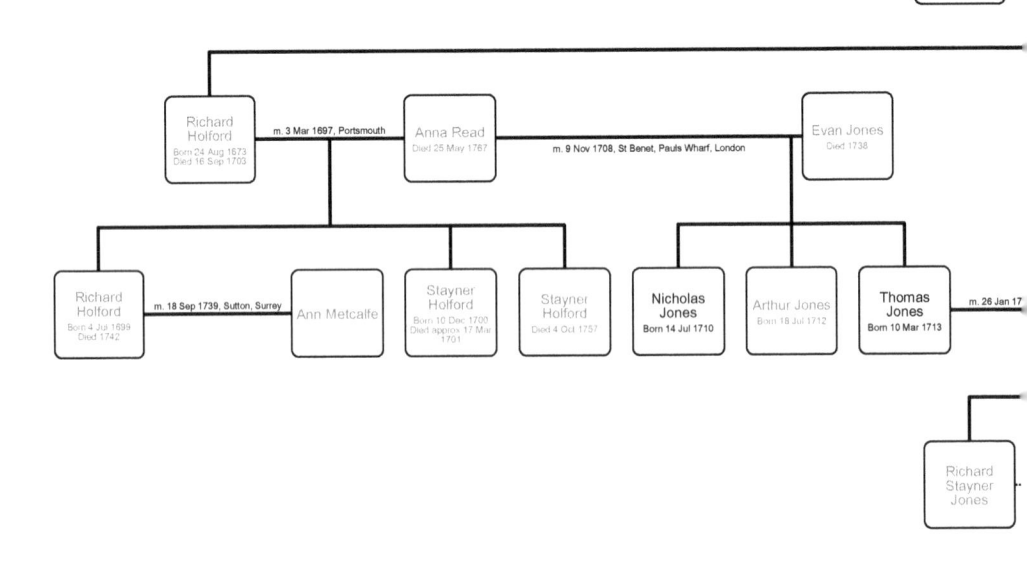

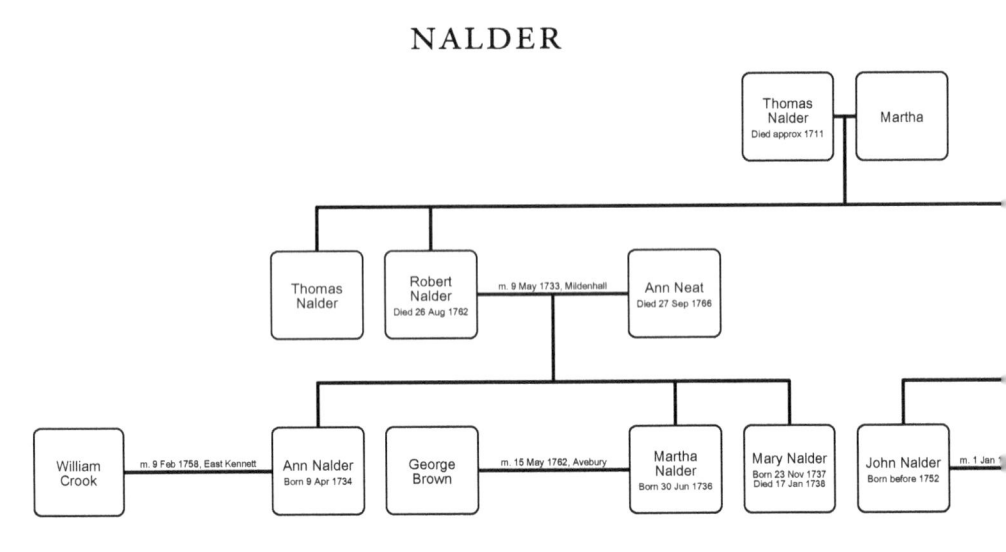

```
Sir Richard Holford
Born 1633
Died 16 May 1718
m.

├─ Richard Holford ── m. 3 Mar 1697, Portsmouth ── Anna Read ── m. 9 Nov 1708, St Benet, Pauls Wharf, London ── Evan Jones
   Born 24 Aug 1673                                  Died 25 May 1757                                                Died 1738
   Died 16 Sep 1703

   ├─ Richard Holford ── m. 18 Sep 1739, Sutton, Surrey ── Ann Metcalfe
   │  Born 4 Jul 1699
   │  Died 1742
   ├─ Stayner Holford
   │  Born 10 Dec 1700
   │  Died approx 17 Mar 1701
   ├─ Stayner Holford
   │  Died 4 Oct 1757
   ├─ Nicholas Jones
   │  Born 14 Jul 1710
   ├─ Arthur Jones
   │  Born 18 Jul 1712
   └─ Thomas Jones ── m. 26 Jan 17..
      Born 10 Mar 1713
      │
      └─ Richard Stayner Jones
```

NALDER

```
Thomas Nalder ── Martha
Died approx 1711

├─ Thomas Nalder
└─ Robert Nalder ── m. 9 May 1733, Mildenhall ── Ann Neat
   Died 26 Aug 1762                               Died 27 Sep 1766

   ├─ William Crook ── m. 9 Feb 1758, East Kennett ── Ann Nalder
   │                                                  Born 9 Apr 1734
   ├─ George Brown ── m. 15 May 1762, Avebury ── Martha Nalder
   │                                              Born 30 Jun 1736
   ├─ Mary Nalder
   │  Born 23 Nov 1737
   │  Died 17 Jan 1738
   └─ John Nalder ── m. 1 Jan ...
      Born before 1752
```

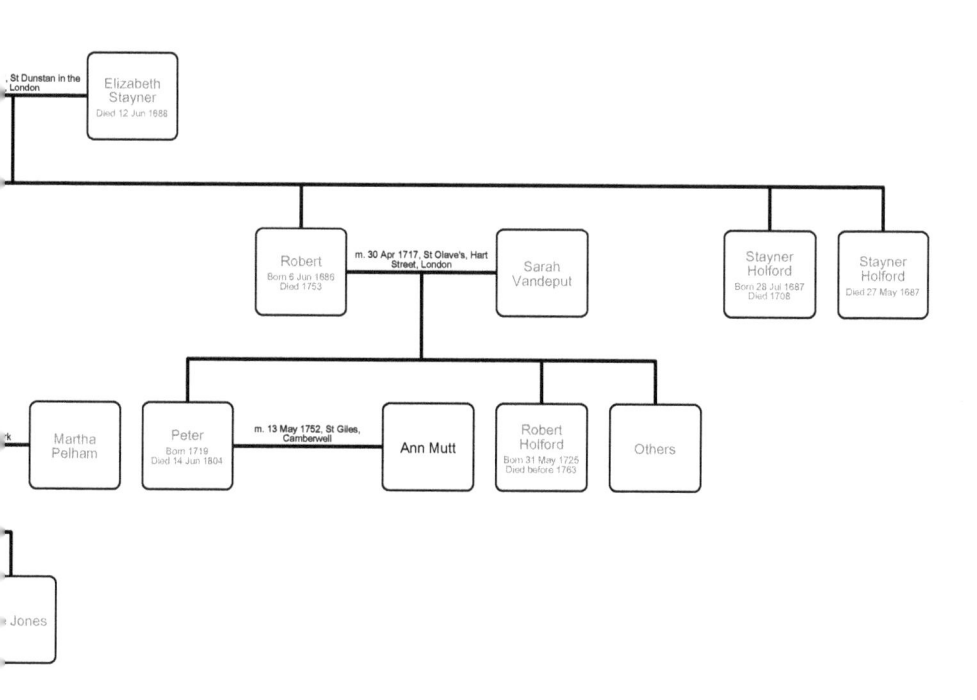

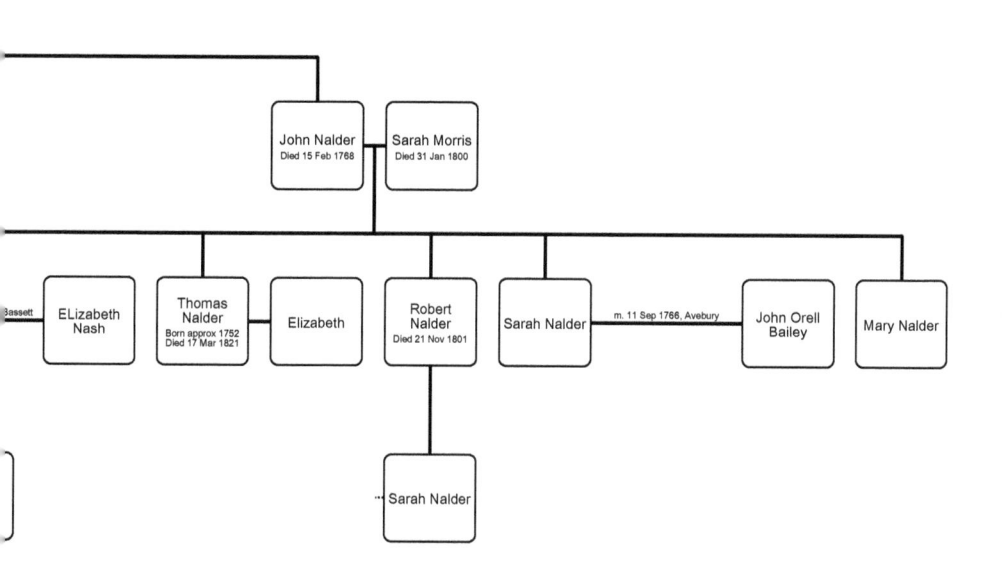

PEDIGREES

- , St Dunstan in the London
- Elizabeth Stayner — Died 12 Jun 1688
- Robert — Born 6 Jun 1686, Died 1753
  - m. 30 Apr 1717, St Olave's, Hart Street, London
- Sarah Vandeput
- Stayner Holford — Born 28 Jul 1687, Died 1708
- Stayner Holford — Died 27 May 1687
- Martha Pelham
- Peter — Born 1719, Died 14 Jun 1804
  - m. 13 May 1752, St Giles, Camberwell
- Ann Mutt
- Robert Holford — Born 31 May 1725, Died before 1763
- Others
- Jones
- Bassett
- John Nalder — Died 15 Feb 1768
- Sarah Morris — Died 31 Jan 1800
- ELizabeth Nash
- Thomas Nalder — Born approx 1752, Died 17 Mar 1821
- Elizabeth
- Robert Nalder — Died 21 Nov 1801
- Sarah Nalder
  - m. 11 Sep 1766, Avebury
- John Orell Bailey
- Mary Nalder
- Sarah Nalder

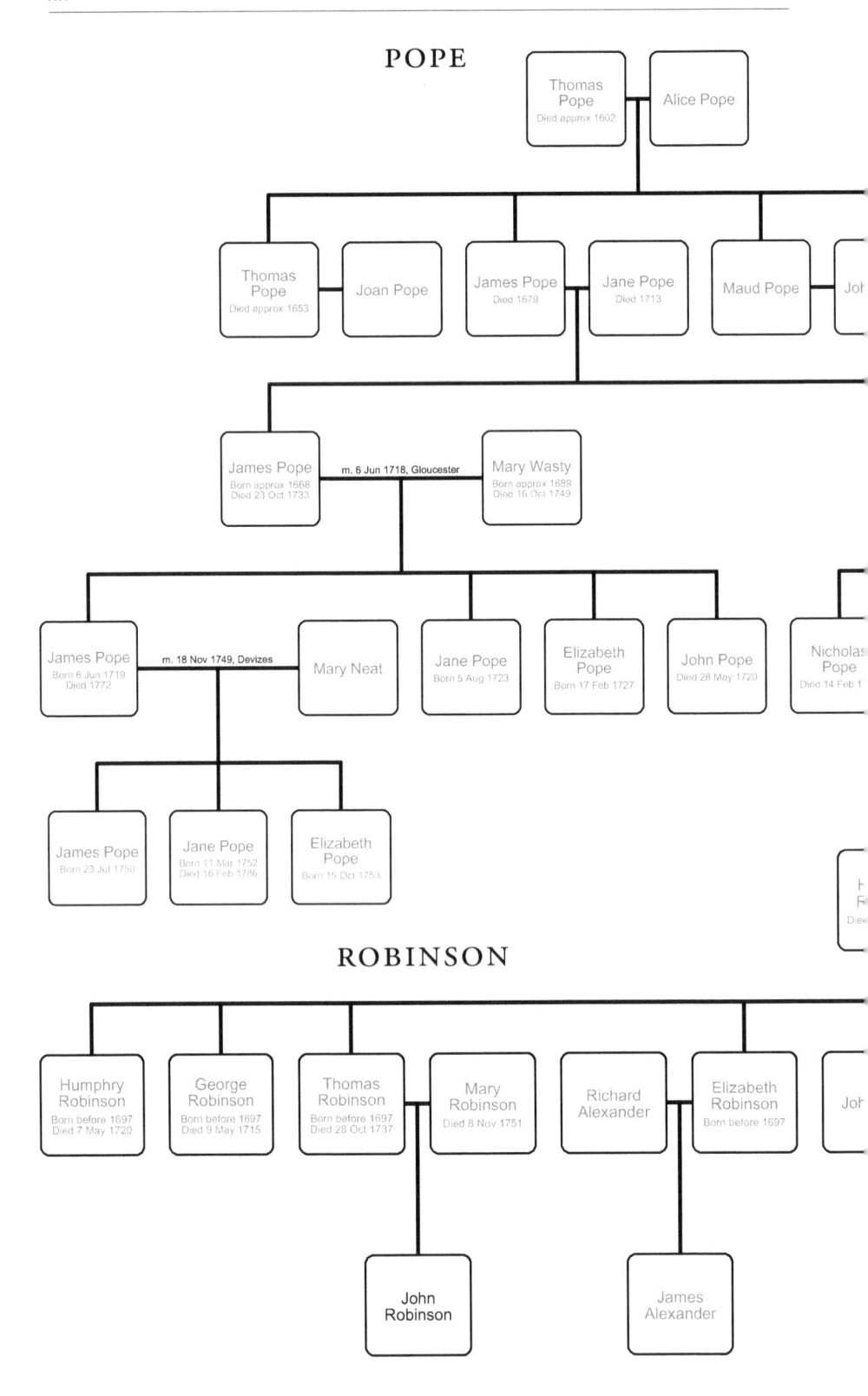

PEDIGREES

POPE

- Thomas Pope — Died approx 1602
- Alice Pope

Children:
- Thomas Pope — Died approx 1653
- Joan Pope
- James Pope — Died 1679
- Jane Pope — Died 1713
- Maud Pope
- Joh[n]...

- James Pope — Born approx 1668, Died 23 Oct 1733
  m. 6 Jun 1718, Gloucester
- Mary Wasty — Born approx 1689, Died 16 Oct 1749

Children:
- James Pope — Born 6 Jun 1719, Died 1772
  m. 18 Nov 1749, Devizes
- Mary Neat
- Jane Pope — Born 5 Aug 1723
- Elizabeth Pope — Born 17 Feb 1727
- John Pope — Died 28 May 1720
- Nicholas Pope — Died 14 Feb 1...

Children of James Pope and Mary Neat:
- James Pope — Born 23 Jul 1750
- Jane Pope — Born 11 Mar 1752, Died 16 Feb 1786
- Elizabeth Pope — Born 15 Oct 1753

ROBINSON

- Humphry Robinson — Born before 1697, Died 7 May 1720
- George Robinson — Born before 1697, Died 9 May 1715
- Thomas Robinson — Born before 1697, Died 28 Oct 1737
- Mary Robinson — Died 8 Nov 1751
- Richard Alexander
- Elizabeth Robinson — Born before 1697
- Joh[n]...

- John Robinson (child of Thomas Robinson and Mary Robinson)
- James Alexander (child of Richard Alexander and Elizabeth Robinson)

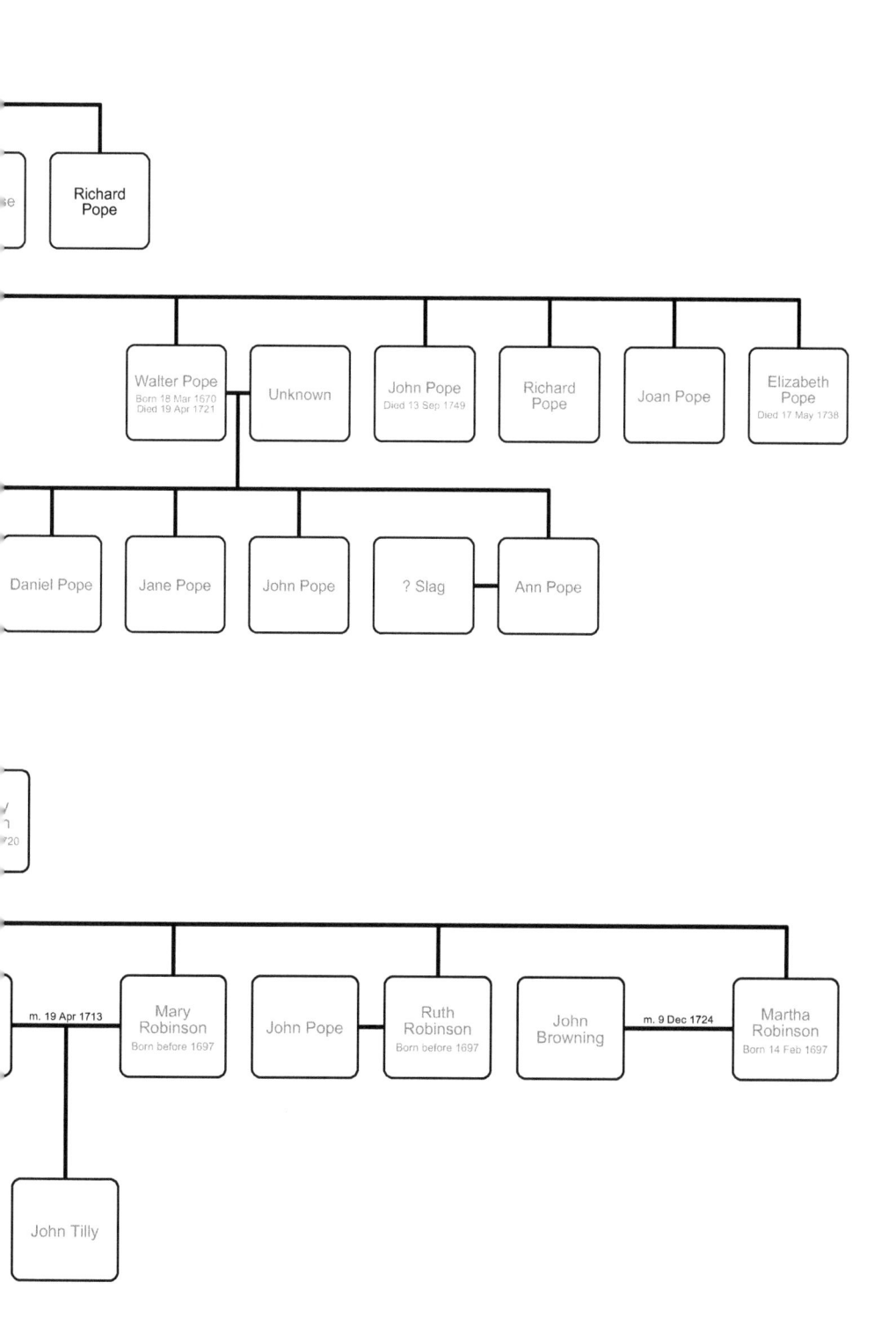

PEDIGREES   *xiii*

Richard Pope

Walter Pope
Born 18 Mar 1670
Died 19 Apr 1721

Unknown

John Pope
Died 13 Sep 1749

Richard Pope

Joan Pope

Elizabeth Pope
Died 17 May 1738

Daniel Pope

Jane Pope

John Pope

? Slag

Ann Pope

m. 19 Apr 1713

Mary Robinson
Born before 1697

John Pope

Ruth Robinson
Born before 1697

John Browning

m. 9 Dec 1724

Martha Robinson
Born 14 Feb 1697

John Tilly

SMITH, PART ONE

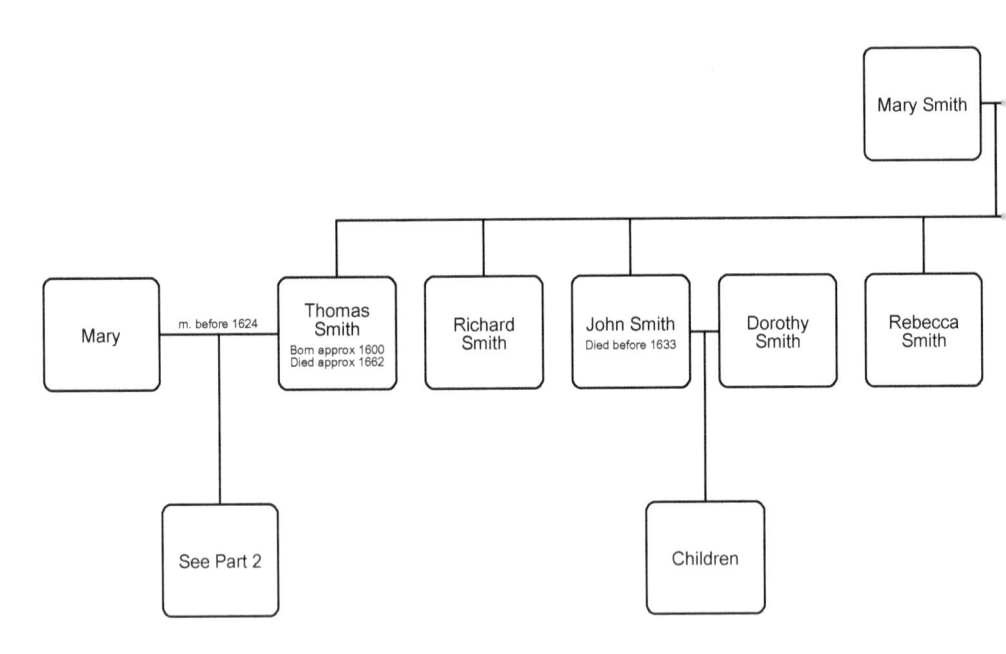

- Mary Smith
  - Mary — m. before 1624 — Thomas Smith (Born approx 1600, Died approx 1662)
    - See Part 2
  - Richard Smith
  - John Smith (Died before 1633)
    - Children (with Dorothy Smith)
  - Dorothy Smith
  - Rebecca Smith

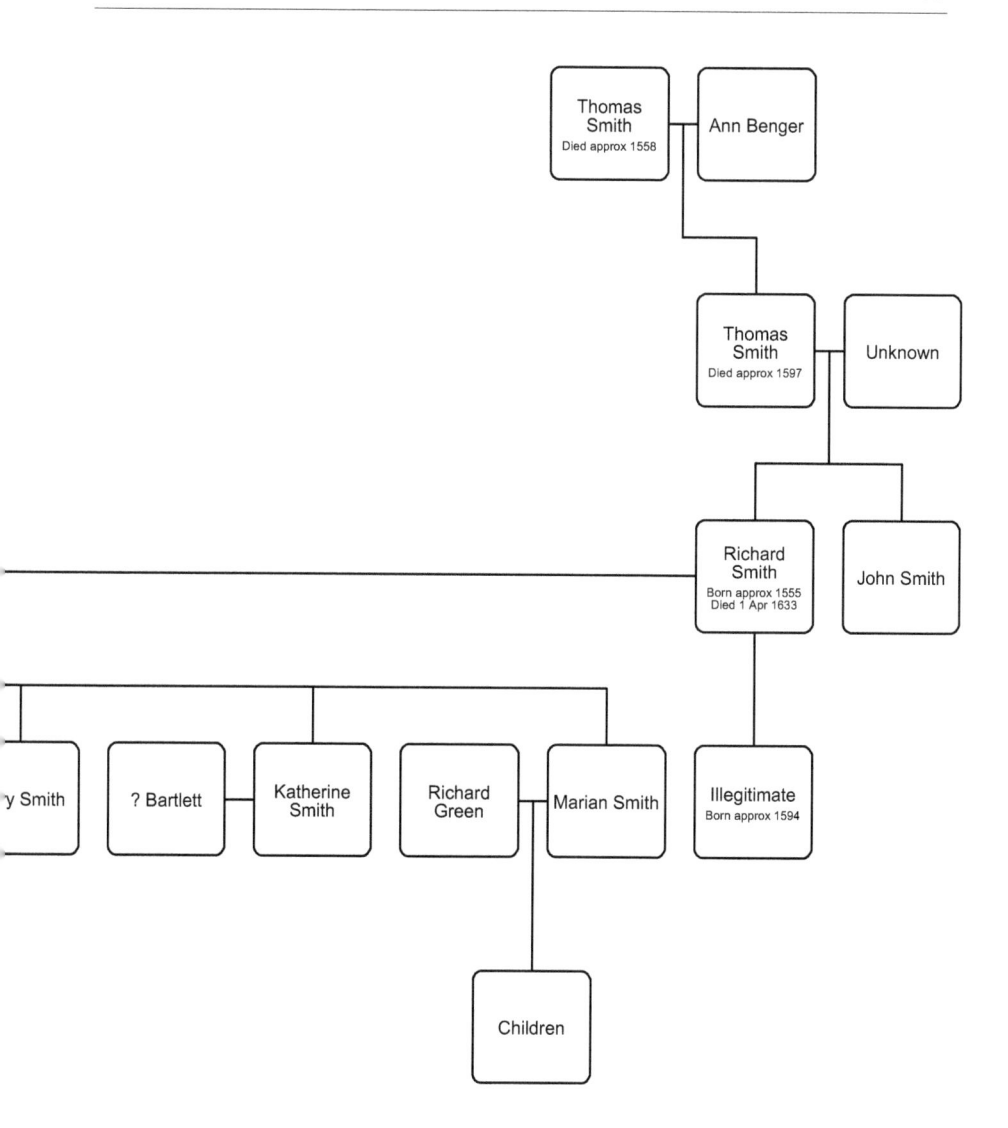

PEDIGREES

```
                    ┌──────────────┬──────────────┐
                    │ Thomas Smith │  Ann Benger  │
                    │ Died approx  │              │
                    │    1558      │              │
                    └──────────────┴──────────────┘
                                │
                    ┌──────────────┬──────────────┐
                    │ Thomas Smith │   Unknown    │
                    │ Died approx  │              │
                    │    1597      │              │
                    └──────────────┴──────────────┘
                                │
                    ┌──────────────┬──────────────┐
                    │Richard Smith │  John Smith  │
                    │Born approx   │              │
                    │   1555       │              │
                    │Died 1 Apr 1633│             │
                    └──────────────┴──────────────┘
                                │
 ┌─────────┬──────────┬──────────────┬──────────────┬──────────────┐
 │ y Smith │?Bartlett │  Katherine   │   Richard    │ Marian Smith │ Illegitimate
 │         │          │    Smith     │    Green     │              │ Born approx 1594
 └─────────┴──────────┴──────────────┴──────────────┴──────────────┘
                                       │
                                  ┌─────────┐
                                  │Children │
                                  └─────────┘
```

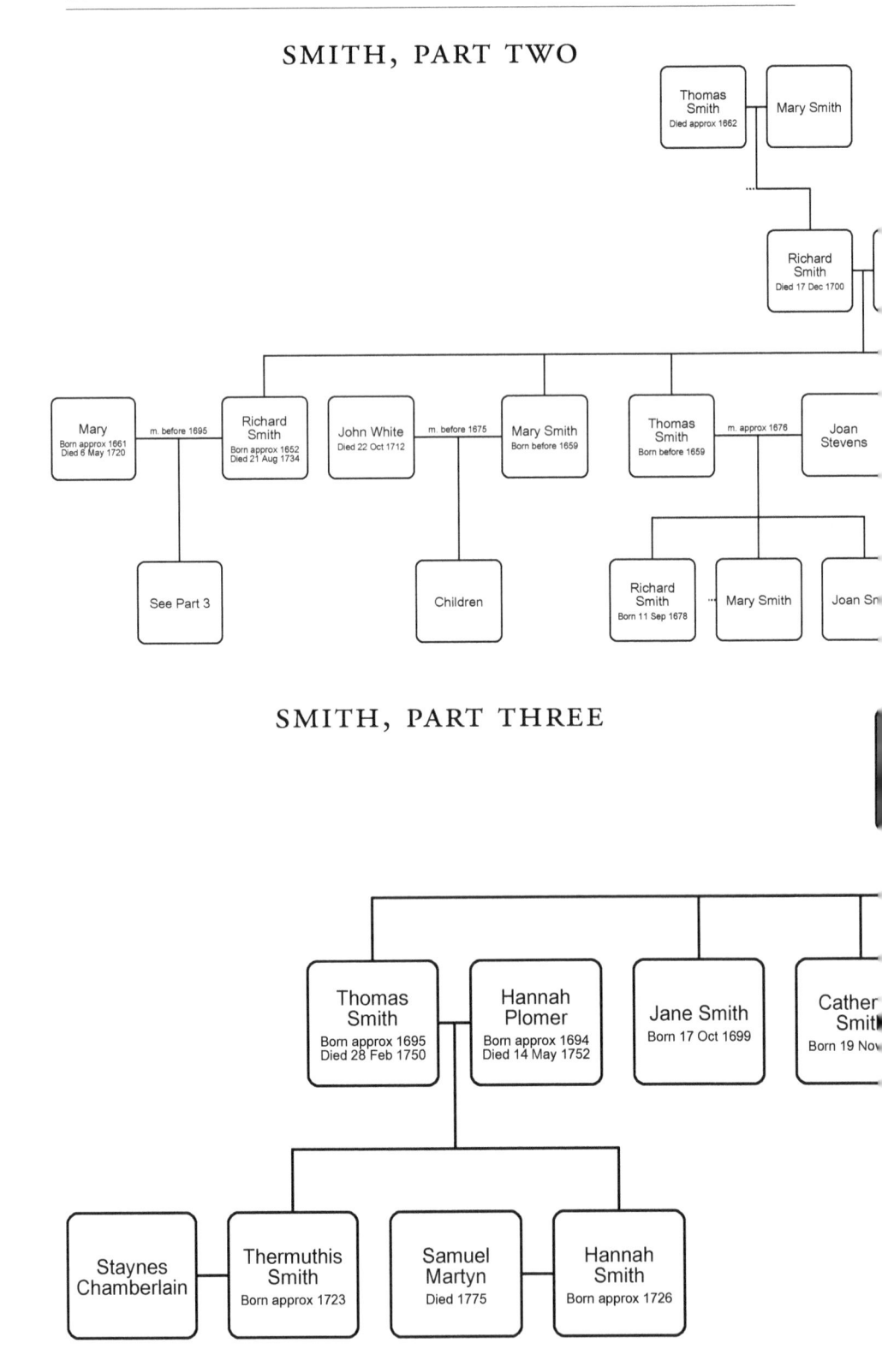

SMITH, PART TWO

- Thomas Smith (Died approx 1662) — Mary Smith
  - Richard Smith (Died 17 Dec 1700)
    - Mary (Born approx 1661, Died 6 May 1720) — m. before 1695 — Richard Smith (Born approx 1652, Died 21 Aug 1734)
      - See Part 3
    - John White (Died 22 Oct 1712) — m. before 1675 — Mary Smith (Born before 1659)
      - Children
    - Thomas Smith (Born before 1659) — m. approx 1676 — Joan Stevens
      - Richard Smith (Born 11 Sep 1678)
      - Mary Smith
      - Joan Sm...

SMITH, PART THREE

- Thomas Smith (Born approx 1695, Died 28 Feb 1750) — Hannah Plomer (Born approx 1694, Died 14 May 1752)
- Jane Smith (Born 17 Oct 1699)
- Cather... Smit... (Born 19 Nov...)

  - Staynes Chamberlain — Thermuthis Smith (Born approx 1723)
  - Samuel Martyn (Died 1775) — Hannah Smith (Born approx 1726)

PEDIGREES · xvii

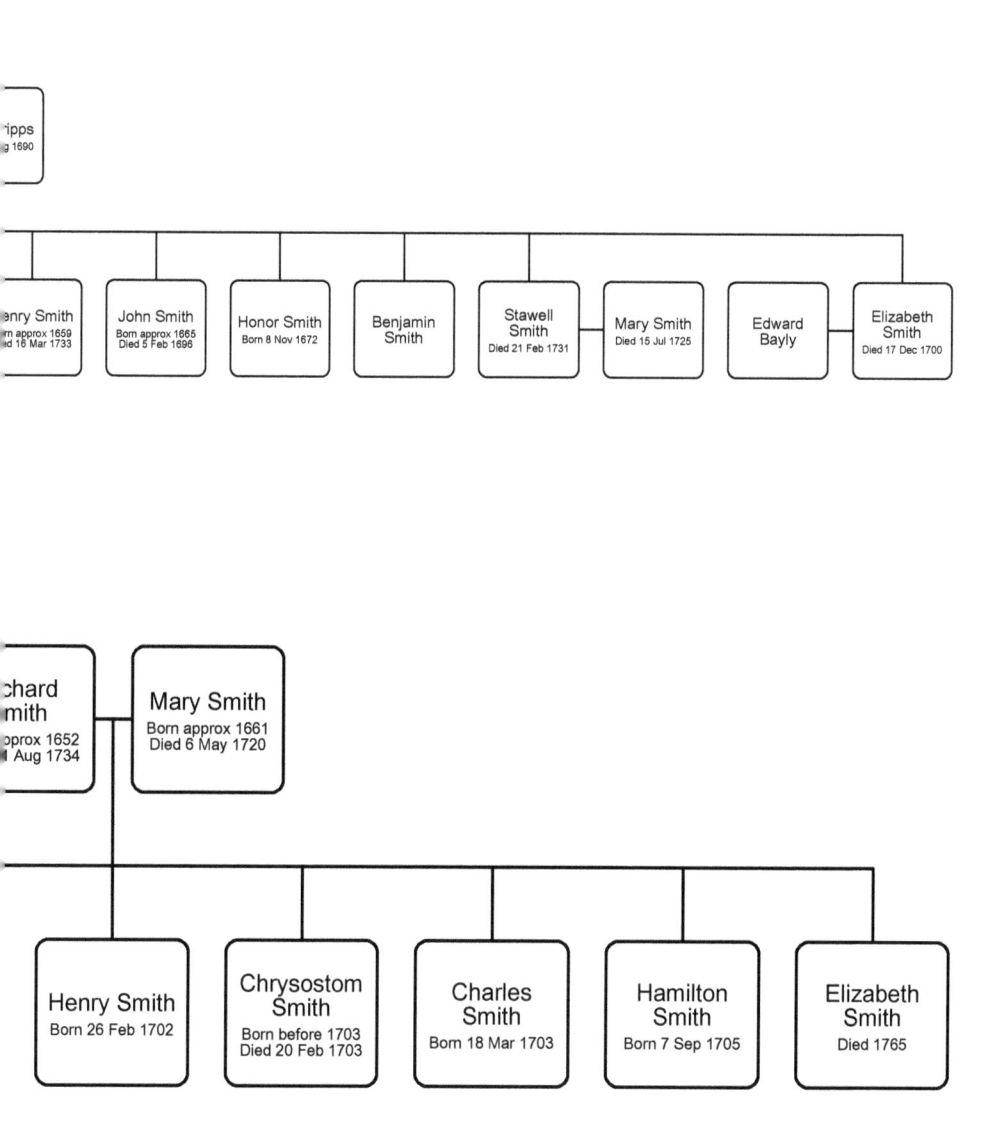

- ...ripps, ...g 1690
- ...enry Smith, ...n approx 1659, ...d 16 Mar 1733
- John Smith, Born approx 1665, Died 5 Feb 1696
- Honor Smith, Born 8 Nov 1672
- Benjamin Smith
- Stawell Smith, Died 21 Feb 1731
- Mary Smith, Died 15 Jul 1725
- Edward Bayly
- Elizabeth Smith, Died 17 Dec 1700

- ...chard ...mith, ...pprox 1652, ...Aug 1734
- Mary Smith, Born approx 1661, Died 6 May 1720

- Henry Smith, Born 26 Feb 1702
- Chrysostom Smith, Born before 1703, Died 20 Feb 1703
- Charles Smith, Born 18 Mar 1703
- Hamilton Smith, Born 7 Sep 1705
- Elizabeth Smith, Died 1765

TRUSLOW, 17-18TH CENTURY

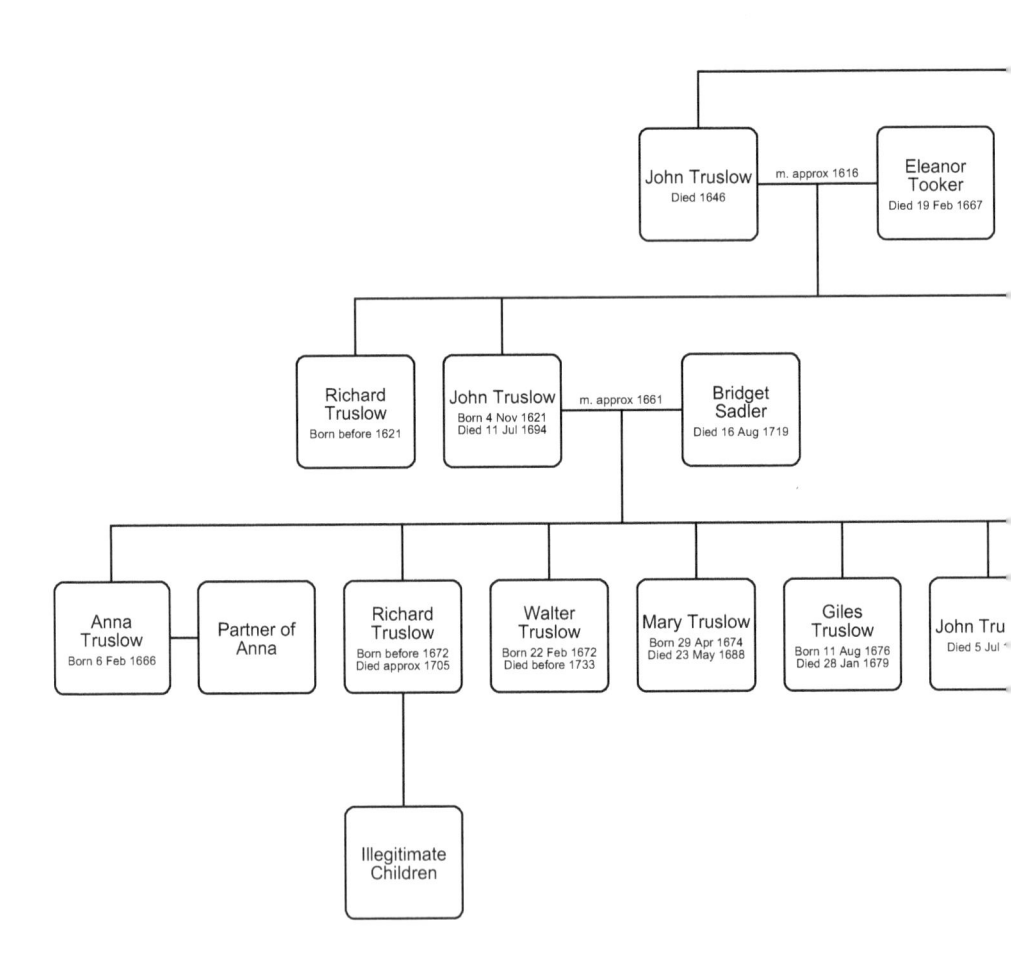

John Truslow — Died 1646 — m. approx 1616 — **Eleanor Tooker** — Died 19 Feb 1667

- **Richard Truslow** — Born before 1621
- **John Truslow** — Born 4 Nov 1621 — Died 11 Jul 1694 — m. approx 1661 — **Bridget Sadler** — Died 16 Aug 1719

Children:
- **Anna Truslow** — Born 6 Feb 1666 — **Partner of Anna**
- **Richard Truslow** — Born before 1672 — Died approx 1705
  - Illegitimate Children
- **Walter Truslow** — Born 22 Feb 1672 — Died before 1733
- **Mary Truslow** — Born 29 Apr 1674 — Died 23 May 1688
- **Giles Truslow** — Born 11 Aug 1676 — Died 28 Jan 1679
- **John Tru...** — Died 5 Jul ...

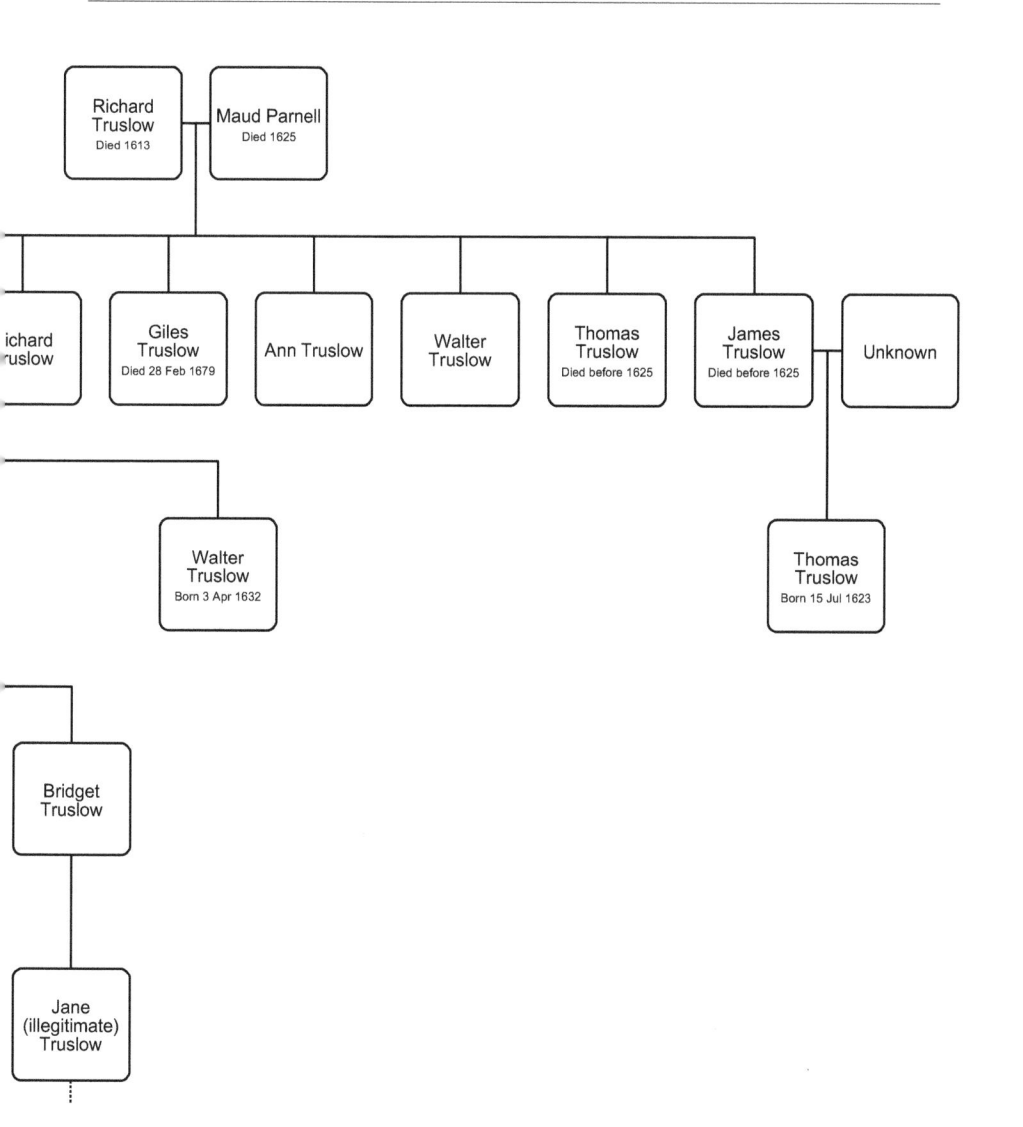

PEDIGREES   xix

- Richard Truslow (Died 1613) — Maud Parnell (Died 1625)
  - ichard ruslow
  - Giles Truslow (Died 28 Feb 1679)
    - Walter Truslow (Born 3 Apr 1632)
      - Bridget Truslow
        - Jane (illegitimate) Truslow
  - Ann Truslow
  - Walter Truslow
  - Thomas Truslow (Died before 1625)
  - James Truslow (Died before 1625) — Unknown
    - Thomas Truslow (Born 15 Jul 1623)

Introduction

In Wiltshire, the heritage industry frequently places the emphasis on prehistory, and particularly on Stonehenge and Avebury. Admittedly the sixteenth century manor house at Avebury does get some attention, and is well worth a visit. But, in general, the history of the parish has been overshadowed by the history of the megaliths, just as the history of medieval Wessex has been overshadowed by the wealth of prehistoric evidence.[1] What about the ordinary people who lived amongst the stones in the two centuries or so after the manor house was built? Notice has been taken of the fact that some of them were stone destroyers,[2] but otherwise they are ignored by visitors to Avebury, and indeed by archaeologists and historians who ought to know better.[3] For nineteenth century antiquaries, the village became 'little more than an intrusion and obstruction, a vile hamlet at the root of all of Avebury's problems and depredations'.[4] Attitudes since then have changed, but nevertheless the *Archaeological Research Agenda for the Avebury World Heritage Site*[5] almost completely ignores the centuries following the Reformation, as though there is nothing in that period worthy of interest. That is not true even archaeologically, and certainly not historically. Ucko et al ask the question, 'should the display and presentation of the Avebury region continue to be almost exclusively focused on the prehistoric period?'[6]

---

1   Eagles, Bruce. 'The Archaeological Evidence for Settlement in the Fifth to Seventh Centuries A.D.', in Aston, Michael, & Lewis, Carenza, eds., *The medieval landscape of Wiltshire*. Oxbow monograph 46. 1994, p.8.

2   For an excellent and up to date summary of their stone-breaking activities, see Gillings, Mark, & Pollard, Joshua. *Avebury*. Duckworth, 2004, especially p.113-33.

3   The best introduction to Avebury's history, as opposed to its archaeology, is Jane Freeman's 'Avebury', in *VCH Wilts*, 12, p.86-105.

4   Gillings, Mark, & Pollard, Joshua. *Avebury*. Gerald Duckworth & Co., 2004, p.172.

5   Avebury Archaeological and Historical Research Group. *Archaeological Research Agenda for the Avebury World Heritage Site*. Trust for Wessex Archaeology, 2001.

6   Ucko, Peter J., et al. *Avebury reconsidered: from the 1690s to the 1990s*. Unwin Hyman, 1991, p.264.

The answer of the present author is a resounding no!' There is much more to Avebury than that.

The aim of this book is to demonstrate that the history of the people of Avebury in the period covered here is very much of interest. It is based on the conviction that men like the schoolmaster, John Clements, the vicar, John White, and the paupers, John and Jane Currier, lived real lives which are worthy of study in themselves. The historian's task is to understand people as they were.[1] For Avebury, their lives are documented by substantial archival and manuscript collections at the Wiltshire and Swindon History Centre, and at the National Archives. Some relevant material is also held by Gloucestershire Archives, the Wiltshire Archaeological and Natural History Society, the Wiltshire Buildings Record, and the National Trust at Avebury. The major collections are the probate records at Chippenham and Kew, and the Holford letters and papers at Chippenham and (to a much lesser extent) at Gloucester. Quarter Sessions and Diocesan archives are also important. Avebury was a parish of dispersed land ownership, so documentation can also be found in many other family collections. I am grateful to the custodians of all these collections for their assistance; in particular, the staff at the History Centre under Steve Hobbs fetched and carried innumerable documents for me, and provided much encouragement. I am grateful too to Ros Cleal and Brian Edwards for checking my text and making helpful comments. My thanks too to the Wiltshire Record Society, which will in due course be publishing my transcripts of journals, letters, accounts, and other memoranda from the Holford papers.

Stuart A. Raymond

---

1 Sharpe, J.A. *Early Modern England: A Social History 1550-1760.* Edward Arnold, 1987, p.353.

I
Introducing Avebury

WE MAY BEGIN our exploration of the history of post-Reformation Avebury[1] with John Sanders, the servant of Sarah Hickes. In 1712, riding on the outside of her coach, he accompanied his mistress, together with Sir Richard Holford (Sarah's brother)[2] and his lady (Susanna, nee Trotman), on their journey from Holford's house at Lincolns Inn to his house in Avebury. Avebury was on the main London to Bath road; even so, the journey took from 11th August until 18th August. Perhaps they stayed at least one night at the Bear in Reading, where Holford had lodged on a previous coach trip.[3] Sanders gives an interesting description of Avebury[4]:

> We came to Sir Richard Holford's house in Avebury. It is a noble larg antient seat, built with whit larg stone, it did belong to Lord Stoil[5], ye late noble Lord Stoil was born thare, and our Queen Anne dined thare. Avebury is compased about with a Wall Ditch,[6] which was thrown up in wars they say 1000 years before Christ. There is two large stons as ye enter ye Town, which they call gates, thare is many larg stons standing up as big as those at Stone edge … Thar lies thick on ye downs many larg stons which they call grey wathers.[7]

1 For a briefer account, see Edwards, Brian. 'Changing Avebury', *The Regional Historian*, 12, 2004, p.3-8.
2 WSHC 184/8; GA D1956/E2/8
3 WSHC 184/8.
4 Sanders, John. 'John Sanders, his book, 1712: the account of my travils with my Mistress', *Records of Buckinghamshire*, 3, 1870, p.93-4. This is reprinted in Meyrick, O. 'An early 18th century visitor to Avebury', *WAM* 57, 1958-60, p.225-6.
5 Lord John Stawell.
6 The ditch around the henge.
7 The stones looked like flocks of sheep, that is, grey wethers, when viewed from a distance.

Sanders was not the first to draw attention to the stones at Avebury, and Queen Anne was not the first monarch to visit. It is just possible that that honour belonged to James I.[1] Charles II certainly paid a visit, as we will see. Some sixty-three years before Sanders' visit, in 1649, John Aubrey came across the village whilst hunting with Colonel John Penruddock and others. The stones distracted Aubrey's attention from the hunt, which continued without him. He 'reined back his horse and dismounted in wonder', and spent the afternoon 'marvelling at the bank and ditch and strange stone circles'.[2]

Aubrey came back repeatedly, several times accompanying James Long of Draycot Cerne on hawking expeditions[3]. After the Restoration, in 1663, he showed the megaliths to no less a personage than Charles II. Whilst travelling to Bath, Charles 'diverted to Avebury, where I [Aubrey] showed him, with a view whereof, he and His Royal Highness the Duke of York were very well pleased'[4]. They rode into the yard of the Catherine Wheel to see the Cove, and then climbed Silbury Hill. The Duke of Monmouth was with them; in 1743, a few of the older inhabitants still remembered their visit[5]. Samuel Pepys[6], visiting in 1688, was surprised by the 'prodigious' size of the stones, not just in the monuments, but also on the surrounding downs. He was struck 'to see how fulle the downes are of great stones; and all along the valley, stones of considerable bigness, most of them growing certainly out of the ground'. Pepys was told that 'most people of learning coming by do come and view'. Local people benefited. The man who escorted Pepys around the stones was paid a shilling for his pains – and a little way further on the diarist gave another shilling to 'the poor and menders of the highway'. One wonders how many other 'people of learning' contributed to the income of Avebury's poor.

Despite these comments, Stukeley expressed his surprise that 'such a place in the Bath road from London should have escapd the survey of the curious when travellers & stage coaches every day pass thro the very midst of the town & cannot but see many of the stones that compose this work which

1 Ucko, Peter J. *Avebury Reconsidered: from the 1660s to the 1990s*. Unwin Hyman, 1990, p.9.
2 Aubrey, John. *Monumenta Brittanica*, ed. John Fowler. 2 vols. Milborne Port: Dorset Publishing, 1980. Vol.1, p.26. See also Scurr, Ruth. *John Aubrey: My Own Life*. Chatto & WIndus, 2015, p.75.
3 Aubrey, *Monumenta*, op cit, vol.1, p.20.
4 Aubrey, *Monumenta*, op cit, Vol.1, p.21; *Life*, p.142-3.
5 Stukeley, William. *Abury: a temple of the British Druids … .* 1743, p.43.
6 Pepys, Samuel. *The Diary of Samuel Pepys*, edited by Robert Latham & William Matthews. *Vol.IX: 1668-1669,*. Bell & Hyman, 1976, p.240-41.

are enough in my apprehension to astonish the most vulgar beholder'.[1]

It was the stones which stood out for all of these visitors. But the title of this book is *Avebury without the stones*. None of the visitors we have mentioned fully realised it, but in fact Avebury was without quite a number of the original stones when they visited[2]. Many were buried between the fourteenth and sixteenth century, before the antiquarians arrived. Destruction proceeded again in the late seventeenth century and early eighteenth century, after Aubrey had visited. Aubrey reported that 'the houses are built of the frustrums [fragments] of those huge ... stones', and that 'the church is likewise built of them'[3]. He did not actually witness destruction of antiquities, but it is probable that the 'frustrums' he mentioned were derived from stone lying in the fields. It was only after the nearby downs had been cleared of recumbent stones that local people turned their attention to the monuments.[4] Stukeley claimed that 'the custom of destroying them is so late that I could easily trace the obit of every stone, who did it, for what purpose, and when, and by what method, what house or wall was built out of it, and the like'.[5] The whiteness of Sir Richard Holford's mansion house, as observed by Sanders, was derived from sarsen stones.

William Stukeley recorded the destruction that was proceeding when he visited in the early 1720s. Although Thomas Twining, sometime curate of the neighbouring parish of East Kennett, was the first to publish a description of the stones,[6] Stukeley has left more evidence of his activities than other antiquaries, and mentions several stone destroyers. He tells us that nine or ten of the stones were destroyed by Tom Robinson c.1700, 'for the sake of the

1 Quoted by Ucko, op cit, p.161.
2 For detailed discussions of the burial and breaking of the stones, see Gillings, Mark, Peterson, Rick, & Pollard, Joshua. 'The destruction of the Avebury monuments', in Cleal, Rosamund, & Pollard, Joshua, eds. *Monuments and material culture: Papers in honour of an Avebury Archaeologist: Isobel Smith*. Hobnob Press, 2004, p.139-63; Gillings, Mark, & Pollard, Joshua. *Avebury*. Bloomsbury, 2004, p.113-53. Gillings, Mark, Pollard, Joshua, Wheatley, David, & Peterson, Rick. *Landscape of the Megaliths: excavations and fieldwork on the Avebury mnuments 1997-2003*. Oxbow Books, 2008, p.252-364.
3 Aubrey, *Monumenta*, vol.1, p.38.
4 Gillings, et al. *Landscape*, op cit, p.326.
5 Cited by Gillings, et al. *Landscape*, op cit, p.332.
6 Twining, Thomas. *Avebury in Wiltshire: the Remains of a Roman work*. 1723. See also Edwards, Brian. 'The "most useful inteligences & observations of Thomas Twinning, c.11664-1739, author of the first publication dedicated to the Avebury Monuments', *Redhorn News*, September 2014.

pasturage'[1]. The destruction of two of them cost Robinson £8[2]. Very expensive pasturage! He also accused Robinson of destroying many other stones – although it has subsequently been discovered that some of those he identified had in fact been buried centuries earlier[3]. More stones were lost between 1718 and 1720.[4] Stukeley's plan shows that stones in the north-east quadrant were 'taken away' in 1718. 'All the neighbours (except the person that gain'd the dirty little profit) were heartily grieved', when Farmer Green took away the stones in Mill Field, and Farmer Griffin ploughed up the ground, in 1724[5]. Green used the stones to build his house at Beckhampton.[6]

Stukeley anathematized Robinson 'and other such sacriligious rascals'; he hoped there would be 'a pitt deeper than ordinary destined for the reception of such villains and sordid rascals'.[7] When he wrote, Stukeley may have forgotten precisely who these men were: to him they were merely farmers. In fact three of the men he named were innkeepers, two were minor landowners, and Robinson himself was a carpenter. Their status was such that Stukeley felt able to condemn them freely. However, given his status as an Anglican clergyman, he avoided condemning others of higher status who were equally guilty. Between 1685 and 1695, John Lord Stawell had a substantial portion of the bank north of the western entrance levelled for the construction of a barn (which is still there) and the planting of trees.[8] Stawell's actions were not condemned, nor were those of Sir Richard Holford, who levelled 'all the way from the north round the top of the vallum on the other side of the ditch'[9]. Indeed, Holford was eulogised: his 'name ought ever to be mentioned with honor and his memory dear to Antiquarians for his great care in preserving these glorious remains'. Holford himself had tried to defend the stones: he

1 Stukeley, *Abury*, op cit, p.22; Ucko, op cit, p.135, 144, 149, 182, & 210-11. The date is questionable; see below, p.129, note 2.
2 Stukeley, *Abury*, op cit, p.25.
3 Gillings, et al. *Landscape*, op cit, p.341.
4 Ucko, op cit, p.272.
5 Cited by Long, William. *Abury illustrated*. 1862, p.20. Little information on the Green family is available, other than the fact that Richard Green served as churchwarden in 1704, cf. WSHC D1/50/6, f.9v; D1/41/1/50, and that he occupied a meadow at Silbury in 1714, cf. WSHC 184/4.
6 Ucko, op cit, p.274.
7 Lukis, W.C., ed. *The Family Memoirs of the Rev. William Stukeley, M.D., ... vol.III.* Surtees Society 80, 1885, p.429.
8 Gillings, et al. *Landscape*, op cit, p.291. Ucko, op cit, p.171.
9 Quoted by Ucko, op cit, p.277. See also Gillings, Mark, Peterson, Rick, & Pollard, Joshua. 'The destruction of the Avebury monuments', in Cleal, & Pollard, op cit, p.155.

noted in 1710 that the vicar, John White, had 'wrongfully broke & carried away a great stone, which I would not have parted with for 5^{li} in the place where hee broke it'.[1] Caleb Bailey, lord of the manor of Berwick Bassett, and a Justice of the Peace, was anathematized in verse at the instigation of the Royal Society, almost certainly because he had been 'responsible for the wholesale destruction through burning of Avebury stones'. But he escaped Stukeley's attention altogether[2]. So did the fact that a megalith was used to mark Rev. Brinsden's grave in neighbouring Winterbourne Monkton.[3]

Stukeley also mentions people keen to preserve them. Reuben Horsell, the parish clerk (dubbed by Stukeley as the 'Antiquarian of Avebury')[4], Mr Robert Holford, and Charles Tooker, esq., of East Kennett, all objected to the destruction going on around them. The destruction of other stones on the road 'was much resented' by Robert Holford.[5] Dr Toope of Bath[6] was also interested, but may have destroyed some evidence in his pursuit of human bones capable of healing his patients[7].

After the 1795 enclosure, Charles Lucas, the curate, expressed the hope that:

> A better lot, I trust, awaits the few
> Remaining stones. No more in common lie
> The fields, each has its separate owner
> Nor longer needs to fear the visionary schemer
> Or hare-brained Speculatist, whose wild plans,
> More mischief did than rustic ignorance … '[8]

His hopes, unfortunately, were not entirely well founded. Sir Richard Colt Hoare discovered, in 1812, that at least a dozen stones had disappeared

1 WSHC 184/1, pt.2. Letter, Sir Richard Holford to John Rose, 23rd November 1710.
2 Gillings, et al, *Landscape*, op cit, p.342. For the verse, and for Bailey's status as a Justice of the Peace, see Law, Alexander. 'Caleb Bailey, the Demolisher', *WAM*, 64, 1969, p.100-106.
3 Meaden, Terence. *The Secrets of the Avebury Stones: Britain's Greatest Megalithic Temple.* Souvenir Press, 1999, p.118.
4 Long, William. *Abury illustrated.* 1862, p.96.
5 Cited by Ucko, op cit, p.273.
6 Long, William. 'Abury', *WAM* 4, 1858, p327, says he was living at Marlborough.
7 Aubrey, *Monumenta*, op cit, vol.1, p.52-3; Piggott, Stuart. *The West Kennet Long Barrow: excavations 1955-56.* HMSO, 1962, p.4.
8 Lucas, Charles. *A descriptive Account in blank verse of the Old Serpentine Temple of the Druids at Avebury in North Wiltshire.* 2nd ed. 1801.

since Stukeley's time.[1] William Long reported further destruction in 1858.[2] Two recently fallen stones were re-erected in 1912.[3] When H.St George Gray undertook his excavations in the early twentieth century, he counted 19 stones in the Kennett Avenue. Stukeley had counted 72.[4]

Many stones, as noted above, had been buried in the centuries before Avebury was 'discovered' by the antiquarians. Chapel Field at Beckhampton is full of buried stones[5], probably from this period. Stukeley recorded these burials in the eighteenth century, and noted the great cost involved, but did not realise that at least some of the stones had been buried as long ago as the fourteenth century[6]. Serious destruction lapsed for several centuries. Aubrey noted in 1684 that 'the great stone at Avebury has fallen and broken into two or three pieces (it was but two foot deep in the earth)'[7]. He also depicted stones at West Kennett as having fallen, or at least lying flat[8]. But these falls seem to have been caused naturally. Stukeley too noted a stone which had fallen and broken in two, probably in the 1670s. It was not broken up for building stone until the mid-1720s[9].

It has been conjectured that religion provided a reason for medieval destruction of the stones, but it is argued below that it had little relevance to the destruction which occurred in Stukeley's time.[10] The destruction he witnessed almost certainly took place for practical reasons – unless, of course, Thomas Robinson was merely out to spite Stukeley, an interfering outsider (hence Stukeley's animosity towards him?).

Some stones simply fell over in inconvenient places. When one fell in 1694 outside of the Catherine Wheel, the innkeeper, Walter Stretch determined to break it up, and to use the pieces to build a new dining room.

1 Hutton, Ronald. 'Modern Avebury', in Leivers, Matt, & Powell, Andrew B., eds. *A Research Framework for the Stonehenge, Avebury, and Associated Sites World Heritage Site: Avebury Assessment*. Wessex Archaeology, 2016, p.136.
2 Long, William. 'Abury', *WAM* 17, 1858, p.331.
3 Cunnington, M.E. 'The re-erection of two fallen stones, and discovery of an interment with drinking cup, at Avebry', *WAM* 38, 1913, p.1-11. See also 45, 1931, p.300-35.
4 Gray, H.St. George Gray. 'The Avebury excavations 1908-1922', *Archaeologia* 84, 1935, p.100.
5 Stukeley, *Abury*, op cit, p.48.
6 Stukeley, *Abury*, op cit, p.15.
7 Aubrey, *Life*, op cit, p.339. For post-medieval destruction, see Gillings, Mark, & Pollard, Joshua. *Avebury*. Gerald Duckworth & Co., 2004, p.141-53 & 157-158.
8 Piggott, *West Kennet*, op cit, p.3.
9 Gillings, et al. *Landscape*, op cit, p.292.
10 Below, p.435

Stukeley thought he was the first to discover how to destroy the stones using fire[1], although Aubrey had described the process earlier.[2] Stukeley, no less, subsequently probably dined in the new dining room! Not only that, but he gave his drawings (including his etching of Reuben Horsell, the parish clerk) to be hung on the Catherine Wheel's walls; John Loveday, another visitor, viewed them in 1729.[3]

Another stone which also stood in the road outside the inn had 'many a slash ... given it & great pieces knocked off'.[4] Yet another stone stood 'in the middle of our landlord's garden'. Similarly, Reuben Horsell remembered how a passing loaded cart had so shaken a stone near the north entrance to the circle that it fell over, 'it being almost undermined by wearing away of the road which is hard chalk.'[5] At roughly the same time, Lord Stawell, the then lord of Avebury manor, levelled the vallum in order to build the barn which now serves as a museum[6]. And in 1723, Richard Fowler, of the Hare and Hounds, emulated Stretch's example by burning one of the long stones at Beckhampton,[7] perhaps using the stone to extend his inn. Stukeley called him a 'horrid depopulator' and 'sacrilegious wretch'.[8]

Stukeley famously claimed that 'covetousness of the little area of ground each stood on' was the chief motivation for stone destruction.[9] Piggott has subsequently argued that 'improvements in agricultural techniques were leading to destruction and vandalism in an ominously modern fashion'.[10] These claims, however, are dubious. Gillings, et al, have shown that 'the stones themselves need not have been viewed as impediments to cultivation'.[11] Furthermore, many of the pits in which the stones stood were left open, and filled with nettles and rubbish. Indeed, they can still be seen as hollows in the

1   Stukeley, *Abury*, op cit, p.25.
2   Aubrey, *Monumenta*. op cit, vol.1., p.38. See also Gillings, Mark, & Pollard, Joshua. *Avebury*. Duckworth, 2004, p.148; Ucko, op cit, p.177.
3   Markham, Sarah. *John Loveday of Caversham, 1711-1789: the Life and Tours of an Eighteenth-Century Onlooker*. Michael Russell, 1984, p.41 & 480-1; Hearne, Thomas, ed. *Remarks and Collections of Thomas Hearne*, vol.10, ed. H.E.Salter. Oxford Historical Society, 67. 1915, p.187.
4   Stukeley, cited by Ucko, op cit, p.278.
5   Stukeley, cited by Ucko, op cit, p.278.
6   Stukeley, *Abury*, op cit, p.27.
7   Cited by Burl, Aubrey. *Prehistoric Avebury*. Book Club Associates, 1979, p.51.
8   Lukis, op cit, p.247.
9   Stukeley, *Abury*, op cit, p.15.
10 Piggott, Stuart. 'William Stukeley: Doctor, Divine, and Antiquary', *British Medical Journal*, 3, 1974, p.725-727.
11 Gillings, Peterson & Pollard, op cit, p.148.

ground.[1] That does not fit with the idea of land reclamation. There is also the point that standing stones were used as boundary markers:[2] one close to the Parsonage House was so used by John Truslow.[3]

The chief motivation for stone destruction in our period was to obtain stone for building. There was much building activity in the parish, perhaps promoted by the fact that dissenters were attracted to the area by virtue of the fact that it was a 'five-mile' village[4]. One megalith had to be destroyed because it stood on the site proposed for the new dissenting chapel.[5] Its stone is probably in the chapel walls. In 1701, a sarsen from the Beckhampton avenue was used to construct a bridge and causeway over the Winterbourne.[6] According to Stukeley, one stone was used as 'a stall to lay fish on, when they had a kind of a market here'[7]. He also noted that Farmer Green 'took most of the stones [of the Sanctuary] away to his buildings at Bekampton, and in the year 1724 Farmer Griffin ploughed half of it up'.[8] Freeman suggests that Green's farm buildings were those at Galteemore, just south of the hamlet.[9] In the 1740s, Reuben Horsell could remember the fate of three stones which had once stood in pasture fields. One lay on the floor of the house in the churchyard, the others could be seen in a number of houses in the street.[10] All of these were evidently built in the early eighteenth century.

Destruction continued. When the level of the Bath to Marlborough coach road was raised in 1762, the bank of the earthwork was quarried to provide material. Towards the end of the eighteenth century, stones in the Kennett Avenue were removed by Mr Nalder in order to build a farmhouse and other houses at West Kennett. In 1794, more stones from the Avenue were taken by Mr Tanner[11]. In the nineteenth century, many more stones were

1   Gillings, Peterson & Pollard, op cit, p.159.
2   Gillings, Peterson & Pollard, op cit, p.140.
3   TNA E134/41/Eliz/Hil8.
4   See below, p.421.
5   Furlong, David, & Gunter, Jim. A*vebury: Carpenter Cottage: Geophysical Survey.* 2014, p.10-11. www.davidfurlong.co.uk
6   Gillings, Mark, & Pollard, Joshua. *Avebury*. Duckworth, 2004, p.142. See also King, Bryan. 'Avebury: the Beckhampton Avenue', *WANHM* 18, 1879, p.382; Stukeley, *Abury,* op cit, p.34.
7   Cited by Ucko, op cit, p.177.
8   Cited by Cunnington, M.E. 'The Sanctuary on Overton Hill near Avebury', *WANHM*, 45(152), 1930, p.321.
9   *VCH Wilts.*, 12, p.90.
10 Smith, A.C. *Guide to the British and Roman Antiquities of the North Wiltshire Downs ... .* Marlborough College Natural History Society, 1884, p.147.
11 Long, William. *Abury illustrated.* 1862, p.64.

cleared. Three stones which stood in the highway, and which made horses shy, were removed by the turnpike trustees in the 1820s.[1] In 1858, William Long noted that 'a farmer cut a waggon drive through this barrow [West Kennett], some time ago, much to the annoyance of his landlord'[2]. When the A4 was widened c.1960, much of the sarsen stone from demolished buildings at West Kennett was used to build roadside walling.[3]

The stones were not the only feature in the parish which attracted antiquarian interest. Silbury Hill, and the West Kennett long barrow,[4] were in the south of the parish. Windmill Hill, on the northern boundary, should also have stood out, but attracted surprisingly little attention until it was excavated by Alexander Keiller in the early twentieth century.[5] Robert Holford had trees planted on top of Silbury Hill in 1723, and in so doing evidently disturbed the soil to the depth of six feet[6]. His trees, however, failed to grow; there were no trees there in the 1790s, when Mrs Williamson was trying to persuade her bailiff to plant some (presumably unaware of previous attempts).[7] John Fowler, who was one of the workmen involved in 1723, subsequently sold Stukeley an 'iron chain', which he had supposedly dug up, and which Stukeley deduced was a bridle which had been buried with the 'great king' whose remains had also been dug up[8]. In 1773, some servants of Arthur Jones, the then lord of Avebury manor, were ploughing in a field close to Silbury Hill when they supposedly unearthed 2,000 Roman coins.[9] One wonders if this discovery

[1] Long, op cit, p.22. See also Smith, op cit, p.142 & 146.
[2] Quoted by Piggott, *West Kennet*, op cit, p.4.
[3] *Appraisal of Buildings on the Avebury Estate, part 1. Conservation Plan, for the National Trust.* Ferguson Mann Architects, 1999. Unpublished report held by WBR.
[4] Their histories are recounted by Leary, et al, op cit, and by Piggott, *West Kennet*, op cit.
[5] Smith, Isobel Foster. *Windmill Hill and Avebury: Excavations by Alexander Keiller, 1925-1939.* Oxford: Clarendon Press, 1965.
[6] Edwards, Brian. 'Silbury Hill: Edward Drax and the excavations of 1776', *WAM* 103, 2010, p.259; Lukis, W.C., ed. *The Family Memoirs of the Rev. William Stukeley, M.D., ... vol.III.* Surtees Society 80, 1885, p.245. One wonders if Robert Holford is mistakenly credited for planting these trees. Sir Richard Holford recorded in his journal that he had five trees planted on Silbury Hill in 1712; cf. GA D1956/E2/8. Perhaps Robert tried again.
[7] See, for example, WSHC 184/6. Letter, Richard Hickley to Mrs Williamson, 5th August 1793.
[8] Cited by Leary, et al, op cit, p.6.
[9] *Reading Mercury*, 16th August 1773; *Bath Chronicle and Weekly Gazette* 12th August 1773.

helped to prompt the excavation of the hill by Edward Drax, in 1776. He could easily afford the expense,[1] but may nevertheless have been supported by a 'subscription set on foot for opening Silbury Hill', as advertised in the *Bath Chronicle*.[2] He recruited a band of coalminers to do the work[3]. Richard Hickley, the bailiff of Avebury manor, was present at the excavation of Silbury, and of a nearby barrow[4]. One hopes that the finds made were not as spurious as the pitcher of milk which a poor boy accidentally dropped as he carried it along the road past Silbury. As he lamented his bad fortune, a tailor chanced to meet him just as a coach was about to pass. He told the boy to cry out as the coach passed, and was able to pass the pitcher off as an urn which his father had dug out of a barrow, and which was therefore very valuable. The travellers gave the tailor a crown (five shillings) for the broken pieces, and he gave the boy a shilling. The transaction was related many years later in the *Bath Chronicle*.[5]

Avebury originally lay to the west of the stone circle, and perhaps partly to the north of the manor house.[6] It was, however, encroaching on the circle even in Aubrey's day. When he undertook his survey of the monument, he found that, due to 'the cross-streets, houses, gardens and several small closes, and the fractures made in this antiquity for the building of these houses, it was no very easy task for me to trace out the vestigia and so make this survey'[7]. Perhaps that was one of the reasons why so few travellers noticed the megaliths. Buildings even made use of the stones in situ: 'one of the monuments in the

1 Edwards, Brian. 'Imagining 'Silbury and Parnassus the same': Edward Drax and the Batheaston Vase Adventure', *Regional Historian*, 26, 2013, p.23.
2 *Bath Chronicle and Weekly Gazette* 19th September 1776. See also *Kentish Gazette* 18th September 1776, & *Chester Chronicle* 20th September 1776.
3 They have been variously described as being from Mendip, Kingswood, and Cornwall; see Edwards, Brian. 'Silbury Hill: Edward Drax and the excavations of 1776', *WAM* 103, 2010, p. 259; Cannon, Jon, & Constantine, Mary-Anne. 'A Welsh Bard in Wiltshire: Iolo Morganwg, Silbury, and the Sarsens', *WAM*, 97, 2004, p.78-88; Whittle, Alasdair. *Sacred Mound, Holy Rings: Silbury Hill and the West Kennet Palisade Enclosures: a later Neolithic complex in North Wiltshire*. Oxbow Monograph 74. 1997, p.8; Merewether, John. *Diary of a Dean, being an account of the Examination of Silbury Hill*. 1851, p.10.
4 Edwards, Brian. 'A Missing Drawing and an Overlooked Text: Silbury Hill Archive Finds', *WAM* 95, 2002, p.91; Edwards, Brian. 'Silbury Hill: Edward Drax and the excavations of 1776', *WAM* 103, 2010, p. 263.
5 *Bath Chronicle and Weekly Gazette* 14th November 1776.
6 Fretwell, Katie. *Avebury Manor: Park and Garden Survey*. National Trust, 1992 (unpublished report), p.29.
7 Aubrey, *Monumenta*, op cit, v.1, p.38.

street ... that runs east and west, is converted into a pigstye or cow house'.[1] By the early eighteenth century, there were perhaps thirty buildings fronting the roads that crossed through the henge.[2] The monument had become 'a confusing patchwork of roads, houses, outbuildings, hedgerows, closes, and orchards'.,[3] it had ceased to be merely an adjunct to the village, as it had been in the medieval period, but had become imbedded in it. And right at the centre, beside the Cove, and on the north-east corner of the road junction, stood the Catherine Wheel,[4] the inn which Stukeley used as his base to explore the henge. The dissenters' meeting house was built on the opposite side of Green Street. By c.1724, building in the stone circle had reached its greatest extent.[5]

It was not until the twentieth century that an effort began to disentangle the stone circle from the village.[6] When Alexander Keiller purchased the manor, and began his archaeological investigations, he intended to remove all vestiges of the village from the circle. He had little interest in the period covered by the present work, except perhaps in his own house. His concern was with the megaliths. In the late 1930s, he supervised much demolition work. After the war, this work was continued by the National Trust. The present shape of the village is consequently not what it was in our period. The dilapidated houses that the numerous poor of the late eighteenth century had lived in, together with many more recent buildings, have disappeared from both the henge, and from the centre of the village. Even the Great Barn, built partially over the Wall Ditch, came under threat. These buildings were not regarded as 'key historic monuments'.[7] However, many better quality houses of the seventeenth and eighteenth century do survive, and the destruction of the barn was averted.

We do not, unfortunately, have any evidence relating to the perambulation of the parish boundaries in our period. The boundaries were, however, important.[8] Everyone who lived within them was automatically

---

1 Ibid, p.41.
2 For a discussion of the number of houses, see Ucko, op cit, p.165.
3 Gillings, Mark, & Pollard, Joshua. *Avebury*. Duckworth, 2004, p.135-6.
4 It was not on the site of the present inn. See *VCH Wilts.*, 12, p.90.
5 Ucko, op cit, p.565.
6 Gillings, Mark, & Pollard, Joshua. *Avebury*. Gerald Duckworth & Co., 2004, p.182-3.
7 On their destruction, see Edwards, Brian. 'Avebury and other not-so-ancient places: the making of the English heritage landscape', in Kean, Hilda, Martin, Paul, & Morgan, Sally J., eds. *Seeing History: Public History in Britain Now*. Francis Boutle, 2000, p.65-80.
8 See Raymond, Stuart A. 'Crossing the Avebury Parish Boundary', *Local Historian*,

assumed to be part of the parish community which assembled at church every Sunday (even if they actually attended the dissenters' chapel), and were entitled to poor relief from the parish if they fulfilled the legal criteria for being 'settled'. When Henry Howson junior, a native of the parish, was accused of vagrancy in London, he was still eligible for support from the overseers of Avebury.[1] Boundaries were inclusive. But they were also exclusive. Several poor people not legally 'settled' were removed from the parish when they threatened to become a charge on the poor rate.[2]

The parish is shaped like a lozenge. It is bounded by Cherhill, Yatesbury, Winterbourne Monkton, Overton, East Kennett, All Cannings, Bishops Cannings, and Calstone Wellington. In total, it occupies 4,690 acres,[3] extending from the Ridge Way on the eastern boundary, to West Down, which lies between the roads to Cherhill and Devizes, and from Windmill Hill in the north towards the Wansdyke in the south (although not quite reaching it). The hamlets of Beckhampton and West Kennett lie on what was the turnpike (now the A4) to the south of the village.

The parish of Avebury occupies the South-West corner of the Marlborough Downs. This is a region of nucleated settlements, which are concentrated in the valleys of chalk streams, and which are surrounded by wide expanses of open down.[4] Most of Avebury lies above 152 metres.[5] One of the head streams of the River Kennett (anciently known as the Winterbourne, and probably referred to locally as 'the Brook'),[6] flows through Avebury in a southerly direction. It passes just west of the village, where it is joined by another stream flowing from Yatesbury. Proceeding away from the river on either side, one passes successively through water meadows, permanent pasture, arable land, and hill pasture.[7] In the valley the soil is heavy and sticky, but readily drainable, and therefore particularly suitable for wheat and oats.[8] The Downs had been grazed by sheep for at least two millennia. In our period, the large

---

53(4), 2023, p.300-311. See also Rumsey, Andrew. *Parish: an Anglican Theology of Place*. SCM Press, 2017, especially p.146.

1 See below, p.176.
2 See below, p.180-1.
3 *VCH Wilts.*, 12, p.86.
4 Bettery, J.H. *Rural Life in Wessex, 1500-1900*. Alan Sutton, 1987, p.7.
5 Ibid, p.86.
6 Ucko, op cit, p.175. This surmise is strengthened by the fact that the area west of the Winterbourne, and north of Trusloe Manor, is known as Westbrook.
7 Stedman, A.R. *Marlborough and the Upper Kennet Country*. [Marlborough School?], 1960, p.5.
8 Stedman, op cit, p.3.

flocks greatly impressed visitors. They were characteristic of the Downs.[1] Defoe noted that 'the Downs are an inexhausted store-house of wooll, and of corn' when he visited North Wiltshire in the 1720s.[2] The grazing of sheep created the characteristic short, springy turf of the Downland, with its distinctive flora.[3] At the beginning of the nineteenth century, Arthur Young commented that he had 'never seen so good sheep-walks in all this country: the verdure is good, and the grass, in general, fine pasture'.[4] The Downs were covered in large sarsen stones, some 650 of which had been used by prehistoric man to build the henge, and perhaps another 40 for Stonehenge.[5] In 1752, a coach carrying an Irish gentleman stopped to view them,[6] and it is likely that coach drivers regularly did so; they may have stopped at Avebury too. Sarsens were used by seventeenth and eighteenth century local people to build some of Avebury's houses and barns, and to erect gateposts. Much local sarsen was used in the rebuilding of London after the Great Fire.[7] In the nineteenth and early twentieth centuries, sarsen was used to provide building stone, tramway supports, and kerbing, on an industrial scale, for the railway town of Swindon. Indeed, the latter activity transformed the landscape, as many of the fields to the east of Avebury were cleared of stone.[8] The 'grey wethers', as the stones were called, almost disappeared from the landscape which they had once covered.

Parson Gilpin castigated Avebury's eighteenth-century landscape as 'one of the most dreary of scenes' – but he himself has been described as 'a rather strange man'![9] By contrast, Alfred Williams has described the Downs as 'bareness, simplicity, and spaciousness, coupled with a feeling of great strength and uncontrolled freedom, an infinity of range, and an immortality

1 Hare, John. 'Agriculture and Settlement in Wiltshire and Hampshire', in Aston, Michael, & Lewis, Carenza, eds., *The medieval landscape of Wiltshire*. Oxbow monograph 46. 1994, p.160.
2 Defoe, Daniel. *A Tour through England and Wales, divided into Circuits or Journies*. J.M.Dent, 1927. v.1, p.284; Stedman, op cit, p.3.
3 Bettey, Joseph. 'Downland', in Thirsk, Joan, ed. *The English Rural Landscape*. Oxford University Press, 2000, p.30 & 43-44.
4 Cited by Massingham, H.J. *English Downland*. B.T.Batsford, 1936, p.20.
5 Brentnall, H.C. 'Sarsens', *WAM 51*, 1946, p.421-2.
6 Huth, Henry, ed. *Narrative of the Journey of an Irish gentleman through England in the year 1752*. Chiswick Press, 1869, p.135.
7 Fowler, Peter, & Blackwell, Ian. *The land of Lettice Sweetapple: an English countryside explored*. Tempus, 1998, p.143.
8 Gillings, Mark, & Pollard, Joshua. *Avebury*. Gerald Duckworth & Co., 2004, p.158-9; King, N.E. 'The Kennett Valley sarsen industry ', *WAM 63*, 1968, p.83-93.
9 Watts, Kenneth. The *Marlborough Downs*. Ex Libris Press, 2003, p.22.

of purpose'[1]. They could also be dangerous. William Skeat told Sir Richard Holford that 'pore John Cue' had been found dead on the Downs due to the 'extremety of this could wether' in November 1698.[2] In 1776, Stephen Stevens, a young boy aged under eight, lost his way, 'rambled about', and was found dead the next day.[3] When, in February 1784, Sarah Eallys set out to walk south from Berwick Bassett to Avebury, she failed to make it; the coroner recorded 'bad weather'.[4] In 1799, James Taylor of Maidenhead was found 'frozen to death', and buried in Avebury churchyard. When Archibald Robertson crossed Beckhampton Down early one morning in 1792, he 'was suddenly encompassed by a thick fog'; he commented that 'the deception caused by vapour … will hardly be credited by a person who has not had ocular demonstration'.[5] The road between Beckhampton and Shepherds Shore was thought by coachmen (who ought to know) to be 'the coldest spot on all the road between London and Bath'.[6]

The Downs to the south were even more isolated. Waden Hill, between Silbury and the West Kennett Avenue, was admittedly close to the village, but it was a two mile walk from Beckhampton to Tan Hill, just across the parish's southern boundary. There were no houses on the way. Tan Hill was the site of a great sheep fair every August, which was regularly attended by farmers,[7] yeomen, husbandmen, and shepherds from all over the Marlborough Downs and further afield.[8] Farmer Skeat, the tenant of Avebury Great Farm, was planning to visit a fair in August 1711; it was probably Tan Hill.[9] Gypsies came too, to trade in horses. The fair was not held in 1637, when plague was prevalent.[10] In 1794, Richard Hickley took his lambs there; they 'sold tollerable

1 Cited by http://www.wshc.eu/blog/tag/Alfred%20Williams.html
2 WSHC 184/1. Letter, William Skeat to Sir Richard Holford, 23rd November 1698.
3 Hunnisett, R.F., ed. *Wiltshire Coroners' Bills, 1752-1796*. Wiltshire Record Society 36, 1980, no.990.
4 Hunnisett, op cit, no.1396.
5 Robertson, Archibald. *A topographical survey of the Great Road from London to Bath and Bristol*. Pt.2. 1792, p.38-9.
6 Harper, Charles G. *The Old Inns of Old England*. Chapman & Hall, 1906, vol.1, p.236.
7 This word was used solely for the very substantial 'farmer' of the demesne for most of our period. Therefore I normally refer to yeomen or husbandmen.
8 Parslew, Patricia. *Beckhampton: time present and time past*. Hobnob Press, 2004, p.26-7, 32, & 52-3; *VCH Wilts.*, 10, p.29; Watts, op cit, p.81.
9 WSHC 184/8.
10 Waylen, James. *A History, Military and Municipal, of the ancient Borough of Devizes*. Longman Brown & Co., 1859, p.192.

INTRODUCING AVEBURY 17

well'.[1] The last fair there was held in 1932; it was almost impossible for motorised traffic to drive there.[2] Tan Hill was crossed by the ancient defensive ditch known as Wansdyke, which ran for many miles in an east-west direction. North of Wansdyke, and to the west of the village, were Beckhampton and Cherhill Downs.

Avebury lay mid-way between Devizes and Marlborough. Both were garrisoned by the opposing forces during the Civil War, and Avebury did not escape the impact of the plundering, the forced conscription, the extortionate taxation, and the sheer instability of those years.[3] For example, William Dunch's house (probably Avebury Trusloe manor house), with his goods, were 'burnt and spoyled', during the conflict.[4] We do not know where responsibility for that particular incident lay, but it is clear that neither side was innocent of making excessive demands on the territory they controlled. We know, for example, that the Royalists demanded unspecified sums from the Hundred of Selkley in early 1644 to help support Colonel Thomas Howard's regiment, and that they were recruiting troops in Marlborough and Calne – and hence probably in Avebury – in the summer of that year.[5] In January 1645, a parliamentary news-sheet reported that in Wiltshire and Somerset, 'the country people suffer exceedingly by the oppressions of the Cavaliers' . A Saturday market continued to be held in Marlborough, but in June 1645, a Parliamentary cavalry regiment from Devizes regularly lay on the Marlborough Downs waiting to rob country people carrying their produce to market.[6]

The only direct evidence of 'plundering' in Avebury itself is provided in the Chancery bill filed by John Forsyth, the vicar. Unlike the Royalist majority of Wiltshire clergy,[7] Forsyth was probably a puritan; his son served in the Parliamentary army. Forsyth claimed that, in 1643, cavaliers from the King's garrison at Devizes (or possibly Oxford or Lacock) had seized all his goods, to the value of £400+, and that he himself had been imprisoned for ten months in Oxford.[8] Given that the Lord of the manor, Sir John Stawell, was a prominent

1   WSHC 184/6. Richard Hickley to Mrs Williamson, 31st August 1794.
2   Gurney, Peter. *Shepherd Lore: the last years of traditional shepherding in Wiltshire.* Wiltshire Folk Life Society, 2010, p,18-19.
3   Wroughton, John. *An Unhappy Civil War: the experience of ordinary people in Gloucestershire, Somerset and Wiltshire, 1642-1646.* Lansdown Press, 1999.
4   TNA C5/426/43; C8/316/12.
5   Harrison, George Anthony. *Royalist Organisation in Wiltshire, 1642-46.* London Ph.D., 1963, p.227 & 259.
6   Ibid, p.354 & 362-3.
7   For the royalist sympathies of Wiltshire clergy, see ibid, p.274-8 & 488-9.
8   TNA C2/Chas1/A9/39.

royalist commander, it is evident that the parish was divided in its loyalties. Indeed, Forsyth accused a number of his creditors of having persuaded the cavaliers to plunder him, in order to avoid paying their debts. Two of them bore names well known in Avebury: Richard Mortimer and William Phelps. The others came from surrounding villages, and from Devizes.

In the neighbouring hundreds of Potterne and Cannings, constables were constantly having to face demands for money, supplies, and men.[1] Some of those supplies, including cheese and wheat, actually passed through Avebury in November 1644, on their way to supply the King's army at Marlborough. The town changed hands six times during the war,[2] and it is probable that some Avebury men were caught up in the fighting there. That was particularly likely on the day in November 1642 when the Royalists stormed the town on a market day, when it would have been full of people from surrounding villages.[3] It is likely, too, that some Avebury men were present when Devizes was besieged at the end of the war.[4] There is no evidence that any Avebury men were involved in the supposedly neutralist 'Club' movement, although it is known to have been active in Marlborough and Calstone. The likelihood is that some Avebury men did endeavour to oppose the depredations of soldiers.[5]

Wroughton describes Wiltshire as a 'corridor county' for marching armies, and Avebury saw a number of armies passing through, seizing supplies as they went, and, indeed, fighting. When Lord Wilmot, in July 1643, led 1,800 cavalry from Marlborough to the relief of the Royalist garrison in Devizes they passed through Beckhampton.[6] Some of them had passed the other way a few days before, as they retreated to Oxford to seek reinforcements. Those reinforcements included an ammunition convoy guarded by dragoons under the Earl of Crawford. It was intercepted and seized by Parliamentary forces in a skirmish near Beckhampton – the only fighting actually recorded in Avebury parish.[7] The defeat of the Parliamentarians at the Battle of Roundway Down, a few days later, must also have had some impact on Avebury. It is probable too that Sir John Stawell, the then lord of Avebury manor, rode from his house in Avebury[8] when, in 1644, he went to petition the King at Hungerford to

1 Waylen, *History*, op cit, p.195-201 & 210-12.
2 Wroughton, op cit, p.203.
3 Wroughton, op cit, p.229-30.
4 Waylen, *History*, op cit, p.139-45.
5 Harrison, op cit, chapter 6.
6 UK Battlefields Resource Centre www.battlefieldstrust.com/resource-centre/civil-war/battleview.asp?BattleFieldId=36
7 Waylen, *History*, op cit, p.161.
8 Although the Stawell estates were centred on Cothelstone (Somerset), Sir Richard

remove unwelcome royalist troops from the county.[1] Stawell had served as royalist governor of Taunton, and had raised and successfully commanded several regiments in Somerset on behalf of the Crown (although he had little involvement in the war in Wiltshire).[2] He was imprisoned in the Tower between 1649 and 1653; his property was seized and sold.[3] It was purchased in 1651 by Sir Edward Bayntun, a prominent – if somewhat disreputable - local Presbyterian, who had been the commander of the Parliamentary forces in Wiltshire at the outbreak of war, and whose house at Bromham, described as 'the famousest buildings in these Western parts', containing 'great store of very rich furniture', had been burnt to the ground by Royalist forces in 1645.[4] It was said to have been worth over £50,000. Bayntun's house at Bremhill was also destroyed.[5] He therefore moved into Avebury manor, although whether he did so before he actually purchased it from the sequestrators is not clear. He resided there until his death in 1657.[6] His encouragement of Presbyterianism probably contributed to the strength of dissent, not just in Avebury, but also in Bremhill and Bromham, after the Restoration. However, Stawell regained his Avebury property following the return of Charles II. Baynton's heir built Spye Park to replace his father's Bromham mansion.[7]

In our period, Avebury was an open field parish, at least until enclosure in 1795.[8] West and North Fields lay respectively west of the village, and to the north. South Field, which was smaller, probably lay between the village and

Holford thought that Sir John had actually resided in Avebury; cf. WSHC 184/1, pt.1. Letter, Sir Richard Holford to John Gardiner, 21st August 1701.

1 Underdown, David. *Revel, Riot and Rebellion: Popular Politics and Culture in England 1603-1660.* Clarendon Press, 1985, p.147 & 155.
2 Stawell, George Dodsworth. *A Quantock Family: the Stawells of Cothelstone and their Descendants, the Barons Stawell of Somerton, and the Stawells of Devonshire and the County Cork.* Barnicot & Pearce, 1910, p.87-94. Victor, David. 'The Fall of the Stawell Family', *Notes & Queries for Somerset & Dorset*, 39(393), 2021, p.127; Knowles, Francis, Sir. 'Avebury manor', WAM 56, 1955, p.364. His limited involvement with Royalists in Wiltshire is evidenced by the fact that his name is not even mentioned in Harrison, op cit.
3 Green, M.A.E., ed. *Calendar of the Proceedings of the Committee for Compounding, &c., 1643-1660.* HMSO, 1890, vol.2, p.1427; Stawell, op cit, p.94-9.
4 Wroughton, op cit, p.143.
5 Ryland-Epton, Louise. *Bremhill parish through the Ages: the Heritage of a Wiltshire community.* Bremhill Parish History Group, 2021, p.17
6 The History of Parliament 1622-1649. Member Biographies: Sir Edward Bayntun www.historyofparliamentonline.org/volume/1604-1629/member/bayntun-sir-edward-1593-1657
7 Waylen, *History*, op cit, p.282.
8 *VCH Wilts.*, 12, p.97 & 99.

Waden Hill. Beckhampton had its own open field. The demesne of Avebury lay to the east of the village. Meadow lands lay along the river, and there were extensive common pastures on East Down, West Down, and to the south of Beckhampton and West Kennett. East Down was at the southern end of the great expanse of downland known as Hackpen Hill, which extended through several parishes; the Ridgeway ran north/south along its top, forming the parish boundary. Throughout our period, the process of enclosure occasioned constant nibblings at the edges of the downland, culminating in the 1795 enclosure act.

When James Sutton compiled a terrier of the land he owned in 1788, he had many small pieces of land, especially in Tenantry Field. He also had a share of 315 acres in Furze Down, which had just been ploughed up (presumably for the first time). He was entitled to run 336 sheep out of the total flock of 1192 which pastured there.[1] Sheep and corn were intertwined. Sheep were folded on the arable at night in season, thus increasing the land's fertility, and run on the downs by day all year. That was possible because the downs were well-drained and usually dry.[2] Farmers did, however, need to ensure that there was water for the sheep. In February 1792, the manorial bailiff had to spend 19s 10d, 'my part for repairing the common wells on the Downs'.[3]

Surface water is scarce on the downland. Even the Winterbourne is not totally reliable. The name Winterbourne gives the clue: it indicates a stream that flows in the winter, but is inconstant. It could overflow, with disastrous results. In November 1725, the manor house was flooded. Peter Griffin gave an account of it to his landlord, Samuel Holford: 'the water rusht and came into every room of your worship's house that has its flour on ye ground. It came so suddenly that we were put hard to it, or had scarce time to get your beer out of the cellars, where the water was afterward as deep as a man's middle. I've set the beer on wooden horses in the great hall till the water were sunk, and since that have carried it into the cellars again'.[4] Presumably the whole village was flooded. The same thing happened again in 1792: Richard Hickley wrote to Mrs Williamson that 'Bar Close, the new garden, pleasure ground and every part was underwater. All the lower rooms in the house up to my knees'. Fortunately, the grass in South Meadow had not been mowed. It was

1 WSHC 248/195.
2 Wilson, Avice R. *Forgotten Labour: the Wiltshire Agricultural Worker and his Environment, 4500 B.C. – A.D. 1950.* Hobnob Press, 2007, p.122.
3 WSHC 184/7.
4 WSHC 184/1, pt.2. Letter, Peter Griffin to Samuel Holford, 22nd November 1725.

cut four days later; however, Hickley thought that it had been 'sanded', and that it was 'so full of grist' the sheep would refuse to eat it.[1]

Flooding did not prevent the creation of water meadows on the eastern side of the Winterbourne, just west of the village,[2] and also between Avebury and Silbury Hill. Traces have been found in the present National Trust car park.[3] William Morris as a schoolboy at Marlborough walked through those near Silbury Hill in 1849, and wrote a brief description, just before they went out of use.[4] Water meadows were an innovation in the early seventeenth century. The aim was to cover meadows on either side of a stream with about an inch of running water. The lime rich water would deposit fertile silt, and encourage early growth.[5] The technique, pioneered in Wiltshire by the Earl of Pembroke (who owned the neighbouring manor of West Overton)[6], and by the St John family of Lydiard Tregoze, helped to solve the problem of finding fodder early in the year for increasing numbers of stock, and also provided a good hay crop in June or July for winter feed.[7] They enabled the keeping of much larger flocks

1 WSHC 184/6. Richard Hickley to Mrs Williamson, 4th September 1792.
2 McOmish, David, et al. 'Fieldwork in the Avebury area', in Brown, Graham, Field, David, & McOmish, David, eds. *The Avebury Landscape: aspects of the field archaeology of the Marlborough Downs*. Oxbow Books, 2005, p.18 & 33.
3 Last, Jonathan. *Avebury Southern Car Park (Glebe Field): a desk based assessment*. Centre for Archaeology Report 29/2002. English Heritage, 2002, p.4, 5, 8, & 13.
4 Watts, op cit, p.85.
5 Parslew, Patricia. *Beckhampton: Time Present and Time Past*. Hobnob Press, 2000, p.29; Stedman, op cit, p.5. Water meadows in Wessex are briefly discussed in Bettey, J.H. *Rural Life in Wessex 1500-1900*. Alan Sutton,1987, p.26-9. For more detailed discussions, see Cowan, Michael. *Wiltshire Water Meadows: Understanding and Conserving the Remains of a Farming and Engineering Revolution*. Hobnob Press, 2005; Atwood, George. 'A Study of the Wiltshire Water Meadow', *WAM*, 58, 1963, p.403-13.
6 Fowler, P.J. *Landscape Plotted and Pieced: Landscape History and Local Archaeology in Fyfield and Overton, Wiltshire*. Society of Antiquaries of London, 2000, p.148. See also the detailed discussion of West Overton's water meadows, p.140.
7 Thirsk, Joan, ed. *The Agrarian History of England and Wales, vol.IV*. 1500-1640. Cambridge University Press, 1967, p.180-82; Bowie, G.G.S. 'Northern Wolds and Wessex Downlands: Contrasts in Sheep Husbandry and Farming Practice, 1770-1850', *Agricultural History Review* 38(2), 1990, p.120-1. Smith, Nicola. 'Medieval and later sheep farming on the Marlborough Downs', in Brown, Graham, Field, David, & McOmish, David, eds. *The Avebury Landscape: aspects of the field archaeology of the Marlborough Downs*. Oxbow Books, 2005, p.193. Aston, Michael, & Bettey, Joe. 'The post-medieval rural landscape c.1540-1700: the drive for profit and the desire for status', in Everson, Paul & Williamson, Tom, eds. *The Archaeology of Landscape: studies presented to Christopher Taylor*. Manchester University Press, 1998, p.127-31.

of sheep than would otherwise have been possible, and hence enhanced the productivity of arable land on which those flocks were folded.

Trenches were cut to hold water from the stream; oaken hatches which could be opened and shut at will were installed to control the flow of the water. The sheep would be put into the meadows in mid-March, long before grass was available anywhere else. They would soon have eaten it close: Massingham likened the sheep to 'living lawnmowers ... whose teeth created the very tapestry of the Downland surface', the 'velvety resilient turf'.[1] By the end of April, they would be moved onto the Downs, allowing the drowner to briefly float the meadows again. A good crop of hay followed in June. Thereafter, cattle could be let into the meadow, or perhaps another crop of hay grown. In the late autumn, the hatches would be raised again to allow the water to flow in preparation for the spring crop of grass.[2] Farmers were able to obtain yields of hay perhaps four times as great by floating meadows. Arable yields from the fields on which sheep were folded at night also increased.[3] Water meadows meant more sheep, and more cattle. Aubrey noted that 'watering of meadows about Marleburgh ... was, I remember about 1646'.[4] The right to erect weirs and dig water courses was mentioned when William Dunch sold the manor to Sir John Stawell in 1639.[5] In 1669, John Worlidge described water meadows as 'one of the most universal and advantageous improvements in England within these few years'.[6] Whether William Skeat would have agreed is debatable; in December 1698 he complained that the water 'hant ben bayd up ... since May', and that consequently coaches and wagons had to divert across his open fields, and were ruining his crops, despite being expected to pay 12^d each time they passed by.[7] One of his successors dealt with the problem by moving the hatches and building a bridge, so that the water could flow under the road. But that caused problems with neighbouring Mr Smith, whose land suffered when Holford's tenant watered his meadow.[8] Water meadows continued in use until the great agricultural slump towards the end of the nineteenth century.

After passing the village, the Winterbourne runs south to Silbury, where it is fed by the Swallow Head spring. From thence, it is re-named the

1 Massingham, H.J. *English Downland.* B.T.Batsford, 1936, p.19.
2 Stedman, op cit, p.5.
3 Kerridge, E. 'The floating of the Wiltshire water meadows', *W.A.M.*, 55, 1953, p.106-9.
4 Cited by Ucko, op cit, p.170.
5 WANHS.Genealogy, v.A-A, p.113.
6 Quoted by Aston & Bettey, op cit, p.129.
7 WSHC 184/1.
8 WSHC 184/1, pt.2. Letter, John Cures to Richard Holford, 5th May 1739.

Kennett, and flows east to join the Thames at Reading. Stukeley regarded the Swallow Head spring as the true source of the Kennett; the Winterbourne 'affords but little water, except in wet seasons'.[1] Before leaving the parish, the river passes through more water meadows at the foot of Silbury.[2] In 1720, a great storm flooded these meadows, destroying their crops.[3] The hatches for watering South Mead were moved c.1730 to prevent the water flooding the road, and became a subject of dispute in 1739.[4] In 1781, William Norris paid Stephen Crook for repairing the water hatches on his farm, presumably at Brunsden.[5] Richard Hickley had to pay £9 16s in 1793 for 'cleansing 98 pole of the water course in South Meadow'.[6] When the open fields and downs were enclosed in 1795, the Enclosure Commissioners ordered that hatches or floodgates should be erected to control the water in Silbury Meadow, and that the proprietors were to keep the drains and ditches in repair. The cost was to be divided between Peter Holford, the Duke of Marlborough, and James Sutton, all of whom received allotments in the Meadow.[7] Similarly, hatches newly set up in Bar Close, with the associated water course that ran across the lands of Adam Williamson and Robert Nalder, were to be repaired by these two proprietors. Their use of the water was regulated by the enclosure award. These arrangements subsequently led to much dispute between the proprietors.[8]

The water meadows continued to be floated until the late nineteenth century, when the combination of agricultural depression, high labour costs, and increasing availability of alternative sources of early spring feed, caused the system to be abandoned.[9]

1 Stukeley, *Abury*, op cit, p.19.
2 For archaeological discussions of the water meadows at Silbury, see Leary, Jim, Field, David, & Campbell, Gill, eds. *Silbury Hill: the largest Prehistoric Mound in Europe*. English Heritage, 2013, p.276-9. Crosby, Vicky, & Hembrey, Nicola. 'An evaluation in the Fields South of Silbury Hill in 2010: Romano-British settlement, later alluviaton and water meadows', *WAM*, 106, 2013, p.115-6 & 157. See also Watts, Kenneth. *The Marlborough Downs*. Ex Libris Press, 2003, p.85.
3 Mayo, Charles Herbert. *A genealogical account of the Mayo and Elton families of the counties of Wilts and Hereford*. Chiswick Press, 1882, p.43.
4 WSHC 184/1, pt.2. John Cures to Richard Holford, 5th May 1739. Cures was perhaps Holford's steward.
5 WSHC 473/277.
6 WSHC 184/7.
7 WSHC A1/EA 95. See also Wadsworth, op cit, p.lxix.
8 Wadsworth, op cit, p.cxii-cxiv.
9 Bettey, Joseph. 'Downland', in Thirsk, Joan, ed. *The English Rural Landscape*. Oxford University Press, 2000, p.43.

Wells were also important, and are frequently mentioned in deeds. Most houses probably had one, and some can still be seen. In 1778, Arthur Jones paid Thomas Fowler 2s 6d for 'going into the well and mending the pump'.[1] This was probably the same well that is noted in the 1548 survey of Avebury's manor house.[2] In 1723, there was a newly constructed well and pump at West Kennett.[3] There were three wells at Westbrook Farmhouse, and one in the garden of Westbrook Cottage. Carpenter's Cottage had one which was seventy feet deep, but is now beneath an extension.[4] So is the well at Hitchcock's Farm (now Manor Farm House).[5] In 1765, James Cary was paid £1 2s 2d for digging a well at Avebury manor.[6] Well buckets for it were purchased from Daniel Fry, cooper, in 1781.[7] When Anthony Allen purchased two tenements at West Kennett in 1772, he was to have the shared use of a well in the adjoining farm.[8] Like the Downs, wells could be dangerous if proper precautions were not taken: in 1780, a two-year old named Jonathan Bailey 'fell into a deep well and was instantly killed'.[9]

There was also a pond at Eastbrook, on the south side of Green Lane, discovered by Keiller in the course of his excavations.[10] It probably provided water to the neighbouring houses, and was also used for watering livestock. Sir Richard Holford had a horse trough and a horse pool in his barton, presumably for the latter purpose, although there was a pump beside them.[11] His successor, Richard Holford, paid Walter Emly £11 2s 8d for 'making a pond' in 1742.[12] This was probably a dew pond on the Downs for sheep and cattle to drink from. In January 1792 Richard Hickley had to pay 19s 10d towards repairing the common wells on the Downs, which were provided for the same purpose.[13]

The downs were mostly open grassland. Some woodland did, however, exist. When Avebury Manor was sold by the Parliamentary Commissioners

1 WSHC 184/5. Statement, Arthur Jones to Samuel Fowler, 1778-9.
2 WSHC 2664/1/2D/8.
3 Somerset Heritage Centre. DD/PO/6/ Lease, 3rd September 1723, Richard & Thomas Smith to Francis Popham.
4 WBR.
5 Appraisal ..., op cit.
6 WSHC 184/5.
7 WSHC 184/5. Daniel Fry's invoice, 1781.
8 WSHC 118/88. Draft indenture, Chamberlayne to Allen, 1772.
9 Hunnisett, op cit, no.1216.
10 Keiller, Alexander. 'Avebury: a summary of excavations, 1937 and 1938', *Antiquity* 13(50), 1939, p.230.
11 WSHC 184/4. Plan of the house, gardens and barton.
12 WSHC 184/5. Walter Emly's bill, 1742.
13 WSHC 184/7.

in 1652, the 'woods, underwoods and timber trees' on the estate were valued at £44 8s (although that included eighty acres of wood at Catcomb in Hilmarton).[1] William Skeat, the farmer of the manor, received detailed instructions for the planting of all sorts of trees on Sir Richard Holford's estate in 1695.[2] He reported in early 1696 that he had 'set 2 okes & elm & aishes according to your order'.[3] In 1708 he purchased a 'decayed elm growing 'in the sheep barton', together with a wood pile, from his landlord.[4] Skeat was allowed to take half an acre of coppice every year to maintain the bounds of his farm,[5] although, according to Sir Richard, there was 'a lack of timber upon the farme'.[6] Nevertheless, oak, ash and elm trees were mentioned in his agreement with John Rose in 1710.[7] Sir Richard 'planted a little parterr of trees' on the end of the terrace which he had created by levelling part of the vallum, and also planted that part of the ditch with trees.[8] He also had a walnut tree and sycamores, probably in the garden of Avebury Manor.[9] More walnut trees were planted in 1717.[10] The tenant was expected to 'overlook the new planted trees'.[11] Withies grew along the Winterbourne; they provided rods used in thatching.[12] At the end of our period, spruce and firs were being planted: General Williamson received a bill for 90 spruce and 50 Scotch firs from Hugh Lavington in 1791. More were required in 1792.[13] The following year, Richard Hickley commented that Mrs Williamson's plan to plant trees on the top of Silbury Hill, would 'cost a deal of money to make a fence round it, that is, I mean the top of it', although, admittedly, 'a plantation on the top

1 WANHS. Genealogy v.A-A, p.119. For the Catcomb wood in 1548, see WSHC 2664/1/2D/8.
2 Ucko, op cit, p.259.
3 WSHC 184/1, pt.2. Letter, William Skeat to Sir Richard Holford, 4th January 1695/6.
4 WSHC 184/4/1. Account of Sir Richard Holford with Farmer Skeat, 1708.
5 WSHC 184/1. Letter, 9th November 1704, Sir Richard Holford to John White.
6 WSHC 184/1, pt.2. Letter, Sir Richard Holford to Richard Chandler, 2nd June 1709.
7 WSHC 184/4/1. Articles of agreement, Sir Richard Holford and John Rose, 1710.
8 Stukeley, quoted by Ucko, op cit, p.277.
9 WSHC 184/4/1. Articles of Agreement, Sir Richard Holford & John Rose, 1710; 184/1, pt.2. Letter, Sir Richard Holford to John Rose, 23rd November 1710; Fretwell, Katie. *Avebury Manor: Park and Garden Survey*. National Trust, 1992 (unpublished report), p.41 & 46.
10 Fretwell, op cit, p.8.
11 WSHC 184/1, pt.2. Peter Griffin's proposals for taking Avebury Farm.
12 WSHC 435/24/1/7.
13 Fretwell, op cit, p.56.

of that hill in a few years would look beautiful'.[1] He took a similarly dim view of her desire to plant trees in the hedges on the Down: 'think that will not do, as I have known many planted since I have been at Avebury, but none of them came to anything'.[2] Hickley had to go to a coppice at Standley (perhaps in Bremhill parish) to obtain the poles needed to make his hurdles.[3] But it may be that the clumps of beech which now stand on the Downs east of Avebury were planted by him: they are not native trees.[4] No documentary evidence for this suggestion has been found, but they probably date from the late eighteenth or early nineteenth centuries.

There were also trees on smaller estates. When John Truslow leased a Beckhampton tenement to John Pontin in 1692, he reserved to himself the elms and ashes growing on the property.[5] Half a century earlier, there were also oaks on Beckhampton Farm.[6] In 1702, there were 108 ash trees, and 38 elms, on the 395 acres owned by William Norris.[7] Thomas Smith had walnut trees on his West Kennett farm in 1729.[8] He planted more trees in a plot of ground there, probably in the early 1740s.[9] When John Amor leased Avebury Trusloe manor in 1795, he was allowed to lop the pollards on his farm after eight years growth.[10] Stukeley notes that trees were sometimes planted where stones had once stood.[11] He also noted elm trees embracing a megalith in his landlord's garden.[12] Elms were characteristic of the Kennett Valley.[13] There were willow and ash trees on West Kennett Farm in 1724,[14] and willows were planted on islands in the river there in 1772.[15] They were also planted south of Avebury manor at roughly the same time,[16] and in Bar Close, north of the manor house,

1   WSHC 184/6. Letter, Richard Hickley to Mrs Williamson, 5th August 1793. One wonders what had happened to the trees planted there by Mr Holford in 1723, as mentioned above.
2   WSHC 184/6. Letter, Richard Hickley to Mrs Williamson, 30th July 1794.
3   WSHC 184/5. Bill for coppice poles from William Gale, 1786.
4   Watts, op cit, p.31 & 102-3.
5   WSHC 371/1, pt.3. Lease 16th April 1692.
6   WSHC 212b/104. Lease, Richard Truslow to Thomas Smith, 10th June 1647.
7   WSHC 473/274.
8   WSHC 568/7.
9   WSHC 568/7. Lease, Thomas Smith to Ambrose Lanfear, 6th November 1745.
10 WSHC 873/262. Lease, Sir John Hopkins to John Amor, 16th April 1795.
11 Ucko, op cit, p.272.
12 Stukeley, cited by Ucko, op cit, p.278.
13 Stedman, op cit, p.5.
14 WSHC 568/7. Lease, Thomas Smith to John Beake, 13th October 1724.
15 WSHC 118/88. Draft Indenture, Chamberlayne to Allen, 1772.
16 VCH Wilts., 12, p.87.

in 1792.[1] Avenues of lime trees were planted in the Park north of Avebury manor, and perhaps in the Plough Way (leading from the village street to the manor barton) in the late eighteenth century.[2] In 1797, timber on the farm at Brunsden was valued at £94.[3] When the turnpike trustees wanted to widen the road outside of the Catherine Wheel in 1797, trees of ash and lime had to be taken down.[4] Firewood from oak, ash, elm, willow and poplar was used in burning stones[5]. Ash trees were planted in pits left by burnt stone in the southern inner circle, but elsewhere pits were left to the nettles[6]. The planting of trees was evidently encouraged by the landholders, as the parish was sparsely wooded, at least in the eighteenth century.[7] In 1796, William Norris, esq., paid Thomas Sartain for valuing timber and underwood on his estates, including those in Beckhampton and Avebury (although probably there was more at Sheldon and Bromham).[8] It is probable that timber for building had to be obtained elsewhere.

To the west of the village, across the Winterbourne, lay the hamlet of Westbrook, whose farm and seven cottages (which are still standing) were depicted on one of Stukeley's maps.[9] Immediately to the south of these lay Avebury Trusloe manor house. Eastbrook, to the east of the Winterbourne, covered the village and the stone circle, and included both the original Catherine Wheel and the Meeting House, on opposite sides of Green Street. There were also, in 1709, six outlying cottages on Hackpen, and another six on Thornhill, together worth a mere twelve shillings per annum.[10] The other two important hamlets were Beckhampton and West Kennett, both of which lay on the turnpike, and both of which had substantial inns for travellers – the new Catherine Wheel (for the coaching trade) and the Bear (now the Waggon and Horses) at Beckhampton (for drovers),[11] the White Hart at West Kennett.

For local government purposes, Beckhampton and West Kennett were separate tithings in their own right. There were perhaps only four houses in Beckhampton in 1724, but by 1773 buildings lined both sides of the street

1 WSHC 184/6. Letter, Richard Hickley to Mrs Williamson, 6th March 1792.
2 Fretwell, op cit, p.29-30.
3 Somerset Heritage Centre DD/PO/6.
4 WSHC 1371/1.
5 Gillings, et al. *Landscape*, op cit, p.324.
6 Gillings, et al. *Landscape, op cit*, p.325.
7 *VCH Wilts.*, 12, p.87.
8 WSHC 473/78.
9 Gillings, et al. *Landscape*, op cit, p.371.
10 WSHC 184/1/1. 'Rental' (actually a count of sheep) 1709.
11 For other names, see below, p.320.

(which is now hidden away to the south-east of the roundabout).[1] A road from Beckhampton led directly south across the Downs to the Wansdyke, and on to Wilcot; the section in Alton Priors parish was sufficiently important in 1792 to be presented as in need of repair, although now it is merely a byway.[2]

The few houses at West Kennett, which included West Kennett farm, and which mostly incorporated sarsen stone from the Kennett Avenue, stood to the south of the turnpike.[3] There was a malt house at West Kennett Farm in 1745 (the building still survives),[4] and the development of a brewery, probably in association with the White Hart, caused West Kennett to expand on the northern side of the road towards the end of the eighteenth century.[5]

The road through the village was more important before the days of the turnpike; Aubrey's 'survey' of Avebury shows 'the way to Marlborough' passing directly through the centre of the stone circle[6]. It was part of an ancient Anglo-Saxon 'herepath', that is, army path, leading from Wroughton, via Yatesbury, to Marlborough[7]. Welsh drovers may have used that route on their way to the cattle market at Smithfield, or perhaps drove their sheep along the Ridgeway to the great fairs at East Ilsley,[8] leaving great clouds of white dust from the chalk in their wake.[9] Coaches between Bristol, Bath, and London also travelled this way: the earliest known service was mentioned in 1657.[10] The *London Evening Post* reported in 1737 that, in the previous five months, 200 coaches had passed between Sandy Lane and Beckhampton.[11] The road through Shepherds

1 Crawford, O.G.S. 'Notes on Fieldwork round Avebury, December 1921', *WANHS* 42 (137), 1922, p.52; *VCH Wilts.*, 12, p.90.
2 WSHC A1/110, 1792M.
3 *VCH Wilts.*,12, p.90.
4 *Appraisal of Buildings on the Avebury Estate, part 1. Conservation Plan, for the National Trust.* Ferguson Mann Architects, 1999. Unpublished report held by WBR.
5 *Appraisal of Buildings on the Avebury Estate, part 1. Conservation Plan, for the National Trust.* Ferguson Mann Architects, 1999, pt.1.2. Unpublished report held by WBR.
6 Aubrey, *Life*, op cit, p.152-3.
7 Reynolds, Andrew J. 'Avebury, Yatesbury, and the archaeology of communications', *Papers from the Institute of Archaeology* 6, 1995, p.21-30.
8 Bonser, K.J. *The Drovers: who they were and how they went: an epic of the English Countryside.* Macmillan, 1970, p.197-8.
9 Jones, E.L. *Landscape History and Rural Society in Southern England: an economic and environmental perspective.* Palgrave Macmillan, 2021, p.101.
10 Gerhold, Dorian. *Carriers and Coachmasters: Trade and Travel before the Turnpikes.* Phillimore, 2005, p.198; Phillips, Daphne. *The Great Road to Bath.* Countryside Books, 1983, p.70.
11 Phillips, op cit, p.80.

Shore was the only turnpiked road at that time. To the east of Avebury, coaches had to travel up Green Street[1] and over Hackpen. The hill was difficult for coaches, especially in the vicinity of Old Eagle. Thomas Smith told the House of Commons in 1743 that waggoners travelling towards Marlborough were obliged to hire four or five horses at Cherhill to pull their waggons over the Downs.[2] The Marlborough postmaster, Walter Gilmour, added in his evidence that he had known the mail lost due to the 'badness' of the road. There was an alternative route via Silbury, but part of that ran through a 'deep hollow way', with no room for carriages to pass, and tended to be too foundrous for coaches, especially in winter (although it was used by waggons and pack horses). Petitioners from Marlborough thought it would be easier to turnpike the road over the Downs, and more expensive to turnpike this lower road,[3] but in the event their objections were over-ridden. The turnpike past Beckhampton and Silbury was created in 1745.[4]

Sir Richard Holford and his footman travelled by the 'Bath flying coach' when they visited Avebury in June 1712; in his journal, he recorded a number of other occasions on which he travelled on regular coach services.[5] Servants, however, sometimes found themselves relegated to travelling with the carrier.[6] The 'caravan' in which Bratton's schoolmaster travelled through the night from Devizes to Marlborough on 25th May 1740 either went that way, or passed under Silbury.[7] The higher route avoided the pre-turnpike winding route through the villages on the south bank of the Kennett, which occasionally flooded in winter.[8] John Loveday, however, thought that 'it is very considerably nearer to leave Avebury on the left hand and go close by Selbury Hill'.[9] He was probably riding on horseback. The cost of maintaining the road was contentious. In 1717, users of the road (including some from Avebury)

1 The name 'Green Street' is a 20th century invention; see Fowler, Peter, 'Moving through the landscape', in Everson, Paul, & Williamson, Tom, eds. *The Archaeology of Landscape: studies presented to Christopher Taylor*. Manchester University Press, 1998, p.32.
2 *Journals of the House of Commons*, 43, p.265.
3 *House of Commons journal* 24, p.413.
4 Watts, op cit, p.122.
5 GA D1956/E2/8.
6 GA D1956/E2/8.
7 Reeves, Marjorie, & Morrison, Jean, eds. *The Diary of Jeffery Whitaker, Schoolmaster of Bratton, 1739-1741*. Wiltshire Record Society, 44. 1989, p.36-7.
8 Fowler, Peter, & Blackwell, Ian. *The Land of Lettice Sweetapple: an English countryside explored*. Tempus, 1998, p.81 & 115.
9 Markham, Sarah. *John Loveday of Caversham, 1711-1789: the Life and Tours of an Eighteenth-Century Onlooker*. Michael Russell, 1984, p.315-6.

petitioned the House of Lords, complaining that 'the inhabitants of the parishes through which the highways run have neglected the highways with the design of exempting themselves and laying the burden upon petitioners and other travellers'.[1] Their petition was against a bill to turnpike a part of the London to Bath road closer to the capital, which would force them to pay tolls. There was much opposition to the introduction of turnpikes, including in Avebury, but it ultimately failed to achieve its object.

When the turnpike bill for the portion of the road passing through Beckhampton[2] was before Parliament in 1742/3, Robert Holford expressed his concern that the proposed change in route, which diverted the road from the village, would prejudice his nephew Stayner's estate. He thought that 'it will do your estate a great deal of prejudice, for it turns ye road quite from Abury, which must be a great disadvantage to ye village, & consequently I think to you, besides that what of your land may bee gone over in ye new road'.[3] Stayner sought the advice of his tenant, Peter Griffin, who laid his fears to rest, expressing to his landlord the opinion that it would 'be both to your advantage and mine', although he advised his landlord to attend the first meeting of the trustees.[4]

According to Stukeley, Griffin followed up the turnpiking by attempting (unsuccessfully) to stop traffic on the old route: 'they have of late endeavor'd to exclude travellers going upon it, by inclosing it at both ends with ditches, but the badness of the lower road has defeated their purpose, and made people still assert the public right'.[5] But the diversion did have an impact on the village. As we will see, the landlord of the Catherine Wheel, where Stukeley had stayed, removed his inn to the cross-roads at Beckhampton.

The old road had been used by Civil War armies. Mention has already been made of the Battle of Roundway Down, and the movements of Royalist troops preceding it. In April 1644, the Royalist army encamped for one night at Ogbourne, just a few mile to the east; later in the year they were at Fyfield.[6] In early 1645, the Lords Hopton and Goring led 3,000 men through

1 *Manuscripts of the House of Lords* N.S.12. HMSO, 1977, p.424.
2 It included the road from Marlborough to Shepherds Shore, from the Hare and Hounds to the top of Cherhill Hill, and from Beckhampton to the village of Avebury; cf. *London Gazette*, 22nd March 1742.
3 WSHC 184/1, pt.2. Robert Holford to Stayner Holford, 10th February 1742/3.
4 WSHC 1841/1, pt 2. Letters, 10.2.1742/3 & 6.3.1742/3. His conclusion was supported by Holford's successor several decades later; cf. WSHC 271/2. Valuation of Avebury property, 18th September 1780.
5 Cited by Ucko, Peter J., op cit, p.173.
6 Long, Charles Edward, ed. *Diary of the Marches of the Royal Army during the Great*

Devizes (and probably through Beckhampton) on their way to Bristol.[1] The 150 Parliamentarians who soon after marched from Marlborough to relieve Rowden House in Chippenham must also have passed through.[2] So, probably, did Sir James Long and his 400 dragoons when he was accompanying the Prince of Wales from Oxford to Bristol.[3] In 1685, James II's army marched through Avebury on its way to deal with Monmouth's rebellion.[4] It may be that James II's army marched this way when William of Orange invaded in 1688: one contingent was stationed at Marlborough.[5] A late eighteenth century commentator noted that, when 'the road to London, Bath &c was over the Downs [it was] much to the injury [of adjoining property] & often times breaking out upon the lands'.[6] That was a common problem: it was the 'good passage', rather than the 'beaten track' which legally constituted the highway, and consequently travellers were entitled to use the fields on either side of the road if the road itself was 'foundrous'.[7] Consequently, even fences and standing corn could be ridden over. William Skeat threatened to sue John Griffin in 1699 'for driveing over my grass'.[8] Damage may have been made worse as a result of the gradual extension of cultivation onto the Downs.[9] In 1794, the turnpike trustees recognized the damage that droving could do; they agreed to fence Mill Field at Kennett 'to prevent cattle trespassing therein'.[10] One can be sure that when Farmer Skeat, at the beginning of the eighteenth century, regularly drove cattle up to London,[11] he avoided damage to his own land on either side of Green Street. One wonders whether Richard Hickley, the bailiff, drove his sheep along Green Street when he took them to Marlborough market in November 1793. He paid 3s for sheep pens to hold them when

---

Civil War kept by Richard Symonds. Camden Society old series 74. 1859, p.3 & 151.

1 Waylen, James. *Chronicles of the Devizes, being a History of the Castle, Park, and Borough of that Name.* Longman & Co., 1839, p.145.
2 Waylen, *History*, op cit, p.147.
3 Waylen, *History*, op cit, p.215.
4 WSHC A1/110, 1685M, f.163.
5 Waylen, *Chronicles*, op cit, p.362. One contingent of James II's army was stationed at Marlborough.
6 WSHC 271/2. Note re Avebury estate.
7 Webb, Sidney & Beatrice. *The Story of the King's Highway.* English local government, 5. Frank Cass & Co., 1963, p.6.
8 WSHC 184/1, pt.1. Letter, William Skeat to Sir Richard Holford, 30th January 1698/9.
9 Jones, E.L. *Landscape History and Rural Society in Southern England.* Palgrave Macmillan, 2021, p.115-6.
10 WSHC 1471/1.
11 WSHC 184/8.

they arrived, but there is no accompanying toll recorded in his accounts for the turnpike.[1] In April 1797 Hickley paid toll of 4s to drive sheep along the turnpike. It must have been a large flock, but no corresponding sale price is recorded.[2]

A century earlier, in 1668, Pepys crossed the Downs with some trepidation, fearing that the coachman might lose his way – there were few tracks, and no signposts.[3] Even so, he recorded five coaches on it in one day.[4] Even in 1690, four coach services were available from Marlborough.[5] Some of the coaches on the road were private coaches. Sir Richard Holford usually travelled in his own coach when he came down from London in the early eighteenth century.[6] His coach house stood to the north of the present barn.[7] When he was suffering from a sore toe in 1717, and wanted to return from Bath to Avebury, he had to pay £3 for a horse litter.[8] His grandson, another Richard Holford, had his own coach when he died in 1742.[9] So, when he made his will in 1766, did his brother, Stayner Holford, who also had a 'post chariot'.[10] A 'chariot' was also mentioned by Stayner's half-brother in 1780.[11] There was a coach house at West Kennett in 1772,[12] which may still have housed the 'mourning coach' used to transport the body of Hannah Smith to Great Amwell (Hertfordshire) when she died in 1752.[13]

It was not just passenger traffic that was important. Even in the seventeenth century carriers were operating regular services. By the end of the seventeenth century, pack-horse services were dying out, although one was still operating from Marlborough in 1690. Waggon services were much more numerous; no fewer than nine operated from both Chippenham and Devizes.[14] Some of these services passed through Avebury; In 1695, for example, Daniel

1 WSHC 184/7.
2 WSHC 184/7.
3 Pepys, op cit, p.240-41.
4 Parslew, op cit, p.37.
5 Gerhold, Dorian. *Carriers and Coachmasters: Trade and Travel before the Turnpikes.* Phillimore, 2005, p.181.
6 WSHC 184/8.
7 WSHC 184/4. Plan of the house, gardens and barton, 1695.
8 GA D1956/E2/8.
9 TNA PROB 11/721/329.
10 TNA PROB 11/932/345.
11 WSHC 271/2. Valuation of Avebury property, 18th September 1780.
12 WSHC 118/88. Draft indenture, 1772.
13 TNA PROB 11/795/275.
14 Gerhold, Dorian. *Carriers and Coachmasters: Trade and Travel before the Turnpikes.* Phillimore, 2005, p.181.

Want of Devizes almost certainly travelled through Avebury on his weekly service to London.[1] The road had long been used by clothiers to transport their goods to London. At the beginning of the Civil War, John Ashe of Freshford regularly organized convoys of carriers to take cloth up to London;[2] they would have passed through Beckhampton. That was dangerous; at least one clothiers' convoy suffered the depredations of both Royalist and Parliamentary troops on their journey.[3] It is probable that Ashe suspended his own trading between 1643 and 1645.[4]

Cheese was another important commodity regularly sent to London. When the lord of the manor became governor of Jamaica in the early 1790s, his bailiff, Richard Hickley, frequently sent goods such as food, beer, garden seeds, shoes, and even dogs, to go on board ship at Bristol. He also purchased wine and coal in Bristol to bring back to Avebury. Hickley occasionally drove the waggon himself, thus saving the cost of carriage. He frequently had business to attend to in Bath, and, in the other direction, in Hungerford.[5]

Carriers regularly travelled the roads in all directions. Letters from London were frequently left for collection at shops and inns in Marlborough. For example, Sir Richard Holford directed that a 1706 letter for John White, the vicar, was to be left with Mr Bailey, a Marlborough mercer. In 1709 Holford could not remember whether he had directed a letter for Richard Chandler to be left at the Half Moon or the Post House in Marlborough.[6] In 1710 he promised to direct letters to his new tenant to be left with Mr Kimber, a Marlborough grocer.[7] In July 1791, Richard Hickley 'paid the postmaster for letters forwarded to London' 1s 9d.[8] Sometimes, letters were taken by local people visiting London; for instance, a letter from Sir Richard Holford to Archdeacon Yeate in 1698 was carried by Humphry Wall, who was a Marlborough attorney.[9] Mr Norris, a local landowner, similarly carried letters

---

1   Ibid, p.19 & 53-4, citing TNA C8/556/7.
2   Wroughton, op cit, p.154 & 156.
3   Waylen, *History*, op cit, p.228-9.
4   Gaisford, John, ed. *Clothiers and Merchants in Spanish Cloth:1627-1665: the Ashe family of Somerset, Wiltshire and London, and their account books.* Somerset Record Society, 101. 2023, p.21.
5   WSHC 184/6.
6   WSHC 184/4, pt.2. Sir Richard Holford to Richard Chandler, 21st July 1709.
7   WSHC 184/1, pt.2. Sir Richard Holford to John Rose, 7th June 1710.
8   WSHC 184/7.
9   WSHC 184/1, pt.1. Letter, Sir Richard Holford to Archdeacon Yates, 14th July 1698

for him.[1] That was safer than sending them by carrier. Letter writers could be cautious in what they wrote: William Smith commented that 'I have not wrought everything distinctly for fear of miscarriage'.[2] And letters sometimes never arrived. Indeed, Peter Griffin was extremely concerned in 1743 when an important letter did not arrive. He had sent his landlord, Stayner Holford a letter with a bill for £50, and 'expected to hear in your last letter that you receved it, but as you said nothing of it, I fear it is fawlen into bad hands through the neglect of some postmaster'.[3] By 1788, the postal service had improved, so much so that post could be delivered to Avebury Manor every morning.[4]

A wide variety of other goods were also carried; for example, in 1781 Arthur Jones bought a box of 'best crown soap' in Bristol, and had to pay 10d for its carriage to Avebury.[5] The accounts of Richard Hickley in the 1790s are full of payments for carriage of goods; for example, in September 1792 he paid 11s 3d for 'carriage of two hampers from London'; the following month he paid 5s 10d for the 'carriage of 2 tables from Portsmouth'.[6] We may assume that when he 'gave the coachman' 2s 'to forward a box to Falmouth' In January 1795, it was being sent to his master, General Williamson, in Jamaica.[7]

Like letters, goods sometimes mis-carried. Sir Richard Holford complained in 1711 that a basket sent by coach from Mr Green had not arrived. What was in it we do not know.

Carriers were operating on the Marlborough to Bristol road at least as early as 1614, when John Parker, travelling towards Devizes, met Mr Johnson, a Bristol carrier, on his way to London.[8] Carriers were also operating between local market towns; in 1622, John Weaver, a labourer of Coate (in the neighbouring parish of Bishops Cannings), applied to Quarter Sessions for permission to be a carrier, since he could not find any other work. It is unlikely that he had sufficient money to purchase one of the substantial waggons that were by then being increasingly used.[9] Carriers in the sixteenth century had used two wheeled carts. By the early seventeenth century, they were being replaced by heavy four wheeled waggons with broad wheels and hooped canvas

1   WSHC 184/1, pt.1. Letter, Sir Richard Holford to William Skeat, c.1698.
2   WSHC 184/1, pt.1. Letter, William Smith to Sir Richard Holford, 6th July 1700.
3   WSHC 184/1, pt.2. Letter, Peter Griffin to Stayner Holford, 23rd April 1743.
4   WSHC 271/2. Note re Avebury manor, c.1788.
5   WSHC 184/5. Bill for soap from Robert Fletcher of Bristol, 1781.
6   WSHC 184/7.
7   WSHC 184/7.
8   WSHC A1/110, 1614M, f.132.
9   WSHC A1/110, 1622M. f.149.

tops;[1] one led by three horses is depicted on Stukeley's 1724 plan of Avebury. Waggons were generally drawn by a number of horses walking in single file, with the wagonner walking beside them. The roads were generally too narrow for horses to walk side by side with the wagonner beside them,[2] as can be seen even today by walking westward along the (now deserted) turnpike road from Shepherd's Shore.

In 1698/9, William Skeat intended to send bacon and turkey to Sir Richard Holford in London by the Calne carrier, but discovered they had actually been sent by the Marlborough carrier. He evidently had a choice of carriers.[3] Carriers needed good roads. Waggoners travelling from Bristol to London in 1708 complained of the 'badness of the roads, and petitioned Quarter Sessions for permission to use an extra two horses to pull their waggons on hills. 'Cherill Hill' and 'Graywethers Hill', on either side of Avebury, were particularly named.[4] A heavy wagon drawn by perhaps a dozen horses was likely to take five days on the journey from Bath to London, perhaps taking a day to travel from Pickwick, through Beckhampton, to Marlborough.[5] The fact that the earliest turnpikes on the Bath Road were at the clothing towns of Devizes, Bath and Calne emphasizes the importance of roads to the cloth trade.[6] Roads and tracks in Avebury were probably similar to those at Kington St Michael, a few miles away, which were experienced by the antiquary, John Britton, in his youth. 'Being only used by wagons and carts, they were worn into two deep ruts by the wheels, and another equally deep by the horses'.[7]

On leaving Avebury, the coach road turned south-west towards Beckhampton, rather than going straight on down Bray Street and through Westbrook.[8] The area immediately to the west of the village was marshy and frequently inundated, and so unsuitable for coach traffic, despite the bridge erected in 1701. Indeed, the road to Devizes, probably where it crossed

1 Wilson, Avice. *Forgotten Harvest: the Story of Cheesemaking in Wiltshire*. The author, 1995, p.97. Gerhold, op cit, p.4.
2 Gerhold, Dorian. *Carriers and Coachmasters: Trade and Travel before the Turnpikes*. Phillimore, 2005, p.50 & 116.
3 WSHC 184/1, pt.1. Letter, William Skeat to Sir Richard Holford, 23rd February 1698/9.
4 WSHC A1/110, 1708M. Petition of Francis Braithwaite, Henry Norman, and Francis Done.
5 Stedman, op cit, p.293.
6 Buchanan, Brenda J. 'The Great Bath Road, 1700-1830', *Bath history* 4, 1992, p.73-4.
7 Britton, John. *The autobiography of John Britton*. 1850, p.33.
8 For a detailed account of the Bath Road, placing Beckhampton and Avebury in their context, see Phillips, op cit, passim.

the Winterbourne, was so inundated with water that it was said to be very dangerous in 1715.[1] Other local roads were also important. The Ridgeway had once been an important long distance route. Even in 1919, there were men who could still remember the day when 'coal came from South Wales along the Ridgeway by waggon'.[2] Nevertheless, it had declined to importance, and its traffic in Avebury had largely diverted to the road in the valley running due north from the Megalith. This was turnpiked in 1767.[3] Sir Richard Holford occasionally used local roads to travel to his other manors at Westonbirt and Wells, and to Bath, where he could meet 'Society'.[4] He noted that the route to Westonbirt via Christian Malford and Sutton Draycott was 'somewhat nearer & at summer a better way than by Calne & Chipenham'. Presumably in winter that route was less easy to pass in a coach.

The new turnpike, authorised by Act of Parliament in 1743,[5] provided the final link in the road to the West, from London to Bristol; it joined Marlborough to Cherhill.[6] It was not, however, a new road. It was in fact roughly on the line of the old Roman road. In 1705 it had been described as the 'great road'.[7] It seems likely that it was the increasing amount of wheeled traffic in the late seventeenth and early eighteenth century that caused it to be out of repair.[8] Stukeley noted that 'this was the post and coach road to the Bath, til for want of reparation they were forc'd to find a new one, more northward upon the downs, and farther about thro' the town of Abury'.[9] It was not until the more southerly route was turnpiked that it began to be used again as the main coach road. By 1755, coaches to Bath had deserted Green Street; much of it became a mere trackway.[10] That portion in West Overton and Fyfield was officially described as 'a public bridleway and private … carriage road' in 1814.[11]

1 WSHC A1/110, 1715M. Grand jury presentment.
2 Vincent, James Edmund. *Highways and byways in Berkshire*. Macmillan & Co., 1919, p.193.
3 *VCH Wilts.*, 12, p.89.
4 WSHC 184/8.
5 16 George II, c.10. See *VCH* 4 for later acts.
6 Albert, William. *The Turnpike Road System in England, 1663-1840*. Cambridge University Pres, 1972, p.37.
7 Fowler, P.J. *Landscape Plotted and Pieced: Landscape History and Local Archaeology in Fyfield and Overton, Wiltshire*. Society of Antiquaries of London, 2000, p.22.
8 Cochrane, C. *The Lost Roads of Wessex*. David & Charles, 1969, p.112.
9 Ucko, op cit, p.173.
10 Parslew, op cit, p.42.
11 Bowen, H.C., & Fowler, P.J. 'The Archaeology of Fyfield and Overton Downs, Wilts', *WAM*, 58, 1962, p.115

To the west, the original route to Bath led from Beckhampton through Shepherd's Shore and Sandy Lane. This had been turnpiked in 1713.[1] Its trustees were naturally opposed when a new road across Cherhill Down was proposed several decades later. They advertised in the *Bath Journal*, complaining that the Sandy Lane route had been 'falsely and maliciously represented … as being in a bad condition', when in fact it was 'in the best repair imaginable'.[2] Their opposition was vigorously supported by Walter Grubbe, lord of the manor of Cherhill,[3] but nevertheless did not succeed. After the new turnpike across Cherhill was opened in 1745, and joined up with the new turnpike from Beckhampton to Marlborough, the old route lost most of its traffic; its trustees ceased to operate in 1755.[4]

The Beckhampton trustees initially erected gates outside of the Hare and Hounds; its proprietor collected the tolls. In 1765, however, it was decided that this was unacceptable, and the innkeeper had to resign as collector.[5] A new tollhouse was built on the opposite side of the road. By the early nineteenth century – possibly earlier – the tolls were being let by the trustees. There were also two tollhouses in the village of Avebury, one on the corner of the road leading to Berwick Bassett, and the other at the entrance to the village from West Kennett.[6] The trustees of the Beckhampton turnpike erected milestones along the whole length of their roads; a few are still in situ.[7]

When Rev. John Whitaker rode through the parish in 1772, he 'expected the Bath Road to have gone through' the village, but discovered the diversion just mentioned.[8] He asked for the 'little inn' that Stukeley had stayed in, but discovered that 'it had long since been shut up', and that the nearest inn was at Beckhampton. It was evidently not explained to him that, in 1745, the innkeeper at the old Catherine Wheel had built a new inn at the Beckhampton cross-roads, also called the Catherine Wheel, to take advantage

---

1 Phillips, op cit, p.36.
2 Cited by Baines, Richard. *A History of Chippenham from Alfred to Brunel*, ed. Tony Pratt, Mike Stone, & Kay Taylor. Chippenham Civic Society, 2009, p.149.
3 Waylen, *History*, op cit, p.406.
4 Phillips, op cit, p.81.
5 See below, p.319.
6 WSHC A1/205/3. See also Haynes, Robert, & Slocombe, Ivor. *Wiltshire toll houses*. Hobnob Press, 2004, p.6-8. A fourth tollhouse was erected at Beckhampton in 1857. See also Wadsworth, Alan, ed. *The Farming Diaries of Thomas Pinniger, 1813-1837*. Wiltshire Record Society 74. 2021, p.cxxi-iii.
7 Described by British Listed Buildings https://britishlistedbuildings.co.uk
8 Nichols, John. *Illustrations of the literary history of the eighteenth century, vol.IV*. John Nichols & Son, 1822, p.855.

of coaches passing along the turnpike. They needed accommodation and food for travellers, and changes of horses. There was sufficient traffic to justify two inns: the Bear[1] was built in 1669, before the turnpike, to cater for drovers; its accommodation included pasture for cattle.[2] This is presumably the field called Folly Hill Inclosure on the 1795 enclosure map. Iolo Morganwg, the Welsh bard, probably stayed in one of these inns on his journey to Bristol in December 1776 or January 1777. Silbury Hill aroused his interest, and he asked 'an intelligent shepherd' for information about the Duke of Northumberland's recent excavation.[3]

Both inns continued to operate into the nineteenth century. In 1835, the conversion of the Catherine Wheel into racing stables began, although it continued to operate until at least 1849.[4] Its final closure as an inn was probably due to the opening of the railway from London to Bristol in 1841, which put an end to the coaching trade.[5] The Bear (by then the Hare and Hounds), however, survived, and is still open as the Waggon and Horses.

The turnpike attracted an increasing amount of traffic. It facilitated, for example, the introduction of fast Royal Mail coaches from Bath to London in 1784.[6] At least one Avebury man found employment on them: Stephen Dean was described as a 'guard to the night coaches' when he married in 1786.[7] In the late eighteenth century, the road from Cherhill to Silbury became 'crowded with coaches, post-chaises, private carriages, express waggons, slow waggons, etc'.[8] By 1798, three coaches left the Castle Inn in Marlborough every day for Bath. Coaches also ran daily from both the Duke's Arms and the Black Swan; there were a number of less frequent services from other inns, as well as the mail coaches.[9] Nineteen passenger coaches, and four mail coaches, were passing through Reading every day, traveling between London and Bath.[10] All of these coaches presumably ran through Beckhampton. It was also possible to hire a

1 See above, p.320, for its later names.
2 See below, p.320.
3 Cannon, Jon, & Constantine, Mary-Ann. 'A Welsh Bard in Wiltshire: Iolo Morganwg, Silbury, and the Sarsens', *WAM* 97, 2004, p.78.
4 Wadsworth, Alan, ed. *The Farming Diaries of Thomas Pinniger, 1813-1837.* Wiltshire Record Society 74. 2021, p.lxxii-lxxiii.
5 Wadsworth, op cit, p.cxxiii.
6 Postal Museum: Mail Coaches. www.postalmuseum.org/discover/collections/mail-coaches
7 Parish register.
8 Marsh, A.E.W. *History of the Borough and Town of Calne.* Calne: Robert S. Heath, 1903, p.283.
9 *VCH Wilts.,* 12, p.209.
10 Dils, Joan. *Reading: a History.* Carnegie Publishing, 2019, p.161.

chaise (a small closed carriage for two passengers) to travel privately.[1] In 1778, Arthur Jones did so on several occasions to travel to Bath and Chippenham.[2] The coaching trade expanded considerably in the late eighteenth century; the invention of steel springs for coaches, together with continually improving turnpike roads, meant that coaches could go faster.[3] One day journeys between Bath and London were established in 1761.[4] The popularity of Bath as a resort meant that the number of services on the road through Beckhampton were steadily increasing; by 1768, Glasier & Co., the Bristol coachmasters, were running no fewer than twelve services per week to London.[5]

In the nineteenth century, we know that many carriers passed through Avebury on their way to market in Devizes, Marlborough, and further afield; they carried many small packages for their customers[6]. Many purchases made by the owners of Avebury manor required separate carriage; for example, the load of tiles purchased by Arthur Jones on 16th June 1781 had to be carried from Marlborough, at the cost of 14s.[7] In June 1793, Richard Hickley paid 'James Porter the carrier's bill', amounting to 12s 6d; it is not clear what that was for.[8] The road was frequently used to attend official and other meetings at the Catherine Wheel, situated at the cross roads.[9] Other venues for meetings were further away: the creditors of John Griffin Grant, another Avebury bankrupt, had to travel to the Black Bear,[10] in Devizes, to receive their dividends from his estate in 1771[11] and 1772.[12] Drovers probably preferred not to use the turnpike.[13] They may have used the pasture provided at the Bear in Beckhampton, but their cattle preferred to walk on un-metalled roads, perhaps via Green Street, or along the Ridgeway. The idea of paying to use the road also deterred them.

1   Phillips, op cit, p.87.
2   WSHC 184/5. Bill of J.Williams, 1778.
3   Gerhold, Dorian. *Bristol's stage coaches*. Hobnob Press, 2012, p.44-6.
4   Ibid, p.44.
5   Ibid, p.60.
6   Greening, Alan. 'Nineteenth century carriers in North Wiltshire', *WAM*, 66, 1971, p.163 & 166.
7   WSHC 184/5. Thomas Palmer's bill for tiles, etc., 1781.
8   WSHC 184/7.
9   *Northampton Mercury* 25th October 1779. See also below, p.150.
10 One of the principal inns in Devizes; cf. Maudlin, D. 'The urban inn: gathering space, hierarchy and material culture in the eighteenth-century British town', *Urban History*, 46(4), p.617-48. Digitised at http//hdl.handle.net/10026.1/1291.
11 *Northampton Mercury*, 30th December 1771.
12 *Kentish Gazette* 18th July 1772.
13 Webb, Sydney & Beatrice Webb. *The Story of the King's Highway*. Longmans Green & Co, 1920, p.69.

Nevertheless, in 1830, no fewer than 14,500 Irish pigs passed through the turnpike gate at Beckhampton on their way to London.[1]

The open road could be dangerous, especially in bad weather. Parslew notes that 'more than once villagers have toiled up the hill to rescue the occupants of an overturned coach, sometimes, sadly, arriving too late to save the lives of horses or travellers'.[2] In February 1770, the wind was so strong on Cherhill Hill that a coachman was blown off his box.[3] On February 2nd, 1836 (admittedly after the end of our period) the coaches from London were 'nearly buryed' by snow near Beckhampton, so much so that two ladies were forced to remain in one of them overnight. There was 'no possibility of getting to the coach with any conveyance to bring them away'.[4] Between 1764 and 1788, six deaths on the road were reported to the coroner.[5] Most were not local men: in 1768, 'a man unknown fell from the limber of a broad-wheel waggon, as was imagined asleep. The waggon went over him and killed him on the spot'.[6] The only local man to suffer in this way was James Pope in 1772; he 'fell from his horse and was instantly crushed to death by the wheels of a stage waggon'.[7] The death of William Hinton of Shepton Mallet does not seem to have been reported to the coroner. His cart overturned between Beckhampton and Shepherds Shore in 1788, and he was found dead under the cart.[8] Working with horses was a dangerous occupation; it resulted in nine of the fifteen Avebury deaths which the coroner investigated in the second half of the eighteenth century.[9]

There was also a danger from thieves, despite the ominous presence of a gibbet on the Downs between Beckhampton and Cherhill.[10] In 1783, John Brookes, travelling 'on the highway in the parish of Avebury', was assaulted and robbed of four shillings in silver. His supposed assailant, Stephen Powell (who also went by the name of Charles Coleman), was charged and committed

---

1 Bonser, op cit, p.57.
2 Parslew, op cit, p.38.
3 *Bath Journal* 12th February 1770, cited in *Beckhampton: a Village through Time.* [Jane Brunning], 2000, p.18., and in Phillips, op cit, p.68-9.
4 Wadsworth, Alan, ed. *The Farming Diaries of Thomas Pinniger, 1813-1837.* Wiltshire Record Society 74. 2021, p,264.
5 Hunnisett, op cit, passim.
6 Hunnisett, op cit, no.603.
7 Hunnisett, op cit, no.785. This is probably the death referred to in the *Salisbury and Winchester Journal* 30th November 1772.
8 *Salisbury and Winchester Journal* 9th June 1788.
9 Hunnisett, op cit, passim.
10 Stedman, op cit, p.296.

to Fisherton Gaol.[1] The Royal Mail was robbed in 1770 somewhere on this road, and the supposed perpetrator – John Franklin – was executed and hung in chains, despite maintaining his innocence to the end.[2] The *Bath Chronicle* reported that thousands assembled on the Downs to watch his execution. In 1790, two carters taking corn to Devizes market were robbed and 'very ill treated' by two footpads whilst crossing Beckhampton Down.[3] In 1798, a mare was stolen from Mr Jefferys's stables at Beckhampton. He offered a reward of five guineas for the apprehension of the thief. [4]

There were a number of other trackways connecting Avebury to surrounding villages. Some of these were disputed. There was, for example, a track through the fields at Beckhampton, which in 1711 was regularly being used by 'heavy carriages', travelling between Devizes and Marlborough. Sir Richard Holford thought that use was 'very injurious' to the growing crops; he claimed it was an 'ancient pack and padway', not a 'common wagon and cartway', and wanted to stop its mis-use. [5] We do not know whether he was able to do so, but it is likely that the turnpike solved the problem. Perhaps this was the 'French Way' which (presumably) bypassed the Bear, and which the rector, James Mayo, threatened to re-open in 1753 when he thought the innkeeper was in a 'state of damnation'.[6]

The turnpike was not the only improved means of communication projected for Avebury in our period. The projectors of the Kennett and Avon Canal (who included, in 1789, Arthur Jones, the lord of Avebury manor)[7] were also considering a route through Avebury when they advertised their intention to seek an act of Parliament in 1790.[8] Adam Williamson was asked for his consent for the route to pass through his lands,[9] but, in the end, the canal followed a more southerly route. That was described by John Ward, Williamson's agent (and also the principal clerk of the Canal company)[10] as 'a great disappointment to us'.[11] Ward, however, was conflicted in his loyalties,

1 *Bath Chronicle and Weekly Gazette* 17th April 1783.
2 *Bath Chronicle* 26th April 1770. See also WANHS mss.2628.
3 *Reading Mercury* 26 April 1790
4 *Reading Mercury* 09 April 1798
5 GA D1956/E2/8.
6 WSHC 184/1, pt.1. Letter, James Mayo to William Fowler, 10 July 1753.
7 Berry, Warren. *The Kennet and Avon Navigation: a History.* Phillimore, 2009, p.12.
8 *Reading Mercury* 30th August 1790; 13th September 1790; *Bath Chronicle and Weekly Gazette* 9th September 1790; 16th September 1790; 23rd September 1790.
9 WSHC 184/6. Letter, Adam Williamson to Richard Hickley, undated.
10 Berry, Warren. *The Kennet and Avon Navigation: a History.* Phillimore, 2009, p.18.
11 WSHC 184/6. Letter, John Ward to General Williamson, 20th September 1793.

and also acknowledged in a letter to the Earl of Ailesbury that 'the superiority of the Pewsey line in every point of view is apparent'.[1] Williamson's bailiff, Richard Hickley, had no doubts: he thought that 'wee country farmers want no canals near us'.[2]

The manor of Avebury, extending to over 1400 acres, consisted mainly of Avebury Great Farm, which occupied much of the parish, especially in the east. It included the 211 acres of Hackpen Common, and a number of other extensive commons in the east of the parish. From there it extended through the village, and then mostly along the southern side of Bath Road towards Beckhampton. There were a number of out-lying fields south of Beckhampton, and another outlying area of downland on the far western side of the parish[3].

In 1788, the manor of Avebury was described as 'situated in one of the most favoured countys in the Kingdom for to have landed property in & for residence within four score miles of London, surrounded with turnpike roads which lead to every part of the Kingdom', including 'three or four market towns at small distances'.[4] The commentator, like most antiquarians, and, more recently, most archaeologists, paid little attention to the people who actually lived there.

Local history is about local people. What, then, of the people who lived in the houses built of sarsen stone? What of the Robinsons, the Griffins, and others whose hard work destroyed the stones? What of Reuben Horsell, the parish clerk, and Mr Robert Holford, neither of whom were happy with the destruction?[5] What of the other landlords, who, according to Stukeley, could have easily put a stop to the 'vile' destruction?[6] What of the farmers, the clergy, and the labourers, who carried on with their daily lives oblivious to the destruction? We have heard a great deal from numerous writers about prehistoric man at Avebury. Not a lot has been written about the people who actually lived there when the prehistoric monuments were being destroyed.[7] This book is devoted to their stories.

1 Corfield, Michael. 'John Ward and the Kennett and Avon Canal', *BIAS Journal* 14,1981 p.32
2 WSHC 184/6. Letter, Richard Hickley to Mrs Williamson, 4th June 1793.
3 WSHC 1553/71.
4 WSHC 271/2.
5 Stukeley, *Abury*, op cit, p.25.
6 Lukis, op cit,p.247.
7 The most substantial work covering our subject is Jane Freeman's chapter on Avebury in *VCH Wilts.*, 12.

John Aubrey, from Britton's Memoir of John Aubrey

William Stukeley (courtesy Wikimedia)

Reuben Horsell, parish clerk

Thomas Robinson, stone destroyer

Stukeley's view of Avebury

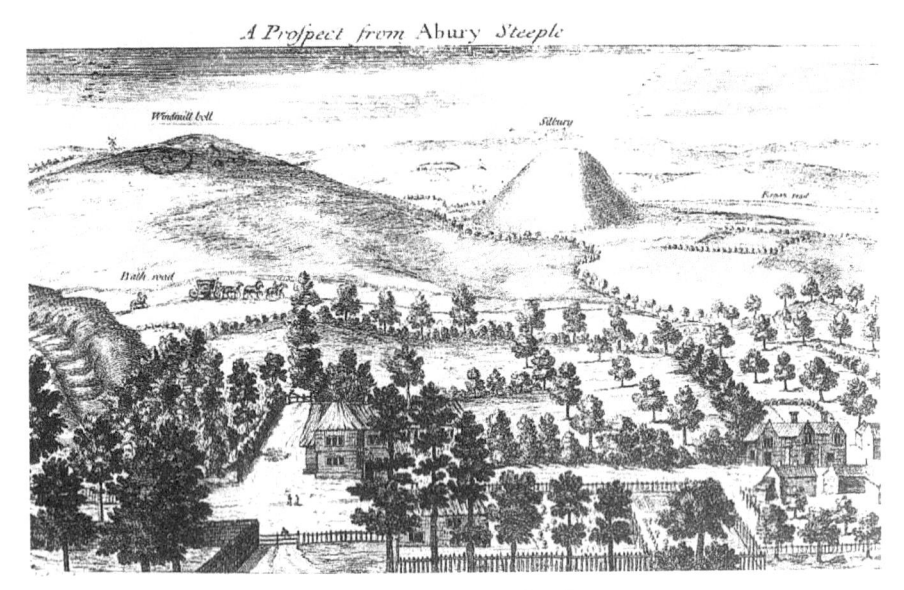

Stukeley's view from the Church Tower

Avebury Manor

The Bear (now the Waggon and Horses)

The Dovecote at Avebury Manor

Green Street

Sheep at Avebury: the mainstay of the economy

The 15th century rood screen

The Dissenters' Chapel

2
THE DEMOGRAPHY OF AVEBURY: PEOPLE AND POPULATION

REASONABLY ACCURATE STATISTICS of population are not available to the Avebury historian until 1801. In that year, the census reveals there were 115 houses in the parish, occupied by 291 males and 299 females (although the enumeration district did not cover the whole parish).[1] It was the second largest parish in the Hundred of Selkley; numbers were only exceeded by Aldbourne, which had a population of 1280. Certainly, throughout our period, Avebury's population was larger than that of most other parishes on the Marlborough Downs.

There are earlier estimates, although the 1662 hearth tax figures may be discounted[2] in the light of the 1676 Compton census. This states that there were 181 conformists and 25 dissenters in the parish, making a total of 206.[3] These were probably adults aged over 16. Assuming that children under 16 constituted 40% of the population, the total population would have been c.417. In the mid-1730s, the inhabitants were counted again in order to petition the bishop against the vicar's non-residence. The population of Avebury was said to be 329, of Beckhampton, 64, and of West Kennett, 51, making a total

---

1 www.histpop.org. There were also 5 unoccupied houses.
2 TNA E179/259/29. This is almost certainly incomplete, and enumerates only 16 taxpayers in Avebury and Beckhampton. It does not include those who were exempt. A decade later, the numbers who were exempt exceeded the number of taxpayers. The 1670 exemption certificate (TNA E179/348) lists 19 exempt households, and another undated list (of roughly the same date) identifies 8 paupers whose names do not occur on the certificate. There were 24 names on the 1674 exemption certificate.
3 Whiteman, Ann, ed. *The Compton Census of 1676: a Critical Edition*. Records of Social and Economic History new series 10. Oxford University Press, for the British Academy, 1986, p.129. Turner, G.Lyon. *Original records of Early Nonconformity under Persecution and Indulgence*. T.Fisher Unwin, 1911, p.132. WSHC D1/27/1/4/66, f.16.

of 444.[1] The only other evidence for population in our period is provided by the parish register. Unfortunately, only a few entries survive from before c.1665. However, dissent in the parish after the Restoration means that the parish register evidence for baptisms and marriages appears to be incomplete, even for those periods when dissenting baptisms (1694-1705, and 1783-94) should have been entered to comply with the government's demand for taxes on baptisms. Only after the 1753 Marriage Act, which ended legal recognition of dissenting marriages, are marriage entries likely to include all marriages. The number of marriages registered does increase dramatically after this date. There were a mere 11 marriages in the 1740s, but 36 in the 1750s – including 9 in 1759 alone. In the following years there were at least 38 marriages in each decade until 1800.

The number of burials registered provides a more useful guide to demography than marriages registered. Dissenters had no alternative to burial in the churchyard, so registered burials can be used to calculate decadal death rates between 1670 until 1800. The number of deaths in this period were as follows:

1670s	55	1720s	139	1760s	135
1680s	82	1730s	82	1770s	107
1690s	100	1740s	90	1780s	133
1700s	88	1750s	94	1790s	107
1710s	74				

Despite the fluctuations, the long-term trend revealed by these figures was upwards; after the 1670s, burials always exceeded the number recorded in that decade; in the last four decades of the eighteenth century they always exceeded 100 per decade. The numbers reflected a population increasing in fits and starts towards the numbers recorded in 1801. Unfortunately, they are too late to reflect the impact of dearth and famine in the late sixteenth and early seventeenth centuries.[2] But they do reflect the impact of plague (probably smallpox).

We know very little about disease in Avebury in the sixteenth and seventeenth centuries, although it is unlikely to have escaped the impact of the plague outbreak which hit Marlborough, Calne, and Devizes in 1603. There

1   WSHC D1/47/3.
2   On this, see Gray, Todd, ed. *Harvest Failure in Cornwall and Devon: the Book of Orders and the Corn Surveys of 1623 and 1630-31*. Institute of Cornish Studies, 1992.

were several other severe outbreaks in Marlborough between 1593 and 1610,[1] and probably later in the seventeenth century. In 1637, plague necessitated the cancellation of the annual fair at Tan Hill.[2] Devizes suffered a particularly severe outbreak in 1644.[3] The Devizes Chamberlain's account book records at least six payments made in consequence of plague between 1627 and 1646, including three payments made in consequence of outbreaks in Calne between 1637 and 1642,[4] which were also mentioned in the Michaelmas 1639 Quarter Sessions roll.[5] Plague had an impact on mobility, as well as on mortality. Restrictions on movement imposed in 1603 had considerable impact on attendance at the ecclesiastical courts.[6] Unfortunately, Avebury's parish register for most of the seventeenth century is lost, so we cannot assess the impact of these epidemics on the parish.

For the eighteenth century, we have slightly more information directly from Avebury, and not just from the parish register. Smallpox was said to be 'very busye in ye country', in January 1701,[7] and 'much increase[d] in ye countery & very mortall' a month later.[8] Although the letters which give us this information were written in Avebury, the parish itself seems to have escaped this epidemic: there were only five burials in 1701. Neither do we hear anything concerning the epidemic of 1717, when Sir Richard Holford avoided staying in Marlborough because 'the small pox is very busye there'.[9] It was, however, hit by an epidemic of plague in 1719. 23 parishioners were buried in that year, and an all time high of 26 in 1720. The epidemic was recorded by the rector, John Mayo, in a letter to Lady Holford dated 20th May 1720. He noted that 'the burials at Avebury are ceas'ed, there having

---

1 Stedman, A.R. *Marlborough and the Upper Kennet country.* [Marlborough College?], 1960, p.131. For Quarter Sessions orders relating to the plague in 1603 see WSHC A1/110, 1603M, f.209.
2 Waylen, James. *A History, Military and Municipal of the Ancient Borough of Devizes.* Longman Brown & Co., 1859, p.192.
3 Waylen, James, et al. *The Annals of the Loyal and Ancient Borough of Devizes 1102-1900.* Devizes, 1988, unpaginated.
4 Waylen, *History,* op cit, p.192.
5 WSHC A1/110, 1639M, f.202.
6 Ingram, Martin. *Church Courts, Sex, and Marriage in England 1570-1640.* Cambridge University Press, 1990, p.350.
7 WSHC 184/1. Letter, William Smith to Sir Richard Holford, 11th January 1700/1.
8 WSHC 184/1. Letter, William Smith to Sir Richard Holford, 11th February 1700/1.
9 GA 1956/E2/8.

been no funeral for a week past, & nobody is dangerously ill'.[1] He was slightly premature; five further deaths occurred in June and July. Thereafter, it seems, the epidemic ceased. However, it may have burst out again in the late 1720s. There were 16 burials in 1727, 19 in 1728, and 22 in 1729. That compares to an average of seven in the previous decade. Plague undoubtedly reduced the number of marriages recorded in the parish register. There were 33 in the first decade of the eighteenth century, and 23 in the 1710s, but the number reduced dramatically to 14 in the 1720s.

Plague did not disappear in our period. Avebury mortality in the 1760s was probably not unconnected to the 1761 outbreak of plague in Devizes, when 80 townspeople died in the first four months of the year.[2]

Mortality from plague depended on contact with those who suffered from it. As has been seen, the constant comings and goings along the road from London to Bath and Bristol brought many people through the village, not least the King. It sometimes also brought the plague, which travelled with them. Although it is over five miles from any town, Avebury even in the seventeenth century was not cut off.[3] Indeed, the very fact that it was five miles from any town attracted dissenting ministers – and a dissenting congregation in consequence - after they were banned from living less than five miles from a corporate town in 1665. Its inhabitants could easily maintain contact with neighbouring towns and villages, and indeed with distant cities. Indeed, some landowners lived many miles away; Sir Richard Holford, who lived in Chancery Lane, London, visited Avebury every year. Credit in the form of mortgages or bonds might be obtained in Bristol. Executors sometimes had to travel to London to obtain probate. Yeomen and husbandmen had to take their produce to markets such as Marlborough, Devizes, or Tan Hill, and sometimes as far as Smithfield Market in London. Many young Avebury men travelled to London to take up apprenticeships. The poor could also travel long distances from or to Avebury seeking work – or begging. Overseas travel was not unknown; people with Avebury connections could be found as far afield as New England and India. Many of these travellers will be identified in the next chapter.

1   Mayo, Charles Herbert. *A genealogical account of the Mayo and Elton families of the counties of Wilts and Hereford.* Chiswick Press, 1882, p.43.
2   Goddard, E.H. 'Smallpox in Devizes in 1761', *WAM* 27(81), 1893, p.314.
3   For a study of the reasons Avebury men and women crossed the parish boundary, see Raymond, Stuart A. 'Crossing the Avebury Parish Boundary', *Local Historian*, 53(4), 2023, p.300-311.

3
AVEBURY PEOPLE AND FAMILIES

THIS BOOK IS primarily about the people of Avebury. It is therefore appropriate, before dealing with their economic and social circumstances, to ask who they were, and how they were connected with each other genealogically. This chapter will recount the stories of a number of families and individuals. Some were lords of manors and/or leading tenants. Some, such as the schoolmaster, the bell founder, and the destroyers of stones, were chosen because of what they did. Others were merely husbandmen or tradesmen. Yet others were labourers or paupers. Some were chosen, at least in part, because they were very well documented; for others the documentation is poor. The lack of documentation does prevent us from considering the lives of some families. For example, all that is known of Robert Heath, an Avebury labourer, is that his wife and daughter were both named Joanna (the younger Joanna was baptised 17th August 1735), that he stole turnips from the proprietor of the Catherine Wheel,[1] and that he was buried 9th December 1763. Similarly, nothing is known of John Chandler, who stole coins from Richard Alexander.[2] Lack of documentation does not necessarily mean that either Heath or Chandler were unimportant in parish life.

Much biographical information is also provided in other chapters of this book; for example, a number of innkeepers are considered in chapter 7, and clergy are dealt with in chapter 9. The families considered here include:

Amor	Cruse or Cuss	Hickley
Bailey	Currier	Hitchcock
Burry	Dunch	Holford
Caswell	Goldsmith	Horsell
Clements	Griffin	Jones
Crook	Hayward	Morris

1 WSHC A1/110, 1742M.
2 WSHC A1/110, 1790M.

Nalder	Rose	Tanner
Phelps als Bromham	Shuter	Tilly
Pontin	Skeat	Tomkins
Pope	Smith	Truslow
Reeves	Stawell	Williamson
Robinson	Stretch	Wiltshire

Amor

The Amor family were amongst the leading yeomen of Avebury in the last three decades of the eighteenth century. They were originally absentee landlords; land tax on 'Mr Amor's estate' was paid in 1751 by John Rose.[1] In 1772, Henry Amor was described as resident at Christian Malford, although his right to vote in the Parliamentary election of that year depended on his freehold property in Avebury. He was probably resident in the following year, when he served as churchwarden. He voted again, described as a yeoman, in 1775, but died c.1777. Henry left no will, but his estate was administered by William Amor, yeoman, of Avebury, who was probably one of his sons. The estate was evidently of substantial value, judging by the fact that William had to enter an administration bond for £3000 (bonds were usually double the estimated value of the estate).[2] Unfortunately, no other probate documents survive. William's bondsmen included John Amor, also described as 'of Avebury', who was probably his brother, together with two members of the Barnes family from Chirton and Manningford Bruce.

William Amor perhaps continued to reside in Christian Malford. His marriage took place there on 19th March 1773, and no further mention of him has been found in Avebury. His brother John, however, tenanted Mr Simpkins' (and subsequently Sir John Hopkins') property in Avebury from 1780 until at least the end of the century. When he renewed his lease in 1795, his rent was set at £250 per annum.[3] One wonders if this was the property his father had once occupied.

John Amor married Elizabeth Axford at St John's, Devizes, on 3rd December 1783. There were at least five children of this marriage, all baptised at Avebury between 1787 and 1802 (although some were baptised when they were five or six years old). Like his father, John served as churchwarden between 1781 and 1784, and again from 1788 until 1790. He served in a variety of other public roles: land tax assessor, Hundred Constable, and Grand Juryman.

1   WSHC 184/3.
2   WSHC P3/A/454.
3   WSHC 873/262.

But he escaped service as tithingman, despite being repeatedly named as a 'proper person' to fill that role between 1782 and 1794.

Richard Amor played a similar role in public life. He was probably related to John, but we know little about him, other than that he was regularly named on the freeholders' list between 1782 and 1799,[1] that in the 1780s and 1790s he was summoned to serve on juries at Quarter Sessions on several occasions, and that he was indicted (but found not guilty) for refusing to serve as High Constable in 1790.

Bailey[2]

When Elizabeth, the daughter of Richard and Ruth Bailey, was born on 1st September 1706, his parents did not ask the vicar, John White, to baptise her. But White did enter her name in his register of dissenters' children, and presumably collected the duty imposed on baptisms at that time by Parliament. Richard, Elizabeth's brother, born 12th February 1708/9, also had his name entered in White's register. Another brother, Moses, was not entered, but his burial is recorded in the parish register on 12th October 1705. Richard senior was buried 16th July 1710, although the vicar, John White, refused to conduct the funeral service of a dissenter.[3]

The children were probably baptised in Avebury's dissenting chapel, in which their parents played an important role. Richard senior was one of the signatories of the certificate applying for a meeting house licence when the chapel was built in 1707.[4] His son, Richard junior, also became a leading dissenter. When Caleb Bailey, lord of the manor of Berwick Bassett, and a prominent dissenter, created a charity for the support of dissenting ministers in his 1749 will,[5] he named Richard as one of the trustees. It is not clear whether Caleb was a relative. When Richard himself made his will in 1780, he bequeathed an annuity of two guineas to 'the present minister of the meeting house in Avebury and his successors'.[6]

1 WSHC A1/265/24-41.
2 There were several families of this name in eighteenth-century Avebury, but only one is studied here.
3 GA D1956/E2/8.
4 Chandler, J.H., ed. *Wiltshire Dissenters' Meeting House Certificates and Registrations, 1689-1852*. Wiltshire Record Society, 40. 1985, p.14.
5 TNA PROB11/782/93. The will was challenged by Caleb's cousin Edward Bailey, his heir at law if no will had been made; see TNA C 11/2124/5.
6 WSHC P3/B/1679.

Richard Bailey senior was a glazier, so described in 1697[1] and 1708.[2] In 1697, he was amongst the defendants against whom the vicar, John White brought a tithe case. In 1713, he was the lessee of a tenement, probably in West Kennett, owned by Richard Smith (the vicar's father in law).[3] In 1708, his wife, Ruth (nee Wallis) with her two sisters, jointly inherited a tenement, backside and garden in Eastbrook from their mother. It seems that, in order to untangle the inheritance, the property was sold to Caleb Bailey, and Richard senior became his tenant. However, when Ruth died in 1743/4, she bequeathed 'all my part, purparty, and proportion of all the tenement or cottage, backside, orchard, stable and garden which did belong to Elizabeth Wallis my mother deceased', to her daughter Elizabeth.[4] The three sisters were also mortgagees of Samuel Morris's tenement in Eastbrook, on part of which the dissenting chapel had been built. In 1724 Thomas Robinson, another dissenter, took over the mortgage, paying them £80.[5] Ruth was also the under-tenant of an orchard on the south side of High Street.[6] In 1738 she paid two shillings land tax.[7] It was probably on the same property that 'Mr Bailey' (probably Richard junior) paid two shillings for the house and window tax in 1757.[8]

Richard Bailey junior became a maltster. In 1775 he was owed £10 9s 4d for malt and hops by the estate of the late Samuel Martyn.[9] His will tells us that he held a copyhold estate in Ogbourne St George, and a freehold estate in Avebury. He also tenanted Mr Nalder's estate (Nalder was another leading dissenter), and paid land tax on his landlord's estate from at least as early as 1766.[10] In 1781, the last year in which he paid, the tax amounted to £1 18s 4d. Between 1747 and 1775 he regularly appeared on the list of freeholders liable to jury service at Quarter Sessions, and eligible to vote in Parliamentary

1   WSHC 1569/5.
2   WSHC 212A/31/3. Lease & release, 17/18th June 1708, by Richard Bailey et al, to Caleb Bailey et al.
3   WSHC 568/5, & 212B/110. Deeds 16/17th November 1713. Smith was the vicar's father in law.
4   WSHC P1/B/1164.
5   WSHC 529/185. Deed, 19th June 1724.
6   WSHC 873/261. Lease & release, 20/21st August 1736, William White to Samuel Morris.
7   WSHC 184/3.
8   WSHC 184/3.
9   WSHC 118/88.
10 WSHC 184/3. Land tax assessment, 1766. A1/345/18A. Land tax assessment 1781.

elections.[1] He served as high constable in 1755.[2] No marriage has been traced, nor have any children. He bequeathed his estate to his sister Elizabeth's children and step-children when he died in 1783.[3]

Elizabeth Bailey married James Thring of Wilton, according to the grant of probate for her mother's will.[4] She was his second wife; he already had other children, who are named in Elizabeth's 1802 will,[5] and also in her brother's will. James was another trustee of Caleb Bailey's charity, which is discussed further below.[6] His trusteeship, and that of Richard Bailey, both descended to James's son Richard Thring, who inherited his uncle's property at Avebury and Ogbourne St George. He probably also inherited through his mother the property once owned by Elizabeth Wallis.

Burry

Not all Avebury families are easy to trace, and very little is known of this family, apart from the fact that there seem to have been four or five individuals all named Adam Burry. Such a distinctive name suggests they were all related, although this cannot be proven. The Burry family can stand as an example of how fragmentary records for a particular family can sometimes be – although it may be that further research in other parishes would enable a more joined up pedigree to be constructed. The Burry's do seem to have crossed parish boundaries.

The first Adam Burry, and Frances his wife, had two daughters baptised at East Kennett, Elizabeth in 1671, and Mary in 1676. Ann Burroughs, described as the daughter of Adam, was buried at Wroughton in 1684, and may perhaps have been another of their children. It is possible that William Burry, husbandman, who leased a cottage in West Kennett from Richard Smith in 1698 for the lives of his wife Alice and his daughter Susanna, was a son.[7]

In 1683, another Adam Burry married Anne Nevil at East Kennett. When Anne died in 1685, she was referred to as the wife of Adam junior, so it is not impossible that this Adam was the son of Adam and Frances, especially in view of the fact that they named their daughter Frances. Sadly, mother and daughter were buried together at East Kennett on the same day, just two years after the marriage.

1 A1/265/16-21 & 23; A1/110, Michaelmas sessions 1747-71, 1774,1777, & 1779.
2 WSHC A1/110, 1755M.
3 WSHC P3/B/1679.
4 WSHC P1/B/1164.
5 WSHC P2/1802/64.
6 P.433-4.
7 WSHC 568/7 & 568/39. Lease, 5th November 1698.

We do not know whether Adam re-married. The next time the name appears in the records is when Adam Burry of East Kennett is named as surety when, in 1689, Thomas Burry of West Kennett had to enter a recognizance to answer accusations being made against him at Quarter Sessions by Joan Hancock of Overton.[1] Adam and Thomas were probably related, but we do not know how.

The Adam Burry who married Temperance Morris at Winterbourne Monkton in 1727 was probably related to his foregoing namesakes. The couple had nine children, born between 1728 and 1745/6. Three were baptised at East Kennett, and six at Avebury. There were three sons, William, Adam, and Thomas, but two died in childhood. Thomas, the survivor, married Susan Milsom in 1757; their children were baptised in Marlborough.[2] Their father owned a dwelling house in Avebury, which he sold to Thomas Hunter some time before the latter made his will in 1746/7.[3] By 1755, Temperance Burry, their grandmother, was probably a widow; her rent of 32s 6d per annum was being paid by the overseers.[4] One wonders whether Betty Burroughs, who had a bastard daughter by William Sumner of Seend in 1756, was a relative.[5]

Yet another Adam Burry, a shepherd married to Martha, joined with others to sell various rights in the common fields to Caleb Bailey in 1727.[6] We know nothing more of him. Perhaps it was his son, another Adam, who was employed as a child to scare birds by Stayner Holford in 1755.[7]

It is evident that the Burry family – if they were one single family – were poor. One was a husbandman, another a shepherd. One had a bastard, and one was a widow whose rent was paid by the overseers. One wonders what happened to the six daughters born to Adam and Temperance.

Caswell

The Caswells were substantial farmers in early eighteenth century Avebury, although they also had interests in other local parishes.[8] They were present

---

1 WSHC A110, 1689M, f.32.
2 Bury, Margaret G. *They came from Wiltshire: a History of the Burry family.* 1987, p.68 (pedigree 17).
3 WSHC P3/H/1256.
4 WSHC 184/3. List of house rents paid by the parish 1755.
5 WSHC 184/9/4.
6 WSHC 212A/31/3; 1409/16/3.
7 WSHC 271/4.
8 Caswell, Michael James. *Our Caswell Relatives, Book 2.* Palmyra: privately printed, 1994.

in Avebury as early as 1633, when Richard Caswell served as tithingman.[1] There is, however, only very limited evidence of the family in the parish before the eighteenth century. It seems likely that they had occupied property at Beckhampton as early as 1664, when Richard Caswell 'of Beckington' (that is, Beckhampton) served on a jury at Quarter Sessions.[2] There is little further evidence of this family in Avebury until 1709, when (probably) another Richard Caswell took a four year lease of Goddard's Farm, Truslow's Farm, the lands of the Free Chapel, and other property from Charles Tooker, paying £210 per annum rent.[3] Tooker retained two rooms and a stable for his own use. It was probably when he took this lease that Caswell married Hester Pope, the daughter of John Pope, a prominent dissenter.[4] In 1711 Richard was named as administrator of his father in law's estate, on his wife's behalf. Pope bequeathed a legacy of £20 to keep the Meeting House in repair; Richard was expected to act as trustee. When the vicar refused to bury Pope, Richard helped to bring an action against him for neglect of duty.[5]

Richard's parents were Robert and Mary Caswell.[6] In 1711, they were living at Cherhill, and described as 'aged'; they were anxious for their son to be closer [7] Richard therefore took another farm, and gave up his lease at Avebury, proposing that his uncle John Caswell of Bishops Cannings[8] should succeed him in his tenancy. By then, Sir Richard Holford had bought Tooker's property.[9] Holford had his doubts about his tenant's proposal,[10] but nevertheless, John Caswell took a lease from 1713.[11] His predecessor, however, was not free of liability for his care of the estate. He had foolishly taken his original lease without making sure that his then landlord, Charles Tooker, ensured that the property was properly repaired. That lease had also stipulated that he should not plough up more than two-thirds of the property in any one year, in order to ensure the farm's continued fertiity. Richard Caswell had not adhered to the

1 WSHC 9/1/153.
2 WSHC A1/110, 1664 M, f.111.
3 WSHC 371/1, pt.4. Lease, 16th April 1709.
4 WSHC P3/P/633.
5 WSHC D1/42/68. See below, p.428.
6 For Robert's 1626 will, see WSHC P3/C/139.
7 GA D1956/E2/8.
8 Holford's journal states he was of All Cannings, but the baptisms of his children at Bishops Cannings, and the property mentioned in his will at Bishops Cannings, suggest that Holford made a mistake.
9 WSHC 184/4/1. Charles Tooker's agreement to produce lease, 1710.
10 Discussed below, p.242-3.
11 WSHC 184/4/1. List of taxes allowed to John Caswell by Sir Richard Holford.

latter condition. Consequently, Holford as the new owner sought damages, and felt compelled to sue to obtain recompense. Eventually Caswell agreed to pay £10, although Holford thought that £50 'will not make mee satisfaction'.[1] Quite what the new tenant, John Caswell, thought of the behaviour of his nephew does not appear.

In addition to his new lease, John Caswell also owned freehold property in Bishops Cannings, which he mortgaged in 1726/7.[2] Seven of his children were baptised there between 1692 and 1704,[3] but he served as Avebury's churchwarden in 1720/21, and for three years from 1730.[4] His lease was regularly renewed, at the same rent, for many years. In 1730, William Caswell, one of John's sons, was said to be in possession,[5] although technically John was still lessee. He was, however, elderly and unwell, and probably unable to work. When he 'attorned' the premises to Samuel Holford, Sir Richard's heir, in 1731, he was unable to sign the deed because he had 'broke his right hand wrist & hurt his left sholder'.[6]

John died in 1735, and made his widow, Elizabeth, his executrix. She was given his freehold estate at Bishops Cannings as her dower; on her death it was to descend to his son Edmund, or, if he died, to Richard (another son). Richard also received a token bequest of five shillings, as did his brother Thomas. John's daughter, Mary Baskerville, received the same, as did her husband Francis. Another son, Michael, received £100, which was to be paid 'when my executrix ... shall think fit for him to have it'. John's grandchildren also received five shillings each. They included the children of two other sons not otherwise named in the will, John and William. John Pope, described as a 'son in law' also received a token bequest of five shillings, 'if he be living', suggesting that he and his un-named wife had moved away from Avebury and could not be easily contacted. It is not clear whether he was related to Hester Pope, who, as has been seen, married John Caswell's nephew Richard .

William was probably John senior's eldest son, which may be why he is not mentioned in John's will (his other children were). Between 1719 and 1739, he served on several Hundred court and Quarter Sessions juries, although he

1 GA D1956/E2/8.
2 WSHC 248/62.
3 Parry, Joseph Henry., ed. *The Registers of Bishops Cannings, Wiltshire.* Devizes: Gazette Printing Works, 1906.
4 WSHC D3/15/11; D1/50/13, f.35.
5 WSHC 371/1, pt.5. Conveyance, Samuel Holford to William Hunt, 17th December 1730.
6 WSHC 371/1, pt.5.

was also presented in 1736 for allowing the highway at West Kennett to flood.[1] Perhaps that was why he was required to serve as highway surveyor in 1737 (if indeed he did so).[2] In the same year, he served as tithingman for West Kennett.[3] In 1733, he succeeded his father as churchwarden.[4] He in turn was succeeded by Robert Caswell,[5] his cousin,[6] who at that time was the lessee of a farm at West Kennett owned by Thomas Smith,[7] although he moved to Yatesbury before his death in 1752.[8]

As already noted, William was 'in possession' of his father's estate in 1730. In 1737, the land tax assessment reveals that he paid £4 17s 2¾d for his own estate in Avebury, and that he also leased Phoebe Grubbe's estate, valued at £220[9] He was also possessed of an estate in Purton worth £20 per annum. When he died, he also had a 'very considerable personal estate ... chiefly consisting of a very large quantity of corn, grain and stock', estimated to be worth as much as £3000.[10] Despite his wealth, the 1785 Close Rolls tell us that he had been a mere husbandman 'of Kennett', where he farmed 106 acres at Brays Farm.[11]

William was buried 29th April 1740. He died intestate; his estate was administered by his wife Mary. She was bound with Robert Caswell of Yatesbury, William's uncle, and with Thomas Nalder, the prominent dissenter.[12] The administration of the estate was, however, challenged in Chancery.[13] According to William's daughter Elizabeth (who had married John Rose), she was the sole heir, her brothers having died before their father. She accused her mother of failing to compile either an inventory or an account. One wonders if her Chancery bill had anything to do with Rose's subsequent bankruptcy.[14]

1 WSHC A1/110, Michaelmas rolls.
2 WSHC A1/165/5.
3 WSHC 9/23/1.
4 WSHC D1/15/12.
5 He served for two years from 1735; cf. WSHC D3/15/11, D1/50/14; D1/41/4/48.
6 He was the son of Robert and Mary Caswell, and therefore the nephew of William's father. For his will, see WSHC P3/C/852.
7 WSHC 568/7. The lease was for 9 years from 1729.
8 For his will see WSHC P3/C/852.
9 WSHC 184/3.
10 TNA C11/382/40.
11 WANHS Genealogy mss v.A-A, p.150.
12 It is worth noting that Nalder in 1752 also acted as Robert Caswell's executor, together with Thomas Neate, who made his affirmation as a Quaker in the Archdeaconry court; cf. WSHC P3/C/916.
13 TNA C11/382/40.
14 See below, p.133-4.

John junior married Elizabeth, but died before his father; his will was proved in 1731.[1] He bequeathed his only 'child' £200, and named his father as a trustee. The child was identified as another John in his grandfather's will.

By 1748, Richard was the occupier of the property at Bishops Cannings which had been bequeathed to Edmund, who then lived in Calstone.[2] The lives of John senior's other children (Thomas, Michael, and Robert), have not been traced, and it is probable that some at least left Avebury.

Clements

John Clements was the eldest of four children born in Avebury to John and Sarah Clements between 1714 and 1725/6. All his siblings had long lives, although their father died c.1738.[3] John the elder was probably illiterate, judging by the fact that he made his mark when he witnessed the will of William Hollery in 1726.[4] Literacy, however, was to prove indispensable to his eldest son. In 1739, soon after his father's death, John Clements was appointed by the vestry as master of the village charity school.[5] That enabled him to marry. His bride was Mary Brokenbrow, who he married at Winterbourne Monkton in 1740.

John was still in post in 1766, when he was fifty-two.[6] Twenty years later, his niece Ann married William Alexander, the schoolmaster of Berwick Bassett. One suspects that, by then, John was ready to retire, and relinquished his position to his niece's husband (although the latter subsequently became gaoler at Devizes).[7] But schoolmastering was not very remunerative: the holder of the post was paid the interest on Lady Holford's £200 legacy,[8] and may conceivably have also received small fees from parents. Schoolmasters did, however, have opportunities to increase their income. For John, that meant serving as clerk of the vestry, a position which was probably paid. We don't know when he first took on that role, but he was certainly in post when the

1 WSHC P3/C/789.
2 WSHC 248/62.
3 WSHC D3/8/2.
4 WSHC P3/H/1039.
5 WSHC D1/41/4/48. See also below, p.171-3.
6 He is described as a schoolmaster in a 1766 bond; cf. WSHC 2664/3/10/1/a. For an earlier mention of his schoolmastership, see the 1746 entry for his son, William Clements, in London Apprenticeship Abstracts, 1442-1850 https://search.findmypast.co.uk/search-world-records/london-apprenticeship-abstracts-1442-1850.
7 According to the 1814 will of Joseph Clements; cf WSHC P1/1814/60.
8 WSHC 184/6.

vestry debated whether Stayner Holford could erect a seat in church for his servants in 1752.[1] The role perhaps resulted in his witnessing two marriages (one with his brother Robert) in 1755, perhaps whilst standing in for the parish clerk. Four decades later, he was still active; in 1793 (and perhaps much earlier), he was responsible for collecting the small amount of tithe owned by the vicar (most tithes had been appropriated). In his old age, Richard Hickley, the bailiff, described Clements as a 'great advocate for the parson'.[2] He was also a surveyor – which was probably much more lucrative.

In 1769, John described himself as a 'land measurer'.[3] Ten years later, in 1779, he used the description 'land surveyor' on the occasion of his second marriage,[4] and also when he claimed a debt of just over £10 from the estate of Samuel Martyn (this was a bad debt; he only received £3 5s 3d).[5] He still described himself as a land surveyor in his 1797 will (he died in 1798).[6] Evidence for his work as a surveyor has been found dating from 1753 to 1789, and it is likely that a more detailed search would find more.[7] Schoolmastering gave him long vacations whilst his pupils were helping to bring in the harvest, so he probably used that time to undertake surveying commissions.

By 1764, he was sufficiently well off to lend £100 on bond to John Talbot of Lacock.[8] Land tax records suggest his increasing prosperity. In 1751 he paid three shillings land tax.[9] By 1780, he was paying four shillings per annum for property occupied by his son, Joseph Clements, and eight shillings for property occupied by Thomas Dixon (his niece Rachel's husband).[10] The 1798 land tax indicates that Mrs Dixon, by then a widow,[11] occupied one of these properties, and William Dixon, presumably her husband's relation,[12] was occupying the other.[13] In 1797, the year before his death, Clements was sufficiently wealthy to

1   WSHC 184/8. Licence for Stayner Holford's seat.
2   WSHC 184/6. Letters, Richard Hickley to Mrs Williamson, 4th December 1792 & 31st March 1793.
3   Jane Rose's bond, in Sarum Marriage Licence Bonds, op cit.
4   Sarum Marriage Licence Bonds. www.findmypast.co.uk
5   WSHC 118/88. Statement of debts of Samuel Martyn, and List of receipts of Martyn's executor.
6   WSHC P3/C/1138. There is a copy at WSHC 1102/2.
7   For details, see below, p.298-9.
8   WSHC 2664/1/2f/3/46. In 1766 Takbit gave him a bond for the payment of £200.
9   WSHC 184/3.
10 WSHC A1/345/18A.
11 Her husband Thomas was buried 1st September 1795.
12 Rachel's son William was probably named after him, but he was only eleven years old.
13 TNA IR 23/96/189. At least one of the brother's was probably a taylor; cf. 184/7.

loan £200 to the Turnpike Trustees.[1] He was not, however, a well man. He had been employed in surveying work for the 1792 enclosure, but was too ill to do the work properly, and an assistant had to be brought in to help him. Richard Hickley reported that 'Clements is in a poor way, don't think he will hold it long. Has been of no sort of use in this business'.[2]

Clements also ran a business as a shopkeeper or grocer, probably when he was no longer fit enough to do any other work. His invoice to General Williamson for goods such as candles, starch, butter, and currants, supplied in 1792, totaled £1 11s 8½d.[3] His wife helped him in the business; Richard Hickley had to pay 'a bill of Mrs Clements for small articles' in 1793.[4]

Other records emphasise the schoolmaster's status in the community. It seems to have fallen to his lot to be called on to witness wills; he witnessed at least twenty-one between 1740 and 1795.[5] One wonders whether he actually wrote any of them (and was perhaps paid for doing so). We do know that, in 1749, he appraised the probate inventory of Thomas Hunter.[6] In 1747, he witnessed pauper apprenticeship indentures for Jane and John Currier, who had perhaps been his pupils.[7] In the 1750s and 1760s he served on several occasions as assessor for the land tax, although on one occasion he made a mistake which had to be rectified by Stayner Holford.[8] The house and window tax was assessed and collected by him in 1757,[9] and probably on other occasions. In 1754 he

1   WSHC 1371/1.
2   WSHC 184/6. Letter, Richard Hickley to Mrs Williamson, 4th September 1792.
3   WSHC 184/5. He was also described as a grocer by Long, William. 'Avebury notes', *WAM* 17, 1878, p.333.
4   WSHC 184/6. Letter, Richard Hickley to Mrs Williamson, 31st March 1793.
5   Including the wills of Edward Taylor 1740 (WSHC P1/T/418), Samuel Fowler 1740 (WSHC P3/F/359), John Fowler 1745 (WSHC P3/F/368), Thomas Hunter 1746/7 (WSHC P3/H/1256), Richard Mortimer 1750 (WSHC P1/M/592), Hannah Smith 1752 (TNA PROB11/795/275), William Philpot 1753 (WSHC P3/P/887), William Crook 1754 (WSHC P3/C/933), Robert Nalder 1758 (WSHC P3/N/257), John Cruse 1760 (WSHC P3/C/971), Samuel Martyn of Kennett 1767 (PROB11/1022/67), Philip Crook 1774 (WSHC P3/C/1048), Richard Bailey 1783 (WSHC P3/B/1679), William Hillier 1774 (WSHC P3/H/1407), William Herbert 1778 (WSHC P3/H/1431), James Smith 1783 (WSHC P3/S/1568), William Philpot 1786 (WSHC P3/P/1027), John Wiltshire 1795 (WSHC P3/W/1066), his brother Robert Clements 1795 (WSHC P3/C/1134), Sarah Dyke Howson (WSHC P3/H/1476).
6   WSHC P3/H/1256.
7   WSHC 184/9/3.
8   WSHC 184/3. Holford's appeal; 184/1, pt.1. Letter, Stayner Holford, to William Norris, 14th June 1761.
9   WSHC 18/3. House and window tax assessment 1757.

witnessed a conveyancing bond entered into by Mary and John Cue.[1] His name is mentioned in the marriage register as witness to two marriages in 1755. He witnessed the bastardy bonds entered into by Charles Giddance in 1754,[2] and by John Rumsey in 1763.[3] In 1756, he witnessed a bond entered into by local farmers endeavouring to extract the maximum amount of work from their labourers.[4] The private apprenticeship indenture of Nanny Moor, probably another of his pupils, was witnessed by Clements (and by his daughter Ann) in 1759.[5] He stood bond when James Norris sought a marriage licence to marry Mary Tilly in 1762,[6] and in 1783 when John Tilly was required to appear at Quarter Sessions to answer a charge of assault.[7] William Fowler, the innkeeper who had been threatened with damnation by the vicar in 1753,[8] named him as joint executor in his 1765 will.[9] That same vicar was joined with John when William Herbert instructed them both to distribute £2 to the poor on his death in 1778.[10] The schoolmaster had already acted in a similar capacity. Hannah Smith's 1752 will[11] gave the poor of Avebury five guineas, to be distributed by him. His knowledge of his pupils would have enabled him to identify easily those most in need. The same will, incidentally, also gave five guineas to his wife Mary, with the caveat that it was for her 'own separate use', that is, her husband was not to have it.

John Clements' property gave him the right to vote in the 1772 Parliamentary election; the pollbook records that his lands were then occupied by Isaac Ball and Joseph Clements (presumably his son).[12] Between 1773 and 1783 (and perhaps earlier) he was regularly placed on the freeholders' list for jury service.[13] His appearance as one of the few mourners when Joseph Brown, one of Arthur Jones's former servants, was buried in 1794 gives us some indication of why he was fairly highly regarded in the parish.[14]

1 WSHC 212A/31/2.
2 WSHC 184/9/4.
3 WSHC 184/9/5. Bastardy bond, Joanna Hall, 22nd July 1763.
4 WSHC 1569/31.
5 WSHC 184/9/3.
6 Sarum Marriage Licence Bonds www.findmypast.co.uk/articles/world-records/full-list-of-united-kingdom-records/life-events-bmds/sarum-marriage-licence-bonds
7 WSHC A1/110, 1783M.
8 WSHC 184/1, pt.1. Letter, 10th July 1753. James Mayo to William Fowler.
9 WSHC P3/F/368.
10 WSHC P3/H/1431.
11 TNA PROB11/795/275.
12 WSHC A1/340/1.
13 WSHC A1/265/21-5; A1/110, Michaelmas rolls, 1773-5,1777, & 1780-83.
14 WSHC 184/6. Letter, Richard Hickley to Mrs Williamson, 1st April 1794.

John had two wives. Mary Brokenbrow has already been mentioned. She gave him three children, William, Ann, and Joseph, but died in 1778. He re-married in 1779, but his second wife, Ann Stroud, bore no more children. His son, William, was apprenticed to a London painter stainer in 1756,[1] and married Martha Allaway at Little Somerford in 1778. No children have been traced. William's sister Ann married William Chapman, a collar maker, and had two children, William and Phoebe, who are mentioned in their grandfather's will.[2] Joseph married twice; his first wife, Hannah, was buried on 35th January 1793. When he made his will at Trowbridge in 1814 he made his second wife, Patience, his executrix, and also named his nephew William as a beneficiary.[3]

In his 1797 will,[4] John bequeathed his house at Avebury to his wife Ann for life, and then to his grand-daughter Phoebe Chapman. His two houses at Beckhampton were left to his son Joseph. William was not mentioned, although according to the 1798 land tax assessment he occupied his father's property at Beckhampton.[5]

The schoolmaster had three siblings. Ruth, his only sister, never married. Nor did his brother, William Clements, who was an innkeeper at Kennett. Licences were granted to William between 1756 and 1761, and probably for much longer.[6] In 1757, he was one of the 'creditors' of George Stretch deceased who brought a (probably collusive) action against James Hitchcock which enabled Hitchcock to wind up his father in law's estate.[7]

Like his brother, William was fairly prosperous. In 1763, he lent £140 on mortgage to his fellow innkeeper, John Dobson;[8] two years later, he took a bond from Dobson to repay £20.[9] In 1779, he purchased a cottage for £105.[10] He witnessed several marriages in the 1760s. In 1772, he voted in the Parliamentary election, although he was then stated to be resident in Clyffe Pypard; his property at Avebury was occupied by William Little.[11] Between

---

1 Webb, Cliff. *London Livery Company Apprenticeship Registers vol.38. Painter-Stainers' Company, 1655, 1666-1800.* Society of Genealogists, 2003, p.13.
2 WSHC P3/C/1138.
3 WSHC P1/1814/60.
4 WSHC P3/C/1138. See also 1102/2. He was actually buried 1st March 1798.
5 TNA IR 23/96/289. f.249-50. This assessment ignores the fact that John Clements had just died.
6 WSHC A1/326/1-2.
7 WSHC P3/S/1306.
8 WSHC 488/1.
9 WSHC 488/12.
10 WSHC 2027/2/1/855.
11 WSHC A1/340/1.

1773 and 1788, he was placed on the list of Avebury freeholders; he was frequently called on to serve on Quarter Sessions juries,[1] and in 1774-5 he served as high constable of Selkley Hundred.[2] Samuel Martyn's 1776 will was witnessed by him.[3]

The schoolmaster's younger brother, Robert, had five children fairly late in life, by his wife Ann. They were born between 1763 and 1786. His eldest son, another John, presumably pre-deceased him; he is not mentioned in his father's 1795 will (he died in 1797). Robert too seems to have been relatively prosperous, although when he paid John Robinson £20 to purchase a cottage in 1755 he was described as a labourer.[4] Like his father, he farmed the vicar's tithes in 1772.[5] He left his cottage to his eldest daughter Leah, who was unmarried.[6] She already occupied the cottage next door, so, in 1799, sold her father's property for the same price that he paid for it.[7] The residue of Robert's estate was to be divided equally between his three other children, Stephen Clements, Rachel Dixon and Ann Alexander.

Despite his designation as a labourer in the 1755 deed, Robert was a yeoman, and regularly appeared at the Hundred Court as a suitor from Beckhampton in the 1740s and 1750s.[8] He served as tithingman from 1752 to 1754.[9] In 1755, with his brother, he signed the register as witness to the marriage of Joseph Sprules and Katharine Shilton. He was employed as a gamekeeper between at least 1768 and 1784.[10] In 1782, when he served as hundred constable, he was also described as a corn chandler.[11]

Crook

When Sir Richard Holford purchased the manor of Avebury, he found much work for masons and other tradesmen. One of them was William Crook, a mason, who undertook various tasks for Sir Richard in the early eighteenth century, and worked closely with the carpenter, Humphry Robinson.[12]

1 WSHC A1/265/21-7; A1/110, Michaelmas rolls, 1773-5, 1779-82, & 1785.
2 WSHC 9/23/1.
3 TNA PROB11/1022/7.
4 WSHC 1102/2.
5 WSHC A1/340/1.
6 WSHC 1102/2.
7 WSHC 1102/2.
8 WSHC 9/23/1.
9 WSHC 9/23/1.
10 WSHC 9/23/1, & A1/305-7.
11 WSHC 9/23/1. See also A/110/, 1782M.
12 GA D1956/E2/8; WSHC 184/8. For a fuller discussion, see below, p.302.

This William was probably the father of three brothers, William, Philip, and Robert. Philip and Robert acted as executors when their brother William died in 1754.[1] William was a carpenter; his brother Philip was a mason.[2] Robert became a tailor, and moved to Mildenhall.[3] The likelihood is that William and Philip worked in conjunction with each other in building work. One wonders whether William was apprenticed to Humphry Robinson, his father's close associate.

The Family of William Crook the younger

William the younger described himself as a carpenter in his 1754 will.[4] The baptisms of three children are recorded in the parish register between 1734 and 1752. However, five are recorded in the will. The testator gave his son John, probably the eldest, a token shilling. He had presumably already been established in his trade, unlike some of his younger siblings. We know that John served as a juror in the Selkley Hundred Court in 1791,[5] and it is possible that he was the John Crook of Marlborough who sent cotton to be spun in the Bristol Workhouse in the 1760s.[6] But we hear no more about him in Avebury.

William bequeathed all of 'my lands and tenements ... with ... all ... my stock in trade, working tools, bills, bonds and book debts, and all goods' to his other four children equally, although Ambrose received an extra £25 to pay for his apprenticeship. In the event, Stephen continued to occupy his father's house and shop, and continued his business as a carpenter and wheelwright;[7] his two sisters' husbands, and his father's executors (on behalf of his brother Ambrose) sold him their interests in it by lease and release in 1761.[8] One wonders if the £30 he borrowed from the blacksmith James Lewis, and which he repaid when Lewis's estate was being wound up in 1793, provided the capital to pay for this purchase.[9] Ambrose, in accordance with his father's will, entered apprenticeship indentures with his brother Stephen. Several of Stephen's other apprentices have

1 WSHC P3/C/933.
2 WSHC P3/C/1048.
3 He was one of the vendors (probably as his brother's executor – see below) who sold Stephen Crook a house and shop in Avebury; cf. WSHC 1102/1. Lease & release by Philip Crook et al to Stephen Crook, 2nd/3rd June 1761.
4 WSHC P3/C/933.
5 WSHC 9/23/1.
6 V.C.H. Wilts 12, p.208.
7 See below, p.303 for his business activities.
8 WSHC 1102/1.
9 TNA PROB 31/840/590.

been recorded.[1]

William's will was witnessed by Jonathan White, who subsequently married the testator's daughter Rachel (they married at Avebury, 22nd January 1759; he was a maltster from Potterne). The other witnesses were John Clements, the schoolmaster, and John Strange. William's other daughter, Susanna, married John Symes of Marden, a stay maker, at Compton Bassett on 6th July 1756.

Stephen himself married Susanna Compton on 6th April 1760; their nine children were baptised between 1760 and 1780. His stature in the community was such that he witnessed the wills of two leading members of the gentry: Henry Howson, gent., in 1775,[2] and Arthur Jones, esq., in 1786.[3] Stephen the elder was buried 13th September 1806; his wife Susanna on 13th September 1797. When his son Stephen took out his marriage bond in 1799, he was described as a carpenter, following the family tradition.[4] The property he either owned or occupied in Avebury made him liable to pay four shillings land tax in 1800.[5]

The Family of Philip Crook

Philip Crook, William's brother, made his will on 9th May 1774,[6] and died in the following December. He owned the freehold of the house he lived in, and let another to William Nurdan in the parish. He also had the lease of a house in Ogbourne Maizey, and paid three shillings land tax on his Avebury property in 1751.[7] He witnessed the will of Ruth Bailey in 1733/4,[8] and signed the 1736 petition to the Bishop protesting at the vicar's residence in Calne.[9]

Philip was a mason, and probably worked closely with his brother, and with his three sons. His bill for masonry work in 1741 included a charge for work done by his young sons,[10] who would have been aged six and eleven at the time. That work stood the children in good stead; the eldest, William was subsequently described as a bricklayer in his marriage bond, and as a mason in the parish register.

Philip bequeathed all his estate to his wife Ann for her life; on her death it was to be divided between his sons William and Richard. His other

1 See p. 280.
2 WSHC P3/H/1476.
3 TNA PROB11/1181/174.
4 Sarum Marriage Licence Bonds www.findmypast.co.uk
5 WSHC A1/345/18A.
6 WSHC P3/C/1048.
7 WHSC 184/3.
8 WSHC P1/B/1164.
9 WSHC D1/47/3.
10 WSHC 184/5. Stephen Crook's bill, 1741.

son, Barnabus, who had married Rachel Smith of Preshute in 1764,[1] is not mentioned. One wonders whether he had recently died. Barnabus's children, Richard and Ann, were mentioned. Richard was just four months old when Philip made his will.

William, Philip's eldest son, married Ann, the daughter of Robert Nalder.[2] Curiously, she was described as of Figheldean in their 1758 marriage licence.[3] The marriage was celebrated at East Kennett on 9th February 1758.[4] William tenanted land owned by the Holford family. In 1761 he admitted ploughing up land which should have been kept as a droveway for Mr. Holford.[5] In 1780, the land tax assessments record him as occupier of lands owned by Mr (Richard) Bailey, Mr Griffin, and Mr Nalder (his wife's uncle), which together were liable to tax just exceeding £38.[6] In 1779 he agreed to be bound with Isaac Ball when the latter was indicted for assault; the recognizance describes him as a yeoman.[7] In 1795, he owned the property now known as Vine Cottage in South Street.[8] This was probably the cottage he had purchased from Joseph Deavin in 1786.[9] When Avebury's landowners petitioned for enclosure in 1792, his was the only name missing from the petition.[10] He became a trustee for his 'brother in law' George Brown (in fact the husband of his wife's sister Martha) when the latter died in 1793.[11]

William Crook was the only member of his family known to have served in public office. He was churchwarden on several occasions between 1767 and 1787,[12] overseer in 1775,[13] tithingman of Kennett in 1761 and 1762,[14]

1 Sarum Marriage Licence Bonds www.findmypast.co.uk.
2 See below, p.109.
3 Sarum Marriage Licence Bonds www.findmypast.co.uk. She is described as being of East Kennett in the parish register.
4 There is also an entry for a marriage of a couple of these names in the Upavon register, 26th January 1758.
5 WSHC 184/4/1.
6 WSHC A1/345/18A. His landlords were probably acting as trustees. of Caleb Bailey's charity.
7 WSHC A1/110, 1779M.
8 WBR. Note by Margaret Parrott, 7th November 2000.
9 WSHC 435/214/1/9.
10 WSHC 184/6. Richard Hickley to Mrs Williamson, 6th March 1792.
11 WSHC P3/B/1742
12 WSHC D1/50/24; D3/15/17; D3/15/18; D1/50/28; D3/15/19; D3/15/20. D3/15/18.
13 WSHC 184/9/5.
14 WSHC 9/23/1.

tithingman of Avebury in 1782 and 1784,[1] land tax assessor for Avebury Tithing in 1785,[2] and high constable of Selkley Hundred in 1788.[3] He was regularly listed in the freeholders' books throughout the 1780s and 1790s,[4] and served on various juries at Quarter Sessions in the 1790s.[5] In 1800, however, he was amerced (fined) 6s 8d for neglecting jury service in the Selkley Hundred court.[6] He died in 1806 aged 74.

Cruse or Cuss

John Cruse was an illiterate blacksmith, whose wife Mary (nee Tomkins) inherited a leasehold estate in East Kennett from her mother in 1727.[7] He and his wife sold rights on Avebury Common to Caleb Bailey in 1726,[8] but still owned sufficient property in 1737 to pay land tax amounting to 2s 1d on property in Avebury.[9] He probably purchased a house in 1749, when Jane Pottow and Rebecca Hillier quitclaimed 'all actions' against him.[10] In the early 1750s he paid land tax on two houses.[11] One was apparently let out to John Nurden in 1752, although the name does not recur in the assessments. The other was probably the cottage and garden that he was leasing in 1756 and 1757 at a rent of thirty shillings per annum.[12] He also leased a tenement from John Coombes of Highworth.[13]

John Cruse died in 1762. With the exception of a token bequest of 1s to his cousin John Dew, he left his whole estate to his widow.[14] She died two years later. Their only son (as far as is known), John, had died ten years earlier,

1 WSHC A1/110, 1782M & 1785M. He was nominated again in 1794, but avoided serving; cf. A1/110, 1794M.
2 WSHC 473/352.
3 WSHC A1/110, 1788M.
4 WSHC A1/265/24-41.
5 WSHC A1/110, 1790M, 1792M, 1793M, 1794M, 1795M, and 1798M.
6 WSHC 9/23/1.
7 His illiteracy is demonstrated by the fact that he made his mark on a petition to the bishop in1736; cf. WSHC D1/47/3. For Mary's mothers will, see WSHC P3/T/497. For his blacksmithing, see below, p.309-10.
8 WSHC 212A/31/3; 1409/16/3.
9 WSHC 184/3.
10 WSHC A1/110, 1749M.
11 WSHC 184/3.
12 WSHC 212A/31//2. Phelps deed, 5th January 1756; Daniel Bull to John Savage, 4th January 1757.
13 WSHC 184/4/1. Agreement between Stayner Holford and John Coombes, 20.2.1764.
14 WSHC P3/C/971.

leaving his widow Edith (nee Penney) to administer his estate.[1] The grant of administration cost her 3s 8d.[2] Edith died within a year of her husband, and left her father-in-law one shilling;[3] again the cost of obtaining a grant of probate was 3s 8d.[4] The couple had no children.

John and Edith had not been badly off. John paid three shillings land tax on his house in 1751,[5] and Edith's will mentioned a feather bed with curtains and a valence, and a gold ring. That marks her out as being, perhaps, on the edge of the village elite. She also had a bible and a *Book of Common Prayer*, despite the fact that she made her mark rather than signing her will. One wonders who read them to her. Perhaps it was her nephew, John Penney, to whom she bequeathed them. Edith inherited her husband's estate, the bulk of which she bequeathed to her Penney brothers, and to their children.

Currier
The poorest families are frequently almost invisible in our records. There are a few scattered entries for the Currier family in local parish registers, but not all of them can be linked together. We know that John Griffin was required to attend Quarter Sessions in 1695, in order to answer for a 'battery committed by him on ye body of Katherine and John Currier'. Katherine was the wife of Henry Currier; John presumably their son.[6] We know too that Henry Currier (another son?) married Mary Burress in 1714, and that the couple probably had three children. There is no baptismal record for Henry junior, but he was buried in 1728. The other two children were daughters, Katherine, baptised in 1717 (and buried in 1719), and Sarah, baptised in 1723. Only Sarah survived into adulthood; she married William Gooff at Winterbourne Monkton in 1744. It is possible that she was named after another Sarah Currier, who gave evidence against John White in the Consistory Court in 1711, and signed her deposition with a mark.[7]

The family was probably related to John Currier, who was apprenticed as a pauper in 1747.[8] There is no record of his baptism, although he clearly had entitlement to poor relief from the Avebury overseers. It is probable that Jane Currier, who was apprenticed five days later, was his sister. John spent

1 WSHC P3/C/922.
2 WSHC D3/2/9.
3 WSHC P3/C/935.
4 WSHC D3/2/9.
5 WSHC 184/3.
6 WSHC A1/110, 1695M, 16, 22, & 54.
7 WSHC D1/42/68.
8 WHSC 184/9/4. See also below, p.281.

three years with his master in Seend, and then another three years with another master in Melksham. It is not clear where he lived in the subsequent decade, but he had returned to Avebury by 1763, when he was examined by the Justices as to his settlement.[1] We do not know the outcome of that examination; however, we do know that he subsequently married Jane Simms, who already had a bastard daughter, Sarah.[2] Jane was present in Avebury in 1775, when she acted as a witness in a dispute between the overseers of Avebury and Yatesbury.[3] John lived until 1800; his widow, Jane, was buried at East Kennett in 1814. Sarah, his step-daughter, married George Scott, another labourer, in 1781.

The Currier family clearly lived on the edge of subsistence. Support from the overseers was required in 1747, 1763, 1775, and probably on other occasions as well, although documentation does not survive.

Dunch

William Dunch of Little Wittenham (Berkshire), auditor of the Royal Mint, purchased the manor of Avebury from Sir William Sharington for £2,200 in 1551.[4] He settled it on his younger son, Walter, on the latter's marriage to Deborah, the daughter of James Pilkington, Bishop of Durham, in 1581.[5] Walter purchased a reversionary lease of Avebury Rectory estate[6] in 1585.[7] He also owned the manors of Leigh Delamere, Sevington and Berwick Bassett in Wiltshire, and the manor of Exford in Somerset.[8] His widow Deborah was left to pay the subsidy on his Avebury lands in 1594; the land was valued at £6 13s 4d, the highest valuation in the parish.[9] He was a practising lawyer, with chambers at Gray's Inn, and served as MP for Dunwich in 1584 and 1589.

Walter's only son, William, was an infant aged four months when his father's inquisition post mortem was taken in 1594. The couple also had four daughters: Deborah, the wife of Sir Henry Moody, who acquired his baronetcy

---

1 WSHC 184/9/2A. Settlement examination of John Currier, 1763.
2 WSHC 184/9/2A. Settlement examination of Sarah Simms, 1775.
3 WSHC 184/9/5.
4 The following notes are based on S., J. 'Notes on Wiltshire Parishes: Avebury', *Wiltshire Notes & Queries* 8, 1914-18, p.214-6.
5 For the Dunch pedigree, see Metcalfe, Walter, ed. *The Visitation of Berkshire 1664-6, by Elias Ashmole, Windsor Herald, for Sir Edward Bysshe, Clarenceaux.* William Pollard, 1882, p.28-9.
6 Sometimes referred to as the Parsonage.
7 History of Parliament Online www.historyofparliamentonline.org/volume/1558-1603/member/dunch-walter-1552-94
8 TNA PROB11/84/49.
9 TNA E179/198/315.

in 1612, and served as MP for Malmesbury in 1626 and 1628,[1] Ruth, the wife of Sir William Button, who served as sheriff of the county in 1614, purchased a baronetcy in 1621, and was elected Member of Parliament for Wiltshire in 1628, but fought on the Royalist side during the Civil War,[2] Mary, who married firstly a Swayne, and then a Philpot, and Anne, who married Thomas Lambert. William's daughter Deborah, as we will see, was an active puritan.[3]

William's wardship was granted initially to his mother, Deborah. She subsequently re-married; her second husband was Sir James Mervyn. The wardship was therefore re-granted, jointly, to Sir John Cooper of Rockbourne (Hants) and Sir Daniel Norton of Southwick (Hants), and William went to live with Cooper, whose daughter Margaret he married.

His aunts' marriages gave William important political connections. He also had literary interests. Kingsmill Long's translation of John Barclay's *Argenis* (an allegory on French religious conflicts) was dedicated to his friend 'the truly noble William Dunch of Avebury'.[4]

Soon after he attained his majority, in 1616, William Dunch purchased the lands of the Free Chapel of Beckhampton for £455.[5] In the early 1620s, he acquired the manor of Avebury Trusloe. He also had a house in St Martins in the Field, London.[6] In 1628, he headed the list of subsidy payers for Avebury.[7] But he died childless in 1630, and his sisters inherited – although he had many debts.[8] He (or, rather, his executors) gave a paten to Avebury church in 1636.[9] The manor of Avebury was subsequently sold to Sir John Stawell; Avebury Trusloe was sold to Sir Edward Bayntun in 1646.[10]

1. History of Parliament Online www.histparl.ac.uk/volume/1604-1629/member/moody-sir-henry-1582-1629
2. History of Parliament Online www.historyofparliamentonline.org/volume/1604-1629/member/button-sir-william-1585-1655
3. See below, p.419.
4. TNA PROB11/321/306; Nicol, Cheryl. *Inheriting the Earth: the Long Family's 500 year reign in Wiltshire*. Hobnob Press, 2016, p.335.
5. WSHC 371/1, pt.2. Indenture, John Truslow to William Dunch, 1st April 1619; 184/4/1. Abstract of title to the Free Chapel of Beckhampton.
6. WSHC 1178/367.
7. TNA E179/199/400, rot.5. The assessment is damaged, and the amount Dunch paid is lost.
8. For a list of debtors, see WSHC 1178/367. It was not until 1670 that William's sisters finally agreed on the settlement of his estate; see Somerset Heritage Centre DD/PO/6.
9. WSHC D1/5/2/31.
10. WSHC 184/4/1. Abstract of title to Avebury Trusloe; WANHS Wiltshire Genealogy v.A-A, p.117.

Goldsmith

John Goldsmith, who died c.1640, owned a variety of small farms and other property scattered across North Wiltshire and elsewhere. He had purchased all of this property from various vendors; none of it was inherited. One wonders if his name derived from his original occupation: goldsmiths were frequently sufficiently wealthy to purchase land. His properties were held by various feudal tenures, including by knight service. Knight service meant that he was a tenant in chief of the Crown, and therefore liable to various feudal dues. His estate was therefore subjected to an inquisition post mortem, which described his lands in detail.[1] The family claimed armigerous status; a hatchment appears in the church.[2]

He actually lived at Rowse's Farm in Avebury, which, together with a messuage in Westbrook, had been purchased from John Shuter after 1611.[3] He also tenanted Avebury Great Farm c.1623,[4] and again in 1640[5] (although not continuously). Goldsmith also leased Warwicks from William Dunch.[6] He had purchased the lease from the previous tenant, Thomas Pope,[7] and also purchased various properties in Beckhampton from John Truslow in 1630.[8] The ownership of Warwicks was challenged at the Assizes in 1631, and then in the Court of Exchequer in 1632; Goldsmith was accused of having paid the Assize jury in order to obtain a favourable verdict for himself.[9]

Goldsmith also owned property in other parishes. His purchase from Truslow included an acre of land and pasture on the west side of the High Street in Hungerford. Other property included a messuage at Hilmarton called Penn, purchased from William Davis, and held by knight service. In his will, Goldsmith also mentioned properties in Marlborough and in Worcester, which were not mentioned by the Wiltshire escheator. The administration

---

1 Fry, George S., & Fry, Edw. Alex., ed. *Abstracts of Wiltshire Inquisitiones Post Mortem*. British Record Society, 1901, p.375-6.
2 Phillipps, Thomas. *Monumental inscriptions of Wiltshire*, ed. Peter Sherlock. Wiltshire Record Society, 53. 2000, p.211.
3 *VCH Wilts.*, 12, p.94.
4 WANHS Wiltshire Genealogy A-A, p.110.
5 WANHS Wilshire Genealogy A-A, p.115.
6 TNA PROB11/321/306. William Dunch's will. See also WANHS Genealogy mss A-A, f.113.
7 TNA E134/8Chas1/Mich53.
8 WSHC 212B/103.
9 TNA E134/8Chas1/Mich53.

bond attached to his will[1] indicates that his administrator was bound in £4000, suggesting that the total value of his estate was c.£2000, although there is no inventory. He was one of the wealthiest inhabitants of the parish.

It is likely that John Goldsmith was a native of Berwick Bassett. He left £1 to the church there, and some at least of his children were baptised there before he moved to Avebury. John's wife, Elizabeth, is named in the entry for the baptism of their daughter Deborah at Berwick Bassett on 4th October 1605.

In his 1640 will, John referred to Thomas as his 'eldest sonne now livinge', suggesting that at least one other son had died. A daughter, Ann, baptised at Berwick Bassett 1st February 1608/9, is not mentioned in her father's will, suggesting she too died before her father. John mentioned five surviving sons (Thomas, Henry, Joseph, George, and Benjamin) and three daughters (Mary Chivers, Deborah Mortimer, and Elizabeth Mauckes). Thomas, the eldest son, was born c.1614.[2] Benjamin, perhaps the youngest, would have been a young teenager when he was apprenticed in 1641.[3] In the same year, Henry was admitted to Barnard's Inn, one of the inns of court.[4] John also had an unknown number of grandchildren, who received 40s each in his will.

At least two sons married. Joseph married Ann Askew at Devizes, 5th February 1640/1, shortly after his father's death. George's wife, Elizabeth, is mentioned in a 1655 deed.[5] No marriages have been traced for the other sons, nor have children been identified for any of the brothers. The grandchildren were probably children of John's daughters. Only one can be identified. Ann was Deborah Mortimer's daughter.

John Goldsmith served as churchwarden in 1623 and again in 1634,[6] as a grand juror in 1620,[7] and as constable of Selkley Hundred in 1626.[8] In 1620, he gave evidence in a Chancery case brought by William Dunch.[9]

1   WSHC P1/G/142.
2   Fry, George S., & Fry, Edw.Alex., ed. *Abstracts of Wiltshire Inquisitiones Post Mortem*. British Record Society, 1901, p.375-6. See also *Alumni Oxonienses* www.british-history.ac.uk/alumni-oxon/: he was said to be 17 when he matriculated in 1631.
3   See below, p.278.
4   Brooks, Christopher W. *The Admissions Register of Barnards Inn, 1620-1809*. Selden Society supplementary series 12. 1995, p.92.
5   WSHC 212B/106.
6   WSHC D3/15/1.
7   WSHC A1/110, 1620M.
8   WSHC A1/110, 1626M, f.133 & 171.
9   WANHS Genealogy mss A-A, f.100.

He appraised the inventories of Katherine Brown in 1622/3,[1] Richard Cue in 1628,[2] and Richard Parr in 1632.[3] He was also was named as an overseer of four wills: Richard Trewman's in 1616,[4] James Baldveen's in 1628[5] John Peart's in 1621,[6] and Thomas Mortimer's in 1639.[7]

One of these testators, John Peart, was the vicar. He had previously been named with Goldsmith as another overseer of Richard Trewman's will. It seems likely that Goldsmith was a keen supporter of the church; that would explain Peart's bequest to him of 'a boke called *Ye Spirituall Warfare*'. It would also explain why he sent his son Thomas to Oxford: most university students entered the church. Thomas studied there between 1631 and 1636, taking his MA in the latter year.[8] John Goldsmith's support for the church is also demonstrated by the small legacies he made to churches: Avebury, Berwick Bassett, St Paul's Cathedral, and Salisbury Cathedral, all benefited. So did the poor of Avebury, and Richard Bray, the parish clerk. The former received £5, which was 'to be putt forth att interest to be given to eight of the poorest people yearelie on St Thomas day twelve pence a peece the five poundes to remaine as a stocke for ever'.

Goldsmith also left bequests to his servants. Freezy Pope received £40 – much more than the five other servants mentioned, who each received £1. One of his servants, however, was not mentioned in his will. Thomas Clarke was tried at Quarter Sessions in 1640 for stealing a pair of boots, a pair of shoes, and two pairs of spurs, from John's sons Joseph and Henry.[9] He was presumably dismissed, and missed out on a bequest.

Another member of the Goldsmith family was again a victim of theft in 1647. In an 'information' provided by John Phelps, the tenant of the Goldsmith's farm at Beckhampton, it was stated that Sarah Duck was found in possession of barley which had been stolen from Phelps and 'Mr Goldsmith'.[10] John's 1639/40 will made detailed provision for the descent of his property, ensuring that all his sons remained property owners. Thomas, his eldest son, was to have Rowses and Warwicks. Henry was given the property in Worcester.

1 WSHC P3/B/236.
2 WSHC P3/K/39.
3 WSHC P3/P/184.
4 WSHC P3/T/50.
5 WSHC P3/B/294.
6 WSHC P3/P/101.
7 TNA PROB11/194/502. In the event, he died before Mortimer.
8 *Alumni Oxonienses* www.british-history.ac.uk/alumni-oxon/
9 WSHC A1/110, 1640, f.104.
10 WSHC A1/110, 1647M, f.424.

Joseph inherited property at Hilmarton, together with £500 (plus another £200 in a codicil). The lands in Beckhampton, which were then leased to the Phelps family, were given to George, who also received £300. The properties at Marlborough and Hungerford were inherited by Benjamin. John's daughters were all given cash legacies: £400 to MaryCheevers, and £50 apiece to Deborah Mortimer and Elizabeth Mauckes.

The name Goldsmith almost disappeared from the parish within a decade or so of John's death, although Henry's wife Mary (daughter of Thomas Smith of West Kennett) was not buried there until 1713, when she was aged 93. Her memorial states that her husband was 'late of Bernard Inn'.[1] She probably lived in London, but returned to her native parish for burial.[2]
John's eldest son, Thomas, married Eleanor, who died without issue c.1650.[3] In 1642, he was paying Sir John Stawell rent of £410 for Avebury Great Farm, although his rent was falling behind.[4] In 1654, he was described as 'of Shalborne' [Shalbourne], and his brother George was 'of Milton', in the Oxfordshire parish of Shipton. The two brothers sold their messuage in Beckhampton to Richard Phelps (probably a relative of the lessee).[5] The sale had been forced due to their inability to pay off a mortgage. Warwicks was leased to Thomas Griffin in 1652, and it seems likely that the freehold was soon after sold to the Norris family, who were in possession in 1726.[6]

John's other sons presumably settled either in the parishes where they had inherited property, or perhaps, in the case of Benjamin, in London, where he was apprenticed to a grocer soon after his father's death.[7] The only daughter who remained in Avebury, as far as is known, was Deborah, who married George Mortimer on 24th February 1623/4.

Griffin

The Griffins were a prominent and prolific family of (mainly) minor landowners and substantial leaseholders in Avebury for most of our period. There were 26 Griffin baptisms, and 41 burials, between 1672 and 1782; most were probably related to each other, although Thomas Griffin, the taylor, who was licenced

---

1   One of the Inns of Court in London.
2   Phillipps, Thomas. *Monumental inscriptions of Wiltshire*, ed. Peter Sherlock. Wiltshire Record Society, 53. 2000, p.211.r
3   TNA C5/128/75.
4   TNA C6/21/114.
5   WSHC 212B/105 & 106.
6   WSHC 2106/5.
7   See below, p.278.

to marry Mary Symes in 1640,[1] may have been from a different family. It is likely that many were descended from, or related to, William Griffin and his wife Edith, who leased what became known as Griffin's Farm at Beckhampton in 1580[2]. William paid the subsidy on goods valued at £7 in 1594, and at £5 in 1598.[3] Several Griffins served as churchwardens, tithingmen, jurors, and in other public offices.

It is not always easy to distinguish between members of this family who bore the same name; there were, for example, several named John, William, Peter and Thomas. Nor is it possible to construct a pedigree linking them all. However, two members of the family who played significant roles in Avebury can be identified.

Peter Griffin, a prosperous yeoman, was aged 33 when he obtained a licence to marry Ann Phelps als Bromham of Fifield in 1665.[4] He was probably a great grandson of William Griffin, and one of five brothers.[5] He frequently appeared in Avebury's manorial court in the 1650s, either as a member of the homage, or as a tithingman. In 1654 he was sworn as a 'teller of beasts',[6] and in 1668 he agreed to reduce the number of beef cattle he kept on the Downs by a third.[7] In addition to his tenancy of land in the manor of Avebury, he also tenanted eight acres of land, part of the manor of East Kennett, sold by Sir Edward Bayntun to Charles Tooker in 1676.[8] In 1681, he owned a property at Westbrook (perhaps Chestermans?)[9] When he died in 1689, he also had the lease of Warwicks, worth £36, which had probably been bequeathed to him by Thomas Griffin, who took out the lease in 1652.[10]

1 Neville, Edmund. 'Marriage licences of Salisbury', *Genealogist*, N.S., 31, 1915, p.183.
2 The lease has not survived, but it is mentioned in WSHC 371/1, pt. 2 (copy at 3724/1). Deed, William Button to Richard Truslow, 1596. William Griffin was still there in 1596 (WSHC 184/4/1. Abstract of title to Truslow's Farm), and in 1613 (TNA WARD 7/57/71).
3 TNA E179/198/315; e179/198/325.
4 Bishops transcript; Nevill, op cit, N.S., 32, 1916, p.20. The WFHS transcript wrongly transcribes this as Anne Hellyar.
5 He named his brother John in his 1687/8 will, WSHC P3/G/413. Other probable brothers can be identified in the1709 will of Timothy Griffin, which names John as a 'kinsman', cf. WSHC P3/G/435.
6 WSHC 473/52, f.7, 37, 49, 83, & 91.
7 WSHC 271/1. Agreement to abate the keeping of beef cattle.
8 WSHC 371/2, pt. 2. Bargain & Sale, Sir Edward Bayntun, et al to Charles Tooker, 1676; WSHC 3724/1. Assignment, 1676.
9 WSHC 435/24/1/4. Deed, 1st June 1682.
10 WSHC P3/G/413; 2106/5. Lease, William Norris to John Wiltshire, 29th December 1726.

In 1670, he was collecting the appropriated tithes[1] of the Free Chapel of Beckhampton from Joseph Griffin (possibly his brother). His tithe collecting activities also extended to Avebury's Parsonage Farm, probably on behalf of Joseph's landlord.[2] In 1688, he sued Thomas Pontin for tithes in the Court of Exchequer.[3]

Peter Griffin's major intervention in the Avebury land market took place in 1681, when he purchased a portion of the manor of Avebury Trusloe from Sir Edward Bayntun,[4] and perhaps raised part of the capital required by mortgaging a Westbrook property[5] to Mary Stephens, another 62 acres at Westbrook to Richard Phelps,[6] and his various tithes to John Phelps.[7] By 1687, he had granted land to twelve manorial tenants, including his brother John.[8]

Peter either served or was nominated to serve on juries at Quarter Sessions in 1660, 1661, 1662, 1667, and 1675.[9] He served as tithingman for both Beckhampton and Kennett on several occasions in the late 1660s,[10] and as constable of Selkley Hundred in 1673.[11] In 1670 he signed the hearth tax exemption certificate for the parish as overseer.[12] His name frequently occurs as a witness, appraiser, bondsman, and overseer in Avebury's probate records.[13]

1 Tithes which had formerly belonged to monasteries, but which had been sold to laymen at the Reformation.
2 WANHS Genealogy mss v.A-A, p.127.
3 TNA E134/3Jas2/East17.
4 WSHC 184/4/1. Abstract of John Griffin's title; S., J. 'Notes on Wiltshire Parishes: Avebury', *Wiltshire Notes & Queries* 8, 1914-18, p.222. 12, p.93 incorrectly states that this property was purchased by John Griffin.
5 WSHC 435/24/1/4. Deed, 1st June 1682.
6 WSHC 212A/31/1. Lease & release, 17/18th February 1681/2. 212A/31/2. Assignment.
7 WANHS Genealogy mss A-A, p.132-3.
8 WANHS Genealogy v.A-A, p.136-7 (extract from Close Rolls 4 James 2, pt.8, n027). Alternatively, it may have been his son John, but he was still a minor.
9 WSHC A1/110, 1660M, 1661M, 1662M, 1667M, & 1675M, f.161.
10 WSHC 192/12K.
11 WSHC A1/110, 1673M.
12 TNA E179/348.
13 Witness for Richard Cue, 1659 (WSHC P3/K/86); Overseer and appraiser for Margaret Hayward, 1661/2 (WSHC P3/K/86); appraiser for Richard Davis, 1668 (WSHC P3/D/130); appraiser for John Hayward, 1670 (WSHC P3/H/433); witness and appraiser for John Jacob, 1670 (WHSC P3/IJ/101); appraiser for Richard Cripps, 1670 (WSHC P3/C/352); witness and appraiser for Joseph Wallis, 1680 (WSHC P1/W/349); appraiser for James Pope, 1680, (WSHC P1/P/317); bondsman for Sarah Mills as administratrix of her husband James Mills, 1681 (WSHC P3/M/239); witness of a renunciation, and appraiser for Thomas

He was probably a dissenter; in 1682, he and his wife (whose name is not known) were presented at Quarter Sessions for failing to attend church.[1]

Peter's personal estate when he died in 1689 was valued at £979 18^s 2^d.[2] That included 'corne of al sorts & tythe corne' worth over £300, together with 'sheepe & lambs & hurdles cages & barrs' worth over £150, plus a variety of other livestock – cattle, horses, and pigs.

His son John, and three daughters, Rebecca, Anne, and Sarah, were named in his will.[3] All were under age. John was named as executor, but his uncle John was named as his guardian and 'executor in trust'. The daughters were each given portions of £300. It seems likely that the purchase of his portion of the manor of Avebury Trusloe over-stretched Peter's budget; his will specified that 'if my personall estate shall not be sufficient to pay my debts and the said legacies that then what shall fall short shall be raised out of my lands'. In the event, his son sold the property in 1703,[4] presumably to pay his sisters' legacies.

This Peter Griffin gave his name to a number of other members of his family, including the son of his brother Joseph. Joseph was the tenant of Higdens in 1676,[5] and also still held two acres of land which his great grandfather William had leased in 1596. He was thus well able to help his children establish themselves. His son, Peter junior, one of three brothers, was baptised 15th December 1676. For many years, Peter worked for John Rose, the tenant of Avebury Great Farm. In 1719, a legacy of £80 from his father provided him with some capital.[6] He was also mentioned in the will of his brother John, and would have benefited financially had his infant nieces died.[7] He probably inherited the common for 'one rother beast' which he sold in c.1723.[8] He was evidently an ambitious agricultural labourer, and proposed to lease Avebury Great Farm from Lady Holford after his employer died. His 1722

Mortimer, 1684 (WSHC P3/M/257); overseer and appraiser for Toby King, 1685 (WSHC P3/K/106); appraiser for John Cue, 1687 (WSHC P3/C/515); witness and appraiser for Thomas Pope, 1688 (WSHC P3/P/465).

1 WSHC A1/110, 1682M, f.90.
2 WSHC P3/G/413.
3 WSHC P3/G/413.
4 WSHC 184/4/1. Conveyance, 9th October 1703.
5 WSHC 568/5. Marriage settlement 18th November 1676, Thomas Smith & Joan Stephens. His tenancy was remembered in 1712; cf. WSHC 568/5. Deed 13th May 1712.
6 WSHC P3/G/465.
7 WSHC P3/G/485.
8 WSHC 488/1. Abstract of John Nalder's title.

proposal was accepted, but stocking the farm required much more than his £80 legacy.[1] That was probably why he sold his common. It is likely, however, that the £1,000+ he borrowed from John Brown provided the major portion of the capital needed.[2] The rent was £360 per annum, and the lease was renewed in 1729[3] and again in 1732.[4] In 1737, his farm was assessed at that level for land tax purposes.[5] Meanwhile, his financial affairs had become tangled up with John Brown's affairs; although he stood bond with his creditor's administrator when Brown died in 1731,[6] he was unable to produce accounts of their joint dealings, and was consequently sued in Chancery by the administrator.[7]

In 1736, he became Samuel Holford's gamekeeper.[8] In the later years of his tenancy, however, he did not enjoy good relationships with his landlord (by then Stayner Holford), who was unwilling to allow him adequate time to pay his rent, and refused to renew his lease in 1743. Griffin told his landlord that 'to be turned out so suddenly it grieves me very much, and for to take one in which is no better than my self.'[9] He did, however, own the lease of another farm. When she died in 1728, his sister in law Joan (his brother Joseph's widow) had bequeathed her brother in law the 'remainder of my lease upon Mr Norris's farm by ye bridge in Avebury'.[10] Peter probably retired to it. In 1757, it was probably this property which made him liable to pay window tax, amounting to 9^s, for 14 windows.[11]

Peter's status as the leading farmer in the parish meant that he was expected so serve as churchwarden. He filled that role for at least four years from 1723.[12] He also served as overseer, and as tithingman, in 1739.[13] His signature can be found on a bond between George Stretch and John Brown in 1728,[14] on

1 WSHC P3/G/465.
2 TNA C11/363/65. This assumes that John Brown's administrator's accusation against Peter Griffin was true. Griffin himself denied that he had borrowed any money; see TNA C11/777/21.
3 WSHC 435/24/1/7.
4 WSHC 184/4/1. Abstract of lease made 1739.
5 WSHC 184/3.
6 WSHC P3/B/1308.
7 TNA C11/363/65.
8 WSHC 184/4/1. Deed poll, 1836.
9 WSHC 184/1, pt.2. Peter Griffin to Stayner Holford, 26th June 1743. See also below, p.235-6.
10 WSHC P3/G/517.
11 WSHC 184/3.
12 WSHC D1/15/9, f.27v.; D1/15/ 9 & 10, f.37v.; D1/50/10, f.31.
13 WSHC 184/9/3. WSHC A1/110, 1739M.
14 WSHC 212A/31/1.

the pauper apprenticeship indentures of Elizabeth and Mary Tompkins in 1730,[1] and on a 1733 receipt by Bridget Truslow for money due from Robert Holford.[2]

Peter Griffin married very late in life. His first wife, Elizabeth (we do not know her maiden name) bore him two children. Ann was baptised 27th December 1735, Peter on 10th September 1738 (and buried 20th September 1738). Elizabeth died soon after her infant son, and was buried 2nd October 1738. Peter senior promptly took a second wife, marrying Mary Phelps of Manningford on 15th November 1738. She did not bear him any more children. Peter himself was buried 22nd June 1762, survived by his son Peter, and his daughter Ann. Ann married a tyler, Henry Orchard, on 5th March 1763. All that is known of Peter in our period is that he served as churchwarden for two terms from 1784 until 1786.[3]

Hayward

Several Avebury Hayward families can be identified in our period, but it is not clear whether they were all related. Our attention here will be concentrated on Joseph Hayward and his family. Joseph was not born in Avebury; his antecedents have not been traced. He arrived in the parish in November 1689, and was then, in his own words, 'in a low and meane condition', probably a day labourer in husbandry. By 1694 he was renting a cottage with a small garden and orchard, paying £4 per annum. In 1695 he exchanged his orchard for a meadow, which he rented for 15s per annum. He was able to take a crop of hay, and to depasture a nag, which he used 'in carrying about some small wares and commodities'. It may be that he had become a pedlar or chapman. If so, that logically led to him becoming a small shopkeeper. By 1697, he had married, moved to another cottage for which he paid £3 rent and opened his shop selling 'tobacco, candles, tape, thread, and other small comodityes'. He became the father of five children – Joseph, Henry, Elizabeth, Benjamin and John – whose births were recorded in the parish register as 'dissenters' children' between 1696 and 1702. In 1729, just before his death, he was the tenant of three tenements with gardens and backsides in Eastbrook, which he leased from John Phelps of Draycot Foliat.[4]

Joseph Hayward was a dissenter. And dissenters were *persona non grata* to John White, the vicar, as we will see. Most of the preceding biographical details

1 WSHC 184/9/3. Apprenticeship indenture, Edward Wait, 1739.
2 WSHC 371/1, pt.5.
3 WSHC DC/15/9; D1/50/31.
4 WSHC 529/125. Lease for a year, John Phelps to William Hunt, 6th November 1729.

are taken from Hayward's answer to an Exchequer bill against him lodged by White.[1] White sued Joseph for his Easter offering in 1697, and forced him to spend £6 in his defence. And all for a sum of under 12d! Sir Richard Holford thought that the suit 'swallowed all the money poore Hayward had in the world'.[2] Holford probably provided support when, in 1700, Joseph and a number of his neighbours entered a Chancery bill to defend themselves against White's excessive demands for tithe.

Despite John White, Joseph Hayward evidently became highly respected in the parish. He was invited to witness four wills,[3] appraised four inventories,[4] and stood as second bondsman when Thomas Jordan's widow took out her administration bond.[5] He also witnessed a receipt for the money which Caleb Bailey – another leading dissenter – paid to purchase four acres in the Avebury common fields from Richard Tomkins in 1723.[6] When the dissenters sought a licence for their meeting house in 1723, his was the first signature on the certificate.[7]

Joseph Hayward was buried on 28th January 1729/30. His widow, Elizabeth outlived him by almost two decades; she was buried 30th August 1747. Little is known about most of their children, except that burials are recorded for all but Henry between 1747/8 and 1785. We know a little more about Joseph junior. He married Elizabeth Mackerell at Preshute, on 30th March 1733, and it is evident that he resided in Preshute for a time, sufficient to give him a legal 'settlement' there. When he returned to Avebury in 1740, the Preshute overseers provided a 'settlement certificate', certifying that they would accept liability if he needed to claim poor relief.[8] We do not know precisely when he was resident in Preshute, but his daughter Mary was baptised by the vicar (or perhaps his curate) at Avebury on 23rd May 1736. One wonders whether the son had given up his father's dissent, or whether he simply thought that the vicar, John Mayo, was more acceptable than his

1 WSHC 1569/5.
2 WSHC 184/1, pt.2. Letter, Sir Richard Holford to John White, 22nd July 1708.
3 Those of Richard Browne, 1695 (WSHC P1/B/646), Thomas Griffin, 1716 (P1/G/391), Richard Bushell, 1716 (P1//B/825), and Joseph Griffin, 1719 (P3/G/465).
4 Those of Thomas Fry, 1691 (P3/F/211), John Pope, 1711 (P1/P/495), William Mills, 1714/15 (P3/M/377), and Thomas Griffin, 1716 (P1/G/391).
5 WSHC P1/IJ/167.
6 WSHC 212A/31/3.
7 Chandler, J.H., ed. *Wiltshire Dissenters' Meeting House Certificates and Registrations, 1689-1852*. Wiltshire Record Society, 40. 1985, p.20.
8 WSHC 184/9/1.

predecessor, John White, had been. There may also, of course, have been the thought that any future claim to poor relief might depend on the goodwill of the vicar. All that we know of Joseph's daughter Mary is that she married William Hayward, who may have been a distant relative, on 3rd December 1758.

Hickley

Richard Hickley, yeoman, was born c.1747, and became a prominent member of Avebury's elite, although his birthplace and parentage have not been identified. By 1781, and perhaps earlier, he was serving as bailiff of Avebury manor.[1] In 1789, he received a legacy of £100 in his master Arthur Jones's will, together with a lease of the house he lived in for his life.[2] Jones recommended Hickley to his niece, who inherited his property: he was 'a sober, honest, sensible, diligent man, and well acquainted with the property & every circumstance of the country'.[3] If his successor decided to let the property, Jones thought that Hickley should be invited to become tenant.[4] In the event, Hickley remained as bailiff whilst the Williamsons were in Jamaica, and received a legacy of £50 in Sir Adam Williamson's 1798 will. Sir Adam expressed the 'desire that he shall be continued and employed as bailiff of my said farm lands and estates at Avebury during his life or for so long as he shall be able to carry on and manage the business of the said farm'.[5] Williamson's successors complied: Hickley remained as bailiff for many years.

The Avebury manorial bailiff occupied an important position in Avebury, and was expected to play a leading role in parish life. Hickley served as churchwarden in 1775,[6] then continuously from 1780 until 1788,[7] and from 1790 until at least the end of the century.[8] In 1778 he served as overseer.[9] In 1792, he may have been the parish constable.[10] And he was a land tax assessor throughout the 1780s and 1790s.[11] We don't have full lists of office holders, so he may have served in some of these offices at other times. He

1 WSHC 184/5. Receipt for a well bucket, 13th January 1781.
2 TNA PROB11/1181/174.
3 WSHC 271/3.
4 WSHC 271/3.
5 TNA PROB11/1315/187.
6 WSHC D1/50/27; D3/15/18.
7 WSHC D3/15/19-20; D1/50/30-31.
8 WSHC D3/15/19-21.
9 WSHC 184/9/5.
10 WSHC 184/6. Letter, Richard Hickley to Mrs Williamson, 31st July 1792.
11 WSHC A1/345/18A.

witnessed a number of wills,[1] and was named as executor by Robert Clements in 1795.[2] As churchwarden, he served as a trustee of the Holford Charity[3]. and 'took a very active part in cleansing the cottages' of the poor[4]. His letters to his mistress, Mrs Williamson, provide us with much information concerning life in Avebury in the 1790s.[5] It is therefore surprising that it has not been possible to trace the family from which he came, although it may be that he or other family members had served either Stayner Holford or Arthur Jones, his successive employers, when they lived in Portsea. It is likely that he was related to Mary Hickley, servant to Stayner Holford, who married John Judd in 1751. Richard Hickley married Mary Mason at Pewsey on 2nd April 1777, despite the fact that Arthur Jones regarded her as 'unfit for the management of the farm business'.[6] The couple had five daughters, all baptised at Avebury between 1778 and 1784; they received legacies of £10 each in Arthur Jones's will.

Richard Hickley lived for many years after the end of our period, although his activities after 1800 have not been researched. He was buried 17th April 1833, aged 87. His wife Mary pre-deceased him, she was buried 7th January 1817, aged 77.

Hitchcock
In 1754, James Hitchcock married Mary Stretch, the owner of the Catherine Wheel. Little is known of him before that date, except that his sister Alice married Thomas Rogers,[7] that he was a haberdasher, and that in 1749 he was living in a house owned by Thomas Hunter, a glazier and plumber. When Hunter died, Hitchcock, acting as appraiser, valued the house (presumably the lease) at £60.[8] Land tax assessments indicate that he was still there in 1754, when he married.[9] His wife brought him the trade of an innkeeper, as well as the house in Eastbrook which Mary's grandmother (another Mary Stretch)

1 Including those of Henry Howson, gent., in 1785, WSHC P3/H/1466; Arthur Jones in 1788 and 1789, TNA PROB11/1181/174 (codicils only); John Clements in 1797, WSHC P3/C/1138. His wife Mary was also witness to the latter will.
2 WSHC P3/C/1134.
3 *Select Committee on Education of the Poor &c.* 1818, p.1018.
4 Bernard, Thomas. 'Extract of an account of the introduction of straw platt at Avebury', *The Reports of the Society for Bettering the Conditions and Increasing the Comforts of the Poor*, 4, 1802-5, p.92.
5 WSHC 184/6.
6 WSHC 271/3.
7 WSHC P3/R/549.
8 WSHC P3/H/1256.
9 WSHC 184/3.

had purchased in 1712.[1] But in 1755, the inn itself had to be sold after a disastrous fire.[2] And Mary herself died in 1756, leaving her husband to sort out his father in law's estate.[3] It does not appear that there were any children, or that Hitchcock re-married. He was licenced as a victualler on several occasions between 1754 and 1761, and tenanted the inn from its new owner (who was perhaps John Hunter, the son of his former landlord). He did not, however, remain there for much longer. He reverted to his old trade of haberdashery. In 1770, he described himself as specialising in 'drapery, hosiery & grocery', and also acting as a funeral director, and advertised that he was moving his business from Avebury to Corsham.[4] It is therefore no surprise that when his brother in law, Thomas Rogers of Avebury died in 1778, and James acted as one of his executors,[5] he arranged to have him buried at Corsham.

By 1779, however, he was back in Avebury, and was described as a maltster when James Lewis, the blacksmith, named him as executor of his will;[6] it took him until 1792, and a law suit in the Prerogative Court, to wind up the estate.[7] He was described as a maltster in 1779,[8] and presented his invoice for malt and hops totalling £19 11s 2d to General Williamson in 1792.[9] In 1797, the Turnpike Trustees compensated him for land which they had taken for road widening; this suggests he had retained the 2½ acres of land adjoining the inn when the latter had been sold in 1755.[10] He had probably also retained his wife's house in Eastbrook. In 1798 he paid land tax of 19s 7d,[11] although it is not clear which property this was due from.

James Hitchcock became a prominent figure in the late eighteenth-century parish. His name regularly appears in the freeholders' books between

---

1   WSHC 1409/16/3. Marriage settlement, 5th March 1754. For the Eastbrook house, see release, William Phelps to Mary Stretch, 23rd September 1712. See also Sarum Marriage Licence Bonds.www.findmypast.co.uk/articles/world-records/full-list-of-united-kingdom-records/life-events-bmds/sarum-marriage-licence-bonds. See also below, p.150.
2   See below, p.152.
3   See below, p.152.
4   *Bath Chronicle* 6th December 1770. The newspaper actually calls him John, not James, but it is probable that the reporter was in error.
5   WSHC P3/R/549.
6   TNA PROB11/1055/301.
7   TNA PROB 31/840/590.
8   WSHC 118/88. Statement of Samuel Martyn's debts.
9   WSHC 184/5.
10 WSHC 1371/1.
11 TNA IR 23/96/189, f.249-50

1760 and 1787,[1] and he held a variety of public offices. That included two terms as churchwarden, from 1772,[2] frequent service as a juror at Quarter Sessions in the 1760s and 1780s,[3] high constable of the Hundred of Selkley in 1769, and land tax assessor for Avebury in the early 1780s.[4] He was twice (in 1782 and 1787) described as a 'proper person' to be tithingman of Avebury, but managed to evade that unwanted responsibility.[5]

Holford[6]

Sir Richard Holford was probably descended from the Holfords of Holford, Cheshire,[7] whose pedigree was recorded in the 1623 visitation of Gloucestershire,[8] and whose arms are displayed on Sir Richard's gravestone and window at Lincoln's Inn Chapel.[9] Unfortunately, it has not been possible to identify his immediate ancestors, although it may be that he had some connection with the Holfords of Edington. We do know that his sister was Sarah Hickes of Imber.[10] He married three heiresses in succession, and became a successful and prominent lawyer, living in the Liberty of the Rolls in Chancery Lane from c.1693.[11] The Holford family are frequently mentioned in the register of St Dunstans in the West. He was one of the Commissioners for collecting the aid levied in 1693/4. He became a bencher of Lincoln's Inn in 1689, was its treasurer in 1696, and undertook various other activities for the Society.[12] Between 1693 and 1788, seven other members of his family were

1 WSHC A1/265/19-29.
2 WSHC D1/50/26; D3/15/18.
3 A1/110, Michaelmas rolls, 1761, 1764, 1766, 1768, 1769, 1782, 1785, & 1787.
4 WSHC A1/345/18A.
5 A1/110, 1782M & 1787M.
6 My thanks to Angela Potter for advice on Holford family matters.
7 Burke, Bernard. *General Armory of England, Scotland, Ireland, and Wales*. Heraldry Today, 1989 (originally published 1884), p.499.
8 Maclean, Sir John, & Heane, W.C., eds. *The Visitation of the County of Gloucester, taken in the year 1623 by Henry Chitty and John Phillipot ...* . Harleian Society 21. 1885, p.83. For a discussion of Sir Richard's ancestry, see Potter, Angela. *Weston Birt House and the Holfords*. 4th ed. Privately printed, 2017, p.7-8.
9 Potter, op cit, p.8. They are also on his widow's monument in Avebury church; cf. Phillipps, Thomas. *Monumental inscriptions of Wiltshire*, ed. Peter Sherlock. Wiltshire Record Society, 53. 2000, p.209.
10 GA D1956/E2/8.
11 Keene, Derek, ed. *Four Shillings in the Pound Aid 1693/4: the City of London, the City of Westminster, Middlesex*. www.british-history.ac.uk/no-series/london-4s-pound/1693-4.
12 *The Records of the Honourable Society of Lincoln's Inn: The Black books, vol.3. from A.D. 1660 to A.D. 1775*. Lincoln's Inn, 1899, passim.

admitted to Lincoln's Inn.[1]

Sir Richard was a master in Chancery from 1693 until 1711, one of the most important offices in that court.[2] He was knighted in 1695.[3] From 1694, he also served as a messenger in the House of Lords, and took evidence under oath on its behalf.[4] It seems probable that he was one of the official doorkeepers, a lucrative position which provided a small salary, but also the opportunity to charge fees and extract gratuities.[5]

As a Chancery master, it was his duty to prepare reports for the judges of the Court. Amongst the cases he reported on was one of local importance, relating to settling the governance of the Froxfield Almshouse.[6] His two reports, in 1698 and 1700, perhaps occasioned John White's accusation that he had defrauded the widows of Froxfield of £100 per annum.[7] Holford had a long and acrimonious relationship with White, the vicar of Avebury, which is further discussed below, and is detailed in the many letters they exchanged.[8] That relationship has to be seen against the background of the fact that he exhibited at least fifteen bills of complaint against various people in his Court of Chancery; they related to Middlesex and Westonbirt as well as Avebury. Spaeth has described him as a 'legal bully'.[9]

Richard Holford's marriage to Sarah Crewe in 1664 brought him the Gloucestershire manor of Westonbirt.[10] He also became patron of the living[11] – an advantage which he did not enjoy at Avebury. Sarah died in childbed. She was buried 21st January 1670/1 at St Dunstans in the West, on the same day that her infant daughter, Sarah Crue, was baptised. The latter was buried 3rd

1 *The Records of the Honorable Society of Lincoln's Inn vol.1. Admissions from A.D. 1420 to A.D.1799.* Lincoln's Inn, 1896, passim.
2 Foss, Edward. *The Judges of England.* Vol.7. John Murray, 1864, p.295 & 376.
3 Shaw, W.A. *The Knights of England.* Servatt & Hughes, 1906. vol.2, p.269.
4 *House of Lords journal*, passim. www.british-history.ac.uk/search/series/lords-jrnl
5 Doorkeepers https://historyofparliamentblog.wordpress.com/2017/03/06/doorkeepers/
6 Crowley, Douglas, ed. *The Minute Books of Froxfield Almshouse, 1714-1866.* Wiltshire Record Society 66. 2013, p.4-5, 8-9, 125-8 & 130-33.
7 WSHC 184/1, pt.2. Letter, Sir Richard Holford to John White, 4th October 1711.
8 WSHC 184/1. These will be published in my forthcoming edition of *The Holford Papers*, to be published by the Wiltshire Record Society. See also below, p.XXXx
9 Spaeth, Donald A. *The Church in an Age of Danger: Parsons and Parishioners, 1660-1740.* Cambridge University Press, 2000, p.89 & 137.
10 VCH Glos., 11, p.286; Fendley, John, ed. *Notes on the Diocese of Gloucester by Chancellor Richard Parsons, c.1700.* Bristol & Gloucestershire Archaeological Society, 2005, p.286.
11 Clergy of the Church of England Database https://theclergydatabase.org.uk

March 1670/1. After their deaths, Richard spent some time touring Europe, and wrote a journal of his travels.[1]

Sir Richard's second wife was Elizabeth, daughter of Vice-Admiral Richard Stayner;[2] they married 8th August 1672. Through her he acquired the Catherine Wheel inn in Bishopsgate (not the inn of the same name in Beckhampton!), which her father had purchased.[3] She also brought to the marriage the emeralds which her father had seized when he captured the Spanish plate fleet in 1656. Elizabeth was buried at St Dunstan's in the West, 12th June, 1688.

Richard's third wife was Susanna Trotman; they married on 29th August 1689 at Siston (Gloucestershire)[4]. The Trotmans were owners of Siston manor; Susanna's brother Samuel, who acted as her executor, served as Member of Parliament for New Woodstock 1722-34.[5] Her portion was £7000, which her husband used to purchase the manor of Avebury in 1695 – although he had to find an extra £500 from his own funds to pay for it.[6] For the rest of his life, he and his wife (who he referred to as his 'Frog'), regularly visited Avebury (and Westonbirt) for a few weeks in the summer, and kept in close touch with local affairs. This book draws extensively on his letters and journal,[7] and on the papers of his successors at Avebury.[8]

Holford thought very highly of his third wife; in his will he noted 'her constant and extraordinary love and care of me and my children and her decent frugality'. Three of the children were actually her step-children. Only one of the three was still alive when Susanna made her will, but she made detailed provision for him, and for her step-grandchildren, as well as for her own son, whom she named as her executor and residuary legatee.

Sir Richard had four sons by Elizabeth, his second wife. Richard II was baptised 24th August 1673, and was admitted to Lincoln's Inn 21st October

1 WSHC 184/8.
2 Crisp, Frederick Arthur, ed. *Visitation of England and Wales. Notes, vol.5.* 1903, p.48. For Stayner see Oxford Dictionary of National Biography www.oxforddnb.com.
3 TNA PROB11/564/122.
4 Phillimore, W.P.W., ed. *Collections relating to the family of Trotman.* 1892, p.64.
5 The History of Parliament www.historyofparliamentonline.org/volume/1715-1754
6 WSHC 435/24/1/6. Indenture, 25th March 1798, reciting grant of 28th January 1695 by the trustees of Sir John Stawell's estate; WANHS Genealogy mss. v.A-A, p.138.
7 His correspondence concerning Avebury is in WSHC 184/1; his journal is mainly in GA D1956/E2/8, but a few sheets are also in WSHC 184/8. These will be published in a forthcoming Wiltshire Record Society volume.
8 In WSHC 184.

1693.[1] His marriage to Ann Read, which took place at Portsmouth on 3rd March 1697, was without his father's 'privity or consent'.[2] The couple had three children. Richard III, the eldest, was baptised at Portsmouth 4th July 1699. His brother, Stayner, followed on 10th December 1700, but died as an infant.[3] The third child received the same name as his deceased brother. The two surviving boys were left fatherless when their father, who had made no provision for them, was buried 16th September 1703 at Portsmouth.[4] Their grandfather consequently took on the responsibility of maintaining them. He apprenticed Richard III to an attorney in 1715, at a premium of £100, and gave him the Bishopsgate Catherine Wheel in his will.[5] He also placed £3000 in trust for Richard and his heirs; Evan Jones, his step-father, was one of the trustees. Stayner, Richard III's younger brother, was to receive £1000, 'to be layd out upon some profitable office or employment' for him. Despite his original opposition to the marriage, Sir Richard had come to appreciate his daughter in law: according to his will, she had proved 'a loving and prudent wife', and 'a tender carefull mother' to the orphaned children. He therefore continued to support her, and bequeathed her an annuity of £20 per annum, despite the fact that she had re-married. Her second husband was Evan Jones, rector of Portsea from 1717[6]. The two children were brought up with their half-brothers, Nicholas, Arthur and Thomas. In 1723, Richard III brought a Chancery case against his uncle Robert, complaining that he had not been paid the cash legacy due to him; Robert simply replied that it was supposed to be invested in property, but suitable property had not yet been found.[7]

Richard III married Ann Metcalfe at Sutton (Surrey), on 18th September 1739, but died childless in 1742. His death was followed by a Chancery dispute between his joint executors, his widow Ann, and his brother Stayner.[8] Richard had inherited Avebury manor when his uncle Samuel (see below) died in 1738. His 1742 will[9] gave his widow possession of the mansion house at Avebury, together with a London property, for her life. She also received an annuity of £100, payable out of Avebury rents. The manor of Avebury itself went to

1 *The Records of the Honorable Society of Lincoln's Inn vol.1. Admissions from A.D. 1420 to A.D.1799.* Lincoln's Inn, 1896, p.347.
2 TNA PROB11/564/122.
3 www.findagrave.com
4 www.findagrave.com
5 TNA PROB11/564/122.
6 Clergy of the Church of England Database www.theclergydatabase.org.uk
7 TNA C11/2384/33.
8 TNA C11/818/16.
9 TNA PROB/11/721/329.

Stayner Holford. Ann (or perhaps her mother, Mrs Metcalfe) did not like the arrangement whereby Peter Griffin, the tenant of the manor, had the use of part of the manor house; nor did she appreciate that although her annuity was to be paid out of the rent from Peter Griffin, it had to be paid by her brother in law as lord of the manor, rather than by his tenant. Stayner Holford had to calm his tenant's fears when Ann seemed to threaten him with eviction for non-payment[1] (it is ironic that he was subsequently evicted by Stayner himself), and eventually sued his co-executor (and her mother) to obtain the deeds of his brother's property. Sadly, Ann herself died before the suit proceeded, and Stayner felt impelled to continue it against her mother. She counter-claimed that, for several years before Richard III's death, he and his wife lived in her house, and that they owed her £300 for their maintenance. The outcome of the suit is not known, although the bad feeling it engendered meant that Stayner was not informed when his sister in law died.[2] Nevertheless, Stayner was left in possession of the manor. By October 1753 (and probably earlier) he was resident there.[3] His half-brother, Arthur Jones, was also resident; indeed, he claimed in 1788 that he had lived there for fifty years, presumably since Samuel's death.[4]

In 1755,[5] on his tenant John Rose's bankruptcy, Stayner took Avebury Great Farm in hand. The two brothers, according to a cousin, lived 'temperately and regularly, and take moderate exercise, and are much in the air'. The cousin therefore thought 'they are in a reasonable way to obtain health and long life'.[6] In fact, they lived together for about a decade. Stayner died in 1767, and bequeathed the manor to Arthur;[7] possession passed out of the Holford family.

Robert, Sir Richard's second son, was baptised at St Dunstan's in the West on 6th June 1686. He matriculated at Trinity College Oxford in 1702, was admitted to Lincoln's Inn in 1703, and was called to the bar in 1710. Like his father, he held various offices as a bencher of the Inn, and served as a master in Chancery from 1712 until 1750.[8] The manor of Westonbirt, together with

1   WSHC 184/1, pt.2. Letters, between Peter Griffin and Stayner Holford, 29th January 1742/3 & 3rd February 1742/3.
2   WSHC 184/1, pt.2. Peter Holford to Stayner Holford, 9th April 1743.
3   WSHC 184/3. Opinion on Stayner Holford's Land Tax Assessment, 12th October 1753.
4   WSHC 271/2. Note on Avebury estate, c.1788.
5   See p.133-4.
6   Quoted by Knowles, Francis, Sir. 'Avebury Manor', *WAM* 56, 1955, p.367. Unfortunately, Knowles does not cite his source.
7   TNA PROB11/932/345.
8   *Alumni Oxonienses* www.british-history.ac.uk/alumni-oxon/; *The Records of the*

various other property, was bequeathed to Robert in Sir Richard's will.[1] It continued to be owned by his heirs until the early twentieth century. Robert was one of his father's three executors, but was expected to play the leading role, since the other two – Sir Richard's widow Susanna, and her brother Samuel Trotman, both suffered from ill health.

Robert married Sarah, the daughter of Sir Peter Vandeput, on 30th April 1717, at St Olave's Hart Street, London. Sarah was descended from Huguenot refugees.[2] The couple had seven children born between 1719 and 1737, most of whom were baptised at St Andrews, Holborn, and one of whom, Robert, died as an infant. Another Robert, with his brother Peter, were mentioned in their grandfather's will. Siblings born after his death included Sarah, Richard Stayner, and Elizabeth.[3] Sarah and Elizabeth both married in London.[4] Peter followed in his grandfather's steps; he was admitted to Lincoln's Inn in 1735,[5] became a barrister in 1740, and held various offices in the Society, whilst serving as a Master in Chancery.[6] Robert was admitted to Gray's Inn on 16th June 1742,[7] but did not complete his studies; instead, he sailed to India in March 1743, aged about fifteen, and became a merchant in the East India Company. He died there before 1763 without returning home.[8]

Sir Richard and Elizabeth had two other sons – both named Stayner, after their maternal grandfather – who also died before their father. One was

---

Honorable Society of Lincoln's Inn vol.1. Admissions from A.D. 1420 to A.D.1799. Lincoln's Inn, 1896, p.361; *The Records of the Honourable Society of Lincoln's Inn: The Black books, vol.3. from A.D. 1660 to A.D. 1775.* Lincoln's Inn, 1899, passim.

1 TNA PROB11/564/122. For the other property see below.
2 Bosanquet, V.O. 'The Huguenot Families in England, III: the Vandeputs', *Ancestor*, 4, 1903, p.37.
3 All were mentioned in their father's will, TNA PROB11/799/123.
4 Sarah married John Edwards at Sts Ann & Agnes, Aldersgate, 29th December 1739; Elizabeth married Anthony Askew, at St Andrew Holborn, 5th March 1757. Askew was a 'Doctor in Physick' according to the marriage licence register, 3rd March 1757.
5 *The Records of the Honorable Society of Lincoln's Inn vol.1. Admissions from A.D. 1420 to A.D.1799.* Lincoln's Inn, 1896, p.411.
6 *The Records of the Honourable Society of Lincoln's Inn: The Black books, vol.3. from A.D. 1660 to A.D. 1775.* Lincoln's Inn, 1899, passim.
7 Foster, Joseph, ed. *The register of admissions to Gray's inn, 1521-1889, together with the register of marriages in Gray's inn chapel, 1695-1754.* Hansard Publishing Union, 1889, p.375.
8 WSHC 184/1, pt.2. Letter, Stayner Holford to Robert Holford, 6th March 1742; 271/2 Memorandum re Peter Holford's title to Beckhampton Farm, 10th September 1780; TNA PROB11/894/337. Note that although the will was dated 1753, it was not proved until 1763.

described in St Dunstans in the West parish register as 'a child from Chancery Lane', and was buried in the chancel, 27th May 1687. The other was baptised in the same church just a few months later, on 28th July 1687. Sadly, he died c.1708. According to his father's will, he was 'dead in the wars in Flanders unmarried and buried in the Dutch church in Courtray', which is now in Belgium.

Sir Richard's third wife, Susanna, who was much younger than her husband (she was born in 1655), bore three children. Two of them, Susanna and Trotman, died in childhood. Samuel was baptised 4th April 1693 at St Dunstan's in the West, matriculated at Magdalen Hall, Oxford, was admitted to Lincoln's Inn in 1712, and was called to the bar in 1719.[1] When his mother died in 1723, he inherited Avebury, although, like his father, he continued to reside in London.

In addition to the manors at Westonbirt and Avebury, Sir Richard acquired other properties, both in Avebury and elsewhere. A letter from Humphry Wall in 1702 suggests that he had expressed an interest in purchasing Truslow's Farm from Richard Truslow, but was pipped at the post by his East Kennett neighbour, Charles Tooker.[2] In 1710, however, he did succeed in purchasing Beckhampton Farm. This descended with the manor of Avebury until 1731, when Richard Holford conveyed it to his uncle Robert,[3] in a transaction which was subsequently regarded as dubious by Richard's successors.[4] Sir Richard had also acquired property adjoining his manor of Westonbirt, together with the manor of St Etheldred's in Wells (also known as Southover, and purchased in 1672),[5] messuages in Shippon, Sherston, and a lease of Symons Inn in Chancery Lane, all of which were bequeathed to Robert. At the end of his life, Sir Richard estimated that his property at Avebury was worth £12,500, at Westonbirt, £5000, and at Siston and Wells, £300.[6]

---

1 *Alumni Oxonienses* www.british-history.ac.uk/alumni-oxon; *The Records of the Honorable Society of Lincoln's Inn vol.1. Admissions from A.D. 1420 to A.D.1799.* Lincoln's Inn, 1896, p.373; *The Records of the Honourable Society of Lincoln's Inn: The Black books, vol.3. from A.D. 1660 to A.D. 1775.* Lincoln's Inn, 1899, p.256.
2 184/1. Letter, H. Wall to Sir Richard Holford, 18th October 1702.
3 WSHC 371/1, pt.5. Lease & release, 24th February 1731/2. See also *VCH Wilts* 12, p.95, & Long, William. *Abury illustrated.* 1862, p.59.
4 WSHC 271/2. Peter Holford's title to the Beckhampton estate.
5 Potter, Angela. *Weston Birt House and the Holfords.* 4th ed. Holfords of Westonbirt Trust, 2017, p.9. See also LMA CLC/B/120/MS15588.
6 TNA PROB11/564/122.

Sir Richard was 'greatly indisposed in his health' in 1717.[1] In August of that year, he was suffering from a sore toe, and was 'constrained to come from Bath in a horse litter', for which he paid £3.[2] Despite the ministrations of a French surgeon in Bath, and of the vicar, John Mayo (who was also an apothecary), it was probably this complaint that led to his death.

He was buried in the chapel of Lincoln's Inn on 16th May 1718, aged 85.[3] After his death, his widow Susanna took possession of the manor of Avebury as her jointure. Her husband left her all his household goods in both London and Avebury (although not at Westonbirt), together with his coach and horses. She was still living in Lincoln's Inn Fields in December 1720,[4] but probably moved to Avebury, where she was buried 29th March 1723, aged 68.[5] Sir Richard will specified that their son, Samuel, was to inherit his Avebury property on Susanna's death. He, however, continued to reside in London. When he died, in June 1738, he was unmarried and left no will. The estate was therefore inherited by his nephew, Richard III. Richard as already noted, had been apprenticed to an attorney, and was admitted to Lincoln's Inn in 1719.[6] He married three times, but all his wives died without children.[7] By 1737, he was in residence at Avebury, but still 'reading law', and concerning himself in the school founded by his grandmother.[8] According to his 1742 will,[9] he also owned a messuage in the Strand let to Widow Fox, which he bequeathed to his wife Sarah. Sarah also received an annuity of £100 per annum charged on the manor of Avebury. He bequeathed further annuities charged on this property: £60 per annum to his step-mother Ann Jones, £20 per annum to his step sister Ann. The manor itself, however, was given to his brother Stayner. He gave rings to his uncle Robert and his wife, 'desiring them to accept the same', and perhaps mindful that they might dispute the inheritance. In the event, his aunt did so, although unsuccessfully.[10]

1 WSHC 184/4, pt.1. Renewal of John Rose's lease.
2 GA D1956/E/2/8.
3 Baildon, Paley, ed. *Records of the Honourable Society of Lincoln's Inn: Admissions from A.D.1420 to A.D.1893 and Chapel Registers*. Lincoln's Inn, 1896. v.2, p.647.
4 WSHC 184/1, pt.2. Letter, Lady Holford to Thomas Alexander, 12th December 1720.
5 www.findagrave.com
6 *The Records of the Honorable Society of Lincoln's Inn vol.1. Admissions from A.D. 1420 to A.D.1799*. Lincoln's Inn, 1896, p.384.
7 WSHC 271/3.
8 WSHC 184/1, pt.2. Robert Holford to Richard Holford, 24th September 1737.
9 TNA PROB/11/721/329.
10 WSHC 184/1, pt2. Peter Griffin to Stayner Holford, 29th January 1742/3.

Stayner was resident in Portsea (Hampshire), where his step-father Evan Jones had been vicar until his death in 1738.[1] That was the same year that he inherited Avebury. It is therefore likely that he immediately took up residence in Avebury's manor house, although we have no evidence of that until 1754, when a letter was sent to him there.[2] He made his will in Avebury,[3] and was buried there 4th October 1767. He bequeathed the property to his half-brother, Arthur Jones, thus ending Holford ownership of the manor.[4] Their mother Ann was buried a few months before Stayner, on 25th May 1767, ending the annuity she claimed from the manor (which would have been £20 per annum greater if she had survived Stayner).

The Holford name did not, however, disappear from Avebury. Mention has already been made of the fact that Robert, Sir Richard's son, who had inherited Westonbirt, also acquired his nephew's farm at Beckhampton in 1731, perhaps by dubious means.[5] When he died in 1753, the Beckhampton farm descended to his son Robert, but, as noted above, the latter had gone to India, dying there before 1763. Robert junior left a will dividing his estate between his brothers and sisters,[6] but it was ruled invalid because it only had two witnesses; it needed three. Therefore his estate descended to Peter, his eldest brother, much to the disgust of his siblings. They accused Peter of having given his brother false advice to stay in India, in the hope of inheriting the Beckhampton farm himself – which he did. The farm at Beckhampton continued to be held by Peter's descendants until 1897,[7] although their major interests continued to be in Westonbirt.[8] A later member of the Westonbirt family, Robert Stayner Holford, was said to be 'the richest commoner in England' in the nineteenth century[9].

Horsell
Reuben Horsell, the parish clerk of Avebury in the early eighteenth century,

---

1. Clergy of the Church of England Database https://theclergydatabase.org.uk
2. WSHC 184/1,pt.1. Letter, Henry Howson to Stayner Holford, 21st March 1754.
3. TNA PROB11/932/345.
4. TNA PROB11/932/345.
5. WSHC 271/2. Memoranda regarding Peter Holford's title to the Beckhampton estate.
6. TNA PROB11/894/149.
7. *VCH Wilts* vol.12, p.95.
8. For more on the Westonbirt family, see Potter, Angela. *Weston Birt House and the Holfords, 1665-2017.* 4th ed. Holfords of Westonbirt Trust, 2017.
9. Jones, E.L. *Landed estates and Rural Inequality in English History from the Mid-Seventeenth Century to the Present.* Palgrave Macmillan, 2018, p.22.

was immortalised by Stukeley as 'a sensible man and lover of antiquities', who had 'a due veneration for these sacred remains'[1]. The stones did not return his veneration: he narrowly escaped with his life when one he was sheltering under was struck by lightning.[2] We know little of his life, although he is mentioned in probate records: Reuben appraised the inventory of Thomas Jordan in 1719,[3] and witnessed the will of John Griffin in 1722.[4] He was buried 15th January 1727/8. Many years later, in 1772, Stukeley's woodcut of Horsell was described by the elderly Avebury schoolmaster, John Clements, as 'a very great likeness'.[5]

The earliest mention of the Horsells in Avebury is the parish register entry for the baptism of Reuben's son Henry, dated 3rd October 1693.[6] It is likely that they were related to the Horsell family of Wootton Bassett, with whom they shared names such as Reuben, Bartholomew, and Nathaniel. The Avebury branch of the family could perhaps best be described as respectable but poor. Reuben was a shoemaker, a trade which two of his sons, Reuben and John, continued.[7] Both these sons (probably) served successively as parish clerk.[8] Reuben and his wife Esther had at least six children, two of whom died in infancy. Henry, the eldest, was sufficiently well off to pay 2s land tax in 1752,[9] but nevertheless undertook casual labouring work. In 1740 he was digging sand and gravel to provide the materials for Richard Holford to undertake building work.[10] His brother John made enough money as a shoe maker to purchase houses from Robert Woodman and George Mortimer, together with land from a third brother, Nathan.[11]

Nathan was a shepherd. During the bankruptcy proceedings against John Rose in 1755, he stated that he had worked on Avebury Farm for 23 years.[12]

1 Stukeley, William. *Abury: a Temple of the British Druids … .* 1743, p.22 & 25.
2 Long, William. *Abury illustrated.* 1862, p.96.
3 WSHC P1/IJ/167.
4 WSHC P3/G/485.
5 Nichols, John. *Illustrations of the literary history of the eighteenth century, vol.IV.* John Nichols & Son, 1822, p.856. Nichols does not actually name Clements.
6 It is possible that a John Horshell paid hearth tax c.1662 (TNA E179/259/29), but the tax roll is almost illegible, and the reading is uncertain.
7 Markham, Sarah. *John Loveday of Caversham, 1711-1789: the Life and Tours of an Eighteenth-Century Onlooker.* Michael Russell, 1984, p.41.
8 See below, p.413-15.
9 WSHC 184/3.
10 WSHC 184/5. Henry Horsell's account, 1740.
11 WSHC P3/H/1388.
12 WANHS mss 692, f. 3. It was thought c.1757 that he had worked as a servant there for 45 years; cf. WSHC 184/1. Necessary remarks.

In 1756, he was re-engaged when Stayner Holford took the farm in hand.[1] He did, however, own two properties on which he paid a few shillings land tax in 1751, 1752, and 1753.[2] In 1754, however, he only paid on one house. Perhaps the other was the property which his brother John had purchased from him.

Two of these three brothers had children. Henry and his wife Susanna had three – John, Reuben and Mary – between 1719 and 1724. Nathan and his wife, Ann Dangerfield, had ten between 1726/7 and 1749. Several of these children married, and by the end of the century there were many Horsells in Avebury. They will not be traced here. However, the possibility that Reuben and Esther had a fourth son should be mentioned. Proof that Bartholomew was another son has not been found, but it does seem likely. His two eldest sons, John and Bartholomew, lived until the ages of 80 and 76 respectively. Bartholomew the younger described himself as a labourer when he stood bond for the marriage licence of John Brown in 1787. He married Elizabeth; their son William was baptised 16th February 1756. He occasionally made his mark in the marriage register as a witness, and perhaps aspired to his (presumed) great uncle's and grandfather's position as parish clerk.

Jones

Anna Holford, the widow of Sir Richard Holford's son Richard and mother of Richard and Stayner Holford, married Evan Jones on 9th November 1708. Jones had become rector of Portsea in the previous year, and remained there until he died in 1738.[3] The two Holford children were presumably raised in his household with their three step-brothers: Nicholas (baptised 14th June 1710), Arthur (baptised 18th July 1712), and Thomas (baptised 10th March 1713). Both Nicholas and Thomas married and had children, who are mentioned in Arthur's will. Arthur, however, remained un-married.

Like his step-brother Richard and other members of the Holford family, Arthur Jones became a lawyer. He was admitted to Lincoln's Inn in 1729,[4] called to the bar in 1738, and held various offices in the Inn between 1754 and 1774.[5] When his step-brother Stayner died in 1767, Arthur inherited Avebury manor, together with The Hare and Hounds at Beckhampton, other Avebury property, and the Catherine Wheel in Bishopsgate. In the following

1   WSHC 271/4.
2   WSHC 184/3.
3   Clergy of the Church of England Database www.theclergydatabase.org.uk
4   *The Records of the Honorable Society of Lincoln's Inn vol.1. Admissions from A.D. 1420 to A.D.1799.* Lincoln's Inn, 1896, p.400.
5   *The Records of the Honourable Society of Lincoln's Inn: The Black books, vol.3. from A.D. 1660 to A.D. 1775.* Lincoln's Inn, 1899, passim.

year, Arthur took on the office of Hundred constable.[1] He had perhaps already been living in Avebury during legal vacations, as he was described as residing there as early as September 1753.[2] He continued in possession until his death in 1789. At first, he intended to bequeath the property to his nephew Richard but changed his mind.[3] His 1786 will bequeathed the property to Anne, daughter of his brother Thomas, and her husband Adam Williamson.

Morris

The Morris family were prominent members of Avebury's dissenting congregation. A 'conventicle' was meeting at the house of Samuel Morris in 1669.[4] Samuel and Richard Morris (who were probably brothers) and their wives were all presented for dissent at the Marlborough Quarter Sessions in 1682,[5] although Samuel served as a juror at Quarter Sessions in 1683 and 1691, and as a Hundred juror in 1685.[6] Despite their dissent, both men made donations towards the rebuilding of St. Paul's Cathedral in 1678.[7] Samuel gave 4d, Richard 2d. Perhaps they still hoped for agreement between dissenters and the Church of England. It may have been with that in mind that Samuel served as churchwarden in 1687 and 1688.[8] Agreement, however, was sadly not to be, although a measure of toleration was introduced after William III ascended the throne.

Both brothers were manorial tenants. Richard Morris served on several occasions as a homager in the manorial court in the 1650s.[9] In 1654 he served on the Hundred jury.[10] In 1651 he sub-tenanted the copyhold of Susanna Griffin, widow, who was ordered to evict him, and fined 10s for having sub-tenants.[11] However, it seems likely that this was merely a money-raising exercise; he was presumably still resident there in 1659 when she died, and the property, which included a cottage, a small garden, three acres of arable, and common of pasture, and had been 'heretofore parcel of a customary tenement

---

1 WSHC 9/23/1.
2 WSHC 185/3. Thomas Jones's Memoranda, 4th September 1753.
3 Knowles, Francis, Sir. 'Avebury Manor', *WAM* 56, 1955, p.367.
4 Turner, op cit, vol.1, p.109 & 812.
5 WSHC A1/110, 1682M,
6 WSHC A1/110, 1683M, f.167; 1685M, f.206; 1691M, f.140.
7 LMA 25565/24, f.18-19.
8 WSHC D3/15/2.
9 WSHC 473/52, f.7, 37 & 91.
10 WSHC A1/110, 1654M, f.153.
11 WSHC 473/52, f.7.

in Eastbrooke called Brunsdons' was granted to him for a fine of £20.[1] A few years later, c.1662, Richard paid hearth tax on two hearths.[2]

Richard's brother Samuel, a yeoman,[3] occupied a customary tenement in the 1680s, from which a rent of 2d per annum was payable.[4] He married Joan Davis on 12th June 1671. Their tenement was probably the 'cottage on the waste' owned by John Griffin, which was amongst the property he was considering selling in 1702.[5] Morris probably also had other property; he frequently served as a juror at Quarter Sessions in the 1680s and 1690s.[6] He may have been a maltster; Richard Cue owed him £1 for malt in 1678.[7] He witnessed the will of Joseph Wallis, and appraised his probate inventory, in 1680[8] He also stood bond with Ann Cue when she was granted administration of her husband John's estate in 1687.[9]

We may conjecture that Samuel and Richard Morris, who were prominent dissenters in the early eighteenth century, were sons of these two brothers, although their precise relationships are not known.[10] The two both had their dwelling houses licenced for dissenters' meetings. Their certificate was dated 31st March 1707, but within two weeks a newly erected meeting house built on Samuel's land was also licenced. Samuel provided the land on which it was erected, and Richard was amongst the signatories of the certificate. In 1723, Samuel signed a fresh certificate for 'the house called the Meeting House'.[11] Both, incidentally, were well regarded by Sir Richard Holford, who asked Samuel for advice on matters relating to bounds, gates and fences in 1711, when John Rose leased Avebury Great Farm,[12] and who also suggested that when Rose needed to write to him, Richard could act as his scribe (Rose

1 WSHC 212A/31/2. Copy of court roll, 3rd October 1659.
2 TNA E179/259/29.
3 According to John Cue's administration bond, WSHC P3/C/515.
4 WANHS Genealogy mss., v.A-A, f.136-7.
5 WSHC 184/4/1. John Griffin's sale particulars. It was sold to Sir Richard Holford in 1703.
6 WSHC A1/110, 1695M, f.75, 1683M, f.167, 1685M, f.197, 1685M, f.206, 1691M, f.140, & 1695M, f.75.
7 TNA C6/98/30.
8 WSHC P1/W/349
9 WSHC P3/C/515.
10 If the property at Brunsdens granted to Richard in 1659 (see above) was indeed the property sold by Samuel to Caleb Bailey in 1738 (see below), that suggests Samuel was Richard 's son.
11 Chandler, J.H., ed. *Wiltshire Dissenters' Meeting House Certificates and registrations, 1689-1852*. Wiltshire Record Society 40. 1985, nos.159, 160 & 235.
12 GA D1956/E2/8.

was unable to write).[1]

Richard married Sarah Furnil of Marlborough at Mildenhall on 20th March 1705. Their children were not baptised by the vicar, John White, but the fact that duty was due on their baptisms meant that their names had to be recorded in White's separate 'register of dissenters' children'. Sarah was born 4th December 1706; Lydia on 6th January 1710/11. Another child was born on 10th May 1712, but died two days later. It seems likely that Richard subsequently moved to Marlborough, as a Richard Morris of Marlborough, yeoman, stood bond with John Robinson (another Avebury dissenter) when Robinson was granted administration of his mother Mary's estate in 1752.[2]

Samuel, whose wife was also named Sarah, had his daughter Sarah baptised by a Church of England clergyman at Bishops Cannings on 25th July 1714, which suggests (assuming this was the same Samuel Morris) that the dissenters of Avebury had no theological objection to Anglican baptism. Perhaps it was merely their own local vicar, John White, to whom they objected. This Samuel Morris was a cordwainer in 1724,[3] although by 1734 he was a maltster, sufficiently wealthy to lend £150 on mortgage in 1734 to his fellow dissenter, Thomas Robinson.[4] The mortgage was extended in 1752, despite the fact that Robinson defaulted on payments.[5] In 1736 Morris lent a further £425 to William White, the son of the late vicar, as a mortgage on various lands which had descended to White from his father. The property included the Malthouse, which Morris himself occupied.[6] It was perhaps the tenement at Brunsdens that Richard Morris had been granted in 1659 that Samuel Morris, maltster, sold to Caleb Bailey in 1738,[7] and which in 1752 came into the possession of the dissenters' charity established by Bailey.[8]

It is probable that Samuel was serving as vestry clerk in 1737.[9] He was returned as a freeholder on several occasions between 1736 and 1745, making him liable to serve on juries at Quarter Sessions, and eligible to vote

---

1 WSHC 184/1, pt.2. Letter, Sir Richard Holford to John Rose, 23rd November 1710.
2 WSHC P3/R/481.
3 WSHC 529/185. Mortgage deed, 19th June 1724.
4 WHC 212A/31/4.
5 WSHC 212A/31/4. Mortgage deed, 2nd January 1752.
6 WSHC 488/1; 873261.
7 WSHC 212A/31/3. Lease and release.
8 WSHC 212A/31/4.
9 WSHC D1/41/4/48.

in Parliamentary elections.[1] In 1737 he served as Hundred constable,[2] and in 1738 as collector and assessor of the land tax. He paid 24s land tax for his estate and his malthouse in 1752.[3] In 1716 he appraised the probate inventory of Thomas Griffin,[4] and in 1746/7 he witnessed the will of Thomas Hunter.[5]

Samuel's daughter Sarah married John Nalder, another noted dissenter, in 1738; Nalder administered his father-in-law's estate when he died in 1753.[6]

Nalder

The Nalder family, who were prominent dissenters in late eighteenth century Avebury, originally came from Winterbourne Monkton. Thomas Nalder was prominent in local affairs, and served as high constable of the hundred in 1683.[7] He and his wife Martha had five children when Thomas made his will in 1711.[8] His will does not name them, but it is probable that Thomas Nalder of Winterbourne Monkton, who made his will in 1756, was one. He died childless, and bequeathed the lands which he had been given in Caleb Bailey's will to his two brothers, Robert and John.[9] Robert received lands in Broad Hinton and Cleeve, although he served as churchwarden of Avebury on five occasions between 1752 and 1760.[10] John was due to receive three-quarters of the manor of Berwick Bassett on the death of Giles Bailey. He would have been able to add that to the reversion of a further portion of the manor already given to him by Bailey's will, but unfortunately died before he actually came into possession. The two brothers were named as joint executors in Thomas's will. Both Robert and John described themselves as 'of Avebury' in their own wills, although John was buried in Winterbourne Monkton.

John Nalder and his family,

John Nalder married Sarah Morris in 1738.[11] She was the daughter of Samuel

1 WSHC A1/265/8-16.
2 WSHC A1/110/1737M
3 WSHC 184/3.
4 WSHC P1/G/391.
5 WSHC P3/H/1256.
6 WSHC P3/M/523.
7 WSHC A1/110, 1683M, f.113.
8 WSHC P1/N/133.
9 TNA PROB11/782/93 (Caleb Bailey's will); WSHC P3/N/250 (Thomas Nalder's will). Bailey was a noted dissenter.
10 WSHC D3/15/15 & D1/50/20-22.
11 The 'event place' given by the IGI is 'Dean of Salisbury, Wiltshire', whatever that might mean. But it does make it probable that the marriage took place in the Church of England.

Morris[1], on whose land the dissenter's meeting house had been built. John acted as administrator of his father-in-law's estate in 1753. Caleb Bailey's will named him as one of the trustees for the dissenting charity he established.[2] Bailey also bequeathed Nalder his lands in 'Kennett'.

Between 1744 and 1774, John Nalder served on numerous occasions as tithingman for East and West Kennett.[3] Despite his nonconformity, he served as churchwarden in 1749, and perhaps in 1750.[4] He also served as overseer in 1755,[5] and again in 1763.[6] As a freeholder, he was frequently summoned for jury service at Quarter Sessions in the 1760s and 1770s.[7] In 1755 and 1756 he helped to appraise the stock of John Rose, the bankrupt, on behalf of Stayner Holford,[8] and also sold some stock to Holford when the latter took the bankrupt's farm in hand.[9]

In addition to the lands mentioned above, John Nalder tenanted both John Norris's 'little farm' in 1751 and subsequent years,[10] and Stayner Chamberlain's farm in West Kennett in 1755; on the latter, he paid rent of £185 per annum.[11] According to his 1762 will, he had purchased property at Clyffe Pypard from Walter Grant 'lately'.[12] He was probably a substantial employer, and endorsed the demand made by Avebury's farmers in 1756 that their labourers should work longer hours[13].

Nalder's dissenting connections involved him in providing financial support to his fellow dissenters. In 1755, he took over the small mortgage on John Robinson's house in Eastbrook from his father in law; [14] two years later he transferred it to his niece Martha's son in law, George Brown. Also in 1757, John Nalder took over his father-in-law's mortgage on Robinson's land at Parsonage Close.[15] In 1758 he bought the property outright. Robinson had

1   See above, p.104.
2   See below, p.433-4.
3   WSHC 9/23/1.
4   WSHC D1/50/19; D3/15/14.
5   WSHC 184/9/3. Pauper indenture for Thomas Burrows, 24th May 1755.
6   WSHC 184/9/5. Bastardy bond of John Rumsey, 22nd July 1763.
7   WSHC A1/110, Michaelmas sessions rolls, passim.
8   WSHC 184/4/1. Account, 4th November 1755 and 11th March 1756.
9   WSHC 184/4/1. Particulars of purchases, 1755-6.
10 WSHC 184/3.
11 WSHC 568/7. Stanes Chamberlayne & Samuel Martyn to John Nalder, 9th November 1755.
12 TNA PROB11/938/220.
13 WSHC 1569/31.
14 WSHC 529/185.
15 WSHC 212A/31/4. Mortgage deed, 21st September 1757.

once lived in the house, which fronted the Meeting House, but had divided the property into two cottages and let them out.[1]

In 1758 John Nalder witnessed the will of his brother Robert.[2] His own will[3] was written in 1762, although he did not actually die until 1768. In it, he bequeathed his widow Sarah an annuity of £20 per annum. In 1795, when the manor was enclosed, she held four acres of arable in Ratland Field.[4] She died in 1800 aged 86. John's will names three sons, John, Thomas and Robert, and two daughters, Sarah and Mary; all were under age when he died. They were probably all baptised in the dissenters' chapel, so are not mentioned in the parish register. Thomas, the second son, was aged 69 when he died in 1821, so must have been born c.1752. His daughter Sarah married John Oriel Bailey, a clothier of Calne. The 1753 Marriage Act required dissenters to be married by an Anglican priest, so their marriage was recorded in the parish register on 11th September 1766.[5]

John the younger probably took up residence in Berwick Bassett when the manor reverted to him soon after his father's death. By September 1768, he was certainly in possession, as he was employing Robert Clements (the Anglican schoolmaster's brother) as his gamekeeper there.[6] He also inherited the remainder of his father's lease of a farm at West Kennet, together with a number of small annuities. It was probably John the younger, rather than his father, who was accused of taking many stones from the West Kennett megalithic avenue. He was supposedly acting under the instructions of his landlord, Mr Grubbe, and used the stones to build a farmhouse and many of the houses at West Kennett[7].

In 1770, John the younger purchased four acres of land in Kennett Fields from John Dobson. The property included two newly erected dwelling houses, with a bake house, malt house, and outhouses, together with common of pasture for one 'rother beast'.[8] In the 1770s, he apparently helped his cousin Martha's husband, George Brown to pay the rent of his farms at Brunsdens and Pophams.[9] In 1780, land tax amounting to £11 9s 2d was paid on the property he let to William Crook, his cousin's husband, £1 18s 4d on property

1 WSHC 529/185.
2 WSHC P3/N/257.
3 TNA PROB11/938/220.
4 WSHC A1/EA95.
5 See also Sarum Marriage Licence bonds www.findmypast.co.uk.
6 WSHC A1/305.
7 Long, William. *Abury illustrated*. 1862, p.64.
8 WSHC 488/1. Abstract of Deeds.
9 WSHC 473/277.

tenanted by Richard Bailey, and 16s on John Strange's tenancy.[1],

In 1790 he occupied property at Avebury valued at £75 for the land tax.[2] Ten years later, its value was said to be £120 – the increase in value was perhaps due to the enclosure. John was buried at Berwick Bassett 8th June 1821, aged 78.

On 1st January 1784 John the younger married Elizabeth Nash at Berwick Bassett. Their three children were baptised there between 1787 and 1794.

Thomas, John the elder's second son, married Elizabeth, but had no surviving children when he made his will in 1821.[3] He had inherited his father's reversionary interest in lands at East Kennett, together with £600.[4] In 1779, he purchased a 'capital messuage' and farm in Avebury, with a tenement in Beckhampton, from Mary Hopkins, the widow of Richard Phelps, paying the substantial sum of £1500.[5] He had formerly rented property at Draycot Foliat from her.[6] In 1794, one of the houses in Kennett Fields was exchanged for a cottage owned by George Hillier.[7] Thomas leased a substantial farm at East Kennett from the Grubbe family, and subsequently from Mr Tanner, from at least as early as 1780 until c.1793.[8] He also leased the vicarial tithes of Kennet[9] from Rev James Mayo for the same period.[10] He paid land tax on various properties in East and West Kennett, including his house in West Kennet which was rated at 12s 8¼d in 1797.

Thomas was frequently listed for jury service at Quarter Sessions between the 1770s and 1790s, and served on the Grand Jury on several occasions.[11] In 1789, he served as land tax assessor for the tything of East and West Kennett

---

1 WSHC A1/345/18A.
2 WSHC A1/345/18A. The taxpayer was named in the assessment as 'Mr Nalder', so he might have been one of John's brothers.
3 TNA PROB11/1645/129.
4 TNA PROB11/938/220. He paid land tax on this throughout the 1780s and 1790s; cf. WSHC A1/345/240A.
5 WSHC 212A/31/4.
6 WSHC 212A/31/1. Lease & release, 17/18th March 1778. Harriet Southby to Mary Hopkins.
7 WSHC 488/13.
8 WSHC A1/345/240A.
9 Probably of West Kennett, although they were listed in the 1780 assessment for the parish of East Kennet.
10 WSHC A1/345/240A.
11 WSHC A1/265/21-41. WSHC A1/110, 1779M, 1781M, 1782M, 1784M, 1787M, 1791M, 1792M, and 1797M.

(he himself paid £1 4s 1d),[1] and also became a trustee of Caleb Bailey's charity.[2] When he died in 1821, he continued his family's support for the meeting house (by then described as Presbyterian) by bequeathing thirty perches of land adjoining to it either for a burial ground, or for the erection of a house for the minister.[3] But that was later than our period.

Robert, John the elder's third son, in contrast to his brother John, was commended by Charles Lewis, the curate of Avebury, for 'his earnest endeavours at preserving the remains of this wonderful stupendous work [the megaliths], and for his general urbanity at all times in communicating the results of his knowledge concerning it'.[4] In the 1795 enclosure award, he was recorded as holding nine pieces of land. That included 168 acres of arable and downland, and a variety of smaller holdings.[5] It also included a third share of land held with Richard Thring, presumably in trust for Caleb Bailey's charity, of which he became a trustee in 1789[6] (or it may have been held in trust for Avebury chapel). In 1792, the Turnpike Trustees paid him six guineas to compensate him 'for the damage done him over many years past in digging and carrying flints from off his Down'.[7] He served on the Grand Jury at Quarter Sessions on several occasions in the 1780s and 1790s,[8] as tithingman of Avebury in 1785,[9] and as land tax assessor on several occasions in the 1790s.[10] Service in the Hundred court, however, was not to his liking. At various times in the 1790s he served as high constable of the Hundred, and as foreman of the Hundred jury, but was repeatedly fined for neglecting jury service.[11] It may be that he was not keen on participating in an institution which challenged his religious and political beliefs. When rioting broke out in the early 1790s, Richard Hickley, the churchwarden, commented that Dr Joseph Priestly, the Unitarian controversialist, was a 'very bad man', and 'at the bottom of the mischief', but nevertheless was 'a great favourite of the Nalders'.[12] This Robert was buried 21st November 1801.

1 WSHC 473/352.
2 Reeves, K.M. 'The Caleb Bailey Charity', *Baptist Quarterly* 26(2), 1975, p.64.
3 TNA PROB11/1645/129.
4 Lewis, Charles. *A descriptive Account in blank verse of the Old Serpentine Temple of the Druids at Avebury in North Wiltshire*. 2nd ed. 1801, p.5.
5 WSHC A1/EA95.
6 Reeves, op cit, p.64.
7 WSHC 1371/1.
8 WSHC A1/110, 1783M, 1784M, 1791M, 1794M and 1796M; See also his name on the freemen's list from 1773, A1/265/21-41.
9 WSHC A1/110, 1785M.
10 WSHC A1/345/18A.
11 WSHC 9/23/1.
12 WSHC 184/6. Richard Hickley to Mrs Williamson, 29th July 1791.

Robert Nalder and his family,

Robert Nalder, John the elder's brother, was living at Draycot Foliat, in the parish of Chiseldon, when he married Ann Neat of Lydiard Tregoze at Mildenhall on 9th May 1733. Their daughters, Ann, Martha, and Mary, were baptised at Chiseldon between 1734 and 1737. Mary died when she was barely two months old. Her father must have moved to Avebury in the 1740s.

In the 1750s, Robert was the tenant of John Norris's property at Brunsdens, referred to in the land tax assessments as Norris's 'Great farm'; his land tax in 1751 amounted to £24.[1] We have already seen that his brother Thomas left him land at Cleeve and Broad Hinton in 1756.[2] In 1756 he joined with his brother John and other farmers in demanding longer hours from his labourers.[3]

Robert served several terms as Avebury's churchwarden, in 1751,[4] 1752,[5] and from 1756 until 1759.[6] In 1751, and again in 1761, he served as land tax collector,[7] and in 1757 he collected the house and window tax, being assessed himself on 19 windows.[8] Like his brother, he was returned as a freeholder in 1760 and 1761, eligible to serve on Quarter Sessions juries, and to vote.[9]

There is little detail in Robert's 1758 will (he died in 1762), except that he left his wife an annuity of £20 per annum, and his daughter Ann was given £100. If she had any children, they were to receive £200, to be divided equally between them. Martha was made her father's residuary legatee and executrix. Robert's will was witnessed by his brother John, his future son in law, George Brown, and by Robert Clements.

Robert's widow Ann was buried at Winterbourne Monkton 26th June 1766. His daughter Ann married William Crook, the carpenter, at East Kennett, 9th February 1758, before her father's death. Martha married George Brown at Avebury 15th May 1762, after her father had made his will, but just before he died. Curiously, her marriage bond stated that she was born in 1741, although she was actually baptised on 30th June 1736.[10]

1 WSHC 415/134. For the land tax assessments see 184/3.
2 WSHC P3/N/250.
3 WSHC 1569/31.
4 WSHC D3/15/15.
5 WSHC D1/50/20; D3/15/15.
6 WSHC D1/50/21-22; D3/15/14
7 WSHC 184/3. Land tax assessment 1751. Appeal against land tax assessment by Mr Holford, 1761.
8 WSHC 184/3. House and window tax assessment, 1757.
9 WSHC A1/265/19-20.
10 Salisbury Marriage Licence Bonds www.findmypast.co.uk

Phelps als Bromham[1]

The Phelps als Bromham family of Avebury were a prolific family (or perhaps 'families'; it is not clear that all who bore this name in the parish were related), who were present in the parish from the beginning of our period until the mid-eighteenth century, although some of them moved away to places such as Draycot Foliat, Chiseldon, and even London. They claimed the right to heraldic arms, which were inscribed on the memorial stone of John Phelps in 1731.[2] In the late sixteenth century, they were substantial tenants of the manor, but some members of the family subsequently became landowners in their own right; our knowledge of them mostly concerns their land holding and their public service.

The family is first mentioned in the survey of the manor made in 1548,[3] when Richard Phelps I held at will a small cottage, with 22 acres of arable in the West Field, 22 acres in the North Field, a few small pieces of pasture and meadow, and common for 80 sheep, 6 'rother' beasts, and 2 horses. He – or perhaps his son – is next mentioned in 1589 and 1590, when he served as churchwarden for two years.[4] A Richard Bromham paid the subsidy on goods valued at £4 in 1594 and 1598.[5] Nicholas Bromham, who was rated at £6 in the 1563 subsidy, was probably related.[6]

It is not possible to be certain, but it is probable that Richard II, who served on Quarter Sessions juries on several occasions between 1603 and 1616,[7] was the son or grandson of Richard Phelps I. He was a yeoman, and in 1601, took a three-life lease of c.25 acres of arable, with a close of pasture and a dwelling house, at Beckhampton. It was granted by Richard Truslow, gent., on payment of an entry fine of £100, and a rent of 16s per annum.[8] Richard II named his two sons, John I, and Timothy I, as lives. Thomas Phelps of

---

1 So many members of this family bore the names John, Richard and Timothy, that it has been necessary to number them below in order to distinguish them. Their surname has been abbreviated here to Phelps, except in those few instances where they are only called Bromham in the sources.
2 Phillipps, Thomas. *Monumental inscriptions of Wiltshire*, ed. Peter Sherlock. Wiltshire Record Society, 53. 2000, p.210. They are not, however, mentioned in Squibb, op cit.
3 WSHC 2664/1/2D/8.
4 WSHC D3/7/1, f.35 & 50.
5 TNA E179/198/315; E179/198/325
6 TNA E179/198/276.
7 WSHC A1/110. Michaelmas rolls, 1603, 1605, 1607, & 1609-16.
8 WSHC 212B/102. Lease, 30th April 1601.

Overton served as Truslow's attorney in this transaction; he may have been a relative.

John I, in 1631, was granted a reversion of his tenement – presumably, that is, the tenement which his father had leased – in favour of his son John II.[1] In 1634, he was forty years old, so must have been born c.1594. It is probable that he was buried in late 1686, in his nineties. He married Ann,[2] and had at least four children, John II, Richard III, Timothy II, Anne, and Sarah. Sarah died as an infant, on 19th April, 1632. His daughter Anne's 1652 marriage settlement notes that she was to marry John Hopkins of Clyffe Pypard.[3] As part of the settlement, Hopkins enfeoffed John the elder with a messuage in Bushton, Clyffe Pypard. Both John I and his brother Timothy I served as churchwardens for two terms, Timothy in 1629 and 1630,[4] John in 1638 and 1639.[5] John also served as a juror at Quarter Sessions on several occasions between 1624 and 1654,[6] as high constable of Selkley Hundred in 1634,[7] and as tithingman of Eastbrook on several occasions in the 1650s.[8] He was named overseer of William Plummer's will in 1631/2,[9] and appraised several probate inventories: Thomas Bray (1639),[10] John Jacob (1670),[11] John Hayward (1670),[12] and Nathaniel Power, the vicar (1670).[13] In 1647 he accused Sarah Duck of stealing his barley.[14] In 1662 he stood bound with Joseph Eatall for the latter's appearance at Quarter Sessions.[15] He was assessed to the hearth tax on three hearths c.1662,[16] and to the subsidy on lands valued at £2 in 1663.[17] The lands

1 TNA E134/9and10Chas1/Hil1.
2 Her name is given in the baptismal entry for their daughter Sarah.
3 WSHC 212B/1921.
4 WSHC D3/15/1.
5 WSHC D3/15/1
6 WSHC A1/110, Michaelmas rolls, 1624-6, 1630, 1635, 1639-40, 1647, 1654. Timothy served as juror in 1632 and 1647; cf.A1/110, 1632M, f.201, & A1/110, 1647M. f.12.
7 WSHC A1/110, 1634M, f.209 & 272.
8 WSHC 473/52, f.7, 37, 49, 83, & 91.
9 TNA PROB11/161/422.
10 WSHC P3/B/420.
11 WHSC P3/IJ/101.
12 WSHC P3/H/433.
13 WSHC P3/P/329.
14 WSHC A1/110, 1647M, f.424. His 'information' names two of his sons, John II and Richard
15 WSHC A1/110, 1662E.
16 TNA E179/259/29.
17 WANHS mss.140.

concerned were probably those at Beckhampton which he occupied with his brother Timothy I, and which were the property of John Goldsmith.[1]

Timothy I married Mary Mortimer, 19th November 1621; their daughters Catherine and Margerie were baptised on 26th December 1623 and 28th December 1632 respectively. He held a copyhold tenement, which he surrendered to Sir Edward Baynton as lord of the manor in 1654.[2] When Frissy Baldveen died c.1631, £35 of her money was in his 'hanes & custody'.[3] He witnessed the nuncupative will, and appraised the inventory, of Christopher Battington in 1636.[4]

The Family of John Phelps als Bromham II

John II never obtained the reversion of the tenement originally leased by his grandfather; he died in 1662, before his father. He, or perhaps his son John III, paid tax on three hearths c.1662.[5] He left an estate valued at £491 3s 8d. His will[6] indicates that he was a tenant of Alexander Popham, lord of the manor of Winterbourne Monkton.[7] He made his elderly father, and his brother Richard II, joint guardians of his son John III (born c.1656)[8] and of his four daughters, Ann, Mary, Sarah and Elizabeth. His wife was not mentioned, so presumably died before him. Ann was named after both her grandmother, and her aunt. Mary obtained a marriage licence to marry John Bryant of Hilmarton, 3rd February 1663/4.[9] Her sisters were buried un-married, on 2nd January 1691/2 and 23rd June 1699 respectively.

John Phelps III married another Ann; their son Robert was baptised 15th August 1677. In 1681 John and Ann were presented by the vicar, John White, for 'not coming to church to hear divine service'.[10] Ann was buried 28th February 1682/3. A couple of years later, on 28th June 1685 at Woodborough, John III took Mary Dyke as his second wife.[11] Their daughter, again named Ann, was registered as a 'dissenters child' when she was born on 1st December 1700.

1. WSHC P1/G/142
2. WSHC 473/52, f.55.
3. WHSC P1/B/230.
4. WSHC P3/B/368.
5. TNA E179/259/29.
6. WSHC P1/B/416.
7. *VCH Wilts* 12, p.194.
8. He was said to be aged 31 when he gave evidence in an Exchequer case in 1687; cf. WANHS Genealogy v.A-A, p.135.
9. Neville, op cit, 32, 1916, p.202.
10. WSHC D3/12/2.
11. It is possible that she was the first wife of John IV.

John III was a clothier,[1] and was sufficiently wealthy (with Peter Griffin) to become one of Robert Baynton's mortgagees in 1683,[2] although he had to assign other mortgages he held in order to raise the capital.[3] In 1697, he purchased the freehold of several copyhold tenements in Eastbrook from Peter Griffin, some of which were tenanted by members of his family.[4] As a freeholder, he was paying a 'high rent' of 3s to John Griffin in 1703, probably for some of these properties.[5]

John Phelps III occupied several public offices: churchwarden, with Thomas Phelps, in 1689;[6] constable of Selkley Hundred in 1695;[7] tithingman for Beckhampton in 1700.[8] He served on many Quarter Sessions juries between 1678 and 1700.[9] In 1688 he appeared as a witness for Peter Griffin when he sued Thomas Pontin for tithes.[10] He appraised several probate inventories in the 1680s,[11] and witnessed the will of Peter Griffin in 1687.[12] In 1678, he contributed 1s to the fund for rebuilding St Paul's Cathedral,[13] despite his dissent. In 1698 he was asked to act as surety when William Skeat was bound over to keep the peace against John Griffin.[14] Between 1701 and 1703 he took the oath as a dissenting minister.[15]

The entry in the parish register recording the burial of 'John Phelps gent' in 1729, probably refers to John III, although that would make him a centenarian, and no mentions of him have been traced in the previous two decades. If that is correct, he outlived his son Robert, who was buried 14th

---

1 WSHC 212A/31/1. Lease and release, 17/18th February 1681/2. Another copy at 435/24/1-3.
2 WSHC 184/4/1. Abstract of title to the manor and rectory of Avebury.
3 WSHC 212A/31/1. Lease and release, 17/18th February 1681/2. Another copy at 435/24/1/1-3 See also 435/24/1/4
4 WANHS Genealogy, v.A-A, p.136-7.
5 WSHC 184/4/1. Proposed conveyance, John Griffin to Sir Richard Holford, 1703.
6 WSHC D1/50/3, f.29; D3/15/2.
7 WSHC A1/110, 1695M, f.75.
8 WSHC 192/12K.
9 WSHC A1/110, Michaelmas rolls, 1678-1700. It is possible that some of these entries refer to John IV.
10 TNA E134/3Jas2/East17.
11 John Tomkins, 1680 (WSHC P3/T/284); Joseph Wallis, 1680 (WSHC P1/W/349); Toby King, 1685 (WSHC P3/K/106); Thomas Mortimer, 1684 (WSHC P3/M/257); John Cue, 1687 (WSHC P3/C/515).
12 WSHC P3/G/413.
13 LMA 25565, f.18-19.
14 WSHC A1/110, 1698M, f.51.
15 WSHC A1/239.

June 1728. Robert served as a juror at Quarter Sessions in 1700 and 1712.[1] No other evidence for him has been found.

The family of Richard Phelps als Bromham

Richard Phelps III (the son of John I), who was described as a yeoman in his will,[2] married Anne Cooke of Coate, a widow, at Bishops Cannings, 1st May 1664.[3] Anne's jointure was a dwelling house in Beckhampton, with 'several parcels of arable dispersed in the common fields of Beckhampton'.[4] Her husband already owned the property at Beckhampton – perhaps thirty or forty acres, with a dwelling house – which had previously been tenanted by his father and Timothy Phelps I.[5] He had, in 1654, purchased it for £320 from Thomas and George Goldsmith, the sons of his father's landlord.[6] He also possessed another property in Avebury, on which he paid tax on two hearths c.1662.[7] In 1681, he purchased a tenement in Eastbrook, including sixty-two acres of arable in the common fields, and common for one hundred sheep, six 'rother beasts', and two horses.[8] This was probably the portion of the manor of Avebury Trusloe formerly owned by Robert Baynton.[9] His 'new enclosure' was tenanted by Thomas Mortimer in 1682.[10] In the 1680s Richard III was also a copyholder of land owned by Peter Griffin and John Phelps III.[11] In 1685, he purchased an estate at Stockley, in Calne[12]. And at some stage he acquired property at Draycot Foliat, which he bequeathed to his wife Anne for her life.[13] Richard Phelps III was nominated for jury service at Quarter Sessions on several occasions in the late 1660s but only actually served once.[14] He did however, serve as constable of Selkley Hundred in 1662 and 1665, and

---

1. WSHC A1/110, 1700M & 1712M (unfoliated).
2. WSHC P1/P/432.
3. For their marriage licence, see Neville, Edmund. 'Marriage licences of Salisbury', *Genealogist*, N.S., 32, 1916, p.204.
4. WSHC 212B/107.
5. WSHC P1/G/142.
6. WSHC 212B/105. Deed, 16th May 1654.
7. TNA E179/259/29.
8. WSHC 212A/31/2. Release 18th February 1681/2. Copy at 529/125.
9. *VCH Wilts* 12, p.93.
10. Hobbs, Steven, ed. *Wiltshire Glebe Terriers, 1588-1827*. Wiltshire Record Society 59. 2003, p.17.
11. WANHS Genealogy v.A-A, p.136-7.
12. *VCH Wilts* 17, p.73.
13. WSHC P1/P/432.
14. WSHC A1/110, 1664M, f.180; 1665M, f.132; 1666 M, f.67; 1668M, f.128.

presented John Jacob at Quarter Sessions for not coming to church.[1] He also served as churchwarden in 1666,[2] and as parish constable c.1670.[3]

Two of Richard and Ann's children were baptised at Avebury: John IV, baptised 3rd December 1666, Mary, baptised 15th March 1670/1. There were other children, possibly baptised elsewhere, whose baptisms have not been traced. Richard III bequeathed £500 each to his daughters Eleanor and Honour, and substantial sums to other children. His will also refers to his 'daughter West', his 'daughter Stratton', and his son Richard IV. He was buried at Avebury on 16th May 1701, although his will describes him as being of Burderop, Chiseldon.

Richard IV became the best known bearer of the family name, as the proprietor of the famous Whitechapel bell foundry in London.[4] It may be that he had been apprenticed to James Bartlett, whom he succeeded there in 1701.[5] We know that he was a native of Avebury, since a bell hung in Avebury church in 1719 is inscribed 'Richard Phelps, London, nat. par.'[6] Many of his bells still survive, including the great hour-bell of St Pauls Cathedral. His father left him £100,[7] which would have helped to establish him in the bell founding trade. He made his will in Whitechapel, and died in August 1738.[8]

John Phelps IV of Draycot Foliat and his family

John IV inherited his father Richard III's portion of Avebury Trusloe manor.[9] His marriages, however, brought him property at Chiseldon, and at Draycot Foliat. He also held land at Calston and Blackland.[10] His first wife was Mary, the daughter of John Turke of Chiseldon; they married at Charlton on 22nd

1 WSHC A1/110, 1662M, f.113; 1665M, f.137.
2 Bishops' transcript.
3 TNA E179/348.
4 Page, William, ed. *A History of the County of Middlesex: Volume 2, General; Ashford, East Bedfont With Hatton, Feltham, Hampton With Hampton Wick, Hanworth, Laleham, Littleton.* London, 1911, pp. 165-168. www.british-history.ac.uk/vch/middx/vol2/pp165-168.
5 Page, William, ed. *A History of the County of Middlesex: Volume 2, General; Ashford, East Bedfont With Hatton, Feltham, Hampton With Hampton Wick, Hanworth, Laleham, Littleton.* London, 1911, pp. 165-168. www.british-history.ac.uk/vch/middx/vol2/pp165-168.
6 Mayo, Charles Herbert. *A genealogical account of the Mayo and Elton families of the counties of Wilts and Hereford.* Chiswick Press, 1882, p.43.
7 WSHC P1/P/432.
8 TNA PROB11/691/110.
9 *VCH Wilts* 12, p.93-4.
10 TNA PROB11/653/24.

April 1694. She was buried 2nd June 1705 at Avebury, but John IV kept her dowry: Drayton Farm at Chiseldon.[1] He married again in 1706; his second wife was Mary Moore, who brought him property in Draycot Foliat.[2] Land tax on his Avebury property was assessed at £5 7s 8d in 1738, and was paid by his tenant, Robert Rose.[3] He apparently settled in Draycot Foliat, although his body was returned to Avebury for burial on 3rd December 1731; the Avebury parish register recorded that he was 'of Draycot Foliatt, gent'. A son, John V, had already been buried there 15th January 1713/14. His widow outlived him by almost thirty years; on 18th October 1760, she too was buried at Avebury, but described as 'of Draycot Foliat'. He was survived by his first wife's two daughters, and by four daughters and a son by his second. The first two had already married, and been given dowries of lands in Draycot Foliat.[4] They each received a token shilling in their father's will.[5] The other four daughters were each to receive annuities of £36 whilst they remained single, and a portion of £800 upon marriage.

Richard V, John IV's only surviving son, inherited his freehold property, including the farm at Avebury, although, when he also died (at Bath, 24th May 1744) his executors had to sell off part of the estate to meet his sisters' legacies. Various law suits followed, which are outside of the scope of this book.[6] Property at Avebury, Calne, and Blackland was advertised in the *London Gazette* on 1st February 1755; it was then let for £110 8s 8d per annum. Ultimately, much of the estate was sold to John Bull of Calne in 1756[7]. The reversion of some property at Avebury was purchased by John Savage of Marlborough in 1757,[8] and ultimately became the property of Caleb Bailey's dissenting charity. Other property at Avebury had been left to Richard V's widow, whose second husband, Thomas Hopkins, claimed it; it was sold to John Nalder for £1500 in 1779.

1 WSHC 212B/1790.
2 WSHC 1840/1/5.
3 WSHC 184/3. Land tax assessment 1738.
4 *VCH Wilts* 9, p.47.
5 WSHC 212A/31/2. Common recovery 7th November 1729; TNA PROB11/653/24.
6 See WANHS Genealogy v.A-A, p.148. There are many relevant bills and answers in TNA C11 and C12.
7 WSHC 212a/31/2.
8 He was the widower of Eleanor, one of John IV's daughters; cf. *VCH Wilts* 12, p.94; WSHC 212A/31/2. Lease & release, 4th January 1757.

Pontin

Between 1671 and 1713, Thomas Pontin frequently served as a juror at Quarter Sessions, and on the Selkley Hundred court,[1] although some of the later mentions may refer to his son, another Thomas. He served as churchwarden in 1686,[2] and again in 1710,[3] He or his son is also mentioned in the 1712 freeholders' book.[4]

The evidence suggests that Thomas was not the most popular person living in Avebury at the beginning of the eighteenth century. It was said that the bailiff of the manor of Avebury Trusloe refused to allow him to serve on the manorial jury, because he was 'soe troublesom a person amongst his neighbours'.[5] His financial dealings were probably at the root of his troublesomeness. It seems likely that he was a money lender. His occasional involvement in the process of probate can probably be attributed to the fact that he was owed money by the deceased. In 1693, he was the 'principal creditor' of the late Elizabeth Styles, and as such administered her estate.[6] He took on the same role as 'principal creditor' of Frances Pope, in 1712.[7] Thomas also stood bond with John Tomkins in the administration of Tomkins' father's estate in 1680,[8] and with John Pope in the administration of John Mills's estate in 1701.[9] In 1709 he appraised the estate of Richard Tomkins.[10] The executors of Andrew Mills in 1672 paid him 15s 7d for ploughing the deceased's lands.[11]

Thomas also appraised the probate inventory of Richard Cue in 1678, and stood bond with Cue's widow, Mary, for the administration of his estate.[12] This was more significant, since, four year's later, he married Cue's widow, and brought up her infant daughter Joan as his step-daughter. She was the heir to her father's leasehold property, but her step-father took it over. He also had a

1 WSHC A1/110, 1671M, f.162; 1672 M, f.94 & 155; 1679M, f.135; 1685M, f.206; 1687M, f.189 & 203; 1695M, f.75; 1701M, unfoliated; 1702M, unfoliated; 1703M, unfoliated; 1713M, unfoliated. But later mentions may refer to his son Thomas.
2 WSHC D1/50/2; D3/15/2.
3 WSHC D3/15/8.
4 WSHC A1/265/2.
5 TNA E134/3Jas2/Hil2.
6 WSHC P3/S/782.
7 WSHC P3/P/637.
8 WSHC P3/T/284.
9 WSHC P3/M/324.
10 WSHC P3/T/421.
11 WSHC P3/M/60.
12 WSHC P3/K/92.

number of other leasehold estates in Avebury, Berwick Bassett, and Calne.[1] In the early 1680s he was running between forty and seventy sheep on his stepdaughter's estate.[2]

Thomas Pontin's possession of his step-daughter's property eventually led to a law suit. Many years later, after Joan had married Nathan Cooper, and had subsequently died in childbed, her widower husband sued Thomas and Joan's mother to obtain possession of the leasehold.[3] Thomas responded by pointing out that his costs in raising Cue's daughter and heiress exceeded the value of her father's estate. It seems that Cooper lost his case; at least, Pontin held a leasehold estate known as 'Kewes' when he made his will in 1720.[4] The question remains, was Joan the victim of her step-father's rapaciousness, or was her widower without justification in bringing the Chancery case? It is certainly true that Thomas was disliked by his neighbours, and considered to be an exceptionally awkward individual to deal with. Several witnesses in an Exchequer case in 1688[5] complained of his litigiousness. Thomas Griffin noted that, in the twenty years of his acquaintance, he 'had never knowne him to be out of suites in law'.[6] Walter Cue, Joseph Griffin, and Edith Arnold all accused him of having them imprisoned for debts they did not owe.

Thomas was also reluctant to pay his debts. When William Bray sold him cattle and other goods worth over £100 in 1669, he had to sue in order to obtain payment.[7] Similarly John Griffin sued him in the Exchequer in 1687, in order to obtain payment of tithes from the leasehold estate his stepdaughter had supposedly inherited.[8] He was also sued for non-payment of tithes by the vicar, John White, in 1710.[9] He countered that by joining with Richard Caswell to accuse White of neglecting his duties.[10] He had earlier been involved in a suit concerning tithes against John White; in 1700 he had been one of several 'complainants' in Chancery who challenged the vicar's claim to tithes.[11]

1   TNA PROB11/585/280.
2   TNA E134/2and3Jas2/Hil2.
3   TNA C6/98/30.
4   TNA PROB11/585/280.
5   TNA E134/3Jas2/East17. See also E134/2and3Jas2/Hil2.
6   The only suits for which evidence survives are those mentioned here.
7   TNA C8/185/8.
8   TNA E134/2and3Jas2/Hil2. This is abstracted in WANHS Genealogy v.A-A, p. 134.
9   WSHC 184/8.
10 WSHC 184/8; D1/39/1/67, f.106-69, passim; D1/42/68.
11 TNA C10/534/43.

Later mentions of Thomas Pontin are likely to relate to Thomas Pontin the younger, who is mentioned in his father's 1720 will.[1] In 1706 he was required to answer an accusation from John Brinsden, vicar of Winterbourne Monkton, that he had stolen several cattle, and also 'touching his clandestinely keeping a gate post from him' (whatever that might mean!). An accusation of affray was made against him in 1713, and a *billa vera* (a true bill) was found against him in 1714.[2] Three years later, he was again in trouble before Quarter Sessions, this time for probably begetting a bastard (although there is no evidence of an actual birth). According to Martha Robinson, he had twice had 'carnall knowledge of her bodie', once 'in an outhouse belonging to Humphry Robinson', and then in his house.[3] Humphry Robinson, her father, was one of the leading lights in Avebury dissenting congregation,[4] and would have been greatly embarrassed. The issue still rankled when he made his will in 1720. Although he bequeathed Martha a house and an annuity, the annuity was to cease if she married Pontin.[5]

Thomas Pontin the elder was buried 23rd November 1720. In his will, he described himself as a yeoman. He mentioned his wife Mary, his son Thomas, and his two daughters, Frances and Charity.[6] We may assume that they were all adults at his death. The will reveals him as a minor landowner. He had a copyhold estate called Fowlers at Berwick Bassett, which he bequeathed to his son. Charity was given his leasehold estate at Axford in Avebury, together with property he had purchased from a member of the Phelps family. She was still paying land tax of 4s 1d for this property in 1738.[7]

The property at Axford was probably leased from John Griffin. Pontin is mentioned as a leaseholder in the 1703 sale of Griffin's estate to Sir Richard Holford,[8] and probably had two lives remaining.[9] It is likely that this is the property his widow was still occupying in c.1731.[10] She was buried 11th January 1731.

1 TNA PROB11/585/280; copy at WSHC 1075/001/410, pt.2.
2 WSHC A1/110, 1713M & 1714M, unfoliated.
3 WSHC A1/110, 1717M.
4 See below, p.127.
5 WSHC P1/R/275.
6 TNA PROB11/585/280; copy at WSHC 1075/001/410, pt.2.
7 WSHC 184/3. Land tax assessment 1738.
8 WSHC 184/4/1. Deed, 9th October 1703.
9 There had been a year earlier; cf. WSHC 184/4/1. Particular of John Griffin's estate, 1702.
10 WANHS Genealogy v.A-A, p.147; WSHC 371/1, pt.5. Draft deed, c.1730, between R.L., & Robert Holford.

Frances received his freehold lands in Calne, together with leasehold property which had been purchased from Thomas Baskerville, gent. The daughters never married; Charity was buried 2nd July 1741, Frances 26th April 1734. Thomas the younger was still paying land tax of 1s 6d in 1752,[1] but there is no further evidence for his life.

There were other Pontin families in Avebury; between 1666 and 1784 there were twenty-one baptisms. However, the evidence is fragmentary, and it seems probable that there were several unrelated families.

Pope

The Popes were another prolific family in seventeenth and eighteenth century Avebury. Thomas Pope, who made his will in 1601/2,[2] was probably the brother of James Pope, whose inventory he appraised just before his own death.[3] Elizabeth Pope, who made her will in 1618,[4] may have been related, perhaps their sister in law. The wills of Thomas and Elizabeth enable us to trace their descendants. James left no will, but his widow Alice did, so his descendants too could be traced. Most, but not all, Avebury Popes were descended from these three.[5] Here, we will confine ourselves primarily to Thomas and his family.

Thomas Pope I was a moderately prosperous husbandman, who employed his own shepherd, and also had a maidservant. In c.1595 he leased Warwicks, and paid the subsidy on goods valued at £4 in 1594 and 1598.[6] In 1598 he was said to be aged 62.[7] His 1601/2 will[8] provides some indication of the basis of his prosperity. He had a flock of more than forty sheep, at least two bullocks and a calf, and at least two hives of bees, together with several acres of wheat and barley. He was the lessee of the farm at Warwicks, and also of property at Highway and Manton (in Preshute). He made bequests to Salisbury Cathedral, and to his parish church.

Thomas I's will identifies three sons, Thomas II, the eldest, James II, and

1   WSHC 184/3. Land tax assessment, 1752.
2   WSHC P3/1Reg/95.
3   WSHC P1/P/11. Both James and his wife Joan gave evidence in an Exchequer case in 1599; he was about 70 years old, she about 60. See TNA E134/41Eliz/Hil8.
4   WSHC P3/P/78.
5   John Pope, a dissenter, who married Ruth Robinson, and was buried without the rites of the established church in 1711, was related to this family, but the precise relationship cannot be established; see his will, WSHC P1/P/495. For his burial, see GA D1956/E2/8. See also below, p.411.
6   TNA E179/198/315; E179/198/325.
7   WANHS Genealogy mss., v.A-A, p.91.
8   WSHC P3/1Reg/95.

Richard I. James and Richard were both bequeathed flocks of sheep and other livestock. Thomas had the lease of Warwicks. Their sister Maud, had married John Skuse; her daughter, Edith Skuse was given £10 in her grand-father's will (although it was money which Edith's father owed to the testator). Thomas I also made bequests to each of his three sisters, Isobel, Constance and Joan. He was survived by his wife Alice, whom he named as joint executrix with his son Thomas II. John Pope, probably his nephew, was named as overseer.

Thomas II inherited his father's lease of Warwicks, which he sold to John Goldsmith some years later.[1] An un-dated survey of Avebury Farm, which probably refers to Thomas I's sons, names Thomas II as the tenant of thirty acres of arable in Pickedstone Piece, and James II as the tenant of 27 acres of arable in three separate pieces, one of which he shared with Thomas.[2] They are also probably mentioned as neighbours of William Dunch in 1639.[3] Both brothers paid 3s in the subsidy of 1611.[4] Their other brother, Richard I, receives no further mention in available records.

Thomas II, and his wife Joan, were presented in 1593 for 'not receivinge at Easter', that is, refusing to take communion.[5] Five years later, he (or perhaps his father) appeared in the Consistory Court accused of defaming John Balden by describing him as a 'whore master knave'.[6] The couple do not seem to have had any children. Thomas II's brother, James II, served as churchwarden in 1613,[7] 1621,[8] and again (possibly) in 1633;[9] on the latter occasion he was presented for negligence in his office. Both brothers were free suitors of the manor of Avebury in the 1650s, and appeared (or defaulted) regularly at the manorial court; Thomas was nominated to serve as tithingman for Westbrook in 1653, but the entry in the court book is deleted, suggesting that he died before he could take office.[10] The appointment of his brother to succeed him is not recorded. That he did so, however, is evident by the fact that, at the following court, James II came and 'desired to be discharged of his office'. He was succeeded by James III, 'the younger', presumably his son.

1 TNA E134/8Chas1/Mich53.
2 WSHC 184/4/1. Survey of Avebury Farm.
3 WANHS Genealogy mss, v.A-A, p.113.
4 TNA E179/199/369.
5 WSHC D3/7/1, f.97v.
6 WSHC D1/42/16, f. 189r-191v. I owe this reference to Steve Hobbs.
7 WSHC D1/42/28, f.35-37r & 61r-62r. I owe this reference to Steve Hobbs.
8 WSHC D3/15/1.
9 WSHC D1/39/2/12, f.10v.
10 WSHC 473/52, f.6, 7, 37, 83, 91 & 98.

James III and his brother, Richard I, who died respectively in 1679 and 1685, were both relatively young men when they died; one of James III's sons was barely ten years old when he was orphaned, and both widows survived their husbands for several decades. As a young man, James III served in Captain Colley's militia company in 1660.[1] He witnessed the will of John Hayward in 1661,[2] and served as churchwarden in 1672.[3] He donated 6d towards the rebuilding of St Paul's Cathedral in 1678.[4] His 1680 inventory lists the goods of a moderately wealthy husbandman; it was valued at just over £372.[5] Like most Avebury yeomen/husbandmen, he practised sheep/corn husbandry. His 350 sheep and lambs were valued at £100, his 'corne in the barnes & ricks' at £136. He also had eleven 'rudder beas' (cattle), four horses, and eleven pigs. That may be compared with his widow Jane's 1712/13 inventory,[6] which records 347 sheep valued at £150, 'wheat drashed & undrashd in riks & barnes' worth £100, and 'barly in the barnes' valued at £72. She also had nine horses, twelve cows, four heifers, six calves, and seven pigs, and had managed to increase the value of her estate in her many years of widowhood to over £641. It is likely, however, that she vacated the marital home after her husband's death, as in 1681 she was renting a cottage from Peter Griffin for one shilling per annum.[7] One of her sons probably lived in his father's house.

That may have been James III. In 1673, he (or perhaps his father) tenanted three yardlands from Mary Narborne and Robert Baynton.[8] This property probably gave him the right to pasture his 'beef' on Hackpen and West Down. In 1668/9, he agreed to 'abate' a third of this entitlement for the ensuing year.[9]

Neither James Pope III nor his widow Jane left a will. Their children are named in the 1685 will of James's brother, Richard Pope I, who had no children of his own, and described Jane as his sister-in-law[10]. They included Walter, James IV, John, Richard II, Jane, and Elizabeth.[11] Richard II had paid

1 WSHC 1178/48-9.
2 WSHC P3/H/339.
3 Bishop's transcript.
4 LMA MS 25565/24 f.18-19
5 WSHC P1/P/317. His status is inferred rather than stated.
6 WSHC P3/P/644.
7 WANHS Genealogy mss v.A-A, f.136-7.
8 WSHC 3724/1.
9 WSHC 271/1. Abatement agreement, 11th March 1668/9.
10 WSHC P1/P/1006.
11 Baptismal entries for all but Walter (see below) do not survive.

tax on three hearths c.1662.[1] His estate was valued at £249 (including £180 in bonds, and £34 10s in sheep), and was bequeathed to his widow for her life; she survived him for 25 years.[2] His sister in law, Jane, owed him £110 when he died; most of that money was bequeathed to her children. They all received £10 in Richard II's will, with the exception of Richard III who received £60. Richard II made a few other minor legacies,[3] but the residue of his estate was left to Frances, Richard II's widow, although in the event she renounced the executorship in favour of Richard's nephew, James Pope IV. Richard's will was witnessed by John White, the rector, suggesting that he was no dissenter. That is suggested too by the fact that, in 1678, he gave 4d towards the fund for rebuilding St Paul's Cathedral.[4] A John Pope, possibly Richard's son, was named in 1700 as likely to give evidence for John White in an Assize case he was bringing.[5]

Three of James IV's children married and had children. Walter Pope was baptised 18th March 1669/70. By 1694, he was one of the tenants of property at Beckhampton owned by Richard Truslow, which was subsequently sold to Charles Tooker in 1702, and to Sir Richard Holford in 1710. He was still there when he died in February 1720/21. In 1697, Walter was one of those sued by John White, the vicar, for small tithes on cattle and horses.[6] When Mary Rose administered her husband John's estate in 1699, Walter witnessed the bond.[7] Walter's lease named his sons Nicholas and Daniel as lives. Nicholas, described as a labourer in Susanna Pope's 1734 will,[8] surrendered the lease in order to obtain a re-grant in 1740.[9] He was named as a suitor in the Selkley Hundred

1   TNA E179/259/29.
2   She was buried 28th January 1709/10.
3   To his three cousins (a term which then included nephews and nieces): Thomas and Elizabeth Pope, both of Avebury, and Mary Horton of Quemerford (in Calne). He also mentioned Ruth Eatall (nee Pope) of Winterbourne Monkton. Mary Pope had married John Horton in 1681; cf. Nevill, Edward. 'Peculiars of the Dean & Chapter of Sarum', *Wiltshire Notes & Queries* 6, 1908-10, p.565.
4   LMA MS 25565/24 f.18-19.
5   WSHC 184/1, pt.1. Letter, William Skeat to Sir Richard Holford, 29th January 1699/1700
6   WSHC 1569/5.
7   WSHC P3/R/295.
8   WSHC P3/P/807. Her relationship to Walter and Daniel has not been determined; perhaps she was Walter's sister. She occupied a cottage on Richard Smith's estate in 1712; cf. WSHC 568/5. She is also mentioned as a 'kinswoman' in John Pope's 1711 will, WSHC P1/P/495, and was probably Peter Griffin's servant; see TNA C11/363/65.
9   WSHC 371/1, pt.5.

Court in 1738.[1] Daniel was also mentioned in Susannah's will: he was a blacksmith, living at Chiseldon. Several of Walter's other children – James VI, John, and Ann (nee Slag) - were mentioned in the will of their aunt Elizabeth, who died single in 1738/9.[2] Nicholas was buried 14th February 1750/51, probably unmarried; nothing further concerning his siblings has been traced. Little is known of James III's son John. It is possible that he was a Hundred juror in 1690,[3] and churchwarden in 1695.[4] It may be that he was the 'John Pope' who signed the petition of c.1736 on behalf of his sisters and his four children.[5] According to his sister Elizabeth's 1738/9 will,[6] he was still alive then, and had a daughter Jane. Information relating to any other children has not been traced. It was probably this John Pope's burial that was recorded on 13th September 1749.

John and Walter's brother, James IV, was a fairly prosperous yeoman,[7] probably born in the 1660s.[8] In 1701, he was running 100 sheep on Thornhill and Westdown.[9] In 1713, he was said to be the tenant of 100 acres of arable in the Beckhampton common fields, together with 24 acres of arable at Chestermans and other small fields, all of which he held from Richard Smith of West Kennett.[10]

James IV served as churchwarden in 1686,[11] 1693,[12] 1710,[13] 1719[14] and 1729.[15] In 1701 he served as sidesman.[16] During his term of office in 1719, a new tenor bell was cast, and his name as churchwarden was placed upon it.[17] He signed the pauper indenture for Elizabeth Tompkins at the end of his last

1   WSHC 9/23/1.
2   WSHC P3/P/806.
3   WSHC A1/110, 1690M, f.116.
4   WSHC D1/50/5, f.12v.
5   WSHC D3/47/3. For this petition, see below p.402.
6   WSHC P3/P/806.
7   According to his will, WSHC P3/P/779.
8   His marriage allegation, GA, GDR/Q3/35, dated June 1718, states he was aged 50.
9   WSHC 184/4. Estimate of the rent of Avebury, by Farmer Skeat, 1709.
10 WSHC 568/5; 212B/110.
11 WHC D1/50/2; D3/15/2.
12 Bishops' transcript.
13 WSHC D3/15/8.
14 WSHC D1/50/9, f.15. Mayo, p.151.
15 WSHC D1/50/12, f.31; D3/15/11.
16 WSHC D1/54/17/3/69.
17 Lukis, William Collings. *An account of church bells, with some notices of Wiltshire bells and bellfounders.* J.H.Parker, 1957, p.110.

term of office.[1] James was sufficiently well informed to be called on to provide evidence relating to the value of Avebury vicarage in 1707.[2] He also served on a number of Quarter Sessions juries,[3] and on the Hundred jury.[4] When he died in 1733 he was serving as parish constable.[5] He was accused at Quarter Sessions of failing to make a return of jurors, but was probably on his deathbed at the time. He appraised the inventory of Richard Garroway in 1687/8,[6] and John Mills in 1701/2,[7] as well as administering the estates of both his mother and his uncle.

James IV married late in life; his bride was Mary Wasty of Hampton Road, Gloucestershire, who he married in 1718.[8] He was aged 50, she was aged 30. Despite their ages, children quickly followed. James V, John, Jane, and Elizabeth were all baptised between 1719 and 1726/7. James's will, made in 1732,[9] named his widow, Mary, as executrix, and his brother John as a trustee. The children were all minors. James V inherited his father's freehold lands, subject to paying his mother one-third of their profits, to the payment of £100 to his brother John, and of £50 to each of his sisters. His mother Mary was buried 16th October 1749.

We may presume that the freehold James V inherited included Chestermans and Higdens, on which he paid £3 13s 6d land tax in 1738; he also paid a total of £2 6s 5d, for two smaller properties.[10] In 1751 he paid a total of £21 6s 6d; he seems to have accumulated leasehold property from several different estates, as well as his freehold.[11] In the 1750s he joined with others in 'the affair of the moles', contributing 2s 2½d, presumably for the eradication of pests.[12]

Like his father, James V served in a variety of public roles. He was named in the freeholders' books as eligible to serve on Quarter Sessions juries throughout the 1740s and 1750s.[13] He served as collector of the land tax in

1 WSHC 184/9/3.
2 WSHC D1/3/5/1.
3 WSHC A1/110, Michaelmas rolls.
4 WSHC A1/110, 1689M, f.98 &106; 1692M, f.145.
5 WSHC A1/165/4.
6 WSHC P3/G/327.
7 WSHC P3/M/324.
8 GA GDR/Q3/35.
9 WSHC P3/P/779.
10 WSHC 184/3. Land tax, 1738.
11 WSHC 184/3. Land Tax, 1751.
12 WSHC 184/3.
13 WSHC A1/265/13-18. After 1747 there is only one freeholders' book until 1774. A1/110, Michaelmas session rolls 1742-54M.

1742,[1] overseer in 1746,[2] and as churchwarden in 1750.[3] In 1749, he obtained a marriage licence to marry Mary Neat of Yatesbury;[4] the couple married at Devizes on 18th November 1749. Three children – James VI, Jane, and Elizabeth – were born between 1750 and 1753. Sadly, however, their father was killed when he fell from his horse and was crushed by the wheels of a waggon in 1772.[5] Thereafter, this family disappears from Avebury records, although a Jane Pope was buried 16th February 1786.

Reeves

The Reeves are only briefly mentioned in Avebury records, but are worth mentioning here as an example of an eighteenth century labouring family. Robert Reeves and Ann Hillier were married 20th October 1714; four children were baptised between 1716/17 and 1725. One of them, William, probably had a wife named Mary; their three children were baptised between 1744/5 and 1753. In 1755, William had been 'servant on Avebury Farm upwards of six years and employ'd in every branch of the business', and was prepared to give evidence regarding its stock when John Rose went bankrupt.[6] In 1767, he (or perhaps his son) was accused of poaching at Wroughton Coppice; he 'had in his possession one hare'.[7]

William's eldest son, another William, married Ann Pickett, 2nd November 1766; he was a labourer, although also a suitor in the Selkley Hundred court throughout the 1770s.[8] Their four children were baptised between 1767 and 1781. John the eldest, also a labourer, married Dinah Collins, 10th April 1788. The couple had no children; Dinah was buried 6th January 1793.

Robinson

The Robinson family played an important role in Avebury's dissenting history. That is why their marriages and baptisms were not recorded in the parish register. Humphry Robinson, carpenter and wheelwright,[9] who was buried

1 WSHC 184/3. Receipt, 22nd November, 1742.
2 WSHC 184/9/5. Bastardy bond of Thomas Moss 1746.
3 WSHC D1/50/19; D3/15/14.
4 Sarum Marriage Licence Bonds www.findmypast.co.uk
5 Hunnisett, R.F., ed. *Wiltshire Coroners' Bills, 1752-1796*. Wiltshire Record Society, 36. 1980, no.85.
6 WANHS mss 692.
7 WSHC A1/260/1767/Reeves.
8 WSHC 9/23/1.
9 On his carpentry activities, see below, p.301.

17th May 1720, had at least seven children. They were all mentioned in the will of his son in law, John Pope, who died in 1711.[1] Two of them, Humphry and George, died before their father, in Humphry's case just ten days earlier. One wonders if father and son succumbed to the same disease. Thomas married Mary; like his father, he was a carpenter. Three of the four sisters married; the children of Elizabeth Alexander, Mary Tilly, and Ruth Pope were all remembered in their father's will.[2] So was Martha, who, subsequently (in 1724) married John Browning. Her previous dalliance with Thomas Pontin,[3] so offended her father that, in his will, he forbade her to marry him, on pain of losing her inheritance of 50s per annum for ten years – although she was also given two houses without condition. John Pope, Ruth's husband, made his father in law his executor and residuary legatee.

Martha's birth in 1696/7 was recorded in the separate list of dissenters' children compiled by the vicar, John White. He evidently did not baptise her, but did record her name in the parish register for tax purposes. A few months after the vicar had entered Martha's name, he sued her father (and several other tradesmen and smallholders, at least some of them dissenters) for Easter offerings and small tithes.[4]

A decade later, in his 1711 will, John Pope, Humphry's son in law, provided a £20 loan for fifteen years in order to keep the recently erected meeting house in repair.[5] That may have been why the vicar, John White, refused to bury him.[6] When the loan was repaid, the money was to be given to two of Humphry Robinson's daughters, Elizabeth and Martha. Their brother Thomas, Humphry's sole surviving son, signed the certificate in 1723 when application was made for a meeting house licence.[7]

---

1 WSHC P1/P/495.
2 WSHC P1/R/275.
3 See above, p.119. It is not clear whether she had an illegitimate child; the parish register records the baptism of Thomas the 'spurious' son of Mary Robinson on 28th October 1717, and it is possible that the scribe wrote Mary rather than Martha.
4 WSHC 1569/5.
5 WSHC P1/P/495.
6 GA D1956/E2/8. See below, p.411, for the vicar's refusal to bury dissenters. The lack of a funeral service for Pope was probably one of the factors which persuaded Humphry Robinson to give evidence against John White when he was accused of not burying the dead before the Consistory Court later in 1711, although Pope himself was not mentioned in that case; see WSHC D1/42/68.
7 Chandler, J.H., ed. *Wiltshire Dissenters' Meeting House Certificates and Registrations, 1689-1852*. Wiltshire Record Society, 40. 1985, p.20.

The Robinsons had standing in the community, despite Martha's indiscretions in an outhouse. Humphry's will[1] mentions four houses that he owned (and which he may have built). Most of them were probably within the henge, although it is not clear whether they were freehold or leasehold. As early as 1690, he appraised the inventory of Robert Rogers.[2] When John Truslow died in 1694, he owed Humphry £7, perhaps for carpentry work.[3] He was frequently consulted by Sir Richard Holford, and not just on carpentry matters. In 1713, for example, he was brought in to arbitrate between Holford and the Caswell family concerning dilapidations at their Beckhampton farm.[4] He also gave evidence in the Consistory Court when John White, the vicar, was accused of neglecting his duties in 1711.[5]

Despite his dissent, Humphry Robinson served as churchwarden in 1704/5,[6] and again in 1716/17.[7] He was one of the nine parishioners who voted in the 1705 general election,[8] and was one of the freeholders nominated to serve on the county's grand jury in 1713.[9]

Humphry's son, Thomas Robinson, was also a carpenter, but he diversified into property development.[10] He was the *bete noir* of the antiquarian, Stukeley, who regarded him as another 'Herostratus of Avebury' (the first was Walter Stretch),[11] and the destroyer of the megaliths. He was 'particularly eminent for this kind of execution, and he very much glories in it'. He stood accused of destroying no fewer than forty stones,[12] although the accusation was

1 WSHC P1/R/275.
2 WSHC P3/R/254.
3 WSHC 371/1, pt.3. Deed, Bridget Truslow to Richard Truslow, 26th December 1694.
4 GA D1956/E2/8.
5 WSHC D1/42/68.
6 WSHC D1/50/6, f.9v.; D3/12/13; D1/41/1/50.
7 WSHC D3/12/21.
8 WSHC 931/1. Poll book, 17th February 1705.
9 WSHC A1/265/2.
10 For his activities as such, see below, p.302.
11 Stukeley, William. *Abury: a Temple of the British Druids* .... 1743, p.15. Herostratus was accused of destroying the Temple of Artemis in Ephesus, one of the wonders of the ancient world.
12 Gillings, Mark, et al. *Landscape of the Megaliths: excavation and fieldwork on the Avebury monuments, 1997-2003*. Oxbow Books, 2008, p.340.

probably exaggerated.[1] Nine or ten of them, supposedly demolished c.1700,[2] had stood along the eastern boundary of the henge, just south of Green Street.[3] Most of his destruction took place in that segment of the stone circle which he owned. But he found that the cost of destruction was greater than the value of the houses he built with the rubble. He was supposedly ruined when they were burnt down,[4] although in fact, as we will see, his son John did inherit some of his property.[5] In 1772, Rev. Whitaker asked after him, and heard him described as a 'silly ideotish dissenter'[6]. Thomas was still remembered in nineteenth-century Avebury as 'the stone-breaker'.[7]

Like his father, Thomas was nominated to serve on the Grand Jury at Quarter Sessions in 1731 and 1732,[8] and again in 1737.[9] He served as juror in the Hundred court in 1731 and 1737.[10] In 1727, he witnessed the will of Mary Tompkins.[11] He was buried 28th October 1737.

The absence of information from the parish register means that we know little about Thomas's wife and children, other than that his widow, Mary paid 11s 7d land tax in 1738,[12] and that his son, John, continued the family trade. In both 1751 and 1755 he had been described as a 'shopkeeper',[13] but

---

1 Gillings, Mark, Peterson, Rick, & Pollard, Joshua. 'The destruction of the Avebury monuments', in Cleal, Rosemary, & Pollard, Joshua, eds. *Monuments and material culture: Papers in honour of an Avebury Archaeologist: Isobel Smith*. Hobnob Press, 2004, p.153.
2 The date is questionable. We do not know Thomas's age, but his sister was born in 1696/7, so he would have had to be much older than her to demolish stones in 1700. That of course is not impossible. It is also, of course, possible, or even probable, that Thomas's father was involved in the demolition: he would have been the leaseholder.
3 Stukeley, *Abury*, op cit, p.22; Ucko, Peter J., et al. *Avebury reconsidered: from the 1690s to the 1990s.* Unwin Hyman, 1991, p.135, 144, 149, 182, & 210-11.
4 Lewis, Charles. *A Descriptive Account in blank verse of the Old Serpentine Temple of the Druids at Avebury in North Wiltshire*. 2nd ed. Marlborough: E. Harold (printer), 1801.
5 See p.130.
6 Nichols, John. *Illustrations of the literary history of the eighteenth century, vol.IV*. John Nichols & Son, 1822, p.856.
7 Long, William. *Abury illustrated*. 1862, p.65.
8 WSHC A1/265/4-5.
9 WHSC A1/265/8.
10 WSHC A1/110, 1731M & 1737M.
11 WSHC P3/T/497.
12 WSHC 184/3. Land tax assessment.
13 WSHC 1102/2; P3/R/481.

was identified as a carpenter in 1757,[1] He probably married Anne Paget of Bishops Cannings in 1745.[2] He was assessed to the land tax on six tenements adjoining his house, plus his own estate, paying a total of 25s 6d.[3] Mortgage deeds record that there was a mortgage on a part of the land he inherited from his father.[4] They also indicate that either he or his father had erected buildings on that land (probably including those which burnt down). In 1755 he sold one of his six tenements to Robert Clements, a labourer,[5] the brother of John Clements the schoolmaster. Probably his other tenements were let to labourers. He had once occupied a house 'fronting the Meeting House door', although by 1758 it had been divided into two separate tenements and let out. In 1758 he sold much, if not all, of his property to John Nalder, and paid off his mortgage.[6] That, incidentally, included the field where his father had destroyed nine or ten of the stones.[7] By this time he was living elsewhere, and may have moved out of the parish. His name is not recorded again in eighteenth-century sources, although his descendants were said to be living in the parish, and working as masons, in the late nineteenth century.[8]

Rose
The Family of John Rose
John Rose was described as a labourer in 1689,[9] and was illiterate, as most labourers were. He was probably related to Joshua Rose, who leased a messuage and garden at Beckhampton in 1669.[10] John himself had tenanted Richard Smith's property at Higdens,[11] and it was probably the tithes on this property which were the subject of his dispute with John White in 1699. Rose 'would not suffer him [White] to take it [tithes] where hee pleasd at harvest last', as

1 WSHC 312a/31/4. Lease & release, John Robinson to John Nalder, 23rd/24th September 1757.
2 Sarum Marriage Licence Bonds www.findmypast.co.uk
3 WSHC 184/3.
4 See p.323.
5 WSHC 1102/2. Conveyance, John Robinson to Robert Clements, 10th March 1755.
6 WSHC 529/185. Lease & release, John Robinson to John Nalder, 20th/22nd July 1758.
7 The field is shown as Robert Nalder's property on the 1794 enclosure map, WSHC EA/95.
8 King, Bryan. 'Avebury: Archaeological Varia', *WAM* 14, 1874, p.229.
9 WSHC A1/110, 1689M, f.32.
10 WSHC 371/1, pt.2.
11 WSHC 184/1, pt.2. Letter, John Rose to Sir Richard Holford, 23rd February 1711/12.

William Skeat put it. White responded by suing Rose for riotous assembly at Quarter Sessions.[1] Skeat thought that the case might go to the Assizes, but was aware that White had also launched a suit in Chancery. When he wrote to his landlord, Sir Richard Holford, Skeat noted that Rose 'humbly intreateth your assisting advice in this matter'.[2] We do not know how the dispute was settled, but we do know that, subsequently, Rose rented John White's tithes.[3]

John Rose's former tenure of Higdens meant that he was able to provide useful information about that property to Sir Richard Holford when the latter was considering purchasing it.[4] By that time, he had (in 1710) succeeded William Skeat as the tenant of Holford's Avebury Great Farm, for which he paid rent of £350 per annum.[5] His illiteracy was seen as a drawback by Holford, who even before Rose took over the tenancy noted that he did 'now find in part the inconvenience I feared by John Rose's not being able to write.[6] Holford advised him to ask his 'Uncle Smith' to act as his scribe.[7]

Rose renewed his lease when it expired in 1718; when he died in 1720, he owned no less than 1,304 sheep, together with a herd of thirty cows, and an inventory valued at just over £1865.[8] The lease expired on his death. Thomas Alexander thought that he 'left so much wealth … that his family can scarce slep in their beds for fear of being robbed'.[9]

In 1698 and 1699 John Rose served as tithingman of Beckhampton.[10] He served as churchwarden on several occasions between 1705 and his death,[11] and his name was inscribed on the new bell when it was cast in 1719.[12] William Skeat, his brother in law,[13] and his predecessor as Holford's tenant, witnessed his will. So did his brother Robert, and his daughter

1   WSHC A1/110, 1699M, f.113.
2   WSHC 184/4, pt.1. Letter, William Skeat to Sir Richard Holford, 29th January 1699.
3   WSHC 188/8.
4   WSHC 184/1, pt.2. Letter, John Rose to Sir Richard Holford, 23rd February 1711/12.
5   WSHC 184/4, pt.1.
6   WSHC 184/1, pt.2. Sir Richard Holford to William Skeat, 23rd February 1709/10.
7   WSHC 184/1, pt.2. Letter, Sir Richard Holford to John Rose, 7th June 1710.
8   WSHC P3/R/365.
9   WSHC 184/1, pt.2. Letter, Thomas Alexander to Lady Holford, 12th December 1720.
10 WSHC 192/12K.
11 WSHC D3/15/4-5; D3/12/15; D3/50/8, f.27; D3/12/20; D3/12/21; D1/50/9, f.15.
12 WSHC D1/5/2/31.
13 WSHC 184/1. Letter, William Skeat to Sir Richard Holford, 19th February 1699.

Rebecca Stretch. He named Joseph Rose (probably another brother), and his wife Jane, as joint executors.

John's widow, Jane (nee Skeat), who he married at South Broom on 29th November 1694, died just a year after her husband, in 1721. Six children were born between 1698 and 1710; all except one received £120 in their father's will. Rebecca, the exception, had already married. She had evidently already been provided for, and received a token bequest of 1s, although she witnessed the will. Her husband was George Stretch, proprietor of the Catherine Wheel. Similarly, she only received 1s in her mother Jane's will in 1721, although her husband was named as Jane's joint executor, and her baby daughter Mary was given £20.[1]

William was John and Jane's only son. He was still under age in 1721, when his mother died. She bequeathed him a further £200, which was to be 'to be placed out at interest on good security & the interest thereof to be paid him by halfe yearly payments for and towards his mainteynance'.[2] William evidently died a bachelor, or perhaps a widower without any children. When he made his will in 1749/50,[3] he divided his estate between his surviving siblings. The will describes him as a gentleman, 'late of Avebury', ... 'but now of Yelden in the County of Bedford'.

Only a limited amount is known of the four other daughters of John and Jane. Their mother bequeathed them the residue of her estate in equal portions. Jane married Thomas Wylde in 1739/40 and received a bequest of £100 in her brother William's will (or, rather, her husband received it). Elizabeth probably died before her brother, as she received no mention in his will. The will mentions that Mary married a Pinfold; William forgave her a debt of £35. Similarly, he forgave his sister Ruth a debt of £130. She was living in Hungerford in 1756;[4] when she died in 1796, aged 87, she was brought back to Avebury for burial.

Robert Rose and his son John

Robert Rose, John's brother, was a prominent figure in Avebury; he served as overseer in 1714[5] and as churchwarden on several occasions in the 1720s and 1730s.[6] In 1729, he was the tenant of fifty-six acres of arable in Avebury's

1 WSHC P3/R/364.
2 WSHC P3/R/364.
3 TNA PROB11/786/41.
4 According to the will of Mary Hitchcock, who described Ruth as her aunt; cf. WSHC 1409/16/3.
5 WSHC 184/9/3. Apprenticeship indenture of William Fry.
6 WSHC D3/15/9, f. 17v, 27v & 37v; D3/15/10, f.31; D1/50/12, f.31; D1/50/16;

common fields, common of pasture for 180 sheep and other animals, and a variety of small closes in Avebury and Beckhampton.¹ His landlord was Richard Phelps of Hinton, who named Rose as his tenant in his 1741 will.² Robert also owned a cottage and a small amount of land, which he had purchased from William White, the son of the vicar, but which he sold to Sarah Deavin of Marlborough in 1755.³

Robert married Jane, who died in 1737. Three children are known: Jane died in 1704 as an infant, Robert was baptised 8th October 1706 and died thirty years later, and John, baptised 28th December 1710. Their father, Robert, was buried 24th February 1765.

John had two wives. His first was Elizabeth Caswell, who he married at Heddington, 10th March 1740/41; their children were Elizabeth, baptised 25th May 1743 and Jane, baptised 26th June 1745. Elizabeth was buried 1st February 1747/8, and John married Mary Payne of Bremhill at Seagry, 20th July 1749.⁴ No children of the second marriage are known.

John Rose took the tenancy of Avebury Great Farm c.1744, and went bankrupt after over a decade as tenant. The land tax assessment for 1751 show that he held a number of tenancies.⁵ His own lands were assessed at £4, Mr Savage's estate at £3 14s, Mr Howard's and Mr Roberts' estates together at £3 4s, and his brother Robert Rose's at 9s 6d. His property included a lease of Bray's Farm at Kennett (106 acres), which his wife Elizabeth had inherited from her father, William Caswell.⁶ On John's bankruptcy, it was assigned in trust for the use of creditors, together with other property in Porton and Tytherton.⁷ But Avebury Great Farm, by then the property of Stayner Holford, was his principle tenancy, valued at £400 per annum.⁸

John Rose, like his uncle, was unable to write, although he could probably – just – manage to read his landlord's letters. Consequently, he called

---

D3/15/11 & 13. It is possible that some of these entries relate to one of the other Robert Roses mentioned below.
1 WSHC 212A/31/2. Deed, 7th November 1729, John Phelps als Bromham to William Hunt.
2 TNA PROB11/734/263.
3 WSHC 435/24/1/8. In 1786 it was purchased by William Crook; cf. WSHC 435/24/1/9.
4 For her abode, see Sarum Marriage Licence Bonds www.findmypast.co.uk/articles/world-records/full-list-of-united-kingdom-records/life-events-bmds/sarum-marriage-licence-bonds
5 WSHC 184/3.
6 WANHS Wiltshire Genealogy, v.A-A, f.150. TNA C11/382/40.
7 WANHS Wiltshire Genealogy, v.A-A, f.150. TNA C11/382/40.
8 WSHC 184/3.

on the services of the vicar, John Mayo, to be his amanuensis.[1] His service as churchwarden gave him another point of contact with Mayo; Rose served in that office in 1729, and for most years between 1744 and 1755.[2] He also served as constable of the hundred in 1744,[3] and as overseer in 1754.[4] In the 1740s and early 1750s he was frequently placed on the freeholders' list for jury service at Quarter Sessions.[5] In 1743, he served as collector of the land tax.[6] In 1754 he was named as a trustee in the marriage settlement of James Hitchcock and Mary Stretch[7] (his cousin).

Bankruptcy proceedings were begun against John Rose in 1755, and a commission against him was recorded in the *London Gazette*.[8] He was officially described as a 'dealer and chapman', but that was a legal fiction in order to ensure that he could be made bankrupt rather than imprisoned for debt. Proceedings against him were not completed until at least 1761.[9] His farm servants accused him of bad husbandry; John Bridgeman stated that 'no part of the stock kept on this estate either as to the numbers, or quality, or any husbandry utensils, were equal to what the occupation of such large property as this estate only required, nor equal to the stock always kept on this estate before it was occupied by John Rose'.[10] His landlord, Stayner Holford, bought much of his stock and farming implements, and was forced, reluctantly, to take the farm in hand himself. Despite his bankruptcy, however, Rose was able to retain some land. An assessment to church and poor rates from the 1760s shows that his estate was then valued at £24.[11] However, no more is heard of him in Avebury.

Shuter or Suter
John Shuter, together with his son John, leased the demesne lands of Avebury manor in 1530, for their lives.[12] In the mid 1530s they were sued in Chancery

1 WSHC 184/1, pt. 2. James Mayo to Staynor Holford, 27 April 1746.
2 WSHC D1/50/12, f.31; D1/50/17-18; D3/15/14-15.
3 WSHC A1/110, 1744M.
4 WSHC 184/9/4. Bastardy bond, Charles Giddance.
5 WSHC A1/265/13,14, 16 & 18; A1/110, 1746M, 1747M, 1748M, 1751M, 1752M, 1753M & 1754M.
6 WSHC 184/3.
7 WSHC 1409/16/3, pt.2. Marriage settlement, 5th March 1754; Mortgage deed, James and Mary Hitchcock to William Stone, 4th June 1755.
8 Issue 9549, 24th January 1756, p.6.
9 *London Gazette*, issue 10088, 17th March 1761, p.5.
10 WSHC 184/4/1. Rose's servants: their particulars about the stock.
11 WSHC 184/3.
12 WSHC 26641/2D/8. The date c.1535 is given in *V.C.H. Wilts* 12, p.98, but its

by Thomas Truslow. Truslow possessed rights of common by virtue of a lease from Fotheringhay College, which he had let to tenants; Shuter, presumably believing that Truslow had no such rights, had been 'detaining' the tenants' cattle pasturing on that commmon.[1]

John I also owned tenements at Yatesbury, at Compton Bassett,[2] and at Kellaways.[3] He served as churchwarden in 1587/8.[4] He was the highest rated parishioner in both the benevolence of 1545, and the subsidy of 1576, being rated at £4 in the former, and £24 in the latter.[5] However, he was not of sufficient status to bear a coat of arms; John disclaimed the name of a 'gentleman' during the 1565 herald's visitation.[6]

John I had at least eight children by his first wife: his sons John II, Richard (born c.1548[7]), Christopher, and Philip, his daughters Ann Laynes and Constance Tythener, and another un-named daughter who married Edmund Pike. It seems likely that Ann, his second wife, married John when all, or at least most, of his children were already of age. It was her second marriage too; her previous husband had been a member of the Griffin family.[8] The Shuter household was augmented by the presence of Henry Woodrose, Anne's nephew, whom she brought up.

John II, in addition to the lease of the manor farm he held with his father, was also granted a copyhold holding of 45 acres in 1545.[9] When he died, he was lord of the manor of Winterbourne Dauntsey, and of various

---

source, TNA SC6/HenVIII/3931, rot.1, has not been checked by the present author.
1 TNA C1/912/53.
2 TNA PROB11/124/472.
3 TNA STAC 8/269/32. £4 of the 1576 levy could perhaps have been the amount his son John was assessed on.
4 WSHC D3/7/1, f.6v.
5 Ramsay, G.D., ed. *Two sixteenth Century Taxation lists, 1545 and 1576*. Wiltshire Archaeological and Natural History Society records Branch 10. 1954, p.23 & 103. In 1576 the bulk of this assessment - £20 - was in the tithing of Beckhampton, and the remainder in the tithing of Avebury. It is possible, of course, that John Shuter the elder was assessed in one tithing, and John Shuter the younger in the other. The subsidy list gives no clue on this point. In the 1563 subsidy, he was rated at £50; see TNA E179/198/276.
6 Metcalfe, Walter C., ed. *The Visitation of Wiltshire, 1565, by William Harvey, Clarenceaus King of Arms ...* . William Pollard & Co., 1897, p.54.
7 He was 50 in 1598; cf.WSHC D1/42/16, f.189r-191v.
8 Her 1596/7 will mentions her sons John Suter (who was deceased) and Thomas Griffin; cf. WSHC P5/1597/104.
9 WSHC 26641/2D/8.

other properties.[1] It may be that he was the lessee of property in the manor of Avebury Trusloe, which was in his son John III's hands c.1592.[2] Like his father, he paid the 1545 benevolence mentioned above; he was assessed at 12s. He pre-deceased his father, and was buried at Winterbourne Gunner on 28th December 1578. In his will,[3] he named his wife, Bridget, and his son John III, as joint executors. He also made provision for 'a childe which is yet unborn', which he thought his wife was expecting – although that child's baptism has not been traced, if in fact one was born. John III became the ward of his uncle, Edmund Pike,[4] and in due course (in 1615) was named his executor.[5]

Two wills of John senior were proved in the Prerogative Court of Canterbury after he died. Both, curiously, were witnessed by John Peart, the vicar. The first,[6] dated 2nd March 1588/9, bequeathed 'the halfe deale of all my plate of silver not onlie guilte but also unguilt and parcel guilt houshould stuffe ymplements of houshould ploughebeasts harses oxen kyne sheepe and of all maner of cattell ymplements of husbandrie stockes stores and moueable goodes and chattels of whatsoeuer sorte or nature they be of called or knowne by and whersoeuer they shalbe founde', to John III, with the residue, including all his lands, and the executorship, to his widow Ann. She made her will at Calne in 1596/7.[7] John III and his brother Philip were mentioned in this will, but none of John senior's surviving sons.

John senior's second will,[8] dated 17th September 1591, bequeathed Rowse's Farm to his son Richard, the lands in Yatesbury and Compton Bassett to Philip, small sums to Ann Laynes and Constance Tythener, his daughters, and the residue to Richard and Christopher Shuter. This will was purportedly proved in the Prerogative Court, 4th October 1591, and the estate was distributed accordingly. John had also, in 1582, supposedly made a fifty year lease to both of his sons of the properties they were to inherit, which were to take effect on his death.[9] At least, that is what Richard and Philip claimed; they were held to be fraudulent in the subsequent court case.

John III was probably barely a teenager when his uncles proved their

1 TNA C142/187/105. Inquisition Post Mortem.
2 TNA C142/237/132. Inquisition post mortem of John Truslow.
3 TNA PROB11/61/160.
4 TNA STAC8/269/32. See also TNA C21/S32/14.
5 TNA PROB11/127/12.
6 TNA PROB11/124/472.
7 WSHC P5/1597/104.
8 TNA PROB11/78/167.
9 TNA REQ2/92.

father's will. He was not in a position to object, although his guardian, unsuccessfully, tried to do so on his behalf.[1] It is not surprising that he took exception to the second will when he came of age. He had the advantage that he had been admitted to the Inner Temple in 1600, and was probably called to the Bar in 1609.[2] He soon after brought a case in Star Chamber against his three uncles, Richard, Christopher, and Philip,[3] alleging that two of them, Richard and Christopher, had married against their father's will. Richard had also upset his father by entering a copyhold tenement which the latter had purchased for his own use. Similarly, Christopher defrauded his father of the profits from his property at Kellaways. They had both been dis-inherited by their father; indeed, Christopher had been turned out of doors; his father would not endure the sight of him. Richard and Christopher, incidentally, had been prosecuted at Quarter Sessions in 1584 for a trespass against Edith Mortimer.[4] In 1603, however, Richard was called to serve on a Quarter Sessions jury.[5]

John III also claimed that John senior was severely incapacitated when he made his last will. The Star Chamber interrogatory implies that it was made under duress, or at least without the proper consent of the testator – despite the fact that the vicar was present. John senior was said to have been 115 years of age. One may doubt that, but he was certainly very aged, and he may have been both deaf and blind; he probably died as a result of a fall, in which he broke his ribs. The interrogatory suggests that his 'sences and understanding with extremitye of age [were] much decayed & almost cleane gone'. He did not know what he was doing when he signed his second will, consequently, that will was invalid, and the inheritance rightfully belonged to John III.

John III won his case; his uncles were declared contumacious by the Prerogative Court, and the earlier will was proved on 4th November 1614. He soon after sold Rowse's Farm to John Goldsmith.[6] That may have been the end of the Shuter family's sojourn in Avebury, although we do not know when John III's tenancy of land in the manor of Avebury Trusloe ceased (his

---

1 TNA REQ2/92.
2 Inner Temple Admissions Database www.innertemplearchives.org.uk
3 TNA STAC 8/269/32. A bill of complaint was also proved in Chancery, which ordered that the defendants should be tried at common law in Kings Bench; see TNA C21/S32/14.
4 John son, H.C., ed. *Wiltshire County Records: Minutes of Proceedings in Sessions, 1565 and 1574 to 1592*. Wiltshire Archaeological & Natural History Society Records Branch, 4. 1949, p.107.
5 WSHC A1/110, f.203.
6 *VCH Wilts* 12, p.94.

name is recorded as a tenant in 1613).[1] John III was described as being 'of Winterbourne Gunner', c.1612, when he was thought able to lend £20 to James I.[2] Richard Shuter was perhaps buried in West Lavington on 13th January 1610/11, although he was named as an Avebury assessor for the subsidy of that year.[3] He had previously, in 1594 and 1598, paid the subsidy on goods valued at £6.[4] Philip Shuter made his will[5] on 12th September 1612, when he was probably of Bremhill. He had no issue, so left his entire estate to his brother Christopher. Christopher was also without children. He was of Kellaways when he made his will a few months after receiving his inheritance, on 22nd May 1613,[6] and left all his estate to his widow, Bridget.

Skeat

William Skeat tenanted Avebury Great Farm from 1689 until 1710, but was not a native of Avebury, nor did he (as far as we know) die there. He was the son of John Skeat, of Ramsbury, and his wife Jane, nee Pontin, and was baptised at Wootton Bassett, 17th January 1654. His sister Jane married John Rose, on 27th November 1794 at South Broom.[7] William Smith was another kinsman.[8] When he agreed with Lord Stawell to become his tenant, Skeat was living at Rockley, in Ogbourne St Andrew.[9] He will appear in subsequent chapters in a variety of different roles.

Skeat married Elizabeth Michael; their children were Jane, baptised at Ramsbury 1st May 1682, John, baptised at Ramsbury 18th October 1685,[10] and Emanuel, who was probably baptised as a dissenter at Avebury.[11] Jane was characterised by Sir Richard Holford, when he visited in 1699, as being of a 'very quiet & good disposition'.[12] In contrast, Skeat himself was described as

1   TNA WARD 7/51/71.
2   Murphy, W.P.D., ed. *The Earl of Hertford's Lieutenancy papers, 1603-1612*. Wiltshire Record Society, 23. 1969, p.182.
3   TNA E179/199/369.
4   TNA E179/198/315; E179/198/325.
5   WSHC P3/5/90.
6   TNA PROB11/122/270.
7   In addition to the parish register, see WSHC 184/1. Letter, William Skeat to Sir Richard Holford, 19th February 1699. Skeat describes John Rose as his brother in law.
8   WSHC 184/1. Letter, William Smith to Sir Richard Holford, 20th November 1700.
9   WSHC 184/4/1. Agreement, Lord Stowell and William Skeat, 1689.
10 https://gw.geneanet.org
11 Emanuel is named in Sir Richard Holford's diary, c.1709; see WSHC 184/8.
12 WSHC 184/1. Letter, Sir Richard Holford to William Skeat, 26th November 1698.

being 'of no very obliging temper'.[1] His letters to Holford (who had succeeded Stawell as his landlord) support that characterisation. Holford was, for example, deeply embarrassed at the way Skeat treated the son of a neighbouring landlord who was hunting on Holford's property.[2] His 'temper' was probably also the reason why he 'detained' the wages of one of his servants, Roger Dorchester, in 1695, and had to be forced to pay them by entering a recognizance.[3] It may also lie behind the accusation of assault and battery laid against him by John Griffin in 1698, and the writ in which he riposted that Griffin damaged his grass by driving over it, presumably whilst avoiding ruts on the road.[4]

Skeat was a yeoman, the most substantial farmer in Avebury. His name frequently appears on Quarter Sessions jury lists between the 1680s (even before he became Stawell's tenant) and the 1700s.[5] In 1692 he was the Hundred constable.[6] He served as churchwarden for two years from 1690,[7] despite the fact that he was a leading figure amongst the dissenters, and the *bête noire* of the vicar, John White. White subsequently described him as 'my profest enemy', and accused him of setting up 'a hellish, factious, scandalous, & schismatical conventicle'.[8] The vicar probably exaggerated Skeat's role in the dissenting congregation. Their enmity played a major role in fomenting the dispute over tithes between Sir Richard Holford and John White. These matters will be discussed in more detail in chapter 9.[9]

Skeat gave up his farm in 1710, much to Sir Richard Holford's disgust. Holford commented that 'now hee pretends that hee is groweing old & is infirme, and his wife very crazy, and not fit for soe much troble'.[10] He had been seriously injured in 1698/9, when the limb of a tree fell on him, and it is possible that he never fully recovered.[11] He was succeeded by his brother in

1   WSHC 184/1. pt.2. Letter, Cornelius Yeate to Sir Richard Holford, c.9th March 1698.
2   See below, p.374.
3   WSHC A1/110, 1695M, f.21.
4   WSHC 184/1, pt.1. Letter, William Skeat to Sir Richard Holford, 30th January 1698/9.
5   WSHC A1/110, Michaelmas rolls
6   WSHC A1/110, 1692M, f.127 & 145.
7   WSHC D3/15/3; D3/12/5.
8   WSHC 184/1, pt.1. Letter, John White to Sir Richard Holford, undated; c.25th January 1695.
9   See below, p.397-400.
10 WSHC 184/1, pt.2. Letter, Sir Richard Holford to Richard Chandler, 2nd June 1709.
11 WSHC 184/1, pt. 1. Letter, William Skeat to Sir Richard Holford, 30th January 1698/9.

law, John Rose. After he left Avebury, no more is heard of him, except that his former landlord called on him at Rowden,[1] near Chippenham, on 13th April 1711, and that he visited Holford in London in March 1715/16.

His son John was apprenticed in London in 1708;[2] he described himself as a carpenter when he made his will in Devizes in 1743.[3] His son Emanuel was buried in Bishops Cannings on 3rd November 1739.

Smith

The Smith family were lords of the manor of West Kennett, which extended into Lockeridge and Overton. In the late sixteenth century their farm was known as Barbor's Court, and subsequently as West Kennett Farm. The early sixteenth-century heiress of the property, Anne Benger, married Thomas Smith. Anne outlived her husband, who died c.1558. When she died the property passed to the Henshaws, probably her relations. In 1594, they sold it to Thomas Smith II, who was probably Anne & Thomas's son. The conveyance described him as a yeoman,[4] although his descendants described themselves as gentlemen. In the same year, Thomas paid the subsidy on goods valued at £15. That was probably assessed before the conveyance took effect.[5]

Thomas Smith II died in 1597.[6] The property was inherited by his son, Richard Smith I, who held it until he died in 1633 aged 78.[7] He paid the subsidy on goods valued at £7 in 1598.[8] The manor was held from the Earl of Hertford's Selkley Hundred, paid 12d rent, and owed fealty and suit at the hundred court. Richard was constable of the Hundred in 1613 and 1614,[9] at the same time as he was churchwarden.[10] He also served on various juries at Quarter Sessions between 1612 and 1632.[11] In addition to the property acquired from the Henshaws, Richard purchased a messuage with sixteen acres

1 Skeat also wrote to Sir Richard Holford from Rowden in 1705; he probably had family connections there; cf. WSHC 184/1, pt.1. Letter, 20th June 1705.
2 GA 1956/E2/8.
3 WSHC P1/9Reg/252.
4 WSHC 568/4.
5 TNA E179/198/315.
6 VCH 12, p.97.
7 Phillipps, Thomas, Sir. *Monumental Inscriptions of Wiltshire*, ed. Peter Sherlock. Wiltshire Record Society, 53. 2000, p.210. Phillipps gives the date of death as 22nd August 1733, but this seems to be incorrect, as his will was proved 21st May 1633.
8 TNA E179/198/325.
9 WSHC A1/110, 1613M, f.121, 1614M, f.158.
10 WSHC D1/42/28, f.35-37r & 61r-62r.
11 WSHC A1/110, Michaelmas rolls, 1612-32.

in Lockeridge and Overton from John Harding. In 1623, he was named as an under-tenant of lands in Beckhampton owned by the Truslow family.[1] This was presumably the half moity of Beckhampton Farm which he leased from John Truslow in 1638, and which his son, Thomas Smith III purchased outright in 1647.[2] He was also a tenant of William Dunch's manor of Avebury, for which he paid 13s 4d rent per annum.[3]

Richard owed suit at Selkley Hundred court; in c1610, the court fined him for neglecting to repair the highway.[4] He was also fined for not attending the court in 1627.[5] In 1601 and 1611, he served as one of the 'sessors' for the subsidy, and in 1611 he paid on goods valued at £16 – the highest assessment in the parish.[6] John Peart, the vicar, named him as one of the overseers of his will in 1621, and bequeathed him a copy of 'Dod's book', probably a theological tome; he appraised Peart's inventory.[7] Peart set a trend: Richard was subsequently named as an overseer in four wills [8] and appraised six inventories[9]. He served as churchwarden in 1622, and again in 1627-8.[10] In 1632, he gave evidence concerning the ownership of Warwicks in the Court of Exchequer.[11]

In September 1623, Richard claim to armigerous status was publicly and humiliatingly disclaimed during the heraldic visitation at Salisbury; they were said to have 'usurpt the name or title of gentleman without authoritie'.[12] Despite the heralds' disclaimer (which his successors ignored), Richard owned lands that were liable to feudal dues, and an inquisition post mortem was

1   WANHS Genealogy mss., v.A-A, p.99.
2   WSHC 212B/104. Conveyance, Richard Truslow to Thomas Smith, 1647.
3   Fry, op cit, p.183.
4   WSHC 192/12I, f.41l
5   WSHC 9/15/324.
6   TNA E179/266/15 & E179/199/369.
7   WSHC P3/P/101.
8   Thomas Andrews (1622) TNA PROB11/141/197; Edith Pope (1624) WSHC P3/P/126. Edith Mortimer (1628 – but he died before she did) WSHC P3/M/117, and Frissy Baldveen (1630/31WHSC P1/B/230.
9   Those of Katherine Brown (1622/3) WSHC P3/B/236; Edith Pope (1624), WSHC P3/P/126; Richard Harding (1627), WSHC P3/11/210; Bridget Dyer (1629), WSHC P3/D/76; Richard Cue (1629) WSHC P3/K/39; and Richard Parr (1632) WSHC P3/P/184.
10 WSHC D3/15/1; D3/4/6, f.2.
11 TNA E134/8Chas1/Mich53
12 Marshall, George W., ed. *The Visitation of Wiltshire 1623*. George Bell & Sons, 1882, p.103.

accordingly taken in 1633.[1] It recorded that Richard had died on 1st April 1633, that his widow, Mary was 'dowered in all the said premises', and that his son Thomas III was aged '32 years and more'. Richard also had an illegitimate child, whose name is unknown; the churchwardens presented him as its father in 1594.[2]

His 1632/3 will[3] mentions his wife Mary, and his seven children. The eldest, Thomas III, inherited the farm and was made executor and residuary legatee. Thomas's brother Richard Smith II, a minor, was given £950 in his father's will. A third son, John, received nothing, although his wife Dorothy and her children received legacies of 20s each; perhaps John had died. Four daughters were named, two were minors: Rebecca and Mary both received £500. The other two were already married: Katherine Bartlett and Marian Green received token bequests of 20s each, as did their children, and as indeed did Thomas III's children, and his wife Mary. The latter received an annuity of £40 per annum, together with the 'use and occupaton of the chamber wherein I doe usuallie lodge' in the West Kennett farmhouse. This former churchwarden also left £1 for the repair of Avebury church, and £1 for the relief of the poor. His will was witnessed by his brother John, his son in law (presumably) Richard Greene, and William Smith, probably either another brother, or a cousin.

Thomas III leased Avebury Great Farm for four years in 1632, paying £310 per annum, and serving as manorial bailiff.[4] In 1647, he paid Thomas Truslow £260 for half of the freehold of Beckhampton Farm.[5] He evidently still held land within Avebury manor in 1654, when he was amerced for failure to attend its court.[6] In 1634 he served as churchwarden;[7] in 1646 and 1647 as high constable.[8] He also served on a number of Quarter Sessions juries.[9]

Thomas Smith III's 1662 will names his sons Richard III and Francis, and three daughters, Alice, Lucy, and Mary. Richard (probably) entered Gray's Inn

1 Fry, George S., & Edw. Alex, eds. *Abstracts of Wiltshire Inquisitiones Post Mortem returned into the Court of Chancery n the reign of King Charles the First.* Index library, 23. 1901, p.183.
2 WSHC D3/7/1, f.121.
3 TNA PROB11/163/542.
4 WANHS Genealogy mss., v.A-A, p.109.
5 WSHC 212B/104. Conveyance, 10th June 1747.
6 WSHC 473/52, f.50.
7 WSHC D3/15/1.
8 WSHC A1/110, 1646M, f.159; 1647M, f.237.
9 WSHC A1/110, Michaelmas rolls, 1634-6, 1638, 1641, & 1643.

23rd May 1653.[1] Mary married Henry Goldsmith of Barnard's Inn (another of the inns of court),[2] and one of her sisters married William Spackman. In their father's will, Lucy received a portion of £450, Alice £350. He had borrowed £95 from Mary, and £100 from Alice; both were to be repaid. His widow Mary was to live in the house in Avebury where Richard III lived; presumably Richard was expected to move into the West Kennett farmhouse. Thomas III named his son Francis, and his son-in-law William Spackman as his executors.

Richard Smith III served as tithingman of Kennett on several occasions between 1662 and 1674.[3] In 1671 he served as churchwarden, and signed the hearth tax exemption certificate.[4] His second term was served in 1682, when he signed the controversial glebe terrier which his son in law, the vicar, had prepared[5] - and found himself caught up in the great dispute between White and Sir Richard Holford.[6] In that year, he also served as High Constable of Selkley Hundred, and nominated himself to serve as a juror at Quarter Sessions.[7] A few years earlier, in 1679, he had presented his son in law to the vicarage of Manningford Bruce (which White was to hold in plurality with Avebury vicarage); Smith had probably purchased the right to present for one time only, with that purpose in mind.[8]

He tenanted Avebury Great Farm in 1652,[9] and paid the subsidy on lands valued at £2 in 1663.[10] In 1682 he was granted a messuage at Chestermans, in Westbrook, to be held by copy of court roll.[11] In 1696, he purchased a further two yardlands in West Kennett, although he had to mortgage this property for £300 just before he died in 1700.[12] He contributed two shillings to the fund for

1 Foster, Joseph, ed. *The Register of Admissions to Gray's Inn, 1521-1889.* Hansard Publishing Union, 1889, p.264.
2 Phillipps, op cit, p.211.
3 WSHC 192/12K.
4 TNA E179/348
5 Hobbs, Steven, ed. *Wiltshire Glebe Terriers 1588-1827.* Wiltshire Record Society 56. 2003, p.18. Smith is frequently referred to by White as 'Father Smith' in White's letters; cf. WSHC 184/1. See also 184/1, pt.2. Necessary Remarks on the Dispute depending on tithes.
6 See below, p.395-6, 398-9.
7 WSHC A1/110, 1682M, f. 151.
8 *VCH Wilts* 10, 1975, p.117.
9 WANHS Wiltshire Genealogy, v.A-A, p.119.
10 WANHS mss.140.
11 WSHC 435/24/1/4. Mortgage deed, 1st June 1682; WANHS Genealogy mss., v.A-A, p.136-7.
12 WSHC 568/40. Lease & release, Richard Harding to Richard Smith, 28/29th September 1696; Mortgage deed, Richard Smith & Stawell Smith to Ann

re-building St Paul's Cathedral in 1678 – the largest contributor in the parish, apart from the vicar (Richard's son Thomas IV gave one shilling).[1] When he gave evidence for Thomas Pontin in a 1687 Chancery case, he was said to be of Berwick Bassett.[2]

Richard III and his wife Jane (the daughter of Thomas Cripps)[3] had six sons: Thomas IV, Benjamin, Henry (died 16th March 1732/3 aged 74),[4] Richard IV, John (baptised 27th June 1665) and Stawell. Stawell became a linen draper in London,[5] although he was described as 'of Overton' when he was buried at Avebury 21st February 1731. Stawell's wife, Mary, was buried at Avebury 15th July 1725.[6] She shared her name with her sister-in-law, Mary, who was probably Richard oldest child. She married John White, the vicar, before 1675. Her sister Honor was baptised 8th November 1672. Another sister, Elizabeth married Edward Bailey, a Bristol grocer, but was buried at Avebury 2nd June 1698.[7] Richard III was buried 17th December 1700. Jane, his wife, pre-deceased him; she died 25th August 1690.[8]

All Richard III's offspring are mentioned in the family settlement made in 1676, when Thomas IV married Joan Stephens.[9] In 1695, Thomas agreed to stand surety for none other than William Skeat – his brother-in-law the vicar's bête noir – when Skeat was accused of withholding one of his servant's wages.[10] The couple only had one son: Richard V, baptised 11th September 1678, who sadly died as a child. Their daughters were Mary, who married Edward Scoles of Wanting (Berkshire), and Joan.[11]

Richard V's death meant that his father died with no male heir. Consequently, the estate descended to his brother Richard IV.[12] In 1703 and

---

    Goulding, 22nd October 1700.
1 LMA 25565/24, f.18-19.
2 WANHS Genealogy mss., v.A-A, p.137; TNA E 134/2and3Jas2/Hil2.
3 According to his will, WSHC P3/C/245.
4 Phillipps, op cit, p.210.
5 WSHC 568/40. Mortgage deed, Richard & Stawell Smith to Anne Goulding, 22nd October 1700.
6 Phillipps, op cit, p.210.
7 Phillipps, op cit, p.210.
8 Phillipps, op cit, p.210.
9 WSHC 568/5. Settlement, 18th November 1676. This is incorrectly dated 1666 in VCH 12, p.97. See also WSHC 118/88. Abstract of Samuel Martyn's title.
10 WSHC A1/110, 1695M, f.21.
11 WSHC 568/5. Mortgage deed, Edward Scoles et al, Richard Smith, & Humphry Wall, 21st June 1704.
12 Two successive mortgage deeds in WSHC 568/5, dated 2nd June 1703, and 1st June 1704, describe him respectively as Richard III's eldest son, and as his second

1704 he borrowed £1000 by mortgaging his farm at West Kennett.[1] He also mortgaged lands which had been purchased from Richard Harding to his two sisters. At about the same time, he exchanged lands with Walter Grubbe, presumably to make a more compact holding.[2] Richard IV served four terms as churchwarden between 1708 and 1712;[3] in 1709 he appraised Thomas Fry's estate, and acted as surety for his widow when she took out letters of administration.[4]

Richard IV married Mary. Thomas V, their eldest son, was born c.1695.[5] Their daughter, Elizabeth, was not recorded in the parish register. Other children included Jane, baptised 17th October 1699, Catherine baptised 19th November 1700, Henry, baptised 26th February 1701/2, Charles, baptised 18th March 1702/3, Chrysostom, buried 20th December 1703, and Hamilton, baptised 7th September 1705. Henry was still present in the parish when he witnessed the will of William Spackman, in 1763.[6] Elizabeth was remembered in her brother Thomas V's will,[7] and was still living in the parish when she made her own will in 1765.[8]

According to his memorial stone in the church, Richard IV died 22nd August 1734 – although the parish register states that he was buried 21st August! He was aged 78. His wife Mary died 5th May 1720, and was buried 6th May, aged 59.[9] The mis-dated memorial stone was presumably set up in accordance with his daughter Elizabeth's will; she instructed her executor to 'set up a decent monument' to her father.[10] A number of slab memorials in the south aisle and elsewhere in the church record other Smith family burials.

In 1712, when the entail on the estate was broken, Thomas V was described as 'of London',[11] and presumably met his wife there. According to Stukeley, he was a lawyer, so probably studied at the Inns of Court. In 1723, he

---

son. Perhaps eldest <u>surviving</u> son is meant.
1 WSHC 568/5. Deed, 17th November 1713, Richard and Thomas Smith to Walter Stocc and Thomas Grinfield.
2 WSHC 568/5. Deed, 2nd June 1703, between Walter Grubb of Potterne and Richard Smith.
3 WSHC D3/15/5; D1/50/7, f.25.
4 WSHC P3/F/266.
5 He died in 1750 aged c.55, and is memorialised at Great Amwell; see www.findagrave.com/memorial/116105253.
6 WSHC P3/S/1401.
7 TNA PROB11/786/436.
8 WSHC 118/88.
9 Phillipps, op cit, p.210.
10 WSHC 118/88.
11 WSHC 568/5. Deed, 13th May 1712.

described himself as an attorney.[1] His great-aunt's husband, Henry Goldsmith, was described as of Barnard's Inn on his wife's tomb-stone, and it may be that the young lawyer attended his great-uncle's inn. His uncle Stawell would also have welcomed him to London. Stukeley was interested in him because he 'lives in Monument Yard [London] and desires to take away the stones of S long barrow', that is, West Kennett long barrow.[2] One wonders whether his seven-year lease of the capital messuage at West Kennett in 1719, and again in 1724, was due to his intention to stay in London.[3] In 1727, he was described as 'of St Margarets, now Fish Street, London'.[4] Nevertheless, he frequently served on the Hundred jury in the 1730s,[5] and was named in the Wiltshire freeholders' books on several occasions in the 1730s and 1740s.[6] In c.1736, he signed the petition to the bishop concerning the vicar's non-residence.[7] And in 1742 he gave evidence in the House of Commons in support of the proposal to turnpike the Bath Road at Beckhampton.[8]

Thomas V's marriage with Hannah, daughter of William Plomer, in 1719 brought with it payment of the outstanding mortgage on the family estate.[9] The Plomers came from Great Amwell (Hertfordshire),[10] where Hannah was baptised 8th January 1694. Thomas and Hannah had two children, Thermuthis (a Plomer family name) and Hannah. Thomas was presumably still living in London when Thermuthis was baptised at St Magnus the Martyr on 10th April 1723. Hannah was baptised at Wilcot 27th November, 1726.

Thermuthis married Stayner Chamberlain at St Stephen Walbrook (London) on 22nd August 1745, and lived in Essex for most of her life, probably rarely if ever seeing her family. Her father's will[11] left her sister Hannah 'my own picture and my daughter Chamberlains both drawn in miniature and set up together in one frame'. He made no bequest to Thermuthis herself, although

1 Somerset Heritage Centre. DD/PO/6/ Lease, 3rd September 1723, Richard & Thomas Smith to Francis Popham.
2 Gillings, et al, 'Destruction', op cit, p.153.
3 Somerset Heritage Centre DD\PO/6. Lease, Thomas Smith to Francis Popham, 1723; WSHC 118/88. Lease, Thomas Smith to John Beake, 24 August 1727.
4 WSHC 118/88. Elizabeth & Jane Smith to Thomas Smith, 24th August 1727.
5 WSHC A1/110, Michaelmas rolls.
6 WSHC A1/265.
7 WSHC D1/47/3. See below, p.402.
8 *Journals of the House of Commons*, 24, p.365.
9 WSHC 118/88. Abstract of Mr Martyn's title.
10 Although one wonders whether the family were connected to Richard Plomer, who was a tenant at will in Avebury when the 1548 survey was taken; WSHC 2664/1/2D/8.
11 TNA PROB11/786/436.

half his freehold property descended to her – and hence to her husband. In 1755, he was the joint owner, with Samuel Martyn, his sister in law's husband, of a property in West Kennett which commanded a rent of £185 per annum.[1] In 1772, it was let for £220 per annum.[2]

Hannah junior married Samuel Martyn. Her dowry included property in Clifton, Bedfordshire which her maternal uncle, Robert Plomer had once owned, and which was sold in 1748 to raise capital for re-investment.[3] Hannah's father, Thomas Smith V, bequeathed to her husband 'all and singular my lands tenements and hereditaments whatsoever', probably meaning his leasehold property; also 'all my household goods household furniture, plate linen Implements of household and all and singular other my goods chattels and personal estate whatsoever'. Martyn was named joint executor together with Thomas V's cousin, another Thomas Smith, gent., of Marlborough, who received £20.[4] Thomas V also remembered his sister Elizabeth, who was given a guinea to buy a mourning ring, and his wife, who received 'her brothers picture'. Two servants were also given 30s each to buy mourning clothes.[5]

In her 1752 will Hannah senior made provision 'that I may be buried in my father's vault in the parish of Amwel Magna in the County of Hertfordshire and also that my late husband shall be taken up at the same time and with all imaginable care be put into a lead coffin without being exposed to view and carried with me in a hearse attended with one mourning coach into the same vault'.[6] Her family's memorial stone at Great Amwell records both her burial there, and that of her husband.[7] Her will does not mention either of her daughters, but it does mention her two grand-daughters, both of them named Thermuthis.

The death of Hannah Smith senior marked the end of the Smith family's long ownership of the manor of West Kennett. A few scions of the family continued to live in the parish. Elizabeth, Thomas V's sister, was buried on 1st June 1766. In her unproven will she bequeathed diamond rings to both her

---

1 WSHC 568/7. Lease, Stanes Chamberlain and Samuel Martyn to John Nalder, 9th November 1755.
2 WSHC 118/88. Draft lease, Stanes Chamberlain and Samuel Martyn to Anthony Allen, 1772.
3 WSHC 568/5. Indenture tripartite, 7th December 1748.
4 *VCH Wilts* 12, p.97, incorrectly states that Thomas V devised his manor to this cousin.
5 Elizabeth and the two servant were not mentioned in an earlier unproven will; WSHC 118/88, 18th January 1750/51.
6 TNA PROB11/795/275.
7 www.findagrave.com

nieces.[1] Her bequest to Mrs Smith of Gutton Lane, London, shows that there were still Avebury Smiths in London at this date. Mary Smith, who witnessed the will, was presumably a relative.

The Stawell Family

The Stawells were major landowners based at Cothelstone in Somerset, with a rent roll said to yield between £4000 and £5000 per annum in 1643.[2] On the eve of the Civil War, in 1639, Sir John Stawell purchased the manor of Avebury, paying £8550.[3] He served as Member of Parliament for Somerset in the Long Parliament, and, as we have seen became a prominent Royalist commander during the Civil War, serving as governor of Taunton. His estate was confiscated and sold during the Interregnum, but was restored to Sir John at the Restoration.[4]

It is unlikely that Sir John Stawell ever actually lived at Avebury, although he may have used it as his base when he rode to meet King Charles at Hungerford in 1644.[5] He died in 1662, and the estate descended to his eldest son, George.[6] Avebury was a very minor part of his estate, indeed, so insignificant that the family regarded it as a mere farm.[7] Nevertheless, George's brother, Ralph, moved into Avebury manor house.[8] It was Ralph who paid the hearth tax in 1662.[9] He married Anne Ryves in 1667; in the marriage settlement he was described as being 'of Aubery'.[10] Their son John was baptised in Avebury on 6th August 1668. He needed his own house, and it was probably thought desirable that a member of the family should live there in the light of the

1 WSHC 188/88.
2 TNA C2/Chas1/A9/39. This estimate was made by John Forsyth, the Parliamentarian vicar of Avebury.
3 WANHS. Wiltshire Genealogy, v.A-A, f.113, citing the Close Rolls. *VCH Wilts.*, 12, p.91, states 1640, but is probably mistaken.
4 For his activities during the Civil War and Interregnum, see Stawell, George Dodsworth. *A Quantock Family: the Stawells of Cothelstone and their Descendants, the Barons Stawell of Somerton, and the Stawells of Devonshire and the County Cork.* Barnicot & Pearce, 1910, p.87-99.
5 Underdown, David. *Revel, Riot and Rebellion: Popular Politics and Culture in England 1603-1660.* Clarendon Press, 1985, p.147 & 155.
6 TNA. PROB/11/307/336.
7 Stawell, op cit, p.349.
8 According to Sir Richard Holford, who noted that Ralph and his son lived there; see WSHC 184/1, pt.1. Letter, Sir Richard Holford to John Gardiner, 21st August 1701.
9 TNA E179/259/29.
10 Stawell, op cit, p.376.

family's Royalism, and of the fact that the parish had been heavily influenced by Puritanism during the Interregnum.

George Stawell died in October 1669,[1] and Ralph succeeded to the family estate.[2] He probably moved out of Avebury at this stage, and took up residence at Cothelstone. Ralph subsequently, in 1685, became a baron.

It is not known whether Avebury Great Farm was let whilst Ralph was resident, or whether it was kept in hand.[3] John Baskerville was named as the previous tenant when William Skeat took a lease in 1689; Baskerville's lease may well have been granted by Ralph after George died. When Ralph in turn died in 1688, Avebury became his widow's dower. But so did Hartley Wespall (Hants), together with lands at Fitzhead and Wiveliscombe in Somerset.[4] Her 1690 will implies that she actually lived at Hartley Wespall, where she was buried in 1692.[5] When William Skeat leased the farm from Lord John Stawell in 1689, he was granted the occupation of most of the manor house, but provision was made so that the Stawell family could use it for occasional visits.[6] Baskerville had probably had a similar arrangement.

Ralph Lord Stawell died in 1688. He was succeeded by his son John, who lived long enough to run up enormouse debts, but nevertheless died in 1692 when he was just 23. According to Collinson, Cothelstone was 'thought to be one of the best houses in the West of England' when Ralph died.[7] Despite that, the new Lord began to tear down the old house, and set about building a new one.[8] He died in the middle of the building work. His debts were so great that an Act of Parliament had to be obtained in order to pay them off. One of the properties which had to be sold was the manor of Avebury, which thus passed out of Stawell ownership and was purchased by Sir Richard Holford.

Stretch
Walter Stretch, yeoman, was probably the son of Christopher and Alice Stretch of Preshute. If this identification is correct, he was baptised in 1657, and his brother William was baptised in 1663. His brother resided in Overton in

---

1 Stawell, op cit, p.111.
2 Stawell, op cit, p.111.
3 For tenants in 1642 and 1652, see below, p.231.
4 Stawell, op cit, p.349.
5 Stawell, p.114 & 349.
6 Wiltshire & Swindon History Centre. 184/4.
7 Cited by Stawell, op cit, p.120.
8 Victor, David. 'The Fall of the Stawell Family', *Notes & Queries for Somerset & Dorset,* 39(396), p.261-2.

1707.[1] Christopher, incidentally, was described as 'of Avebury' in 1654, when he served as a hundred juror.[2] Walter himself was described as 'of Lockeridge' in 1691. He married Mary Stephens at Marlborough in 1684. Two years earlier, she had purchased a messuage in Eastbrook, which the couple mortgaged in 1691[3]. She also brought to the marriage a small portion of land, formerly the property of Robert Bayntun, which she had purchased three years earlier. It had formerly been a copyhold of Avebury Trusloe manor,[4] and Walter was still paying a 'high rent' of 8d to John Griffin in 1703.[5]

The couple built their inn, the Catherine Wheel, on one of these pieces of land.[6] Walter notoriously used stone from a megalith to build his dining room.[7] Stukeley described him as one of the Herostratus's of Avebury, and credited him with having discovered the way to demolish the standing stones by fire, c.1694[8]. It was probably in his inn that the long-drawn out dispute over tithes between Sir Richard Holford and John White was settled in 1701: Walter Stretch witnessed the final agreement.[9] A variety of other meetings were also held there.[10] Walter was sufficiently prominent to be frequently nominated for jury service c.1701-7.[11] He voted in the 1705/6 Parliamentary election.[12]

The couple had two children, George and Mary. George was born 1696;[13] Mary was baptised 16th August 1700, but probably died young; only George is mentioned in Walter's 1707 will.[14] Walter bequeathed the whole of his freehold estate (presumably including the Catherine Wheel) to his widow for life. In 1712, she paid £850 for an Eastbrook tenement which included 50 acres of pasture, as well as various common rights.[15] Mary was buried 13th

1   WSHC P1/S/709.
2   WSHC A1/110, 1654M, f.153.
3   WSHC 212A/31/1. Mortgage deed, 1691.
4   WSHC 212A/31/1. Lease & release, 1681; *VCH Wilts* 12, p.94;
5   WSHC 184/4, pt.1. Proposed conveyance, 1703, John Griffin to Sir Richard Holford; Conveyance, 9.10.1703. John Griffin to Sir Richard Holford.
6   For his inn-keeping activities see Raymond, Stuart A. 'The Inns of Avebury, c.1600-1800', *WAM*, 117, 2024, p.159-67.
7   Stukeley, William. *Abury: a Temple of the British Druids ... .* 1743, p.25.
8   Stukeley, *Abury*, op cit, p.25.
9   WSHC 184/4, pt.2. Agreement between Sir Richard Holford & John White, 2nd October 1701.
10 For these, see Raymond, 'Inns', op cit.
11 WSHC A1/110, 1701M, 1702M, 1704M, 1705M, & 1707M; A1/265/1.
12 WSHC 931/1. Poll book, 17th February 1705.
13 Wiltshire Memorial Inscriptions Index www.findmypast.co.uk
14 WSHC P1/S/709.
15 WSHC 1409/16/3.

May 1720, and George inherited. He mortgaged the Eastbrook property for £160 in 1726,[1] and sold part of the land attached to Caleb Bailey in 1727.[2]

George continued to run his father's inn; his licence for 1741 is recorded.[3] In 1726, he was described as a maltster.[4] He married Rebecca, the daughter of John and Jane Rose,[5] probably after his mother's death, but before her father's death in September 1720.[6] The couple's only daughter, Mary, was baptised on 17th May 1721. She received a bequest of £20 in her grandmother Rose's will, entrusted to her father during her minority. George was also named as one of his mother-in-law's executor. When her other executor, John Brown, died in 1731, George stood bond for his administrator.[7] As an innkeeper, he was occasionally called upon to assist in probate business. He had already witnessed the will of John Griffin in 1715[8], and appraised his father in law's inventory in 1720.[9] He similarly stood bond for Peter Griffin as administrator of Joseph Griffin's will in 1732/3,[10] and appraised the inventory of his fellow inn-keeper, John Fowler, in 1745.[11] He served as hundred constable in 1734,[12] as tithingman in 1739 (probably) and 1744,[13] and as churchwarden in 1744 and 1745.[14] He was also frequently nominated for jury service, c.1730-47.[15]

George died 7th June 1748, aged 52.[16] However, his legacy lived on. When the turnpike came to Beckhampton, George and Rebecca had closed down the Catherine Wheel in the village,[17] and built a new inn at Beckhampton, giving

1 WSHC 1409/16/3. Mortgage deed, George Stretch to John Browne, 28th February 1726/7.
2 WSHC 1409/16/3. Lease & release, William Phelps to Mary Stretch, 22nd/23rd September 1712; also John Cue et al to Caleb Bailey, 1st June 1727.
3 WSHC A1/325/4.
4 WSHC 1409/16/3. Mortgage, George Stretch to John Browne, 28th February 1726.
5 According to their wills, cf. WSHC P3/R/365 & WSHC P3/R/364.
6 WSHC P3/R/365.
7 WSHC P3/B/1308.
8 WSHC P3/G/454.
9 WSHC P3/R/365
10 WSHC P3/G/556.
11 WSHC P3/F/368.
12 WSHC A1/110, 1734M.
13 WSHC A1/110, 1739M & 1744M.
14 WSHC D1/50/17, D3/15/13.
15 WSHC A1/265; A1/110, Michaelmas rolls.
16 Phillipps, Thomas, Sir. *Monumental Inscriptions of Wiltshire*, ed. Peter Sherlock. Wiltshire Record Society, 53. 2000, p.210.
17 The property was sold to Richard Bailey, James Thring, and John Nalder, probably as trustees for Caleb Bailey's charity, in 1755; cf.*VCH Wilts* 12, p.94.

it the same name. It attracted land tax; in 1752, Rebecca had to pay the large sum of £2 1s 2d.[1] By then, the inn was sometimes known as Beckhampton House.

Rebecca, incidentally, received a bequest of £145 in her brother's 1749/50 will.[2] It was not, however, actual cash, but rather money which she had borrowed from him on bond, perhaps used to finance the cost of building. Rebecca's daughter, Mary, also received £50. The two also received legacies of ten guineas each in Hannah Smith's 1752 will.[3] When Rebecca herself died in February 1754, she bequeathed the whole of her estate to Mary.[4]

Mary had already inherited her father's inn, together with the house her grandmother had bought in 1712, together with 29 acres of pasture[5] She did not, however, possess the inn for long. In the early 1750s it suffered a disastrous fire,[6] and was consequently sold in 1755. By then, her mother Rebecca had died, and she had married James Hitchcock, a haberdasher.[7] The marriage did not last long; Mary herself was buried 4th December 1756.[8]

Her death left a problem for her husband. When George Stretch died, his widow Rebecca had taken out an administration bond.[9] She had failed, however, to administer the estate. On her death, responsibility for the administration descended to her daughter, and thence to her son in law. It may be that George had left debts outstanding which had never been paid. Alternatively, the case brought against James Hitchcock in the ecclesiastical court may have been a collusive action to secure safe title to his estate. However that may be, James Mayo, the rector, and William Clements, George's fellow innkeeper, claiming to be creditors, questioned the administration. After nine years, and after the fire, it was felt to be impossible to compile an inventory, so James had to make a declaration that none of his father-in-law's goods had come into his hands.

1 WSHC 184/3. Land tax assessment 1752.
2 TNA PROB11/786/41.
3 TNA PROB11/795/275.
4 WSHC P3/S/1352.
5 WSHC 212A/31/4/. Conveyance, James Hitchcock to John Merriman, 6th May 1755.
6 WSHC 212A/31/4. Lease & release, 5th & 6th May 1755.
7 Sarum Marriage Licence Bonds www.findmypast.co.uk/articles/world-records/full-list-of-united-kingdom-records/life-events-bmds/sarum-marriage-licence-bonds See also *VCH Wilts,* 12, p.94.
8 Phillipps, Thomas, Sir. *Monumental Inscriptions of Wiltshire,* ed. Peter Sherlock. Wiltshire Record Society, 53. 2000, p.210.
9 WSHC P3/S/1306.

Tanner

William Tanner, gent., married Sarah Gammon at Great Bedwyn 25th April 1774; the couple had two sons, William (1778) and John (18th May 1780). Sarah was buried at Avebury 1st July 1816 at the age of 81; he outlived her, being buried 7th July 1826 aged 96.[1] It is possible that William was related to Daniel Tanner of Urchfont who served as one of the Avebury enclosure commissioners in the 1790s.[2]

The family came to live in Avebury when William purchased a farm at West Kennett, c.1778.[3] He also held property in East Kennett, on which he paid land tax of £28 10s 3d in 1784. Tanner also leased the rectorial tithes from Rev. James Mayo in 1794.[4]

William Tanner and his wife were amongst the few in Avebury to pay hair powder tax in 1796,[5] perhaps an indication of their social standing. He served as overseer of the poor in 1795,[6] and was a turnpike trustee in 1798.[7] From 1794, his name regularly appears on the freeholders' lists.[8] The farmhouse he lived in was built of sarsen from the megaliths destroyed by Mr Nalder, the previous tenant. Tanner himself destroyed several Kennet Avenue megaltiths in 1794.[9]

Tilly

The earliest mentions of the Tilly family in Avebury are the marriage of John Tilly and Mary Robinson (the daughter of Humphry Robinson, the prominent carpenter and dissenter) on 19th April 1713, and the baptism of their eldest son, John, on 26th September 1713/14. The couple went on to have eight children by 1730, one of whom died as an infant. In 1720, Mary was bequeathed a large 'brewing kettle' by her father, who also gave her son John £5 'to bind him apprentice when he do attaine to age for ye same'.[10]

The family all crammed into what was probably a tiny cottage, newly built on a small plot of land which had formerly been part of an East Kennett

---

1 For his will, see TNA PROB11/1730/102.
2 WSHC A1/EA95.
3 *VCH Wilts XII*, p.97; WSHC 1366/8.
4 WSHC A1/345/240A.
5 WSHC A1/395.
6 WSHC A1/125/46N.
7 WSHC 1371/1.
8 WSHC A1/265/36-40.
9 Long, William. *Abury illustrated*. 1862, p.64.
10 WSHC P1/R/275.

farm owned by the Grubbe family. It was described in their 1715 lease as 'newly erected'[1], although they had to surrender a former lease, probably purchased from the Hillier family. They paid a small entry fine of forty shillings, plus rent of 2s 6d and two 'well fatted capons' every year, so it is unlikely that the accommodation was anything more than basic. John the elder was described in the lease as a 'yeoman', although it is likely that the family had problems maintaining that status, and at least one daughter (Mary) married a labourer, James Norris, in 1762.

John the younger (the eldest son) renewed the lease in 1752, although his father was still alive[2]. Whether he had been apprenticed in accordance with his grandfather's bequest is not known; however, like his father he was described as a yeoman in the lease. He married Elizabeth Day at Yatesbury on 5th October 1750; that was probably why his father enabled him to take over the lease.

John and Elizabeth had four children, two of whom died in infancy. Their son Thomas renewed the lease again in 1785[3]. This time he had to pay an entry fine of £11, although the rent did not change. He married Mary Butler of Wolcot (Somerset) at Berwick Bassett on 4th February 1779. The lease described him as a cordwainer (that is, a shoemaker), so it is likely that he had served an apprenticeship, but unlikely that he was regarded as a yeoman. The lease named his two children, John (then aged 6) and Thomas (aged 2). Subsequently, two other children were born, both named Elizabeth. One was buried on 14th August 1791, at East Kennett; the other was baptised just 3 months later, on 13th November 1791.

Thomas and Mary, both aged 73, were buried together at East Kennett on the same day, 7th November 1820, at East Kennett; Thomas was described as 'of Overton'.

John the younger's brother, Richard, also had a large family; he and his wife Mary had six children. One of them, another John, was a turnpike keeper when he married in 1780.

Tomkins[4]

John Tomkins served as constable of Avebury in 1651, was ordered to repair his house in 1655, and served as a member of the manorial homage in 1655

[1] WSHC 212B/112.
[2] WSHC 212B/115.
[3] WSHC 212B/117.
[4] Sometimes spelt 'Tompkins'.

and 1656.[1] He was a husbandman, although his 1669/70 probate inventory[2] shows minimal evidence of his occupation. His furniture, clothing, and other household goods, together with a small quantity of wheat, were valued together at £6. But he also had £60 in cash, perhaps the proceeds of the sale of his 1669 wheat crop.

Elizabeth Tomkins, who was buried 3rd March 1676/7 was probably John's widow. Ruth Tomkins, who married John Pope on 25th July 1672, was a daughter.[3] So was Mary Tomkins, whose estate was administered by her sister Ruth when she died in 1681. It was valued at £25, including bonds worth £15.[4]

John's estate was administered by his son John, who was described as a yeoman in his administration bond, and as of East Kennett in his burial entry. In 1681/2 he occupied a copyhold tenement with a house, garden, and backside, probably in Eastbrook.[5] He was sufficiently wealthy to loan John Truslow £10, which Truslow's son Richard agreed to repay in 1694.[6] John junior married Mary; their son Richard was baptised on 21st July 1678, and their daughter, another Ruth, was baptised 12th May 1693, and buried 2nd October 1698. The baptismal entries for three other daughters, Mary and Elizabeth, do not survive, although their mother's will tells us that they all married.[7] Mary married John Cue, the blacksmith.[8] Elizabeth married an Arnall, although his christian name has not been traced. The third daughter is not named, but she married into the Poore family. All three daughters had children who are mentioned in their grandmother's will. John junior was probably the John Tomkins of East Kennet who was buried in Avebury 22nd June 1708.

Richard Tomkins did not outlive his father for very long. He was buried 7th August 1709. His will[9] mentions his son Richard junior, and his daughter

1 WSHC 473/52, f.7, 72 & 83.
2 His inventory is dated 7th January 1669/70, although administration was not granted until 7th May 1680; cf. WSHC P3/T/284.
3 John I's grandson Richard was described as a 'kinsman' in John Pope's will; cf. P1/5Reg/31.
4 WSHC P3/T/288.
5 WSHC 529/125.
6 WSHC 371/1, pt.3. Deed, 26th December 1694, Bridget Truslow to Richard Truslow.
7 WSHC P3/T/497.
8 WSHC 212/31/3. Deed to lead the uses of a fine, John Cue et al to Caleb Bailey, 1st June 1727.
9 WSHC P3/T/421.

Mary. In a deed of 1752 he was described as a husbandman.[1] His estate was valued at a mere £16 3s. It included 'twoe ackers of corne' worth £4. That was presumably grown on the four acres of freehold land which had been granted to John II in the 1680s at a rent of 4d per annum.[2] The rent was still being paid in 1708,[3] and had given Richard the entitlement to vote in 1705.[4]

Richard senior bequeathed to his son 'all my wholl estate', although making a few provisions for his wife and daughter. The will does not say so, but the freehold land was to be retained by his wife (or perhaps his grandmother) for life before descending to his son. In 1723, however, Richard junior sold his interest in the property to Caleb Bailey for £150.[5] The whole of the property reverted to Bailey in 1727, when Richard, Mary his sister, and Mary his grandmother, were all buried within three months of each other. Perhaps they all succumbed to the same disease.

As far as is known, Richard junior did not marry. He did, however, have a bastard daughter, Hannah, who was baptised 9th January 1721/2. Her mother's name is merely given as 'Chiverson'. One wonders whether Mary and Elizabeth Tompkins, who were both apprenticed as paupers in 1730,[6] were also Richard's daughters. Their master was John Chivers of Yatesbury, who may perhaps have been related to Hannah's mother.

Truslow

The Truslows came to Avebury in the early sixteenth century. The historian of Marlborough tells us that Thomas Truslow was 'by repute a Yorkshire butcher' who was then 'recently arrived'.[7] A witness in a court case remembered, in 1599, that Thomas Truslow had been a butcher seventy years earlier.[8] John and Edward Truslove, successive mayors of Beverley in the 1580s and 1590s[9] (John was also Member of Parliament for Beverley in 1589),[10] were probably cousins of the Avebury family. The Truslows were one of the few Avebury

1 WSHC 212A/31/4, Deed, John Nalder et al to John Brown, 15th February 1752.
2 WANHS Genealogy mss., v.A-A, p.136.
3 WSHC 184/4/1. Sale Particulars, 1702; Rental, 1708.
4 WSHC 931/1. Poll book, 17th February 1705.
5 WSHC 212A/31/3. Receipt, 28th January 1723/4.
6 WSHC 184/9/3.
7 Stedman, A.R. *Marlborough and the Upper Kennet country.* [Marlborough College?], 1960, p.107.
8 TNA E134/41Eliz/Hil8.
9 Allison, K.J., ed. *A History of the County of York East Riding: Volume 6, the Borough and Liberties of Beverley.* Victoria County History. London, 1989, p.202-3.
10 www.historyofparliamentonline.org/research/members/members-1558-1603

families who claimed entitlement to their own coat of arms. Edward Truslow's claim was humiliatingly 'disgraded' by William Harvey, the herald, in 1565.[1] In 1623, however, another herald accepted that the family were descended from the Beverley Trusloves,[2] and recorded their coat of arms. That decision rebounded on John Truslow in 1631, when he was fined £14 for failing to seek knighthood at Charles I's coronation.[3]

The Avebury family is first mentioned in 1524, when Thomas Truslow appears in the lay subsidy rolls.[4] In the mid-1530s, he was engaged in the Chancery suit against John Shuter mentioned above.[5] In 1545, he was assessed to the benevolence at £3, the second highest assessment in the parish after John Shuter.[6] Thomas's second wife[7] was Joanna Trugge; her will[8] names their children as John, Alse (who died before her mother), Elizabeth, and Ellen. John was born c.1527. Ellen (Eleanor) was aged c.78 in c.1598, so was born c.1520.[9] Thomas, Joanna, and their son John, leased the manor of Avebury Trusloe,[10] together with the Rectory, from Cirencester Abbey, in 1533. In 1535, the rent was £41 per annum.[11] In 1563 Joanna was rated at £30 in the subsidy.[12] For sixty years (and perhaps much longer), the property was administered as a single unit. However, Joanna's purchase of the manorial freehold in 1563 separated ownership of the Rectory and the Manor, causing problems when the

---

1. Metcalfe, Walter C., ed. *The Visitation of Wiltshire, 1565*, by William Harvey, Clarenceux King of Arms … . William Pollard & Co., 1897, p.54. Edward was presumably the head of the family at this date, although he is not otherwise mentioned in our sources.
2. Squibb, op cit, p.198.
3. Fry, E.A. 'Knighthood Compositions for Wiltshire', *Wiltshire Notes & Queries* 1, 1893, p.106. See also Raymond, Stuart A. 'The Armigerous Status of the Truslow Family', *The Recorder*, 22, 2023, p.11.
4. Gover, et al, op cit, p.295.
5. See p.134-5, and TNA C1/912/53.
6. Ramsay, G.D., ed. *Two sixteenth Century taxation lists, 1545 and 1576*. Wiltshire Archaeological and Natural History Society Records Branch 10. 1954, p.22 & 103.
7. Acording to S., J. 'Notes on Wiltshire Parishes: Avebury', *Wiltshire Notes & Queries* 8, 1914-18, p.218.
8. TNA PROB11/51/51.
9. TNA E134/40and41Eliz/Mich7; S., J. 'Notes on Wiltshire Parishes: Avebury', *Wiltshire Notes & Queries* 8, 1914-18, p.217.
10. The family gave its name to the manor, differentiating it from the manor formerly owned by Fotheringhay College.
11. *Valor Ecclesiasticus*, vol.2. 1814, p.466.
12. TNA E179/198/276.

lease of the more valuable Rectory ran out in 1593.[1] Joanna's three daughters all married; in her 1567/8 will, she mentioned no fewer than nineteen grandchildren. None bore the Truslow surname.

On Joanna's death, both the manor, and the lease of the Rectory lands, descended to John. In 1576, he was assessed for the subsidy at £4.[2] In 1587, he contributed the substantial amount of £25 towards a Marlborough muster in preparation for the Armada.[3] He served as churchwarden in 1594.[4]

John's property included the right to tithes which had formerly belonged to Cirencester Abbey. Tithes were contentious. John's tenants contended that the tithes from the Rectory estate belonged to the vicar, and in 1585 he sued them in Chancery to obtain payment.[5] It is not clear whether this had anything to do with the fact that he was presented at visitation c.1591 'for withholding xls from the churche'.[6]

John was not content with leasing the Rectory and owning the Manor. The lease of the Rectory was due to run out in 1593, so he sought other property for his portfolio. In 1580, he purchased four closes and three yardlands from Chideock Wardour.[7] In 1584 the estate of Beckhampton Chapel in Beckhampton and Stanmore was purchased.[8] A farm at Beckhampton, then known as Griffin's farm (it was tenanted by William Griffin) was purchased from William Button in 1588.[9]

John died childless 18th April 1593 aged 67.[10] His manor (but not the Rectory lands) passed to a relative, Richard Truslow of Teffont Evias, who described himself as John's 'adopted heir and executor' when he erected his

1 *VCH Wilts* 12, p.92 & 98; TNA LR2/191, f.141.
2 Ramsay, op cit, p.103.
3 Stedman, op cit, p.116. Noble, T.C., ed. *The names of those Persons who Subscribed towards the Defence of this Country at the time of the Spanish Armada, 1588, and the amounts each contributed.* A.R.Smith, 1886, p.67.
4 WSHC D3/7/1, f.126v & 135.
5 WANHS Genealogy mss., v.A-A, f.84.
6 WSHC D3/7/1, f.89.
7 TNA C2/Eliz/T1/22. This Chancery case was brought against Thomas Smith and George Mortimer, who had probably formerly had an interest in the land, in order to protect his title.
8 VCH Wilts 12, p.96; WSHC 371/1, pt.2. Indenture, Robert Howse to John Truslow, 4th February 1584.
9 WSHC 5724/1. Indenture, William Button et al to Richard Truslow, 20th September 1588. Subsequently known as Truslow's Farm, later as Beckhampton Farm.
10 Phillipps, Thomas, Sir. *Monumental Inscriptions of Wiltshire*, ed. Peter Sherlock. Wiltshire Record Society, 53. 2000, p.209.

memorial stone.[1] The deed of settlement naming him as heir was executed just eight days before John's death.[2] Almost immediately, he was forced into a dispute with Sir James Mervyn, whose wife, formerly Deborah Dunch, had inherited a reversionary lease of the Rectory lands. It was unclear which land belonged to Truslow's manor, and which to the Rectory. The dispute lasted for two decades, and was continued under his heir.[3] It seems likely that the loss of the Rectory lease, which provided a major portion of the Truslow's income, contributed to the subsequent decline in the family fortunes.

Richard married Maud Parnell, the daughter of John Parnell of Winterbourne Monkton.[4] In 1597/8 he was named as overseer in Robert Rychards' will;[5] in 1609/10 he appraised the probate inventory of William Hayward.[6] Between 1604 and 1612, he was frequently called for jury service.[7] In 1611, he was one of the 'sessors' for the subsidy, assessing himself on goods valued at £8 – the second highest assessment in the parish – although in 1594 he had paid tax on goods valued at £16.[8]

Soon after coming into his inheritance, Richard purchased Beckhampton Chapel tithes in 1594,[9] and the manor of Beckhampton in 1596. The latter cost £1000.[10] These purchases were probably financed by a mortgage of £300 by Oliver St.John. Richard's failure to repay this debt resulted in St John seizing the manor of Beckhampton to obtain repayment. That was probably why Richard took a substantial entry fine - £100 – when he granted a three-life lease on a Beckhampton farm of just over 20 acres in 1602. The rent to be paid by Richard Phelps als Bromham was just 16s per annum.[11] Charging high entry fees and low rents was one way to raise money quickly.

The manor did not stay in the possession of St. John for long. When Richard Truslow died in 1613, his successor was a minor, the estate was found

1 Squibb, op cit, p.198; Philipps, op cit, p.209.
2 It is transcribed in his inquisition post mortem, TNA C142/237/132.
3 See below, p.211-12 for this dispute.
4 Squibb, op cit, p.199.
5 WSHC P3/R/3.
6 WSHC P3/H/56.
7 WSHC A1/110, Michaelmas rolls, 1604-8 & 1610-12.
8 TNA E179/199/369; E179/198/315. The assessment had been reduced to £8 in 1598; TNA E179/198/325.
9 *VCH Wilts* 12, p.96.
10 *VCH Wilts* 12, p.95; WSHC 371/1, pt.2. Indenture, William Button et al to Richard Truslow, 20th September 1596; WSHC 184/4/1. Abstract of title to Truslow's Farm.
11 WSHC 212B/102. Lease, 30th April 1601.

to be held as of the manor of East Greenwich by knight service[1], and the manor was seized for wardship by the Crown.[2] St. John had to wait until the heir came of age before pursuing his claim in Chancery.[3]

Richard's widow, Maud, made her will in 1625.[4] In it, she mentioned five children – John, Richard Giles, Walter, and Ann, all of whom were probably adults at her death. Two other sons probably died before their mother: Thomas is mentioned in the 1623 heraldic visitation,[5] James in his son's baptismal entry in the parish register. Maud also mentioned three grandchildren, John, Thomas, and Richard. Nothing more is known of Richard. John, baptised 4th November 1621, was the son of John and his wife Eleanor. Thomas was probably the son of James, baptised 15th July 1623; James was not mentioned in his mother's will, probably because he had died.

John, Richard and Maud's son, inherited his father's estate. He took out a licence to marry Eleanor Tooker, the daughter of Thomas Tooker of Shrewton, in 1616.[6] The couple had at least three children, Richard the eldest, John, and Walter.

John served on the grand jury at Quarter Sessions in 1620, 1628, and 1632,[7] appeared as a suitor at Selkley Hundred court in 1627,[8] and served as tithingman in 1637 and 1638.[9] He appraised the inventories of both George and Margery Brown in 1619 and 1620.[10] Katherine Brown, probably a relative of this couple, made him overseer of her 1623 will.[11] So did Edith Mortimer, in 1628.[12] And so did John Peart, the Vicar, whose 1621 inventory he also appraised. Peart evidently had a high opinion of him, as he bequeathed him a copy of one of Martin Luther's books.[13] John's brother, Walter, as Peart's godson, also received a theological tome: a copy of 'on book called Bullenger'. Bullenger was a prominent Calvinist, who led the church in Zurich. One

1 Many properties of the dissolved monasteries were held by this tenure.
2 TNA WARD 7/51/71. See also WANHS Genealogy mss, v.A-A, p.98-9, citing TNA C3/324/3.
3 S., J. 'Notes on Wiltshire Parishes: Avebury', *Wiltshire Notes & Queries* 8, 1914-18, p.219.
4 WSHC P3/T/86.
5 Squibb, op cit, p.199.
6 Nevill, Edward. 'Marriage licences of Salisbury', *Genealogist* N.S., 24, 1908, p.32.
7 WSHC A1/110, 1620M;1628M, f.172; 1632M, f.206.
8 WSHC 9/15/324.
9 WSHC 9/1/155-6.
10 WSHC P3/B/179 & 195.
11 WSHC P3/B/236.
12 WSHC P3/M/117.
13 WSHC P3/P/101.

wonders whether their theological readings caused the family to fall out with Peart's successor. In 1633-4, John served as churchwarden – and was presented by Peart's successor, John Forsyth, for negligence![1]

One wonders also whether John's 'negligence' says anything about the fact that he sold so much of his inheritance. He began the process in 1616, when the lands of the Free Chapel of Beckhampton were sold to William Dunch for £455.[2] He sold the manor of Avebury Trusloe in 1623.[3] The tithes of Beckhampton Chapel were sold at about the same time.[4] In 1630 he received £130 from the sale of the tenement at Beckhampton then occupied by John Pope.[5] He also sold a portion of the manor of Beckhampton in c.1638.[6] John Goldsmith's 1639/40 will mentions land in Hungerford that he had recently purchased from John Truslow.[7] John Truslow died in 1646.[8] His inventory was valued at a mere £21 5s 2d, although he was still described as a 'gent'.[9] However, when his widow's inventory was taken in 1666/7, it was valued at £100.[10]

Richard Truslow was John's son and heir. Just over a year after his father's death he sold half of Beckhampton Farm to Thomas Smith for £260, presumably to raise money to pay off his father's debts.[11] Richard presumably died young; the rest of the estate passed to his brother John.

John Truslow, yeoman, took out a marriage licence to marry Bridget Sadler, the daughter of John Sadler of Chilton (Wroughton) in 1661.[12] The couple had seven children. Anne, Walter, Mary, and Giles, were baptised in Avebury between 1665 and 1676. Baptismal entries are missing for Richard, John, and Bridget.[13] John was called on to act as administrator of his mother's

---

1 WSHC D1/39/2/12, f.10v.
2 WSHC 371/1, pt.2. Indenture, John Truslow to Wiliam Dunch, 1st April 1619; 184/4/1. Abstract of title to the Free Chapel of Beckhampton.
3 *VCH Wilts* 12, p.93.
4 *VCH Wilts* 12, p.96.
5 WANHS Genealogy mss., v.A-A, p. 105.
6 *VCH Wilts* 12, p.95; WSHC 184/4/1. Abstract of title to Truslow's Farm, Beckhampton.
7 WSHC P1/G/142.
8 WSHC P1/T/108.
9 WSHC P1/T/108.
10 WSHC P3/T/207
11 WSHC 212B/104. Indenture, 10th June 1647. This may have been a mortgage, as it was technically a permanent lease with a rent of 12d per annum.
12 Nevill, Edmund, ed. 'Marriage licences of Salisbury', *Genealogist*, 31, 1915, p.260.
13 They are mentioned in his will, WSHC P3/T/356.

estate in 1666/7.[1] In 1670, Richard Cripps' will named him as overseer.[2] A decade later, in 1680/81, he appraised the inventory of John Mills.[3] John served three terms as churchwarden, in 1649/50, 1670, and 1671.[4] In that capacity, he signed the 1671 hearth tax exemption certificate.[5] He served as a constable of Selkley Hundred in 1670,[6] on the Hundred Jury in 1660,[7] and on various juries at Quarter Sessions between 1659 and 1685.[8] He paid tax on three hearths at Beckhampton c.1662,[9] and was assessed at £1 in the 1663 subsidy – a sixth of the amount on which Ralph Stawell (lord of Avebury manor) was assessed.[10] In 1678, he contributed 6d towards the rebuilding of St Paul's Cathedral after the Great Fire of London.[11]

Little evidence relating to John's ownership of land survives. He retained his father's half of Beckhampton Farm, and probably tenanted Rectory and/or Free Chapel tenements which his predecessors had formerly owned: their tithes in 1670 were held by Robert Baynton, who sued John for payment.[12]

John made his will 8th July 1694, making his widow, Bridget, his executrix.[13] Two of their children, Mary and Giles, died before their father. The other children, apart from Richard all received £50. Anne had married a Harrison;[14] her bequest was to go to her husband if she died. However, the estate was so laden with debt that Bridget, John's daughter, did not actually receive her money until 1721.[15] Her two brothers were both dead before their bequests were paid in 1733.[16] Walter was apprenticed to a carman in

1 WSHC P3/T/207.
2 WSHC P3/C/352.
3 WSHC P3/M/239.
4 Marsh, A.E.W. *A history of the Borough and Town of Calne.* Calne: Robert S.Heath, 1903, p.297; WSHC Bishops' transcript 1671; D1/50/1.
5 TNA E179/348.
6 WSHC A1/110, 1670 M, f.84.
7 WSHC A1/110. 1660 M.
8 WSHC A1/110, Michaelmas rolls.
9 TNA E179/259/29.
10 WANHS mss 140.
11 LMA 25565/24, f.18-19.
12 WANHS Genealogy A-A, p.127.
13 WSHC P3/T/356.
14 His surname is given in her brother Richard will, WSHC P3/T/410.
15 WSHC 371/1, pt.5. Acknowledgement by Bridget Truslow, 6th November 1721.
16 WSHC 371/1, pt.5. Acknowledgement by Bridget Truslow, as administrator, 3rd September 1733; schedule of payments due, undated but c.1730s.

London in 1705,[1] but subsequently went as a soldier to Portugal. He was never heard of again. Another brother, John, went to Jamaica, but came back to be buried at Avebury, 5th July 1719. It was not until 1727 that his sister, Bridget, took out an administration bond.[2] At the same time, she also took out an administration bond for her missing brother Walter.[3] She probably did so in order to receive the legacies still due to them from her father's farm. By then, Tooker had sold it to Robert Holford.[4]

Richard the eldest son, inherited his father's estate. He also inherited his debts. Although these had to be met by his mother as executor, he agreed to help with payment by leasing Beckhampton Farm from her. She received an annuity of £20. The lease[5] lists twenty-two creditors. Although he was able to mortgage Truslow's Farm to John Merryweather in 1695,[6] Richard was eventually forced to sell it to Charles Tooker in 1702.[7] Tooker was required to continue paying the annuity of £20 to Bridget Truslow the elder, but the legacies due to Richard's siblings remained as a charge on the property, and were not to be paid until after her death.[8]

Richard served on the Grand Jury in 1697,[9] and as churchwarden 1698-9.[10] He gave evidence in one of Sir Richard Holford's court cases, c.1701.[11] In 1701 he was under-tenant of land at Beckhampton leased by Edmund Goddard of Marlborough.[12] He died a bachelor, although we are told he had several bastard children.[13] When he made his will, on 26th March 1705, he was 'bound on a voiag to sea'.[14] He gave a shilling to his brother Walter, and

1 Webb, Cliff. *London Livery Company Apprenticeship Registers. Vol.29: Carman's Company, 1668, 1678-1800.* Society of Genealogists, 2000, p.47.
2 WSHC P3/T/498.
3 WSHC P3/T/499.
4 WSHC 371/1, pt.5. Acknowledgement by Bridget Truslow, as administrator, 3rd September 1733.
5 WSHC 371/1, pt.3. Lease, Bridget Truslow to Richard Truslow, 26th December 1694.
6 WSHC 371/1, pt.3. Mortgage, 30th May 1695.
7 WSHC 184/4/1. Abstract of title to Truslow's Farm; *VCH Wilts* 12, p.95.
8 WSHC 371/1, pt.4. Charles Tooker's bond, 1702; 371/1, pt.5. Discharge of Dame Susannah Holford by Richard Webb, 2nd November 1719.
9 WSHC A1/110, 1697M, f.184.
10 WSHC 54/16/3.
11 WSHC 184/1. List of witnesses.
12 WSHC 371/1, pt.4. Mortgage, Edmund Goddard to Thomas Smith, 2nd June 1701.
13 Markham, op cit, p.41.
14 WSHC P3/T/410.

to his sister Ann Harrison. His sister Bridget was to receive £5, but only after the money due to him on their mother's death had been paid. He left the more substantial sum of £55 to be used to apprentice the four children of Frances Hillier, widow, who divided the residue of his estate between them. Perhaps they were his bastards.

Bridget was the last legitimate member of the family, as far as we know, to live in Avebury. She was unmarried, but had a bastard daughter, Jane. In 1694 her father instructed that her legacy was to go to Jane if she were to die. Jane subsequently also bore two bastard children, baptised in Avebury in 1713/14 and 1721. The parish register describes her as 'of Calne'. She stood bound with her mother in the administration bonds for her two uncles. Jane was buried 7th August 1763.

Frances Truslow, widow, who made her will on 9th December 1728, was probably a cousin. Her son Thomas[1] died before her, and she asked to be buried beside him. Three other children, Henry, Richard and Frances, were mentioned in her will, although none are mentioned in the parish register. Frances was named as executrix. Subsequently, in 1738, she witnessed the will of Benjamin James.[2]

Frances the younger renewed her lease[3] of two cottages at Beckhampton in 1734, naming her brother Richard as one life, and her son John, aged two, as the other. She was then aged 34, and was described in the three life lease as a spinster. Presumably she was unmarried, so her son was a bastard. Her tiny cottages – one room and a buttery each – were probably amongst those which had formerly been owned by Richard Truslow, and which had come into the possession of Robert Holford. He took an entry fine of £25, and a rent of 2s 6d.

The Truslows had declined from being amongst the leading gentry in the parish, to being one of the poorer and less respectable families. Thomas Truslow, probably a scion of the family, was serving Lady Holford as a footboy when she died in 1723. In her will, she gave him £5 'to be secured for his advantage'.[4] Nevertheless, Frances still had glass in her windows; Holford had spent 11s 1d 'for work done at Frances Truslowe at Beckhampton' in 1731.[5]

1 His siblings were adults; hence he was not the Thomas son of James mentioned above.
2 WSHC P1/IJ/195.
3 WSHC 371/1, pt.5. Lease, Robert Holford to Frances Truslow, 6th March 1734.
4 TNA PROB11/590/280; S. J., 'Notes on Wiltshire Parishes: Avebury', *Wiltshire Notes & Queries* 8, 1914-18, p.272.
5 WSHC 371/1, pt.5. Account, 15th January 1731.

Williamson

When Arthur Jones died in 1789, his heir was his niece Anne, wife of Adam Williamson.[1] Jones wished her to be his executrix (and probably heiress) 'apart from every controul by her husband'.[2] Ann's husband was a senior army officer; he owned two houses in Hungerford,[3] and a house in Bath occupied by Mrs Jenny,[4] before acquiring the manor of Avebury, through his marriage.

Sir Adam did not spend much time in Avebury. In 1790, he was appointed as Lieutenant Governor of Jamaica, and became its governor on the death of his predecessor in November 1791. His wife followed him to the colony, arriving on 31st October 1791.[5] She kept up a lengthy correspondence with her bailiff, Richard Hickley. Ann sadly died of yellow fever on 19th September 1794, and was buried in St Catherine's Cathedral, Spanish Town; the Jamaican Assembly erected a sculptured memorial to her.[6] One wonders whether that had anything to do with the fact that her husband was in the process of installing British government in St Domingue.[7] In late 1794, Hickley received the news that Williamson had been appointed governor of St Domingue 'with much pleasure'.[8] He was appointed a Knight of the Bath on his appointment, in order to impress the colonists.[9] His policies as governor were sound, and he was highly regarded in the colony; however, he proved to be lax as an administrator, and a poor judge of men. His endeavours did not go well: yellow fever and desultory fighting decimated the forces he commanded. He had not sought the appointment in the first place, but had hoped for the governorship of Bengal. He was re-called in late 1795. But his successor was no more successful, and eventually British forces had to abandon the island.

1. This account of Sir Adam Williamson's life is based on the *Oxford Dictionary of National Biography* www.oxforddnb.com
2. WSHC 271/3. Arthur Jones's memorandum.
3. The letting and/or sale of these properties are frequently mentioned in WSHC 184/6 letters.
4. WSHC 271/3.
5. Jamaican Family Search www.jamaicanfamilysearch.com/Members/Barcheo3.htm
6. Jamaican Family Search, op cit; Knowles, Francis, Sir. 'Avebury Manor', *WAM* 56, 1955, p.368.
7. Now known as Haiti.
8. WSHC 184/6. Richard Hickley to Mrs Williamson, 2nd November 1794.
9. The following paragraph is based on Geggus, David Patrick. *Slavery, War, and Revolution: the British Occupation of Saint Domingue, 1793-1798*. Clarendon Press, 1982, passim.

Two of Ann Williamson's nieces resided with Sir Adam at Avebury; they had perhaps lived there whilst he was in Jamaica. He regularly invited young officers stationed nearby to meet them.[1] One of them, Jemima Belford, eloped to Gretna Green to marry Sir Robert Wilson, on 8th July 1797. Another ceremony was subsequently held at St George's, Hanover Square, on 10 March 1798. Both parties were under age, and wards in Chancery; Jemima was one of Sir Adam's co-heirs, as he had no children. According to Wilson's biographer, the marriage (perhaps the marriage at Hanover Square is meant) had the consent of both families.[2] Nevertheless Sir Adam's will disinherited her.

It is possible that the Rennald ladies were also relatives. They occupied the manor house during its owners' absence, and are frequently mentioned in Hickley's letters.

Sir Adam was promoted lieutenant-general, on 26th January 1797, but died as the result of a fall on 21st October 1798. He was buried in the parish church, and bequeathed his estate in trust to his wife's nephew, Richard Jones,[3] a minor.

Wiltshire

John Wiltshire, maltster, made his will in 1734. He had a tenement with a malt house, garden, and orchard, which he had leased from William Norris in 1726,[4] and which he bequeathed to his wife Sarah for life on condition that she did not re-marry.[5] She also presumably became the leaseholder of the thirteen acres of arable in the common fields which he had leased from Caleb Bailey in 1728/9, but which is not actually mentioned in the will.[6] His children, Joseph (baptised 17.2.1720) and John (baptised 13.10.1722) were still minors when he died. His brother in law, Thomas Griffin, with Joseph Griffin, were to act as guardians if Sarah did re-marry.

Joseph Wiltshire died before 1766, when his brother John sold land which Joseph had formerly owned.[7] John married Lucy in the early 1750s. She gave birth to ten children between 1755 and 1770. Sadly, four members of this family, including their mother, died of smallpox in 1770.

1   Ditto. For Jemima Belford at Avebury in 1790, see WSHC 271/16. Letter, Adam Williamson to Ann Williamson, 8th September 1790.
2   *Oxford Dictionary of National Biography* www.oxforddnb.com.
3   Grandson of Thomas Jones, Arthur Jones's brother.
4   WSHC 2106/5. Lease, 29th December 1726.
5   WSHC P3/W/808.
6   WSHC 212A/31/3. Lease, Caleb Bailey to John Wiltshire, 5th March 1728/9.
7   WSHC 3887/9. Release, John Wiltshire to George Brown, 26th March 1766.

John, however, was seventy three when he died in 1795. Aaron was named as executor and residuary legatee; his siblings received a token legacy of one shilling.[1] They were all in their twenties or thirties, and had presumably been helped by their father to establish themselves. Perhaps the expense of doing so had impoverished their father, who was a butcher; his executor was instructed to sell off his 'freehold house and premises' in Avebury to pay his debts.[2]

[1] WSHC P3/W/1066.
[2] See below, p.315.

4
Avebury's Local Government

The Parish Officers

Surviving evidence for local government in Avebury is limited. We know that the parish had its churchwardens and its overseers. The offices were rotated around the leading yeomen and minor gentry of the parish. Stayner Holford, the lord of Avebury manor, served as overseer himself in 1763.[1] Generally, however, lords avoided taking office themselves, but encouraged – or directed – their tenants to do so. The 1732 lease of Avebury Great Farm required the tenant (Peter Griffin) to hold parish office when required.[2] In 1739, he served as overseer.[3] His successor as tenant, John Rose, served as both churchwarden and overseer in 1755.[4] The churchwardens can be listed for most of our period.[5] About thirty overseers can also be identified.[6] Presumably the parish also had its highway surveyors or waywardens; mostly, their names are lost.[7]

Avebury's constables and tithingmen were appointed by the courts of Selkley Hundred (probably) and Avebury Manor. The Hundred court nominated tithingmen for the tithings of Beckhampton and Kennett (which included East Kennett, a separate parish). King Richard I granted Avebury Priory exemption from Hundredal jurisdiction in the tithing of Avebury, which probably explains why no tithingmen for this tithing are mentioned in

1 WSHC 184/9/5. Bastardy bond, Joanna Hall, 22nd July 1763.
2 WSHC 184/4/1. Abstract of lease, Holford to Griffin, 1732.
3 WSHC 184/9/3.
4 WSHC 184/9/3. Thomas Burrows' apprenticeship indenture, 24th May 1755.
5 Mostly in WSHC D1/41, 50, & 54; D3/4, 7, 12, & 15; also in Avebury parish register and bishops' transcripts.
6 Mostly in WSHC 184/9/1-5. For Peter Griffin and Richard More in 1670 see TNA E179/348. For John Long, 1740, see WSHC 473/52, f.83. For William Brewer and Isaac Green in 1758, see WSHC 206/56.
7 Mathew Mortimer served in 1649; cf. WSHC A1/110, 1649M, f.156. Robert Rose and Edward Robins served in 1736; cf. Fowle, J.P.M., eds. *Wiltshire Quarter Sessions and Assizes 1736*. WANHS Record Series 11. 1955, p.125. In 1737, William Caswell was probably the surveyor; cf.WSHC A1/165/5.

AVEBURY'S LOCAL GOVERNMENT

the records of Selkley Hundred Court.[1] They are however, listed in the mid-seventeenth court rolls of the Manor.[2] There were normally three such tithings: Eastbrook and Westbrook were within the parish, but the tithing of Catcomb (which was in Avebury Manor) lay in the parish of Hilmarton. In 1654, there were four tithings: Back Street, Nether Street, Westbrook, and Church.[3] In the 1650s, the manorial court nominated tithingmen for each tithing, but, usually, a single constable.[4] By 1734, nominations were being made by Justices of the Peace. Three names were put forward by Lord Hungerford for Quarter Sessions to choose one.[5] Tithingmen were expected to take their oath before a Justice of the Peace.[6] We know little of their activities, although they did identify those 'qualified to serve' as jurors at Quarter Sessions. Avebury tithingmen were presented in 1735, and again in 1762, for 'not bringing in his list of persons qualified to serve'.[7] Richard Amor, appointed high constable in 1790, was presented for refusing to take up office.[8] It is possible that Richard Hickley, the manorial bailiff, was serving as constable in 1792, when, referring to an Avebury labourer accused of murder, he says he 'took him up' to Salisbury for trial, and 'was on his trial' – presumably serving as a juror, or perhaps as a witness.[9]

The parish officers worked closely together; indeed, churchwardens were ex officio overseers of the poor. Richard Hickley served as churchwarden almost continuously from 1780 until the end of the century; he was also overseer in 1780, and perhaps in other years as well.[10] He was responsible for collecting rates. In the early seventeenth century, the church rate was set by parishioners. On 10th May 1613, morning worship was followed by a parish meeting, which considered the need for repairs to the windows, south porch, bells, clappers and wheels of the church, and set a rate of £5. About thirty parishioners were liable to contribute. John Rosewell was present at the meeting, but failed to pay the 8s 4d due. He was presumably presented by the churchwardens, and brought before the Consistory Court in the following

1 Round, J.H., ed. *Calendar of Documents preserved in France, 918-1206.* HMSO, 1899, p.70.
2 WSHC 473/52.
3 WSHC 473/2, f. 50.
4 WSHC 473/52. In 1654 (f.50) two constables were elected.
5 WSHC A1/110, 1735M.
6 WSHC 473/52, f.37.
7 WSHC A1/110, 1735M, 1762M
8 WSHC A1/110, 1790M.
9 WSHC 184/6. Letter, Richard Hickley to Mrs Williamson, 31st July 1792.
10 WSHC 184/9/5. Receipt for payment of militiaman, 14th December 1780.

year.[1] A few years later, in 1621/2, Thomas Pope, was similarly presented in the Archdeaconry Court.[2] Churchwardens did not always find it easy to collect rates, even though they could sue non-payers in the courts.

In the eighteenth century, church and poor rates were collected together.[3] Both were set by the parish vestry, which met regularly to discuss parish affairs. In April 1711, Farmer Skeat dined with Sir Richard Holford before having to leave early because, as Holford put it, 'it was their day for passing their parish accompts'.[4] In the 1730s, on at least one occasion, the poor rate was set at four pence in the pound.[5] In 1789, it was set at 6d in the pound, and £61 15s 6d was raised.[6] By 1794 the rate was one shilling in the pound, and had been increased again by 1797.[7] A report to Parliament in 1804 records that, overall, poor rates collected in Avebury increased from £250 12s 2d in 1776 to £710 12s 4d in 1803.[8] In 1792, Richard Hickley paid poor rates on behalf of the Williamsons on three occasions, totalling the considerable sum of £38.[9] In 1793, he paid double that amount. In December 1794, he recorded the expenditure of £10 in his bailiff's accounts on 'bread given to the poor people', evidently mixing up his duties as bailiff and as a parish officer.[10] Church rates were much lower. In the 1790s, they were collected every April; Hickley paid amounts ranging between £3 3s 4d and £8 10s 0d.[11]

Churchwardens, overseers, and highway surveyors, were appointed by the vestry,[12] who also appointed other parish servants, including the vestry clerk and the schoolmaster. We have already noted that, in 1752, John Clements, the schoolmaster, was serving as 'clerk of the vestry',[13] and was probably paid. It is possible that Samuel Morris was serving in this role in 1737; he signed the

1 WSHC D1/42/28, f.35-7r & 61r-62r.
2 WSHC D3/4/5, f.80v.
3 WSHC 184/3. Assessment, undated, but probably 1760s.
4 GA D1956/E2/8.
5 WSHC 184/3. Poor rate, undated, but probably 1730s.
6 WSHC 473/352. Poor rate, 1789. This probably just covered the tithing of Avebury, and not the other tithings in the parish.
7 WSHC 184/7.
8 *Abstract of the Answers and Returns ... [to] ... an Act for Procuring Returns relative to the Expence and Maintenance of the Poor in England.* 1804, p.568-9.
9 WSHC 184/7.
10 WSHC 184/7. He was churchwarden; as such, he was ex officio overseer.
11 WSHC 184/7.
12 Manorial courts appointed parish constables, at least in the sixteenth and seventeenth centuries.
13 WSHC 184/8. Licence to Stayner Holford to erect a seat.

vestry book regarding Clements' predecessors as schoolmasters.[1]

The vestry exercised responsibility on a wide range of topics. It would, for example, have been involved when the parish chest was made in 1634,[2] when the tenor bell was commissioned for St. James's in 1719, and when the royal arms of George III were erected later in the century. Sadly, the vestry book has been lost.[3]

Lady Holford's School

Despite that loss, we do have evidence relating to schooling. For the seventeenth century, we have the names of two schoolmasters. Philip Hunton served as schoolmaster in the late 1620s, whilst he was curate at Clyffe Pypard.[4] And in 1698, Jonathan Rashley, the dissenting minister, kept school (probably for the children of his congregation).[5]

It was not until the 1730s that a village school for the poor received a permanent endowment. This was established under the will of Susanna Holford, the lady of the manor. She bequeathed £200 for the purpose.[6] 'The minister and officers were named as trustees; they were to invest the money in land or some other 'security', and apply the profits 'towards the education of such poor children of the said parish whose parents are not able to teach them to read and be instructed in the principalls of the Protestant religion'. Only children whose parents 'often frequent the church' were eligible. Lady Holford also bequeathed £5 to Mr Mayo, the vicar, perhaps in anticipation of the fact that he would be expected to take a close interest in the school.

The capital was not paid to the churchwardens and overseers until 1733.[7] The first master was probably James Exall, but in 1736 he was failing to give satisfaction. Consequently, Robert Liddall was appointed in his place.[8] He 'did educate some of the poor which came from Kennet', presumably privately; that may be why he was offered the appointment. But he did not take up the position, and soon after 'did withdraw himself from the parish ... and hath not returned since'. The children were without a master for a year, until Exall was

1   WSHC D1/41/4/48.
2   WSHC D1/5/2/31.
3   The 'parish book' was in existence in 1752, when it was used to record details of a seat to be erected by Stayner Holford; cf. 184/8.
4   *Oxford Dictionary of National Biography* www.oxforddnb.com. Hunton was subsequently vicar of Westbury, but was ejected in 1662.
5   WSHC D1/54/14.
6   TNA PROB 11/590/280.
7   WSHC 184/8.
8   WSHC D1/41/4/48.

re-instated in September 1737.[1] That was probably at the insistence of Richard Holford, the then lord of the manor, who was in residence in Avebury at the time. His uncle, Robert Holford, told him that he was 'perfectly right in what you have done about the schoolmaster, it will give you that authority in the parish which you ought to have'.[2]

When Exall resumed his duties in 1737, and took his oath, he described his duties as being to 'teach an English school, & the art of writing & arithmetick'.[3] He did not, however, remain in post for long. The following August the poor petitioned the vestry, complaining of Exall's 'neglect of his duty'. The vestry concluded that the complaints were justified, and dismissed Exall a second time, appointing John Clements – 'a sober honest man, & in all respects qualified for educating the poor' - in his stead. As noted above, Clements subsequently served as clerk of the vestry. Exall complained about his dismissal to the bishop, who promised an investigation if he submitted a complaint 'in due form'.[4] Whether he did so is not known, and no further information relating to him survives.

No more is heard of the school until 1775, when Samuel Martyn died. It is not clear whether Martyn had been involved in the administration of the charity, or whether he had simply borrowed its capital. He died, however, owing the charity £221 4s 3d. Rev John Mayo had to swear to the fact that the money was due.[5] It took many years to recover this debt; we know that in 1805 Martyn's executors paid over £137 5s 8d.[6] Martyn had many other debts; for example, he owed £340 to the Broad Town apprenticeship charity. The school, however, continued. The money was invested in 'Navy Five per cents', the interest on which complemented the rent of £6 which had been received for many years from four cottages in South Street.

In 1783 there were sixteen pupils, who were 'taught and instructed in reading, writing and in the grounds and principles of the Christian religion'. The master regularly brought them to church.[7] Little had changed by 1818, when there were 15 children, although 27 attended on Sundays. The poor were said to be 'desirous of having their children educated', but the schoolmaster only

1 He took his oath on 1st November 1737; cf. WSHC D1/22/8.
2 WSHC 184/1, pt. 2. Letter, Robert Holford to Richard Holford, 24th September 1737.
3 WSHC D1/22/8.
4 WSHC D1/41/4/48.
5 WSHC 118/88. Statement of debts of Samuel Martyn.
6 *Reports from Commissioners [concerning charities]*. 1835. Vol.XII, pt.2, p.1339.
7 Ransome, Mary, ed. *Wiltshire returns to the Bishop's Visitation Queries 1783.* Wiltshire Record Society 27. 1972, p.29.

received c.£10-£11 per annum, and it was thought that a better schoolmaster could not be obtained for this salary.

In 1835, the Charity Commissioners' report states that education in reading was free. Writing was also taught, but the churchwarden who responded to the Commissioners' inquiries was not sure whether that was also free. One suspects that it was not, and never had been. Despite Exall's comment noted above, Lady Holford's will only made provision for the teaching of reading. The extent of illiteracy in the parish indicated by the signatures and marks of labourers in the parish marriage register after 1753 suggests that most pupils did not learn to write. Most labourers would probably have attended the school. Between 1754 and 1789, ninety-three labourers married in the parish church. Only eighteen (19%) were able to sign their names. Illiteracy amongst their brides was even higher. Reading and writing were taught separately, and, if it had to be paid for, the art of writing was unaffordable for the poor.

If blame for illiteracy is to be assigned, the fact that attendance of children was probably brief and spasmodic would not have helped. In 1783, the few children in neighbouring Winterbourne Monkton were described as being 'so poor, so badly clothed, and obliged to work for their bread so young', that the vicar, James Mayo, had been unable even to catechise them.[1] It is likely that the same description applied to Avebury children. Nevertheless, Mayo was hoping to put the Winterbourne Monkton children 'under the care of the schoolmaster in Avebury'. We do not know whether he succeeded.

Lady Holford's school was for poor Anglicans. The dissenters also tried to provide education, although we know little about it. Mention has already been made of the school kept by the dissenting minister in 1698. A later minister, William Griffin is said to have 'kept school' from 1788.[2] We do not know where – or whether – other Avebury people sent their children to school, although perhaps some went to Calne where their vicar was master. We can, however, determine that of the 276 marriage partners (including labourers) recorded in the register, only 117 (42%) signed their names.

Poor Relief: Paupers and Vagrants

It is likely that the vestry was also involved in the administration of poor relief, but we have little proof. We do know that 'the money given at the offertory' was 'disposed of by the minister, chiefly to the aged poor and needy, particular

---

1 Ransome, op cit, p.238.
2 Surman Index Online https://surman.english.qmul.ac.uk

regard being had to those who frequent the communion', although 'not absolutely excluding the sick'.[1]

Most poor relief was administered by overseers, whose office was no sinecure. It was the duty of the overseers to relieve the poor – but also to protect the parish rates. Genuine local paupers did receive support. In the early 1670s, eight paupers were in receipt of 'weekly almes' from the parish.[2] In 1755, the parish paid the house rents of seven paupers. Their rents varied between 10s for Martha Chivers, and 32s 6d for Temperance Burry.[3] It may be that some lived in one of the houses owned by the school, for which the parish paid rent of £1 10s per annum.[4]

Paupers' housing sometimes involved overseers in other ways. For example, when the future of the derelict hovel formerly occupied by the deceased pauper James Cue was under discussion, it was the overseer, William Crook, who was asked to arrange its sale on behalf of its supposed owner.[5]

Little evidence survives for the payment of poor rates, but it is recorded that John Caswell paid 12s 6d for 'the vagrant money' in 1733.[6] In 1789, the overseers received £61 15s 6d from a rate paid by 22 ratepayers.[7] After the 1792 enclosure, parish rates had to be 'regulated', that is, reviewed; Richard Hickley reported on progress in several of the letters he sent to Mrs Williamson.[8] He was responsible for paying her assessment: a double assessment on the estate amounted to £19 between 1791 and 1794 (increased to £21 in 1797), and was demanded twice, or even three times, each year.[9]

The vestry were frequently concerned about 'how the poor will be maintained next winter'. Richard Hickley noted in June 1794 that 'we have got a little work for them at present at spinning of cotton. Tis but a trifle for doing it, but still something is better than nothing.'[10] Industrialisation, however, meant the rapidly approaching end of that type of work. At the end of the eighteenth century there was 'a large body of women and children', previously engaged in spinning, who had 'been deprived of their spinning work by the manufactories

1 Ransome, op cit, p.29.
2 TNA E179/348.
3 WSHC 184/3.
4 *Reports from Commissioners [concerning charities]*. HMSO, 1835, p.1339.
5 WSHC 184/9/5; Raymond, Stuart A. 'A Pauper's Hovel in 1775', *The Recorder*, 22, 2023, p.7-8.
6 371/1, pt.5. John Caswell's accounts, 1733.
7 WSHC 473/352.
8 WSHC. 184/6. Letters, Richard Hickley to Mrs Williamson, passim.
9 WSHC 184/7.
10 WSHC 184/6. Richard Hickley to Mrs Williamson, 30th March 1794.

in the neighbourhood'.[1] Richard Hickley, the churchwarden, was busy making broth for the poor, complaining that 'the cloathers manufacture almost all their wool with machines, which deprive the poor people of their bread. Indeed, tis not the poor that suffers, but the landholders, as it makes the poor rates run very high'.[2] Hickley thought that there were 'not less than 250 women and children in this small parish without employ all this winter'.[3] That amounted to almost half of the parish's population. It is likely that when, in 1790, and again in 1799, Avebury's highway surveyors were contracted to undertake minor repairs for the Beckhampton Turnpike trustees, they recruited paupers to do the work.[4] One wonders whether any Avebury poor found work as navvies building the Kennet and Avon Canal, which was to pass just a few miles south of the parish boundary.[5]

Vagrancy was an issue, although only a limited amount of evidence survives. Tithingmen were responsible for 'watching and warding', which included the duty of keeping an eye out for vagrants. In 1636, the high constables of Selkley Hundred presented that 'watching and warding hath been duely kept'.[6] Many vagrants were whipped by the Marlborough beadle.[7] In 1603, plague caused Quarter Sessions to order a more stringent watch to be kept for vagrants throughout the county: they were to be apprehended and constables were 'to execute the statute in that behalf'. If they were found to be infected they were to be prohibited 'from lodginge or abydinge there'.[8] At the same time, Quarter Sessions ordered that parishes in Sir James Mervyn's Division were to contribute to the relief of the plague stricken town of Westbury. Mervyn resided in Avebury, so probably kept a close eye on how this order was carried out in his own parish. Unfortunately, little documentation survives. It is likely that many vagrants were whipped and 'removed' to their parishes of settlement throughout our period without record being kept. We do know that several vagrants apprehended by the constable of Selkley Hundred were

1 Bernard, Thomas. 'Extract of an account of the introduction of straw platt at Avebury', *The Reports of the Society for Bettering the Conditions and increasing the Comforts of the Poor*, 4, 1802-5, p.90.
2 WSHC 184/6. Letter, Richard Hickley to Mrs Williamson, 31st December 1792.
3 WSHC 184/6. Letter, Richard Hickley to Mrs Williamson, 8th November 1793.
4 WSHC 1371/1.
5 Berry, Warren. *The Kennet and Avon Navigation: a History*. Phillimore, 2009, p.19-20.
6 WSHC A1/110, 1636M, f.236.
7 Stedman, A.R. *Marlborough and the Upper Kennet country*. [Marlborough College?], 1960, p.132.
8 WSHC A1/110, 1603M, f.209.

punished 'according to the statute' in 1612.[1] In the 1630s, Charles I required much more detailed reports on vagrant activities, and consequently we learn that, in July 1632, three vagrants, William Jones, Arise Evens, and Umverie Jones (all perhaps from Wales), 'weare tacken wandering at Backhampton ... and theare were punished according to the law'.[2] Six vagrants were punished by whipping, and then 'removed' in 1633.[3]

The names of two Avebury vagrants are known. Henry Howson, on 1st July 1779, was 'removed' from a House of Correction in Middlesex as a vagrant, and carried to Colnbrook on his way back to Avebury by the Middlesex vagrant contractor.[4] He was then aged 35.[5] Unusually, his father was a gentleman. Henry senior almost cut the vagrant out of his will completely, commenting that 'whereas my son ... has for many years behaved both to myself and his mother in a very undutiful and disobedient manner, I therefore give him one shilling'.[6] Henry senior died on 9th May 1779. When his son arrived back in Avebury under escort a few months later, the overseers would have expected his mother to maintain him. She was probably forced to relent from her husband's strict attitude. She gave her son an annuity of £50 per annum in her 1787 will,[7] although she had not 'found any reason to be of a different opinion in respect to the conduct and behaviour of my said son than had been conceived of him by his said late father ... and am moreover of opinion that my said son is liable to be imposed upon and incapable of managing his own affairs'. Perhaps he was suffering from mental illness. The money was placed in the hands of trustees under strict conditions. The only other sufferer from mental illness that we know about was Mary Underwood, the eleven year old daughter of the widow Jane Underwood, who was assaulted by John Tilly in 1783. According to the recognizance by which Tilly was bound, Mary was 'non compos mentis'.[8]

Another Avebury vagrant, John Cary, was a mere child, twelve years old in 1740. He had been a beggar since he was aged eight, when he absconded from his master in Devizes. In 1740, he was examined in Bedminster (Somerset), and sent back to Avebury via the Houses of Correction en route.[9]

1   WSHC A1/110, 1612M, f.160.
2   WSHC A1/110, 1632M, f.154.
3   WSHC/A1/110, 1633M, f.154. For a 1635 vagrant, see A1/110, 1635, f.167.
4   LMA MJ/SP/1779/07.
5   According to his mother's will, WSHC P3/H/1476.
6   WSHC P3/H/1466.
7   WSHC P3/H/1476
8   WSHC A1/110, 1783M.
9   Somerset Heritage Centre Q/SR/308/397-8. See also below, p.281-2.

Vagrancy, technically, was a crime. Pauperism was not, although the boundary between vagrancy and pauperism was ill-defined. Paupers too suffered removal. They could only be relieved by their parish of settlement. If they claimed relief elsewhere, they would be examined, and escorted to their parish of settlement by parish constables. Some of their journeys have already been discussed. Unlike Howson, most migrated within Wiltshire. In 1722, for example, William Ealy and his wife Mary were sent back to Avebury from Huish.[1] Alice Church, a 'single woman', was removed from Overton in 1727.[2] The 'settlement' of Benjamin Gully, his wife, and four children in 1742/3 was found to be Winterbourne Monkton; the Avebury constable escorted the family across the parish boundary.[3] Concern about settlement led the parish officers to complain that Nicholas Edwards kept 'a strange childe likely to become chargeable to the said parish', and that he refused 'to give security of indempnifying of the parish'. He was required to enter a recognizance to appear at Quarter Sessions.[4] When Richard Hickley wanted to evict a tenant named Beaven in 1793, he thought 'he shortly will be starved out. He has a wife and two small children, & he not able to work. Of course he must go to his own parish'.[5]

The poor did not always suffer at the hands of officialdom. In early seventeenth-century Marlborough, poor travellers on the Bath Road frequently received a few pence to help them on the way; they must have passed through Avebury. In 1800, an Avebury overseer was fined for improper conduct towards a poor woman who was walking to Bristol en route for Ireland. He, together with a local lodging house keeper, was convicted of sending her away, presumably without relief, 'in rainy weather when much indisposed'.[6] The bureaucracy of the settlement system meant that poor people had to obtain certificates from parish officers in order to work in another parish. Hence Joseph Hayward, the son of Avebury's shopkeeper, who had (presumably) been working in Preshute when he married a Preshute bride, and therefore gained a settlement there, deposited his settlement certificate in the Avebury parish chest when he returned to the parish of his birth.[7] A settlement certificate was required even when a poor man simply moved across the parish boundary; hence Richard Alexander, with his wife

1 WSHC A1/110, 1722M.
2 WSHC A1/110, 1728M.
3 WSHC 184/9/2B.
4 WSHC A1/110, 1677M.
5 WSHC 184/6. Letter, Richard Hickley to Mrs Williamson, 4th February 1793.
6 *The Times* 30th October 1800.
7 WSHC 184/9/1.

and two daughters, had to obtain one when they moved into Avebury from neighbouring East Kennett in 1765.[1]

Some parishes maintained a workhouse for their settled paupers. Avebury did not possess one. Richard Hickley, the churchwarden, commented in November 1793 that 'a workhouse can be of no sort of service unless there was something for them [the poor] to do. Wee must send them out on the Downs to dig flints to mend the roads, or something of that sort, to keep them out of idleness.'[2] In return, they received between 1s 6d and 3s per week, varying in accordance with the price of a half gallon loaf of bread.[3]

In the final decades of our period, as has been seen, expenditure on the Avebury poor rapidly increased.[4] The winters of 1800 and 1801 were very severe, and the poor of the parish were 'in a state of considerable distress'. Reference has already been made to the fact that spinning had been mechanised, putting many spinsters out of work. They were unable to afford decent living conditions: 'their bedding and linen were worn out, and nothing remained in some of the families but a few patched rags'. Clothing was frequently verminous. The consequence, according to Hickley in early 1793, was that there were 'thousands ripe for rebellion at this time', despite the widespread 'shows of loyalty' displayed by the burnings of Tom Paine in effigy.[5] Towards the end of that year, he was expecting that the poor 'in the great clothing towns' would rebel, 'and destroy those spinning machines, which think will be so much the better'.[6]

Destruction of the new inventions did not, however, solve the problem. Rather, for Avebury, an inventive solution was proposed. The art of straw plaiting was introduced in 1801 at the suggestion of a Mr Douggan.[7] In the process the cottages of the poor – and the poor themselves - were cleaned up. The parish found £10 to fund instruction for the poor, and also paid for fresh bedding and 'a little clothing'. Hickley 'took a very active part in cleansing

1 WSHC 184/9/1.
2 WSHC 184/6. Letter, Richard Hickley to Mrs Williamson, 8th November 1793.
3 Bernard, Thomas. 'Extract of an account of the Introduction of Straw Platt at Avebury', *The reports of the Society for Bettering the Conditions and Increasing the Comforts of the Poor,* 4, 1802-5, p.90.
4 *Abstract of the Answers and Returns ... [to] an Act for Procuring Returns relative to the Expence and Maintenance of the Poor in England.* 1804, p.568-9.
5 WSHC 184/6. Letter, Richard Hickley to Mrs Williamson, 4th February 1793.
6 WSHC 184/6. Letter, Richard Hickley to Mrs Williamson, 8th November 1793.
7 Bernard, op cit, p.90-111. The art of straw plaiting subsequently spread widely; see Armstrong, Alan. *Farmworkers: a Social and Economic History, 1770-1980.* B.T.Batsford, 1988, p.54-5.

the cottages, by whitewashing them with quicklime in every part'. Farmers such as Messrs Jefferys, Brown, Tanner, and Nalder gave their best straw gratis, and encouraged the enterprise. The instruction, by a person brought from London, was entirely successful. Her students were required to practise cleanliness: that was the only qualification for admission to her classes. By 1802, their work was being purchased by a merchant from Bath, who visited monthly and regularly paid them £300+. Almost 100 women and children, most of whom had formerly been dependent on the parish pay, were working at home, and earning between 3s and 10s per week. Indeed, one of the former female pupils was sent to Devizes as a teacher so that their poor too could benefit. Nevertheless, the stigmatisation of the poor continued:[1] concern was expressed that the women would earn too much, and spend it on drink and other dissolute habits.

Despite the success of straw plaiting, poor relief continued to be expensive for the ratepayers. In 1803, 68 adults, with 37 children, had to be relieved. That included sixteen paupers who were aged or disabled. It also included four relieved 'not being parishioners'. They were probably vagrants.[2] One of the houses owned by the Holford charity was rented by the parish for 30s per annum in the early nineteenth century, in order to house a pauper[3]. One wonders if the c.200 men 'employ'd' to dig out the heavy snow-fall on the road between Cherhill and Marlborough in January 1830 – admittedly slightly later than our period - were paupers required to undertake the task by the overseers.[4]

The cost of relief frequently drove the policy of overseers. We have already seen that many paupers claiming poor relief – and possibly others who were thought likely to make a claim – were removed to the parish where they were legally 'settled'. The law of settlement dictated that poor relief could only be claimed in the parish where the claimant had his or her legal 'settlement'. Overseers could therefore be keen to prevent paupers from obtaining that status in their parish, and to remove those who had no legal claim on them. In practice, however, the law was not rigorously applied. If it had been, far more settlement examinations would have survived in parish chests.

---

1 Jones, E.L. *Landed Estates and Rural Inequality in English History, from the mid-seventeenth century to the Present.* Palgrave Macmillan, 2018, p.115.
2 *Abstract,* op cit, p.568-9.
3 *The Charities of the County of Wilts … 1817-1836.* James Newman, 1839, p.1389.
4 Wadsworth, Alan, ed. *The Farming Diaries of Thomas Pinniger, 1813-1837.* Wiltshire Record Society 74. 2021, p.lxxvi & 123.

Those examinations which do survive amongst Avebury's parish records provide interesting information on how the law was applied by local overseers and Justices of the Peace.[1] Examination before a Justice of the Peace determined where a pauper or potential pauper was 'settled', and therefore whether they could be 'removed'. Sometimes the examinee was able to avoid removal: the fact that Robert Chivers[2] possessed freehold land worth £40 when he was examined in 1739 meant that he was able to stay in Avebury.

Thomas Burris, by contrast, despite being born in Semington, never met the criteria for establishing his settlement there. Instead, his settlement was determined by his father's settlement certificate, brought from Avebury when he moved to Keevil perhaps four or five decades earlier. Settlement certificates confirmed the possessor's eligibility for poor relief in his parish of settlement, and were intended to allow the possessor to remain in a parish where he was not 'settled'. In 1756, that certificate was still in Keevil parish chest, presumably proving that Burris was 'settled' in Avebury. The fact that his settlement examination is now with other Avebury parish records implies that he was removed to Avebury. He may, however, have subsequently moved on; a will which may be his, proved in 1763, describes him as a serge weaver of Whitley, Melksham.[3]

Edward West was born in Bishops Cannings, which he left when he was aged seventeen in order to 'go abroad in severall services'. The 'last place where he lived for one whole year' (one criteria for determining settlement) 'was with one Farmer John Rose of Avebury'. Hence his presumed removal to Avebury in 1748. Was he the Edward West whose wife Martha bore William and Ann, baptised respectively on 25th March 1750, and 11th March 1753? If so, he was probably also the Edward West buried 1st April 1784. Had Avebury gained a long-term resident as the result of a removal order?

A Marlborough settlement examination of 1803 provides us with details of another pauper removed to Avebury.[4] Thomas Wiltshire's examination states that he was born in Avebury fifty years earlier, and spent most of his life in either Avebury or Marlborough. When he was twenty, he had served Mr John Nalder at West Kennett for a year, and received wages of about three guineas. That, apparently, gave him settlement. Since then, he had had 'no fixed service' that gave him a settlement. On leaving Mr Nalder's service he had worked

1 The settlement examinations discussed in the following paragraphs are in WSHC 184/9/2A.
2 WSHC 184/9/2A.
3 WSHC P1/12Reg/116 & P1/B/1365.
4 WSHC 2027/2/1/995.

for Arthur Jones, and for various other Avebury masters, as a day labourer, although he also worked in Marlborough during the 'annual malting seasons'. There he met Elizabeth Ball, who lived in the parish of Marlborough St Peter. They were married in Avebury on 17th April 1780 – just one month before the birth of their son John on 17th May (baptised 18th June). In 1793, he rented a house in Marlborough – one in a row of four houses owned by John Hammond. Although the parish register entry for his marriage describes him as a labourer, his settlement examination states that he was a sack weaver, so he probably earned sufficient working at this trade to support himself. In 1803, he claimed that he had constantly paid the rates, and had never sought relief from the overseers until forced to do so as a result of illness. On a technicality, he was adjudged to be 'settled' in Avebury: although he had actually paid the rates in Marlborough, he had never actually been charged with payment, so was sent back to Avebury to obtain poor relief.

Dealing with pauper children was, perhaps, more of a problem. If they had settled status, they could be a drain on the rates for a decade or more. The aim was usually to apprentice them to learn a trade at the youngest age possible. We only have seven pauper apprenticeship indentures, but it is noticeable that none of them mention an Avebury master.[1] Apprenticeship was a criteria for determining settlement, so it was advantageous to find masters in other parishes, which would then become liable if they should claim poor relief again.

Providing for bastard children was also a problem. Giving birth to a bastard was frowned on in our period: it cost the parish money. Fortunately for the overseers, the rate of bastardy was fairly low, and declining in most parts of the country in the early seventeenth century[2] (although increasing at the end of the eighteenth century). Bastardy was not always easy to avoid. Young women needed to marry in order to survive, and it was inevitable that some would 'fall' in the effort to find a husband. The increasing numbers of poor in Avebury at the end of the eighteenth century probably resulted in an increase in the incidence of bastardy. In the last three decades of the century, there were far more baptisms recorded in the parish register where no fathers' names were recorded in the register than previously.

In the seventeenth century, bastards' parents were frequently presented by churchwardens at visitations. Ecclesiastical courts, however, could not bind the men involved to pay maintenance. Consequently, bastardy business was

1 WSHC 184/9/3. For a discussion of where they were sent, see Raymond, Stuart A. 'Crossing the Avebury Parish Boundary', *Local Historian*, 53(4), 2023, p.300-311.
2 Ingram, Martin. *Church Courts, Sex, and marriage in England 1570-1640*. Cambridge University Press, 1990, p.166.

increasingly heard before Justices of the Peace rather than ecclesiastical judges. Overseers, concerned to ensure that the parish was not unduly burdened by bastard children, tried to identify their fathers, and to bring them before the secular arm. Justices could require fathers to pay a regular weekly sum until their children were old enough to be apprenticed, and then to pay the apprenticeship premium. George Piddle was examined by a Justice of the Peace in 1614, accused of 'getting of Margarett Fulmer with child', but denied the accusation, instead accusing a fellow servant, Leonard Edmunds, of being responsible. All three were servants in the household of Christopher Pope.[1] Thomas Gilbert was presented at Quarter Sessions by the jurors of Selkley Hundred as the father of Christian Lawrence's bastard, who was then three weeks old, and who 'lieth upon the chardg of the parish'.[2] The authorities had greater difficulty when Andrew Mills was accused of fathering Joan Pope's child in 1641. He was committed to the tithingman of Beckhampton, Christopher Spencer, to bring before Sir William Button – but he was also Spencer's servant. The high constable, Robert Phelps, accused Spencer of permitting Mills to 'slippe away' instead of bringing him before the Justice of the Peace.[3] He evidently thought he could get away with protecting his servant. Since he was sworn as a juror at the same sessions as he was required to answer the accusation,[4] he may have been justified in the assumption! Spencer, incidentally, had served as high constable of Selkley Hundred in 1633.[5] One wonders if he was related to Ambrose Spencer of Winterbourne Monkton, who in the early 1670s was called on to act as a witness when John Brinsden, vicar of Winterbourne Monkton, was accused of fathering a bastard child.[6]

In November 1754, Charles Giddance, labourer, was charged with being the father of Martha Bailey's unborn child.[7] He was required to meet all the costs of the overseers, and to remove the child from the parish on notice being given. If he failed to do so, the penalty would by £40 – a huge amount for a labourer, but a standard penalty imposed in Avebury's bastardy bonds. The child, Betty, was baptised in February 1755. Similarly, in 1778, William Stiles of Huish was required to pay 6d for Hannah Briant's 'lying in', and 1s 6d per week whilst the child was chargeable.[8]

1 WSHC A1/110, 1614M, f.129.
2 WSHC A1/110, 1615M.
3 WSHC A1/110, 1641M, f.141.
4 WSHC A1/110, 1642M, f.34 & 173.
5 WSHC A1/110, 1633M, f.204.
6 WSHC D1/42/61, f.48.
7 WSHC 184/9/4.
8 WSHC 184/9/4.

The overseers in both these cases were able to intervene before babies had been born. They were not always able to do so, especially if the child had been conceived elsewhere. We do not know why, in 1731, Elizabeth Bunts gave birth to her bastard daughter in Avebury, eleven miles from her home in Wootton Rivers. But the fact that she did so gave the Avebury overseers – who were liable to provide poor relief - a problem. They brought her before two local justices, John Smith and Edward Freke, who determined that George Kingston of Wootton Rivers was the father. He was ordered to pay 18d weekly to the Avebury overseers until the child was ten, and then to pay an additional £10 in order to apprentice her. The mother was ordered to 'keep and nurse the said child until it attains the age of ten years', or to pay 6d weekly. The child is not mentioned in the Avebury parish register.

Sometimes more drastic action was taken, although little evidence of whipping or incarceration has been found. Such action was only thought to be necessary in exceptional circumstances.[1] It may be presumed that the authorities were unable to determine the father of Penelope Bailey's bastard child, who was 'now living and chargeable to the parish'. In August 1795, she was committed to Marlborough Bridewell for a year as punishment for her sin.[2] The child, Sarah, had been baptised on 31st March 1793, so presumably the overseers waited until she was not quite as dependent on her mother before inflicting the punishment.

Ideally, of course, at least from the overseer's point of view, the parents of a bastard child would marry, and thus relieve the parish of any claim to poor relief on its behalf. Indeed, it is probable that, in the early years of our period, couples contracted to marry, who had not actually taken their marriage vows in church, considered that it was perfectly licit to have sexual relationships, fully intending to marry.[3] There was only a narrow dividing line between bridal pregnancy and bastardy.[4] When Christian Killing of Bremhill became pregnant with John Goodcheap's child in 1750, the overseer of Bremhill stood bond in order to ensure that the couple were able to obtain a licence to marry at Avebury.[5] Such procedures did not, of course, always work out; there is no record of this marriage in Avebury parish register. Similarly, when John Brinsden, vicar of neighbouring Winterbourne Monkton, obtained a licence

---

1 Ingram, op cit, p.340.
2 WSHC A1/125/46N.
3 Ingram, op cit, p.219.
4 Ingram, op cit, p.230.
5 Sarum marriage Licence Bonds www.findmypast.co.uk/articles/world-records/full-list-of-united-kingdom-records/life-events-bmds/sarum-marriage-licence-bonds

to marry the girl who was bearing his child, he absented himself before doing so.[1]

The Highway Surveyor

The vestry probably also took responsibility for road maintenance, at least in the eighteenth century, although technically this was the responsibility of the highway surveyor. Little is known about the activities of Avebury's highway surveyors, although, in 1736, they were before Quarter Sessions accused of not properly maintaining a 'cartway' between Beckhampton and Avebury.[2] We have already seen that the parishes along the route of the London to Bath road were accused of neglecting their responsibility for road maintenance in 1717; that probably included Avebury.[3] Thomas Smith told the House of Commons in 1742 that although the parish had constantly done its 'statute work', and levied a highway rate of 9d in the pound, nevertheless, it had several times been indicted for the 'badness' of the highway, and fined £100.[4] His evidence is supported by Arthur Jones's 1780 survey of his Avebury property, which noted that 'the statute labour for the highways which was before a burthen to the occupation of the farm of twenty pounds a year' was now 'reduced to a trifle'.[5] Turnpiking drastically reduced both highway rates, and the need for compulsory and unpaid 'statute labour'. Nevertheless, highway rates continued to be levied; Richard Hickley paid £4 15s in June 1791 on behalf of Mrs Williamson.[6]

Manorial Courts

The Vestry gradually replaced manorial courts in the seventeenth and eighteenth centuries. There were four manors in the parish: Avebury, Avebury Trusloe, Beckhampton, and West Kennett. Court rolls survive for the manor of Avebury during the Interregnum, whilst Sir Edward Baynton claimed ownership.[7] Sir Richard Holford's court was still being held in 1700, when he found the jury 'lamentable troblesome'; they 'made their presentments but very imperfectly', at least through the eyes of a leading lawyer. Nevertheless, his farmer, William Skeat, invited them for dinner, and they were 'all of them

1 WSHC D1/42/61, f.47v.
2 Fowle, J.P.M., eds. *Wiltshire Quarter Sessions and Assizes 1736*. WANHS Record Series 11. 1955, p.125.
3 See above, p.29-30; *Manuscripts of the House of Lords* N.S.12. HMSO, 1977, p.424.
4 *Journals of the House of Commons* 24, p.365.
5 WSHC 271/2. Valuation of Avebury property, 18th September 1780; 271/3.
6 WSHC 184/7.
7 WSHC 473/52.

very cheerful'.[1] Sadly, Holford's court roll has not survived; perhaps he decided that the imperfections made it not worth keeping!

Courts were also held for the manor of Avebury Trusloe, but records do not survive. It is not clear whether manorial courts were held for the manors of West Kennett or Beckhampton.[2]

A wide range of topics were dealt with by the Avebury manorial court. Frequently, its jurisdiction overlapped with other institutions. Roads, as just mentioned, were legally the responsibility of the highway surveyor, but in the sixteenth and seventeenth centuries the manorial court regularly ordered obstructions to be removed, hedges trimmed back, and necessary repairs to be carried out. In 1590, fifteen years after he had enclosed a garden, Robert Richards was ordered to make the footpath which passed through it passable.[3] In 1653, Richard Smith and Richard Greenway were both accused in the manorial court of not having 'done their service towards the reparation of the highway according to the order of the last court', and fined 20s each.[4] In the following year, William White was fined 40s for failing to repair the 'Churchway', despite having been ordered to do by the previous court.[5]

The manorial court kept an eye on the presence of 'inmates', and 'suspicious persons', that is, strangers to the parish who had no ties of kinship or service.[6] John Crook was presented for receiving 'suspicious persons' in 1578.[7] When John Pontin received an 'inmate' as an under-tenant in 1612 he was fined ten shillings; six months later, at the following court,[8] he still had not 'put away his tenant Richard Symes' and was fined a further ten shillings for every month he had been in default[9]. Similarly, in 1651 Susan Griffin, widow, was presented in the manorial court for having Richard Morris as her sub-tenant, and fined 10s.[10] Eight years later, she surrendered her copyhold so that it could be re-granted to Morris.[11] In 1655, the offenders having 'inmates' were

---

1 WSHC 184/8.
2 But see 184/9, which may refer to a court being held for Beckhampton in 1700.
3 WSHC 192/12F, f.45.
4 WSHC 473/52, f.37.
5 WSHC 473/52, f.50.
6 Underdown, David. *Revel, Riot and Rebellion: Popular Politics and Culture in England 1603-1660*. Clarendon Press, 1985, p.37.
7 WSHC 192/12C, f.7.
8 WSHC 43/52, f.50.
9 WSHC 192/12L, f.5v.
10 WSHC 473/52, f.7.
11 WSHC 212A/31/2.

Thomas Burgeman and John Harper.[1] Even relatives could be illegal 'inmates'. We do not know their precise relationship, but in 1652 Margery Plomer was ordered to remove Elizabeth and John Plomer from her house.[2] Similarly, Nicholas Pope was ordered to remove Thomas Pope from his house in 1656.[3] He was still there the following year, when a fine of £3 was imposed.[4]

New cottages erected without having four acres of land attached were also banned. In 1655, John Hiscock was presented in the manorial court for having erected such a cottage 'contrary to the statute in such case provided'. The manorial court also concerned itself with the repair of tenants' houses. In 1655, John Tompkins was required to 'sufficiently repair his house before the next court', under penalty of 10s.[5] Similarly, in 1656, Elizabeth Romayne had failed to comply with an order to repair her barn, so 'forfeited the payne' of 40s.[6] By the following year, the barn had fallen down, and she was ordered to re-erect it 'upon payne' of £5.[7] Her house and a chimney were also 'in decay'; the chimney was described as 'very dangerous for fire'. She was ordered to repair that too, within two weeks. And she was also accused of cutting down twenty trees without the consent of the lord of the manor, and without using them for repairs to her tenement.

The court had cognizance over the care of animals: an order of 1583 required the inhabitants of Beckhampton to ring their pigs,[8] presumably to stop them from digging up grassland. Stray animals were another problem. They were supposed to be impounded in the common pound. The Wall Ditch was used for this purpose by the lord of the manor of Avebury Trusloe until late in the sixteenth century;[9] whether it was used by the tenants of other manors is not clear. In 1584, two strays were being kept by Thomas Smith[10], and in 1604 John Mortimer had one in his keeping worth 2s 6d.[11] In 1599, John Hooper of Avebury was accused of breaking open the pound (where stray animals were impounded) and 'taking out a mare and colte', which had presumably been

1　WSHC 473/52, f.72.
2　WSHC 473/52, f.???
3　WSHC 473/52, f.83.
4　WSHC 473/52, f.98.
5　WSHC 473/52, f.72.
6　WSHC 473/52, f.83.
7　WSHC 473/52, f.98.
8　WSHC 192/12D, f.8.
9　TNA E134/40and41Eliz/Mich7; E134/41Eliz/Hil8.
10　WSHC 192/12D, f.17.
11　WSHC 192/12G, f.74d.

seized as strays.[1] He presumably failed to pay the fine to get them released. At the same time, the inhabitants were ordered to 'make a sufficient pound', presumably because Hooper had destroyed the old one (or perhaps because the Truslows had fenced off the Wall Ditch for other purposes)[2]. In 1655, the court thought the lord of the manor 'ought to erect a sufficient pownd ... for the use of the inhabitants'.[3] The observation was probably occasioned by the fact that Andrew Mills 'did commit a pownd breach'; he was amerced 2s 6d. A half century later, Sir Richard Holford noted that the pound had again been destroyed, and that he might have been more vigorous 'in presenteing the pound breakers, in hopes the actors might be sensible of their follies & make some reasonable satisfaction, without being exposed' and that he was 'not unmindfull that the pound is wanting'.[4]

The manor court also exercised jurisdiction over the pasturing of beasts. In 1654 two men, Peter Griffin and Walter Alexander, were sworn as 'tellers' with the responsibility of ensuring that no tenant pastured more sheep or cattle on the common land than they were entitled to. Those who exceeded their 'stint' were to be fined 2s 6d per sheep, or 10s per 'beast'.[5] The following year Andrew Mills was presented for keeping his sheep 'on the Cowlese contrary to the custom of this manor', and amerced another 2s 6d.[6] The court also exercised jurisdiction over the boundaries between tenants' holdings. In 1656, the manorial court ordered all tenants to meet at the Cowdown in order to 'sett meerestones between every man's downe'.[7]

Cognizance was also taken of moral crimes. John Gilbert was fined for 'drinking and tippling' in John Hulbert's house at midnight in 1655; Hulbert himself was presented for selling ale without a licence. So were Thomas Hancock and Richard Sidfall.[8] Such men might be placed in the 'sufficient paire of stocks' that the manorial court ordered to be erected in 1655[9]

The manorial court regularly appointed a hayward to serve for a year. Robert Gough served in 1654, but it is not clear what his duties were.[10] Tellers of beasts were also occasionally appointed; Peter Griffin and Walter

1   WSHC 192/12G. f.18d.
2   TNA E134/40and41Eliz/Mich7; E134/41Eliz/Hil8.
3   WSHC 471/52, f.72.
4   WSHC 184/1, pt.1. Letter Sir Richard Holford to John White, 6th March 1706/7.
5   WSHC 473/52, f.49.
6   WSHC 471/52, f.72.
7   WSHC 473/52, f.83.
8   WSHC 473/52, f.50.
9   WSHC 473/52, f.72.
10 WSHC 473/52, f.49.

Alexander were appointed at the same time. Presumably they ensured that the commons were not over-stocked. The court also appointed the constables and tithingmen for Eastbrook, Westbrook, and Catcomb. In the 1650s, the constables included John Tompkins (1651), William Bray (1653), Richard Greenway (1654), William White (1654) and John Haworth (1656).[1] A few constables' names are recorded in other sources: James Pope (1633),[2] Richard Phelps (1670),[3] Richard Amor (possibly) in 1790[4], Richard Hickley (possibly) in 1792,[5] William Philpot (1799).[6]

The Selkley Hundred Court

The court of Selkley Hundred was regularly held throughout our period, and its court books survive for most of our period.[7] It was attended by all the men from the tythings of Beckhampton, and of East and West Kennett.[8]. The court met twice yearly, although there was also a 'three week court' for which records have not survived. The court books give the names of suitors, describing them as 'resiants or inhabitants'.

The half yearly court was attended by the men of each tithing. A tithingman was selected for each tithing, and was expected to attend the 'three week court' as well as the half yearly one. The office was probably not popular. When Thomas Gilbert, in 1606, was ordered to appear 'at the next three week court' to be made tithingman, it was grudgingly conceded that he could avoid the duty 'if Mr Richard Truslowe discover another to assume the same'.[9] In 1611, Robert Weston was ordered to 'fynd a sufficient deputy to performe the said office'.[10] The influence of manorial lords was demonstrated in 1614, when the court indicated that it was prepared to defer to Richard Smith, lord of West Kennett manor, in the appointment of the next tithingman.[11] In the eighteenth century, those elected, if not present in court, were expected to appear before a

1 WSHC 473/52.
2 WSHC A1/165/4.
3 TNA E179/348.
4 WSHC A1/165/8.
5 WSHC 184/6. Letter, Richard Hickley to Mrs Williamson, 31st July 1792.
6 WSHC A1/165/8.
7 WSHC 192/12A-M and 9/23/1 (for 1737 onwards)
8 East Kennett was a separate parish, but it is difficult to distinguish between entries relating to East Kennett and West Kennett in the court books. Some of what follows may actually relate to East Kennett, not to Avebury parish.
9 WSHC 192/12G, f.94.
10 WSHC 192/12L, f.2.
11 WSHC 192/12L, f.9v.

Justice of the Peace to be sworn. It may be that ownership of property bestowed the duty of serving. Women could not serve, so Joseph Griffin's widow was ordered 'to find a sufficient person to serve the office of tithingman' when her turn came in 1751.[1] By the end of the century, tithingmen were nominating three different individuals to serve as their successors, the final choice being made at Quarter Sessions.[2]

It is not clear whether the offices of tithingman and constable were identical or separate. In 1604, although John Smith was presented to be constable of Kennett tithing, the inhabitants were ordered to 'nominate and bring unto the next three weeke court a sufficient person to serve the office of tythingman'.[3] The Constable of the Hundred was appointed by the Hundred Court, and we know the names of at least ten Avebury men who served between 1670 and 1794.[4] In 1791, Robert Nalder was appointed, despite - or perhaps because – he failed to appear to serve on the jury. In 1790, Richard Amor was accused of refusing to serve, but was found not guilty.[5]

Business proceeded by presentments from the jury. Jurors were presumably selected by the steward, who summoned them to appear through the bailiff; they were then sworn in court. In 1795, Thomas Lavington of Kennett served as foreman of the jury; in 1797, Robert Nalder served.[6] By this time, however, business in the court was minimal. Presentments two centuries earlier had been much more frequent. For example, defects in the butts used for target practice were regularly presented; so were defects in the stocks used as punishment[7]. Pigs had to be ringed,[8] stray sheep dealt with[9] and a pound (for stray animals) provided,[10] hedges maintained,[11] ditches scoured[12], and roads protected from encroachment,[13] John Rosewell was in trouble in 1599, and frequently in the following decades, for not repairing Port Bridge and the highway;[14] indeed, such was his neglect that 'ther was a man licke to be

1 WSHC 9/23/1.
2 WSHC A1/110, Michaelmas session rolls 1782 onwards.
3 WSHC 192/12G, f.75.
4 WSHC A1/110; 9/23/1.
5 WSHC A1/165/8
6 WSHC 9/23/1.
7 WSHC 192/12D, f.12.
8 WSHC 192/12D, f.8.
9 WSHC 192/12D, f.12; 192/12G, f.74d.
10 WSHC 192/12g, f.18d.
11 WSHC 192/12D, f.45; 192/12G, f.79d.
12 WSHC 192/12G, f.49.
13 WSHC 192/12D, f.45.
14 WSHC 192/12G, f.12, 79d, & 94; 192/12L, f.5v & 6.

drowned by the insufficiency'[1]. He was fined several times for his neglect.

In the eighteenth century, business slowed down. In 1738 the court ordered Long Bridge to be jointly repaired by William Caswell and the tithing of East Kennett.[2] During the second half of the eighteenth century, the only Avebury presentments concerned the appointment of tithingmen and hundred constables, and the non-attendance of those summoned. Business fell away, and suitors from our two tithings ceased to attend. Even John Nalder, the then tithingman for East and West Kennett, was fined 2s 6d in 1773 for not being present. In 1783 the bailiff of the Hundred, Charles Gibbons, personally summoned Anthony Allen, who had served as tithingman of East and West Kennett since 1776, but he too failed to appear, and was amerced five shillings. In 1788, Thomas Brown, who had been summoned to serve on the jury, was fined five shillings for failing to appear. John Rider's 'neglecting to appear' as a juror in 1789 and 1798 cost him 6s 8d both times. At courts held in the 1780s and 1790s, it was frequently noted that no-one from the tithings of Kennett and Beckhampton appeared.[3] Business was done at Quarter Sessions instead; in 1765, for example, the absence of stocks and a pound were presented there rather than in the Hundred Court.[4]

Quarter Sessions

Much business was transacted at Quarter Sessions, except when its proceedings were interrupted by civil war. Most sessions between 1643 and 1646 were not held, and when sessions began again in 1646 the Grand Jury presented 'a great want of Justices for the Peace' in many hundreds, including Selkley, giving 'great charge & trouble of the inhabitants & the greate encouragement of offenders'.[5]

That, however, was exceptional. For most of our period Quarter Sessions business continued as normal. A number of gentlemen with Avebury connections served as sheriff of the county:[6] Sir James Mervyn (1596; he was also a deputy lieutenant in 1597-8),[7] Sir Edward Baynton (1664), William

1 WSHC 192/12L, f.11.
2 WSHC 9/23/1.
3 WSHC 9/23/1.
4 WSHC A1/110, 1762M.
5 WSHC A1/110, 1646M, f.151.
6 Jackson, J.E. 'Sheriffs of Wiltshire', *WAM* 3(8), 1857, p.216-31.
7 www.geni.com/people/. Whilst in office he was in dispute with the Truslows, and the coroner had to be involved in selecting the jury (normally the sheriff's task) needed to hear the dispute; cf. WANHS Wiltshire Genealogy v.A-A, f.87.

Norris of Nonsuch (1759). Sir John Stawell, lord of the manor before the Civil War, was a Somerset Justice and Deputy Lieutenant.[1] In 1758, Stayner Holford made inquiries to ensure that he avoided the troublesome office of sheriff.[2] He had just seen at close quarters some of the problems faced by the sheriff and his under-sheriffs. They had been involved in levying distresses against Holford's tenant, John Rose, when the latter was declared bankrupt.[3]

Several lords of Avebury manor, and other local gentry, served as Justices of the Peace, although Charles Tooker of East Kennett is the only Justice of the Peace whose activities in Avebury are frequently mentioned in surviving documents. The constables of the Hundred regularly submitted lists of freeholders eligible to serve on Quarter Sessions juries, and to vote in Parliamentary elections.[4] Service on a Quarter Sessions jury was almost a rite of passage for Avebury's freeholders; many jurymen have already been identified in chapter 3. Both Hundred constables and Hundred juries made presentments concerning issues requiring the attention of Quarter Sessions. Many concerned routine administrative matters, such as determining the rates levied to support county gaols and bridges, and the Marshalsea.[5] Highway repairs were supervised by the bench, and the inhabitants of Avebury were presented on a number of occasions for neglecting their duty in this regard.[6] In 1683, 'the highway there from Spanswicks house to the ford, being the highway leading from Marlborough to Calne', was 'out of repair & dangerous for travellers'.[7] In 1715, the Grand Jury presented that the Swindon to Devizes road south of the village (probably where it crossed the Winterbourne) was 'so annoyed by water as to be very dangerous', and ought to be repaired by Avebury's inhabitants'.[8] The water was 'still standing very deep' in 1719;[9] perhaps there had been ineffectual attempts to deal with the problem.[10]

1 www.historyofparliamentonline.org/volume/1604-1629/member/stawell-john-1600-1662
2 GA D1956/L1. Letter, Stayner Holford to Peter Holford, 19th December 1758.
3 GA D1956/L1. Letter, Stayner Holford to Peter Holford, 10th June 1756.
4 Chapter 3 has already mentioned many who served on juries.
5 These are all recorded in Sir Richard Holford's 1708-9 accounts; cf. WSHC 184/4/1.
6 That, at least, is my interpretation of the indictments made against the inhabitants of Avebury in 1728 (WSHC A1/165/4), 1736 (WSHC A1/165/5, f.131), 1739 (WSHC A1/165/6), and 1758 (A1/165/7). These process books do not actually record the nature of these presentments.
7 WSHC A1/110, 1683M, f.105.
8 WSHC A1/110, 1715M.
9 WSHC A1/110, 1719M.
10 For other Avebury presentments relating to roads, see A1/110, 1725M & 1729M.

Individuals who failed to provide labour for road maintenance might also find themselves in court. John Rosewell, who we have already encountered in the Hundred Court, was presented at Quarter Sessions in 1613 because he had failed to 'scour' his ditch, and thereby presumably flooded the highway.[1] He was in trouble again in both 1616 and 1618; a causeway passing through his grounds was 'in decay', and he was expected to 'amend' the highway 'betwixt London & Bristol' in West Kennett.[2] The Selkley Hundred jurors were asked by Mathew Mortimer in 1649 to present a number of individuals who had failed to carry loads of stones to repair the highways; they included Thomas Cripps of Berwick Bassett, Richard Smith of West Kennett, Edith Griffin, and John Hopkins.[3] Smith was again in trouble in both 1651 and 1652 (and Griffin in 1652), when they were presented in the manorial court for failing to do their service 'about the reparation of the highwayes'.[4] In 1693, William Skeat was presented because a brook on his farm was inundating the highway between Silbury Hill and the ford.[5] In the following year, he was accused before Quarter Sessions of doing nothing to prevent this inundation.[6] Skeat himself, as constable of the Hundred, had presented John Pope for a 'water cors' at Avebury that was in default' in 1692.[7] In 1736, William Caswell was accused at Quarter Sessions of dumping forty loads of dung in the highway! The accusation was exaggerated, but he probably had inadvisedly stopped up a ditch which caused the road to flood.[8] The Hundred jurors presented him for 'setting bounds [on the highway] two feet further out than usual'.[9]

Presentments for failure to mend roads was generally, however, not due to negligence, but rather to the unwillingness of highway surveyors to rate their neighbours to pay for road maintenance; they preferred the odium of imposing taxation to fall on Quarter Sessions. On presentment, the bench would order a rate to be levied. As we have seen, the creation of the turnpike in 1745 reduced the burden on the highway surveyors; in 1752 the hundred constables were able to present that 'the roads of the weste side of the Hundred are in good repair'.[10]

1 WSHC A1/110, 1613M, f.117.
2 WSHC A1/110, 1616M, f.166, & 1618, f.34.
3 WSHC A1/110, 1649M, f.156.
4 WSHC 473/52.
5 WSHC A1/110, 1693M. f.6.
6 WSHC A1/165/3, f.40.
7 WSHC A1/110, 1692M, f.127.
8 WSHC A1/110, 1736M.
9 WSHC A1/110, 1731M.
10 WSHC A1/110, 1752M. A similar presentment was made in 1753; cf A1/110, 1753M.

Further turnpike acts in 1769 and 1790 enlarged the powers of the trustees.[1] The neglect of constables and tithingmen sometimes came before the court; in 1710 Thomas Andrew, tithingman of 'Kennett' was accused of 'not appearing to make return of juremen according to law'.[2] The same accusation was made against James Pope in 1733,[3] William Philpot in 1757,[4] and against another William Philpot in 1799.[5] It was sometimes difficult to appoint tithingmen: in both 1756 and 1757 the hundred constables presented 'no tythingman for the tything of Avebury'.[6]

Charles Tooker, lord of the manor of East Kennett,[7] served as a Justice for many years. Sacrament certificates record him taking communion at Overton and (probably) East Kennett respectively in 1702 and 1703, and again at East Kennett in 1714; in 1703 he also took the oath against transubstantiation.[8] Both were required in order for him to hold office.

Holding office may not have been easy; in 1691 Richard Garroway of Avebury was required to enter a recognizance to keep the peace against Tooker.[9] On the other hand, many duties of the office were routine. Tooker was occasionally called upon to take the oaths of those making affidavits concerning burial in woollen.[10] Much of his time was probably occupied with minor disputes amongst his neighbours, and petty crime. In 1695, for example, Roger Dorchester complained to him that William Skeat had withheld his wages.[11] In 1699, both John Rouse of Beckhampton, yeoman, and William Rivers, servant, came before him accused of 'prophane swearing'.[12] No doubt many similar cases that came before him were resolved without a record being made.

Tooker's name does, however, occasionally appear in the Quarter Sessions records dealing with more serious matters. In 1685, he had to deal with the case of Ann Bray, who had struck Christopher Axford, a blacksmith,

---

1 https://archives.parliament.uk
2 WSHC A1/110, 1710M.
3 WSHC A1/165/4.
4 WSHC A1/110, 1757M.
5 WSHC A1/165/8.
6 WSHC A1/110, 1756M, 1757M.
7 *VCH Wilts* 12, p.120.
8 WSHC A1/110, 1702M, 1703M., & 1714M
9 WSHC 1/110, 1691M, f.38.
10 Parish register.
11 WSHC A1/110, 1695M, f.21.
12 WSHC A1/265/1699.

with her fist several times on the head.[1] She must have been a strong woman to take on a blacksmith! Tooker bound over Ann's husband, William Bray, to appear at Quarter Sessions, and to answer 'matters ... which shall be objected against her'. He also took 'informations' from Grace Alexander, Joseph Rose, and Ann Mortimer, and bound over Rose and Mortimer, together with the victim, to give evidence at the trial. The two women involved, that is, Ann Bray and Grace Alexander, were presumably to be represented by their husbands.[2] It may be that Tooker was more concerned with the accusation that, when James II's army had marched through Avebury three weeks earlier, Ann had remarked that 'when they was at thwick and thwack she could afforde to kill two or three of her neighbours'. Curiously, both William Bray and Christopher Axford were nominated to serve on a jury at Quarter Sessions in that year.[3] Another Avebury inhabitant, John Truslow, gent., was a member of the Grand Jury which would have considered any indictment.

Tooker also became embroiled in a dispute over tithe between John Rose and John White, the vicar, in 1700. When White sent his reapers to take the tithe he claimed, they were repelled by Rose's reapers, who were working in the same field. White accused them of riot, and Tooker bound them over to keep the peace.[4] The case was eventually tried at the Assizes, although the outcome is not known.[5]

Other Justices of the Peace also took cognizance of Avebury crime. The records sometimes record a trial, but do not state the nature of the crime. For example, in 1757, three members of the Cary family of Avebury were found guilty of an offence, but we do not know what it was.[6] Perhaps it was poaching, which was probably common although infrequently detected. A few cases concerning poaching are mentioned in chapter 8.[7]

A number of cases concerning theft and assault are recorded. In 1640, Thomas Clarke admitted to the theft of boots, shoes, and spurs from his master, Mr. Goldsmith.[8] Goldsmith was also one of the victims of Sarah Duck, who was accused of stealing barley from both him and John Phelps in 1647.[9]

1   For the following paragraph, see WSHC A1/110, 1685M, f.26-9 & 163.
2   Assuming that Grace was Christopher's wife, which is not actually stated.
3   WSHC A1/110, 1685M, f.206.
4   WSHC 184/1, pt.1. Letter, William Smith to Sir Richard Holford. 6th July 1700.
5   WSHC 184/1, pt.1. Letters, William Smith to Sir Richard Holford, 6th July 1700 & 11th January 1700/01
6   WSHC A1/165/7.
7   See below, p.369.
8   WSHC A1/110, 1640M.
9   WSHC A1/110, 1647M, f.424.

In 1697, Hillier's wife was said by William Skeat to have 'stole clothes of the hidge', and would have been whipped on Justice Tooker's order had she not been pregnant.[1] Skeat's allegation was, however, disputed by others.[2] There were few highway robberies,[3] although it was not unknown, as has already been seen. Another case occurred in 1783, when Stephen Powell, alias Charles Coleman (not known to be an Avebury resident) was committed to Fisherton Gaol accused of robbing John Brookes of four shillings in silver.[4]

Theft was frequently simply due to hunger (as was poaching). There was a striking upsurge of prosecutions for theft at Wiltshire's Quarter Sessions in the dearth year of 1623.[5] There were several local thieves with the same motive in the eighteenth century. In 1739, for example, Thomas Maccabee, a labourer, was accused of stealing half a bushel of peas from Joseph Griffin.[6] In 1742, Robert Heath of Avebury, labourer, was fined 6d for 'pulling' and stealing two turnips worth ½d.[7] Sarah Gale, in 1766, was accused of stealing cheese and bacon from her master, John Nalder.[8] In February 1785, a Justice committed Daniel Head of Calne to Fisherton Gaol for stealing ten fowl, the property of William Philpot of Avebury.[9] Philpot appears to have been unpopular: in the following year Elizabeth Reeves was accused of assaulting him, and spent a month in Devizes gaol in consequence.[10] Reeves, incidentally, had claimed to have been the victim of assault a few years earlier; several recognizances in the Quarter Sessions rolls for 1779 relate to her accusation against Isaac Ball of Beckhampton.[11] In 1790, another labourer, John Chandler, was presented for the theft of two half crowns and five shillings from Richard Alexander.[12]

These crimes were not felonies, as the value of the goods stolen was too small. Other crimes were more serious. Some thefts on the highway have

1   WSHC 184/1, pt.2. Letter, William Skeat to Sir Richard Holford, 26 February 1697/8.
2   WSHC 184/1, pt.2. Letter, Sir Richard Holford to Cornelius Yeate, c.9 March 1697/8.
3   Gerhold, Dorian. *Bristol's Stage Coaches*. Hobnob Press, 2012, p.33-6.
4   *Bath Chronicle and Weekly Gazette*, 17th April 1783.
5   Ingram, Martin. *Church Courts, Sex, and marriage in England 1570-1640*. Cambridge University Press, 1990, p.78.
6   WHC A1/110, 1739M, 1740M.
7   WSHC A1/165/6; A1/110, 1642M.
8   WSHC A1/110, 1766M.
9   *Bath Chronicle* 24th February 1785.
10 WSHC A1/165/8.
11 WSHC A1/110, 1779M.
12 WSHC A1/110, 1790M.

already been mentioned, as has the gibbet which stood on the road west of Beckhampton.¹ The latter was used to hang the bodies of the notorious Cherhill Gang of highwaymen, who were executed in Devizes.² In the 'information' taken from John Balden of Yatesbury in November 1661, John Pontin of Beckhampton was accused of stealing five sheep. Pontin confessed, admitting that he had taken them to market in Devizes and sold them to John Emot of Blackland. That was a felony, punishable by death, but whether Pontin suffered the ultimate penalty is not known. One of the labourers employed in the gardens at Avebury manor was sentenced to death for highway robbery in 1792, and may have suffered at the Beckhampton gibbet.³ Richard Hickley escorted him to his trial (perhaps as constable), and served on the jury.

Theft was not always detected. In 1798, John Brown of Avebury advertised a reward for the arrest of a burglar who had stolen, amongst other things, a 'Chippenham bank note' valued at ten guineas, three other notes drawn for five guineas each, and a 'large old silver watch, marked on the case in a cypher J.B'. That would have been a capital offence.

English society was much more violent in the early modern period than it is today,⁴ and assault was regarded as a much less serious crime, requiring the Justice to compose the difference between the parties, rather than to inflict punishment. In 1671, John Curr was bound over to 'keep the peace' against John Hedges of Clatford.⁵ Richard Smith of West Kennett was bound with him. Similarly, a recognizance was taken from John Griffin in 1731, when he was accused of 'beating' Sarah Clements; he was required to appear at the ensuing Quarter Sessions.⁶ So were Mary White, widow, Mary Phelps, and Elizabeth Woodman, who were accused in 1719 of 'beating and assaulting' Elizabeth Phelps.⁷ More accurately, it was the husbands of the latter two who had to answer for their wives crimes. In 1765, two prominent Avebury yeomen, Isaac Godwin and John Griffin Grant, were prepared to stand bond for the appearance of Robert Voysey of Winterbourne Bassett when he was accused of assault.⁸

1 Above, p.40.
2 Philips, op cit, p.139.
3 WSHC 184/6. Letter, Richard Hickley to Mrs Williamson, 31st July 1792. His surname was Bailey.
4 Sharpe, J.A. *Early Modern England: A Social History 1550-1760.* Edward Arnold, 1987, p.114.
5 WSHC A1/110, 1671M, f.16.
6 WSHC A1/110/1731M.
7 WSHC A1/110.1719M.
8 WSHC A1/110, 1765M.

Thomas Pontin came to the attention of the law on two occasions. In 1713 he was accused of assaulting and injuring Thomas Baskerville at Berwick Bassett; a 'true bill' (meaning that the case went to full trial) was found against him in 1714.[1] When Martha Robinson was examined by Thomas Bennett, J.P., in 1717, she claimed that Pontin had 'carnal knowledge' of her in an outhouse belonging to her father, Humphry Robinson.[2]

In dealing with serious disputes, Justices were generally more concerned with keeping the peace, rather than punishing offenders. When a large number of poor women from Calne came to glean in Avebury's open fields, they were resisted by the Avebury poor, and violence broke out.[3] Sir Richard Holford evidently thought that the Calne women were the aggressors, but they nevertheless obtained a warrant from Charles Tooker, the Justice of the Peace at Kennett, against Avebury people. He took no further action, although Sir Richard did send his coachman, Richard Bradney, 'to indeavor to preserve the peace'. The right to glean was a serious matter (at least for the poor), which could lead to rioting, but disputes were to be settled by arbitration, not by course of law.

Quarter Sessions were supervised by judges from the central courts sitting at Assizes. Unfortunately, few Assize records for Wiltshire survive, although we do occasionally find mention of cases from Avebury tried at Assizes; reference has already been made to a case concerning John White's tithe. In 1603, Richard Truslow's title to West Down was disputed at the Assizes by Sir James Mervyn; the verdict went in Truslow's favour.[4] A dispute concerning the tithes of Warwicks came before the Salisbury Assizes in 1631; John Goldsmith was subsequently accused by John Pope of having 'payd the jury' to obtain a favourable verdict, although another witness deposed that the case never came to trial[5] Many civil cases from Avebury were also heard in the central courts, especially in Chancery, but also in the Exchequer and other courts. Sometimes the same case was heard in several different courts. For example, Mervyn's challenge to Truslow's ownership of the Rectory estate was not only heard at Assizes, but also in both the Exchequer,[6] and in Star Chamber.[7]

1   WSHC A1/110, 1713M & 1714M
2   WSHC A1/110, 1717M.
3   For the following paragraph, see GA D1956/E2/8.
4   TNA STAC8/5/1; STAC 8/281/25.
5   TNA E134/8Chas1/Mich53. By one of the witnesses, John Pope. The case was subsequently tried in the Court of Exchequer.
6   TNA E134/40and41Eliz/Mich7; E134/41Eliz/Hil8.
7   TNA STAC8/5/1.

The Militia and Soldiering

The militia was under the direction of the county Lieutenancy. Constables at musters acted under the direction of Deputy Lieutenants, mediated through high constables. In 1604 and 1605, Sir James Mervyn, then resident in Avebury, was serving as Deputy Lieutenant.[1] He was responsible for raising money to pay the muster master, for issuing precepts to the Hundred constables for the necessary rates, and for advising them how to deal with refusal to pay. He was also busy with Quarter Sessions. It was probably his influence which resulted in Richard Sutton being presented at Quarter Sessions in 1608 for 'deniing to marche', that is, refusing to attend musters, despite being 'warned' by the constable.[2]

Few Civil War soldiers from Avebury are recorded, although Avebury men must have served. One wonders whether the John Griffin who served in the Parliamentary garrison at Devizes, and was killed there, belonged to the Avebury family.[3] We know that the son of the vicar, John Forsyth, served in the Parliamentary army, and that consequently his father was 'plundered' and imprisoned at Oxford.[4] The lord of Avebury manor, Sir John Stawell, was a prominent commander in the King's army.[5] John Mortimer was 'resolved to goe and serve as a souldier in the warrs', according to his nuncupative will, but probably died before he could do so.[6] His 1645 will was proved in the Prerogative Court of Canterbury immediately after that of his father Thomas[7]. A 'list of Captain Colley's Company' in 1660 lists the names of six Avebury soldiers and six from 'Kinnetts', presumably both East and West Kennett.[8]

Later in the seventeenth century, Sir Edward Baynton was commissioned to raise a regiment of foot militia in Selkley Hundred; he required four men from Avebury tithing, and three each from the tithings of Beckhampton and West Kennett.[9] It was the duty of the parish constable to ensure that they

---

1   Murphy, W.P.D., ed. *The Earl of Hertford's Lieutenancy Book 1603-1612.* Wiltshire Record Society, 23. 1969, p.37-8 & 89-90.
2   WSHC A1/110, 1608M, f.105.
3   Slocombe, Ivor, ed. *Wiltshire Quarter Sessions Order Book 1642-1654.* Wiltshire Record Society, 67. 2014, p.109.
4   TNA C2/Chas1/A9/39.
5   *Oxford Dictionary of National Biography* www.oxforddnb.com.
6   TNA PROB 11/194/503.
7   TNA PROB 11/194/502-3.
8   WSHC 1178/48-9.
9   Freeman, Jane, ed. *The Common Place Book of Sir Edward Bayntun of Bromham.* Wiltshire Record Society, 43. 1988, p.36.

attended musters in Marlborough.

In 1715, Sir Richard Holford and Mr Norris were expected to provide a horse, presumably when troops were being raised to repel the Jacobite invasion of that year. Foot soldiers were also required: three from Avebury, and one each from Beckhampton and East and West Kennett.[1] In 1766, constables may have been called upon to help suppress rioting in the district. We do not know whether the complaints of the poor at the price of bread were heard in Avebury, but a letter from Peter Holford, who was at Westonbirt, and serving as a Deputy Lieutenant of Gloucestershire, to his nephew Stayner, concerns the threat of rioting in the district.[2] The threat of riot was always present when the price of bread rose: high prices at Devizes market in 1801 'occasioned the populace again to show a disposition to riot'.[3] In 1793, Richard Hickley feared that the introduction of spinning machines would prompt the poor to rebel.[4] His fears were not unjustified; there had been serious riots at Bradford on Avon and Trowbridge in 1791 and 1792.[5]

There is a brief reference to the militia in 1778, when Thomas Phillipps (subsequently a personal servant of Arthur Jones) was chosen by lot to serve.[6] He appointed a substitute, Thomas Dixon, whose wife was living in Brinkworth. In 1780, the Avebury overseers were ordered to pay Phillipps £1 8s for his service, which he presumably used to pay Dixon. But the Brinkworth overseers were ordered to pay Dixon's wife an additional 2s per week for her maintenance. A similar arrangement was made by John Blake, who had also been chosen by lot, and had appointed Robert Painter, a taylor of Devizes, as his substitute. Blake, however, was to be paid £1 14s for his services.

It is probable that many Avebury men fought in the Napoleonic wars. Local people were well aware of the war and its progress; Richard Hickley was 'happy to hear the Duke of York has gained a complete victory over those hell hounds the French' when he wrote to Mrs Williamson in May 1794.[7]; he was presumably referring to the Battle of Willems. A month later he supposed 'you have heard that Lord Howe has given the French a handsome drubbing at last [at Ushant]. Pray God they had such a one every week till they were

---

1 WSHC 84/41.
2 WSHC 271/14.
3 Waylen, James. *A History, Military and Municipal, of the ancient Borough of Devizes.* Longman Brown & Co., 1859, p.476.
4 WSHC 184/6. Letter, Richard Hickley to Mrs Williamson, 8th November 1793.
5 Bettey, J.H. *Rural Life in Wessex, 1500-1900.* Alan Sutton, 1987, p.43.
6 WSHC 184/9/5.
7 WSHC 184/6. Letter, Richard Hickley to Mrs Williamson, 6th May 1794.

conquered.[1] An Avebury constable was almost certainly in attendance when, in 1798, the Wiltshire Yeomanry Cavalry mustered on Beckhampton Down, and were presented with their colours by Lady Bruce.[2] So were thousands of spectators. And so, probably, was William Philpot, who was named in 1799 as a member of the Devizes Troop.[3] Perhaps the muster took place on his land. Richard Hickley was also involved; he thought that 'one may spare three or four hours once in the week without much inconvenience'. He was very concerned at the threat posed by the 'great number of villains in this Kingdom' and thought that 'we want half a hundred guillotine fixed in different parts of the Kingdom, and some considerable use to be made of them'. The purpose of the volunteer cavalry, in his view, was 'to keep those Jacobin scoundrels in order'.[4] He was very firmly in support of the establishment of the day, and joined in a rousing chorus of 'God save the King' at a sumptuous dinner held in August 1794.[5] It is therefore no surprise to find him paying out £2 9s 6d for 'cloathing for Miles in the cavelry', and advancing this cavalryman £1 4s.[6]

Despite the probability that many Avebury men served during the Napoleonic wars, only two names are known. Jacob Horsell enlisted in 1797, aged 37, and served in various foot regiments (including the Royal Bengal Fusiliers) until 1816[7]. Thomas Wait, labourer, aged 32, enlisted at Hythe in 1805, and was sent to serve in Canada[8].

Visitations and the Church Courts

Some aspects of what we would now call secular government were administered in our period by the church through the visitation process, and through the ecclesiastical courts. The seventeenth-century Archdeacons of Wiltshire conducted visitations at six-monthly intervals, except once every three years, when the visitation was carried out by the Bishop. Archdeacons had visited even more frequently during Elizabeth's reign.[9] Matters needing 'correction' were sent to the Archdeacon's and Consistory courts unless they could be

1 WSHC 184/6. Letter, Richard Hickley to Mrs Williamson, June 1794.
2 *Bath Chronicle* 21st June 1798.
3 Graham, Henry. *The Annals of the Yeomanry Cavalry of Wiltshire* ... . Liverpool: D.Marples & Co., 1886, p.216.
4 WSHC 184/6. Letter, Richard Hickley to Mrs Williamson, June 1794.
5 184/6. Letter, Richard Hickley to Mrs Williamson, 31st August 1794.
6 WSHC 184/7.
7 TNA WO 97/1069/238 (digitised at www.findmypast.co.uk)
8 TNA WO 35/409 (digitised at www.ancestry.co.uk)
9 Ingram, Martin. *Church Courts, Sex and Marriage in England, 1570-1640*. Cambridge University Press, 1987, p.44-5.

dealt with immediately at visitation. These matters have been described by one writer as 'sin, sex, and probate'.[1] The ecclesiastical courts were seen as an important means of enforcing 'Godliness'.[2] The purely ecclesiastical aspects of their activities will be dealt with in chapter 9 (although the word 'purely' is a little dubious in this context – some matters, such as recusancy, were of great interest to the secular government as well as to the church).

The probate function of ecclesiastical courts involved acting as registries of wills. Executors, and administrators of intestate estates, were expected to apply for probate soon after the deaths of testators. If they did not, they were liable to find themselves cited to appear in court to explain themselves. The names of the 'possessors of the goods' of deceased persons were regularly taken cognizance of at visitation; for example, on 4th August 1738, Mary James was said to hold the goods of her father Benjamin.[3] In this case, however, the will had already been proved before a higher authority – the Chancellor of the Diocese – on 11th July 1738.[4] Similarly, when Lucy Bushell was prosecuted for not proving her husband's will in December 1716, the act book records 'this mistake – done in the visitation'.[5] The court also sought to ensure that inventories were exhibited: Margaret Mathews als Andrews, for example, was instructed to exhibit her husband John's inventory in 1601/2.[6] If she complied, it does not survive.

Much of the information in this book is based on the wills, inventories, and other probate documents lodged in the registries of the Archdeacon of Wiltshire, the Bishop of Salisbury, and the Prerogative Court of Canterbury. Avebury executors usually had to visit Marlborough or Salisbury to prove their wills, although some of the local gentry preferred to use the Prerogative Court in London. Occasionally, wills were proved in Chippenham or Devizes, and, on at least one occasion, in Avebury itself (probably in the Catherine Wheel)[7]. The fees levied on executors and administrators are recorded; for example, the administrator of Walter Truslow's estate paid fees amounting to 3s 8d in

---

[1] Chapman, Colin. *Sin, Sex and Probate: Ecclesiastical Courts, Officials and Records.* Lochin Publications, 1997.
[2] Sharpe, J.A. *Early Modern England: A Social History 1550-1760.* Edward Arnold, 1987, p.234.
[3] WSHC D3/8/2.
[4] WSHC P1/IJ/195.
[5] WSHC D1/39/2/16. The will was actually proved 14th September 1716; cf WSHC P1/B/825.
[6] WSHC D3/4/1, f.44.
[7] The 1720 will of Humphry Robinson, WSHC P1/R/275.

1727.[1] So did the executor of William Crook in 1754.[2] On occasion, probate disputes came before the courts; the challenge to the will of John Shuter in 1614 was heard in the Prerogative Court of Canterbury.[3] Sometimes, executors or administrators had to explain themselves to the court; for example, in the 1620s, John Pope, administrator of William James, claimed that the deceased had given him all his goods several years earlier, on condition that James provided diet for himself and his wife, plus forty shillings per annum. Pope claimed that the forty shillings per annum was not due to the widow.[4]

The church courts also interested themselves in the morals of parishioners. So did the parishioners, especially if they were slandered. When John Balden was accused in 1598 of being 'a whore master knave', he challenged his accuser in the Consistory Court.[5] That accusation severely damaged his reputation. Whores, of course, produced bastards, and might cost the parish money on the poor rates, unless they could impose maintenance orders on fathers. Bastardy was frequently dealt with in sixteenth and seventeenth century church courts. In the early 1550s, for example, the vicar and churchwardens presented that the 'party' who fathered Joan Reeves' bastard child 'is fled', and that both Richard Payne and Robert Coffe had been living 'incontinently'.[6] In 1594, William Mayne promised to obtain a copyhold and marry Alice Smyth; he 'obteyned his pleasure of her & hath begotten her with child'. He, however, 'betaketh himself as before to his said war & service'.[7] In other words, he was thought to have abandoned Alice. In 1623, Ann Pope was presented 'for having a bastard by Nicholas Pinnell of Brinckworth'.[8] Similarly, in 1632/3, Mary Pontin claimed that Richard Chesterman had 'dyverse hundred tymes promised this examinant marriage' before he had 'carnal knowledge' of her, a claim which he denied.[9] Thomas Gilbert was accused, c1617/18, of being the father of several bastards.[10] In 1634, Richard Mathews, was prosecuted as 'the reputed father of a bastard child begotten on the body of Anne Dymer of the parish of Overton'.[11] If the name of the father was not known, the courts were

1   WSHC D3/2/6.
2   WSHC D3/2/8.
3   TNA PROB 11/124/472.
4   WSHC D3/4/5, f.110.
5   WSHC D1/42/16, f.189r-191v. I owe this reference to Steve Hobbs.
6   WSHC D1/43/1, f.144.
7   WSHC D1/39/2/2, f.39.
8   WSHC D3/4/6, f.10v.
9   WSHC D3/4/7, f.9.
10 WSHC D3/4/3, f.7v.
11 WSHC D1/39/2/12, f.18v

eager to discover them; in 1601, Avebury's churchwardens were instructed to 'learne out who is the father of Beverstone's child'.[1]

Even parents who married when they discovered a child was on the way could be presented for incontinence before marriage. In 1614, John Holmes and his wife obtained a licence to marry in Marlborough, probably because they wished to avoid the bride's pregnancy being noticed. But the Avebury churchwardens nevertheless did notice, and presented the couple in 1614.[2] In the same year, Rose Green was presented for having a bastard by John Hatherall, and compelled to do penance.[3] That was a humiliating ordeal, which usually meant appearing in church dressed in nothing more than a white sheet, and begging the forgiveness of the congregation. For overseers, however, a sentence of penance did not pay the cost of maintaining an illegitimate child. They had to meet that cost if all else failed. Consequently, they increasingly sought to obtain maintenance payments through Justices of the Peace, as discussed above.

The Turnpike Trust

In addition to the secular and ecclesiastical courts, an important Quango concerned itself with Avebury. The Beckhampton Turnpike Act of 1742 established a board of trustees on which many Justices of the Peace and other local landowners sat. They included Stayner Holford. His tenant, Peter Griffin advised him that the first meeting would take place in April 1743, 'at which time it will be propper for you & all gentlemen haveing estates in the parish to be present, & you in particular having so considerable an estate'.[4] Apparently, Holford did not attend; Griffin subsequently wrote that 'the trustees met about fifty of them on Munday last but did but little business, onely chose a number that should act. They meet again next Munday and the Munday following, when they are to fix the pleaces for the gates'.[5]

By 1751, there were two toll gates in the parish.[6] Initially, one of them was manned by the innkeeper at the Hare and Hounds. That, however, changed when a Justice of the Peace decided that it was inappropriate, and refused to renew the innkeeper's licence.[7] Consequently, a new tollhouse had to be built on the other side of the road. In 1797 a third tollhouse was built at the toll bar

1 WSHC D3/4/1, f.26v.
2 WSHC D1/39/2/7, f.95.
3 WSHC D1/39/2/7, f.84v.
4 WSH 184/1, pt.2. Letter, Peter Griffin to Stayner Holford, 6th March, 1742/3.
5 WSHC 184/1, pt.2. Letter, Peter Griffin to Stayner Holford, 23rd April 1743.
6 WSHC 184/3. Land tax assessment 1751.
7 For toll-gate keepers, see below, p.319-20.

in Weedon Field.[1] The trustees had the power to alter the route of the road; when the enclosure of open fields at Beckhampton was under consideration in 1743, the desirability of asking them to close a part of the 'general way' known as French Way, which ran through them, was discussed.[2] In 1793, they were in negotiation with Richard Hickley to purchase the corner of a field beside Silbury Hill in order to straighten the road.[3] They agreed to plough up the disused road and return it to Hickley, but then realised that could not be done, as it gave access to the Duke of Marlborough's property.[4]

The earliest extant minute book for the turnpike trustees commences in 1790. The only Avebury residents who attended meetings were John Nalder[5] and (after he had returned from his governorship of Jamaica) Sir Adam Williamson. The attendance of James Sutton, who owned land in Avebury, but was resident in Devizes, is recorded once, on 29th June 1791. Both Joseph Mighell, who had purchased the neighbouring manor of East Kennett in 1789,[6] and William Tanner, who purchased the Grubbe family's estate in West Kennett in 1788,[7] also attended once each, in 1795 and 1799 respectively. Rev Charles Mayo, rector of Beechingstoke, and cousin to Avebury's non-resident vicar James Mayo, was one of the few regular attenders in the 1790s.[8] Attendance at meetings was fairly dismal; despite the large number of trustees, on many occasions meetings could not proceed because they were inquorate. Nevertheless, the trustees (or their officers, a clerk and a treasurer) were active in maintaining and widening the roads. During the 1790s roads were either newly built, diverted, or widened, on Cherhill Hill, at Beckhampton beside the Catherine Wheel, at Silbury Hill, beside the White Hart at West Kennett, and beside Mr Tanner's farmyard at West Kennett. The tollhouse at Beckhampton was raised to two stories, a shed at the back for coal or wood was built, and a garden created. Another tollhouse was erected at Avebury, under the direction of Sir Adam Williamson. And application was made to Parliament for a fresh act, so that the road from West Kennett to Avebury could be turnpiked. It took

1 WSHC 1371/1. See also A1/205/3.
2 WSHC 184/1, pt.2. Letter, Thomas Smith to Stayner Holford, 29th May 1743.
3 WSHC 184/6. Letter, Richard Hickley to Mrs Williamson, 8th November 1793.
4 WSHC 184/6. Letter, Richard Hickley to Mrs Williamson, June 1794.
5 He was also a trustee of the Calne Turnpike Trust; cf. Tyler, P.J. *Some aspects of the roads of the Calne Turnpike Trust 1773-1871*. Undergraduate dissertation. University of Birmingham Dept of Archaeology, 1980, p.A7.
6 *VCH Wilts* 12, p.120.
7 *VCH Wilts* 12, p.97.
8 James Mayo served as trustee of the Calne Turnpike Trust from 1792; cf. Tyler, op cit, p.A5.

many years before that happened; the requisite act was finally passed in 1840.[1]

Land Tax Commissioners and other Taxes

Turnpike property was liable to the land tax. In 1751 the tollgates were assessed at £15.[2] The land tax was regularly collected in Avebury, although only a few assessments survive for our period. The tax was supported by Sir Richard Holford, who wrote in 1702 that 'Wee are likely to have our taxes continued, which is of absolute nescessity for carrying on the warr against France and Spaine'. But he did object to 'the inequality of Avebury taxes', which was 'more grivious than the tax itselfe', and which he tried to correct.[3] One of his successors, Stayner Holford, similarly objected to his property being more highly taxed than he thought it should have been.[4] In 1738, the tithings of Avebury, West Kennett, and Beckhampton, were rated separately for land tax purposes, although rated together for church and poor rates.[5] By 1780, there was a separate assessment for the parish of East Kennett, although this was described as the 'tythings of East and West Kennett' in 1785 and 1788 without any change in the amount assessed. From 1794, the assessment specified lands in the two separate tythings.[6] Tenancy agreements specified whether landlord or tenant should pay taxes; frequently, as in the case of William Skeat's 1689 lease for Lord Stawell, the tenant paid them, but sought reimbursement from his landlord.[7] Farmer John Caswell, tenant of a farm at Beckhampton in 1708, paid all local taxes, but land tax was 'allowed' to him by Sir Richard Holford.[8]

The Land Tax Commissioners, appointed by Parliament, appointed collectors every year; the latter were drawn from those liable to pay. For example, John Rose, tenant of Avebury Farm (and subsequently a bankrupt), served in 1742 and 1743.[9] Henry Howson, the owner of land at Brunsdens, served with Robert Nalder, his neighbour, in 1751.[10] Richard Hickley, in addition to his other duties, served as collector almost every year between 1780 and 1800.[11]

1 *VCH Wilts* 12, p.89.
2 WSHC 184/3. Land tax assessment 1751.
3 WSHC 184/1, pt.1. Letter, Sir Richard Holford to John White, 23rd December 1702.
4 WSHC 184/1, pt.1. Letter, Stayner Holford to William Norris, 14th June 1761.
5 WSHC 184/3. Statement of yearly value of the lands in Avebury, c.1738.
6 WSHC A1/345/240A.
7 WSHC 184/4/1.
8 WSHC 184/4/1.
9 WSHC 184/3. Land tax receipt, 1743.
10 WSHC 184/3. Land tax assessment, 1751.
11 WSHC A1/345/18A. See also 473/55 & 352.

The Commissioners heard appeals against assessments. A specific amount had to be raised from the parish, so a reduction in the assessment on one person would lead to an increase in assessment on another. That was a recipe for conflict between neighbours. Disputes frequently threatened. In 1695, Sir Richard Holford wrote to his neighbour, Mr Smith, who served as a local Commissioner, asking him 'to make the rates as equall as you can, for that, if I have harder measure than others, I must make complaine in the Exchequer'.[1] Three years later, he was moved to thank Charles Tooker, J.P., 'for standing up soe heartily & effectually for setting the tax in the most equall method for the service of the King and country'.[2] On several subsequent occasions, the Commissioners heard appeals relating to Holford property.[3] In 1753, Stayner Holford objected to the fact that 'it had been customary to load the great estates with sums larger than in proportion on smaller properties'. He was prepared to assist the poorest households, but was not prepared to pay more proportionally than others who could afford to pay. It is not clear whether he won his appeal. However, in 1761, a number of neighbouring landlords appealed against the assessment made on Stayner's property. They argued that the rent ought to be based on the rent which had been paid in the past. And they included in that figure the interest of £20 which a previous tenant had paid on a £500 loan, making a total of £380. But the tenant who had paid that interest had left, and his successor (John Rose!) had failed. Holford had therefore been forced to stock the farm himself, and successfully argued that the assessment should be based on what he had been offered for the farm, ie £340 per annum. The appellants were unsuccessful, and although they tried again in the following year, their appeal was thrown out.

Land tax was not the only levy imposed on Avebury inhabitants. Collectors were also appointed for the subsidy, the hearth tax, and a variety of other impositions. A window tax inspector visited Richard Hickley in 1792, and pointed out that the cart Mrs Williamson had ordered to be made would be liable to pay duty of £3 10s; Hickley asked his mistress if that would cause her to reconsider her order.[4] Hickley also blocked up some of the windows in the mansion house, in order to save £4 on the window tax. He thought it was 'abominable to pay so much tax and no family in the house'.[5]

1 WSHC 184/4/1, pt.1. Letter, Sir Richard Holford to Mr Smith, 22nd February 1695.
2 WSHC 184/1, pt.2. Letter, Sir Richard Holford to Cornelius Yeate, 5th May 1698.
3 WSHC 184/3. Cases stated, 1753 & 1761.
4 WSHC 184/6. Letter, Richard Hickley to Mrs Williamson, 4th September 1792.
5 WSHC 184/6. Letter, Richard Hickley to Mrs Williamson, 4th June 1793.

An excise officer was stationed in Avebury, but we know nothing about him other than the fact that he was rated to the land tax at £7 10s in 1751,[1] and that William Spackman held the office in the early to mid-seventeenth century.[2]

[1] WSHC 184/3.
[2] WSHC 4381/2/1, f.165-6 & 167-8. He was not one of the Avebury Spackman family.

5
Landowners, Tenants, and Wealth

Avebury in the early modern period had several landowning families of gentry status. There were also many moderately wealthy yeomen. We have already noted that there was also a great deal of poverty, especially towards the end of our period. William Skeat, the tenant of Avebury Great Farm, appears to have been sufficiently well-off when his lease expired to refuse to renew it and retire. His experience was a far cry from that of the cottagers on John Griffin's land, who were threatened with eviction when the vicar purchased Griffin's property, and demanded that they take out leases and pay hefty entry fines.[1] The divide widened in the course of the eighteenth century: the rich got richer, and the poor got poorer. Larger farms tended to grow at the expense of the small farmer.[2] One's role and standing depended on the amount of land that one possessed.[3] Local yeomen who were able to accumulate land were elevated to minor gentry status, and what Ingram has described as a 'parochial sub-aristocracy' developed.[4] On the other hand, there were hundreds of poor by the end of the eighteenth century. Avebury, like the rest of England, became a more polarized society.[5] Nevertheless, Avebury was not a 'closed' parish; Sir Adam Williamson, the major landowner in 1798, only paid roughly a fifth of the land tax demanded in the parish.[6] There were other substantial landowners.

1. WSHC 184/1, pt 1. Letter, John Jerome & Christopher Page to Sir Richard Holford, 18th April 1707.
2. Wordie, J.R. 'The South: Oxfordshire, Buckinghamshire, Berkshire, Wiltshire and Hampshire', in Thirsk, Joan, ed. *The Agrarian History of England and Wales,. Vol.V: 1640-1750, pt.1. Regional Farming Systems.* Cambridge University Press, 1984, p.332.
3. Hey, David G. *An English Rural Community: Myddle under the Tudors and Stuarts.* Leicester University Press, 1974, p.86
4. Ingram, Martin. *Church Courts, Sex, and marriage in England 1570-1640.* Cambridge University Press, 1990, p.76.
5. Langford, Paul. *Eighteenth-Century Britain: a Very Short Introduction.* Oxford University Press, 1984, p.40.
6. TNA IR23/96/189, f.249. Williamson paid £52 16s 1d; the total amount levied in Avebury (including the tithing of Beckhampton) was £252 11s 0d.

Landowners after the Reformation

The landowners and tenants of Avebury property played central roles in the life of the parish. The prime focus here is to examine their social structure and interactions rather than to trace the descents of properties (although that has been done to a limited extent).[1] The Reformation led to dramatic changes in land ownership. Changes in the succeeding centuries were not as dramatic, but landownership and occupation was far from being static. Enclosure at the end of our period brought further changes. These were more concerned with the landscape and the distribution of land than with the landowners themselves. Few landowners sold up in the immediately succeeding years.

Before the Reformation, various ecclesiastical establishments owned much of Avebury. The manors of Avebury and (at least in part) Beckhampton were held by Fotheringhay College. Cirencester Abbey held the Rectory and the manor of Avebury Trusloe (although whether the latter property was a 'manor' was questioned at the end of the sixteenth century)[2]. Avebury church owned enough land (including Higdens) to support a light. The chantry at Bromham possessed Rowses Farm, and Beckhampton Chapel owned tithes on two farms, a messuage, and other minor property[3]. There were a few laymen who also owned property. Warwicks was a part of the manor of Cherhill, which was owned by the Bayntun family of Bromham, although it owed its name to the fact that the Beauchamps, Earls of Warwick, had once been manorial lords[4]. The manor of West Kennett was owned by Anne Benger, who married Thomas Smith[5]. A moiety of Beckhampton was owned by William Button.[6]

The structure of ownership in the parish dramatically changed as a consequence of the Reformation[7]. The Crown confiscated the ecclesiastical properties, but failed to consolidate holdings, and sold them off piecemeal as it had received them. Several speculators, such as Sir William Sharington, and Thomas Brown of Winterbourne Bassett,[8] purchased land in the parish,

---

1 For more detailed descents, see *VCH Wilts.*, 12, p.91-7.
2 TNA E134/40and 41Eliz/Mich7; E134/41Eliz/Hil8.
3 *VCH Wilts.*, 12, p.91-7.
4 Blackford, J.H. *The Manor and Village of Cherhill: a Wiltshire village from early times to the present day.* 1941, p.65-8 & 75.
5 *VCH Wilts.*, 12, p.97.
6 *VCH Wilts.*, 12, p.95.
7 The following discussion is based on *VCH Wilts.*, 12, 91-7, except where otherwise stated.
8 He purchased the estates of the Free Chapel of Beckhampton; see the abstract of title to Chapel lands in WSHC 184/4/1.

but did not retain them for long. In the long term, no one family achieved total dominance, although the lords of the manor of Avebury – the Dunches, followed by the Stawell and Holford families - usually had close connections at Court, and liked to think that they were the leading landowners in the parish. Their influence was reduced, however, when they were not resident in the parish. The Stawell family, as we have seen, were thought by Sir Richard Holford to have lived there after their 1639 purchase. Provision for occasional use of the manor house were made in Sir John Stawell's lease to William Skeat. Sir Richard Holford and his heirs, however, were absentee landlords, at least until Stayner Holford took the farm in hand in 1755. They were absentees again in the early 1790s, when General Williamson was governor of Jamaica. Absentee landlords gave greater scope for families of minor gentry to establish their positions, and some continued to be Avebury landowners for more than a century after the Dissolution (although few if any families resident in the late sixteenth century were still there in 1800). Unlike other parishes in the chalk district, manorial control was fairly weak,[1] and not helped by the fact that there were several distinct manors. Underdown's comment that 'parochial gentry frequently emerged from the ranks of the more successful yeomen, by incremental accumulation over several generations'[2] has its Avebury exemplars. Some members of both the Griffin and the Phelps family, as we saw in chapter 3, were active in the land market, and described themselves as 'gent'. So did members of the Truslow family, although they disappeared from the parish in the early eighteenth century.

The manor of Avebury was acquired, in 1547, by Sir William Sharington, a prominent courtier, who also purchased Lacock.[3] But, shortly after, his peculations at the Bristol Mint led to his being attainted, and his properties were seized. He was very soon pardoned, and regained his estates. However, his needs for money were great, probably as a consequence of his building activities at Lacock, and his need to pay a substantial fine to the Crown[4]. Consequently, in 1551, he sold the manor of Avebury to William Dunch.[5] It remained in the Dunch family until 1640, although Sir James Mervyn married the mother of the Dunch heir in the 1590s, and acquired her life interest.[6]

1   Davis, T. *A General View of the Agriculture of Wiltshire*. 1811, p.xiv.
2   Underdown, David. *Revel, Riot and Rebellion: Popular Politics and Culture in England 1603-1660.* Clarendon Press, 1985, p.21.
3   WSHC 2664/1/2A/5.
4   www.historyofparliamentonline.org/volume/1509-1558/member/sharington-william-1495-1553
5   WSHC 184/4, pt.1. Abstract of deeds.
6   www.historyofparliamentonline.org/volume/1558-1603/member/marvyn-

When he died it reverted to William Dunch, whose 1630 will granted it to three trustees – Thomas Lambert, Ellis Swayne, and Kingsmill Long - to pay off his debts.[1]

The lands of the manor of Avebury Trusloe,[2] and of the Rectory or parsonage (both of which had been appropriated by Cirencester Abbey before the Reformation) were closely inter-mixed. It seems likely that they were farmed together even in late medieval times, as the particulars taken for Henry VIII's surveyors described them as indivisible.[3] For example, the western part of the Wall Ditch was said to belong to Avebury Trusloe, whilst the nearby Parsonage House was built on the Rectory estate.[4] The Crown, as already noted, could have consolidated holdings before selling them after the Dissolution, but failed to do so. At the dissolution, both properties were held by the Truslow family on a sixty year lease, due to expire in 1594.[5] Joan Truslow bought the freehold of the manor in 1563,[6] but the more valuable Rectory estate continued to be held on the old lease.[7]

Joan was succeeded by her son John in 1568,[8] who was in turn succeeded by a cousin, Richard Truslow, in 1593. As has been seen,[9] his son John sold off much of the estate. By 1628, the manor was in the hands of the Dunch family, who were evidently further consolidating their estate.[10]

The Rectory c.1598 was said to be worth between £100 and £200.[11] When the lease fell in c.1593, its land was claimed by Sir James Mervyn, whose wife (the widow of Walter Dunch) held the reversion. However, Richard Truslow failed to vacate it fully. He claimed not to know where the boundary between the manor and the Rectory estate lay. Neither did some of the witnesses in the ensuing Exchequer suit. Much of the Exchequer

james-1529-1611

1. TNA PROB11/321/306.
2. The sources, confusingly, frequently use the name, 'the manor of Avebury' for two distinct manors. The distinguishing name 'Trusloe' was not added until the seventeenth century. The lack of clarity is ignored In Knowles, Francis. 'Avebury Manor', *WAM*, 56, 1955, p.363-4.
3. TNA LR2/191, f.141
4. TNA E134/41Eliz/Hil8.
5. Wilkinson, Louise J., ed. *Calendar of Patent Rolls, 27 Elizabeth I (1584-1583)*. C66/1254/1270. List & Index Society, 293, 2002, p.36.
6. *VCH Wilts* 12, p.92 & 98.
7. TNA LR2/191, f.141.
8. *VCH Wilts.*, 12, p.93.
9. Above, p.XXXX.chapter 3
10. *VCH Wilts* 12, p.93.
11. *VCH Wilts* 12, p.98.

documentation concerns the right of way into Truslow's barn, and the dovecote (which Joan Truslow had built on the Rectory estate).[1] We do not know how the case was settled, but Truslow subsequently claimed that his right to West Down as part of his manor had been accepted by the Court of Exchequer.[2] That claim emerged after an altercation between the servants of the two manorial lords on West or Knoyle Down led to another case in Star Chamber c.1603.[3]

Two years later, there was another altercation on West Down (which Mervyn called Parsonage Down in order to establish that it was part of his Rectory estate). Mervyn's men, on the instructions of his wife, attempted to depasture about 100 sheep on the Down. Truslow also accused them of stealing four cart loads of hay. The dispute again went to Star Chamber.[4] It may not have been finally settled until both men had died: it was ended when William Dunch acquired the manor of Avebury Trusloe in the 1620s, thus uniting ownership of both properties.[5]

The lord of the manor of Beckhampton seems to have lost control of much of the manor in the medieval period. Part of it was sold by Lord Stourton to William Button before 1549, and remained in the Button family until 1586, when it was sold for £1000 to Richard Truslow[6]. Another portion of the property (known as Goddard's Farm) was purchased by Thomas Goddard of Upham (Aldbourne), in 1573, and stayed in his family until 1702, when it was purchased by Charles Tooker.[7] At the same time, Tooker also purchased the other portion of the farm from Richard Truslow.[8] On both properties, Tooker had to continue paying annuities. £20 per annum had been settled on Thomas Goddard's brother Edmund. Bridget Truslow, Richard's mother, similarly had her annuity of £20. These annuities continued to be paid after Tooker subsequently sold the properties to Sir Richard Holford.

1 TNA E134/40and41Eliz/Mich7; E134/41Eliz/Hil8; WANHS Genealogy v.A-A, f.86-95; S., J. 'Notes on Wiltshire Parishes: Avebury', *Wiltshire Notes & Queries* 8, 1914-18, p.217-9.
2 According to John Jennings, a Star Chamber witness, the issue had also been considered at length by the Assizes at Salisbury in 1603; their verdict had also favoured Truslow. See TNA STAC8/281/25.
3 TNA STAC8/5/1.
4 TNA STAC8/281/25.
5 *VCH Wilts.*, 12, p.93.
6 WSHC 371/2, pt.2. Indenture 20th September 1596. See also *VCH Wilts* 12, p.95.
7 WSHC 184/4/1. Abstract of title.
8 WSHC 371/1, pt.4. Lease & release, Richard Truslow to Charles Tooker, 29/30th October 1702.

The manor of West Kennett was one of the few properties in the parish which had not been in ecclesiastical hands. After the death of Thomas Smith in 1558, it was settled on his wife Anne, and thereafter on Ralph Henslow and his wife. In 1594, the Henslows sold it to Thomas Smith, who was probably a relative of their predecessors. The property remained in the possession of the family throughout our period, although it was not until 1713 that the then head of the family managed to buy out an annuity of £31 with which the Henslows had encumbered the property.[1]

The Crown took several decades to dispose of the property which had funded a light in the church. We know that from 1547 it was leased to John Chesterman, but it was probably not sold by the Crown until c.1575. At least part of this property, three yardlands at Higdens, was sold by Thomas and Catherine Henslow to Richard Smith in the early 17th century[2]. The Smith family subsequently acquired another portion of the estate, Chestermans; they sold both in 1713.

The possessions of the Bromham chantry were granted to Edward Cary in 1564; by 1582, Chantry Farm, also known as Rowses Farm, was held by John Shuter, who described himself as a gentleman in his 1591 will. He bequeathed the farm to his son Richard [3], and described the property as lying in 'Beckhampton and Kennett'.

The small estates of Beckhampton chapel were granted in 1549 to its former chaplain, John Warner, Regius Professor of Medicine at the University of Oxford.[4] They constituted the tithes on two farms in Beckhampton, plus a messuage, an acre of pasture, and a yardland, some of which lay at Stanmer (in Clyffe Pypard)[5]. He sold the property in 1561; it passed through a number of owners, but in 1584 it was purchased for £320 by John Truslow[6], whose grandson sold the property for £455 to William Dunch in 1619.[7]

---

1   WSHC 568/4. Deed, Richard Grinfeild to Richard & Thomas Smith, 14th November 1713.
2   Fry, George S., & Fry, Edw. Alex., eds. *Abstracts of Wiltshire Inquisitiones Post mortem ... in the reign of King Charles the First.* Index Library. British Record Society, 1901, p.183. Abstract of TNA C142/517/16.
3   TNA PROB 11/78/167.
4   He was subsequently Vice-Chancellor. For his other preferments, see 'The Good Old Days of Pluralism', *Wiltshire Notes & Queries* 7, 1911-13, p.94.
5   WSHC 371/2, pt.2.
6   WSHC 371/1, pt.2.
7   WSHC 371/1, pt.2. Deed, 1st April 1619.

Seventeenth Century Manorial Lords: the Stawells

The manors of Avebury and Avebury Trusloe were both sold after William Dunch died in 1630. His trustees had to pay off his debts, a process which took a number of years. Sir John Stawell of Cothelstone (Somerset) purchased the manor of Avebury in 1639, paying £8550.[1] He was already a major landowner; Stawell's estate was said to yield him between £4000 and £5000 per annum in 1643.[2]

Sir John Stawell became a prominent Royalist soldier during the civil war. After his surrender at the siege of Exeter, and after his refusal to take loyalty oaths to Parliament, Sir Edward Baynton promised to 'bring him [Stawell] upon his knees'.[3] Parliament's subsequent sequestration of Stawell's estate meant that Baynton could occupy and purchase Stawell's's manor house at Avebury. He thus came into possession of both Avebury manors, and resided there between 1651 and 1657.[4] The manor was actually sold to George Long of Preston Candover (Hants) in 1652[5], but the probability is that Long was acting as Baynton's agent.

After the Restoration, Stawell recovered possession of his manor, and it descended to his sons and grandson. The property included 'the capital messuage, farm, and demesne of Awbury', including Avebury Farm, Parsonage Barn, and 'the curtilage, backside and wall-ditch thereunto adjoyning, sometime belonging to the farm called Trusler's Farm', with common of pasture for 900 wethers, 340 lambs, and 30 'rother beasts' on the downs of Hackpen, West Down, South Down, Houndsplot, and Waden Hill. Mortimer's Tenement and Griffin's Close gave him common of pasture for a further 53 sheep and 3 rother beasts. He also held the impropriate rectory of Avebury, giving him the right to tithes in Avebury, Beckhampton, Kennett, and Winterbourne Monkton. These details are taken from the Act of Parliament which authorised the sale

1 WANHS Wiltshire Genealogy, v.A-A, f.113, citing the Close Rolls. *VCH Wilts.*, 12, p.91, states 1640, but is probably mistaken.
2 TNA C2/Chas1/A9/39. This estimate was made by John Forsyth, the Parliamentarian vicar, who had been imprisoned by Royalist troops.
3 Stawell, George Dodsworth. *A Quantock Family: the Stawells of Cothelstone and their Descendants, the Barons Stawell of Somerton, and the Stawells of Devonshire and the County Cork*. Barnicot & Pearce, 1910, p.395.
4 *VCH Wilts.*, 12, p.91.
5 Green, M.A.E., ed. *Calendar of the Proceedings of the Committee for Compounding &c. 1643-1660.* [vol.2]. HMSO, 1890, p.1429. WANHS. Genealogy v.A-A, p.119. George was the brother of Kingsmill Long, literary friend of Walter Dunch, see above, p.76, & Nicol, Cheryl. *Inheriting the Earth: the Long Family's 500 year reign in Wiltshire.* Hobnob Press, 2016, p.339.

of John Lord Stawell's extensive estates in Somerset, Dorset, Wiltshire, and Gloucestershire in order to pay his debts, after his death in 1694.[1]

The Baynton Family and the Partition of the Manor of Avebury Trusloe

Sir Edward Baynton purchased the manor of Avebury Trusloe, together with the Rectory lands, in 1646.[2] During the Interregnum, he also acquired (temporarily) the manor of Avebury. When Sir Edward died in 1657, his illegitimate son Robert inherited both manors.[3] Robert, as lord of the manor (it is not clear which one) granted a copyhold tenement on 3rd October 1659.[4] Two decades later, he sold Avebury Trusloe piecemeal.[5] Like the manor of Avebury, much of it eventually came into the hands of the Holford family.

One portion of the manor was purchased by Peter Griffin in 1681.[6] It became the subject of a dispute between Griffin and the vicar, John White, who had been granted the copyhold in 1677.[7] Sir Richard Holford had articles drawn up in 1703 to purchase this property, but discovered that the title was not to his liking, and desisted.[8] John White, however, had retained the copyhold, and purchased the property outright in 1704. He and his son William remained in possession for most of the first half of the eighteenth century.

Another portion of Baynton's purchase, known as Pophams, or Little Avebury Farm, was sold to George Popham c.1675.[9] He in turn sold it to a neighbouring landowner, William Norris of Bromham, in 1691. Norris was paying a 'high rent' of 4d, probably for this property, to the lord of the

---

1 GA D678/2/F6/17. See also Victor, D. 'The Fall of the Stawell Family', *Somerset & Dorset Notes & Queries* 39(396), p.262-3.
2 WSHC 184/4/1. Abstract of title to Avebury Trusloe; WANHS Wiltshire Genealogy v.A-A, p.117. For the Rectory, see TNA C8/316/12. The date of 1633 given in *VCH Wilts* 12, p.93, appears to be incorrect.
3 For his illegitimacy, see TNA C6/18/26.
4 WSHC 212A/31/2.
5 *VCH Wilts.*, 12, p.93-4. See also S., J. 'Notes on Wiltshire Parishes: Avebury', *Wiltshire Notes & Queries* 8, 1914-18, p.223-4.
6 WSHC 184/4/1. Abstract of John Griffin's title.
7 TNA C5/577/76.
8 WSHC 184/4/1. Articles of agreement, John Griffin to Sir Richard Holford, 9th October 1703; 184/1, pt.1. Letter, Sir Richard Holford to John White, 6th March 1706/7.
9 It may be that it had originally been purchased by the Spencer family, and that it is identical to the farm at Beckhampton sold by them to Alexander Popham in 1666; cf. WANHS Wiltshire Genealogy, v.A-A, p.123.

manor in 1703.[1] It remained in the hands of the Norris family for most of the eighteenth century.

A third portion was sold to Richard Phelps in 1681, and again remained in his family, and in the family of his grand-daughter's husband, Richard Savage, throughout the rest of our period.[2]

In 1681, Robert Baynton also sold several pieces of land formerly held by copy of court roll from the manor of Avebury Trusloe. John Griffin purchased one of these properties at the same time as he purchased the portion of the manor mentioned above. This land, however, remained in his family, and in the family of John Banning, his son in law, throughout the eighteenth century. Brunsden's Farm, probably another former copyhold tenement of Avebury Trusloe, was retained by Robert Baynton when he sold the rest of his manor. His nephew sold it to William Norris in 1691, for £3500.[3]

The free chapel of Beckhampton had also been purchased by Robert Baynton, and came into the possession of his half-brother, Sir Edward Baynton.[4] In addition to Sir Edward's Avebury property, he was also lord of the manor of East Kennett; when he sold the latter to Charles Tooker in 1676 (for £5200), the Free Chapel was included in the deal, as was the Rectory of West Kennett, forty acres of land in Beckhampton open fields, and various other small pieces of land in Avebury.[5] In 1702, as has been seen, Tooker purchased another property at Beckhampton from Richard Truslow. All these properties were joined together as Beckhampton Farm (sometime known as Griffins or Truslows, and now as Galteemore) and sold to Sir Richard Holford in 1710.[6] In addition to the farm, which was let to Richard Caswell for four years,[7] the property also included small tenements let to the widows Edith Pontin and Mary Rose, Walter Pope, and John Bradfield. The first three paid 30s per annum rent; Bradfield paid £1.[8]

1 WSHC 184/4/1. Proposed conveyance, John Griffin to Sir Richard Holford, 1703.
2 *VCH Wilts* 12, p.84.
3 WSHC 1259/41.
4 WSHC 184/4/1. Abstract of title to the Free Chapel.
5 WSHC 371/2, pt.2. Bargain and sale, 13/14 June, 1676.
6 *VCH Wilts* 12, p.95; WSHC 371/2, pt.2. Indentures 13/14th June 1676; 371/1, pt.4. Lease & release, Charles Tooker to Sir Richard Holford, 31st November/1st December 1710. For its later descent, see WSHC 271/2. Peter Holford's title to the Beckhampton estate. S., J. 'Notes on Wiltshire Parishes: Avebury', *Wiltshire Notes & Queries* 8, 1914-18, p.272.
7 WSHC 184/4/1. Charles Tooker's statement, 1710.
8 GA D1956/E2/8.

Some Eighteenth Century Landlords

Sir Richard Holford

Sir Richard Holford, like the Dunches and the Stawells, was an outsider. As has been seen, he was a successful lawyer who had married an heiress, thus acquiring lordship of the manor of Westonbirt (Gloucestershire). Marriage to his third wife, Susanna Trotman, enabled him to purchase the manor of Avebury in 1695.[1] It was not sold again for the remainder of our period, although it did pass out of the Holford family's possession.

Sir Richard's acquisition of Avebury manor was not his last intervention in the land market. In the early decades of the eighteenth century, he was actively seeking to expand his landed estate, for example, purchasing the Minchin estate at Westonbirt in 1707.[2] In 1702, he was in the market bidding for two local estates.[3] It appears that neither of his bids succeeded immediately, although he did obtain one of the properties eventually. Charles Tooker pipped him at the post in purchasing the property at Beckhampton mentioned above. However, eight years later, as has been seen, Tooker sold that property to Holford.[4] The other property was purchased by Holford's *bête noir*, the vicar, John White.

Sir Richard had to make provision for several sons, and split his estates between them when he died in 1718. Consequently, his property at Westonbirt and Wells ceased to be in the same ownership as the manor of Avebury. Beckhampton, however, descended with Avebury until 1731, when Robert Holford of Westonbirt bought it from his nephew Richard.[5] The Holford policy seems to have been to extinguish rights of pasture on the common. In 1726, When William Philpot renewed his lease in 1726. he lost his pasture rights.[6] So did Walter Pope's son, Nicholas, when he renewed his lease in 1740.[7] Holford was prepared to buy out pasture rights where possible; in 1740 he exchanged half a cottage in Beckhampton for rights to a 'cow pasture for one beast.[8]

---

1 WSHC 435/24/1/6. Indenture, 25th March 1798, reciting grant of 28th January 1695 by the trustees of Sir John Stawell's estate.
2 GA D1956/12/1.
3 WSHC 184/1, pt.1. Letter, H. Wall to Sir Richard Holford, 18th October 1702.
4 *VCH Wilts.*, 12, p.94.
5 See above, p.98.
6 WSHC 371/1, pt.4. Lease, Robert Holford to William Philpot, 17th September 1726.
7 WSHC 371/1, pt.5. Lease, 6th August 1740.
8 WSHC 371/1, pt.5. Exchange, Robert Holford and John Rose of Calne, collarmaker, 19th September 1740.

The Norris Family of Nonsuch

The Norris's were prominent Wiltshire gentry based at Nonsuch House, Bromham. William Norris, who purchased Brunsden's (sometimes referred to as his 'great farm, and not to be confused with Avebury Great Farm) in 1691,[1] and Pophams, in 1709[2] would have been well known to his neighbour, Sir Richard Holford. Both were frequently described as 'of Lincoln's Inn', and were eminent practitioners in Chancery. Sir Richard dined at Nonsuch on 19th November 1714.[3] Brunsdens and Pophams both remained in the Norris family until 1796, although a small portion of Brunsdens was leased to George Stretch on 25th Mary 1745/6 in order to build the Catherine Wheel.[4] These properties remained in the hands of the family for almost a century. However, when another William Norris inherited in 1794, he was encumbered with debt, and in 1796 was forced to sell Brunsdens and Beckhampton House (as the Catherine Wheel was then known). Brunsdens was purchased by the sitting tenant, John Brown.[5] The Catherine Wheel (which yielded a chief rent of £5 per annum) was sold to the lessee, William Edmunds.[6]

Caleb Bailey and his Trustees

In the early eighteenth century, Caleb Bailey, the lord of the manor of Berwick Bassett, was another active player in the Avebury land market. Between 1708 and 1726 he bought up at least eight small properties in the parish; for example, in 1708 he purchased one beast leaze, that is, right of pasturage, from Richard Bailey and his family; in 1725, he purchased the 1½ acre field called Long Close from John Beake; in 1720, he purchased four acres in the common field, with common of pasture for three beasts, from Richard Tomkins.[7] When he died, much of this property was bequeathed to the charity he established to fund dissenting preachers. It was vested in trustees in 1752.[8] The trustees – John Nalder, Richard Bailey, and James Thring – added to the

1. See above, p.216
2. WSHC 1259/41.
3. WSHC 184/8.
4. WSHC 415/134. Abstract of William Norris's title to the Catherine Wheel.
5. WSHC 473/278; Somerset Heritage Centre, DD/PO/6. Common recovery, 1797.
6. 'Nonsuch House, Bromham', *Wiltshire Notes & Queries* 2, 1896-8, p.199.
7. For the full schedule of the properties purchased, see WSHC 212A/31/4. Trust deed, 15th February 1752. Some of the relevant deeds are in WSHC 212A/31/3. See also WSHC 1409/16/3.
8. WSHC 212A/31/4. John Nalder et al to John Brown and Ambrose Lanfear, 15th February 1752.

charity's property by purchasing copyhold land at Home Close, in Eastbrook, from John Cue of Calne in 1754.[1] In 1770, they also purchased 43 acres in the common fields which had been the property of the recently deceased John Savage of Marlborough.[2] The lease of the Catherine Wheel came into their possession in the late 1750s.[3] John Nalder, incidentally, was the tenant of West Kennett farm in 1752[4]. When he made his will in 1762,[5] he bequeathed this lease to trustees for his son Thomas.

The Grubbes of Eastwell

The Grubbes were another local gentry family who owned property in Avebury but did not actually live there[6]. They had lived at Eastwell, Potterne, since the fifteenth century. Henry Grubbe purchased the manor of Cherhill for the use of his son John in 1631[7]. It included the property in Avebury then known as Warwicks, which was subsequently named either Pophams or Brunsdens. In the late sixteenth century, the property had been detached from the manor, and came into the possession of the Dunch family; however, their claim was challenged in 1632, and ownership seems to have reverted to the lords of Cherhill manor.[8] The Grubbe family continued to claim quit rents from Warwicks in 1796, when John Brown, as tenant of William Norris, paid 10s 8d[9].

In 1682, John Grubbe's grandson Walter was also in possession of lands in West Kennett enumerated in the glebe terrier: Lower Cow Leaze, Upper Cow Leaze, Bell Close, and Broad Close.[10] These all became part of West Kennett Farm, after various properties which had previously been held in common with the Manor farm, including pasture close to the Kennet Avenue, were

1 WSHC 212A/31/4. Release, 4th April 1754.
2 WSHC 212A/31/4. Lease and release, Richard Ewens to John Nalder et al, 4/5 July 1770.
3 WSHC 212A/31/1 & 4.
4 WSHC 212B/115.
5 TNA PROB11/938/220
6 For the Grubbe family pedigree, see Blackford, J.H. *The Manor and Village of Cherhill: a Wiltshire village from early times to the present day.* 1941, p.76-83.
7 *VCH Wilts* 17, p.139.
8 TNA E134/8Chas1/Mic53. Mary Goddard had been granted a copyhold tenement of Warwicks in 1551, but a lease had been granted to Thomas Pope by William Dunch c.1595.
9 WSHC 473/78.
10 Hobbs, Steven, ed. *Wiltshire Glebe Terriers, 1588-1827.* Wiltshire Record Society, v.56. 2003, p.18.

enclosed.[1] The two farms were separated by agreement in 1703 (confirmed in 1714).[2]

In 1715, the Grubbe property in Avebury descended to Walter's brother William, then to his sister in law Phoebe (of London, and later of Mitcham), in 1753, to Walter's grandson William Hunt, who adopted the additional surname Grubbe, and, in 1772, to his son Thomas. Thomas sold West Kennett Farm to William Tanner c.1784.[3]

The Grubbes also held one or two small cottages in East Kennett; we have already traced the three successive leases held by the Tilly family (above, p.153-4). The Avebury property was only a small portion of their landholdings. Warwicks was only a small part of their manor of Cherhill; they also owned the manor of Potterne, together with other lands elsewhere[4].

The Churchills, Dukes of Marlborough

Coles Bargain was a 180 acre farm in Beckhampton, presumably once a part of the manor of Beckhampton. It was owned by Francis Hawes, one of the unfortunate directors of the South Seas Company, whose lands were sold by Parliamentary directive in 1726.[5] The purchaser was Sarah Churchill, Dowager Duchess of Marlborough. It remained in her family's possession throughout our period[6]. Both Hawes and the Churchill family were absentee landlords: Hawes had houses in London and Reading;[7] the Churchills were given their palace at Blenheim (Oxon), and their dukedom, in reward for the first Duke's successes on the battlefield. One wonders whether Sir Richard Holford was acquainted with either of them.

Landowners in 1751

Landownership in 1751 Avebury can best be studied from the land tax assessment for the tithing of Avebury, although admittedly it does not cover the smaller tithings of Beckhampton and West Kennet.[8] The assessment lists landowners, as well as some tenants, although it does not locate the property on which tax was paid. Most tenants paid tax on behalf of their landlords. Three of them – John Rose, James Pope, and Stephen Browning - all had multiple

1 WBR. Notes on West Kennett Farm by Dorothy Treasure.
2 Ditto.
3 *VCH Wilts* 12, p.97.
4 Blackford, op cit. See also V.C.H. vols.7 & 17.
5 WSHC 3724/2. Act, 7 George I, c.28. *London Gazette*, 21st January 1723, p.2.
6 WSHC 371/1, pt.1. Abstract of title. See also 623/1.
7 Carswell, John. *The South Sea Bubble*. Cresset Press, 1961, p.279.
8 WSHC 184/3.

tenancies; Rose and Pope had their own estates, as well as the properties they tenanted.

Stayner Holford, the lord of the manor of Avebury, was the most heavily taxed; his tenant John Rose paid £40 on his behalf. John Norris had two separate farms, on which his tenants paid a total of £34 10s. James Pope paid £11 on Mr Grant's estate. And Stephen Browning paid £8 1s 6d for Mr Hopkins estate. These were the four largest estates in the parish, although the toll gates, and the (un-named) excise officer, both paid £15. None of these landlords actually lived in the parish, although Stayner Holford probably took up residence in 1754, after he was forced to take his property in hand by his tenant's bankruptcy.

There were 47 smaller landowners. Some estates were let to tenants, as we will see, but many were owner occupied. For example, the vicar, James Mayo, paid £2 8s for his vicarage, and William Fowler, alehouse keeper at the Hare and Hounds, paid 12s 'for his estate'. Henry Howson, one of the assessors, collected £5 from himself. Most, however, were assessed at under £1. John Robinson, the carpenter, paid 15s 6d 'for 6 tenements adjoining his house;' one wonders if he or his father had built them. No fewer than eighteen householders paid 3s each for their houses. That included, amongst others, John Clements, the schoolmaster, Nathan Horsell, the shepherd, and Philip Crook, the mason.[1]

Enclosure

In 1788, Beckhampton Farm was owned by James Sutton, esq. A survey[2] conducted by Richard Richardson of Devizes shows that it covered 208 acres (including a share in 315 acres of Down equivalent to 88 acres), and was worth £118. The property had been improved recently by exchanges (presumably in the common fields), but Sutton argued that it would be 'very much improved if the same were late [sic] out in severalty'. That argument applied equally to the lands of other proprietors in Avebury, and had frequently been made. Before the enclosure act of 1792, much enclosure and exchange of lands took place piecemeal. In the late sixteenth century, for example, John Truslow had the Wall Ditch fenced.[3] In the late seventeenth century, Walter Grubb enclosed pasture near the Kennett Avenue, which became part of West Kennett

---

1 For their families, see above, chapter 3.
2 WSHC 248/195.
3 WANHS Wiltshire Genealogy, v. A-A, f.90-91.

Farm.[1] He and Richard Smith exchanged lands in 1703.[2] Four acres of land in Kennett Fields were newly enclosed in 1720.[3] Land close to the new Catherine Wheel inn had been recently exchanged and enclosed in 1754.[4] When Stayner Holford inherited his estate in 1742, Thomas Smith wrote to him that 'Mr Norris desired me to acquaint you that several proposals had been made to your relations that were last possest of your estate in order to exchange such lands as lay in Avebury, that each estate might be in several, by which meanes both his and your estate would be the more valuable by a great many hundred pounds'.[5] Holford was suspicious; he thought that 'the exchange of land as now transacted may lay a foundation for many litigations amongst the representatives or successors of the several proprietors now negotiating as there is no Act of Parliament to give sanction to such procedures'.[6] Nevertheless, it was obvious that some consolidation was needed. Robert Rose informed Stayner Holford that one estate he was considering purchasing was 'far from being compact, that some of the lands lie near three miles distant from the other ... The largest piece of ground belonging to this estate contains about eight acres, which is just without the Wall Ditch. The other pieces lie scattered all over the fields in single acres & halfs at a mile & a half distances on each side of the village'.[7] Holford was advised, if he did purchase, that he should also purchase two other small estates which lay contiguously, which could then be merged as a single farm. A few years late, in 1749, John Norris wrote to Stayner Holford, observing that 'there seems now to be a general spirit amongst ye landholders of ye tithing of Avebury to throw their estates into severalty by making mutual exchanges, & to this they are very much engaged by seeing the advantages their neighbours hope from an agreement of ye same nature'.[8] Norris thought that the exchange of land would be attended with little expense, since enclosure (that is, fencing) would not be necessary.[9] However, he thought that action was needed immediately, because his neighbours were 'very fickle & inconstant'. Stayner Holford was approached to see if he would agree to

1   Notes in WBR on West Kennett Farm.
2   WSHC 568/5. Deed, Walter Grubbe to Richard Smith, 2nd June 1703.
3   WSHC 488/1. Abstract of title of John Nalder; 488/12. Assignment of mortgage, 19th November 1763 (recites 1720 lease).
4   WSHC 1409/16/3, pt.2. Mary Stretch's marriage settlement, 5th March 1754. See also grant by the devizees of Caleb Bailey, 6th May 1755.
5   WSHC 184/1, pt.2. Letter, Thomas Smith to Stayner Holford, 29th May 1743.
6   WSHC 184/1, pt.2. Undated note by Stayner Holford.
7   WSHC 184/1, pt.2. Letter, James Mayo to Stayner Holford, 12th July 1746.
8   WSHC 184/1, pt.2. Letter, John Norris to Stayner Holford, 24th May 1749.
9   WSHC 184/1, pt. 1. John Norris to Staynor Holford, 24th May 1749.

relinquish his right of feeding sheep on some of the land in question, but gave a very cautious answer, observing that there was no proposal for an act of Parliament to give sanction to the exchange.[1] As it turned out, the fickleness Norris mentioned meant that enclosure was delayed for another four decades, despite continued recognition of the benefits it could bring. In 1772, Arthur Jones thought that enclosure would increase the value of his estate by between £60 and £100. The only reason he did not pursue the idea was that he was too unwell to give it the 'pains attention & expence' it required.[2] When James Sutton had a terrier of his land compiled in 1788, he noted that 'the estate has in some small degree been benefitted by exchanges, but would be very much improved if the same were late out in severalty'.[3]

When Adam Williamson came into possession of the manor of Avebury, he took the initiative. First, he obtained advice from John Ward, the Marlborough attorney, on how to obtain an enclosure act.[4] He then presumably called a meeting of the freeholders, although we have no record of the actual meeting. We do know that Ward posted a notice on the church door, and that he personally attended the church on three successive Sundays in order to explain Williamson's proposals.[5] There was evidently some debate, with both Mr Peter Holford and Charles Simpkins offering some objections.[6] In the end, however, only William Crook refused to sign the petition to Parliament.[7] The act for 'dividing and allotting several open and common lands and grounds within the parish of Avebury' was passed in 1792, and the Commissioners met regularly before making their award in 1795.[8] Richard Hickley, who attended most of their meetings, described their work as 'a very troublesome business, so many customs & rights to set forth, requires great care'.[9]

The act did not cover the whole parish, but only those lands which had not previously been enclosed. It omitted the land north-west of the village, and the whole of West Kennett. The fourteen landowners it mentions did

1 WSHC 184/1. Letter, Staynor Holford, probably to Peter Holford, 29th May 1750.
2 WSHC 271/2. Arthur Jones's Advice to his Sucessors, 11th December 1772.
3 WSHC 248/195.
4 WSHC 184/6. Memorandum of John Ward.
5 WSHC 184/6. Letter, Richard Hickley to Mrs Williamson, 22nd August 1791.
6 WSHC 184/6. Letter, Richard Hickley to Mrs Williamson, 3rd August 1791.
7 WSHC 184/6. Letter, Richard Hickley to Mrs Williamson, 6th March 1792.
8 WSHC 212A/31/4 & A1/EA 95
9 WSHC 184/6. Letter, Richard Hickley to Mrs Williamson, 8th June 1792. Hickley's expenses attending meetings are recorded on a number of occasions in his accounts, WSHC 184/7.

not, therefore, include everyone owning property in the parish. The greatest landowner was Sir Adam Williamson, who owned 714 acres. His connection by marriage, Peter Holford, owned 419 acres. Charles Simpkins and James Sutton both had just over 200 acres. Farms of between 100 and 200 acres were held by Thomas Webb Dyke (147 acres), the Duke of Marlborough (171 acres), James Sutton (201 acres), Richard Thring (133 acres), and Robert Nalder (182 acres). All except Nalder were non-residents. As has been seen, Thring and Nalder were trustees of a dissenting charity; it may be that their lands were actually vested in them as trustees. Nalder probably farmed both properties himself.

Sarah Nalder, Robert's widowed mother, was another proprietor; she held four acres of arable. Four others, including the non-resident vicar, James Mayo, together with William Crook, John Griffin, and John Dore, also had small acreages. John Dore was the smallest proprietor; he owned just over an acre of arable in Folly Hill Field, just behind the inn, which had probably once been used to accommodate drovers' cattle. His name recurs in no other source that has been traced, although it is possible that he was related to the Dore family of Burbage. The letters of John Ward, Williamson's agent, and Richard Hickley, his bailiff, together with Hickley's accounts, describe the process of enclosure in some detail.[1] Both attended the Commissioners' meetings, but Hickley thought that Ward was there merely so that he could send in a bill for his attendance: writing to Mrs Williamson, he commented that Ward was 'of no more use with regard to the exchange of your property'.[2]

Enclosure cost much money. The expenses of the commissioners and surveyors, etc., totalled £891 6s 2d; Williamson was expected to pay £266 12s 4d. That was not all. The land had been divided up between the proprietors, but they still had to be bounded and prepared for farming in severalty. Hickley's accounts in the following years are full of payments for planting hedges, making banks, and levelling land.[3] In August 1793, the Commissioners paid him £49 towards the building of a bridge across the Winterbourne, between Waden Hill and Silbury Meadow, which was required by the enclosure process.[4]

A memorandum probably prepared (apparently) for William Norris notes that the even greater sum of £2017 10s was 'expended on account of

---

1 WSHC 184/6 & 184/7.
2 WSHC 184/6. Letter, Richard Hickley to Mrs Williamson, 4th September 1792.
3 WSHC 184/7.
4 WSHC 184/7. See also 184/6. Letter, Richard Hickley to Mrs Williamson, 4th December 1792.

the several exchanges of lands for the further advancement of said estates'.[1] This presumably refers to the 1795 enclosure, although it is possible that it concerns earlier enclosures. The same memorandum also notes £156 10s spent on 'inclosing and fencing a great part of said lands, which before was common field, and subject to others right of feed'. Norris was dis-satisfied with the results; he complained that his estates were 'now lett, at a less rent than they have been for fourscore years past', and that the enclosure had not been advantageous to him.[2]

Tithes

It has already been pointed out that most of the parish had been under monastic ownership prior to the Reformation. That meant that most of the great tithes had been paid to ecclesiastical institutions, rather than to the incumbent, although the latter retained the small tithes. Great tithes were, however, due to the incumbent on a piece of land beside the church, and on lands in Eastbrook, Beckhampton, and West Kennett.[3] The amounts due to the vicar from some of these were disputed.[4] A composition of £4 per annum was, however, still being paid by the lord of the manor in the 1790s for some of the disputed tithes.[5]

The impropriated tithes were sold off by the Crown, and passed to lay impropriators. Many landowners bought up the tithes payable on their own lands, thus effectively extinguishing them. However, others owned tithes payable by other landowners. In 1632, Thomas Smith, appointed bailiff of Avebury manor, became responsible for collecting tithes worth £300 per annum.[6] In the 1630s, John Pope took a two-year lease of Avebury manor's tithes in Winterbourne Monkton for £47 per annum.[7] In 1701, the tithes of West Kennett, owned by Charles Tooker, were valued at £90.[8] In 1789, Mr Amor was assessed to the poor rate on tithes valued at £60.[9] The 1795 enclosure award[10] identifies tithe liabilities; the Commissioners did not extinguish them,

1 WSHC 1259/41.
2 WSHC 184/1, pt.1. Letter, William Norris to Stayner Holford, 2nd March 1762.
3 Hobbs, Steven, ed. *Wiltshire glebe terriers 1588-1827.* Wiltshire Record Society 56. 2003, p.17-18.
4 See below, p.397.
5 WSHC 184/7.
6 WANHS Genealogy mss., v.A-A, p.109.
7 TNA E134/9and10Chas1/Hil1.
8 WSHC P3/2/392.
9 WSHC 473/352.
10 WSHC A1/EA 95.

but rather transferred the liability to pay of specific landowners to the new allotments made to them. Thus Richard Thring and Robert Nalder had their liability transferred to new allotments in Ratland Field. Similarly, William Crook's liability to pay tithes were transferred to his new allotments in Houndsplot Field.

Landowners at the end of the Eighteenth Century

At the end of the eighteenth century, the pattern of land ownership was similar to that in 1751, although there were fewer small proprietors. In 1790,[1] Adam Williamson, heir to the Holford estate, paid land tax on lands valued at £380. William Norris's estate was valued at £307, and Charles Simpkins at £230. Robert Nalder occupied the estate of Caleb Bailey's Charity[2], valued at £118, and there were thirteen other estates valued at between £5 and £75. Three others paid on lands valued at £3 or £4, but there were eight who paid tax of four shillings each on property which they occupied. These figures seem to cover the whole parish, rather than just the tithing, and suggest that the number of owner occupiers was decreasing.

In 1798, the land tax return[3] indicates that Avebury property was in the hands of 27 landowners, excluding those whose property was worth less than £1 per annum. The returns (for Avebury and West Kennett) do not indicate which properties individual landowners held, but that may be worked out from other sources, and the tax paid provides a rough indication of the extent of their landholding (although it ignores property held in other parishes). Sir Adam Williamson, heir to Arthur Jones, and to the Holfords, and lord of the manor of Avebury, was the greatest proprietor. He paid £50 19s 5d for his main property – presumably the manor - plus £1 16s 8d for the inn tenanted by Mr Hatchett[4], and another 12s for a property let to his bailiff, Richard Hickley. Beckhampton Farm (now Galteemore), which had been purchased by Sir Richard Holford in 1710[5] was in the possession of his grandson Peter Holford, who paid £28 6s 8d.

The Norris family estate has already been discussed. By 1798, their Avebury property had been reduced in size, and their tenant, John Brown, paid £14 15s 7d land tax. He also paid £28 18s 2d on that portion of the Norris estate he had purchased in 1796. The Duke of Marlborough's estate has

1 WSHC A1/345/18A.
2 Described as 'Mr Thring's estate' in the 1790 land tax assessment.
3 TNA IR23/96/189, f.249-50 & 255.
4 See below, p.241 & p.320 for the Flying Waggon.
5 See above, p.216.

also already been mentioned; he paid a mere £8 3s 6d on his Beckhampton farm.

William Hopkins paid £28 18s 2d land tax. Hopkins' father, Sir John, had purchased a part of the former manor of Avebury Trusloe from his brother in law, Charles Simpkins (whose family had owned it for at least twenty years) just after the enclosure, c.1795, but died the following year.[1] He was a London alderman (and former lord mayor), who also owned a share in the Verdigris works (for dyeing or medicinal purposes) at Newnham (Gloucestershire), and an estate in Monmouthshire, in addition to his London interests.[2]

James Sutton, who was assessed to pay £11 10s in 1798, inherited his Avebury estate (another portion of the old manor of Avebury Trusloe), as well as other substantial estates, from his father, Prince Sutton, a wealthy clothier of Devizes, who described himself as 'esquire' in his will. Prince had purchased it in 1749, and died in 1779.[3] James Sutton served as MP for Devizes 1765-80, and as sheriff for the county in 1785.[4] He owned property in 15 local parishes in 1796, and had a rent roll totalling £5,584 18s 6d; his tenant at Beckhampton, William Philpot, paid him £125 per annum.[5] When he died in 1801, James Sutton was seated at New Park, Devizes;[6] his estate was valued at £52,483 10s 10d.[7]

Thomas Webb Dyke (probably of Winterbourne Dauntsey)[8] paid £15 4s 1d for one of his properties, and £1 11s 9d for another. These were presumably the farms at Chestermans and Higdens respectively, which had been bequeathed to him by Sarah Dyke Howson in 1787.[9]

The Duke of Marlborough was a major landowner, although his estate in Avebury was small. He paid a mere £8 3s 6d land tax for a 180 acre farm at

1 VCH Wilts 12, p.93. It was purchased before he leased it to John Amor, 16th April 1795, cf.WSHC 873/262, but he did not begin paying land tax until 1796, cf. A1/345/18A. For the relationship, see Howard, Joseph Jackson & Crisp, Frederick A., eds. *Visitation of England and Wales. Notes*, vol.1. 1896, p.1.
2 Howard & Crisp, op cit, p.1-2.
3 VCH Wilts 12, p.96; TNA PROB 11/1058/346. Prince also purchased the Caswell family's property at Bishops Cannings in 1748; cf. WSHC 248/62. For his family, see Waylen, James. *A history, Military and Municipal, of the ancient Borough of Devizes*. Longman Brown & Co., 1859, p.554.
4 History of Parliament Trust www.historyofparliamentonline.org
5 GA D1571/E56. Rental.
6 TNA PROB 11/1365/39.
7 Baynes, Simon. *The Forgotten Country House: the Rise and Fall of Roundway Park*. Quiller, 2009, p.30.
8 See will of Thomas Webb Dyke, 1822, TNA PROB 11/1660/225.
9 WSHC P3/H/1476.

Coles Bargain in Beckhampton, which, as has been seen, had been acquired by a former Duchess in 1726.[1]

Mr Griffin, who paid £12 16s 7d land tax in 1798, and whose property was tenanted by Mr Mundy (it had previously been in the tenancy of William Crook), was probably John Griffin of West Lavington, who may have been related to the Avebury family of that name.

All of the foregoing were absentee landlords. A few other owners lived locally. Mrs Martyn and William Tanner were the most substantial landowners in West Kennett. Martyn paid land tax amounting to £17 17s 11¾d; Tanner's two properties paid £41 0s 4d. All of their properties were tenanted by Robert Lavington.

A number of properties in 1798 were owner occupied. That included Avebury manor, which, had been taken in hand by Stayner Holford in 1754 and never re-let – although it was run by a bailiff whilst General Williamson was in Jamaica. Several other large properties, as well as many of the smaller ones, were also owner occupied. John Brown, William Crook, and Robert Nalder, were all substantial landowners (in Avebury terms) who farmed their own lands. William Crook (the son in law of Robert Nalder, and perhaps the brother in law of John Brown's father[2]), who paid £8 11s 7d, was probably the owner of Rowses, which had once been owned by the Goldsmith family.[3] Rowses was not included in the enclosure award, but he also owned ten acres of arable in Houndsplot Field. Crook may also have occupied a part of his wife's grandmother's property.[4]

Robert Nalder was a substantial owner occupier, who paid £14 14s 4d land tax in 1798, plus 14s 8d on land let to Mrs Rennald. He also held a property jointly with Richard Thring, which was probably (as noted above) vested in them both as trustees of Caleb Bailey's charity, which Nalder tenanted, and on which he paid £12 5s 3d tax.[5] Thring had a house in Avebury (presumably the Dissenters' chapel), which was licenced for dissenting worship,[6] but probably

1 *VCH Wilts* 12, p.96. See above, p.220.
2 WSHC P3/B/1742.
3 *VCH Wilts* 12, p.94.
4 The land tax assessment refers to 'Mr Cook', which may perhaps be in error for Crook. And there were other Crooks in the parish who may have been intended; cf. chapter 3.
5 See chapters 3 and 9.
6 Chandler, John, ed. *Wiltshire Dissenters' Meeting House Certificates and Registrations, 1689-1852*. Wiltshire Record Society 40. 1985, p.35 & 38. In 1790 it was referred to as being owned jointly by Richard Thring and Robert Nalder, who were probably acting as trustees.

actually lived in Wilton. He paid £12 5s 3d on this land.

Fifteen of the 1798 taxpayers were assessed at under £5. That included Thomas Nalder, Robert's brother, whose lease of West Kennett Farm (on which he paid 16s 3¼d), had been bequeathed to him in his father's 1762 will.[1] It also included the vicar, Rev James Mayo, who let his glebe (on which he paid £1 11s 9d) to his curate, Rev. Charles Lucas. He was also said to 'occupy' property at Beckhampton on which he paid 11s 10d. In fact, he lived in Wimborne Minster (Dorset).[2] In addition, he had a small property in West Kennett, let to William Tanner and Robert Lavington, on which he paid 19s.

Three properties on which land tax of 4s each was paid were probably occupied by relatives of their owners. Jonathan Russell's property was occupied by his sister. Two of John Clements' properties were occupied by his son William, and his niece, Rachel Dixon.[3] Another son, Joseph, occupied his father's property at Beckhampton from at least as early as 1782, and inherited it in 1798. Widow Clements (presumably his mother) became the occupier.[4] Michael Wiltshire, who was probably related to Thomas Griffin, occupied the latter's property. John Strange, another small landowner, let his property to Mr Mills. In previous years he himself had been tenant to John Nalder (in 1780) and Sarah Nalder (in 1790).[5]

Eight other small landowners occupied their own property. Most were tradesmen, who owned the houses they lived in and not much more. Samuel Fowler, who paid 8s land tax in 1798, and who died shortly after, was a carpenter when he married Sarah Rogers in 1770.[6] John Clements, the former schoolmaster, was one of the few 1798 taxpayers who had also been assessed in 1751; he paid 4s. He actually died before the assessment was raised, but these assessments were frequently out-dated when they were made. Stephen Crook was a carpenter, who had purchased his house in 1761.[7] It had a shop and a saw-house where he could practice his trade. Joseph Caswell, the village blacksmith, had been paying his 4s land tax regularly since 1791.[8] James Strugnell, who paid £1 5s 5d, and redeemed his land tax in 1799, was innkeeper at the White Hart, and served as high constable in 1797.[9] The will

1 TNA PROB 11/938/220.
2 See below, p.xxxx.
3 John died the year before, but land tax assessments were frequently outdated.
4 WSHC A1/345/22A.
5 WSHC A1/345/18A.
6 Sarum Marriage Licence Bonds, 1770 www.findmypast.co.uk
7 WSHC 1102/1.
8 WSHC 473/277; A1/345/18A.
9 WSHC 9/23/1; P1/1808/39 (1808 will).

of James Paradise, proved in 1837, tell us he was a yeoman; he also paid 4s land tax. Mr Hitchcock, who paid 19s 7d, was probably the former innkeeper at the Catherine Wheel.

The Tenants

What of the tenants? The earliest evidence for them is William Sharington's survey of Avebury manor in 1548. It lists twenty-one tenants, as well as the 'farmers' of the demesne, John Shuter and his son.[1] The word 'farmer', incidentally, had a narrower meaning at the beginning of our period than it does today; it referred to substantial leaseholders, such as the tenants of Avebury Great Farm, rather than smaller agriculturalists. Here the term is generally used in the modern sense. The majority of tenants were copyholders holding a house, out-buildings, and a yardland amounting to forty or fifty acres. Those acres were scattered across the manor, in different fields. Richard Plomer, for example, in addition to his house and outhouses, had 'a barton a garden and orchard and a close lying byhynde the said tenement conteynyng di[2] acre of pasture a close called Northehey conteynyng i acre of mede, a quarter of an acre of mede in the west mede, a quarter of acre of mede in brode mede, a quarter of an acre of mede in the northe mead, and ii severall leses for shepe apon borden hyll conteynyng iiii acres of pasture, xxii acres of arrable land in the west feld, and xxii acres of arrable land in the Northe feld', in all amounting to 50¼ acres.[3] Plomer was one of the more substantial tenants. By contrast, Henry Godman merely held a two-roomed house, a barton, a garden, an orchard and half an acre of meadow, for which he paid 12d rent per annum. Nicholas Bromham and John Pope both had cottages in addition to the houses in which they lived; presumably they sub-let them.

Copyhold tenants' entry fines were almost all below £2; their rents were similar. Andrew Smith, whose father John had been admitted to his copyhold in 1517, paid 33s per annum. Most had paid their entry fines to the Shuters (the farmers of the demesne), to whom they also owed labour dues at harvest time.

There were also six tenants at will. John Colby was a mere cottager, with a barton, a garden, and a quarter of an acre pasture. All the others were roughly on a par with the other copyholders in terms of their holdings and common

1   WSHC 2664/1/2D/8. The manor included property at Catcomb (in Hilmarton) and Barbury (in Ogbourne St Andrew), whose tenants are excluded from this discussion.
2   Half.
3   WSHC 2664/1/2D/8.

rights. Those rights included not just pasture for sheep; tenants could also use the Downs to pasture five or six 'rother best', that is, oxen, and one or two horses.

The farmers, John Shuter and his son John, leased Avebury Great Farm from Fotheringhay College in 1531.[1] John the elder died in 1598, although his will was not proved until 1613.[2] His son (who was also one of the manorial tenants) died before him. William Dunch sometimes kept the demesne in hand in the early seventeenth century,[3] although John Goldsmith was the tenant c.1623,[4] c.1630,[5] and again in 1639 (when the manor was sold).[6] Thomas Smith leased the farm for four years from 1632, at a rent of £310 per annum; he also acted as bailiff, and rented his landlords' impropriate tithes for £130 per annum.[7] After Sir John Stawell had purchased the property, Smith acted as the new manorial lord's agent in negotiation with Goldsmith over the latter's debts.[8] In 1638, presumably after the expiry of his lease from Dunch, Smith took a life-lease of a substantial farm in Beckhampton, which he subsequently (in 1647) purchased outright.[9] As has been seen, he was also lord of the manor of West Kennett.

Thomas Goldsmith, John Goldsmith's son, was the tenant in 1642, paying a rent of £410 per annum.[10] By 1652, the tenant was Richard Smith, Thomas's son.[11] The farm may have been taken in hand in the 1660s, when Ralph Stawell lived in the manor house;[12] the next known tenant was John Baskerville, who gave up his lease in 1689.[13] Twenty years later, Sir Richard Holford commented that his 'ill husbandry' had 'very much abused both the land and the landlord', adversely affecting the value of the farm.[14]

1   WSHC 2664/1/2D/8.
2   TNA PROB 11/124/472. See above, p.136-7, for the dispute concerning this will.
3   *VCH Wilts.*, 12, p.98.
4   WANHS Wiltshire Genealogy A-A, p.110.
5   TNA E134/9and10Chas1/Hil1.
6   WANHS. Wiltshire Genealogy A-A, p.115.
7   WANHS. Wiltshire Genealogy A-A, p. 109. See also TNA E134/9and10Chas1/Hil1.
8   TNA C6/21/114.
9   WSHC 212B/104. Conveyance, Richard Truslow to Thomas Smith, 10th June 1647.
10 TNA C6/21/114.
11 WANHS. Wiltshire Genealogy A-A, p.119.
12 See above, p.148-9.
13 Perhaps the son of Thomas Baskerville, lord of the manor of Winterbourne Bassett. See *VCH Wilts* 12, p.187-8, & the will of Thomas's widow Mary, WSHC P3/B/1234.
14 WSHC 184/1, pt.2. Letter, Sir Richard Holford to Richard Chandler, 2nd June

Avebury Great Farm was, according to Sir Richard Holford, 'too big for ordinary tennants'. He frequently complained of the 'great troble' ... 'of changing a tenant in such a farme'.[1] That was why he was reluctant to lose the tenant who had leased the property from his predecessor. John White, the vicar, did suggest two other tenants, but neither proposal went any further.[2] Another potential tenant was a Quaker teacher: that would never do if contention was to be avoided.[3] Holford's negotiations when his tenant refused to renew his lease were difficult. He had hopes that Richard Chandler of Woodborough would take the farm, but in the end Chandler refused to pay the rent that Holford demanded.[4]

At the end of the seventeenth century, the tenant of Avebury Great Farm was undoubtedly the leading tenant in the parish. That followed the usual pattern on the chalk downs. Elsewhere in Wiltshire, when lords withdrew from direct cultivation, they usually split their lands into multiple farms. On the Downs, however, demesnes were, as in Avebury, usually let to a single tenant.[5] Indeed, as we have seen, some other properties were joined together to be farmed as single units: John Brown's tenancy of Brunsdens and Pophams before 1796 being a case in point.

John Lord Stawell let Avebury Great Farm to William Skeat in 1689[6]. When Sir Richard Holford purchased the estate, Stawell's steward, John Bennett, offered him 'a substantiall tenant', but Skeat's lease had some years to run.[7] He remained there until 1710. Sir Richard Holford regularly compiled accounts of his dealings with Skeat. The rent was originally £350 per annum, although when Holford became landlord Skeat sought to use him as a go-between with the Lord Stawell's trustees; he claimed that Stawell had promised to 'allow mee £100 out of my rent in consideraton of the bad times & my

1709.
1   WSHC 184/1, pt.2. Letter, Sir Richard Holford to Richard Chandler, 2nd June 1709.
2   WSHC 184/1, pt.2. Letters between John White & Sir Richard Holford, 20th & 30th October 1708.
3   WSHC 184/1, pt.2. Letter, Sir Richard Holford to Richard Chandler, 15th June 1709.
4   WSHC 184/1, pt.2. Letter, Sir Richard Holford to Richard Chandler, 15th June 1709 & 21st July 1709
5   Hare, John. 'Agriculture and Rural Settlement in the Chalklands of Wiltshire and Hampshire, from c.1200-c.1500', in Aston, Michael, & Lewis, Carenza, eds. *The medieval landscape of Wiltshire*. Oxbow monographs 46. Oxbow Books, 1994, p.162.
6   WSHC 184/4. Lease, Lord Stawell to William Skeat, 1689.
7   WSHC 184/1, pt.2. Sir Richard Holford to John White, 30th October 1700.

loses'.[1] Similarly, in 1701, when renewal was due and the price of corn was low, the landlord was forced to reduce the rent to £320 per annum.[2] Had he not done so, he could have lost a good tenant, and possibly not been able to find another. Despite the abatement, rent was not always paid on time. However, Holford was prepared to accept a bond when Skeat did not have ready cash. In 1708 two bonds, for £350 and £200, were outstanding.[3]

The vicar, John White, accused Skeat in 1700 of sub-letting parts of the farm, unbeknown to his landlord. That might have had deleterious effects on the farm, as sub-tenants were less likely to obey conditions in Skeat's lease affecting fertility and the course of husbandry. Holford thanked White for his information, but may well have suspected it, given the animosity between White and the dissenting Skeat.[4] Nine years later, he noted that 'I don't know that the farmer [Skeat] hath been an ill husband upon it'.[5] Nevertheless, landlord and farmer were unable to agree on terms when Skeat's lease came to an end. Holford's letters[6] trace their 'discourses' (as Holford described them) in detail. In the end, Holford accused Skeat of having 'left all the bounds, fences &c in great disorder and defective'.[7]

Skeat's original 1689 lease from John Lord Stawell [8]made provision for Stawell's occasional visit to his Avebury manor house. Skeat had to ensure that Stawell's horses were provided with 'wheat, straw, and lytter', and also with 'good and sufficient hey and other provinder'. Holford similarly relied on his tenant to provide various services. Horses had to be fed; a 1708 account reveals expenditure on 'horse meale', including hay, for 72 nights. Putting horses out to grass overnight cost 4d per night, and incurred expenditure of 7s. Skeat provided food and drink for his landlord's table. Expenditure on 'butchers meate, fowle, bacon, butter, cheese, small beere, &c' totalled £5 13s; 'of drinks, halfe hogsheads, 16 bushells of malt & 2 of hopps' cost £2 15s 4d. Holford's manor also provided for his London establishment: in 1707, Skeat sent up 103 pounds of cheese. He also sold his landlord a 'fine younge coach horse', which had to be delivered to London. Part of the £25 paid for the horse was

1   WSHC 184/1, pt.2. William Skeat to Sir Richard Holford, 17th May 1695.
2   WSHC 184/4/1. Agreement re abatement of rent, 1701.
3   WSHC 184/4/1. Account 22nd September 1708.
4   WSHC 184/1, pt.2. Letters between John White and Richard Holford, 20th & 30th October 1708.
5   WSHC 184/1, pt.2. Letter, Sir Richard Holford to Richard Chandler, 2nd June 1709.
6   WSHC 184/1.
7   GA 1956/E2/8.
8   WSHC 184/4/1.

discounted by Holford's sale of a wood pile to Skeat. Holford commented that 'I did think the wood pyle wold have yielded much more', and hoped that his tenant would have a 'profitable bargain to him'. He evidently sought good relations with his tenant.

When Holford was not in residence, Skeat acted as his agent, paying various local taxes, including the land tax, and seeking re-imbursement from Holford. He even paid the bell ringers 5s; for what purpose is not stated. Holford also employed his tenant to supervise building work. Skeat paid various tradesmen: glaziers, tylers, masons, and a 'helper in the stable'. He carried bricks and lime, and paid the Calne lime burner's bill. He even weeded the hedges in Holford's garden — or at least paid one of his servants to do so. And he and his successor, John Rose, acted as guides when Holford wanted to take his coach to Westonbirt, or across the Downs.[1]

John Rose probably first had dealings with Sir Richard Holford when the latter was considering purchasing Higdens, the farm which Rose then tenanted. Rose provided him with much useful information, and thus placed himself in a position to take over Avebury Great Farm when Skeat gave up his lease.[2] Rose died in 1720. Confusingly, he shared his name with a relative who became tenant in 1733.

It may be assumed that Rose continued to provide the services which Skeat had provided to his landlord. Certainly, similar arrangements continued when Peter Griffin became tenant to Holford's widow in 1722. Griffin had to renew his lease in 1729, after Richard Holford inherited his grandfather's estate[3]. He paid rent of £360 per annum, and, like his predecessor, had to ensure that when his landlord visited he was well supplied with food for himself and his horses. He was also required to spread dung annually on the Old Orchard; in return, he was granted the right to the fruit grown there and in the Cherry Court, provided he looked after the trees. Like his grandfather, Richard was tolerant of arrears of rent; indeed, when Holford died Griffin was owing £124 in arrears.[4] His lease was presumably renewed again on similar terms in 1736, when his seven year term came to an end. Peter Griffin paid

1   WSHC 184/8.
2   WSHC 184/1, pt.2. Letter, John Rose to Sir Richard Holford, 23rd February 1711/12.
3   WSHC 435/24/1/7. Lease, 1st March 1729/30. But his original lease in 1722 had been for seven years anyway; WSHC 184/1, pt.2. Peter Griffin's Proposals for taking Avebury Farm. According to Stayner Holford, Griffin took another lease in 1732, but he may have mistaken the date; cf. WSHC 184/4, pt.1. Abstract of lease made 1739.
4   WSHC 184/4/1. Receipt, 16th November 1742.

him in 1743 for produce supplied to the manor house: eggs, pigeons, bread, chickens, cheese, milk and cream.[1] Griffin had to provide five loads of dung for the garden, and to sell fruit from the orchard on behalf of his landlord.[2] He even had to purchase a horse on behalf of his landlord.[3] In 1741, he was instructed to pay no fewer than twelve bills, totalling over £79, for items as various as malt, gloves, beer, labourers' wages, a mason's bill, and a blacksmith's bill.[4] Griffin's disbursements for his landlord amounted to over £655 in 1743.[5]

Stayner Holford, who inherited the estate in 1742, was not quite as easy a landlord. He was insistent on his need to receive overdue rent. 'I would not be so pressing upon you for mone, but that my late brother's creditors are pressing on me, which cannot be paid but out of the arrears of rent due from you, as particularly directed by my brother'.[6] That raised difficulties for Griffin, who was liable to lose money by selling his produce when prices were too low: he commented that 'corn sells very low and a £100 is a great while a raising and must desire you not to be so pressing on me for money at a time when corn is so very cheap. In some time it may double prise'.[7] The money could not be raised 'without some considerable disadvantage, corn being so cheap'.[8]

Griffin's difficulties in raising money probably caused his new landlord to refuse to renew his lease, which had fallen in on Robert Holford's death. Word of Griffin's unruly servants,[9] and doubts concerning his upkeep of the farm, may also have been relevant. James Mayo noted that 'the walls of the pond and the yard are very much out of repair' in 1744, and that the new tenant wished his landlord to 'give orders to Peter Griffin to put them into such repair as they ought to be at the expiration of his time'.[10]

Holford's refusal to renew the lease elicited Griffin's response that, considering 'how many years I have lived in it, what care and paine I have taken, and to be turned out so suddenly it grieves me very much, and soe to take one in which is no better than my self'.[11] Griffin hoped that the new

1 WSHC 184/5. Peter Griffin's bill, 1743.
2 WSHC 184/4, pt.1. Abstract of lease, 1732 (made in 1739).
3 WSHC 184/5. Peter Griffin's disbursements, 1741.
4 WSHC 184/4/2. List of 'bills left with Farmer Griffin', 5th November 1740.
5 WSHC 184/5. List of Peter Griffin's disbursements on behalf of Stayner Holford, 1743.
6 WSHC 184/1, pt.2. Letter, Stayner Holford to Peter Griffin, 21st January 1742/3.
7 WSHC 184/1, pt.2. Letter, Peter Griffin to Stayner Holford, 28th January 1742/3.
8 WSHC 184/1, pt.2. Letter, Peter Griffin to Stayner Holford, 23rd March 1742/3.
9 WSHC 184/1, pt.2. Letter, T.H., to Samuel Holford , 26th August 1723.
10 WSHC 184/1, pt.2. Letter, James Mayo to Stayner Holford, 31st March 1744.
11 WSHC 184/1, pt.2. Letter, Peter Griffin to Stayner Holford, 18th October 1743.

tenant, John Rose, 'may prove as good a tennant as I have been. If so, it's more than any of our neighbours take as well acquainted with us both do think, excepting those who have consolation in it'.

Griffin's comment was prescient. John Rose went bankrupt in 1755, much to the astonishment and dismay of his landlord. Holford dismissed the reasons given in the bankruptcy petition as very slight, and thought that since Rose was a farmer, he was not really entitled to be described as a 'dealer and chapman', and therefore not strictly eligible to receive the protection of the bankruptcy laws from imprisonment for debt. Holford himself was subsequently sued in Chancery by Rose's creditors.[1] Worse, from Holford's point of view, was the fact that he was unable to find a suitable tenant. He 'treated with three different persons about it, but they refusing it' on the conditions he sought.[2] The rent he demanded was too great; indeed, that had been part of the reason why Skeat had refused to renew his lease in 1710. One potential tenant had offered £340, but on conditions that Holford thought too onerous.[3] Another had offered £320, but that was thought to be insufficient. Holford felt compelled to take the farm in hand, and stock it himself. The bailiff in 1756 was John Scane.[4] It remained in hand for the rest of our period. In 1776, Arthur Jones, successor to the Holfords, thought that it should not be let for less than £420 per annum.[5] The accounts of Richard Hickley in the 1790s demonstrate why it could not be. In 1792 – the only year for which they are complete – they record a loss of £137 14s 08¼d.[6] Admittedly that was a bad year; Hickley complained at the end of July, just as harvest was due to begin, that 'the weather is very cold and wet, the corn don't ripen'.[7] But the following year's profit (omitting the December account, which is missing) was only £91 17s 04d – not enough to justify a high rent.

Smaller tenants held by a variety of tenures, and had to abide by a variety of conditions.[8] Copyholds were still being granted in the sixteenth century. At the Dissolution of the monasteries, Cirencester Abbey had five copyhold tenants on their manor (Avebury Trusloe), who owed customary

1 See above, p.xxxx, & GA D1956/L1. Letters, Stayner Holford to Peter Holford, 1756-8. Unfortunately, the relevant Chancery records have not been located.
2 WSHC 184/4, pt.1. Letter, Stayner Holford to William Norris, 14th June 1761.
3 WSHC 184/3. Stayner Holford's statement on oath, c.1761.
4 WSHC 184/1, pt.1. Letter, John Mayo to John Scane, February 1756.
5 WSHC 271/16.
6 WSHC 184/7.
7 WSHC 184/6.
8 Conditions of tenancy agreements relating to the maintenance of property are discussed below, p.257-8.

dues to the manorial lord. They were liable to undertake one day's harvest work for every yardland in their tenure, and were also called on to help with haymaking in various specified meadows (although their help was not always requested).[1] The copyholders in the mid-sixteenth century included Richard Brown, Richard Davis, Richard Clifford, and John Brunsden. Richard Davis held by grant from the Abbot, but when he died his son Thomas received a grant from the Crown. The Truslows kept two tenements in hand.[2]

Copyholds continued to be granted on both manors in the early seventeenth century. The Avebury manorial court roll for 1651-7 records a number of grants.[3] For example, in 1653, John Mortimer was admitted to the tenancy of a cottage formerly held by Constance Parker, who had just died. In 1654, Christopher Pope died; the court ordered that his widow Edith was to hold the tenement during her widowhood, according to manorial custom, but she was to pay a heriot of 'the best beast'. At the same court, the homage presented that James Miles had also died, but they did not know who had the right to succeed him.

It is probable that the twelve 'grants' made by John Phelps and Peter Griffin (owners of a small portion of the manor of Avebury Trusloe) between 1681 and 1687 were copyhold; the rents recorded were very small, ranging from 2d to 2s.[4] However, the three life lease, which could be surrendered and renewed, became common in the seventeenth century.

Copyhold, from the landlord's point of view, was inflexible, and rents could be much more easily increased by converting to leasehold tenures.[5] In Avebury, that process was under way as early as 1607, when John Spencer leased Goddard's Farm from Richard Goddard. He paid an entry fine of £145, plus rent of £4 per annum, on a three-life lease.[6] By the end of the century, such leases were more common. For example, in 1692, John Pontin, husbandman, surrendered his lease to John Truslow and renewed it for the lives of himself,

1 TNA E134/41Eliz/Hil8.
2 TNA E134/40and41Eliz/Mich7. According to the evidence of George Brown, Richard's son, half a century later. Another witness in the same Exchequer case, Roger Whithorn, remembered seven tenants, but that may have been some decades later.
3 WSHC 473/52.
4 WANHS Wiltshire Genealogy, v.A-A, p.136-7. Names of tenants are also given in WSHC 184/4/1. Proposed conveyance, John Griffin to Sir Richard Holford, 9th October 1703.
5 Sharpe, J.A. *Early Modern England: A Social History 1550-1760*. Edward Arnold, 1987, p.133.
6 WSHC 371/1, pt.2. Lease, Richard Goddard to John Spencer, 10th July 1607.

Edith his wife, and Mary his daughter[1]. The property was merely a messuage or tenement, with a backside and garden, with common rights on Beckhampton Common for one 'rother beast'. He paid an entry fine of £5 10s, and annual rent of 10s per annum. Similarly, five leases for lives on the manor of West Kennett were granted by the Smiths between 1663 and 1729.[2] Walter Grubbe was another landlord who preferred the three life lease, although in his case he insisted on including 'two grand and well fatted capons' as part of the rent due from the cottage and meadow in West Kennett granted to John Tilly in 1715. Tilly also paid 2s 6d per annum; there was no entry fine.[3] Robert Holford was another landlord who was willing to let small tenements on three life leases. In 1726, he renewed William Philpot's lease of a tenement in Beckhampton without an entry fine, for a mere six shillings per annum.[4] Philpot was to hold the tenement for the lives of his wife and his two sons. Frances Truslow did pay a substantial entry fine - £25 - when she leased two cottages at Beckhampton from Holford in 1734, but her rent was a mere 2s 6d per annum.[5]

The practice of leasing for lives rarely applied to larger holdings, and by the mid-eighteenth century, such leases were ceasing to be made. In 1713, Richard Smith and his son Thomas leased the capital messuage of West Kennett to William Spackman, taking an entry fine of £700, and rent of £55.[6] That was one of the last leases for lives that Thomas Smith made. In 1723, he leased the new building adjacent to his manor house to Francis Popham of Littlecote (Ramsbury) for just seven years, at a rent of £20 per annum.[7] Popham was himself a major landowner.[8] In 1724 Smith leased part of his farm to John Beake for nine years, at a rent of £200 per annum, without an entry fine. In 1729, the same property (probably) was let to Robert Caswell for 9 years at £220 per annum, and in 1745 Ambrose Lanfear succeeded Caswell, paying a rent reduced to £180, but again for nine years.[9] Such arrangements were becoming more typical. Short leases gave landlords greater flexibility in increasing rents. In 1765, for example, John Brown was paying William Norris

1   WSHC 371/1, pt.3.
2   WSHC 568/39.
3   WSHC 212B/112.
4   WSHC 371/1, pt.4. Lease, 17th September 1726.
5   WSHC 371/1, pt.5. Lease, 6th March 1734.
6   WSHC 568/7.
7   Somerset Heritage Centre. DD/PO/6/ Lease, 3rd September 1723, Richard & Thomas Smith to Francis Popham.
8   For his pedigree, see Popham, Frederick W. *A West Country Family: the Pophams from 1150*. The Author, 1976, p.66.
9   WSHC 568/7.

rent of £280 per annum for his two farms in Avebury. Norris increased that by £5 per annum in 1766, by £15 per annum in 1772 (although he attempted to increase it by £35), and by a further £20 in 1777. Brown's rent then stood at £320 per annum.[1]

Tenants at will were in a more precarious position. When John White, the vicar, purchased part of John Griffin's property c.1707, he demanded that the tenants of cottages on his waste take out leases and pay entry fines of £10 each. Christopher Page and John Jerome had lived there for twenty years or more, but were unable to afford to pay, and were threatened with eviction. Their response was to write to Sir Richard Holford and ask for his advice. They evidently thought of him, with some justification, as being on their side.[2]

White's property was sold by his son to Robert Rose, who in turn sold it to Sarah Deavin in 1755.[3] The lease and release recorded that it had been tenanted by John Smith, but a cottage had been divided into two, and let to Joseph Moore and Edward Mazey. It consisted of a cottage and backside, with an orchard and garden. There were five acres of arable dispersed in Hackpen Field and West Field, half an acre of meadow or pasture in Church Close (in Hackpen Field), plus more arable in the marsh in Hackpen Field. There was also common of pasture for three 'rother beasts'.

The 1798 land tax assessment is useful for identifying more substantial tenants. We have already identified several who were also landowners: Robert Nalder, John Brown, and William Crook. We have also identified three small landowners whose property was occupied by their own relatives: John Clements, Jonathan Russell, and Thomas Griffin.

In addition to the three landowners doubling as tenants, there were a number of other substantial tenant farmers: John Amor, William[?] Mundy, Sarah Jefferys and William Philpot. John Amor, yeoman, was the lessee of a farm which had formerly been part of the manor of Avebury Trusloe. He had been the tenant of the Simpkins family, but Sir John Hopkins purchased the freehold in 1795, and Amor renewed his lease at the substantial rental of £250 per annum.[4]

Mr Mundy was another substantial tenant, probably to be identified with the William Mundy who served as high constable of the Hundred in

---

1 WSHC 473/277.
2 WSHC 184/1, pt.1. Letter, Christopher Page & John Jerome to Sir Richard Holford, 18th April 1707.
3 WSHC 435/24/1/8.
4 WSHC 873/262.

1795.[1] His landlord, Mr Griffin, paid land tax of £12 16s 7d on the land he occupied, but nothing more is known of him. Perhaps he sub-let the land.

Sarah Jefferys occupied Peter Holford's estate at Beckhampton, which paid £28 6s 8d land tax annually, throughout the 1780s and 1790s.[2] She was the widow of William Jefferys, and presumably took over the lease when he died in 1778. His estate was probably worth c.£400.[3] Sarah was the daughter of Hannah Griffin, who bequeathed her £175 in her 1777 will.[4] Her husband was a native of Chippenham, but it is likely that he moved to Avebury when, in 1769, he married into a prominent Avebury family,[5] and presumably became Holford's tenant. He served as churchwarden in 1774.[6]

William Philpot was a member of a long established and prolific Avebury family, but was one of ten children of a ninth child, and was described as a labourer when he married Betty King in 1779.[7] In 1786, however, his wealthy husbandman uncle (also named William) bequeathed seven of his siblings £300 each, but gave his nephew 'all my stock of sheep, horses, and all other my cattle, corn, grain, hay, and impliments of husbandry used in the farming business, together also with my household goods'.[8] That enabled him to become a substantial tenant farmer. He occupied the properties of both the Duke of Marlborough and James Sutton at Beckhampton throughout the 1780s and 1790s, and was also described as the 'proprietor' of other land at Beckhampton between 1782 and 1788, although the land tax assessments suggest that this property was purchased by James Sutton c.1789. The farm he tenanted from the Duke of Marlborough was still held on an annual tenancy in 1800.[9] His two Beckhampton tenancies covered c.372 acres in total, and paid land tax of £8 3s 6d and £11 10s respectively.

A little is known of the tenants of Mr Dyke's properties, Chestermans and Higdens. Mr Rider was the tenant of Chestermans, which, as we have seen, was a substantial farm. He was also the innkeeper at Beckhampton House

---

1 WSHC 9/23/1.
2 WSHC A1/345/22A
3 She was bound in £800 as administrator of his estate, cf. WSHC P1/IJ/273. Administrators were usually bound in sums roughly double the presumed value of estates.
4 WSHC P3/G/711.
5 Sarum Marriage Licence Bonds www.findmypast.co.uk
6 WSHC D3/15/18.
7 Sarum Marriage Licence Bonds www.findmypast.co.uk
8 WSHC P3/P/1027.
9 WSHC 623/1.

in 1783,[1] although he had left by 1795.[2] Dyke's tenant at Higdens, Thomas Hatchett was also an innkeeper; he ran the Flying Waggon (now the Waggon and Horses).[3] Both men were named as victuallers of Beckhampton in the 1783 Hundred court rolls. They also both served as constable of the Hundred, Rider in 1787, Hatchett in 1794.[4]

The Flying Waggon was actually owned by the lords of Avebury manor; it was probably the property which Hatchett was said to 'occupy' in 1780, and on which land tax of £1 18s 0d was paid.[5] In 1798, Hatchett was described in the land tax assessment as 'occupier' of a property – presumably the same property – owned by Sir Adam Williamson on which land tax of £1 16s 8d was paid.

West Kennett Farm was tenanted by Richard Green in 1715[6]. In the 1730s (probably) land tax for it was paid by William Caswell.[7] By 1752 the lease was held by John Nalder[8]. When Nalder made his will in 1762[9]; he bequeathed this lease to trustees for his son Thomas.

Three other tenants are discussed in more detail elsewhere. Richard Hickley[10] was the bailiff of Sir Adam Williamson, and leased a cottage from him. Rev Charles Lucas[11] was employed as a curate by the non-resident vicar, and was therefore the 'occupier' of the vicarage. John Russ, Mr Edmunds' tenant, ran the Catherine Wheel.[12]

There are two other tenants recorded in the land tax assessment concerning whom little is known. Mrs Mary Rennald was the tenant of Mr Nalder, and had been so since at least 1790.[13] She was evidently of some status,

1 WSHC P3/C/1078. Will of William Chilcot. He was probably a sub-tenant of Thomas Hatchett; see below.
2 *Bath Chronicle* 1st January 1795.
3 WSHC IR 2.96/189, f.249-50.
4 WSHC 9/23/1. His name is spelt 'Hatchyard', but we may assume he was the same person.
5 WSHC A1/345/18A.
6 WSHC 212B/112.
7 WSHC 184/3. Undated land tax return for West Kennett tything.
8 WSHC 212B/115.
9 TNA PROB11/938/220
10 See p.87-8
11 Moody, Robert. 'The Reverend Charles Lucas (1769-1854) of Avebury and Devizes – a forgotten novelist, miscellaneous writer and crusading clergyman', *WAM*, 104, 2011, p.221-36. See also below, p.407-8
12 Raymond, Stuart A. 'The Inns of Avebury, c.1600-1800', *WAM*, 117, 2024, p.159-67.
13 WSHC A1/345/18A.

as she paid hair powder tax in 1796.[1] Richard Hickley regularly mentioned her in his letters to Mrs Williamson. She was buried 14th March 1804 aged 69. Otherwise, she has not been traced. Neither has Mr Mills, who tenanted the small property owned by Mr Strange, and who bore a common Avebury name.

At the end of the eighteenth century, we know that there were hundreds of poor in Avebury, but little is known of their role as tenants. At this level, the land tax returns are of little use, since they do not record property worth less than £1 per annum. Nor do they record details of labourers who occupied cottages owned by their employers. There are few other sources recording the poor as tenants. We do, however, have some information concerning the Beaven family.

The Beavens were a family of four, including two small children. Their tenure was very insecure, and when the head of the household found himself unable to work, and to pay his rent, the family were in a very vulnerable position, facing an unsympathetic bailiff. Richard Hickley wrote to Mrs Williamson, fearing that 'I shall have some trouble to get Beaven out of the house, tho think he shortly will be starved out … Of course he must go to his own parish'.[2] But it was not until four months later that he was able to report 'have got Beaven out of the house at last, but not a farthing of money, nor ever shall'.[3] Presumably the overseers (perhaps Hickley himself?) had 'removed' them.

What did landlords look for in choosing tenants? We get some clues from Sir Richard Holford's journal. When, in 1711, Richard Caswell wanted to give up his tenancy of Holford's Beckhampton property, he proposed his uncle John as a replacement. Holford was not particularly impressed. John Caswell was 'antient, & haveing 5 or six sons at home with him, several of them very much impaired in their health, & not likely to employ the poor labouring neighbors'.[4] Tenants had to be fit, and Holford thought that one who was elderly, and had several children with poor health, was not desirable. Another consideration was that, if Caswell's children had been fit, they would have reduced the tenant's need to employ labour. That meant there would be less employment for the poor, who would therefore be more likely to claim poor relief. Poor rates were a burden on landlords, so it was desirable that tenants should employ labourers rather than rely on family labour. Holford

1 WSHC A1/395.
2 WSHC 184/6. Letter, Richard Hickley to Mrs Williamson, 4th February 1793.
3 WSHC 184/6. Letter, Richard Hickley to Mrs Williamson, 4th June 1793.
4 GA. D1956/E2/8.

also thought that Thomas Nash of Cannings[1] might prove a better tenant. He was 'liked much better than either of the Caswells, he being a sensible faishionable man & reputed a very honest man and a good husband and about £60 per annum office on estate incomings and a more desirable tenant'. When Richard Caswell said he would not give up his tenancy unless his uncle could take the farm, Holford took umbrage and 'expressly refused', saying that he 'would not have a tennant forct upon mee'. Despite all these considerations, however, John Caswell succeeded his nephew as tenant at Lady Day 1713.[2]

Credit and Mortgages

Not many people in early modern England had much money in their pockets. The scarcity of coin in England is demonstrated by the small number of Avebury people whose appraisers recorded cash in their probate inventories. Coinage was not the primary means of exchange: credit was.[3] There was no banking system; money was either spent, lent to neighbours, or kept in a chest under the bed. Over 41% of Avebury's probate inventories between 1700 and 1850 record credit. That was roughly average nation-wide.[4] Bills, bonds, specialties, and desperate debts are frequently mentioned[5]. These terms encompass two types of loan. The bill without specialty was a promissory note without security, and usually for a small amount, intended as a short loan. Such loans are frequently referred to in the inventories as 'desperate debts', and might prove difficult to recover after the death of the lender, a fact which John Cruse recognised in 1760 by specifying that 'my executor shall not be responseable for any moneys which shall be lost on account of bad security'.[6] The term 'bill' might also include tradesmen's debts recorded in their shop books, and which may not have had any legal paperwork. The bond, by contrast, had security.

1 It is not clear whether this was All Cannings or Bishops Cannings.
2 GA. D1956/E2/8.
3 Muldrew, Craig. *The Economy of Obligation: the Culture of Credit and Social Relations in Early Modern England.* 1998, p.100-3.
4 Raymond, Stuart A. *Seventeenth Century Week St Mary, Cornwall, including an edition of the probate records, 1598 to 1699.* Adelaide MA thesis, 1988, p.123. Available at https://digital.library.adelaide.edu.au/dspace/handle/2440/122518
5 The various types of credit available are discussed in Holderness, B.A. 'Credit in English rural society before the nineteenth century, with special reference to the period 1650-1720', *Agricultural history review*, 24, 1976, p.97-109, and by Spufford, P. 'Long term rural credit in seventeenth-century England', in Arkell, Tom, Evans, Nesta, & Goose, Nigel, eds. *When death us do part: understanding and interpreting the probate records of early modern England.* Local Population Studies, 2000, p.213-28.
6 WSHC P3/C/971.

Money lent by bond could normally be easily recovered. Even bonds, however, involved risk: Andrew Mills' executor in 1674 was unable to recover £15 'due on bond' from John Stevens. Nevertheless, several decedents had substantial sums due on bonds.

We have already discussed Thomas Pontin's dubious money lending activities.[1] Two vicars, John Forsyth and John White, both lent money extensively. In Forsyth's situation, that proved very risky; his bonds for repayment of £215 were lost when his house was plundered during the Civil War; indeed, he thought his debtors bore some responsibility for that plundering, and he had to pursue them in Chancery to obtain repayment.[2] John White's 1712 probate inventory was valued at £531 12s; of that, £450 was 'money due to the deceased, and £50 was described as 'desperate'. A few others had also lent major portions of their wealth. In 1616, Richard Trewman, the blacksmith had lent £88 on 'obligacon' to Christopher Pope, out of an estate valued at £97 17s 10d.[3] Maud Truslow's estate, valued at £189 7s in 1625, included 'desperate debts' valued at £100, and 'good debts' at £25.[4] That included 'all such moneys as are due unto mee from Mr Perkyns of London' (however much that was), which was to be divided between two of her sons. John Griffin, innholder, was owed £230 out of a total estate valued at c.£398 in 1715.[5] Richard Chesterman evidently made a business out of money lending; his 1639 probate inventory identifies thirteen borrowers, who had borrowed small sums ranging from 2s 4d to £24.[6] The widow Deborah Mortimer in 1650[7] bequeathed £400, made up of debts owed by three borrowers, to her daughter Elizabeth. A number of other testators similarly gave relatives moneys which they had borrowed. In 1601/2, for example, Thomas Pope gave his infant grand-daughter, Edith Skuse, £10 which her father had borrowed from him. Similarly, in 1686, the £110 which Jane Pope had borrowed from her father in law, Richard Pope was bequeathed to her children[8]

The probate inventories also record many smaller sums on loan. In 1688, for example, Richard Garroway, whose estate was valued at £151 11s

1 Above, p.117.
2 TNA C2/Chas1/A9/39. See Raymond, Stuart A. 'A Plundered Minister at Avebury', *Recorder: the Annual Newsletter of the Wiltshire Record Society*, 23, 2024, p.3-4
3 WSHC P3/T/50.
4 WSHC P3/T/86.
5 WSHC P3/G/454.
6 WSHC P3/C/239.
7 TNA PROB11/219/402.
8 WSHC P1/P/1006.

6d, had 'good debts of 14s and 'bad debts' of 7s 6d.[1] John Cue, who died in 1687, was a substantial yeoman, whose estate was valued at £429 12s 6d; he had 'good debts and bad debts' worth a mere £6.[2]

Debts to tradesmen were also frequently mentioned in probate records. A high proportion of the 1706 estate of George Arnold, a collar maker[3], was made up of £52 3s 6½d 'due on the shopbook'. He also had 'desperate debtes' of £11 1s, out of a total inventory of £88 4s 6½d. The blacksmith Richard Cripps (1670), had £30 due on his shop book, of which £10 was desperate.[4] Thomas Fry, innkeeper of the White Hart at West Kennett, also had a small amount – under £10 - due on his 'book', although he also had £82 due 'uppon several bands', and had loaned £41 to two brothers in law. His estate was valued at £219 11s.

Several wills made provision for moneys to be lent at interest; for example, in 1662 John Phelps als Bromham left the residue of his substantial estate 'for the present maintenance' of his three daughters, the money to be placed at interest by his executors.[5] Peter Griffin in 1687/8 left his three daughters portions of £300 each, and told his executors to lend the money at 5% interest.[6] In 1712 the vicar, John White bequeathed each of his three daughters £200, 'to be put or kept out at interest'; the interest was 'to be divided between them for their present maintenance'.[7] The innkeeper, John Griffin in 1715 left legacies totalling £200, which was to be 'put out to interest dureing the minority of my said children'.[8] John Nalder made bequests to a number of trustees, who were to pay the interest raised on the capital to his children.[9] Thomas Rogers in 1778 ordered his executor to sell 'my house, lands, stock and implements in trade with my household goods; they were to be 'converted into money', which was to be added to 'the money due to me on book or otherwise', and put out at interest in order to provide an income for his widow to live on.[10]

Charitable bequests might also be invested to yeild an income. Lady Holford's school was funded by the interest on the capital of £200 she

1 WSHC P3/G/327.
2 WSHC P3/C/515.
3 i.e. collars for horses.
4 WSHC P3/C/352.
5 WSHC P1/B/416.
6 WSHC P3/G/413.
7 WSHC P3/W/671.
8 WSHC P3/G/454.
9 TNA PROB11/938/220.
10 WSHC P3/R/549.

bequeathed in 1623.[1] That, as has been seen, was enough to pay a schoolmaster.[2] John Goldsmith's 1639/40 legacy of £5 to the poor was also 'to be putt forth att interest'.[3]

Two testators specified the rate of interest that was to be charged: Peter Griffin expected 5%; a century later, in 1787, only 4% was demanded by Sarah Dyke Howson.[4]

It was often thought more desirable to lend substantial sums by way of mortgage, which gave the security of property. That was why the widow, Jane Rose, specified that the residue of her substantial estate, given to her daughters, was 'to be placed out at interest by my executors on good land security', in other words, lent by way of mortgage.[5] When the blacksmith, James Lewis, died in 1779, he had already placed £250 on bond with Mr West of Bath, and had provided a mortgage of £150 on houses in Marlborough: his wife was to receive the interest.[6]

Larger loans were frequently secured by taking out a mortgage. Many landowners required substantial mortgages in order to meet their commitments. They were frequently arranged through local attorneys, such as Humphry Wall of Marlborough, who might also invest themselves. Professional men sometimes amassed capital which could be lent to gentlemen who owned property but needed ready cash. John Merewether, a Devizes 'batchelor in physicke', was one such. When Richard Truslow's father died in 1694, he left his son to pay debts ranging in value from 9s to £100, owed to 22 different people.[7] Truslow borrowed £250 on mortgage from Merewether, on the security of Griffin's Farm.[8] However, when he sold the farm to Charles Tooker in 1702, he himself became a mortgagee, lending Tooker £400 to make the purchase. Interest on the money was to be paid to his widowed mother Bridget Truslow. The mortgage remained in place when Sir Richard Holford purchased the farm, and was not finally discharged until Lady Holford paid off the capital to Truslow's executor in 1719.[9]

1 TNA PROB 11/590/280.
2 See above, p.171-3.
3 WSHC P1/G/142.
4 WSHC P3/H/1476.
5 WSHC P3/R/364.
6 TNA PROB11/1055/301
7 WSHC 371/1, pt.3. Deed, Bridget Truslow to Richard Truslow, 26th December 1694.
8 WSHC 371/1, pt.3. Mortgage deed, Richard Truslow to John Merewether, 30th May 1694.
9 WSHC 371/1, pt.5. Receipt, 2nd November 1719.

Wealthy widows and spinsters frequently invested in mortgages. When John Merewether needed his money back, the mortgage was taken over by Bridget Madox of Tidenham, Gloucestershire.[1] The widow Anne Goulding of Chippenham was another mortgagee; she loaned £309 to Richard Smith secured on his West Kennett estate in 1700. She too re-claimed her money, in 1703, by transferring the mortgage to Humphry Wall; he provided an additional £140 to Smith. The mortgage was then transferred again to Richard Lewis of Corsham.[2] It was probably paid off after Smith's death, when his son (another Richard) suffered a common recovery to free his estate from the constraints of a settlement, and, in 1713 and 1714, raised another mortgage of £1000. This time, the mortgage was provided by two local gentlemen, Walter Stott of Chippenham, and Thomas Grinfield of Clyffe Pypard.[3]

On a smaller scale, in 1690, Samuel Morris mortgaged his cottage and tenement at Eastbrook to Elizabeth Wallis for £80. Subsequently, the 'meeting house for protestant dissenters', was built on part of the premises. When, in 1724, Thomas Robinson (a prominent dissenter) took over the mortgage, and paid off Elizabeth's daughters, the meeting house was excluded from the deed.[4]

In 1755, Robinson's son John himself borrowed a small amount of money on mortgage, on two properties which lay beside the meeting house, and which he had leased to John Strange. Initially, he borrowed £33 12s from William Heath, a shopkeeper of Wootton Bassett, but in 1758, he found that he needed more cash, and borrowed another £81 5s from his fellow dissenter, John Nalder.[5] Nalder also paid off William Heath's capital.

In 1691, George Stretch took out a mortgage for £210 from Elizabeth Dowdeswell of Pool Court, Worcestershire. When she died c.1722, the mortgage was transferred to Elizabeth Lewis, who in 1725 transferred it to John Brown, a London saddler from Avebury. He in turn transferred it to Joseph Merryman of Newbury (Berkshire) in 1734.[6]

Mortgaging a property was not always straightforward, and could give rise to dispute. In 1667, the heirs of William Dunch brought a Chancery case against Sir Edward Baynton concerning his purchase of the manor of Avebury Trusloe in 1646. Baynton had agreed to pay off Dunch's debts, which exceeded £10,000, in return for the manor. However, Dunch's heirs claimed that the

---

1   WSHC 371/1, pt.4. Mortgage deed, 27th January 1700/01.
2   WSHC 568/5, pt.2. Mortgage deed, 12th April 1706.
3   WSHC 568/5, pt.2. Mortgage deed, 17th November 1713.
4   WSHC 529/185.
5   WSHC 529/185.
6   WSHC 1409/16/3, pt.2. Assignment of mortgage, 18th August 1734.

'bargain and sale' had merely been a mortgage.[1] It seems that they lost their case. Baynton's heir, as has been seen, was still in possession in the early 1680s, when he began to sell.

Thomas Goldsmith was another landowner who lost his estate due to his inability to pay off a mortgage. He was already having difficulties paying his rent for Avebury Great Farm in 1642.[2] He mortgaged his own property, Rowses Farm at Beckhampton, for £500, c.1645, but when the mortgagee called in the debt nine years later, he was unable to obtain access to the deeds, and therefore lost two opportunities to re-mortgage the property. He sued the London lawyer who held the deeds in 1655, and presumably won his case; the property was sold in the following year.[3]

Wealth Distribution

There are two sources which can be used to study the distribution of wealth in the parish: tax lists, and probate inventories. Unfortunately, prior to 1700 there are only two useable tax lists. These record the collection of the subsidy in 1576[4] and 1663.[5] For the late eighteenth century, there are many land tax returns, which have already been discussed. The sums assessed were, of course, notional, and do not reveal the real values of estates. They do, however, reflect the way in which the wealth of landowners was distributed.

The 1576 subsidy lists sixteen subsidy men in the Tithing of Avebury, five in the Tithing of Beckhampton, and eight in the Tithing of Kennett (two or three of whom lived in the parish of East Kennett, rather than in Avebury).[6] Most, if not all, were assessed on goods, rather than on lands.[7] John Shuter, the farmer of Avebury manor demesne, was given the highest assessment, as has already been noted. He paid on £20 in the tithing of Beckhampton, and another £4 in the tithing of Avebury. Thomas Smith of West Kennett had the next highest assessment: £15.[8] George Mortimer of Kennett (probably West Kennett) was assessed on £12, nine others at between £5 and £10, and twelve at under £5.

The descendants of many of those taxed in 1576 escaped assessment in

1 TNA C5/426/43.
2 TNA C6/21/114.
3 TNA C5/128/75; WSHC 212B/105 & 106.
4 Ramsay, G.D., ed. *Two sixteenth Century taxation lists, 1545 and 1576*. Wiltshire Archaeological and Natural History Society Records Branch 10. 1954, p.103.
5 WANHS mss 140.
6 East Kennett, which was a separate parish.
7 The two exceptions to this rule were probably residents of East Kennett.
8 Richard Franklin was assessed at £28, but lived in East Kennett.

1663. Nevertheless, a similar pattern appears. The subsidy collected in 1663 named eleven taxpayers taxed on land, and only one on goods. Ralph Stawell (then brother of the lord of the manor), and Margaret Dunch, were both assessed at £6. Dame Mary Baynton was assessed at £3, four others at £2, one at 30s, and three at £1.

Tax assessments, as already noted, were notional, and not based on actual values. Probate inventories, by contrast, do state the actual values of the goods they list. However, they only list personal estate, not real estate, as the latter was not under the jurisdiction of the ecclesiastical courts which administered probate. Inventories do not value freehold or copyhold property, although leases are included. Consequently, they cannot be used to establish total wealth. The reliability of the work of appraisers may occasionally be questioned. When John Truslow, gent., the former lord of the manor of Avebury Trusloe, died in 1646, there may have been a probate dispute, as two separate inventories were taken. The first was valued at a mere £21 5s 2d.[1] Truslow had admittedly sold his manor, and was heavily in debt, but even so he was still the owner of a farm at Beckhampton, and other properties. One wonders whether his appraisers failed to list all of his goods, or whether some had been removed before they arrived. Perhaps he had retired from active involvement in farming activities; the six pigs and three cows listed in the inventory were not many to stock his substantial farm. His widow's estate was valued at £100 twenty years later.[2]

Wealth levels in Avebury were increasing in our period. Between 1621 and 1640 fourteen inventories were exhibited. Their average value was just over £75, but three of them recorded wealth between £100 and £500. After the Civil War, eighteen inventories were exhibited between 1661 and 1680; their average value was just over £360; nine recorded wealth levels between £100 and £500. Thereafter, average values fluctuated between c.£195 in 1701-20, and c.£441 in 1721-40; the numbers valued at over £100 always equalled, and sometimes out-numbered, those valued at below £100, and at least one inventory in every twenty year period recorded wealth levels in excess of £500. In 1720, John Rose's inventory was valued at £1865 12s 0d.[3]

Much of this wealth was invested in crops and livestock, especially sheep. Most Avebury inhabitants were dependent, to some extent, on agriculture. In the next chapter we will investigate the nature of agriculture in Avebury.

---

1   WSHC P1/T/108.
2   WSHC P3/T/207.
3   WSHC P3/R/365.

6
SHEEP, DUNG, AND WHEAT: AVEBURY'S AGRICULTURE

SHEEP AND CORN husbandry was the basis of agriculture in Avebury throughout our period, and, indeed, had been since a much earlier date.[1] Wheat was the prime cash crop, but sheep were kept primarily for their dung – although of course wool sales also provided a useful income.[2] The Truslows in the late sixteenth century usually kept several hundred sheep on the Downs, sometimes more.[3] In 1791, Richard Hickley, Adam Williamson's bailiff, had 1220 sheep and lambs on Avebury Great Farm,[4] but, after the 1792 enclosure, he hoped to run over 1,500 sheep.[5] Sheep farming continued to be important throughout our period, although, as we will see, agricultural practices were beginning to change at the end of the eighteenth century. Much depended on the price of corn and wool. Low prices when Sir Richard Holford was seeking a new tenant meant that he had to let his farm at a lower rent than he had hoped.[6] Farmers were always dependent on the weather. They needed rain to grow the seeds, and sun to harvest their crops. Sometimes their needs were contradictory; Hickley complained in the summer of 1794 that he

---

1 For a discussion of sheep farming at Avebury, see Smith, Nicola. 'Medieval and later sheep farming on the Marlborough Downs', in Brown, Graham, Field, David, & McOmish, David, eds. *The Avebury Landscape: aspects of the field archaeology of the Marlborough Downs*. Oxbow Books, 2005, p.191-201. See also Wordie, J.R. 'The South: Oxfordshire, Buckinghamshire, Berkshire, Wiltshire and Hampshire', in Thirsk, Joan, ed. *The Agrarian History of England and Wales,. Vol.V: 1640-1750, pt.1. Regional Farming Systems*. Cambridge University Press, 1984, p.329-34.
2 Bettey, J.H. *Rural Life in Wessex, 1500-1900*. Alan Sutton, 1987, p.10-11.
3 TNA E134/40and41Eliz/ Mich7; E134/41Eliz/Hil8. The actual number fluctuated during their long occupation of the Rectory and manor of Avebury Trusloe; different witnesses, giving evidence from different years, gave a variety of figures.
4 WSHC 184/4/1. List of stock, 1791.
5 WSHC 184/6. Letter, Richard Hickley to Mrs Williamson, 4th September 1792.
6 WSHC 184/4/1. Letter, Sir Richard Holford to Richard Chandler, 2nd June 1709.

wanted 'fine weather and rain at the same time'. There had been a prolonged drought; consequently, turnips had refused to grow, and recently planted trees threatened to die, but on the other hand he was in the middle of haymaking, which needed sun.[1] The amount of hay that could be reaped was, of course, dependent on rain during the growing season. He thought that 'wee must take chances, wet or dry'. When turnips failed in 1793, the sheep did not thrive; consequently Hickley feared a bad market for them.[2] Similarly, a poor hay crop meant that he might have to purchase hay. In the spring of 1797, 28 tons of hay cost him £100.[3]

Sometimes farmers were fortunate: 1695 was a 'uery great coren yeare'.[4] Sometimes they were not. There was a serious threat of famine between 1595 and 1597. As has been seen, prosecutions for theft increased as a consequence of bad harvests in the early 1620s. There were several bad harvests in the 1740s. Peter Griffin noted in 1743 that 'I have suffered very much by dry summers; for severall years past it hath cost me scores of pounds a year for hay. Now this year there is a plentiful crop not onely of English grass, but upwards of sixty acres of very good clover'.[5] But his eviction from the farm meant that he would be unable to benefit from the new season's crop. Heavy rain in the spring and summer of 1766 resulted in very low yields – and protests from the poor.[6] 1792 proved to be another year of heavy rain, floods, and a poor harvest.[7] In 1794, blight threatened to be ' very hurtful to the yield' of the wheat crop, and Hickley complained about the lack of rain.[8]

The open fields close to the village were cultivated for corn (predominantly wheat), whilst there was common grazing on the Downs, where vast flocks of sheep were pastured during the day. At night they were folded on the arable. Until the late eighteenth century, emphasis was placed on the production of wool from wethers (castrated rams).[9] Bowie

1 WSHC 184/6. Letter, Richard Hickley to Mrs Williamson, June 1794.
2 WSHC 184/6. Letter, Richard Hickley to Mrs Williamson, 8th November 1793.
3 WSHC 184/7.
4 WSHC 184/1, pt.1. Letter, Robert Smith to Sir Richard Holford, 7th February 1695/6.
5 WSHC 184/1, pt.2. Letter, Peter Griffin to Stayner Holford, 26th June 1743.
6 Wilson, Avice. *Forgotten Labour: the Wiltshire Agricultural Worker and his Environment, 4500 B.C. – A.D. 1950.* Hobnob Press, 2007, p.150.
7 WSHC 184/6. Richard Hickley to Mrs Williamson, 4th September 1792.
8 WSHC 184/6. Richard Hickley to Mrs Williamson, June 1794.
9 Bowie, G.G.S. 'Northern Wolds and Wessex Downlands: Contrasts in Sheep Husbandry and Farming Practice, 1770-1850', *Agricultural History Review* 38(2), 1990, p.119.

states that surplus lambs were killed off at Michaelmas, but we know that in 1755 Stayner Holford sent 50 lambs for wintering to Rowd, and another 50 to Corsham.[1] Similarly, in 1781 Richard Hickley paid several people for wintering sheep away from the Downs: 78 were sent to James Willis, 56 to Daniel Hitchcock, 20 to Edward Long, and 79 to John Hiscock.[2] He was still wintering sheep off the Downs in the winters of the early 1790s; in April 1792, for example, he paid five different farmers over £52 in total for wintering 241 sheep.[3] By 1794, he had determined to 'get rid of that cursed affair of putting the sheep out to wintering'. It was expensive, and the sheep were not properly looked after. Instead, he proposed to 'raise turnips enough to keep them all at home'.[4] By contrast, Richard Cue, when he died in 1678, owed John Mills £1 'for summering of sheep'; presumably he did not have enough downland for his forty sheep to keep them during the summer.[5]

The custom of Avebury manor allowed the tenants to winter 950 sheep on Hackpen Down. They were allowed pasture for another 950 sheep in the common field all the year round.[6] The numbers of sheep on Avebury farms far exceeded numbers in other parts of the country; in sixteenth century Leicestershire, for example, there were a mere 30 sheep per farmer.[7] In 1548, nineteen tenants of Avebury manor had the right to common for between 40 and 170 sheep each[8]. In 1709, nine farmers who kept their sheep on the Downs belonging to Avebury Great Farm were listed; seven had 1106 sheep between them on Hackpen, although it had previously accommodated 1570. A further 430 were pastured on Thornhill and West Down, by three farmers[9]. In 1639, Sir John Stawell's purchase of the manor gave him the right to pasture 920 wethers (castrated rams), 400 ewes, 340 lambs, and 30 kine on the Downs and in the common fields of Avebury.[10] In 1730, Samuel Holford had the right to feed 400 sheep in the West Field; Mr Grant had the right to feed 200, and Farmer Pope had the right to feed 40.[11] The value of these rights was a

1 WSHC 271/4.
2 WSHC 184/5. Receipts for wintering sheep.
3 WSHC 184/7.
4 WSHC 184/6. Letter, Richard Hickley to Mrs Williamson, 2nd May 1794.
5 TNA C6/98/30. His sheep are counted in his inventory; WSHC P3/K/92.
6 WSHC 1553/71.
7 Hey, David. *An English Rural Community: Myddle under the Tudors and Stuarts.* Leicester University Pres, 1974, p.63.
8 WSHC 2664/1/2D/8.
9 WSHC 184/4/1. Rental (sheep count) 1709.
10 WANHS Genealogy v.A-A, p.115.
11 WSHC 184/4/1. Account of the feed of stubble, 1730.

mere 15s in total, but the advantage for the land when they were taken up was considerable.

In our period the value of the Downs for grazing was regarded as so important that restrictive covenants in some tenants' leases prohibited ploughing. The terms of John Beake's 1724 lease of West Kennett Farm included this prohibition.[1] A later owner of the same estate required John Nalder to pay £8 for every acre of downland he ploughed up, and £10 for every acre of pasture.[2] Landowners sought to prevent tenants ploughing up permanent pastures at the end of their leases: tenants would benefit from their high fertility, but growing wheat would much reduce fertility for future tenants.[3] When Richard Caswell vacated his tenancy at Beckhampton, having ploughed up more land than his lease permitted (and also having left the property in a bad state of disrepair) Sir Richard Holford sued him for damages. He thought that '£50 will not make mee satisfaction', although in practice he was prepared to settle the dispute for a mere £10 'in compassion'.[4]

The fertility of arable land also had to be protected. When George Mortimer left his grandson Richard forty sheep in 1613, he did so on condition that they were always to be penned on his father's land.[5] Towards the end of the seventeenth century, John Baskerville's poor husbandry as tenant of Avebury Great Farm 'had very much abusd both the land and landlord. Sir Richard Holford thought 'that the land was then much wors for a tenant than it is now … or else it would have brought a better rent'.[6] Robert Caswell's 1729 lease of Thomas Smith's farm at West Kennett included a prohibition on ploughing or sowing any of the arable lands 'out of the usual course of husbandry'.[7] In 1791, John Brown's lease of Brunsdens required him to pay £20 for every acre of meadow, pasture or downland he ploughed up, plus an additional £5 if his landlord refused to give his consent.[8] When John Amor leased a portion of the former manor of Avebury Trusloe in 1795, he covenanted not to plough up more than two-thirds of the arable land each year, so that one-third could be

---

1   WSHC 568/7. Lease, Thomas Smith to John Beake, 13th October 1724.
2   WSHC 568/7. Lease, Stayner Chamberlayne & Samuel Martyn to John Nalder, 8th November 1755.
3   Jones, E.L. *Landscape History and Rural Society in Southern England: an economic and environmental perspective*. Palgrave Macmillan, 2021, p.146.
4   GA D1956/E2/8.
5   TNA PROB 11/122/637.
6   WSHC 184/1, pt.2. Letter, Sir Richard Holford to Richard Chandler, 2nd June 1709.
7   WSHC 568/7.
8   WSHC 473/72. Draft lease, William Norris to John Brown, 3rd November 1791.

left fallow. He was also instructed not to sow 'the same sort of corn or grain for two years in succession'.[1]

Most sheep were of the Old Wiltshire Horned breed, also known as 'Wiltshire Crocks'.[2] The breed, as the name suggests, were horned, both rams and ewes; they had arched white faces, were short fleeced, with high heads, long straight backs, and long bony legs. They required little water, and could survive on scanty herbage, whatever the weather, and their great stamina enabled them to be driven long distances daily to fold on the arable, where they could feed on the stubble, and fertilise the soil. They were, however, slow to fatten, and their mutton was not of the best. Sheep were kept primarily for their wool, which was short and coarse; their fleeces weighed perhaps two pounds. The sheep had to be washed in early June, and were sheared a week or so later.[3] In 1791, shearing was late: Richard Hickley paid out 17s 6d for washing sheep on 27th June; on 29th June he paid £3 4s for shearing.[4] Shearing was a major event in the farmer's life. The wool was used to produce a hard-wearing broadcloth, for which Wiltshire was renowned.

When John Rose was negotiating a lease of Avebury Great Farm in 1710, his predecessor, William Skeat, estimated that it would cost between £1200 and £1400 to stock it fully.[5] That included a substantial sheep flock. Rose died possessed of the tenancy in September 1720. He had a flock of 1,304 sheep, worth £690.[6] He also had 2008 fleeces, suggesting that he had sold many sheep after the spring shearing in that year. It is probable that other tenants of this property also had substantial flocks. At the end of the century, in November 1798, the bailiff noted that there were 840 sheep on the farm – but that, of course, was before the spring lambing.[7]

Other farms were not as large; however, some farmers still had substantial numbers of sheep. Six probate inventories between 1602 and 1749 record flocks of between 200 and 400 sheep. Christopher Battington, for example, had 367 sheep worth £100 when he died in 1636.[8] John Jacob

1   WSHC 873/262. Lease, Sir John Hopkins to John Amor, 16th April 1795.
2   Wilson, *Forgotten Labour*, p.122; Stedman, A.R. *Marlborough and the Upper Kennet Country.* [Marlborough School?], 1960, p.236.
3   Wadsworth, Alan, ed. *The Farming Diaries of Thomas Pinniger, 1813-1837.* Wiltshire Record Society 74. 2021, p.xlii. See also Wordie, op cit, p.329.
4   WSHC 184/7.
5   WSHC 184/8.
6   WSHC P3/R/365.
7   WSHC 271/6.
8   WSHC P3/B/368.

had about 200 sheep, plus 20 lambs, valued at £73 in 1670.[1] He also had wool worth £20. Fifty years later, in 1722, John Griffin's herd numbered 220 sheep and 40 lambs, worth £82.[2] He also had four dozen hurdles, with iron bars, worth 15s., used to fold the sheep on the arable at night. It is likely that John Bromham als Phelps sold some sheep after his 1662 shearing; his clip of wool was valued at £39, which was more than the £37 at which his 120 sheep were valued.

There were many smaller flocks. The probate inventories reveal that, between 1601 and 1620 the average number of sheep in a flock was 61. That increased in subsequent decades; between 1661 and 1680 the average was 168. For the whole period from 1602 to 1748, there were nine farmers with between 100 and 200 sheep each; thirteen had fewer than 100. Smaller men included, for instance, William Hayward, who described himself as a shepherd in his 1610 will,[3] and probably ran his own flock of nine ewes with those of his employer. Several were widows, like Edith Pope in 1624, whose ten sheep were valued at a mere £2;[4] her total inventory was valued at a mere £19 1s 6d. It is likely that, before enclosure, Avebury's farmers ran their sheep together in a single flock, and employed a shepherd through the manorial court.[5] This arrangement is hinted at in the early 1680, when Thomas Webb and John Plummer both served as 'sheepward'.[6]

The sheep played a major role in fertilizing Avebury's arable fields. Defoe noted that the Downs produced 'prodigious' quantities of corn, despite their poor soils; 'all which has been done by folding their sheep upon the plow'd lands, removing the fold every night to a fresh place, till the whole piece of ground has been folded on'.[7] The sheep fold, according to Davis, was 'the sheet-anchor of its [Wiltshire's] husbandry'.[8] Many hurdles are mentioned in the probate inventories. Stayner Holford ordered eight dozen to be made in 1755, at a price of 5s per dozen. He already had a large number.[9] It is probable that the 147 'poles of wood' purchased by Richard

1 WSHC P3/IJ/101.
2 WSHC P3/G/485.
3 WSHC P3/H/56.
4 WSHC P3/P/126.
5 Bettey, op cit, p.13.
6 TNA E134/2and3Jas2/Hil2.
7 Defoe, Daniel. *A Tour through England and Wales, divided into Circuits or Journies.* J.M.Dent, 1927. v.1, p.285.
8 Davis, T. *A General View of the Agriculture of Wiltshire.* 1811, p.152. See also Wordie, op cit, p.333.
9 WSHC 271/4.

Hickley in 1781 were used to make hurdles. They cost 14s 10d.[1] Hickley also purchased eight dozen hurdles from Edmund Goatley at the same time.[2] Goatley continued to supply them; he provided no fewer than 480 more hurdles in 1790.[3] Hurdles were generally made of hazel; they were generally four feet six inches long, three feet six inches high.[4] They were used to pen the sheep on arable fields, to fertilise the next year's crop. Fifteen dozen of them were needed to enclose a statute acre, with sufficient room for twelve or thirteen hundred sheep. Hurdles were moved daily, so that eventually sheep's dung covered the whole field.[5] It was one of the most highly valued product of sheep-keeping in our period,[6] essential for growing crops in the open fields. The custom of the manor required tenants who had sheep to pen them on the Downs at night, so that they could fertilise the soil. When Richard Smith, the widow Edith Griffin, and James Pope all 'brought away' their sheep from West Down in 1651, they were all fined by the manorial court.[7] A century later, John Rose, the tenant of Avebury Great Farm who went bankrupt in 1755, had no fewer than 211 hurdles.[8] A substantial amount of labour was obviously needed to move them regularly. Where there were large flocks, wethers, ewes, and hogsters or yearlings were penned separately. Sheep bells, perhaps purchased from dealers at Tan Hill fair, helped the shepherd to keep track of where his flock were.[9]

There were 'pennings' or sheep cotes on the Downs, where sheep could shelter from bad weather, or be penned overnight.[10] The remains of two of these have been identified: one on Avebury Down, the other on Horton Down.[11] Thomas Truslow built one on West Down in the late sixteenth century.[12] John Beake's landlord expected him to 'keep a good dead hedge or fence round the

1   WSHC 184/5. Two bills for poles of wood, 1781.
2   WSHC 184/5. Bill of Edmund Goatley, 1781.
3   WSHC 184/5. Bill of Edmund Goatley, 1790.
4   Bettey, op cit, p.12-13.
5   Parslew, Patricia. *Beckhampton: Time Present and Time Past.* Hobnob Press, 2004, p.29.
6   Thirsk, op cit, p.56 & 65; Gandy, Ida. *The heart of a Village: an intimate history of Aldbourne.* Alan Sutton, 1991, p.56.
7   WSHC 473/52.
8   WSHC 184/4/1. Account of John Rose's stock sold, 15th November 1755.
9   Gurney, Peter. *Shepherd Lore: the last years of traditional shepherding in Wiltshire.* Wiltshire Folk Life Society, 2010, p.32.
10 For pennings in neighbouring parishes, see Fowler, Peter, & Blackwell, Ian. *The land of Lettice Sweetapple: an English countryside explored.* Tempus, 1998, p.56.
11 Smith, op cit, p.195 & 200.
12 TNA E134/40and41Eliz/Mich7.

ground called ... Pennings', and was prepared to remit 40s in rent to pay him to do so.[1] Beckhampton Penning is still marked on the Ordnance Survey map. Even when pennings had to be used, the dung was still important enough to be carried to the fields and spread. Dung from sheep – and from cattle – was carried out to the fields in 'dung pots' or dung carts. The work of spreading it has been described as 'one of the most arduous and miserable jobs on the farm'.[2] In November 1765, William Stevens spent 5½ days spreading dung, and was paid 4s 7d for his efforts.[3]

Landlords and tenants alike were concerned to maintain good husbandry and the fertility of the soil. Buildings and fencing also had to be kept in order. When William Skeat vacated his farm, Sir Richard Holford accused him of having 'left all the bounds, fences &c in great disorder and defective',[4] despite the fact that Skeat had repeatedly promised to get the hedging done.[5] John Rose, apparently, did no better: when Stayner Holford took the farm in hand, he found that Rose's failure to maintain fences meant he could not keep cattle in Bar Close.[6] Deeds and leases frequently reflect a concern with fertility. Many tenancy agreements specified that the 'soil, dung and compost' arising on the premises were to be spread on the land.[7] A witness in a court case, c.1605, remembered seeing West Down 'for the most part covered with orth made with strawe given to sheep'.[8] In 1708, John White took Sir Richard Holford by surprise when he accused Holford's tenant of sub-letting parts of Avebury Farm, and thereby imperilling the fertility of his property.[9] When Charles Tooker leased a farm at Beckhampton to Richard Caswell in 1709, his tenant was expected to 'carry forth, lay, and spread on some parte of the demised premises' all 'the compost soyle and dung thereof made and comeing'.[10] In his 1729 lease of Avebury Great Farm, Peter Griffin was obliged to spread dung

1   WSHC 568/7. Lease, Richard Smith to John Beake, 13th October 1724.
2   Wilson, Avice. *Forgotten harvest: the Story of Cheesemaking in Wiltshire*. The author, 1995, p.71.
3   WSHC 271/4.
4   GA 1956/E2/8.
5   See, for example, letters William Skeat to Sir Richard Holford, c.23 November 1698 & 21 December 1698.
6   WSHC 271/4.
7   See for example, WSHC 568/7. Lease, Stanes Chamberlayne & Samuel Martyn to John Nalder, 9th November 1755.
8   TNA STAC8/281/25. Deposition of Walter Gybbes.
9   WSHC 184/1, pt.2. Letter, John White to Sir Richard Holford, 20th October 1708.
10 WSHC 371/1, pt.4.

in the old orchard, which otherwise Samuel Holford kept in hand.[1] In 1729, when John Wiltshire leased thirteen acres in the common fields from Caleb Bailey, he was expected 'to carry out, spread and bestow in an husbandlike manner all the dung compost and soil that shall be made arise or be of or from all the straw chaff and other issues … that shall arise or grow on the said land'.[2] Bailey inserted similar clauses into leases made to Robert Woodman in 1733,[3] and to John Beake in 1734.[4] Similarly, the Allen family's lease of the farm at West Kennett in 1772, required that 'all hay, straw, muck, dung, soil, and compost' arising on the farm was to be used there. The tenant was to 'keep depasture and feed a full and sufficient stock of sheep', and to 'penn and fold' them on the farm, so that their dung would fertilise the fields. The lease specified that, when linten corn was sown, clover was to be sowed with it.[5] John Amor, when he leased Avebury Trusloe manor in 1795, was required not to sow 'the same sort of corn or grain' in the same fields 'two years in succession'.[6] Mention has already been made of the water meadows which encouraged spring growth.

This concern with fertility was a consequence of the fact that wheat and barley earned farmers large slices of their incomes. The value of these and other arable crops was much greater than the value of sheep. In 1636, Christopher Battington had sheep worth £100, but arable crops valued at £348.[7] Margaret Hayward's sheep were valued at £38 in 1663, but her corn was worth £127 10s. John Rose had sheep valued at £690, plus fleeces worth another £90, but his arable crops – wheat, barley, oats, vetches, and hay – were valued at £810 in 1720.[8] Stayner Holford's accounts record his purchases of wheat and oats seed from various sources in the winter of 1755.[9] Richard Hickley paid £15 12s for seed wheat in 1781.[10] In May 1791, he had 95 acres of wheat in the ground, together with three stacks of wheat. He also had 91 acres of barley and oats, a stack of oats, and a stack of barley, in addition to his 1220 sheep.[11] But he

1   WSHC 435/24/1/7.
2   WSHC 212A/31/3. Lease, 5th March 1728/9.
3   WSHC 212A/31/3. Lease, 22nd September 1733.
4   WSHC 212A/31/3. Lease, 12th September 1734.
5   WSHC 118/88. Draft indenture, 1772.
6   WSHC 873/262. Lease, Sir John Hopkins to John Amor, 16th April 1795.
7   WSHC P3/B/368.
8   WSHC P3/R/365.
9   WSHC 271/4.
10 WSHC 184/5. Bill for seed wheat from Thomas Stockwell, 1781.
11 WSHC 184/4/1. List of stock, 1791.

suffered badly from the weather in 1792, so sowed oats in 1793.[1] In November 1798, he had wheat stored in ricks from about 90 acres, together with barley and oats from about seventy acres. He had already sown 96 acres of wheat for the following year's crop.[2]

The usual course of cropping on the Downs was to grow wheat after the summer fallow.[3] It was sown broadcast from mid-September onwards. After the wheat harvest, the ground would be ploughed, and barley, or perhaps some other crop would be sowed. Fallowing would follow. It was considered essential every second or third year.

Moles could be a problem, although one that is rarely mentioned by historians.[4] An account of c.1760 found amongst the Holford papers is headed 'the affair of the moles', and lists thirteen local farmers who clubbed together to raise £5, presumably to employ a mole-catcher and eliminate the problems caused by mole-hills.[5] Vermin also included rats; the manorial bailiff in the early 1790s regularly had to pay 10s 6d 'for half a year's rat catching'.[6]

All of the substantial farmers who grew crops also ran sheep. Only a few small proprietors decided not to both run sheep and cultivate crops. Some of them were tradesmen whose primary interests lay elsewhere. For example, in 1670 Lemuel Fowler, the innkeeper, had corn and hay worth £8, but no sheep.[7] Richard Cripps, the blacksmith, had sheep and lambs valued at £32 10s, but no crops.[8]

Probate inventories frequently mention 'corn', without distinguishing between wheat, barley, oats and rye. However, it is clear that wheat and barley predominated. Defoe emphasised the importance of barley, and the fact that it was sold for malting and sent to London.[9] Peter Griffin's malt in 1689 was worth £75, and evidently intended for more than just home consumption.[10] There were a number of moderately substantial maltsters in the parish, as we will see in the next chapter; they must have been supplied with barley grown

1 WSHC 184/6. Richard Hickley to Mrs Williamson, 30th April 1793.
2 WSHC 271/6.
3 Bettey, op cit, p.15.
4 Jones, E.L. *Landscape History and Rural Society in Southern England: an economic and environmental perspective.* Palgrave Macmillan, 2021, p.151.
5 WSHC 184/3. List, c.1750.
6 WSHC 184/7.
7 WSHC P3/F/135.
8 WSHC P3/C/352.
9 Defoe, op cit, p.284.
10 WSHC P3/G/413.

locally. Malt is frequently mentioned in other inventories, but is rarely valued at over £5, and was evidently used for home brewing. Malt mills and other brewing equipment receive frequent mention in the probate records.

Oats were also grown occasionally; a 'mow of oats' is mentioned in the 1699 inventory of William Bray,[1] and may be hidden under the generic term 'corn' in other inventories. Richard Hickley was sowing oats in April 1793, although he had an 'indifferent' crop, and was forced to buy some in the following year.[2] At the end of the eighteenth century, they were probably more important than they had been earlier; they were the only cereal crop mentioned by the curate when he reported that there had been a very good crop in 1801.[3]

There is no mention of rye, either in Hickley's letters, or in the inventories, but it too may be similarly hidden in the inventories. William Skeat also grew rape and hemp; the vicar claimed tithe on it.[4]

Farmers generally grew grass and made hay. In 1636 Christopher Battington had 'good hey' worth £50, and also 'some hey & grase in Brinkworth parishe' worth £13.[5] Peter Griffin in 1689 had hay worth £60.[6] Sir Richard Holford encouraged his tenants to grow French grass.[7] We have already seen how the water meadows produced two crops of grass in a year. Sheep were put into the early crop, but summer grass could be used to make hay. In May 1791, at the end of winter, Richard Hickley still had a stack of hay.[8] In September 1793, he commented that he was 'like to have a good crop of after grass, which will help us very much'.[9]

Hay provided winter feed for both cattle and sheep. It was an important crop, and if farmers were unable to make enough they had to buy it in. Either that, or stock had to be sold before winter. Richard Hickley thought that 'buying hay is a dreadful thing for a farmer', and complained in March 1792 that he had been forced to spend 23 guineas to buy a small rick.[10] The

1 WSHC P3/B/986.
2 WSHC 184/6. Letter, Richard Hickley to Mrs Williamson, 30th April 1793, 5th August 1793 & 30th July 1794.
3 [Turner, Michael, ed.] *Home Office Acreage Returns (HO67). List and analysis part III: Staffordshire – Yorkshire, 1801.* List & Index Society, 195. 1983, p.81.
4 WSHC 184/1, pt.2. Humfry Wall to Sir Richard Holford, 5th June 1698.
5 WSHC P3/B/368.
6 WSHC P3/G/413.
7 WSHC 184/8.
8 WSHC 184/4/1. List of stock, 1791.
9 WSHC 184/6. Letter, Richard Hickley to Mrs Williamson, 9th September 1793.
10 WSHC 184/6. Letter, Richard Hickley to Mrs Williamson, 6th March 1792. See

following month, he was still complaining that the purchase had 'robed me of every bit of cash I could get'.[1] The alternative was to sell off stock before winter. That is what Hickley did the following year. On 20th November 1793 he sold 197 ewes, and 161 lambs, at Marlborough market.[2] Such sales were common in the district.[3]

After the enclosure of Avebury, Hickley intended to grow hay on the Downs, from which he expected a 'tollerable good crop'.[4] Making hay involved a lot of work, and was an important event in the agricultural year. The grass had to be cut with scythes, then allowed to dry in the sun. Hay from grass in the water meadows had to be carried elsewhere to be dried: the ground there was too wet for it to dry properly.[5] Once dried, the hay had to be carried into the rickyard, and built into ricks, which had to be thatched or perhaps covered in some other way to protect them from the weather. Wheat and barley were also stored in ricks, although the wheat had to be protected from rodents by using staddle stones to raise it up away from the ground.[6] Two staddle stones cost Richard Hickley just over £9 in December 1792.[7] In May 1797, he had to pay 11s for 'dressing corn ricks for the mice'.[8]

After harvest, many ricks would have been seen dotted across the parish. In 1680, for example, James Pope had 'in the rick barton two hay rickes one rickstand' together worth fifteen guineas.[9] Many inventories record a rick worth £3 or £4. In the winter, the hay had to be cut from the rick and carried to the animals – another labour intensive task. In 1827, slightly after our period, half a ton of hay had to be cut and carried every winter's day on Thomas Pinniger's farm at Little Bedwyn.[10]

Fodder was also provided by crops such as clover, vetches, and turnips, which were increasingly grown on the downs, replacing permanent grassland.[11]

---

also his February 1792 accounts at 184/7.
1 WSHC 184/6. Letter, Richard Hickley to Mrs Williamson, 30th April 1792.
2 WSHC 184/7.
3 Davis, op cit, p.20.
4 WSHC 184/6. Letter, Richard Hickley to Mrs Williamson, 4th June 1793.
5 Wadsworth, Alan, ed. *The Farming Diaries of Thomas Pinniger, 1813-1837.* Wiltshire Record Society 74. 2021, p.xxxvi.
6 WSHC 184/6. Letter, Richard Hickley to Mrs Williamson, 4th June 1793.
7 WSHC 184/7.
8 WSHC 184/7.
9 WSHC P1/P/317.
10 Wadsworth, Alan, ed. *The Farming Diaries of Thomas Pinniger, 1813-1837.* Wiltshire Record Society 74. 2021, p.xlvii.
11 Jones, E.L. *Landscape History and Rural Society in Southern England: an economic and environmental perspective.* Palgrave Macmillan, 2021, p.119.

Humphry Robinson, the carpenter, had three acres of clover when he died in 1720.[1] Richard Hickley in 1794 commented that 'the clover grass is very good, but the natural grass is very short'. He attributed the latter to the dry summer.[2] Vetches grown as cattle fodder are occasionally mentioned in inventories. When John Rose became bankrupt in 1756, he had six acres of vetches.[3] In 1791, Hickley was considering feeding his cows with potatoes – but his letters say no more about this.[4]

Turnips were used as supplementary feed for livestock, rather than as a full course of rotation.[5] They were generally grown in small quantities, and served as a useful fallow crop on lighter soils. They had originally been grown in gardens, but their popularity as a field crop increased after c.1730.[6] George Stretch was growing turnips in 1742, perhaps to feed his guests or their horses at the Catherine Wheel. A labourer was caught feloniously 'pulling' two of them for his table.[7] John Rose had fourteen acres of turnips when he was made bankrupt in 1756.[8] Four decades later, Richard Hickley also tried to grow them, but complained that he had 'sowed a great many, but the weather continuing dry so long they never came up. Have got about nine or ten acres, which believe will be tollerable good.'[9] Nevertheless, he intended to grow them in the following year.[10] The spring of that year was dry too, but he hoped to pull ten acres, and promised to sow another twenty acres 'as soon as rain comes'.[11] However, a few months later he complained that 'the grub worm is got among the turnips'. He was, as mentioned above, hoping to feed turnips to his sheep, but he thought the infestation might 'hurt the sale of sheep'.[12] In the event, he had a 'tollerable good crop of turnips'.[13] However, he noted that, had that not been the case, he would not have been able to buy any: 'every one has work enough to raise them for himself', without growing them for sale.

1 WSHC P1/R/275.
2 WSHC 184/6. Letter, Richard Hickley to Mrs Williamson, June 1794.
3 GA D1950/L1. Letter, Staynor Holford to Richard Holford, 22nd June 1756.
4 WSHC 184/6. Richard Hickley to Mrs Williamson, 3rd August 1791.
5 Jones, E.L., ed. *Agriculture and Economic Growth in England 1650-1815*. Methuen & Co., 1967, p.155.
6 Wordie, op cit, p.331; Bettey, op cit, p.30.
7 WSHC A1/110, 1642M. Examination of Charles Chappell & Thomas Andrews, witnesses, 24th September 1742.
8 GA D1950/L1. Letter, Staynor Holford to Peter Holford, 22nd June 1756.
9 WSHC 184/6. Letter, Richard Hickley to Mrs Williamson, 9th September 1793.
10 WSHC 184/6. Letter, Richard Hickley to Mrs Williamson, 8th November 1793.
11 WSHC 184/6. Letter, Richard Hickley to Mrs Williamson, June 1794.
12 WSHC 184/6. Letter, Richard Hickley to Mrs Williamson, 31st August 1794.
13 WSHC 184/6. Letter, Richard Hickley to Mrs Williamson, 2nd November 1794.

They entailed too much work; perhaps that is the reason why there is no other evidence for them in Avebury.

Although, prior to enclosure, the Downs were the preserve of sheep during the winter, cattle were also grazed there during the summer.[1] Oxen, sometimes referred to as 'rother beasts', were kept for the plough. Cows were probably longhorns by the eighteenth century; they were good for both milk and beef.[2] Calves were reared for beef, but some cows were kept for their milk, which was used to make cheese and butter. Sheep could also provide milk, and sheep's milk had been produced in earlier centuries, but that had ceased in our period.[3]

Herds of cattle in Avebury were generally small, although their numbers were similar to those in other parts of England. In sixteenth and seventeenth century Myddle (Shropshire), for example, there were an average of 13.4 cattle per farmer.[4] In Avebury, as in Myddle, even the largest farmers had no more than twenty or thirty beasts. Cattle ate much more grass than sheep; indeed, some farmers did not have sufficient pasture for their beasts, and so practised agistment, that is, renting pasture to feed them. The vicar claimed tithe on cattle agisted on Avebury Great Farm.[5] Nevertheless, most farmers kept some cattle. In the late sixteenth century the Truslows kept 12 'kine' and a bull on East Down.[6] A century later, in 1689, Peter Griffin had 'seven oxen twelve cowes & one bull, three yearlings & three weanelings' together worth £57. He also had his own 'dayry house', where he kept 'one cheese presse, one silt, one cheese cowle, one churne & cheese fats, one powderinge tubb, milke pans & kevers with other utensils', together worth £2.[7] These were all used in cheese-making.[8] In his cheese loft he had 'cheese of all sorts' worth £6, together with cheese racks for storage. John Rose was another substantial farmer who kept cattle. Thirty cows and oxen were recorded in his 1720 inventory.[9] Unfortunately, his cheese making equipment is hidden under the term 'All ye houssell goodes'.

1 Smith, Nicola, op cit, p.192.
2 Wilson, *Forgotten Harvest*, op cit, p.63.
3 Wilson, *Forgotten Harvest*, op cit, p.28-9.
4 Hey, op cit, p.67.
5 WSHC 184/1/2. Letter, Humfry Wall to Sir Richard Holford, 5th June 1698.
6 TNA E134/41Eliz/Hil8.
7 WSHC P3/G/413.
8 For a discussion of the cheese-making process, see Wilson, *Forgotten harvest,* op cit, passim.
9 WSHC P3/R/365.

Richard Hickley, another century later, had 22 'cows of different sorts' in 1791[1] In May 1791 he purchased a bull for six guineas to serve them.[2] By November 1798 his herd had been reduced to eight cows.[3]

Others specialised in either 'rother beasts' (bullocks or oxen) or milking cows. In 1636, Christopher Battington (1636) had twenty 'rother beasts', worth £51.[4] Similarly, John Hayward (1661) had 'fifteen rudder beast and nine calves' valued at £50.[5] Others kept cows for their milk. John Jacob's thirteen cows (1670) were worth £26,[6] and were accompanied by 'cheese and cheese racks' worth £3. John Mills (1681) had 'nine cow beas & six pigs' together worth £30. He also had cheese and bacon in his kitchen, together with other 'lumber goods', worth £6 10s.[7] A yeoman or husbandman who could make cheese had a potential stream of income.

It has been suggested that the average number of cows kept in the cheese country of North Wiltshire was between ten and twelve.[8] In Avebury, however, many kept just a few cows. Sometimes their produce was just for domestic consumption, but it is likely that the eleven cheeses valued at 3s 8d recorded in Charles Summers' probate inventory in 1682 were for sale (although it is doubtful that they were produced from the milk of the one cow that was in his possession when he died).[9] Richard Trewman, the blacksmith (1617), similarly had just one cow.[10] Richard Cue, husbandman, had two cows and two pigs, together worth £5.[11] John Peart, the vicar (1621), had three 'kine', which had presumably provided the milk needed to make his 'butter & cheese with other provision' worth £2[12]. Poor cottagers with just one cow could graze it on the unploughed land between cultivated strips in the open fields, or on the strips themselves after harvest, when they were fallow.[13] Richard Hickley, on the other hand, raised twelve calves, which he sold. The five cows he still had in April 1794 continued to provide butter and cheese for two households, his own, and

---

1 WSHC 184/4/1. List of stock, 1791.
2 WSHC 184/7.
3 WSHC 271/6.
4 WSHC P3/B/368.
5 WSHC P3/H/339.
6 WHSC P3/IJ/101.
7 WSHC P3/M/239.
8 Wilson, *Forgotten Harvest,* op cit, p.51.
9 WSHC P3/S/634.
10 WSHC P3/T/50.
11 WSHC P3/K/92.
12 WSHC P3/P/101.
13 Wilson, *Forgotten Harvest,* op cit, p.67.

that of the Rennald family.[1] In the following month he intended to visit Calne fair to buy another one,[2] although he was reluctant to keep too many cows. In April 1792, he hoped to sell some of the 'worst old cows' and to reduce the number he milked to just five or six.[3] By June he only had eight cows, and milked five of them; he intended to 'make what cheese I can', but did not think he would make much unless more grass grew on the Downs.[4] In 1793, he had no cheese suitable to send to Mrs Williamson in Jamaica, and had decided to 'make no chees, at least but very little', just enough for the family. That also applied to butter.[5] Butter is mentioned in the inventories much less frequently than cheese, probably because little was made for sale, and appraisers thought that its value meant that it did not warrant a mention.

The dairy products listed in inventories were probably for sale; inventories do not normally record perishable food kept for home consumption. John Aubrey described Marlborough as 'one of the greatest markets for cheese in the West of England',[6] and it is likely that Avebury cheeses were sent there.[7] Cheese sales are, however, rarely recorded in our sources. We do know that farmers of Avebury Great Farm frequently made cheese for their landlord. When Peter Griffin negotiated his tenancy, he promised 'one hundred of the best new milk cheese made about the month of May' would be reserved for Lady Holford. His successor, John Rose, promised in 1744 that a cheese 'shall be made according to your orders as good as possible in the month of May'.[8]

Cows were usually kept in the fields all year, and milked there.[9] Wooden milk pails or buckets were used by the dairy maids to carry milk back to the dairy (frequently termed white house or dey house) on yokes. Sir Richard Holford was one of the first to realise that shelter kept cows in better condition, and needing less food. As a result of the persistent urging of his tenant, John Rose,[10] he erected 'extraordinary' cow stalls 'for sheltering & comfort of

1   WSHC 184/6. Letter, Richard Hickley to Mrs Williamson, 1st April 1794.
2   WSHC 184/6. Letter, Richard Hickley to Mrs Williamson, 2nd May 1794.
3   WSHC 184/6. Letter, Richard Hickley to Mrs Williamson, 30th April 1792.
4   WSHC 184/6. Richard Hickley to Mrs Williamson, 5th June 1792.
5   WSHC 184/6. Letter, Richard Hickley to Mrs Williamson, 4th June 1793 & 2nd July 1793.
6   Cited by Bettey, op cit, p.19.
7   *VCH Wilts* 12, p.209; Bettey, op cit, p.19.
8   WSHC 184/1. Letter, James Mayo to Stayner Holford, 31st March 1744.
9   Wilson, *Forgotten Harvest,* op cit, p.60.
10 GA D1956/E2/8.

cattle & saving fodder & soyle [dung]'.[1] His house had a 'dairy house' at the northern end of the west wing.[2]

In the inventories, dairy produce is frequently mentioned in conjunction with bacon. Bacon was probably the main source of meat for most people. The pig was cheap, easy to raise, fed on practically anything (including the whey from cheese-making), and matured quickly. It was 'the husbandman's best scavenger, the housewife's most wholesome sink', and its meat kept better than all other flesh.[3] Jean Pope, the widow (1713), was particularly well supplied; she had thirteen sides of bacon in her buttery, as well as a cheese press.[4] She also had 'one fatt pigg' and 'six store pigs', together worth £6 2s. Pigs were kept by most farmers, and also by many tradesmen and labourers. Richard Hickley had 48 'pigs great & small' in 1791 – the largest known herd.[5] A century earlier, in 1689, Peter Griffin had 'tenne hog-pigs & eighteene store pigs' worth £19.[6] He also had six 'flitches of bacon' worth £5 8s. John Rose's eighteen pigs (1720) were valued at £15.[7] The size of these three herds were exceptional. The vicar, Nathaniel Power (1670), was more typical; he had four pigs worth £2 6s. The carpenter Humphry Robinson's single pig (1720) was worth £1.[8] Flitches of bacon are frequently mentioned in inventories; decedents had evidently owned a pig just before they died, and had killed it for bacon. Richard Cripps, the blacksmith (1670), had 'one flitch & a halfe of bacon' in the 'roome that is over the shopp'.[9] Walter Stretch, yeoman (1708), did not have any live pigs. He must have recently killed them, as he did have '8 flitches of bacon' worth £6.[10] He probably died at the beginning of winter, as pigs were frequently slaughtered then in order to provide bacon for the winter.[11] Pigs were also slaughtered to feed harvest workers: Richard Hickley had to buy a side of bacon to feed his harvesters in the autumn of 1794.[12] He evidently had none of his own ready for slaughter.

1   WSHC 184/4/1. John Rose's renewal of lease, 1717.
2   WSHC 184/4. Plan of the house, gardens and barton, 1695.
3   Thirsk, op cit, p.192.
4   WSHC P3/P/644.
5   WSHC 184/4/1. List of stock, 1791.
6   WSHC P3/G/413.
7   WSHC P3/R/365.
8   WSHC P1/R/275.
9   WSHC P3/C/352.
10 WSHC P1/S/709. The inventory is dated 1st August, but the date of burial is not recorded.
11 Wilson, *Forgotten Harvest*, op cit, p.43.
12 WSHC 184/7.

Two inventories value 'swine and powltry' together: George Brown's appraisers (1619) valued his at £2 6s 8d;[1] a year later, his wife Margery's were worth 15s. Poultry were valued for their eggs, which were an important part of the diet of the poor. In 1694, Joseph Hayward kept a cock and two hens; the latter provided him with thirty or forty eggs per year.[2] Very few poultry appear in the inventories; their value was small, and it is likely that most appraisers thought them not worth listing. Thomas Phelps als Bromham (c.1621) had 'powltries of all sortes' worth 6s 8d in 1621.[3] Christopher Battington's poultry were valued with his coarse wool and sacks; together, they were worth £1 16s 8d.[4] John Peart's poultry were valued with his bees at £1.[5] Stayner Holford kept poultry when he took his farm in hand; his accounts for late 1755 record many eggs.[6] Richard Hickley in 1792 was hoping to 'make something of poultry this summer' by selling their eggs.[7] In April and May 1793 he took 15s 6d, and noted that 32 chickens, 16 ducks, and 17 turkeys had hatched.[8] A month later, he advised his landlady that he had a 'tollerable stock of poultry', although few pigeons.[9]

In 1698, William Skeat sent a turkey to Sir Richard Holford in London.[10] Turkeys were introduced to England in the sixteenth century. Turkeys and geese, as well as hens, are all mentioned in John White's Chancery bill claiming tithes.[11]

Bees were also tithable. They provided honey, which must have been a welcome addition to a diet which was otherwise sugarless. John White claimed tithe on honey wax produced on Avebury Great Farm.[12] Hives or stalls of bees are mentioned in twelve inventories. Most had no more than three or four hives, although Richard Cripps, the blacksmith (1670), had no fewer than 22 'stockes of bees'.[13] Like poultry, their value was small; Cripps' hives were valued with a grindstone, a ladder, and other 'lumber' at £7. A substantial number of hives

1 WSHC P3/B/179.
2 WSHC 1669/5.
3 WSHC P3/P/93.
4 WSHC P3/B/368.
5 WSHC P3/P/101.
6 WSHC 271/4.
7 WSHC 184/6. Letter, Richard Hickley to Mrs Williamson, 8th June 1792.
8 WSHC 184/7.
9 WSHC 184/6. Letter, Richard Hickley to Mrs Williamson, 4th June 1793.
10 WSHC 184/1.
11 WSHC 1569/5.
12 WSHC 184/1, pt.2. Letter, Humfry Wall to Sir Richard Holford, 5th June 1698.
13 WSHC P3/C/352.

were also owned by John Mills (1701), a husbandman, whose inventory notes that his personal possessions were worth a mere £12 15s 8d. That included his fourteen hives valued at 35s.[1] Thomas Andrews (1601), another husbandman, owned at least seven hives; he gave one to each of his seven children.[2] Richard Brown, a taylor, had bees worth 10s in his garden.[3] Many of Avebury's apiarists were tradesmen or small husbandmen, rather than substantial farmers. Bee keeping was a useful source of income for the industrious poor.

The poor also benefited from the crops they could grow for themselves in their gardens. Many cottages had small gardens attached. Cottagers grew potatoes, cabbages, onions and beans in their gardens. Lettice Sweetapple's garden in neighbouring West Overton was full of such produce (except for cabbages, which she disliked).[4] It is likely that potatoes and beans were grown more widely in the late eighteenth century than is apparent in most sources;[5] in 1801 the curate reported to the Home Office that there had been a very good crop.[6]

Two gardens at the manor house are mentioned in the manorial survey of 1548;[7] the one adjoining the dovecot was enlarged by John Truslow in the late sixteenth century,[8] but there is no evidence relating to crops grown in them until the eighteenth century. In 1711, Sir Richard Holford planned to replant his orchard with between 80 and 100 trees, and called in William Thomas, a gardener from Broad Town, to undertake the task.[9] Eight apple trees were planted in 1712.[10] In 1717, Holford had apple trees, pears, cherries, plums, gooseberries and currant bushes planted, as well as vegetables including leeks, onions and kidney beans.[11] 'Coucambar glases' were purchased by Richard Holford in 1741, presumably for growing cucumbers.[12] Arthur Jones again bought new cucumber frames in 1781.[13] Jones also had a greenhouse, which

1 WSHC P3/M/324.
2 TNA PROB11/103/328.
3 WSHC P1/B/646.
4 Fowler & Blackwell, op cit, p.145.
5 They were grown extensively in Wessex in the late eighteenth century; Bettey, op cit, p.30.
6 Turner, op cit, p.81.
7 WSHC 2664/1/2D/8.
8 TNA E134/41Eliz/Hil8.
9 GA D1956/E2/8.
10 Fretwell, Katie. *Avebury Manor: Park and Garden Survey.* National Trust, 1992 (unpublished report),
11 GA D1956/E2/8.
12 WSHC 184/5.
13 WSHC 184/5. Stephen Crook's bill, 1781.

his successor needed to replace in 1794.[1] It may be that the water cress Richard Hickley ate for the sake of his health in 1794 was grown there;[2] so, probably, were the bottles of gooseberries sent to Jamaica in July 1794.[3] Grapes were grown in the hothouse in 1794, and 'ripened well', but those planted outside did not ripen at all, and an attempt to grow vines at the farm failed.[4] Potatoes and gooseberries were to be planted in the garden in 1793.[5] In the same year, General Williamson's gardener purchased a range of vegetable seeds: onions, carrots, leeks, cabbage, cauliflower, celery, & beans, amongst others.[6] Apricots were growing in 1794.[7] Some old cherry trees 'bore a fine crop' in 1794.[8] The gardener made ten gallons of cherry brandy from them.[9] Hickley sent damsons, mushrooms, cantilups, and onions to his master in Jamaica the same year.[10] According to the gardener, in 1794 'the garden was as full as can bee of fruite trees'.[11] The bailiff even had to pay £1 10s 6d for 'two tubs for the orange trees' in July of that year.[12] We do not know whether they produced fruit. However, in January 1793 Hickley had to purchase a sack of potatoes costing 3s 6d,[13] presumably to be consumed by the occupants of the manor house, and perhaps his own servants. Receipts from the sale of garden produce frequently appear in Richard Hickley's accounts, although they generally amount to no more than £2 or £3.[14] In 1794, the poor benefited from the many cabbages and other greens that Richard Hickley was unable to sell.[15]

Fruit was also important. The importance of apples is illustrated by the fact that Maud Truslow (1625)[16] had an apple loft. It is probable that the sixteen bottles of cyder Thomas Hunter had in his cellar in 1748/9 were made

1 WSHC 184/6. Letter, Richard Hickley to Mrs Williamson, 31st July 1792.
2 WSHC 184/6. Letter, Richard Hickley to Mrs Williamson, 30th March 1794.
3 WSHC 184/6. Letter, Richard Hickley to Mrs Williamson, 31st August, 1794.
4 WSHC 184/6. Letter, William Richardson to Mrs Williamson, 1st December 1794.
5 WSHC 184/6. Letter, William Richardson to Mrs Williamson, 4th December 1792
6 WSHC 184/6. Hugh Lavington's account.
7 WSHC 271/16. Letter, William Richardson to Mrs Williamson, 5th August 1794.
8 WSHC 184/6. Letter, Richard Hickley to Mrs Williamson, 30th July 1794.
9 WSHC 271/16. Letter, the gardener to Mrs Williamson, 5th August 1794.
10 WSHC 186/6. Letter, Richard Hickley to Mrs Williamson, 30th November 1794.
11 WSHC 271/16. Letter, William Richardson to Mrs Williamson, 5th August 1794.
12 WSHC 184/7.
13 WSHC 184/7.
14 WSHC 184/7.
15 WSHC 184/6. Letter, Richard Hickley to Mrs Williamson, 1st December 1794.
16 WSHC P3/T/86.

from apples grown in the parish's orchards.[1] Some of the less wealthy also had their own apple trees; Joseph Hayward in 1694 had three or four in his orchard.[2]

John White's Chancery bill tells us that, in addition to apples, the fruit grown in the parish included pears, plums, cherries, apricots, and hops. Such produce was not always intended to benefit the poor. In 1698, William Skeat's daughter sent a 'bascat of aples' to Sir Richard Holford's children in London.[3] When Farmer Skeat was preparing to vacate Avebury Great Farm in 1709, Sir Richard Holford asked Skeat's wife 'to sett beans & to sett some parsley & sage, and cabbage or coleworts or other garden stuff at my charge'.[4] In 1717, a new orchard in 'the Shere Barton [was] fully planted with peare trees, apple trees, cherry trees, & plum trees, goosberrys & currants'.[5] When Peter Griffin proposed to lease Avebury Great Farm in 1721/2, he promised to 'take care to preserve the fruit in the new orchard for the landlady's use' – a promise which he may not have fully kept.[6] In August 1723, a basket of apples and peaches was sent up to London for her successor, Samuel Holford, with a letter from 'T.H.', complaining that Peter Griffin's servants had already purloined several bushels of fruit – including raspberries and strawberries - which Holford should have had.[7] Griffin's 1721/2 proposal had included a provision for '5 load of soyle [dung] from the yard to be drawn by the tenant to any parte of the orchards & near it'; this provided the fertiliser for Holford's orchard and garden.[8] The lease to Griffin excluded the orchard. Towards the end of the century, the Williamson's gardener, William Richardson, reported that he had planted gooseberries and currants,[9] and that he had sent '7 dozen of apricots' to London (presumably for sale).[10] In 1794, he harvested 212 lb of cherries, which he made into cherry brandy.[11]

1   WSHC P3/H/1256.
2   WSHC 1669/5.
3   WSHC 184/1, pt.1. William Skeat to Sir Richard Holford, 16th February 1698.
4   WSHC 184/1, pt.2. Letter, Sir Richard Holford to William Skeat, 23rd February 1709.
5   GA D1956/E2/8.
6   WSHC 184/1,pt.2. Peter Griffin's proposals for taking Avebury Great Farm, 9th January 1721/2.
7   WSHC 184/1, pt.2. Letter, T.H., to Samuel Holford, 26th August 1723.
8   WSHC 184/1,pt.2. Peter Griffin's proposals for taking Avebury Great Farm, 9th January 1721/2.
9   WSHC 184/6. Letter, William Richardson to Mrs Williamson, 4th December 1792.
10 WSHC 271/16. Letter, William Richardson to Mrs Williamson, 5th August 1794.
11 Ditto.

Food was also provided by rabbits, by pigeons, by fish, and by deer, all of which were farmed, although also found in the wild. In the medieval period, rabbits became valued for both their flesh and their fur, and were increasingly nurtured in artificial burrows called warrens.[1] The well-drained, steep lands of the chalk provided congenial habitats.[2] Rabbit warrens provided a good use for poor soils, and a means of meeting the growing demand for meat and rabbit skins. In nearby Aldbourne, perhaps 5,000 rabbits were sold every year in the late medieval period.[3] We do not know how many were sold at Avebury, but we do know that the lord of the manor had his warren in the mid-sixteenth century.[4] It was perhaps replaced by the rabbit house which formed part of the manor house in 1711.[5] In 1793, Richard Hickley promised to look out for some rabbits to send to Mrs Williamson in Jamaica.[6] Some rabbits escaped from the warrens, but few survived in the wild until the eighteenth and nineteenth centuries, when gamekeepers launched an assault on natural predators such as stoats, weasels, and polecats, and when fodder crops began to be planted in place of winter fallows, providing winter feed for them.[7]

Pigeons were another source of food, sufficiently important for John White, the vicar, to claim tithe on them.[8] Sir Richard Holford denied the claim, but nevertheless thought that his tenant ought to occasionally send some to the vicarage out of neighbourly respect. A contemporary commentator thought that a pigeon house would yield at least £5 per annum.[9] There were at least two pigeon houses in the parish. Joan Truslow built one in the Parsonage Barton in the late sixteenth century;[10] it is still a feature of the National Trust yard. There was another at West Kennett in the early eighteenth century.[11] These

1 Bettey, Joseph. 'Downland', in Thirsk, Joan, ed. *The English Rural Landscape*. Oxford University Press, 2000, p.37.
2 Wilson, *Forgotten labour*, op cit, p.158.
3 Hare, John. 'Agriculture and Settlement in Wiltshire and Hampshire', in Aston, Michael, & Lewis, Carenza, eds., *The medieval landscape of Wiltshire*. Oxbow monography 46. 1994, p.164.
4 WSHC 2664/1/2D/8.
5 Fretwell, op cit, p.29.
6 WSHC 184/6. Letter, Richard Hickley to Mrs Williamson, 4th June 1793.
7 Bond, James. 'Forests, Chases, Warrens and Parks in Medieval Wessex', in Aston & Lewis, op cit, p.146-7.
8 WSHC 184/1, pt.2. Letter, Sir Richard Holford to John White, 2nd April 1710.
9 Markham, Sarah. *John Loveday of Caversham, 1711-1789: the Life and Tours of an Eighteenth-Century onlooker*. Michael Russell, 1984, p.5.
10 WANHS Wiltshire Genealogy, v.A-A, f.91.
11 It is recorded in two of Thomas Smith's leases in 1729 and 1745; cf.WSHC 568/7.

houses provided for the tables of the elite. Pigeons were also sold commercially: Richard Hickley asked 3s per dozen in 1792.[1]

Fish were also farmed in Avebury. In 1729, Thomas Smith had a 'fish pond that is now making' at West Kennett.[2] One wonders whether any of the other manorial lords had a fishpond.

Farmers also diversified by breeding horses. They were owned by the elite, by yeomen, and by the more prosperous tradesmen. Horses were kept for a variety of different purposes. John White's 1697 bill of complaint[3] tells us that horses, geldings, and mares were frequently let out for hire, presumably to travellers on the Bath Road. White thought that such hire generated a substantial profit. Richard Hickley distinguished between his 2 'saddle horses', kept for riding, and his 11 'cart horses' in 1791.[4] Leading landowners like Walter Dunch, Sir John Stawell and Sir Richard Holford owned their own coach horses. William Skeat was able to sell 'a paire of good sound horses' to Alexander Popham, esq., of Littlecote (Ramsbury) in 1700, although he was upset when Popham's servants mistakenly 'drenched' one of them (for medicinal purposes) and so killed it.[5] He asked Holford (his landlord), to speak to Lord Rennell when the latter was seeking a grey gelding for his coach, as he had one to sell.[6] When Holford himself needed a gelding, he asked a neighbour, William Smith, for help, and was advised 'that if ye case wase mine I would espye out a good coulered & well markd young gelding out of a countery mans hand, that hath not been tampered with, xi in hed, handleth his leggs well. I could have him soon perfected for any gentillmans use by an excellent horserider liveing now at Calne, which of late hath shewn his skill in many horses to ye admiration of many'.[7] Holford again needed a 'nag' in 1711. John Rose, his new tenant, promised that 'if your worship will venture my skill I will do the best I can to please you, and if hee prove not according to expectation not to bee blamed afterward'.[8]

When Holford came down to Avebury from London in August 1714,

1 WSHC 184/6. Letter, Richard Hickley to Mrs Williamson, 8th June 1792.
2 WSHC 568/7. Lease, Thomas Smith to Robert Caswell, 3rd September 1729.
3 WSHC 1569/5.
4 WSHC 184/4/1. List of stock, 1791.
5 WSHC 184/1, pt.1. Letter, William Skeat to Sir Richard Holford, 6th July 1700.
6 WSHC 184/1, pt.1. Letter, William Skeat to Sir Richard Holford, 16th February 1698/9
7 WSHC 184/1, pt.1. Letter, William Smith to Sir Richard Holford, 11th Febuary 1700.
8 WSHC 184/1, pt.2. John Rose to Sir Richard Holford, 23rd February 1711/12.

his coach was pulled by 'four fine horses'.[1] He was accompanied by his son on horseback. The horses were refreshed at the end of their journey by the large 'horse pool', outside of Avebury Manor house, which was 'walled round, & very good water'.[2] Holford had some 'very good stables' to accommodate them. His agreement with John Rose in 1710 provided for the care of his horses when he visited; they were to have 'good & sufficient hay, corne and provender' together with straw for litter, 'at moderate and reasonable prices'.[3] Similarly, when Peter Griffin proposed renting Avebury Great Farm from Lady Holford in 1722, he agreed that she could reserve to herself 'the depasturing of a saddle horse at grass 20 weekes'. Her horses were to have 'wheate straw for litter when the family or any of them lie in the County'. Griffin was to sell her hay. She needed to make provision for her horses when she visited.[4] The horses which pulled her coach were probably her own, but she and others of gentry status sometimes needed to hire horses for their coaches, or to ride to London and other distant destinations. Both John Peart and Nathaniel Power, successive vicars, would have used their horses whilst visiting their parishioners;[5] so, doubtless, did their successors – especially the Mayos, who had to ride from their house in Calne to take services. But most horses would have been used for motive power on farms, pulling ploughs or waggons. When General Williamson died in 1798, his bailiff recorded that there were 14 horses on his farm. He also had six wagons, three carts, four ploughs, eleven harrows, one drag, two rollers, and one drag plough – all of which would have been pulled by horses or oxen.[6] George Brown (1619) had 'three cart horses with their harnisse' valued at £8;[7] they were evidently used for haulage purposes, probably on his farm, but possibly also for hire. John Jacob's 'six horse beasts' (1670) were valued with their 'harnesse plows carts & waggons', suggesting that, like oxen, horses were sometimes harnessed to the plough.[8] Like Jacob, other substantial farmers frequently had several horses. Richard Harding (1627), for example, had five, valued, with their harness, at £18.[9] Christopher

1 WSHC 184/8.
2 WSHC 184/1, pt.1. Letter, Sir Richard Holford to John Gardiner, 21st August 1701.
3 WSHC 184/4/1. Articles of agreement, Sir Richard Holford and John Rose, 1710.
4 WSHC 184/1, pt.2. Peter Griffin's proposals for taking Avebury Great Farm, 9th January 1721/2.
5 WSHC P3/P/101; P3/P/329.
6 WSHC 271/6.
7 WSHC P3/B/179.
8 WHSC P3/IJ/101.
9 WSHC P3/H/210.

Battington (1636) had eight horses in his stable, valued at £34.[1] John Hayward (1661) had nine, said to be worth £50 with their harness,[2] although the same nine (probably) were valued at £85 when his widow died two years later.[3] John Rose's ten horses were worth £60 in 1720.[4] In 1794, Richard Hickley had twelve horses, which, with his four oxen, would 'do the work' of ploughing up 'the two large inclosures on the Down'.[5] But he intended to sell the oxen, once the rest of the Downs had been enclosed, as they needed too much hay, and there would be less work for them.

Many others – tradesmen as well as farmers – had just one horse. Joseph Hayward sometimes lent (or hired?) his nag to his neighbours. It may also have carried his stock of trade as a chapman.[6] Richard Cripps, the blacksmith (1670),[7] also had his horse, as did his contemporary, Lemuel Fowler, the innkeeper (and yeoman).[8] Toby King (1685), another blacksmith, had two.[9] Shoeing horses was a major source of income for blacksmiths. They had, of course, to treat them with respect. Three deaths reported to the coroner in the late eighteenth century resulted from a horse's kick. One must have sympathy for the horse which had just been ridden by John Willis; he 'imprudently beating a horse he was unharnessing was kicked by it and killed'.[10]

Blacksmiths would also have made the wide variety of farm implements that were found in Avebury. Richard Hickley's implements in 1791 included five waggons, three carts, two rollers, seven harrows, two drags, and four ploughs.[11] These all required oxen or horses to pull them. He also had a winnowing fan, seven sieves, eighty sacks, and eight corn staddles (used to support stacks of wheat above the ground to prevent rodent damage), amongst other items.

The traditional sheep-corn husbandry at Avebury began to disappear at the end of the eighteenth century, although Defoe noticed the expansion of arable farming on the Downs as early as 1726.[12] The emphasis turned to

1 WSHC P3/B/368.
2 WSHC P3/H/339.
3 WSHC P3/H/369.
4 WSHC P3/R/365.
5 WSHC 184/6. Richard Hickley to Mrs Williamson, 2nd November 1794.
6 WSHC 1669/5.
7 WSHC P3/C/352.
8 WSHC P3/F/135.
9 WSHC P3/K/106.
10 Hunnisett, R.F., ed. *Wiltshire Coroners' Bills 1752-1796*. Wiltshire Record Society 36. 1980, no.1799.
11 WSHC 184/4/1. List of stock, 1791.
12 Cited by Wordie, op cit, p.333. See also p.337.

producing mutton. From c.1770, wethers began to be replaced by breeding ewes.[1] Consequently, new breeds more suited for this purpose were introduced. Joseph Mighell of Kennett was reputedly the first to introduce Southdown and Leicester Cross breeds to Wiltshire, in 1789.[2] In 1793, Richard Hickley 'had a great deal of talk with Mr Mighell about them at different times. Many people are getting into the sort of them, but it is the general opinion, after they becomes plenty in this country, they will not be approved of, that is, they will not sell. Therefore I wish to wait a year or two to see the event, as it would be a sad piece of business to have them to change again if they should not answer.'[3] His caution was justified: unseasonably severe cold in June 1795, just as the sheep had been shorn, caused huge losses of sheep in Wiltshire, especially amongst the new Spanish breed: perhaps one-fourth of the sheep were lost.[4] The new breeds were less hardy than the old Wiltshire Crocks; they were unable to live on coarse grass, or to walk long distances to find fodder.

Enclosure at Avebury took place during the early years of the Napoleonic wars. The enclosure process resulting from the act of 1792 has already been discussed; it remains to be pointed out that it took place against the background of a war which demanded a different type of husbandry. Richard Hickley anticipated that, for his mistress's estate, 'the course of the husbandry will be so altered there won't be near the work to be don as at present', and thought that in consequence he would be able to sell four oxen, and rely solely on horse power. Oxen ate too much hay.[5] Hickley did his best to anticipate the changing nature of farming. The course of husbandry did indeed change, but it is unlikely that Hickley foresaw the full impact of the coming changes; indeed, ploughing up the Downs probably meant more work, not less. The high prices offered for arable produce as a result of war encouraged the plough, and impoverished the soil. War put an end to the old sheep/corn husbandry.[6] The Wiltshire Crocks disappeared in the early nineteenth century. The dominance of sheep was finally ended by the coming of the railways in the mid-nineteenth century.[7]

1 Smith, op cit, p.193.
2 Stedman, op cit, p.363.
3 WSHC 184/6. Letter, Richard Hickley to Mrs Williamson, 8th November 1793.
4 Waylen, James. *A history, Military and Municipal, of the Ancient Borough of Devizes.* Longman Brown & Co., 1859, p.470.
5 WSHC 184/6. Richard Hickley to Mrs Williamson, 6th March 1792.
6 Bettey, Joseph. 'Downland', in Thirsk, Joan, ed. *The English Rural Landscape.* Oxford University Press, 2000, p.44.
7 Bettey, op cit, p.32-3.

7
EARNING A LIVING:
OCCUPATIONS, TRADES, AND PROFESSIONS

THE GREAT MAJORITY of the adult population in early modern Avebury were involved in agricultural activities. At the end of our period, the 1801 census enumerators for the Avebury enumeration district counted 201 'persons chiefly employed in agriculture'. Another 23 persons were 'chiefly engaged in trade, manufactures, or handicraft'.[1] There were also 366 persons – presumably mostly women and children - supposedly engaged in neither. These figures must be treated with a degree of scepticism. It is likely that many tradesmen also kept a cow or two, that many farmers also engaged occasionally in trades such as weaving or thatching, and that many women (and children) were in fact employed part-time.

We have already seen that the plight of the poor was giving much concern in the 1790s. Just after the end of our period, a school to teach straw plaiting was established in Avebury, and a person from London was employed to teach the trade to 'all the females of the parish'.[2] Within a couple of years, there were c.100 women employed earning between 3s and 10s per week.

If we rely on the 1801 census figures to record occupations, we will only gain a simplistic view of occupations in late 18th century Avebury. A much more detailed picture can be gained by investigating what might be called life-cycle occupations, and then examining the specific occupations hidden under the 1801 banners of 'agriculture' and 'trades'.

The first 'occupation' that most people followed was attending school. We have already identified the names of several schoolmasters, and seen that a school for the poor was established in Avebury in the 1730s, in accordance with

---

1 www.histpop.org
2 Bernard, Thomas. 'Extract of an account of the introduction of straw platt at Avebury', *The Reports of the Society for Bettering the Conditions and Increasing the Comforts of the Poor*, 4, 1802-5, p.90-110.

the will of Lady Holford.[1] There is little evidence of other educational provision, although one wonders whether the grammar school run by successive vicars of Avebury in mid-eighteenth century Calne attracted any Avebury pupils. It may be, too, that some Avebury children attended the grammar school at Marlborough; an Avebury landlord, Charles Tooker, J.P., sat on a Commission investigating the school in 1711.[2] It is possible that his son, who subsequently studied at Oxford, had formerly been a pupil.[3] Most children of gentlemen and yeomen were taught reading and writing, but we know little of the educational provision made for them. We can identify a number of illiterates. Sir Richard Holford was concerned that his tenant John Rose was illiterate.[4] John Brown's illiteracy presented his administrator with considerable problems when he died in 1732: he had failed to keep accounts of his extensive financial dealings with his neighbour Peter Griffin. And it is not surprising that Brown's servant (and prospective wife), Susanna Pope, was also illiterate.[5] Even Bridget Truslow, the daughter of a gentleman, had to make her mark when she signed a receipt in 1721.[6]

Until the founding of Lady Holford's school, it is likely that the children of the poor were illiterate, and stayed at home until they could either enter service or take up an apprenticeship. In 1789, Arthur Jones' bequests to the daughters of his bailiff, Richard Hickley, encouraged their parents to 'place them out to be instructed in reading, writing, needlework, etc.'[7] – but probably not in the charity school.

It is not clear whether Joan Cue, the orphaned daughter of Richard Cue, was sent to school by her step-father, Thomas Pontin. However, by the age of twelve she was able to spin, knit, and sew; she 'applied herself thereunto and had what she earned', rather than serving Pontin.[8]

The Statute of Apprentices and Artificers required tradesmen to serve a long apprenticeship before they practiced their trade. Those who had not served an apprenticeship were not supposed to trade. In 1647, Roger Norman,

1 See above, p.171-3.
2 Stedman, A.R. *Marlborough and the Upper Kennet country.* [Marlborough College?], 1960, p.193.
3 WSHC 184/1, pt. 2. Letter, Charles Tooker to Sir Richard Holford, c.29th December 1697, in which he writes, 'My son I have latly taken home from Oxford'.
4 WSHC 184/1, pt.2. Letter, Sir Richard Holford to William Skeat, 3rd February 1709/10.
5 TNA C11/363/65; C11/777/21.
6 WSHC 371/1, pt.5. Acknowledgement by Bridget Truslow, 6th November 1721.
7 TNA PROB11/1181/174.
8 TNA C6/98/30.

a shoemaker of Calne, complained to Quarter Sessions that Robert Morris of Avebury, husbandman, had set himself up as a shoemaker without serving an apprenticeship. He was therefore illegally competing for business with Norman.[1]

Apprentices were required to serve their masters for seven years, and to be totally obedient to them. Masters were usually expected to provide food, clothing, and lodging, and to teach apprentices their trade. Parents frequently paid substantial premiums to secure apprenticeships for their sons. In 1715, John Griffin instructed two trustees to apprentice his two children 'to some convenient trade', and provided £20 each to pay their premiums[2]. In 1720, John Tilly, the grandson of Humphry Robinson, was left £5 'to bind him apprentice when he do attaine to age for ye same'[3]. Apprenticeship indentures recorded the agreements made between masters and apprentices, but only one private indenture from Avebury has survived. That, unusually, was for a girl. In 1759, Nanny Moor apprenticed herself to Elizabeth Spencer of Berwick Bassett, a mantua maker.[4] A premium of £5 was paid by Robert Dangerfield.

Fortunately, the loss of indentures does not mean that the information in them is lost irretrievably. A number of other sources enable us to identify many Avebury apprentices. Those who were sent to London are recorded in the apprenticeship registers of London livery companies. Others can be identified in wills, and in the apprenticeship stamp duty registers of the eighteenth century.[5]

We have already mentioned Richard Phelps, who was probably apprenticed to the master of London's Whitechapel bell foundry.[6] Several other Avebury boys were apprenticed to London tradesmen.[7] Robert Rogers, the son of a mere husbandman, was apprenticed to a vintner in 1633. On the eve of Civil War, in 1641, Benjamin Goldsmith, son of a gentleman, was apprenticed to Thomas Hamor, a member of the elite Grocers Company. By 1700, these two boys had been followed by at least six others: John Bray (1655), Henry Griffin (freedom of London granted 1662),[8] William Plumer (1677), Charles

1 WSHC A1/115. Samuel Morris, perhaps a relative, was a cordwainer in 1724; see WSHC 529/185.
2 WSHC P3/G/454.
3 WSHC P1/R/275.
4 WSHC 184/9/3.
5 TNA IR1.
6 See above, p.115.
7 These are mostly recorded in London Apprenticeship Abstracts, 1442-1850 https://search.findmypast.co.uk/search-world-records/london-apprenticeship-abstracts-1442-1850
8 Radcliffe, F.R.Y. 'List of Wiltshiremen extracted from the minute books of the

Woodford (1683), Richard Cary (1693), and Joseph Rose (1694).[1] Their trades, respectively, were fishmonger, weaver, founder, gunmaker, turner, and armourer. It is likely too that John Brown of London, saddler, the nephew of John Brown of Avebury, tailor, was sent to London as an apprentice.[2]

More boys followed in the eighteenth century. 1705 saw the apprenticeship of Walter Truslow as a London carman; unusually, he was apprenticed to a widow, Mary Slaitch.[3] The vicar's son, Charles White, secured an apprenticeship as clerk to an apothecary in 1707.[4] John, the son of William Skeat, Sir Richard Holford's farmer, was apprenticed to Thomas Tarrant, broderer, in 1708, possibly through Holford's influence. Unusually, in 1711 Skeat was 'turned over' to a former fellow apprentice. When William Spackman, who was from a local family, completed his seven years servitude with Thomas Tarrant, he immediately took Skeat as his own apprentice for the final four years of his term.[5] Curiously, Spackman subsequently described himself as a grocer before returning to live in Avebury.[6] Skeat became a carpenter.[7] Men evidently did not necessarily follow the trade to which they had been apprenticed.

A number of later Avebury apprentices in London were recorded. In 1738, Richard Alexander, the son of Avebury's wheelwright, may have been apprenticed to a relative. His master was William Alexander, a tallow chandler.[8] William Clements, the son of Avebury's schoolmaster, went to serve Thomas Bromwich, painter, in 1756.[9] Alexander Shepherd was apprenticed to Daniel Hutchinson, skinner, in 1772.[10]

Company of Weavers of London, 1653-1674', *WAM*, 38, 1913-14, p.574.
1 Webb, Cliff. *London Livery Company Apprenticeship Registers vol.22. Armourers and Brasiers Company*. Society of Genealogists Enterprises, 2014, p.48.
2 He administered his uncle's estate; cf. WSHC P3/B/1308.
3 Webb, Cliff. *London Livery Company Apprenticeship Registers vol.29. Carmen's Company 168, 1678-1800*. Society of Genealogists, 2001, p.47.
4 Webb, Cliff. *London Livery Company Apprenticeship Registers vol.42. Society of Apothecaries, 1670-1800., with masons Company, 1619-1639*. Society of Genealogists Enterprises, 2006, p.48.
5 Webb, Cliff. *London Livery Company Apprenticeship Registers vol.6*. Society of Genealogists, 1997, p.27.
6 WSHC 568/7. Lease, 10th March 1712/13.
7 WSHC P1/9Reg/252.
8 Webb, Cliff. *London Livery Company Apprenticeship Registers, vol.39. Tallow Chandler's Company, 1633-1800*. Society of Genealogists, 2003, p.2.
9 Webb, Cliff. *London Livery Company Apprenticeship Registers, vol.38. Painter-Stainers Company, 1655, 1666-1800*. Society of Genealogists, 2003, p.13.
10 Webb, Cliff. *London Livery Company Apprenticeship Registers vol.47. Skinners*

A few apprentices served local masters. Four apprentices of Stephen Crook, an Avebury carpenter and wheelwright, can be identified in the apprenticeship stamp duty registers.[1] The first was his brother, Ambrose Crook, who was eight years younger, and entered indentures on 24th June 1756[2] - just after his new master had completed his own apprenticeship. Three others followed at roughly seven year intervals: Thomas Scotford in 1766[3], John Sims in 1772,[4] and Isaac Wheeler in 1777.[5] Others were taken on by George Arnold, a collar maker (1725),[6] Thomas Rogers, the village tailor (1768),[7] and Samuel Fowler, another carpenter (1786).[8] For the seventeenth-century, the names of a number of apprentices are known, but no details of their masters survive. Christopher Dyer's mother Bridget bequeathed forty shillings in 1629 to buy him a cloak when he came out of his apprenticeship[9]. Thomas Fry's father (also Thomas) left him the more substantial sum of £30 in 1691, to be paid when he came out of his apprenticeship.[10] The money was probably intended to enable him to establish himself in trade.

Boys were generally apprenticed in their early teens, although younger apprentices were known. If a child became an orphan, it was likely he would be apprenticed as soon as possible. When, in 1639, Thomas Bray bequeathed his unborn child £20 'to be payed att its full age of seven yeeres', he was anticipating the need for the child to be apprenticed at or soon after that age[11]. In 1705, John Truslow left £55 to the four children of Frances Hillier, widow, so that they could be bound apprentice at the discretion of parish notables[12].

Pauper apprenticeship was a perversion of the traditional system of private apprenticeship, although sometimes it did provide training in useful skills. There was, presumably, good reason for the overseers to send the young Thomas Burrows as far as Trowbridge in 1755, as apprentice to James Smith, broadweaver. The indenture was signed by John Griffin Grant, the churchwarden,

Company, 1604-1800. Society of Genealogists Enterprises, 2014, p.154.
1 TNA IR 1.
2 TNA IR 1/52.
3 TNA IR 1/56.
4 TNA IR 1/58.
5 TNA IR 1/60.
6 TNA IR 1/11.
7 TNA IR 1/56.
8 TNA IR 1/56.
9 WSHC P3/D/76. Will of Bridget Dyer.
10 WSHC P3/F/211.
11 WSHC P3/B/420.
12 WSHC P3/T/410.

whose father came from Trowbridge. Unfortunately, however, the master died, and the apprentice was left reliant on the Trowbridge overseers – who had to assume responsibility for him under the settlement laws, because he had served a Trowbridge master. They arranged to have his original apprenticeship discharged, but did not find another broad weaver to take him on. Instead, they entered into an entirely new indenture with Daniel Bailey, who was described as 'of Bradford', although now residing in Trowbridge. The boy was to learn the art of 'scribling of wool'.[1]

John Currier was another pauper who became the responsibility of the Avebury overseers. He too was sent to learn weaving, this time from James Pincks at Seend, c.1747. Many looms were to be found in the Seend of our period.[2] But Currier was a victim of the many fluctuations in the trade: he too found himself cast adrift. After 3½ years, 'his master turned him away and told him he had no more for him to do'. He found another master in Melksham, and stayed with him for three years. However, by 1763 John had returned to his birth-place, where the Justices interrogated him to determine his settlement.[3] By then he was probably in his late twenties, but does not appear to have been married. He subsequently married Jane Simms, whose illegitimate daughter, Sarah Simms, was examined in 1775.[4]

John Currier probably also had a sister named Jane; the siblings' indentures are both dated December 1747. She too was apprenticed to a broadweaver. Her master lived in Melksham, not far from her brother at Seend.

Fulling was another stage in the cloth-making process. In 1714, William Fry was sent to learn the trade of a fuller from Thomas Smith of Devizes,[5] who may have been related to an Avebury family.

Pauper apprenticeship frequently did not work out. The twelve-year old John Cary believed that he had been born in Avebury, but had been removed to Roundway when he was a mere three years old. At the age of seven – as was usual in pauper apprenticeship – he was bound to his uncle James at Avebury. After a year, however, the latter sent him away, placing him with John Bankard in Devizes. The boy did not know whether the legal paperwork involved in the 'turn-over' of an apprentice had been completed when he was sent to Bankard. Be that as it may, he left (absconded?) after about three months, and in 1740 he was apprehended as a 'rogue and vagabond' wandering and begging at Bedminster,

1 WSHC 206/56.
2 Bradby, Edward. *Seend: a Wiltshire Village past and present.* Alan Sutton 1981, p.72.
3 WSHC 184/9/2A. Settlement examination.
4 WSHC 184/9/2A.
5 WSHC 184/9/3.

in Somerset.[1] One wonders how a twelve-year old child could have survived so long on his own. In the absence of any paperwork, the Justice who examined him was uncertain whether he was legally settled in Avebury or Devizes, but nevertheless ordered the boy to be conveyed via houses of correction to Avebury.

Once an apprentice had served his term, he could set up his own business. That might require an initial expenditure. Alexander Pope had to borrow £40 for this purpose towards the end of the seventeenth century; the money was loaned to him by his step-father, John Mills.[2]

Those who were not bound apprentice – and many of those who were – could look forward to a life of servanthood. The poor were required to have masters. In 1687, the Grand Jury at Quarter Sessions presented that 'severall poore persons both men and maids doe live with theire poore friends ... and take upon them little or noe worke, by reason whereof many disorders and charges doe arise'. Consequently, 'servants are not to be had without great wages more than are usually sett or allowed by the law, which wee conceave to be a great grievance to the subject'.[3] Jurymen, of course, were mostly farmers and employers, who thought of themselves – not the poor – as the subjects.

Sir Adam Williamson's solution to the scarcity of servants, at the very end of our period (1798), was to bring back one of his teenage slaves from the West Indies. Williamson freed him in his will[4] (although slavery in England was illegal anyway!). He also bequeathed him £5 plus an annuity - an income for life - of £5. A month after his master's death, on 2nd December 1798, he was baptised as 'Samuel Avebury', and described as a 'mullato lad'. Williamson also had a 'black' servant, Elizabeth Pierce, to whom he left £10 and an annuity of £20. She too may have been brought back from the West Indies.

Williamson also had several English servants (who may have served him in Jamaica or St Domingue, and returned with him to Avebury), several of whom were given annuities in his will. Daniel Cannington and his wife Maria received £10 per annum, Miles Illingworth £5, and John Brown (servant at the farmhouse) £5, together with a lump sum of £5. Thomas Coxhead, the butler, received all his master's clothes, together with a lump sum of £50. There were also several un-named servants, each of whom was given one year's wages, together with whatever was already owing to them.

Williamson's servants were treated very generously. Usually, life as a servant was precarious. Edith Cruse recognised that when she made her will in 1753. She

1 Somerset Heritage Centre Q/SR/308/397-8.
2 TNA C5/174/72.
3 WSHC A1/110, 1687M, f.200.
4 TNA PROB 11/1315/187.

left her niece, Grace Penney, many of her clothes, but specified that they were not to be given her until she was seventeen, when she would need suitable apparel to be placed 'out to service'.[1] Young men and women were generally employed by the year, and lived in their masters' houses until they married. They were entitled to food and lodging, and received an annual lump sum (likely to increase as they gained skills and specialisms), in return for a varied range of duties.[2] Their diet at their master's table would have been much more reliable than what they could expect once they married and became day labourers. Many would have attended annual hiring fairs in Marlborough, Wootton Bassett, Devizes, or Cricklade, in order to secure a position.[3] Once taken on, they were obliged to work for a full year; otherwise they were liable to be called to account before a Justice of the Peace.

Servants were to be found in many households. They frequently had a precarious existence, although some were relatives of their masters/mistresses. Joan Wyatt, for example, lived with her aunt Joan Truslow for six years in the late sixteenth century.[4] Others developed close relationships with their employers. For example, Roger Whithorn, another of the Truslow's servants, lived with them for twenty years.[5] Susanna Brown only agreed to become John Brown's housekeeper when he promised to marry her. She lent her master £30 to help him lease his farm. And she also took charge of the key to his coffer, and his money.[6]

Masters who were close to their servants were sometimes willing to turn a blind eye to their mis-deeds. For example, Christopher Spencer, yeoman, who had once served as high constable, was quite prepared to permit his servant Andrew Mills to 'slippe away' when he was required to answer a charge of begetting a bastard in 1641.[7] Equally, servants might participate in their masters' mis-deeds. In 1699, four of John Rose's labourers were accused with their master of riotous behaviour when they prevented John White, the vicar, taking his tithe corn at Beckhampton.[8] A different Andrew Mills, together with a number of Sir

1 WSHC P3/C/935.
2 Armstrong, Alan. *Farmworkers: a Social and Economic History, 1770-1980.* B.T.Batsford, 1988, p.22.
3 Chandler, J.E. *A history of Marlborough: the Gateway to Ancient Britain.* White Horse Bookshop, 1977, p.18; Wadsworth, Alan, ed. *The Farming Diaries of Thomas Pinniger, 1813-1837.* Wiltshire Record Society 74. 2021, p.liv.
4 TNA E134/40and41Eliz/Mich7.
5 TNA E134/40and41Eliz/Mich7.
6 TNA C11/363/65; C11/777/21.
7 WSHC A1/110, 1641M, f.141.
8 WSHC A1/110, 1699M, f.113.

James Mervyn's servants, were accused of riotous behaviour c.1605 after they tried to depasture Mervyn's sheep on Downs whose ownership was disputed by Richard Truslow. Mills had been Mervyn's servant for 5 years, but had served his wife for 20 years before that.[1]

Servants could also be called on as witnesses to their masters' actions. When John White came to collect disputed tithes from Richard Caswell at Beckhampton, Sarah Hiscock, Caswell's servant, witnessed the payment her master made, and subsequently gave evidence to the Consistory Court on his behalf.[2] Equally, they could give evidence against their masters. When John Rose became bankrupt, his (former) servants provided evidence of his mismanagement of Stayner Holford's farm.[3]

The elite, of course, employed many servants. Sir Richard Holford had a coachman and a footman with him when he visited Avebury in 1700.[4] In 1711, his wife's maid travelled in the coach, which was driven by the coachman, Richard Bradney. Austin, a footman, travelled behind the coach. Another footman, John Hitchins, may have been on horseback.[5] They travelled in convoy with at least one other coach, which carried friends and relatives. On Sir Richard's 1714 visit, his coach was accompanied by his wife's maid, a cook maid, and his man Thomas, as well as by his son Samuel, on horseback.[6] In August 1717 his visit was similarly accompanied.[7] On his death in 1718, he left his servants £3 each 'to buy their mourning'.[8] His wife bequeathed her servants £5 each.[9]

Almost two decades later, in 1740 and 1741, their grandson, Richard Holford, brought three maids, and Edward, the man servant, with him.[10] In his 1767 will, Stayner Holford bequeathed 'such of my domestic servants as shall be in my service at the time of my decease … who have been in my service upwards of three years' sufficient money to purchase 'suitable and proper mourning'. That was only intended for his domestic servants, not those who were 'employed in the occupation of my farm'.[11] Domestic servants such as these were higher up the social scale than farm servants. There was a sharp distinction between the two.

1 TNA STAC8/281/25.
2 WSHC D1/42/67. White v.Caswell.
3 WSHC 184/4/1. Particular of John Rose's stock, 1755.
4 WSHC 184/8.
5 GA D1956/E2/8.
6 WSHC 184/8.
7 GA D1956/E2/8.
8 TNA PROB 11/564/122.
9 TNA PROB 11/590/280.
10 WSHC 184/4/1. Certificate by Peter and Mary Griffin, 15th December 1742.
11 TNA PROB11/932/345.

At the end of the eighteenth century, whilst the Williamson's were absent in Jamaica, the manor house was nevertheless staffed. Mrs Mitchell seems to have acted as housekeeper (although that word is not used), and was paid seven guineas per annum.[1] Richard Hickley frequently paid bills that she had incurred on household expenses. That included payment for servants. He paid Betty Hacker wages of 19s in December 1791;[2] she was probably Mrs Mitchell's maid. In 1797, '18 weeks pay to the girl at the house' amounted to £1 16s.[3] She probably slept in the servants' room or maids' chamber in the manor house. The latter was equipped in 1798 with a four-poster bed, together with a pillow, two blankets, and a quilt. It was probably quite luxurious for the maid-servant(s) who slept in it.[4] One wonders if these were the two servants' chambers recorded in the 1548 survey.[5]

Some servants were specialists. According to Arthur Jones, John Phillips was a 'useful servant in every branch of domestick life, a most excellent gardiner, & a very useful gamekeeper'.[6] He was described as Jones's butler in 1783,[7] and given £100 in his employer's will. Phillipps had been chosen by lot in 1778 to serve in the militia, but had chosen a substitute.[8] By General Williamson's death in 1798, he had been replaced as butler by Thomas Coxhead.[9]

Other servants might be asked to undertake menial tasks; Sir Richard's servant John Hitchins was asked to deliver a letter to the vicar in 1711.[10] John Cue collected tithes on behalf of Peter Griffin in 1683.[11] Mary Powell answered the door to Sarah Curry when the latter came to request Mary's master, John White, to conduct a funeral service.[12]

We know little about the servants of early lords of Avebury Manor. William Dunch's servant, John Irishman, was presented for absence from

1 WSHC 184/7.
2 WSHC 184/7.
3 WSHC 184/7.
4 WSHC 271/6.
5 WSHC 2664/1/2D/8. The survey's description of the house is transcribed below, p.345-6.
6 WSHC 271/3.
7 WSHC 271/3.
8 WSHC 184/9/5.
9 WSHC 184/6.
10 WSHC 184/1. Letter, Sir Richard Holford to John White, 5th October 1711. Only his first name is given in this letter, but we may assume it was the same servant as is mentioned above.
11 TNA E134/2and3Jas2/Hil2.
12 WSHC D1/42/68.

church in 1624.[1] Another of his servants, Kingsmill Long, a 'gentleman servant', was a scion of one of Wiltshire's leading families.[2] Margaret Chesterman was a servant in the Parsonage House in the mid-sixteenth century[3].

There were good and bad servants. After the Holfords had visited Avebury in the summer of 1698, William Skeat accused Sir Richard servants of having committed various enormities at the house which they shared. [4] Richard Bradney,[5] the manservant, had 'had my men in to ye seller and thare they have drinked what thay had a mind to'. Betty, the maid, had suspiciously stayed up at night; Skeat thought she might have been dallying with his men. One of the servants anonymously wrote back to Skeat, vehemently denying his accusations. 'You had better have sayd what you had a mind to against mee before wee came away. Then I would have spoke to you face to face and vindicated myself'. He also pointed out that his master had not given 'credit to your pittifull letters', and that he had not been dismissed. The letter, however, was probably written by Philip, a servant whom Skeat had not intended to accuse.

Peter Griffin, one of Skeat's successors as tenant of Avebury Great Farm, also had 'unruly servants'. They would 'confound everything they come near', according to one of Samuel Holford's correspondents.[6] Griffin, however, colluded with them. His reapers were 'lodged ... in your [Holford's] blankets, and some in your beds'. Holford was 'dismissed' of much of his small beer, and Griffin's servants took for themselves his plums, peaches, raspberries, strawberries and other fruit. Griffin's 'kind of a Welch housekeeper' was viewed with great suspicion.

Over four decades later, servants were still causing problems. Sarah Gale was a servant of John Nalder in 1766, when she betrayed her master's trust by stealing a cheese weighing 14 pounds, and six pounds of bacon.[7] She gave them to her brother Thomas, a labourer, 'part of which cheese and bacon ... he carry'd to his mother Mary Gale now living in the parish of Calne'. We may presume that Sarah was dismissed, but it was Thomas who

1 WSHC A1/110, 1624M, f.153.
2 Nicol, Cheryl. *Inheriting the Earth: the Long Family's 500 year reign in Wiltshire.* Hobnob Press, 2016, p.335.
3 WANHS Wiltshire Genealogy Vol. A-A, p.94.
4 For the following, see WSHC 184/1. Letters, William Skeat to Sir Richard Holford, 23rd November 1798 & 19th December 1698; anonymouse servant (probably Philip) to William Skeat, c.December 1698.
5 His surname is not stated in the letter.
6 WSHC 184/1, pt.2. Letter, T.H. to Samuel Holford, 26 August 1723.
7 WSHC A1/110, 1766M.

was to be indicted at Quarter Sessions: Nalder had to enter a recognizance to prosecute him.

Sex was another major issue which caused problems. In 1614, Christopher Pope had at least three servants: George Piddle, Leonard Edmunds, and Margaret Fulmer. They fell into a common trap; one of the men (which one was a matter of dispute) made Margaret pregnant.[1] Whilst the two men disputed before a Justice of the Peace (Edmunds entered a recognizance to appear at Quarter Sessions),[2] Margaret left Pope's employ and moved into a house in West Kennett. She was probably dismissed. So, probably, was Sarah Spencer, whose fellow servant in Malmesbury became the father of her bastard child, and who came home to Beckhampton to give birth.[3]

Maid servants were in a vulnerable position, and could find it difficult to deal with lecherous masters.[4] Sarah Hawkins, for example, was perhaps the servant of Samuel Fowler, the carpenter, who fathered a bastard child on her despite already having four legitimate children.[5] Mary, the 'covenant servant' of Richard Brown, a married man, lived in his house for two years, and claimed to have strenuously resisted his advances. To no avail. She was delivered of his child in 1626. According to her, Brown offered her £20 to keep his fatherhood secret, and instead to say that the father was Richard Mills (whom she had subsequently married).[6] That was not enough, however, to prevent her spilling the beans.

We do not know what Brown's wife thought of Mary. It is clear, however, that servants could easily fall victim to the jealousy of their mistresses. One wonders if that was what happened when Mary Hitchcock made her will in 1756.[7] Legally, married women could not make wills without their husband's consent. That may explain why Mary's will was never proved. Her husband was unlikely to approve of its contents! She gave her husband her lands and tenements in Avebury, provided that 'he don't join matrimony to one Ann Seager or hire her for a servant'. Had Mary dismissed Seager as a servant because she was suspicious of her relationship with her husband? She was certainly determined that she would not benefit by her death.

On the other hand, serving in an elite household could be a positive

1 WSHC A1/110, 1614M, f.129.
2 WSHC A1/110, 1614M.
3 See above, p.XXX. See also WSHC D3/4/7, f.64.
4 Ingram, Martin. *Church Courts, Sex, and marriage in England 1570-1640.* Cambridge University Press, 1990, p.265 & 266.
5 WSHC 184/9/5.
6 WSHC D3/4/6, f.46v & 47.
7 WSHC 1409/16/3.

experience. John Judd and Mary Hickley, who married in 1751, had probably met whilst serving together in Stayner Holford's household. Hickley was probably related to Richard Hickley, who subsequently served Stayner's successors as bailiff for many decades. One wonders whether his servants' marriage was one of the reasons why Stayner had a pew built in the parish church in 1752.[1]

Good relationships between servant and master is frequently evident in wills. Indeed, a few servants actually witnessed their master's will, or even served as executor. The wills of both Richard Holford in 1742,[2] and George Brown, yeoman, in 1785[3] were witnessed by servants. Kingsmill Long, William Dunch's servant, was appointed as joint executor of his master's will in 1630.[4] He also received an annuity of £20 per annum. But he was a 'gentleman' servant from an elite family. The household servants of Richard Smith (not his labourers) received a bequest of 2s each from their master in 1632/3.[5] Freezy Pope, servant to John Goldsmith, gent., was given £25 in his will, whilst five of his other servants received £1 each.[6] One wonders if Freezy was a relative.

Another servant of Arthur Jones, Elizabeth Scane, (probably the daughter of John Scane, the former bailiff) received £80, plus £20 in his will. That was made conditional on her being 'in my service at the time of my decease and under no warning to leave such'.[7] A number of Jones's other household servants received £7 each 'to provide themselves decent and proper mourning to be paid as soon as conveniently may be after my decease, although 'my cookmaid and dairymaid' were only given £5 for that purpose. Other wills also made provision for servants to purchase 'mourning'. In 1750/51, Thomas Smith left his two servants, Ann Jones and Susan Godwin, thirty shillings each for that purpose, although only if his wife did not provide it for them.[8]

At a lower social level, Catherine Brown, servant to Thomas Pope, husbandman, received 'one good ewe and one good lambe', in her master's 1601/2 will.[9] Pope also remembered others who had worked for him. His shepherd received a lamb, and Thomas Slie was given 'all the thirds of the

1 WSHC 184/8.
2 TNA PROB/11/721.
3 WSHC P3/B/1742.
4 TNA PROB11/321/306.
5 TNA PROB11/163/542.
6 WSHC P1/G/142.
7 TNA PROB11/1181/174.
8 TNA PROB11/786/436.
9 WSHC P3/1Reg/95.

corne that he did sowe for me in Highwaies feilde'. Thomas Phelps' three servants each received a lamb in his 1621/2 will.[1]

Agricultural labourers and farm servants formed the majority of the adult male population of Avebury. The occupations of most bridegrooms are stated in the marriage register between 1754 and 1790. 94 out of 138 were described as labourers. They were needed. The fact that in 1755 the tenant of Avebury farm had 211 hurdles, which had to be moved daily, suggests the extent to which that was so.[2] Four of John Rose's servants testified to the livestock kept on his farm (probably Avebury Trusloe) before he went bankrupt; they, like the stock, were probably 'not equal to what the occupation of such large property as this estate only required'.[3]

Agricultural labourers were not well paid. In 1793, the wages of a farm servant supervised by the bailiff, Richard Hickley, totalled five guineas, probably for the year.[4] In 1791, the farm maid also received five guineas. The farm boy received two guineas per annum.[5] In return for such wages, labourers were expected to work from six in the morning until six at night, with an hour's break at 10.00 am and 3.00 p.m. Their hours were, however, subject to dispute. Avebury's farmers complained in 1756 that their labourers had 'long established that very bad custom of going out of their business two hours every day at their breakfast time and one hour of their dinner time for the space of nine months in the year, and two hours every day all the other part of the year, to our great detriment'. Nine farmers determined to compel their servants to work an extra hour per day, and entered into an obligation with each other to enforce this requirement[6]. The threat to extend already long hours recurred again in 1794, when Avebury farmers expressed concern about their labourers' lack of output.[7] Illness was not an option for them; the Duke of Marlborough expressed the opinion that 'the lower orders are never ill'. For him, turning up for work was mandatory.[8] As the artisan poet Stephen Duck complained:

1 WSHC P3/P/93.
2 WSHC 184/4/1. Account of John Rose's stock sold, 15th November 1755.
3 WSHC 184/4/1. Particular of John Rose's stock, 1755.
4 WSHC 184/7.
5 WSHC 184/7.
6 WSHC 1569/31. To put this in context, see Armstrong, Alan. *Farmworkers: a Social and Economic History, 1770-1980.* B.T.Batsford, 1988, p.29.
7 Wilson, Avice. *Forgotten Labour: the Wiltshire Agricultural Worker and his Environment, 4500 B.C. – A.D. 1950.* Hobnob Press, 2007, p.154.
8 Jones, Eric L. *Landed Estates and Rural Inequality in English History: from the mid-seventeenth century to the present.* Palgrave Macmillan, 2018, p.40.

Thus, as the Year's revolving Course goes round,
No Respite from our Labour can be found:
Like Sisyphus, our Work is never done.

There were, of course, gradations in the ranks of agricultural labourers. The itinerant shepherd, who stayed with his sheep overnight on the Downs, was an important figure. He would summon the sheep by horn to graze the sheep walks by day, and to return to their folds at night; Blowhorn Street in Marlborough commemorates him.[1] He would move the hurdles used to enclose sheep on the fallow for the sake of their dung every day – no light task when there were perhaps 180 of them to be moved. During lambing time, he followed a solitary life in his rough shelter, and abandoned family life for a few weeks. Sheep runs could be a long way from human habitation. Mention has already been made of the 'pennings' or sheep cotes on the Downs;[2] the shepherd would have slept there with his flock, in a primitive shelter made of hurdles and thatch.[3] The shepherd's hut was only introduced in the mid-nineteenth century. In the spring, shepherd's supervised the annual shearing. Many men would have been needed for casual employment as shearers in the spring, especially on Avebury Great Farm, where over 1,000 sheep had to be sheared every year.[4] In July 1791 a glazier named Stroud – not an Avebury name - was contracted to do the work, and was paid £10. It seems likely that he was a gang master, who brought in a team of shearers.[5] Tradesmen like him could easily turn their hands to casual work.

In July 1792, Richard Hickley paid his shearers three guineas for shearing 800 sheep and 410 lambs.[6] The following year he paid out £3 5s for shearing 1310 sheep, plus another 18s 6d for washing them. We have already mentioned William Hayward and John Pontin, who were shepherds in the seventeenth century. A shepherd was employed by the Truslows on West Down in the late sixteenth century.[7] 'My sheppard that now is' was bequeathed 'one chilver lamb' in the 1601/2 will of Thomas Pope.[8] Robert Spencer served Richard Truslow as a shepherd when he and his master were involved in an

1 Massingham, H.J. *The English Downland*. B.T.Batsford, 1936, p.20.
2 See above, p.256-7.
3 Watts, Ken. *The Marlborough Downs*. Rev ed. Ex Libris Press, 2003, p.160-61.
4 John Rose, the tenant of this farm, had 1,304 sheep when he died in 1720; cf. WSHC P3/R/365.
5 WSHC 184/7.
6 WSHC 184/7.
7 TNA E134/40and41Eliz/Mich7. Evidence of John Jennings.
8 WSHC P3/1Reg/95.

altercation on West Down c.1603.[1] Others included John Romsey, who was a shepherd aged 37 when he sought a marriage licence in 1628,[2] Thomas Pope of West Kennett, who leased a tenement in East Overton from Thomas Smith in 1663 for an entry fine of £11 and a rent of 2s per annum,[3] William Bailey, married in 1758, Adam Burry, who sold rights on Avebury Common to Caleb Bailey in 1726,[4] Nathan Horsell, who was employed on Avebury Great Farm for many years (his pay was 5s 9d per week in 1756),[5] and Edward Cue, who 'entered into Mr Holford's pay' in 1756.[6] As already noted, Thomas Webb and John Plummer probably served as manorial shepherds in the early 1680s.[7]

When Richard Hickley's shepherd, William Harper, died in 1793, Hickley found himself 'at a loss'. Loosing a good shepherd was a serious problem. Harper died from 'a mortification in his bowels'. Hickley consoled himself with 'the satisfaction to know he was properly attended and all the care taken of him that lay in my power', but hoped he could 'soon get a proper person that will answer my purpose as well'.[8] He was eventually able to recruit 'a very good shepherd, which is a great article'.[9] The success or failure of a sheep farm was heavily dependant on the quality of the shepherd, who was perhaps the most important worker on the farm.[10]

Other specialist agricultural labourers included dairymen, ploughmen, and carters, amongst others.[11] When Stayner Holford took his estate in hand after John Rose's bankruptcy, he recruited John Bridgeman as a ploughman; his wage was 5s per week.[12] Charles Underwood was taken on as a ploughman at the same time; his son sometimes worked as a plough boy. Thomas Mortimer, 'the boy that drives oxen', would probably have grown up to be a ploughman. William Young was another labourer whose son worked with him, ploughing,

---

1 TNA STAC 8/5/1.
2 Nevill, Edmund, ed. 'Marriage licences of Salisbury', *Genealogist*, New Series 27, 1911, p.41.
3 WSHC 568/39.
4 WSHC 212A/31/3; 1409/116/3.
5 See above, p.99-100. For his wages, see WSHC 271/4.
6 WSHC 271/4. One wonders whether this was the same Edward Cue who held a victualler's licence in 1741; cf. WSHC A1/325/4.
7 See above, p.255.
8 WSHC 184/6. Richard Hickley to Mrs Williamson, 4th June 1793.
9 WSHC 184/6. Richard Hickley to Mrs Williamson, 1st April 1794.
10 Gurney, Peter. *Shepherd Lore: the last years of traditional shepherding in Wiltshire.* Wiltshire Folk Life Society, 2010, p.10.
11 Most of this paragraph is based on WSHC 271/4.
12 WSHC 184/4/1. Rose's servants' particulars about the stock, 1755.

spreading dung, and carrying wheat to market.[1] He, or possibly his son, was described as 'my carter' by Holford's successor, Arthur Jones. In the codicil to his 1788 will, Jones gave him a legacy of £5 – a substantial sum for an agricultural labourer.[2] The drowner who operated the hatches in the water meadows was particularly important; he had a skilled job.

The permanent staff on most farms were unmarried living in servants, who were engaged by the year. They were likely to occupy unheated and badly lit attics.[3]

Many other agricultural labourers, such as the shearers mentioned above, were employed at peak times of the year on a casual basis. In late summer, the fields were full of harvest workers. Many travelled from the cheese districts of the North Wiltshire claylands in order to bring in Avebury's hay and corn harvests.[4] Their own harvests would have had different timings. Other harvesters were cloth workers from places like Seend and Trowbridge, who found they could earn more working in the harvest. The two men who mowed John Phelps' barley in 1647, John Angell and Thomas Bodham, were casual labourers, who probably did not live in the parish:[5] at least, no other mention of them has been found. Hickley's 'several haymakers' in August 1793 were much more numerous than his permanent work force (we don't know how many), and were paid £18 7s in total. The following month, Hickley paid out various amounts for mowing, forking, raking, and thrashing wheat. [6]Women were frequently employed for the less strenuous tasks, such as raking and gathering.[7] Casuals were also needed at other times of the year. In May 1794, for example, Hickley paid out £9 9s 10d for 'work don by the women on the downs weeding corn &c'. In August 1791, even the former schoolmaster was paid £1 17s 4d 'for work'.

Casual labour could be recruited from amongst three groups. Small husbandmen who farmed perhaps twenty or thirty acres sometimes undertook casual work for larger farmers. Skilled workers such as shepherds, dairymen, or ploughmen, could be recruited on a contract basis. Unskilled workers could be

1 WSHC 271/4.
2 TNA PROB11/1181/174.
3 *Avebury Manor, Avebury, Wiltshire. Historic Building Survey.* Unpublished report. *Wessex* Archaeology, 2011, 5.3.8, & room data sheets 37-8. (held by the National Trust, Avebury).
4 Armstrong, Alan. *Farmworkers: a Social and Economic History, 1770-1980.* B.T.Batsford, 1988, p.25
5 WSHC A1/110, 1647M, f.424.
6 WSHC 184/7.
7 Armstrong, op cit, p.27.

employed casually, just for the day, or perhaps for the harvest.

Casual labourers could be dismissed without much warning. Some found it difficult to secure regular employment; in neighbouring Coate, John Weaver, labourer, complained in 1623 of the 'scarcitie of worke' 'in the extremes of the times present', and sought a remedy by becoming a carrier.[1] In 1741, Mary Fowler, the widow of a carpenter, occasionally sent both her sons, and her 'man', to do casual work for Richard Holford. Their work ranged from cutting down trees to 'taking apart some old doors', from 'making a corn bing' to working in the stable. Her bill, totalling 27 different items between November 1739 and August 1740, came to a mere £1 16s 11½d, but included all their labours; as the head of the household she received their wages.[2] In the late 1750s, Stayner Holford regularly hired labourers for just a few days at a time to undertake specific tasks, such as spreading dung or repairing fences.[3] Thomas Maccabee, for example, was paid 5s for five days of 'shovelling dung' in October 1755.

Even young children might be employed: 'Stephen's boy' was employed for 'keeping the rooks of the lower ground' in November 1756, and paid 3d per day. Holford commented that 'the above boy has been of no use, but I gave his father a pair of breeches'. Nathan Horsell's boy probably performed the task better: he was said to have spent 42 days 'keeping the birds' at the same time. Adam Burry was paid 3s 8d 'for 9 days keeping birds of the wheat & other business'. Stephen Crook, the carpenter, charged seven pence per day for the work of his three young children, aged ten, five and three.[4] Rats also had to be kept down, and it may be that boys were engaged to catch them too: in July 1791, Richard Hickley paid out a guinea 'for killing rats one year'.[5]

If the weather was bad, casual labourers had no work. Regular employees could, however, be re-deployed. John Bridgeman, the ploughman, 'helped at dung cart' in November 1755, the weather 'being too wett to plough'.[6]

In the course of the eighteenth century, the plight of the agricultural labourer steadily worsened.[7] Despite the demand for labour, wages were low, especially on the chalk.[8] Consequently, labourers were not well nourished, well housed, or well clothed, and were not always equal to the tasks farmers

1   WSHC A1/110, 1623M, f.149.
2   WSHC 184/5. Mary Fowler's account, 1740.
3   For the following paragraph, see WSHC 271/4.
4   WSHC 184/5. Stephen Crook's bill, 1741.
5   WSHC 184/7.
6   WSHC 271/4.
7   Wilson, op cit, p.148-9.
8   Bettey, J.H. *Rural Life in Wessex, 1500-1900*. Alan Sutton, 1987, p.67.

required them to do, despite the opinion of the Duke of Marlborough. Their notorious reputation for slowness and sloth was probably due to the fact that they had to pace themselves. The labourer was rarely in a position to bargain, and farmers were quite prepared to come together to impose onerous conditions, as has already been seen. The gap between farmer and labourer steadily widened. By 1650, the labourer's purchasing power had decreased by 50% over the previous century. Thereafter, wages and prices fluctuated, but the labourer was losing access to land where he could grow his own food, or collect firewood; enclosure did not help. More intensive farming methods, and population growth, reduced opportunities. Farmers frequently preferred to employ members of their own families rather than take on a poor labourer. Rises in the price of bread at the outset of the Napoleonic wars meant that the labourer was worse off than ever before. There were occasions when farmers tried to help their workmen: in the winter of 1792 many farmers were buying beef for them.[1] But that only provided temporary support; it did not reverse the long-term decline. By the end of the century, the idea that a farm labourer could rise to become the tenant of a large farm had ceased to be entertained. The career of Peter Griffin, who was a servant on Avebury Great Farm for many years in the early eighteenth century before he became its tenant,[2] was unlikely to be repeated. Nor was it likely that a late eighteenth century labourer could raise £50 to lend on mortgage, as Simon Lambourn did in the late 1730s.[3] Instead, most labourers suffered from poor wages, high insecurity, and the constant threat of pauperism. In the 1770s and 1780s, reapers were paid by piece work, depending on the acreages reaped.[4] Their employers were expected to feed them.[5] In September 1792, Richard Hickley purchased '122 pound of bacon for the reapers'.[6] In a letter to Mrs Williamson, Hickley excused the cost of malt used in brewing, by noting that he had to provide for 'so many people to drink small beer all the summer'.[7] That obviously included his harvesters.

Thomas Wiltshire's employment history was fairly typical. He was employed as a yearly servant by John Nalder c.1772, and received three guineas or a little more for his year's work. When he left Nalder's service, he ceased

1 WSHC 184/6. Letter, Richard Hickley to Mrs Williamson, 31st December 1792.
2 WSHC 184/2. Stayner Holford to Peter Holford, 2nd December 1756.
3 TNA C11/633/24.
4 WSHC 184/5.
5 Armstrong, Alan. *Farmworkers: a Social and Economic History, 1770-1980.* B.T.Batsford, 1988, p.25.
6 WSHC 184/7.
7 WSHC 184/6. Letter, Richard Hickley to Mrs Williamson, 30th November 1794.

to find employment by the year, but worked as a day labourer for various other farmers, including Arthur Jones, during the following twenty years. He married a Marlborough girl in 1780, and rented a cottage in Marlborough in 1792, when he was working as a sack weaver. When he applied for poor relief in 1802, he was sent back to Avebury on the technicality that, although he had paid rates, he had not been charged to them.[1] Edward West was another victim of the poor law. He served Farmer John Rose at Avebury for just one year (the basic requirement to claim 'settlement') before moving on, but when he needed poor relief in 1748 he was 'removed' back to Avebury.[2]

Labourers and servants were also required for non-agricultural pursuits. We have already encountered Stephen Dean, who was employed as a coach guard,[3] but was also described as a labourer when he married in 1786.[4] Some labourers found employment in building work. In 1733, for example, Robert Holford employed several casual labourers to carry out various repairs at Beckhampton. It cost 6s 'for two days 2 men mending ye barns floor'. Two men – possibly the same two – spent a day 'making and hanging ye door of ye barly barne', and were paid 3s. A 'boy' who spent 6 days in ye whole work' received 4s for his trouble. 'John and Robert' received 9s between them for 3 days work. So did 'Adam'[5] and Thomas. 3s was paid 'for a day three men finishing ye house'. Employing 'myself [presumably the bailiff] and 2 men and ye boy 2 days each of us' cost 11s. Another 9s was spent 'for 3 men two days in ye same work'.[6] Various other entries in Robert Holford's accounts record the wages of casual labourers. Similarly, an item in William Norris's building accounts in the early 1760s records that he paid £24 10s 6d for 'nine weeks work by my carts & horses, a man & boy, hauling stone, timber, lime, & other materials'.[7] Labourers were frequently employed in building work.

Labourers were also employed as gardeners. Jacob Heath was Sir James Mervyn's gardener c.1603 and 1605, when he took part in the altercations on West Down discussed above.[8] Nicholas Norris was employed by Sir Richard Holford as a gardener in 1717, when he was criticised for planting walnut trees

---

1 WSHC 2027/2/1/995.
2 WSHC 184/9/2A.
3 Above, p.38.
4 Marriage register.
5 One wonders whether the 'Adam' was one of the Burry family mentioned in chapter 3.
6 WSHC 371/1, pt.5. Account, 20th September 1733.
7 WSHC 473/277. 'Account of monies expended in repairs … 1761, 62 & 63'.
8 TNA STAC8/5/1; STAC 8.251/25. See above, p.212.

in the wrong place.[1] John Wood became Stayner Holford's gardener when he married in 1759.[2]

Gardeners could be of higher status than a mere labourer. Adam Williamson's head gardener, William Richardson, supervised a number of labourers whilst answering to the bailiff, Richard Hickley. Richardson himself was paid £20 per annum in 1792 – a substantial sum.[3] In April 1792, he suggested that if there were to be no 'family' resident in the manor for the year, a different type of cropping might enable him to dispense with one of his men.[4] The opportunity to do so may have come when one of his labourers, named Bailey, was sentenced to death for highway robbery in 1792.[5] John Lovelock, who became Sir Adam Williamson's gamekeeper in 1797, was another gardener, and may have been Richardson's successor.[6] Some gardeners, like William Thomas of Broad Town in 1711, were independent tradesmen.[7]

The breaking up of sarsen stones also relied on labourers. Teams of perhaps twenty men were needed to move the stones into position for burning. A drawing of the process by Stukeley shows five men, some of whom were wearing full frock coats, others wearing merely breeches and blouses. The latter were the labourers.[8] The men in frock coats were obviously supervising. Their presence demonstrates that estates needed more than labourers to run efficiently. They also needed senior staff, and perhaps the landlord himself, to take charge.

The bailiff was an important figure in Avebury, at least when farms were in hand. James Pope was presumably bailiff for Joan Truslow's manor of Avebury Trusloe when he 'warned' the copyholders to undertake their customary harvest work in the late sixteenth century.[9] Edmund Jennings, who was aged c.70 in 1599, was probably one of his predecessors; he too had been responsible for 'warning' the customary tenants of Avebury manor to perform their customary duties at haymaking[10]. William Dunch's bailiff was Richard

1 GA D1956/E2/8.
2 Marriage Register.
3 WSHC 184/7. For his name, see his letters in 184/6.
4 WSHC 184/6. Letter, Richard Hickley to Mrs Williamson, 3rd April 1792.
5 WSHC 184/6. Letter, Richard Hickley to Mrs Williamson, 31st July 1792.
6 WSHC A1/305 & 306.
7 GA D1956/E2/8. See also above, p.268.
8 Gillings, Mark, et al. *Landscape of the Megaliths: excavation and fieldwork on the Avebury monuments, 1997-2003.* Oxbow Books, 2008, p.294.
9 TNA E134/41Eliz/Hil8.
10 WANHS. Wiltshire Genealogy. v.A-A, p.95.

Munday,[1] who was serving when Dunch gave his creditors control of the manor c.1628.[2] His name is mentioned again in the early 1630s, when both manors were in the hands of trustees.[3] Richard Parr was nominated as joint bailiff by the creditors in order to collect debts owed by Dunch. Thomas Smith served as bailiff at the same time as he was tenant of the manor farm in the 1630s, and received the impropriated tithes worth £300 due to his landlord.[4]

John Foster served as bailiff for Robert Baynton's manor of Avebury Trusloe, for a number of years in the 1660s.[5] John Scane became bailiff to Stayner Holford when the latter took in hand Avebury Great Farm, and was responsible for purchasing and paying for farm goods such as the six cart horses with harness he bought in 1756.[6] Scane was succeeded by Richard Hickley, c.1780, who, as we have seen, served Arthur Jones, Adam Williamson, and their successors for many decades.[7] Whilst his employer was in Jamaica Hickley was paid £42 per year.[8] He was also provided with his own house. His letters to his employer in Jamaica demonstrate the importance of his role.[9]

The role of steward was also important. The steward was usually a lawyer, not necessarily resident in Avebury, and was responsible for holding the manorial court. Ellis Swayne served as steward when William Dunch demised Avebury manor; he was 'very angry' when a deed had to be written on paper rather than parchment because his clerk, William Weare, had lost the parchment as he 'rode on the way'.[10] He subsequently became one of the trustees responsible for selling the manor and paying off Dunch's debts.[11] John Taylor was serving as steward for Robert Baynton in 1659,[12] and again in 1677.[13] Mr Francis Bennet served as Lord Stawell's agent in the 1690s, and perhaps earlier.[14] In 1700, the position was held by Mr. Norris, who dined

1   WANHS. Wiltshire Genealogy v.A-A, p.109.
2   WANHS. Wiltshire Genealogy v.A-A, p.110.
3   TNA E134/9and10Chas1/Hil1.
4   WANHS. Wiltshire Genealogy v.A-A, p.109.
5   WANHS Wiltshire Genealogy, v.A-A, p.135.
6   WSHC 184/5. John Scanes bill, 1756.
7   See above, p.87-8.
8   WSHC 184/7. Account January 1793
9   WSHC 184/6.
10 TNA E134/9and10Chas1/Hil1.
11 TNA E134/9and10Chas1/Hil1.
12 WSHC 212A/31/2.
13 WSHC C5/577/76.
14 WSHC 184/1, pt.2. Letter, Sir Richard Holford to Richard Chandler, 2nd June 1709.

with Sir Richard Holford, William Skeat, and the jurors, after holding court.[1] In the 1770s, Mr Hawkes may perhaps have served; he was a Marlborough attorney recommended to his successor by Arthur Jones.[2] After he died in the early 1780s, his son-in-law Thomas Ward served as Jones's steward (he performed the same role for Lord Ailesbury). John Ward, who acted as Adam Williamson's attorney (and probably as steward – he too served Lord Ailesbury) in the early 1790s, was his brother.[3]

Surveying could be an important part of the duties of a steward, but not, as far as we know, in Avebury. The noted surveyor, John Norden, surveyed the neighbouring manor of Cherhill (which included Warwicks in Avebury) in 1616.[4] Otherwise, the earliest surveyor recorded in Avebury was John Overton, a tiler from Devizes. In 1707 he was in negotiation with Sir Richard Holford regarding 'setting about surveying of Avebury', including mapping.[5] Holford put him off temporarily, although he did engage him to tile his new barn. A few years later, in 1714, Overton made a survey of a meadow below Silbury Hill, for which he charged 40s.[6] Richard Richardson of Devizes surveyed Beckhampton Farm for James Sutton in 1788,[7] and Pophams when William Norris bought it in 1791.[8] We have already seen that Avebury itself had a resident surveyor, who combined his surveying with schoolmastering, and also served as vestry clerk. John Clements described himself as a 'land measurer' when he stood bond for Jane Rose's marriage licence in 1769,[9] and as a 'land surveyor' when he claimed a debt amounting to just over £10 from the estate of Samuel Martyn in 1779.[10] The earliest known example of his work was his 1753 survey of the manor of Froxfield, for which he was paid £20 5s 6d.[11] In 1763, he surveyed and mapped various properties at Ogbourne St. Mary.[12] In 1775 he surveyed the

1 WSHC 184/8. Probably William Norris of Bromham and Lincolns Inn.
2 WSHC 271/3.
3 WSHC 184/6; 9/35/261.
4 TNA E134/8Chas1/Mich53.
5 WSHC 184/1, pt.1. Letter, Sir Richard Holford to John Overton, 4th November 1707.
6 WSHC 184/4/1; 184/8. GA D1956/E2/8.
7 WSHC 248/195.
8 WSHC 740/2/2.
9 Sarum Marriage Licence Bonds, op cit.
10 WSHC 118/88. Statement of debts of Samuel Martyn. He is also described as a land surveyor in his 1779 marriage bond; cf. Sarum Marriage Licence Bonds, op cit.
11 Crowley, Douglas, ed. *The Minute Book of Froxfield Almshouse, 1714-1866.* Wiltshire Record Society, 66. 2013, p.181.
12 WSHC 2027/2/3/1/22 & 28.4

churchyard at Compton Bassett.[1] Between 1767 and 1781, he also surveyed the parishes of Bishops Cannings, Chiseldon, Heddington, Mildenhall, and Ogbourne St Andrew, for enclosure commissioners.[2] William Norris of Nonsuch paid him two guineas in 1789, presumably for surveying work.[3] In the 1770s and 1780s, he undertook various administrative tasks for Arthur Jones and Adam Williamson, paying bills, and calculating the wages due to reapers[4] In 1791, he was asked to certify local customs concerning the end of tenancies.[5] He also undertook some surveying on the Downs in advance of the Avebury enclosure in 1792, although he was too ill to attend every meeting, and the Commissioners had to appoint a younger assistant to help him.[6] That was probably B.Haynes, who drew the 1795 enclosure map.[7] Richard Hickley promised to have a rough plan of the Williamson's post-enclosure estate drawn up to send it to Jamaica, but was unsure whether Clements was fit enough to do it.[8] In 1797, the year before he died, Clements was paid ten shillings by the turnpike trustees for measuring lands which they were purchasing for road widening.[9]

Thomas Alexander was another Avebury surveyor. He was sufficiently skilled to draw a coloured ink map of Avebury Farm for Richard Holford in 1733[10]. We know little more about him. Perhaps he was a relative of William Alexander, John Clements successor as schoolmaster. William also doubled as a land surveyor: he took the measurements of William Norris's farms at Avebury preparatory to the sale of one of them in 1796.[11]

The Clements family also had the local gamekeeper amongst its members. Robert, John's brother, was registered as a gamekeeper by Arthur

1 Hobbs, Steve, ed. *Gleanings from Wiltshire Parish Registers*. Wiltshire Record Society 63. 2010, p.72.
2 Sandell, R.E. *Abstracts of Wiltshire Inclosure Awards and Agreements*. Wiltshire Record Society, 25. 1971, p.37, 49, 81, 102, & 107.
3 WSHC 473/277.
4 WSHC 184/5.
5 WSHC 473/52.
6 WSHC 184/6. Letters, Richard Hickley to Mrs Williamson, 3rd April 1792 & 31st July 1792; John Ward to Adam Williamson, 1st October 1792.
7 Ucko, Peter J., et al. *Avebury reconsidered: from the 1690s to the 1990s*. Unwin Hyman, 1991, p.162.
8 WSHC 184/6. Letter, Richard Hickley to Mrs Williamson, 4th September 1792.
9 WSHC 1371/1.
10 WSHC 1553/71. Bendall, Sarah, ed. *Dictionary of Land Surveyors and local mapmakers of Great Britain and Ireland, 1530-1856*. British Library, 1997, v.2, p.7. (no.AO 62.8.). For a brief discussion of the map, see Ucko, Peter J., et al. *Avebury reconsidered: from the 1690s to the 1990s*. Unwin Hyman, 1991, p.162.
11 WSHC 473/352.

Jones esq., in 1768;[1] his services were shared with John Nalder, the lord of Berwick Bassett, who registered him in the same year. Clements was still Avebury's gamekeeper in 1784; however, when Arthur Jones inherited the manor, he was replaced (in 1785) by John Phillipps, who we have already met as Jones's butler. He was subsequently described as a 'menial servant' of Sir Adam Williamson, and was still gamekeeper in 1789. Adam Wiltshire, the son of the butcher, held the position in 1793, but his registration has not been traced.[2] His bill for the year, amounting to £4 4s 6d, was paid in November 1793.[3] His activities were the subject of dispute with the newly formed 'Beckhampton Club' of shooters, who thought that he was interfering with their sport. Gamekeepers ensured that game was available for hunting, and that poachers were deterred, although it may be that they were also called upon to maintain the rabbit warren recorded in the manorial survey of 1548.[4] Wiltshire did not hold his position for long: in 1796, William Ball, taylor, was nominated, and was succeeded in the following year by John Lovelock.

Before Robert Clements, the Holford's tenants of Avebury Great Farm had served as gamekeepers. William Skeat's gamekeeper's warrant was withdrawn when he gave up his tenancy in 1710.[5] His possession of that warrant had probably encouraged him to disrespect his 'betters', and to disrupt the 'sport' of the son of a neighbouring Justice of the Peace – who considered issuing a warrant against him.[6] It is not clear whether John Rose, his successor as tenant, took over his responsibility for game-keeping, but we do know that Peter Griffin, the next tenant, was appointed as gamekeeper by Richard Holford in 1736 at a salary of 3s 4d.[7]

Avebury also provided employment for a wide range of tradesmen. Building tradesmen in particular were much in demand: carpenters (who sometimes doubled as wheelwrights, and may also have made the hurdles that sheep-farmers relied on), masons, glaziers, thatchers, etc. Building activity in Avebury was at its height at the end of the seventeenth century, when many of

1 WSHC A1/305-7. Gamekeepers' deputations.
2 WSHC 184/6. Letters, Richard Hickley to Mrs Williamson, 1st October 1793, 8th November 1793, 31st August 1794, & 27th September 1794.
3 WSHC 184/7.
4 WSHC 2664/1/2D/8.
5 WSHC 184/1, pt.2. Letter, Sir Richard Holford to John Rose, 7th June 1710.
6 WSHC 184/1, pt.2. Letter, Charles Tooker, J.P., to Sir Richard Holford, 4th January 1697/8.
7 WSHC 184/4/1. Deed poll, 1836.

the houses within the stone circle were being built.[1] The Holfords and other landowners were always in need of tradesmen to keep their property in repair. There were also shoemakers, butchers, and other retail tradesmen. It is probable that a market was regularly held in Avebury, although the only evidence is Stukeley's remark that a sarsen stone was used as a fish slab on market days[2].

The earliest carpenter we know of was Roger Whitborne of Kennett, who gave evidence when Deborah Dunch sued Richard Truslow in 1598.[3] John Curr, carpenter, was bound over to keep the peace in 1671.[4] John Cary, carpenter, (perhaps the same person) had his son apprenticed to a London turner in 1693.[5] We only have one inventory of a carpenter, that of Humphry Robinson, who died in 1720, and who combined the trade with that of wheelwright. The journal of Sir Richard Holford, and other papers in the Holford archive, provide much detail of Robinson's work, and of his interaction with tradesmen and farmers. In 1710, for example, Robinson made a wooden gate for Holford's Cherry Court. [6] In the following years, Holford frequently consulted him for advice, not only on carpentry matters. In 1714, Robinson's bill came to the substantial sum of c.£34 for work done at Beckhampton.[7] For a tradesman, Robinson was relatively wealthy; his estate was valued at almost £400. The value of the carpentry 'tooles & other goods' he had 'in ye shop & wellhouse' was £20 – quite a substantial amount. He also had a very considerable amount of 'timber & board & other wood', which he kept in various places: in the street, 'in Mr John Phelpes meddow', 'in ye littell bouse by ye well', 'in ye back side', 'in his owne meddow', 'in ye garden', 'in ye cowe house & skillin', in his barn, and in his woodhouse. That included 'planks & spokes & other od stufe', as well as wheels which he had presumably made; altogether his wood was valued at just over £147. He also diversified into agriculture; he had four cows, with sixty sheep and lambs, and a pig, together worth £33. There were fifteen acres of corn awaiting harvesting (his inventory was taken in June), four quarters of wheat in the barn, and three acres of clover, as well as a small quantity of hay; his arable was valued at £33

1   Ucko, Peter J., et al. *Avebury reconsidered: from the 1690s to the 1990s.* Unwin Hyman, 1991, p.166.
2   Gillings, Mark, et al. *Landscape of the Megaliths: excavation and fieldwork on the Avebury monuments, 1997-2003.* Oxbow Books, 2008, p.291.
3   WANHS Wiltshire Genealogy v.A-A, p.91.
4   WSHC A1/110, 1671 M.
5   Webb, Cliff. *London Livery Company Apprenticeship Registers 45. Turners Company, 1604-1800.* Society of Genealogists Enterprises, 2014, p.24.
6   GA D1956/E2/8.
7   WSHC 184/8.

7s. The substantial sum of £130 was due to him for 'bond depts & booke depts'. In 1694, incidentally, he was due to be repaid £7 which he had loaned to John Truslow.[1]

Humphry Robinson's son Thomas continued his father's trade. He, however, was not as successful as his father. As we have already noted, he was responsible for breaking up many megaliths, and using them to build houses. When some of his houses burnt down, he lost a great deal of money. Perhaps that is why he was forced to take out a mortgage for £150 from Samuel Morris in 1734 on some of his land.[2] The property – and mortgage – was inherited by his son John. The mortgage was transferred to John Nalder in 1752,[3] and to William Heath of Wootton Bassett in 1755.[4] By then, there was a dwelling house, shop, outhousing, and a barn on the land. In 1734 there had only been a barn. The property in 1755 was occupied by John Robinson's lessee, John Strange. One wonders whether one of the stones Thomas Robinson destroyed was used in the foundations of the new buildings.

The Robinsons were not the only entrepreneurial carpenters in the parish. Stephen Browning was sufficiently wealthy to lend £200 on mortgage to John Cue of Westbrook in 1726.[5] William Crook, carpenter, purchased the house and shop where he lived for £40 in 1746.[6] It had a saw-pit, as well as a stable, a cart house and a garden. This was probably the seventeenth-century house now known as Carpenter's Cottage in Green Street, which had a saw-pit in front of its timber-framed workshop.[7] The workshop does not appear on Stukeley's 1724 drawing.[8] Originally, it probably had just two rooms downstairs and two chambers upstairs.[9] Perhaps it was once an ale-house.[10]

William Crook died in 1754, leaving his son Ambrose £25 'towards

1   WSHC 371/1, pt.3. Deed, Bridget Truslow to Richard Truslow, 26th December 1694.
2   WSHC 212A/31/4. Mortgage deed, 1st October 1734.
3   WSHC 212A/31/4. Mortgage deed, Samuel Morris to John Nalder, 2nd January 1752.
4   WSHC 529/185.
5   WSHC 212A/31/3; 1040/108.
6   WSHC 1102/1. Lease & release, James Alexander & Richard Alexander to William Crook, 26/27th April 1746;
7   WBR notes.
8   *Appraisal ... ,* op cit.
9   *Appraisal of Buildings on the Avebury Estate, part 1. Conservation Plan, for the National Trust.* Ferguson Mann Architects, 1999. Unpublished report held by WBR.
10 WBR notes.

breeding him up and teaching him the trade of a carpenter'.[1] We have already seen that Ambrose entered indentures with his brother, Stephen Crook, who was also a wheelwright, and who purchased his father's house in 1761.[2] Nothing more is known of Ambrose. However, his brother appears frequently in our records. In 1775, Stephen took down 'such rotten and fallen parts' of the hovel formerly occupied by James Cue 'as seemed to threaten the lives and limbs of persons passing by'.[3] He received a shilling for his labours. In 1780, Arthur Jones ran up a bill totalling £56 11s 4d for Crook's carpentry work, and had to pay it off by instalments. That included 'putting up post & rails in ye farmyard', 'setting up the fence at the end of ye farmhouse', making '4 stands for the glasshouses', providing 'a handle to a peek axe', making 'a toilet door at Beckhampton', and making 'a mahogany table'.[4] The 'George' mentioned in this bill was probably Stephen's thirteen-year old son, working with his father.

Stephen Crook did much work for William Norris at Brunsdens and/or Pophams; Norris's accounts record several payments to him in the 1780s.[5] In 1782, for example, he provided 460 feet of two inch oak planks, and made Norris (or perhaps his tenant John Brown) a new barn floor. In 1786, he did 'sundry work in repairing the barns, gates, rails &c'. Carpentry remained in the family for the next generation; in 1799, Stephen's son Stephen was described as a carpenter in his marriage bond.[6] A few years earlier, in the early 1790s, either he or his father undertook a substantial amount of work for Richard Hickley, as bailiff of Avebury manor. He was paid over £200 for work done in the previous two years, although whether that was entirely for carpentry work is not clear.[7] In 1795, either father or son was employed by the Turnpike Trustees to erect posts and rails along the road at West Kennett and Silbury Hill.[8] In 1797, he and Samuel Fowler were paid jointly by the trustees for carpentry work. In the following year the two worked together to erect fencing along the newly widened road at Beckhampton, and to repair the trustees' weighing

1 WSHC P3/C/933.
2 1102/1. Lease and release, Philip Crook et al to Stephen Crook, 2nd/3rd June 1761.
3 WSHC 184//9/5. See also Raymond, Stuart A. 'A Pauper's Hovel in 1775', *The Recorder: the annual newsletter of the Wiltshire Record Society*, 22, 2023, p.7-8.
4 184/5. Stephen Crook's bill, 1780.
5 WSHC 473/277.
6 Sarum Marriage Licence Bonds www.findmypast.co.uk
7 WSHC 184/6. Letters, Richard Hickley to Mrs Williamson, 31st July 1792; 31st December 1792
8 WSHC 1371/1.

machine at Beckhampton. Samuel Fowler was also contracted to fence the new garden at the tollhouse, and to build a coal shed.

Samuel was probably the grandson of another Samuel Fowler, who, in 1728, was described as a wheelwright when he purchased property at Eastbrook.[1] Working with wheels was just one aspect of Samuel senior's carpentry business. In 1733, John Caswell accounted for £10 10s 6d for 'a bill paid Fowler ye carpenter'.[2] In 1740 Samuel described himself as a carpenter in his will.[3] Richard his son, followed his father's trade, and was owed the substantial sum of £53 18s 7d for 'work and materials in the business of a carpenter' in 1775, which his son Samuel collected four years later.[4] Samuel junior and his brother James both followed the family trade. James described himself as a carpenter when he married in 1777. So did Samuel, when he married in 1784.[5] A 1779 bill finds Samuel mending well buckets, providing hoops for barrels, and 'going into the well and mending the pump'.[6] The mention of hoops, together with a mention in a 1780 bill of 'hooping a kiver', suggest that he was also a cooper.[7]

Like Stephen Crook, Samuel Fowler also took on apprentices. In 1786, James May paid him an apprenticeship premium of £10.[8] He may perhaps have apprenticed his own son, Richard, who also followed the carpentry trade: Richard was paid 33s 6d for making James Lewis's coffin in 1779.[9]

A number of other carpenters can be identified. John Caswell's 1733 accounts mentioned John Eatwell, whose carpenter's bill amounted to the substantial sum of £30.[10] Eatwell lived in Winterbourne Monkton.[11] William Wilkins was mentioned in William Norris's accounts, in the 1760s. Between 1761 and 1763 he was paid £33 12s 'at sundry times', and in 1767 he received £15 11s 5d for his work 'about the stable & cart house' at Brunsdens.[12] Marriage records identify three other carpenters: Thomas Hillier (1759), Henry Smith

1   WSHC 1040/108.
2   WSHC 371/1, pt.5. John Caswell's accounts, 1733.
3   WSHC P3/F/359.
4   WSHC 118/88. Statement of Samuel Martyn's debts, 1779.
5   Sarum Marriage Licence Bonds www.findmypast.co.uk. The relationship is confirmed by WSHC 118/88 (1779 receipts received by Samuel Martyn's administrator).
6   WSHC 184/5. Bill, Samuel Fowler to Arthur Jones, 1779.
7   WSHC 184/5. Bill, Samuel Fowler to Arthur Jones, 1780.
8   TNA IR 1/64.
9   TNA PROB 31/840/590.
10 WSHC 371/1, pt.5. John Caswell's accounts 1733.
11 WSHC P3/C/820.
12 WSHC 473/277.

(1760), and Thomas Davis (1769) No trace of them has been found in other records, although James Hillier, the carpenter employed by Thomas Pinniger in 1830,[1] may have been a descendant of Thomas Hillier.

A few months after Thomas Davis's marriage, the parish register records that Alexander Dismore, carpenter, also married. He, however, was not from Avebury; his marriage bond describes him as a 'wheeler' from Hungerford.[2] The wheelwright's trade was closely related to carpentry, and we have already seen that both Thomas Robinson and Stephen Crook combined both trades. Richard Alexander was another Avebury wheelwright; he was named as such in 1717.[3] He was still active as wheelwright in 1738, when his son was apprenticed.[4] The trade was an important one for a parish which depended on wheeled traffic.

Coopers practised another trade closely related to carpentry. The barrels needed for brewing had to be made by a cooper. In 1740 and 1741, Samuel Wild, a Marlborough cooper, supplied a variety of hogsheads, tubs and buckets to Richard Holford, and billed him for £2 18s 1d.[5] When John Brown died in 1732 he owed four shillings to a cooper for work done.[6] In the 1790s, Richard Hickley was frequently in need of barrels to send beer to his master in Jamaica. He may well have used them for other purposes; barrels were sometimes used as packing cases for transporting goods such as china or clothes.[7] Amongst the many bills Hickley paid was a 'cooper's bill for hoops', and a 'coopers bill for mending tubs'.[8] Avebury's brewers, however, probably had to obtain their barrels from local towns. The only evidence for coopers in Avebury itself are Samuel Fowler's bills for hoops for barrels, mentioned above.[9]

Carpenters worked closely with masons, sometimes keeping both trades within the family. We have already discussed the Crook family.[10] William Crook, and his brother Philip, were both masons, but William's son, Stephen,

1   Wadsworth, Alan, ed. *The Farming Diaries of Thomas Pinniger, 1813-1837*. Wiltshire Record Society 74. 2021, p.lxxxv.
2   Sarum Marriage Licence Bonds www.findmypast.co.uk
3   WSHC 9/19/180.
4   Webb, Cliff. *London Livery Company Apprenticeship Registers, vol.39. Tallow Chandler's Company, 1633-1800*. Society of Genealogists, 2003, p.2.
5   WSGC 184/5.
6   TNA C11/777/21.
7   Roberts, Hugh D. *Downhearth to Bargate: An Illustrated Account of the Revolution in Cooking due to the use of Coal instead of Wood*. Wiltshire Folk Life Society, 1981, p.66.
8   WSHC 184/7.
9   WSHC 184/5. Samuel Fowler's bills, 1778 & 1780. See above, p.XXXX.
10 See above, p.69-73 & 302-3.

was a carpenter; another son, William was a bricklayer.[1] William the elder was asked to 'pitch' Sir Richard Holford's stable in 1700, but was so busy that he put Holford off several times.[2] In the 1710s, Holford's journal makes frequent mention of him.[3] He worked closely with Humphry Robinson, the carpenter.[4] Philip Crook, William's brother, did some work on Richard Holford's house in 1741. His bill for masonry work included a charge for work done by his young sons.[5] When Holford died in the following year, Philip was made responsible for 'opening the voute [the burial vault] and arching it up again and laying the stones again'.[6] It may well be that the mason who was contracted in 1744 to build an 'oven' for Stayner Holford was a Crook.[7] Philip Crook and his nephew Samuel were both paid substantial amounts for work done at Avebury manor in 1765.[8] Philip also did some work for William Norris in the early 1760s.

Many payments to both masons and carpenters are recorded in Norris's accounts.[9] For example, Walter Long, mason, was paid over £46 for work at Brunsdens in the early 1760s. John Jordan, John Shipway, and John Highway, were all employed as masons by Norris in the 1780s. Shipway had earlier, in 1765, supplied a small quantity of bricks and lime to Stayner Holford.[10] He continued to be involved in lime burning, supplying lime to Arthur Jones in 1781,[11] and to General Williamson in the 1790s.[12] No other Avebury limeburners have been identified, although Sir Richard Holford did pay 13s 4d to a lime burner from Calne in 1708.[13] Shipway's 1792 invoice to Williamson reveals him working with his brother, and employing labourers, whilst engaged in tiling, erecting stone posts, and undertaking repairs to various buildings. In 1794, he was awaiting payment for 'brushing up the old mansion', and for 'putting in some hatches in South Meadow'.[14] The hatches controlled the flow

1 Sarum Marriage Licence Bonds www.findmypast.co.uk. The marriage took place in 1758.
2 WSHC 184/8.
3 GA D1956/E2/8.
4 GA D1956/E2/8.
5 WSHC 184/5. Stephen Crook's bill, 1741.
6 WSHC 184/4. Stephen Crook's bill, 1742.
7 WSHC 184/1, pt.1. Letter, James Mayo to Staynor Holford, 31st March 1744.
8 WSHC 184/5.
9 WSHC 473/277.
10 WSHC 184/5.
11 WSHC 185/5. John Shipway's bill, 1781.
12 WSHC 184/5 & 184/7. Shipway invoices.
13 WSHC 184/4/1. Accounts, 1708.
14 WSHC 184/6. Letter, Richard Hickley to Mrs Williamson, 1st April 1794.

of water in the water meadows. Shipway, described as a mason, purchased a cottage in 1799 which had been 'lately erected' by Robert Clements.[1] One wonders whether he himself had helped to build it.

Like Norris, the Holfords also spent much money on building activities. In 1711, Jonathan Nicholls built Sir Richard Holford a brewhouse and dairy; his bill for £9 10s was paid, but Holford complained that Nicholls' delay in laying a pavement in the garden had 'very much abused mee'.[2] The following June, his complaints continued; the delay had caused 'great defects of the pavement'; 'the frost had torne & shattered it soe that it is scandalous'. Nicholls 'acknowledged it to bee very bad, & beggd mee to excuse it, & promised to make amend & to do it better'.

In 1740, another mason, Thomas Nutt of Box, submitted his bill for just over £25 to Stayner Holford, itemising the many days he had spent working on the manor house.[3] At the same time, Henry Horsell spent 22 days digging sand, 18 days digging earth and gravel, 2 days with the mason, and 5 days cleaning the house.[4] Nutt did more work in 1743.[5]

There was also a role for glaziers in building work. Richard Bailey, glazier, was one of those sued by the vicar in 1697.[6] He remained active as such until at least 1708.[7] Thomas Sadler, glazier, did some work for Sir Richard Holford, in 1712. His bill for £1 13s 6d included work done on 'colloring the stable & garden dores', so he was evidently also a painter (although Holford said the painting was 'not well done' and deducted 6d when he paid).[8] Some glaziers combined their trade with plumbing. Thomas Hunter described himself as a 'glasier & plummer', in his 1746/7 will.[9] 'Hunter ye glazier' was paid 11s 1d by John Caswell for his work at Beckhampton in 1733.[10] However, his will indicates that he ran his glazing business from Lyneham, not from Avebury. He bequeathed 'all that my house, lands, and premises ... in Lineham ... together also with all my glass, led, and working tools in trade as a glasier' to his son John. It seems likely that John had been running the glazing business

1 WSHC 1102/2. Feoffment, Leah Clements to John Shipway, 24th July 1799.
2 GA D1956/E2/8.
3 WSHC 184/5. Nutt's account.
4 WSHC 184/5. Horsell's account.
5 WSHC 184/5. Stayner Holford's instruction to pay Thomas Nutt, 1743.
6 WSHC 1569/5.
7 TNA C10/534/43; WSHC 212A/31/4. Conveyance, John Nalder, et al, to John Brown & Ambrose Landfear, 15th February 1752.
8 GA D1956/E2/8.
9 WSHC P3/H/1256.
10 WSHC 371/1, pt.5. John Caswell's accounts, 1733.

since his father had purchased the White Lion inn at Avebury a few years before his death. Thomas Eacott was another 'glazier and plumber' involved in the renovations at Brunsdens in the 1760s. He also did work for Stayner Holford in 1765.[1] In 1794, Richard Hickley had to pay a glazier's bill that included 'only … such nessacery things as could not be avoided, such as mending windows, garden lights, the gutters on the house, &c'.[2] Perhaps the tradesman concerned was Stroud the glazier, who also undertook shearing. Hickley had already paid him for glazing work on the manor house In January 1792 and February 1793.[3]

Thatching was another building trade that was in demand. In 1733, John Caswell paid 'the thatcher's bill at Goddards', amounting to £1 10s.[4] James Cary (or Carew) and his sons James and Thomas were all thatchers; that is how they were all described when they were found guilty of riotous behaviour in 1757.[5] Despite this verdict, the family were sufficiently well off to be freeholders; James (the elder) paid land tax in the 1750s. He died in 1769; his son, James, was one of the few Avebury freeholders who voted in the 1772 Parliamentary election.[6]

Joseph Chivers and his boy thatched Stayner Holford's granary in 1756, and undertook other thatching work for him.[7] His 'boy' was perhaps Gabriel Chivers, who married Mary Eyles in 1773, describing himself as a thatcher.[8] In 1779, Gabriel was the tenant of a cottage formerly owned by Thomas Rogers, which he had built himself.[9] His father, Joseph was still working in 1784, when he witnessed the marriage bond of Charles Rowe and Sarah Goodship, describing himself as a thatcher.[10] Arthur Jones employed Gabriel's skills on a number of occasions. In 1776, he thatched a wall, the oxhouse, and the cart house.[11] In 1779 and 1780 Gabriel busied himself with thatching ricks of hay, wheat, oats and barley, and with mending hurdles. He was also responsible for 'laying 23 squared 52 feet of thatch on his [Arthur Jones's] buildings at

1 WSHC 184/5.
2 WSHC 184/6. Richard Hickley to Mrs Williamson, 30th July 1794.
3 WSHC 184/7.
4 WSHC 371/1, pt.5. John Caswell's accounts, 1733.
5 WSHC A1/165/7; A1/110, 1757M.
6 WSHC A1/340/1. He was still paying land tax in 1780; cf. WSHC A1/345/18A.
7 WSHC 271/4.
8 Marriage Register.
9 WSHC 2027/2/1/855.
10 Sarum Marriage Licence Bonds www.findmypast.co.uk
11 WSHC 184/5. Gabriel Chivers' thatching bill, 1776.

Avebury and Beckhampton'.[1] A year later, he again thatched a number of Jones's ricks, submitting two bills, one for £1 13s 3d, the other for £1 4s 8d.[2] Hickley's accounts for February 1792 reveal that he was paid a total of £18 11s 8d for thatching a garden wall, farm buildings, Hatchet's house, and a number of hay and corn ricks.[3] In the following year, he billed General Williamson 12s for 'making one dozen of straw hurdles.[4] There was plenty of work for a skilled thatcher to do in our period. When the overseers, in 1739, apprenticed Edward Wait to John Dolman, a Calstone 'chaff cutter and thatcher', they were equipping him with a useful trade.[5]

Tyles, however, were replacing thatch. William Norris in 1768 'paid the thatcher' three guineas; more was to be paid by his tenant.[6] Nevertheless, he was also purchasing tyles for his farmhouse. He paid Henry Archard the substantial sum of £27 8s 4d to lay them.[7] As early as 1707, Sir Richard Holford preferred tiles to thatch, even for his new barn; he engaged John Overton of Devizes to lay them.[8]

Blacksmiths also had some involvement in building work. Sir Richard Holford's building activities gave them much work. In 1710, Thomas Jordan provided the ironwork for the wooden gate made by Thomas Robinson for the Cherry Court.[9] His brother John was also a blacksmith; both were sued by the vicar in the Court of Exchequer in 1698,[10] and in 1700 Thomas responded by joining with others to sue the vicar in the Court of Chancery.[11] If the identification is correct, Thomas died in 1720. His inventory[12] records 'workeing tools' in his shop worth £3, but no other evidence of being a smith. He was worth just over a mere £10.

We have already met John Cruse, Avebury's blacksmith between the 1720s and the 1760s.[13] His 1740 bill itemises a range of goods supplied when Richard Holford, grandson of Sir Richard, was renovating the manor house:

1 WSHC 184/5. Gabriel Chivers' thatching bills, 1780.
2 WSHC 184/5. Gabriel Chivers' thatching bills, 1781.
3 WSHC 184/7.
4 WSHC 184/5. Gabriel Chivers' bill for making hurdles, 1793.
5 WSHC 184/9/3.
6 WSHC 473/277.
7 Archard was described as a 'tyler' when he married in 1760.
8 WSHC 184/1, pt.1. Letter, Sir Richard Holford to John Overton, 4th November 1707
9 GA D1956/E2/8.
10 WSHC 1569/5.
11 WSHC C10/534/43.
12 WSHC P1/IJ/167.
13 See above, p.73-4.

numerous sprigs, cramps, and 'winder bars', a jack, a grate, a fire pan and tongs, keys, and various other items. Cruse's bill totalled over £16.[1] George Webb was paid £19 5s 10d for his work at Brunsdens in the early 1760s, and also provided 'nails, hinges, &c, &c' worth £9 8s 9d.[2] Similarly, in the 1780s, Joseph Caswell, smith, was paid for work at Brunsdens on several occasions.[3]

Meeting the needs of builders was an important element of the blacksmiths' business in Avebury, but meeting the needs of farmers was probably more important. Farmers needed the ploughs, harrows, and other implements blacksmiths made. It is likely that they were responsible for the specially designed rakes used in the process of breaking up sarsen stones, as well as for the sledge hammers and other equipment used.[4] Smiths' goods are described in detail in probate inventories. When Richard Trewman, died in 1616 or 1617, he had eight dozen reaping hooks in stock;[5] he had presumably made them himself. An anvil, a bellows, a vice, tongs, two sledge hammers, a shoeing hammer, and various other tools of his trade are recorded in Trewman's probate inventory; their total value was 32s. The reaping hooks were valued at 30s. The deceased also, incidentally, had 'on blynd horse & on cowe', also worth 30s. But the total value of his estate was almost £98. His wealth was mostly tied up in a bond for £88, owed by Christopher Pope.

By contrast, when Richard Cripps died in 1670,[6] he had £30 'due upon his shopbooke … wherof tenn pounds is desperate debts'. His inventory valued the tools of his trade, together with the materials he was using; he had 'in the shopp one anvill, vice, bickerve, 1 paire of bellowes, 3 sledges, 2 handhamers, 8 paire of tongs, a parcell of cole, a parcell of new iron, a beame & scales, old iron with other lumber there', all valued at £9. But it is clear that he had interests other than his smithy. He had 94 sheep, and 27 lambs, valued at £32 10s. In addition, he had 'one parcell of sheeps wooll one parcel of yarne, a parcel of lambs wooll & loakes, with other lumber', worth £12, 'in a little roome over the buttery'. And outside he had no fewer than 22 hives. He also, as one would expect, had a horse and a pig, presumably for domestic purposes. These other interests meant that he was a little wealthier than Trewman; his inventory was valued at just over £142, including the lease on his house worth £20.

1   WSHC 184/5.
2   WSHC 473/277.
3   WSHC 473/277.
4   Gillings, Mark, et al. *Landscape of the Megaliths: excavation and fieldwork on the Avebury monuments, 1997-2003*. Oxbow Books, 2008, p.294.
5   WSHC P3/T/50.
6   WSHC A1/110, 1642M, f.38.

Toby King was another Avebury blacksmith, whose working tools were similar to those we have just described. When he died in 1685, he had recently made 'new iron gere newly rote yt is to say a new plough share & new boxes & stroudirons & a plough chaine'.[1] Other goods for sale included 'horse shoes lincepins & tacks'. He also had 'new iron in ye shop yt is unrote'[2] worth £20, waiting to be used. Unlike his predecessors, there is no evidence of any crops or animals in his inventory. He did however, have 'five bibls and maney other good books to read'; one wonders whether he was a dissenter. The total value of his inventory was just over £81.

James Lewis's 1779 will[3] reveals that he was the wealthiest blacksmith we have encountered in Avebury. It tells us that he had £410 placed at interest: £250 on bond with an apothecary in Bath, and £160 invested in mortgages on two Marlborough houses. His probate account reveals that each of his six children received £70 when his estate was finally settled in 1793 (after their mother had died).[4] His working tools were similar to those described above; they were sold for £18 9s 3d in 1781.

Some blacksmiths may have specialised as farriers. Everyone who owned a horse relied on blacksmiths for shoeing. That included travellers on the new turnpike, whose horses must have cast their shoes occasionally. The armies that passed through Avebury in the 1640s probably provided good business for Richard Cripps, whose forge was situated on the highway at West Kennett.[5] Some tradesmen, despite the disruption, were able to profit from the Civil War.[6] Avebury blacksmiths also attracted business from drovers, whose oxen required shoeing to protect them from the hard surfaces of the new turnpike.[7] One wonders if William Skeat had his cattle shoed before driving them to London. Coachmen and carriers may also have needed running repairs to be carried out. Richard Hickley had to pay horse farriers' bills totalling over £10 in July 1791 and January 1792, probably reflecting work that had been done over a period.[8]

In 1755, George Webb made an agreement with Stayner Holford, the lord of the manor, to 'shoe and farrier the farm horses' for 7s per year. A

1 WSHC P3/K/106.
2 Unwrought.
3 TNA PROB11/1055/301.
4 TNA PROB31/940/590.
5 WSHC A1/110, 1642M, f.38.
6 Wroughton, John. *An Unhappy Civil War: the experience of ordinary people in Gloucestershire, Somerset and Wiltshire, 1642-1646.* Lansdown Press, 1999, p.165.
7 Bonser, K.J. *The Drovers.* Macmillan, 1970, p.59.
8 WSHC 184/7.

separate agreement was made for the coach horses.[1] There were two George Webbs, father and son. Their shop, 28 feet in length, and 14 feet in breadth, which George senior had leased from Thomas Smith in 1729 for 3s per annum, stood on the south side of the highway in West Kennett.[2] Perhaps it was the same forge used by Richard Cripps in 1642. It was ideally placed to catch the passing trade. George junior stood bond for his father when the latter sought a licence to marry Susan Minty in 1750.[3] He was still smithing in December 1794, when Richard Hickley paid 'Webb the smith's bill' for £14 2s 6d[4] – unless the reference was to his son William, who was described as a blacksmith in his 1795 marriage bond.[5]

There were also forges in Avebury village. A 'smith's shop' is recorded on the south-east corner of the 1695 plan of the manorial barton, which may have been devoted primarily to meeting the needs of Avebury Great Farm.[6] Keiller's excavations in the 1930s found a forge, probably dating from our period, at Eastbrook, on the south side of Green Street.[7]

Farmers also required saddles and harness for horses. In 1739, Francis Batchelur was working as a saddler when he applied for a marriage licence.[8] The large leather collars worn by cart horses were made by collar makers such as George Arnold. When he died in 1706, he had 'six blind halters, four housings, eighteene paire of harness, [and] several peeces of dress leather' in his shop. He also had 'six rawhides'. [9] Another George Arnold (perhaps his son), collar maker, took John Rose, son of Simon and Sisily Rose of Beckhampton, as his apprentice in 1725.[10] By 1734 Rose was living in Calne.[11] He owned common of pasture for one cow in Beckhampton, which he exchanged for half a moiety of a tenement in 1740.[12] William Chapman described himself

1 WSHC 271/4.
2 WSHC 568/39. Lease, Thomas Smith to George Webb, 29th September 1729.
3 Sarum Marriage Licence Bonds www.findmypast.co.uk/articles/world-records/full-list-of-united-kingdom-records/life-events-bmds/sarum-marriage-licence-bonds
4 WSHC 184/7.
5 Sarum Marriage Licence Bonds www.findmypast.co.uk
6 WSHC 184/4.
7 Keiller, Alexander. 'Avebury: a summary of excavations, 1937 and 1938', *Antiquity* 13(50), 1939, p.230.
8 Sarum Marriage Licence Bonds www.findmypast.co.uk
9 WSHC P3/A/259.
10 TNA IR1/11.
11 WSHC 212A/31/3. Reversionary lease, Robert Rose et al to Caleb Bailey, 19th April 1734.
12 WSHC 371/1, pt.5. Exchange, Robert Holford & John Rose, 19th September

as a collar maker when he married Ann Clements in 1764.[1] The same name recurs three decades later, when William Chapman, collar maker, was named as a creditor of Samuel Martyn's estate.[2] It may be that he was the 'collarmaker' whose bills were paid by Richard Hickley in December 1791, and again in May 1793.[3] There were probably more horses needing collars on the Williamson's estate than anywhere else in Avebury.

Collar makers relied on the leather produced by tanners. The earliest potential evidence of tanning in Avebury slightly post-dates our period. There is a tan pit at the rear of Perry's Cottage, which housed a saddler and harness maker soon after the end of our period.[4] One wonders if there were any other (smelly) tan pits in the parish. There was certainly a demand for leather, for both shoes and harness. The fact that a load of bark - used in tanning - was delivered to Beckhampton in 1823 is also suggestive.[5] It seems probable that Avebury workers in leather prior to 1800 obtained their raw materials from tanners in local towns.

Leather workers included shoemakers. Avebury had a number of shoemakers, although there was probably only sufficient work for one at a time. Joseph Wallis was relatively prosperous when he died in 1680; he had money 'due upon bond' amounting to £145, although admittedly £45 of that was 'desperate'. His inventory[6] records 'in the shop lether & showmakers tooles' valued at £2 5s. His moderate wealth may be contrasted with that of Edmund Reazey, cordwainer,[7] who, with his wife and two infants, was 'removed' under the poor law to Woodborough in 1736.[8] Reuben Horsell, the parish clerk, together with his sons Reuben and John, were all shoemakers.[9] Several other Avebury cordwainers or shoemakers can be identified in our records: Thomas

---

1740.
1   Sarum Marriage Licence Bonds www.findmypast.co.uk; see also PR.
2   WSHC 118/88. Statement of debts of Samuel Martyn.
3   WSHC 184/7.
4   http://britishlistedbuildings.co.uk
5   Wadsworth, Alan, ed. *The Farming Diaries of Thomas Pinniger, 1813-1837.* Wiltshire Record Society 74. 2021, p.xxxix.
6   WSHC P1/W/349.
7   The word 'cordwainer' is derived from the Spanish city of Cordoba, once famous for its fine leather.
8   WSHC 184/9/2B.
9   For Reuben junior and senior in the 1720s, see Markham, Sarah. *John Loveday of Caversham, 1711-1789: the Life and Tours of an Eighteenth-Century Onlooker.* Michael Russell, 1984, p.41. For John in 1765, see WSHC P3/H/1388.

Pontin was named in 1694,[1] Samuel Morris in 1724,[2] William Underwood in 1734,[3] Charles Underwood in 1742[4] and 1758.[5] Thomas Tilly, cordwainer, renewed his lease of a small messuage in 1785.[6] Richard Hickley, the bailiff, tried to purchase shoes to be sent to Mrs Williamson in Jamaica, but the shoemaker was too slow, and they missed the ship that Hickley wanted to send them on.[7] Hickley's shoemaker may have been a tenant of General Williamson's named Beaven, who owed three year's rent in 1793, who was unable to work, and who was probably 'removed' when he claimed poor relief.[8] Hickley's order was subsequently placed with a shoemaker in Bath, one Godwin.[9]

Two other retail trades were also found in Avebury: bakers and butchers. Surprisingly, only two bakers are mentioned in our documentation. Thomas Strange was described as such when he married Mary White in 1783. John Dore, maltster and baker, insured his house in 1791.[10] Perhaps bread was one of the commodities that Joseph Hayward sold. Bakers not only sold bread; their ovens could also be used by those who did not have ovens to bake their home-made pies and cakes – and even to roast joints of meat.[11]

Similarly, only a few butchers can be identified. We have already seen that Thomas Truslow had been a butcher in Beverley before he migrated to Avebury.[12] His son (or grandson?) John was practising the trade in the early sixteenth century, according to evidence provided by John Cue in 1599.[13] The buildings on the Rectory estate in the latter year included a slaughter house. 'Vivash the butcher' supplied Richard Holford with beef and mutton

1 WSHC A1/165/3, f.41.
2 WSHC 529/185.
3 WSHC P3/P/807. Will of Susannah Pope.
4 Sarum Marriage Licence Bonds www.findmypast.co.uk
5 He stood bond for William Bailey in 1758, when Bailey sought a licence to marry Martha Bailey, cf. Sarum Marriage Licence Bonds www.findmypast.co.uk
6 WSHC 212b/117. Lease 25th June 1785, Thomas Hunt Grubb to Thomas Tilly.
7 WSHC 184/6. Letter, Richard Hickley to Mrs Williamson, 30th April 1792.
8 WSHC 184/6. Letters, Richard Hickley to Mrs Williamson, 5th June 1792 & 4th February 1793.
9 WSHC 184/6. Letter, Richard Hickley to Mrs Williamson, 2nd June 1794.
10 LMA CLC/B/192/F/001/MS11936/377/581550.
11 Roberts, Hugh D. *Downhearth to Bargate: An Illustrated Account of the Revolution in Cooking due to the use of Coal instead of Wood*. Wiltshire Folk Life Society, 1981, p.60.
12 Stedman, A.R. *Marlborough and the Upper Kennet country*. [Marlborough College?], 1960, p.107.
13 TNA E134/41Eliz/Hil8.

in 1741,[1] but his name does not occur in other records, and he was probably based in one of the local towns. John Wiltshire was identified as a butcher in 1766 when he was accused of assault.[2] In 1780 he sent Arthur Jones a bill for £12 15s 5½d for (mainly) mutton, veal and beef supplied.[3] He was still supplying meat to the manor house in 1793.[4] Wiltshire made his will in 1795.[5] He owned his house, but his executor was instructed to sell it in order to pay debts. His servant, Sarah Perry, was fortunate in her employer; John Wiltshire left her twelve guineas when he died in 1795.[6]

Like the nearby village of Aldbourne, Avebury only had one butcher in the late eighteenth century.[7] It is likely that farmers did their own butchering. Wiltshire's lack of competition was also, at least in part, due to the fact that meat was a luxury for labouring men, unless they had their own pig or poultry - or could poach a rabbit or a hare.

John Wiltshire's business depended to some extent on the sheep he slaughtered. That was one minor aspect of the sheep economy on which Avebury depended. Clothing was much more important. Clothiers, spinners, weavers, and tailors, all depended on sheep. John Phelps was a prosperous clothier, active in the Avebury land market in the 1680s.[8] He probably provided employment for many others. Sarah Nalder married a Calne clothier, John Orrell Bailey, in 1766.[9]

Weaving demanded some skill, and was mostly a male occupation. Surprisingly few weavers have been identified in Avebury, and no looms are identified in the probate records. Nevertheless, it is likely that weaving provided a supplementary income for at least some Avebury husbandmen and labourers. [10] Weavers were able to exercise some independence, and took in wool from any clothier they chose.[11] But Avebury lay at some distance from the fulling mills of the great Wiltshire clothiers, which were to be found west of

1 WSHC 184/5. Vivash the butcher's bill, 1741.
2 WSHC A1/110, 1766M.
3 WSHC 184/5. John Wiltshire's bill for meat, 1780.
4 WSHC 184/5. John Wiltshire's bills for meat, 1793.
5 WSHC P3/W/1066.
6 WSHC P3/W/1066.
7 Gandy, Ida. *The heart of a Village: an Intimate History of Aldbourne*. Alan Sutton, 1991, p.82.
8 WANHS. Wiltshire Genealogy, v.A-A, p.130-34 & 138; WSHC 212A/31/1 & 435/24/1/4.
9 Marriage Register.
10 Wilson, op cit, p.157.
11 Baines, op cit, p.109.

Avebury in the valley of the Avon, and in towns such as Chippenham, Devizes, Melksham, Malmesbury, and Trowbridge.[1] Avebury had no fullers or dyers, as far as is known. A few Avebury boys, as has been seen, were apprenticed to broad weavers and fullers in other parishes.

Spinning was more common in the parish. It was women's work – hence the moniker 'spinster', used in the probate records to describe both Mary Tompkins (1681)[2] and Anne Griffin (1738).[3] Women could frequently be seen spinning outside their doors during the summer. A few 'spinning turns' are mentioned in inventories. In 1609/10, the shepherd William Hayward had one worth one shilling, which had probably been used by his wife and daughter.[4] In 1733, the widow Martha Cue had two.[5]

At the end of the eighteenth century, the introduction of machinery resulted in clothiers becoming factory masters in places such as Trowbridge and Bradford on Avon, and much reduced employment opportunities for the poor. It 'deprived the cottagers' family of the greatest and most profitable part of their domestic employment', and imposed a heavy burden on the poor rates nation-wide. In Avebury, 'a large body of women and children' were deprived of their livelihood as spinsters.[6] In some places, such as Bradford on Avon, Steeple Ashton, and Trowbridge, the introduction of machines met with rioting, leading to their destruction.[7] As far as we know that did not happen in Avebury. But Avebury ratepayers were apt to complain about the cost of poor rates. Richard Hickley in 1792, referring to the new machinery,[8] commented that 'it's more than time some stop was put to it', claiming that 'tis not the poor that suffers, but the landholders, as it makes the poor rates run very high.' A decade later, John Anstie, a clothier, noted that there were still many 'persons of respectability ... who continue to consider the introduction of machinery into the woollen industry as unfriendly to the general interest and particularly injurious to the poor'.[9] In Avebury, the

1   Stedman, op cit, p.238; Baines, Richard, *A History of Chippenham from Alfred to Brunel*, ed. Tony Pratt, Mike Stone, & Kay Taylor. Chippenham Civic Society, 2009, p.108-14.
2   WSHC P3/T/288.
3   WSHC P3/G/584.
4   WSHC P3/H/56.
5   WSHC P3/C/820.
6   Bernard, op cit.
7   Baines, Richard, *A History of Chippenham from Alfred to Brunel*, ed. Tony Pratt, Mike Stone, & Kay Taylor. Chippenham Civic Society, 2009, p.111.
8   WSHC 184/6. Letter, Richard Hickley to Mrs Williamson, 31st December 1792.
9   Cited by Baines, Richard . *A History of Chippenham from Alfred to Brunel*, ed. Tony

EARNING A LIVING

remedy proved to be the introduction of straw plaiting, as we have already seen.[1]

Some of the cloth produced by spinning and weaving was turned into clothing by local tailors. There were usually several tailors working in Avebury in our period. The earliest recorded was William Harper, identified as such in 1633, when he was aged 59.[2] He had previously tried his hand at unlicensed ale selling in the 1620s.[3] In 1623, the Hundred jurors objected to his keeping 'ill rule in his house', 'to the disturbance of his neighbours'.[4]

Thomas Griffin was working as a tailor when he obtained a marriage licence in 1640; he was aged 30.[5] In 1655, the occupation was followed by Richard Bray, who was able to afford to apprentice his son to a London fishmonger,[6] although his 1670 probate inventory valued his goods at a mere £6 8s 6d. One suspects that this was not a complete valuation. Bray also served as parish clerk in the 1640s.[7]

Andrew Mills was a more prosperous tailor; his 1671 inventory valued his estate at just over £147.[8] That included £120 'money on bond'. His will indicates that the house he lived in was leased, but he also owned a tenement which he had purchased from Francis Odyon.

Richard Brown, another tailor, who died in 1695, also owned property, although it is not clear how much. He bequeathed 'all my lands tenements and hereditaments whatsoeuer' in Avebury to his brother to hold 'for ever', so at least some of the property was freehold. But he also owned a lease valued at £60. He had few other possessions; together, they were valued at just over £6. His inventory does, however, record that he had 'in ye shope a tabell board & tow chaires & a paire of sheres & a pressing ier [iron] & other thing' valued at 6s. These were the tools of his trade.

A number of eighteenth century Avebury tailors can be identified, if only briefly. We learn that John Fribbens, deceased, had been an Avebury

---

Pratt, Mike Stone, & Kay Taylor. Chippenham Civic Society, 2009, p.113.
1   See above, p.xxx
2   WANHS. Wiltshire Genealogy v.A-A, p.112.
3   WSHC A1/110, 1621M, f.142; 1627M, un-numbered Selkley Hundred jury presentment.
4   WSHC A1/110, 1623M, f. 148.
5   Nevill, Edmund, ed. 'Marriage licences of Salisbury', *Genealogist*, New Series 31, 1915, p.183.
6   Webb, Cliff. *London Livery Company Apprenticeship Registers vol.44. Fishmongers Company, 1614-1800.* Society of Genealogists, 2006, p.15.
7   According to the will of John Goldsmith, WSHC P1/G/142.
8   WSHC P3/M/60.

tailor from a 1727 deed.[1] A little more information is available concerning Robert Woodman. He charged Richard Holford ten shillings for making a 'sute of close' in the mid-eighteenth century, and was also paid for mending waistcoats, breeches, and a coat.[2] Woodman was another tailor active in the land market. In 1728, Thomas Goddard conveyed two acres of arable to him out of his 'natural love and affection'.[3] Woodman subsequently leased several pieces of arable in the common fields from Caleb Bailey.[4] When John Horsell, shoemaker, made his will in 1765, he noted that he had recently purchased a house from Woodman.[5] Robert Woodman stood bond for the administrator of Elizabeth Phelps's estate in 1730.[6]

The tailor Thomas Rogers married in 1757,[7] and took Harry Bodwell as his apprentice in 1768.[8] Four years later, he paid Thomas Hunter £114 for two cottages, one of which he already occupied.[9] When Samuel Martyn died in 1775, Rogers was owed £9 12s 3d 'for cloth, linninge & making cloths'. It was still outstanding in 1779, by which time Rogers himself had died; his administrator, James Hitchcock, was still trying to collect the debt.[10] Rogers' 1778 will makes a brief mention of his 'stock and implements in trade',[11] but does not record that he was a tailor.

Joseph Johnson and John Holbrook were also Avebury tailors, described as such when they married in 1757 and 1778 respectively.[12] They are not mentioned elsewhere. William Ball, married in 1782,[13] also described himself as a tailor; he lived in one of the houses in the churchyard,[14] and was still working at his trade in 1796, when, as we have seen, he was briefly nominated gamekeeper. Finally, in February 1792, Richard Hickley settled 'Dixon the taylor's bill' for £3.[15] Dixon was probably the tenant of the schoolmaster, John

1 WSHC 212A/31/3. Deed to lead the uses of a fine, 1st June 1727.
2 WSHC 184/5.
3 WSHC 212A/31/3. Lease and release, 16-19th July 1728.
4 WSHC 212A/31/3. Lease 22nd September 1733.
5 WSHC P3/H/1388.
6 WSHC P3/P/742.
7 Sarum Marriage Licence Bonds www.findmypast.co.uk
8 TNA IR 1/56.
9 WSHC 2027/2/1/855.
10 WSHC 118/88. Statement of debts of Samuel Martyn.
11 WSHC P3/R/549.
12 Marriage Register.
13 Marriage Register.
14 WSHC 184/6. Letter, Richard Hickley to Mrs Williamson, 4th February 1793.
15 WSHC 184/7.

Clements, and perhaps his niece's husband. [1]

Wool was not the only clothing material which provided opportunities for Avebury craftsmen in our period. The growth of the cotton industry in the late eighteenth century was not without its impact on Avebury, although all we know is that Joseph Shepherd described himself as a 'manufacturer of cotton' when he apprenticed his son to a London skinner in 1772. [2] It is likely that he was the 'Mr Shepherd' who supplied the overseers of Marlborough with the raw materials they needed to spin cotton between 1751 and 1773.[3]

Cotton, and much else, arrived in Avebury via the roads. The turnpiking of the Bath Road in 1754, created many commercial opportunities, especially for the development of the coaching trade and innkeeping. It also created employment for turnpike keepers. Originally, the Hare and Hounds, as it was then known,[4] was used as the toll house, and William Fowler, the innkeeper, was employed as toll collector (or perhaps he leased the tolls[5]). That arrangement was ended in 1765, [6] and a new tollhouse was built on the opposite side of the road. The name of the new toll collector is not known.

There were three tollhouses in the parish at the end of the eighteenth century.[7] Unfortunately, we do not have full details of all the toll-collectors. Stephen Dell, with his wife Mary, was the toll collector at the toll house opposite what was by then the Flying Waggon throughout the 1790s.[8] He was paid 12s per week, although in most years the trustees gave him an additional gratuity of five guineas, 'for his extraordinary trouble diligence and attention in collection the tolls and oversight of carriages'. Tolls at another Avebury toll gate were collected by the Tilly family.[9] When John Tilly married Sarah Stephens in 1780, he was described as a 'turnpike keeper' in the marriage register. 'Sally', identified as John's wife, was appointed as collector of tolls in 1790.[10] She only

1 TNA IR 23/96/189. See also p.65.
2 Webb, Cliff. *London Livery Company Apprenticeship Registers vol.47. Skinners Company, 1604-1800.* Society of Genealogists Enterprises, 2014, p.154.
3 WSHC 871/190.
4 Now the Waggon & Horses. For the various different names of this inn, see below, p.320.
5 Webb, Sidney & Beatrice. *The Story of the King's Highway.* English local government 5. Frank Cass & Co., 1963, p.138.
6 WSHC 184/1, PT.1. William Fowler to Stayner Holford, 6th April 1765.
7 Haynes, Robert, & Slocombe, Ivor. *Wiltshire toll houses.* Hobnob Press, 2004, p.6-8.
8 WSHC 1371/1; Haynes, Robert, & Slocombe, Ivor. *Wiltshire toll houses.* Hobnob Press, 2004, p.7.
9 WSHC 1371/1; Haynes & Slocombe, op cit, p.8. There is no record of his burial.
10 WSHC 1371/1.

merited a wage of 6s per week, but was still in post in 1799, by which time she was a widow: John died 2nd August 1796.

Another toll house was erected at the toll bar in Weedon Field, Avebury, in 1797.[1] Michael Wiltshire was appointed as toll collector. His son, John, had recently married another Sarah Tilly, who was probably a relative of her name-sake.

Toll collectors were not the only people who earned a livelihood from the road. Coach passengers needed accommodation for themselves and their horses. Drovers needed a place to rest and feed their beasts. Before the turnpike, there were two inns for drovers on the Bath Road: the White Hart at West Kennett, and the Bear at Beckhampton (subsequently known as The Folly, the Hare and Hounds, the Flying Waggon, and now the Waggon and Horses). The origins of the White Hart have not been traced, but it was open in the early seventeenth century. The Bear was erected in 1669 by the lord of the manor, in order to cater for the droving trade. It had a field behind it to accommodate livestock. The coaching trade was catered for by the Catherine Wheel, which stood in the village until c.1745, when the turnpike was opened; its proprietor then built a new inn bearing the old name at the Beckhampton crossroads. Sadly, the new building burnt down within a decade of opening, but it was rebuilt under new ownership. Another coaching inn, the White Lion, remained in the village (it is possible that it was the old Catherine Wheel re-named), but was closed down a decade or so later, probably because coaches had ceased to come through the village.

The owners and licensees of all these inns have been traced elsewhere.[2] It is not, unfortunately, possible to identify more than a few of the maids who served their customers, the grooms who looked after horses, or (in the case of the Hare and Hounds) the servant delegated to collect tolls from passing traffic in the 1750s and 1760s. It is evident, however, that the inn-keeping trade prospered, especially in the turnpike era.

Innkeepers required ale. A number of brewhouses and malthouses are recorded in the parish.[3] We have already noted the malt house built by William Spackman at West Kennett.[4] It stood on the Bath Road, and the 'Kennett ale' which was probably brewed there (or perhaps in the brewhouse at West

---

1   WSHC 1371/1.
2   Raymond, Stuart A. 'The Inns of Avebury, c.600-1800', *WAM*, 117, 2024, p.159-67.
3   See below, chapter 8, p.341.
4   Also mentioned in 1745 in *Appraisal ...*, op cit.

Kennett farm)¹ was sampled and appreciated by many travellers. It became nationally famous, especially after 1789. In 1803, Robert Southey was told that he 'must not pass by without tasting the best beer in England'. In the cellar he saw fifty full barrels of beer.² It was mentioned again in 1808, when the coach carrying Rev Francis Witt to Bath stopped for 'beer &c at Kennet'.³

Some farmers malted their own barley. In 1548, Avebury's manor house had 'a fayre loft where they make malt'.⁴ One wonders whether this loft was still being used in the 1790s, when Richard Hickley was making malt. He did not make enough, and had to purchase more from maltsters.⁵ In 1627 Richard Harding had ten bushels of malt worth £1.⁶ The executors of Richard Cue had to pay John White £2 10s 0d for malt in 1679/80.⁷ Malt is frequently recorded in probate inventories, which also list a number of malt mills and malting stones. Thomas Pope, husbandman, bequeathed a malt mill to his son Thomas in 1602.⁸ John Bromham als Phelps, yeoman, had one in his kitchen in 1664.⁹ Humphry Robinson, carpenter and wheelwright, had one in 1720 which, with his cheese press, was worth 15s.¹⁰

For some, malting barley was a full time occupation. Thomas Griffin described himself as a maltster in 1670, when he stood bond for Sarah Hayward as administrator of her husband's estate.¹¹ Bryant Smith of Avebury was a maltster in 1719, when he was ordered to pay maintenance for Frances Chivers' expected child.¹² John Wiltshire was a maltster when he leased land in the common fields from Caleb Bailey in 1728/9;¹³ he had his own malt house when he died in 1734.¹⁴ Samuel Morris was a maltster in 1734,¹⁵ and still had

1   WSHC 568/7. Lease, Staner Chamberlayne & Samuel Martyn to John Nalder, 9th November 1755.
2   Espriella, Don Manuel Alvarez [pseudonym. Actually Southey, Robert]. *Letters from England*. 2nd ed. Longman Hurst Rees & Orme, 1808 vol.3, p.313.
3   Gerhold, Dorian. *Bristol Stage Coaches*. Hobnob Press, 2012, p.99
4   WSHC 2664/1/2D/8.
5   See for example WSHC 184/6. Letter, Richard Hickley to Mrs Williamson, 31st December 1792.
6   WSHC P3/H/210.
7   WSHC P3/K/86.
8   WSHC P3/1Reg/95.
9   WSHC P1/B/416.
10 WSHC P1/R/275.
11 WSHC P3/H/433.
12 WSHC 184/9/4.
13 WSHC 212A/31/3.
14 WSHC P3/W/808.
15 WSHC 212A/31/3. Lease & release, 12/19th July 1738.

his malthouse in 1751 when he was assessed to land tax 6s.[1] Rachel Crook married a maltster (Jonathan White) in 1759, although he lived at Potterne. Richard Bailey was a maltster for at least three decades before his death in 1783.[2] John Strange tenanted a malthouse just to the west of the Catherine Wheel in 1755.[3] John Cleverly, maltster, applied for a marriage licence in 1766.[4] Samuel Martyn owed Richard Bailey, maltster, just over £10 for malt and hops when he died in 1775.[5] James Hitchcock, who had been innkeeper of the Catherine Wheel, was described as a maltster in 1779,[6] and presented his invoice for malt and hops totalling £19 11s 2d to General Williamson in 1792.[7] Henry Hitchcock, maltster (and perhaps a relative), charged the substantial sum of £27 9s 6d for the malt he supplied to Richard Hickley,[8] and served as Hundred Constable in 1798.[9] The maltster was generally a person of consequence in the parish; Richard Bailey in 1783 not only had a substantial freehold estate in Avebury, but also a copyhold estate in Ogbourne St George; he was sufficiently wealthy to leave his nephew £400 in addition to his copyhold estate.[10]

Travelling badgers, pedlars, and chapmen (which were interchangeable terms) also depended on the road network, and benefited from road improvements. From 1563, they required licences, and many 'badgers' from the area between Devizes, Marlborough and Wootton Bassett can be identified in a late sixteenth century licence register,[11] although none who actually lived in Avebury are named. They would have regularly touted their wares to Avebury householders. In the plague epidemic of 1603, constables were ordered to be on the lookout for unlicensed pedlars.[12] In 1717, John Rose paid £40 to a chapman, Mr Joseph Herne.[13] Such men gradually became more respectable (although 'Mr'

1 WSHC 184/3. Land tax assessment 1751.
2 WSHC 212A/31/2. 1754 bond; P3/B/1679. Will; 118/88 Statement of Samuel Martyn's debts, 1779.
3 WSHC 1409/16/3.
4 Sarum Marriage Licence Bonds, op cit.
5 WSHC 118/88. Statement of Samuel Martyn's debts.
6 WSHC 118/88. Statement of Samuel Martyn's debts.
7 WSHC 184/5.
8 WSHC 184/6. 184/7. Account, November 1794.
9 WSHC 9/23/1.
10 WSHC P3/B/1679.
11 Johnson, H.C., ed. *Wiltshire County Records: Minutes of Proceedings in Sessions, 1563 and 1574 to 1592*. Wiltshire Archaeological & Natural History Society Records branch 4. 1949, p.1-13.
12 WSHC A1/110, 1603M, f.209.
13 GA D1956/E2/8.

signifies a higher social status for a chapman than would be usual at this date), and licences ceased to be required. Corn dealers were perhaps from a better social class, but were still regarded with suspicion. They were frequently accused of 'engrossing' corn, in other words, buying it with intent to sell it again. That was against the law. John Baldwin, John Woodcock, and James Odey, all Avebury men, were accused of this offence in 1611 or 1612.[1]

It was one short step from being a chapman to being a shop keeper. We have already seen how, in the late seventeenth century, the chapman Joseph Hayward established his shop in Avebury selling goods such as candles and tobacco.[2] Others followed his example. In 1711, Robert Phelps was described as a grocer when he gave evidence against the vicar in the Consistory Court.[3] In 1752, John Robinson, the son of a carpenter, was described as a 'shopkeeper' when he borrowed money on mortgage.[4] Four decades later, an invoice of 1793 indicates that John Clements, the elderly former schoolmaster, was selling similar goods.[5] James Lewis's probate account reveals that he purchased groceries worth £6 4s from Clements in the late 1770s; he also paid Thomas Rogers (the former tailor?) £10 2s 4d for 'grocery and shop goods'.[6] By then, such activities had become respectable. Clement's brother, Robert, incidentally, was described as a corn chandler (a dealer in corn) when he served as hundred constable in 1782.[7]

Another aspect of the chapman's trade was followed by John Griffin Grant, a substantial yeoman, who was described as a horse dealer and chapman in 1771, when he went bankrupt.[8] He had been imprisoned for debt in Fisherton Gaol, at the suit of a Warminster innkeeper,[9] before he was able to take advantage of the bankruptcy laws to secure his release.

At the beginning of our period, few chapmen actually lived in Avebury. The same applied to medical professionals. Most medics serving Avebury

1 Williams, N.J., ed. *Tradesmen in Early Stuart Wiltshire: a Miscellany.* WANHS Records Branch 15.1960, nos.761 & 798.
2 WSHC 1569/5. See above, p.85.
3 WSHC D1/42/68.
4 WSHC 529/185. Mortgage deed and bond, John Robinson to William Heath, December 1755.
5 WSHC 184/5. Invoice, John Clements to General Williamson, 28th March 1793.
6 TNA PROB 31/840/590. He had also purchased 'shop goods' from the Clements; see previous note.
7 WSHC 9/23/1.
8 *London Gazette*, 17th December 1771. The description may have been exaggerated in order to conform with the requirements of the bankruptcy laws, which only granted bankruptcy to traders.
9 *Salisbury Journal* 2nd May 1768.

actually lived in Marlborough or Devizes; for example, Marmaduke Burde, apothecary of Devizes, may have had patients in the parish; he took as an apprentice Peter Brewer, the step-son of John Forsyth, the vicar, in 1632.[1] As far as is known, there were no physicians or surgeons in Avebury, at least in 1662.[2] In the late eighteenth century, an 'itinerant quack' regularly visited Kington St Michael, a few miles away;[3] one wonders if he also visited Avebury.

Medicine in our period was very much a hit and miss affair; furthermore, the services of professionals was restricted to those who could afford it. At the end of the sixteenth century, John Shuter called for the services of a bone setter named Townsend when he thought he had broken his ribs. Instead, a tailor named Brunsden tried to set them.[4] The Court of Chancery subsequently condemned him for 'counterfeiting' his trade, 'to the great abuse of the older man', and bound him to good behaviour. Shuter died shortly afterwards. Others who are known to have suffered from broken bones include William Skeat in 1698,[5] and John Caswell in 1731. Skeat had called in a surgeon, and it is possible that the vicar, John Mayo, provided Caswell with medical assistance.[6] Clergy were frequently called upon to provide medical advice, but it is rare that we actually read about it. Mayo had appropriate qualifications, as we shall see.

Skeat's surgeon may have been Dr. Toope (or Took) of Bath, who c.1685 dug up prehistoric remains at West Overton, and perhaps at West Kennett, using the bones to make 'a noble medicine that relieved many of my distressed neighbours'[7]. Others were concerned at the sacrilege involved; at a much later date, one of Stukeley's informants claimed that Toope 'never thrived after it'; indeed, 'his daughter went a begging'.[8]

1 Kite, Edward. 'Judge Nicholas, his parentage and birthplace', *Wiltshire Notes & Queries*, 3, 1899, p.510.
2 Grout, Diana, & Grist, Mervyn, eds. *Churchwardens presentments, 1662, for 73 parishes between Bradford on Avon and Devizes*, vol.2. Wiltshire Family History Society, 2014, p.5, transcribing WSHC D1/54/1/2.
3 Britton, John. *The autobiography of John Britton*. 1850, p.38.
4 TNA STAC 8/269/32.
5 WSHC 184/1, pt. 1. Letter, William Skeat to Sir Richard Holford, 30th January 1698/9.
6 WSHC 371/1, pt.5.
7 Aubrey, *Monumenta*, op cit, vol.1, p.52-3, vol.2, p.984. For Toope's 1685 letter on the subject to John Aubrey, see Long, William. *Avebury Illustrated*. 1862, p.21. Other authorities state Toope was resident in Marlborough in 1678; cf. Piggott, Stuart. *The West Kennet Long Barrow: Excavations, 1955-56*. HMSO, 1962, p.4.
8 Ucko, Peter J., et al. *Avebury reconsidered: from the 1690s to the 1990s*. Unwin Hyman, 1991, p.250.

The elite could afford to pay for the best medical assistance available. Sir Richard Holford had to seek help in 1717, when he was visiting his manors at Avebury and Westonbirt. He was suffering 'grievously' from a sore toe (gout?), and called on the services of Monsieur Raniot, an eminent French surgeon.[1] Raniot was probably based in Bath. However, a remedy proposed by the vicar, John Mayo, eventually proved efficacious, Mayo himself dressing Holford's foot. He may have been well qualified: he married Mary Hayward, the daughter of a medical man,[2] and ran an apothecary's shop in Calne (perhaps inherited from his father in law).[3] He probably applied his medical knowledge during the Avebury plague outbreak of 1720.[4]

Others were not so well qualified. In 1780, Arthur Jones's (un-named) medical adviser thought that 'servants are too often a stranger' to the way in which the sick should be cared for. Jones had given orders that, if he succumbed to illness, his coffin was not to be nailed down until 'his corpse shal change', which he thought might take seven days.[5]

A few other medics are named in our records. In 1780, James Lewis's executor paid Mr Christopher Allsop, an apothecary, £3 1s 4d for medicines supplied during his final illness.[6] Lewis, incidentally, was owed £250 by a Bath apothecary.[7] Mr Pinkney was summoned from Marlborough by Richard Hickley when 'poor old Joe' lay dying in 1794.[8] 'Joe' was actually Joseph Brown, who had been a servant of Arthur Jones, and had continued to live in the farm house, and to be maintained there, under Jones's will.[9] Hickley thought his death was 'no great loss'. We do not know whether Henry Willetts, a Trowbridge apothecary, provided any services in Avebury, but he was mentioned in an Avebury will in 1740.[10]

A few local people followed the profession of law. We have already discussed the manorial stewards,[11] who were probably all legally qualified.

1 GA D1956/E2/8.
2 Mayo, op cit, p.44.
3 WSHC D1/47/3. His parishioners thought it gave him an income of £100 per anum.
4 Mayo, op cit, p.43.
5 WSHC 271/2.
6 TNA PROB 31/840/590.
7 TNA PROB11/1055/301.
8 WSHC 186/4. Richard Hickley to Mrs Williamson, 1st April 1794.
9 TNA PROB11/1181/174.
10 WSHC P1/T/418. Edward must have been the son of Henry Taylor; Willett's will left £100 to Henry Taylor's children, cf. P1/9Reg/9.
11 See above, p.297-8.

John Shuter, son of the leading tenant in the parish, was admitted to the Inner Temple in 1600, and probably called to the bar in 1609.[1] The lord of the manor, Sir Richard Holford, himself occupied an important position as a Master in Chancery. In 1737, his grandson Richard was reading law whilst in residence at Avebury.[2] George Popham, described as being of Berwick Bassett and Avebury, was admitted to the Middle Temple in 1676;[3] he was a member of a prominent county family. Thomas Smith, the son of Richard Smith, lord of the manor of West Kennett, was an attorney; when he and his father leased the extension they had built on to their manor house in 1723, he was described as of London.[4] Walter Sloper lived just north of the parish, in Winterbourne Monkton; he was the attorney who, in 1684, acquainted John Aubrey with the fact that the great stone at the Avebury end of West Kennett Avenue had fallen[5]. He gave William Skeat a greyhound in early 1698, probably intending it for Skeat's landlord, Sir Richard Holford,[6] with whom he may have had some business dealings; Holford asked John Brinsden to 'remember us both to your neighbour Mr Sloper'.[7] Humphry Wall, a Marlborough attorney, acted on behalf of Holford when he was negotiating for the purchase of Avebury land.[8] He also acted on behalf of John Griffin when the latter sold his portion of Avebury Truslow to Holford.[9] John White, the vicar, in his legal actions, depended upon 'the ill advice of his lawyer (as hee called Mr Wilkins)',[10] whose residence is not known.

1 Inner Temple Admissions Database www.innertemplearchives.org.uk. See above, p.137.
2 WSHC 184/1, pt.2. Letter, Robert Holford to Richard Holford, 24th September 1737.
3 Popham, Frederick W. *A West Country Family: the Pophams from 1150*. The Author, 1976, p.67.
4 Somerset Heritage Centre. DD/PO/6/ Lease, 3rd September 1723, Richard & Thomas Smith to Francis Popham.
5 Aubrey, John. *John Aubrey: my own life*, [ed.] Ruth Scurr. Chatto Windus, 2015, p.339.
6 WSHC 184/1, pt.2. Letter, Richard Holford to Charles Tooker, 4th January 1697/8.
7 WSHC 184/1, pt.2. Letter, Sir Richard Holford to John Brinsden, 24th January 1711/12
8 WSHC 184/1, pt.1. Letter, Humfry Wall to Sir Richard Holford, 18th October 1702.
9 WSHC 184/4, pt.1. Survey of Griffin's property, 1702.
10 WSHC 184/1, pt.2. Sir Richard Holford to John Brinsden, 24th January 1711/12. In 1700/01, he referred to White's lawyer as 'Watkins'; he probably had a lapse of memory, cf. 184/1, Pt.1. Sir Richard Holford to William Smith, 22nd February 1700/01.

The teaching profession was also represented at Avebury. As has been seen, Philip Hunton, who afterwards became Prebendary of Heytesbury, and preacher at St. John's, Devizes, was the earliest known schoolmaster in the parish.[1] He probably served in the 1630s. He was deprived of his prebend in 1663.

Some sixty years later, a charity school at Avebury was established under a legacy from Dame Susanna Holford.[2] She bequeathed £200 for the support of this school in 1722, although the money was not paid to the churchwardens until 1733. Poor children 'whose parents often frequent the parish church', were to be instructed 'in the principles of the Protestant religion'.[3] This legacy was supplemented by a legacy from Arthur Jones, who gave £5 'for the countenancing and encouraging the school master and school at Avebury' in his 1786 will.[4]

The schoolmaster was licenced to teach 'an English school, & the art of writing & arithmetick'.[5] He was appointed by the minister and churchwardens, and allowed to use the vestry in the church as his schoolroom[6]. We have already discussed the vestry's concern regarding the unsatisfactory appointment of Thomas Exall in the 1730s, and the career of John Clements.[7] In 1772, Rev. Whitaker met Clements, noting that he was old enough to remember Stukeley's visits, and had a copy of his book[8]. In 1786, William Alexander was the schoolmaster;[9] in that year, he married Ann Clements, his predecessor's niece.

The 1818 Charity Commission report[10] implies that Samuel Martyn of Kennett had acted as trustee of the school's funds until his death in the

---

1   Clergy of the Church of England Database www.theclergydatabase.org.uk ; Schomberg, Arthur. 'Wiltshire nonconformists', *Wiltshire Notes & Queries* 8, 1914-16, p.155; *Alumni Oxonienses* www.british-history.ac.uk/alumni-oxon/
2   For most of the information in the following two paragraphs, see *Select Committee on Education of the Poor &c.* 1818, p.1018. *The Charities of the County of Wilts ... 1817-1836.* James Newman, 1839, p.1389. Although our evidence for the use of the vestry dates from the nineteenth century, it had probably been used from the beginning of the charity.
3   WSHC 184/8.
4   TNA PROB11/1181/174.
5   WSHC D1/22/8. Oath taken by Thomas Exall, 1st November 1737.
6   *The Charities of the County of Wilts ... 1817-1836.* James Newman, 1839, p.1389.
7   See above, p.171-2.
8   Nichols, John. *Illustrations of the literary history of the eighteenth century, vol.IV.* John Nichols & Son, 1822, p.856. The book was probably Stukeley, William. *Abury: a temple of the British Druids ... .* 1743.
9   Parish Register.
10 *Select Committee on Education of the Poor &c.* 1818, p.1018

1770s. Unfortunately, his debts considerably exceeded his assets. The vicar, James Mayo, certified that he owed the charity £221 4s 3d, but when funds were distributed in 1779 it only received £69 1s 3d.[1] It may be that more of the debt was recovered at a later date, as, when new trustees took over in 1805, they received a legacy from Mrs (Hannah) Martyn which, together with cash received from the executors of Samuel Martin, totalled £174 19s 4d. This was invested in 'navy five per cents'. The charity also received a legacy of £20 bequeathed to the poor by Mrs. Martyn. In addition to the cash, the endowment in 1805 consisted of four cottages, which together yielded £6 per annum, although the cost of repairs took a substantial proportion of this income.

[1] WSHC 118/88. Statement of debts of Samuel Martyn.

8
LIVING CONDITIONS IN AVEBURY: HOUSING, FOOD AND POSSESSIONS

EARLY MODERN LIVING conditions were spartan by modern standards. Even c.1800, when straw plaiting was introduced to the Avebury poor, their standard of 'personal cleanliness' was very low. Soap was unknown in Avebury, except to the gentry.[1] Lye, made from ashes, provided a very primitive alternative. But straw plaiting required personal cleanliness. It was 'a task of no little difficulty' to improve it. Poverty had induced the poor 'to dispose of the little means of personal accommodation and cleanliness which they possessed'; consequently, verminous children were sometimes refused admittance to the straw plaiting school.[2] As we have seen, the vestry took steps to remedy the situation.

It is likely that in earlier centuries it had not only been the paupers who suffered from lack of cleanliness. Richard Hickley (the churchwarden) and those who joined with him in the effort to clean up Avebury's poor were passing on the results of a clean-up which had been progressing amongst Avebury's yeomen for centuries. Greater comfort, and facilities for relaxation, were gradually introduced from the late seventeenth century onwards, perhaps epitomised by the summer house at West Kennett Farm, which was built before 1755.[3] Probate inventories for Avebury, and, indeed, for the whole country, demonstrate a steady increase in the amount of wealth invested in personal goods, and in the number and variety of those goods.[4] The quality of housing,

1 In 1781, Arthur Jones bought 'one box best Crown soap'; cf. WSHC 154/5. Bill for soap.
2 Bernard, Thomas. 'Extract of an account of the introduction of straw platt at Avebury', *The Reports of the Society for Bettering the Conditions and increasing the Comforts of the Poor*, 4, 1802-5, p.91-2.
3 WSHC 568/7. Lease, Stanes Chamberlayne & Samuel Martyn to John Nalder, 9th November 1755.
4 Hey, David G. *An English Rural Community: Myddle under the Tudors and Stuarts.* Leicester University Press, 1974, p.124.

and of furniture, even for the poor, was beginning to improve by the end of the eighteenth century.[1] Nevertheless, the houses of the lower orders were designed for shelter, work, sleeping, and eating. They were emphatically not designed for relaxation.

Avebury builders had access to the wide range of building materials provided by local geology[2], as well as to a relatively small quantity of timber. Sarsen was widely used;[3] as early as 1644, Symonds noted that the nearby parish of Fyfield was so full of 'a grey pibble stone of great bignes as is not usuall seene; they breake them and build their howses of them and walls, laying mosse betweene'.[4] In 1673, Marlborough Corporation purchased 'two loads of sarszen stones' for its market house.[5] Avebury's stone circle and avenue provided a readily available quarry. In the seventeenth century, John Aubrey recorded that 'the houses are built of the frustrum's [fragments] of those huge stones, which they invade with great sledges'. In 1723, Thomas Twining observed that 'no less than four villages, two parish churches, and a demolish'd chappel, havd in great measure, forst or last, risen out of the ruins of this single work'.[6]

A neighbouring cleric, John Brinsden of Winterbourne Monkton, informed him that 'these mighty stones (as hard as marble), may be broken in what part of them you please, without any great trouble, for, make a fire on that line of the stone where you would have it rack, and after it is well heated, draw over a line with cold water & immediately give a knock with a smyths sledge, and it will break'[7]. William Stukeley gave a more detailed description in 1743: 'The method is, to dig a pit by the side of the stone, till it falls down, then to burn many loads of straw under it. They draw lines of water along it when heated, and then with smart strokes of a great sledge hammer, its prodigious bulk is divided into many lesser parts'.[8] Ashes resulting from the

1 Sharpe, J.A. *Early Modern England: A Social History 1550-1760*. Edward Arnold, 1987, p.149.
2 Watts, Ken. *The Marlborough Downs*. Ex Libris Press, 2003, p.17-18.
3 For a general discussion of sarsen, see Jones, T. Rupert. 'History of Sarsens' *WAM* 23, 1887, p.122-54.
4 Symonds, Richard Diary of the Marches of the Royal Army during the Great Civil War, ed. Charles Edward Long. Camden Society, 1859, p.151.
5 Jones, op cit, p.128.
6 Twining, Thomas. *Avebury in Wiltshire*. Jos Downing, 1723, p.3.
7 Aubrey, John. *Monumenta Britannica*. Milborne Port: Dorset Publishing, 1980, v.1, p.38. See also Aubrey, John. *John Aubrey: my own life*, [ed.] Ruth Scurr. Chatto & Windus, 2015, p.138.
8 Stukeley, William. *Abury: a temple of the British Druids ...* . 1743, p.15-16. For a more detailed discussion of the process, see Gillings, Mark, et al. *Landscape of*

burnt straw used in this process have been discovered by several excavators.[1]

Many stones had been destroyed in the years immediately preceding Stukeley's first visit. Their destruction was 'excessive hard work', and sometimes required the labour of twenty men. One stone would build a house. The stone was excessively hard, so hard that a Mr Ayloffe of Wootton Bassett 'hewed one of them to make a rape-mill stone', employing twenty yoke of oxen to carry it off. But it 'repeatedly broke his tackle, and he was forced to leave it'.[2]

Stukeley tells us that 'most of the houses, walls and outhouses in the town are raised from these materials.[3] His 'most' may have been a slight exaggeration, as he also tells us that it was generally thought that 'they may have them cheaper, in more manageable pieces, from the gray wethers' scattered in the fields.[4] In 1699/1700, two workmen broke 'out of Mr Smith's Down' (that is, Waden Hill) sixty loads of sarsen stones, and hoped to sell them for 1s per load.[5] It was easier to handle smaller stones rather than the gigantic ones found in the monument. Indeed, Thomas Robinson, Stukeley's arch stone-breaker, complained of the cost of breaking up the megaliths.[6] Nevertheless, we know that many were broken up, and have little evidence that any were used for purposes other than building.

The hardness of sarsen made it very suitable for building purposes. The church, the manor house, and a variety of other buildings, were all built from sarsen. Several inns in the parish were built or extended with sarsen stone from megaliths. A megalith close to the Meeting House was used in its construction.[7] In the later eighteenth century, John Nalder used megaliths from the Kennet Avenue in the construction of several houses at West Kennett, at the direction of his landlord, one of the Grubbes.[8] Sarsen was sometimes

---

the Megaliths: Excavation and Fieldwork on the Avebury Monuments, 1997-2003. Oxbow Books, 2008, chapter 10.

1 See, for example, Smith, Alfred Charles. 'Excavations at Avebury', *WAM* 10, 1867, p.209-16.
2 Stukeley, *Abury,* op cit, p.17.
3 Stukeley, *Abury,* op cit, p.25.
4 Stukeley, *Abury,* op cit, p.16.
5 184/1, pt.1. Letter, William Skeat to Sir Richard Holford, 19th February 1699/1700.
6 Gillings, Mark, Peterson, Rick, & Pollard, Joshua. 'The destruction of the Avebury monuments', in Cleal, Rosemary, & Pollard, Joshua, eds. *Monuments and material culture: Papers in honour of an Avebury Archaeologist: Isobel Smith.* Hobnob Press, 2004, p.153.
7 Gillings, et al, *Landscape,* op cit, p.350.
8 WBR. Notes on West Kennet Farm. West Kennett farmhouse itself is dated in these notes to half a century before Nalder's tenancy. One wonders if it was the

used as footing for timber-framed houses,[1] and to rebuild older timber-framed buildings such as the Old Bakery.[2] It was, however, subject to damp. In 1663, John Aubrey noted that the stone 'doth not endure the weather', and ought not to be exposed to sun and rain.[3] Stukeley commented that it was 'always moist and dewy in winter, which proves damp and unwholesome, and rots the furniture'.[4] Richard Hickley, the bailiff, noted that 'the wet is apt to get into those old walls if not don [whitewashed] once a year'.[5]

Sarsen was frequently used as a base for clunch (hard chalk) or cob walls, or in conjunction with them or brick.[6] Cob was a wet mixture of chalk, clay, and straw, which had to be left to dry as it was being built. It required protection from the elements in order to survive rain, and was usually provided with a good capping of thatch. In February 1793, Gabriel Chivers was paid £5 11s 0d for 'thatching the garden wall', which was presumably made of cob.[7] The boundary wall between the churchyard and Avebury Manor is thatched to protect the topping of cob.[8]

Thatch was cheap. The withies that grew beside the Winterbourne provided thatchers with the materials needed; in 1729, the tenant of Avebury Great Farm, Joseph Griffin, was allowed a quarter of the loppings of withies grown on the farm.[9] Alternatively, long straw wheat, a by-product of the wheat crop, could be used.[10] Thatch had important insulating qualities, important in

---

new building adjacent to the manor house which Thomas Smith leased in 1723; see Somerset Heritage Centre. DD/PO/6/ Lease, 3rd September 1723, Richard & Thomas Smith to Francis Popham.

1   Slocombe, Pamela A. *Medieval houses of Wiltshire*. Alan Sutton Publishing, 1992, p.29.
2   Treasure, D., et al. *The Old Bakery, High Street, Avebury: a Historic Buildings Study*. Unpublished WBR report, 2015, p.21-2.
3   Cited by Treasure, Dorothy. *Vernacular Building Survey 1991-2*. Unpublished report, 1992, held by WBR.
4   Stukeley, *Abury*, op cit, p.16. See also Lukis, W.C., ed. *The Family Memoirs of the Rev. William Stukeley, M.D., ... vol.III*. Surtees Society 80, 1885, p.247-8.
5   WSHC 184/6. Letter, Richard Hickley to Mrs Williamson, 31st July 1792. Hickley frequently mentioned whitewashing in his letters. Damp was still a problem in 1999; see *Appraisal of Buildings on the Avebury Estate, part 1. Conservation Plan, for the National Trust*. Ferguson Mann Architects, 1999. Unpublished report held by WBR.
6   Watts, op cit, p.17.
7   WSHC 184/7.
8   https://britishlistedbuildings.co.uk
9   WSHC 435/24/1/7.
10 Davis, Bob, Upson, Anne', & Cleal, Rosamund J. 'Built Heritage', in Leivers, Matt, & Powell, Andrew B., eds. *A Research Framework for the Stonehenge, Avebury,*

wintry weather when firewood might be scarce. In 1709, the new tenant of a farm at Beckhampton was required to keep 'all the housing ... well covered with straw in a good husbandlike manner'.[1] When John Beake leased West Kennett Farm in 1724, he was required to 'keep the pigge stye, woodhouse, rook stadels, barnes, stables, and all and every other outhouses demised well thatched'. But he was also expected to keep such outhouses as were 'covered with tyle well tyled'.[2] Wintry weather could, of course be a threat to thatch. In April 1711, on Sir Richard Holford's Beckhampton property, 'the thatch of the houses' was 'very much out of repair by the late tempestuous wind'.[3]

Thatch was also a fire hazard. When Stayner Chamberlain leased the house at West Kennett Farm to his wife's brother in law, Samuel Martyn, in 1755, he was careful to specify that if the house burnt down he would be under no obligation to rebuild, although no further rent would be payable.[4] He may have been mindful of the fact that the Catherine Wheel had recently burnt down. Thomas Robinson, the stone destroyer, also suffered from fire: some of the houses he built with stone from the megaliths also burnt down.[5] They were probably thatched, and consequently burnt well. It may be that they included some of the buildings facing Green Street in the South-Eastern quadrant of the henge, the foundations of which have been detected by geophysical survey.[6] They lie in a field that was owned by the Robinsons.[7]

Robinson was not the only person to suffer from the inflammable qualities of thatch. It was blamed for the disastrous Marlborough fires of 1655, 1679, and 1690. In the latter year, it was banned altogether in Marlborough.[8] Elsewhere, it was gradually replaced by tiles, following national trends. When Sir Richard Holford was building in 1711, the tiler suggested fetching tiles

---

and Associated Sites World Heritage Site: Avebury Assessment. Wessex Archaeology, 2016, p.129.

1 WSHC 371/1, pt.4. Lease, Charles Tooker to Richard Caswell, 16th April 1709.
2 WSHC 568/7. Lease, Thomas Smith to John Beake, 13th October 1724.
3 GA D1954/E2/8.
4 WSHC 568/7. Lease, Staner Chamberlayne to Samuel Martyn, 1st December 1755.
5 Lewis, Charles. *A Descriptive Account in blank verse of the Old Serpentine Temple of the Druids at Avebury in North Wiltshire.* 2nd ed. Marlborough: E. Harold (printer), 1801.
6 Papworth, Martin. 'Geophysical survey of the northeast and southeast quadrants of Avebury henge', *WAM* 105, 2012, p.25-6 & 39-40. This could probably be confirmed by excavation.
7 See above, p.128.
8 Stedman, A.R. *Marlborough and the Upper Kennet country.* [Marlborough College?], 1960, p.227.

from Corsham, but John Rose, his tenant, though they would be cheaper if fetched from Westonbirt.[1] Thatch did not, however, altogether disappear. Richard Hickley paid out £1 4s 6d 'for thatching Hatchet's house' in March 1792.[2] The four cottages owned by the Holford charity, which were said to be 'very old' in 1833, were thatched[3].

In the eighteenth century, the danger of fire began to be mitigated against by insurance. The accounts of Richard Hickley in the 1790s, show that Avebury Great Farm, 'Hatchet's house', and 'Avebury' (meaning the manor house?) were all insured, as was the Williamson's house at Bath in the tenure of Mrs Jenny.[4] Hickley, as churchwarden, was probably also responsible for ensuring the labourers' cottages owned by the school trustees were insured by the Royal and Sun Alliance in 1782.[5] The only other property in Avebury known to have been insured was owned by John Dore, maltster and baker, in 1791.[6]

Older houses were frequently timber-framed, although the relative scarcity of timber on the Downland meant that fairly thin timbers (scantlings) might be used. Carpenter's Cottage, and the house now known as the Red Lion, are surviving examples from the late sixteenth or early seventeenth centuries. The Old Bakery, and Rose Cottage, were both originally timber framed, although they were subsequently rebuilt with sarsen.[7] Such conversions must have been common in the village in the eighteenth century, as old timber framing of inferior quality began to show its age. Many of the houses cleared in the 1930s from the Henge, and from the centre of Avebury, were of this character. Some surviving houses, re-built in the eighteenth century in brick or stone, retain evidence of timber framing.[8]

Timber was also used to make the rafters on which thatch was laid, and the beams which in some farmhouses had to support tons of cheese.[9] It is likely

1 GA D1956/E2/8.
2 WSHC 184/7.
3 *The Charities of the County of Wilts ... 1817-1836.* James Newman, 1839, p.1389.
4 WSHC 184/7.
5 LMA CLC/B/192/F/001/MS11936/306/468222.
6 LMA CLC/B/192/F/001/MS11936/377/581550.
7 Treasure, D., et al. *The Old Bakery, High Street, Avebury: a Historic Buildings Study.* Unpublished WBR report, 2015, p.21; Treasure, D., et al. *Rose Cottage, High Street, Avebury: a Historic Buildings Study.* Unpublished WBR report, 2015, p.2.
8 *Appraisal of Buildings on the Avebury Estate, part 1. Conservation Plan, for the National Trust.* Ferguson Mann Architects, 1999, pt.1.3. Unpublished report held by WBR.
9 Wilson, *Forgotten Harvest*, op cit, p.133.

that the timber stored in the yard at the parsonage (on the site of the dovecot) in the late sixteenth century had to be brought from a distance.[1] The ground floor of many houses was probably the bare earth; however, John Bromham als Phelps (c.1663) had 'three planck floores', one in his hall, and three in his barn; they were valued at £40.[2] Oak and elm is found in surviving farm buildings.[3] We have already noted Humphry Robinson's extensive store of timber and wood; he was evidently heavily involved in building timber framed houses, as was his son Thomas. In the 1760s oak planks and elm boards, together with 'oaken posts, rails, &c' were brought from Nonsuch for the renovations at Brunsdens.[4] Norris's 'Little Farm' at Avebury provided 'timber, tyle, & stone'.[5]

Flint was also available, as was brick. There was a brick kiln at Totterdown (in Fyfield parish), to the east of Avebury, and it is possible that the brick houses of Avebury were built using its products.[6] In 1732, Robert Holford purchased 1,000 bricks for £1, and paid 10s for their carriage.[7] In 1764, Stayner Holford purchased substantial quantities of bricks and lime. His accounts name a number of brickmakers, but it is probable that they were not Avebury parishioners.[8] Sometimes stone was brought from further afield: the fireplace in Avebury Manor's Great Parlour was made from freestone brought from Compton Bassett c.1601.[9]

In the eighteenth century, new materials, such as plain tile and slate, slowly became more easily available.[10] William Norris paid £4 17s 6d 'for brick & carriage' when he was renovating the farmhouse at Brunsdens in the early 1760s,[11] although his accounts do not tell us where he obtained them. When West Kennett Farmhouse was refurbished at the end of the eighteenth century, brick was used extensively for decorative purposes.[12] High quality brickwork

1 TNA E134/40and41Eliz/Mich7.
2 WSHC P1/B/416.
3 Davis, et al, 'Built Heritage', op cit, p.129.
4 WSHC 473/277.
5 WSHC 473/277.
6 Fowler, P.J. *Landscape Plotted and Pieced: Landscape History and Local Archaeology in Fyfield and Overton, Wiltshire.* Society of Antiquaries of London, 2000, p.191; Watts, op cit, p.18.
7 WSHC 371/1, pt.5. Account of Disbursements, 1723.
8 WSHC 184/5.
9 *Avebury Manor, Avebury, Wiltshire. Historic Building Survey.* Unpublished report. Wessex Archaeology, 2011, room data sheet 6. (held by the National Trust, Avebury).
10 Davis, et al, 'Built Heritage', op cit, p.129.
11 WSHC 473/277.
12 WBR notes on West Kennett Farmhouse, by Dorothy Treasure.

from this period can still be seen at Bannings, Beckhampton House, and Silbury House, and in several houses on High Street.

Housing for the poorer sections of the community was generally rudimentary. It is possible that some who could not afford the proper foundations continued the older tradition of post beams inserted directly into the ground. These usually rotted after a generation, and had to be replaced. Labourers' cottages from our period have generally not survived. That is likely to apply to all the 32 cottages on Richard Smith's estate in West Kennett and Beckhampton in 1770.[1]

Few labourers had chimneys in our period.[2] Until the eighteenth century, a hole was left above the central hearth to allow smoke to escape. Nevertheless, even the poorest hovel might have sarsen foundations. The house of the pauper, James Cue, which was falling down when he died in 1776, had 'sarsen stones in the foundation', although its walls were of mud[3]. It was probably affected badly by damp from the sarsen, and the cob walls would have turned into mud when the house lost its thatch.[4]

The poor – and not just the poor – were frequently confined to just one or two rooms. For example, the property that John Bradfield, husbandman, leased from John Truslow at Beckhampton in 1689 was merely the north end, 'being one rome', of Thomas Mortimer's house. He and his daughter Elizabeth were the only 'lives' in the lease, so he presumably had to share the one room with her. The rent was 3s 4d per annum, and common of pasture for one beast was included in the lease.[5]

William Burry's rent when he leased a cottage from Richard Smith in 1698 was even lower: 2s per annum.[6] His entry fine, £5 was also low, perhaps in consideration of the work that he had done on the cottage before the lease. It had previously been merely two butteries, together with part of a stable, in a house formerly occupied by Richard Harding. Burry had 'lately converted' it 'into a little cottage', where he, his wife Susanna, and his daughter Susanna dwelt. Another member of the family, Elizabeth, was born in 1702. The garden attached to the cottage bordered on the river.

Similarly, the cottage leased by Frances Truslow at Beckhampton in

1   WSHC 568/5. Indenture, 13th May 1712.
2   Wilson, Avice R. *Forgotten Labour: the Wiltshire Agricultural Worker and his Environment, 4500 B.C. – A.D. 1950*. Hobnob Press, 2007, p.134 & 137.
3   WSHC 184/9/5.
4   Raymond, Stuart A. 'A Pauper's Hovel in 1775', *The Recorder: the Annual Newsletter of the Wiltshire Record Society*, 22, 2023, p.7-8.
5   WSHC 371//1, pt. 3. Lease, 6th December 1689.
6   WSHC 568/39.

1734/5 merely had one ground room and one buttery'[1]. She lived in one of them with her (probably) illegitimate two year old son John. Her brother, Richard, was also a life in the lease, but he probably lived elsewhere. Frances also had a garden 62' x 80'.

The earliest written evidence for housing in Avebury is the survey of 1548 conducted when William Sharington purchased the property from the Crown.[2] This survey says nothing about building materials; it does, however, give us brief descriptions of tenants' houses (and also, incidentally, the manor house). Twenty-one tenants' houses are described. Most had a hall, a chamber, and a kitchen, mostly on one floor, although four lacked a kitchen. One tenant, Nicholas Bromham, had a 'bakehouse' instead. The hall was the principal room of the house; chambers were for sleeping, and the kitchen for food preparation. Many tenants had lofts above one or more of their rooms; these were probably used for sleeping and/or storage. Most also had a barn; nine had an 'ox house', ten had a stable; seven had a 'sheep house' or 'shippen'. These were mostly separate from the house and from each other, presumably surrounding the barton (farmyard). A few were attached to the house, or to each other. Most houses had a garden attached; there were also six orchards (although Thomas Smith had two of them). The survey described John Mills' property as including 'a hall, a chamber within the hall, with a lofte over the chamber, a stable, and an oxe stale at thother end of the hall, all lying together under oon ruff, a barne by hym self'. Most stables and ox houses were separate from the house, although some were joined with each other or with a barn.

A century later, the 1662 hearth tax return for Avebury Tithing lists the number of hearths each householder possessed. That provides a rough indication of the size of houses, although of course not every room in a house had a hearth. Of the sixteen taxpayers mentioned, one (George Riddle) had just one hearth, six had two, seven had three, one (Mr Dunch at Beckhampton) had four, and one (Ralph Stawell) had 13.[3] The hearth tax exemption certificates show that all but one of the nineteen poor in 1670 (and 24 in 1674) had just one hearth; the only exception to this rule was John Pontin, who had two.[4]

Probate appraisers frequently listed goods room by room, enabling us to see how many rooms the deceased had, and what they were used for. That was not, of course, always the case, although one may frequently suspect that decedents for whom rooms were not mentioned actually only had one or two.

1   WSHC 371/1, pt. 5. Lease, 6th March 1734/5, Robert Holford to Frances Truslow.
2   WSHC 2664/1/2D/8.
3   TNA E179/259/29.
4   TNA E179/348.

It is unlikely, for instance, that Elizabeth Pope had more than that when she died in 1618. Her goods were valued at a mere £11 8s.[1]

William Hayward's house was probably fairly typical, at least in the early years of our period. He was a shepherd, and his inventory was valued at just over £15 in 1609/10.[2] He had a hall and a chamber. The hall was the main living room in the house, chambers were mostly bedrooms. In Hayward's hall there was a table board and various items of kitchen equipment. His beds and bedding were in the chamber, although it also had his 'spinning torne', which his wife probably used whilst he was up on the Downs looking after sheep.

Hayward's house was a humble dwelling, but it was no smaller than some houses occupied by householders of higher status. George Brown's 1619 inventory[3] suggests that he was a yeoman farmer; he had 128 sheep, as well as cattle and horses, and his goods were valued at just over £150. He too had just a hall and bedchamber, together with a barn for storing his corn and malt. John Hayward, who died in 1661, was much wealthier – his goods were valued at over £557. He was probably William's nephew, and may still have been living in his uncle's house at his death. Only two rooms were recorded in John's house, the kitchen and the buttery, although if that was all the space he had, one wonders where he put his six beds. John Jacob was another wealthy yeoman, worth £438, whose 1670 inventory[4] only identifies three rooms: the hall, the parlour, and the chamber.

The hall was the principal room in the house, and was likely to be the place where visitors were entertained. It was likely to have a hearth, seating, and a table. The yeoman Thomas Phelps als Bromham had 'in the hall on table with formes and stooles and on cubberd on chears' when he died c.1622.[5] Almost a century later. In 1720, Humphry Robinson, the carpenter, possessed 'in ye hall a tabell board & bras & pewter & other lumber'.[6] Was the brass for display?

The kitchen was the room where food was prepared, and was likely to have an open fire, perhaps with built-in ovens. Pearce's Cottage, which was originally built in the seventeenth century, still has two brick ovens in the room that was, presumably, originally the kitchen.[7] It may be that some Avebury kitchens had cloam ovens, manufactured in North Devon, and designed to

1 WSHC P3/P/78.
2 WSHC P3/H/56.
3 P3/B/179.
4 WHSC P3/IJ/101.
5 WSHC P3/P/93.
6 WSHC P1/R/275.
7 http://britishlistedbuildings.co.uk

be built into fire places. Some have been identified in nearby Horton.[1] In his kitchen in 1696, William Bray had '1 furnace [a cauldron], 3 kettles with other brewing vessels, 1 brasse pott, 2 dripping pans, 12 pieces of pewter, with some iron, tin, wooden and ear[t]hen utensills and lumber', worth £10.

The function of the buttery was to store liquor. Toby King, the blacksmith, had four 'halfe hogsheads', two dozen bottles, and a little barrel in his buttery when he died in 1685.[2] In the few inventories where there is a buttery but no kitchen, the buttery is likely to have functioned as a kitchen. No kitchen is mentioned in Thomas Griffin's 1716 inventory, but he did have 'a little ould furnish[3] in ye wall' (whatever that may mean), in a room within his buttery.[4]

Most houses mentioned in the inventories were of two storeys. It is not possible to identify specific houses mentioned in the inventories, but Rose Cottage must have been typical.[5] It had two rooms on the ground floor, one of which was used for living, the other for storage. Upstairs there were another two rooms, which were heightened in the late eighteenth century to give more head-room. There was a bread oven in an external wall.

In the inventories, upstairs 'chambers' are usually described as being 'chambers above' a specific downstairs room. Bridget Dyer, for example, had a 'chamber over the kitchin', a 'parlour chamber', a 'chamber over the buttery,' and a 'chamber over the hall' when she died in 1629.[6] Chambers could, however, be on the ground floor: in 1719, Thomas Jordan had an 'under chamber', in which there were beds and bedding.[7] Chambers were generally what would now be described as bed-rooms. James Pope, for example, had 'two beds, two bedsteds with beding thereunto belonging, one chest, a parcill of chars, one coffer,' in his 'chamber over the passage', c.1680.[8] Sometimes chambers had other contents. Richard Parr's 'inner chamber' in 1632 contained not just 'one bedsteed', but also 'a chese rack butter & cheese & malt & backon & a larking

---

1 Roberts, Hugh D. *Downhearth to Bargate: An Illustrated Account of the Revolution in Cooking due to the use of Coal instead of Wood*. Wiltshire Folk Life Society, 1981, p.59.
2 WSHC P3/K/106.
3 Furnace.
4 WSHC P1/G/391.
5 Treasure, D., et al. *Rose Cottage, High Street, Avebury: a Historic Buildings Study*. Unpublished WBR report, 2015, p.25.
6 WSHC P3/D/76.
7 WSHC P1/IJ/167.
8 WSHC P1/P/317.

nett and a turne'.[1] In 1720, one of Humphry Robinson's chambers, as befitted a carpenter, was used to store 'nailes & timber' worth over £9.[2]

Tradesmen such as the Robinsons frequently had a 'shop' where they could work. This was a work-room, not a shop in the modern retail sense. In 1670, Richard Cripps's blacksmith's shop contained the tools of his trade, as listed in chapter 7.[3] We have already seen that the contents of Joseph Wallis's shop in 1680 tell us that he was a shoemaker,[4] and that the tan pit and rope walk at Perry's Cottage suggest the presence of a saddler and harness maker.[5]

A few of the larger houses had a pantry. This was originally a store room for food, especially bread. Perishable food is not normally included in inventories, but store cupboards and utensils used in preparing food are. In 1689, there was 'one dresser-bord & shelves, one fryeing-pan, five dozen of trenchers, two dozen of glass-bottles, one gratter with other utensils' in Peter Griffin's pantry.[6]

Two garrets are mentioned in the probate inventories. The garret was a habitable attic, often small, dismal, and cramped, perhaps with sloping ceilings, suitable for the accommodation of lowly servants, or simply for storage. Peter Griffin used his garret to store £3 worth of 'plough tember of all sorts';[7] perhaps it was above a barn, rather than the house. In 1722 John Griffin's garret housed 'one bed & bedsteed with the appurtenances', but also four sides of bacon & two pieces'.[8]

A variety of other rooms are mentioned in the probate inventories, many of them related to decedent's livelihoods. The vicar, John White, had a study where he could prepare his sermons, one of only two studies recorded.[9] He also had a 'dayhouse' [dairy] and a cheese loft, although it is likely that his servants made cheese for domestic consumption only.

Most farmers would have had 'dayhouses' or 'white houses', that is, dairies or milkhouses. When she died in 1623, Katherine Bray, who shared a cow with someone else, had a milkhouse,[10] where she may have made cheese.

1 WSHC P3/P/184.
2 WSHC P1/R/275.
3 WSHC P3/C/352. See above, p.310.
4 See above, p.313.
5 See above, p.313. http://britishlistedbuildings.co.uk
6 WSHC P3/G/413.
7 WSHC P3/G/413.
8 WSHC P3/G/485.
9 WSHC P3/W/671. The other study was in Avebury Trusloe manor house in 1625; cf Maud Truslow's inventory WSHC P3/T/86.
10 WSHC P3/B/236.

In 1699, William Bray similarly had a 'dayhouse' where he presumably made cheese, although on his death its contents included '1 hog in salt' as well as 'dairy vessel'.[1] Joseph Griffin kept his cheese press and other dairy utensils in a white house, although he also had a cheese loft where there were twelve cheeses stored on his death in 1719.[2]

Brewing frequently took place in the buttery, or in the kitchen. However, some decedents did have separate brewhouses. We have already noticed the brewhouse where Lemuel Fowler, the innkeeper, brewed beer for his customers.[3] William Dunch probably built a brewhouse soon after he purchased the manor of Avebury in 1551.[4] In 1689, Peter Griffin, the tenant of Avebury Great Farm, had a brewhouse containing brewing equipment valued at £4.[5] He and other tenants regularly brewed ale or beer for the use of the Holford family when they visited.[6] During Adam Williamson's governorship of Jamaica, his bailiff regularly brewed beer to ship out to him.[7]

Toby King, the blacksmith, had a 'brewing roome', where he kept various brewing vessels.[8] John White, the vicar, had a brewhouse; its contents were valued at £5 when he died in 1712.[9]

A variety of other buildings could be found outside the house. The 'backside' was usually a lean-to against the back of the house, used for storing firewood or coal. A variety of other things might also be found there. Lemuel Fowler, the innkeeper, used his as a sty for his 'two hogs [and] five store piggs'.[10] John Bromham als Phelps kept the hurdles which he used for penning sheep in his backside.[11] 'Six rawhides', waiting to be used for making harness, were to be found in George Arnold's backside.[12]

Barns were ubiquitous. Every husbandman and yeoman needed one to store his corn. Some, of course were large, others were quite small. William Bray's barn held '1 stack of wheat, 3 mows of barly, 1 mow of oats and

1 WSHC P3/B/986.
2 WSHC P3/G/465.
3 Above, p.356.
4 Fretwell, Katie. *Avebury Manor: Park and Garden Survey*. National Trust, 1992 (unpublished report), p.5.
5 WSHC P3/G/413.
6 See, for example, WSHC 184/1, pt.2. Peter Griffin to Samuel Holford, 22nd April 1743.
7 WSHC 184/6.
8 WSHC P3/K/106.
9 WSHC P3/W/671.
10 WSHC P3/F/135.
11 WSHC P1/B/416.
12 WSHC P3/A/259.

vetches' in November 1699, together worth £95.[1] By contrast, Richard Parr's 1632 inventory records 'fodder in the barne' worth just £3.[2] Admittedly it was taken in July, when barns would have been relatively empty awaiting an imminent harvest. The barn at West Kennett Farm incorporates a possibly medieval timber frame. In the seventeenth century (or possibly earlier) it was a three-bay structure, but five bays were added later in that century, and further extensions were added in the eighteenth century.[3] Another late seventeenth-century barn was erected by Sir John Stawell,[4] across what had been the ditch surrounding the megaliths, and is timber framed; it originally had eight bays.[5] To the west, there was an older barn, lost by fire.[6] Perhaps that was the old Parsonage Barn, the way to which was disputed in the 1590s.[7] To the south, one of Sir Richard's successors used sarsen and brick to erect a cart house (with a granary over) on the levelled ditch, which is now used as the National Trust shop.[8]

Cart houses were used to store agricultural implements on a few other farms. In 1662, John Bromham als Phelps was using his cart house to store 'one rowler, plow timber, and other timber'.[9] William Bray in 1699 had '1 wagon, 1 dung pott, with the plows, harrows, 1 rowe, a fan, and other instruments belonginging to the barne and field' in his.[10] An early eighteenth-century cart shed still survives at West Kennett Farm; it is a substantial building, originally of seven bays, although now reduced to five, timber framed, with a thatched roof.[11]

1 WSHC P3/B/986.
2 WSHC P3/P/184.
3 *West Kennett Farm, Wiltshire Preliminary Appraisal of Farm Buildings*. Oxford Archaeological Unit, 1992, p.4-5; *Appraisal of Buildings on the Avebury Estate, part 1. Conservation Plan, for the National Trust.* Ferguson Mann Architects, 1999. Unpublished reports held by WBR.
4 Gillings, et al. *Landscape*, op cit, p.291. Ucko, op cit, p.171; Stukeley, *Abury*, op cit, p.27.
5 https://britishlistedbuildings.co.uk/101286423-great-barn-avebury
6 *Appraisal ...*, op cit.
7 TNA E134/40and41Eliz/Mich7.
8 *Appraisal of Buildings on the Avebury Estate, part 1. Conservation Plan, for the National Trust.* Ferguson Mann Architects, 1999. Unpublished report held by WBR. See also https://britishlistedbuildings.co.uk
9 WSHC P1/B/416.
10 WSHC P3/B/986.
11 http://britishlistedbuildings.co.uk; *Appraisal of Buildings on the Avebury Estate, part 1. Conservation Plan, for the National Trust.* Ferguson Mann Architects, 1999, pt.1.2. Unpublished report held by WBR.

Many yeomen kept horses; for them, a stable was a necessity, especially if, like Christopher Battington in 1636, you had eight.[1] Other things might be stored there too: Thomas Hunter, the innkeeper, had 'about a tun of hay' in the stable in 1748/9.[2] One of the properties in the yard of Avebury manor, now occupied by the Alexander Keiller Museum, was erected as stables; it is built of sarsen.[3]

There were a number of malt houses in the parish. Many farmers made their own malt, but not enough to require a separate malt house. There were, however, a few maltsters who made malt in quantity, and required a separate building for the purpose. The names of known maltsters were identified in chapter 7.[4] The former nonconformist manse on Green Street, now known as Silbury House, is said to have been a malthouse before it was purchased to serve as a manse.[5]

Two dovecotes or pigeon houses may also be found in the parish, both built of sarsen, both now owned by the National Trust, and both now listed buildings.[6] The one in the yard of Avebury manor has a tiled roof, a lantern on the roof providing access for the birds, and fifteen tiers of nesting boxes capable of housing c.468 birds. It was built by Joanna Truslow during her widowhood, probably in the 1560s.[7] Another dovecote of two bays existed in 1548, but had probably been demolished a few years before the new one was built.[8] The dovecote at West Kennett farm is probably early seventeenth century, and possibly built by the Grubbe family. It has a conical roof with clay tiles, and originally held c.438 nesting boxes arranged in twelve tiers.

1 WSHC P3/B/368.
2 WSHC P3/H/1256.
3 http://britishlistedbuildings.co.uk
4 See above, p.321-2.
5 www.oodwooc.co.uk/ph_avebury_history2.htm
6 McCann, John & Pamela. *The Dovecotes and Pigeon Lofts of Wiltshire*. Hobnob Press, 2011, p.23-7. S., J. 'Notes on Wiltshire Parishes: Avebury', *Wiltshire Notes & Queries* 8, 1914-18, p.218; *Appraisal of Buildings on the Avebury Estate, part 1. Conservation Plan, for the National Trust*. Ferguson Mann Architects, 1999. Unpublished report held by WBR. Hayek, Tara. *Avebury Dovecote*. Unpublished report, 2016, held by WBR; http://britishlistedbuildings.co.uk; TNA PROB 11/51/51: will of Joanna Truslow, 1567/8.
7 TNA E134/40and41Eliz/Mich7. According to Eleanor Breach, her daughter. Other witnesses said it was built by her son John, but Eleanor, as a family member, is more likely to be reliable.
8 WSHC 2664/1/2D/8. Demolition is conjectured because the space was said to be open before the new dovecote was built; see James Pope's evidence in E134/41Eliz/Hil8.

The housing stock in Avebury was greatly extended and improved in our period. There are many references to houses 'lately erected' in estate papers and other documents. John Shuter built a farmhouse for himself when he was the farmer of Avebury manor in the sixteenth century.[1] Joanna Truslow built the Parsonage House in the late sixteenth century; it had a parlour, a parlour chamber, a buttery, a kitchen, a boulting house, a cheese loft, a malt loft, and a tyled roof.[2] When her workmen dug out a new cellar they uncovered a pile of human bones, including a skull with a nail driven into it.[3] But she did not live in it; the ground floor was used to make malt, and the rooms above served as guest chambers when visitors came. There was not enough room for them in her manor house. Stayner Holford bequeathed three 'new erected tenements' when he died in 1767;[4] Arthur Jones thought the cottages he inherited (which included these) to be worth £150 in 1780.[5] Thomas Hunter (1748/9)[6] bequeathed two houses which he had 'lately built', one to his wife Joan, the other to his grandson Thomas.

Mention has already been made of the houses built by Thomas Robinson which were destroyed by fire. Other houses built by the Robinsons may still survive, although it is difficult to prove with certainty. For example, the house which Leah Clements inherited from her father Robert, and sold in 1799, was described as having been newly erected by Robert. However, it stood beside property described as having formerly belonged to Robinson. When Robert Clements purchased the property from Robinson in 1755, it already had a house on it, possibly built by Robinson.

At least fourteen listed buildings date from the seventeenth century.[7] The majority are cottages, mostly found in pairs, or short linear ranges, with first floor windows below the eaves. Sarsen and thatch predominate in these cottages. Butler's Cottage, at Beckhampton, was originally of two bays. The two cottages at Chapel Corner each had just one bay with an attic. Little Acre, on Bray Street, was originally built of sarsen, which was subsequently painted. So was Rose Cottage, on the High Street. It was originally a single storey house of two bays, with a thatched roof. The two Churchyard cottages were originally of two bays.

The manor house at Avebury Trusloe is perhaps the oldest house in the

1   TNA E134/40and41Eliz/Mich7.
2   Ditto, according to the evidence of John Jennings.
3   TNA E134/40and41Eliz/Mich7. The house is no longer there.
4   TNA PROB11/932/345.
5   WSHC 271/2. Arthur Jones's Valuation, 18th September 1780.
6   WSHC P3/H/1256.
7   http://britishlistedbuildings.co.uk

parish.[1] It was rebuilt in 1520.[2] Maud Truslow's inventory of 1625[3] provides a listing of its many rooms: it had a hall (with wainscot), a parlour, a buttery, a lodging chamber,[4] a little closet, a chamber over the whitehouse, a study, a chamber over the parlour, an 'inner lodgings', and 'over lodgings', an apple loft, a maid's chamber, a lower house, a store loft, a brewhouse, a kitchen, and a mill house. A porch, and perhaps a service room, was added by Thomas Truslow c.1658.[5]

The largest house in the parish was probably Avebury Manor.[6] It was built on the site of the medieval Priory. The house as it was in 1548 is described in a detailed survey made when Sir William Sharington purchased the manor from the Crown: [7]

'the entering into the manor lyethe on the southe syde, at the dore cumyng in there is a porche of stone wall and an entery goyng through the mydde of the seid manor house. And on the right side of the said entery as you cume in ther is a fayre large hall and a fayre chymney in hym, with a large range on the porche syde. And on the lyfte syde of dore as ye come in to the hall ther is a buttery, a parler on the est syde of the hall, and a buttery byhynde the same, a whyte house at the other end of the hall beyng northe, with a larder house by the same whytehouse, a boultyng house by the larder house, a kechyng byhynde the seid larder house, with a fayre well jonyng to the said kechyn backe dore in a certen orchard joyning to the said kechyng. And over the hall a fayre lofte, wherin they make malte. Over the said parler a fayre strong lofte, which is usid for a chamber syelid over with playster. Over the whyte house a lofte used for a chamber not sielid. And over the boultyng house a lofte wherein is a particion, thon half for a chamber and the other half for malt. And in the backe side of the kechyn an oven a neste to drye malte in. And on the lyft syde of the entre cumyng into the manor house, a fayre

---

1 Davis, et al, 'Built Heritage', op cit, p.133-4.
2 http://britishlistedbuildings.co.uk
3 WSHC P3/T/86.
4 The word before 'lodginge' is indecipherable.
5 http://britishlistedbuildings.co.uk
6 Evans, Siân. *The Manor Reborn: the Transformation of Avebury Manor.* National Trust Books, 2011. See also Evans, Siân. *Avebury Manor* , ed. Oliver Garnett. National Trust, 2014. WBR holds a detailed typescript account of the manor's building history.
7 WSHC 2664/1/2D/8. My transcript has been checked against the transcript made by Steve Hobbs in WBR. Abbreviations have been extended, and punctuation modernised. See also *Appraisal of Buildings on the Avebury Estate, part 1. Conservation Plan, for the National Trust.* Ferguson Mann Architects, 1999. Unpublished report held by WBR. Pam Slocombe's modernised version of this survey is in WBR.

litle parler newe buldyd with a chymney in hym syelied over with playster; byhynd the said parler a chamber for his servauntes And by the said chamber a stayre goyng up into a fayre chamber new buldid over, the said parler wherein the mydell of the same chamber is a chimney of fre stone. And on the ryght hand as ye cume up the stayre, a house of office, and by the same house a dore goying in to a fayre chamber syelid with playster on the right hand, and on the other side of the seid house of office another chamber for his servauntes at the stere hed. And a lofte over the said newe parler callid a chese lofte. And on the backe side of the said manor house a little garden, and a litle barton'.

It may be that the house was occupied by John Shuter, who had leased the demesne of Avebury manor from Fotheringhay College in 1530.[1] He claimed to have built a farmhouse on the manor at some time in the late sixteenth century, but this was probably not the manor house.[2] When William Dunch purchased the manor in 1551, he undertook extensive re-building; indeed, the original construction of the house as it now stands has been attributed to him. However, despite many architectural investigations, it is still not clear to what extent the original house is incorporated in subsequent re-buildings;[3] investigators have been perplexed by the 1548 description of the house printed above. Dunch, like many other purchasers of monastic property, had enhanced his status by becoming a manorial lord, and wanted an impressive new house befitting his new status.[4] The present east front was built by him; dendrochronology suggests that the trees used in construction of its ceiling were felled between 1555 and 1580, and its roof between 1574 and 1599. Assuming both were constructed at the same time, that suggests building took place in the late 1570s.[5] Subsequently, c.1600, Sir James Mervyn, who

1 WSHC 2664/1/2D/8. The date c.1535 is given in *V.C.H. Wilts* 12, p.98, but its source, TNA SC6/HenVIII/3931, rot.1, has not been checked by the present author.
2 TNA C21/S32/14.
3 See, for example, *Avebury Manor, Avebury: Historic Building Survey*. Report no. 78060.1. Wessex Archaeology, 2011. Unpublished report held by the National Trust, Avebury. For a discussion of the survey as it relates to the gardens, see Fretwell, Katie. *Avebury Manor: Park and Garden Survey*. National Trust, 1992 (unpublished report), p.4. See also Treasure, Dorothy. *Vernacular Building Survey, 1991-2*. Unpublished report in WBR, p.1.
4 Aston, Michael, & Bettey, Joe. 'The post-medieval rural landscape c.1540-1700: the drive for profit and the desire for status', in Everson, Paul & Williamson, Tom, eds. *The Archaeology of Landscape: studies presented to Christopher Taylor*. Manchester University Press, 1998, p.121.
5 Alcock, Nat., & Tyers, Cathy. 'Tree-ring date lists 2012', *Vernacular Architecture* 43, 2012, p.93.

married a Dunch widow, added an impressive south front in the Elizabethan style, which according to the date stone, was completed in 1601.[1] The house was assessed to pay hearth tax on 13 hearths c.1662.[2]

When Sir Richard Holford purchased the manor in 1695, he did not have his house to himself. He spent most of his time in London, with occasional visits to Avebury and to his other manor at Westonbirt. He was not therefore in need of much accommodation, and was happy to divide his Avebury house between himself and the tenant of Avebury Great Farm. Farmer William Skeat's 1689 lease gave him 'the kitching, the dry larder, the brewhouse, the little cellar, & the chambers that are over the pantry & greate cellar, with the chambers over the dairy house & wett larder house, & the use of the backside' (in common with his lord)[3]. He probably retained this portion of the house throughout his tenure. A similar arrangement initially continued when John Rose succeeded Skeat in 1710[4]; he was to have 'the kitchin, the wett & dry larder, the dairy, the Brewhouse, the orchard celler now devided into two cellars, the chambers, one parie of staires over the great celler, and over the said two cellars, and over the wet larder and dairy house'. However, the house had to be altered to provide separate living accommodation for Rose and his family.[5] Sir Richard was 'at great expence in building a convenient habitacon for him the said John Rose and his family during such time as Sir Richard and his family are here'. John Ladd and John Overton both worked on the house, and Holford asked Rose to let him know of any delays.[6] Rose was also to 'call on Mr Smith to make & fittings the casement for that chamber as soone as may be'. A few months later, a 'little new building' was also being erected.[7] However, when Stayner Holford was forced to take the farm in hand, and to reside at Avebury permanently, he no longer needed a tenant who could look after the manor house whilst he was non-resident, and his bailiff lived in an

1   Stedman, op cit, p.109. It has been suggested that this was the date of success in a legal battle, rather than the date of building; cf. Treasure, Dorothy. *Vernacular Building Survey 1991-2*. Unpublished report, 1992, held by WBR, p.3; *Appraisal of Buildings on the Avebury Estate, part 1. Conservation Plan, for the National Trust*. Ferguson Mann Architects, 1999. Unpublished report held by WBR.
2   TNA E179/259/29.
3   WSHC 184/4/1. Lease, Lord Stawell to William Skeat, 1689.
4   WSHC 184/4/1. Articles of Agreement, Sir Richard Holford & John Rose, 1710.
5   Fretwell, Katie. *Avebury Manor: Park and Garden Survey*. National Trust, 1992 (unpublished report), p.7; GA D1956/E2/8.
6   WSHC 184/1, pt.2. Letter, Sir Richard Holford to John Rose, 7th June 1710; 184/4/1. Renewal of John Rose's lease, 1717.
7   WSHC 184/1, pt.2. Letter, Sir Richard Holford to John Rose, 23rd November 1710. Some of the expenses are itemised in GA D1956/E2/8.

entirely separate house.[1] Perhaps he also thought that living in the same house as his farmer, and having to share his blankets with the farmer's reapers (as Samuel Holford had done),[2] was beneath his dignity. Henceforth, the bailiff was always provided with a separate house; that is made clear in many of Richard Hickley's letters.[3]

When Sir Richard Holford purchased the manor, he had been aware that the house was 'grievously in decay'; 'in truth the mansion house is soe very much out of repair that in several places of the tyleing and wainscot as in the hall & parlour downe'.[4] The tenant, William Skeat, told him that 'the huse is very much out of repair & the ould baren, which if not spedy course tooke they'll drop down'.[5] The new owner seems to have had the necessary repairs carried out, but it is doubtful whether he actually undertook many alterations to the house,[6] other than those needed to accommodate his second tenant. He did, however, floor the barns, and erected the 'extraordinary' cow stalls mentioned above[7]. He also fenced the Great Barton orchard with gates, posts and rails.[8] The plan of 1695 shows a new stable (now the Alexander Keiller Museum) and a new coach house[9] (which Holford reserved for his own use in his 1710 agreement with John Rose).[10] By 1700, Holford had already equipped his farm with most of the buildings which, a century later, Davis was to argue were essential for any chalkland farm: barns, stabling, a granary, and a drinking pool in the yard for cattle.[11]

When Richard Holford inherited the estate in 1740, he undertook major refurbishment of the manor house, constructing the dining room in the latest style, installing a new principal staircase, and re-modelling the roof of the south range.[12] A substantial invoice for sheet lead for the roof indicates a date

1   WSHC 184/3. Appeal against Land Tax Assessment 1761.
2   WSHC 184/1, pt.2. T.H., to Samuel Holford, 26 August 1723
3   WSHC 184/6.
4   WSHC 184/1, pt.2. Sir Richard Holford to John Adams, 28th May 1695.
5   WSHC 184/1, pt.2.
6   This has been argued by *Avebury Manor, Avebury, Wiltshire. Historic Building Survey.* Wessex Archaeology, 2011. Unpublished report held by the National Trust, Avebury, 5.5.
7   See above, p.265.
8   WSHC 184/4/1. John Rose's renewal of lease, 1717.
9   *Appraisal of Buildings on the Avebury Estate, part 1. Conservation Plan, for the National Trust.* Ferguson Mann Architects, 1999. Unpublished report held by WBR.
10 WSHC 184/4/1. Articles of Agreement, Sir Richard Holford & John Rose, 1710.
11 Davis, T. *A General View of the Agriculture of the County of Wiltshire.* 1811, p.10.
12 *Avebury Manor, Avebury, Wiltshire. Historic Building Survey.* Wessex Archaeology, 2011. Unpublished report held by the National Trust, Avebury, 5.7.

of 1741.[1] An oven was being constructed in 1744,[2] and repairs to the house and orchard walls were estimated at £20+ in 1746.

Richard successors, Stayner Holford, and his half-brother, Arthur Jones, built a small two gabled extension in the rear angle of the east and south ranges, but otherwise undertook no further alterations. That continued to be the policy in the 1790s, when Sir Adam Williamson succeeded. His bailiff blocked up a few windows to save window tax; he considered it 'abominable to pay so much tax and no family in the house'.[3] Otherwise, he confined himself to the annual use of whitewash.[4] When Williamson died, his successor was a minor, and the house was advertised to let in the *Times*.[5]

The Holfords were not the only manorial lords in Avebury who shared their manor house with a tenant. Thomas Smith's farmhouse at West Kennett was another substantial seventeenth-century house that was divided up.[6] When Robert Caswell leased a portion of the manor from Thomas Smith in 1729, he lived in a part of the 'capital messuage', occupying a kitchen and a buttery on the ground floor, and three rooms up one pair of stairs with the garrets over them'; he also had a 'milchhouse', the use of a malthouse when his landlord was not using it, stables for six horses, and two-thirds of a cart house.[7] This was probably the new building which Francis Popham had leased in 1723.[8] Unfortunately, we have no description of the rest of the house, which his landlord occupied. Smith retained the pigeon house, the newly constructed fishpond, and a third of the cart house, together with a garden bordered by the river. Caswell was instructed to avoid burning straw in the kitchen; he was not to build ricks too close to the house, or to engage in other activities which might interfere with his landlord's comfort. By 1745, when Caswell was succeeded by Ambrose Lanfear, there was a newly planted orchard, and a small piece of woodland, both of which the landlord reserved for himself.[9]

---

1 *Avebury Manor, Avebury, Wiltshire.* Historic Building Survey. Wessex Archaeology, 2011. Unpublished report held by the National Trust, Avebury, 5.8.2. WSHC 184/5.
2 WSHC 184/1, pt.2. James Mayo to Stayner Holford, 31st March 1744.
3 WSHC 184/6. Letter, Richard Hickley to Mrs Williamson, 4th June 1793.
4 WSHC 184/6. Letter, Richard Hickley to Mrs Williamson, 4th June 1793.
5 *Times*, 24th June 1799, p.1.
6 http://britishlistedbuildings.co.uk
7 WSHC 568/7. Lease, Thomas Smith to Robert Caswell, 3rd September 1729.
8 Somerset Heritage Centre DD/PO/6. Lease, 3rd September 1723, Richard & Thomas Smith to Francis Popham.
9 WSHC 568/7. Lease, Thomas Smith to Ambrose Lanfear, 6th November 1745.

By 1755, Thomas Smith (presumably) had built a summer house, and his heirs, Stayner Chamberlayne and Samuel Martyn, had agreed to build a 'convenient brewhouse' for the new tenant. Martyn, who was living in the house, presumably wished to have exclusive use of the old one.[1] In 1772, the farm had a coach house.[2]

There were several other substantial houses in the parish. Bannings, in Bray Street, is a two-storeyed farmhouse, with a cellar, built of brick in Flemish bond, and dating from c.1690-1720.[3] It was probably built either by John Griffin or by his son in law John Banning. The name Banning has been carved several times in the parlour fireplace. Its central entrance lobby contains a baluster oak staircase, and leads into the two principal ground floor rooms, the hall and the parlour. A through passage leads to service rooms at the back under a catslide roof. There are two chambers above, plus an attic. Flooring is of oak throughout.

The vicarage was probably fairly typical for its period. It was greatly extended in 1841, but the plans prepared then show the original dimensions of a house that was probably constructed in the seventeenth century[4]. It stood across the lane from the church.[5] The house had two parlours, separated by a vestibule or passage way. At the back was a scullery. Upstairs there were three bedrooms, with a small dressing room on the landing (possibly White's 'study'). There was also an attic with loft space. Water may have been supplied by the 'forcing pump' at the back of the house, although this may have been a new feature planned in 1841. Outside, across the kitchen court, was the 'servant's privy'. The 1841 plan shows that a new water closet was to be installed upstairs; there was also to be a 'garden privy'. It is unlikely that toilet facilities existed inside the house (or indeed in any other house, except the manor house, which in 1548 had 'a house of office'[6]) in our period; the outside 'servant's privy' may originally have been used by the whole household. The plan also shows that,

1 WSHC 568/7. Lease Stanes Chamberlayne and Samuel Martyn to John Nalder, 9th November 1755. See also lease, Stanes Chamberlayne to Samuel Martyn, 1st December 1755.
2 WSHC 118/88. Draft indenture, 1772.
3 WBR notes.
4 WSHC D1/11/85.
5 WSHC 184/4. Plan of the manor house, gardens and barton, 1695. The vicarage is marked as 'White's.
6 WSHC 2664/1/2D/8. Even the newly constructed extension to West Kennett manor only had an outside 'bogg house' in 1723; see Somerset Heritage Centre DD/PO/6. Lease, 3rd September 1723, Richard & Thomas Smith to Francis Popham.

in 1841, a variety of new outhouses were planned for the stable yard next to the house, including a stable, a coach house, and a piggery. It seems likely that these replaced existing buildings which were to be demolished, and which are not shown on the plan.

Probably, this house is the one described in the 1670 inventory of Nathaniel Power, the then vicar.[1] His appraisers mention a parlour, a hall, a kitchen, a buttery, and chambers (that is, bedrooms) over the parlour, hall, and buttery.

Most of the inns would have been substantial houses. We only have a detailed description of one of them. Thomas Hunter's appraisers in 1748/9 list all the rooms in the White Lion: it had a kitchen, two parlours, a closet, four chambers, a shop, a cellar, a pantry, a brewhouse, a stable, a woodhouse, a coalhouse, and a 'sealling' (presumably a loft).

Vernacular architecture was ceasing to be the norm towards the end of our period. Eighteenth century houses such as Bannings Farmhouse, West Kennett House, Beckhampton House, Silbury House, and a number of houses along the High Street, display high quality brickwork. Houses became taller, ceilings became higher, attic spaces became more habitable, and there was even a three storey house at West Kennett House.[2] Truslow Farm Cottages were originally a two storeyed farmhouse, built of sarsen, with painted limestone dressings and a tiled roof in the late seventeenth or early eighteenth centuries.[3] It has a (then) fashionable mansard roof, that is, a roof with two slopes, with room for a useable attic in the eaves. The dissenters' Meeting House, although built of sarsen, had brick facings, and a tiled roof, probably dating from when it was built in 1708. Samuel Fowler, despite his trade (he was a carpenter), used colour-washed brick, together with sarsen, to build the three bayed Hollis Cottage c.1710.[4]

Nevertheless, old construction methods could still be used for a new house in the late eighteenth century. Jasmine Cottage, at West Kennett, was built of sarsen, and thatched. Thatch was also used for the two-bayed Brow Cottage, at Avebury Trusloe, although it was built of brick. It was originally of one storey.

It is probable that few houses of the poor had glass in their windows. However, glass was available to the wealthier yeomen and gentry. A number

---

1   WSHC P3/P/329.
2   Davis, et al, 'Built Heritage', op cit, p.135.
3   http://britishlistedbuildings.co.uk
4   http://britishlistedbuildings.co.uk. For his 1740 will, stating his occupation, see WSHC P3/F/359.

of local glaziers have already been mentioned.[1] All of the listed buildings built in the seventeenth and eighteenth centuries probably had glass in their windows.[2] The tax assessment of 1757 reveals that Stayner Holford's manor house had no less than 52 windows.[3] On proposing to lease Avebury Farm in 1721/2, Peter Griffin accepted responsibility for repairing the windows in his part of the manor house.[4] When Richard Caswell took a lease of the farm at Beckhampton from Charles Tooker in 1709, he was expected to keep 'all the windows well glazed'.[5] So was John Beake when he leased West Kennett Farm in 1724.[6] In 1731, 8s 6d was paid for new glass installed at Frances Truslow's house at Beckhampton, probably by her landlord.[7] Richard Holford in 1741 purchased '212 foot of new glas', at 7d per foot, for his renovations at the manor house.[8] The same tradesman also supplied lead, and undertook to paint twelve casements, plus '155 yardes of painting', at 7d per yard.

In 1757, thirteen taxpayers paid window tax. Holford paid the most, but Mr Hitchcock (at the Catherine Wheel) had 46 windows, and most of the others had more than ten.[9] Window glass had become common; that, of course, was why a tax had been imposed on it. Other windows are subsequently mentioned. Jane Pope's windows are mentioned in the indictment of the Cary family in 1757.[10] In 1795, when John Amor leased Avebury Trusloe manor, he was expected to 'keep in repair the glass windows.'[11]

Furniture
Behind the windows, what of the contents of the house? Most sixteenth and seventeenth houses were bare by modern standards; furniture was sparse. For Avebury, there are seven inventories which record no furniture at all, but it is probable that they belonged to decedents who lived in other people's houses.[12]

1 See above, p.308.
2 http://britishlistedbuildings.co.uk
3 WSHC 184/3. Window Tax Assessment 1757.
4 WSHC 184/1, pt.2. Peter Griffin's proposals for taking Avebury Great Farm, 8th January 1721/2
5 WSHC 371/1, pt.4. Lease, 16th April 1709.
6 WSHC 568/7. Thomas Smith to John Beake, 13th October 1724.
7 WSHC 371/1, pt 5.
8 WSHC 184/5.
9 WSHC 184/3. Window Tax Assessment 1757.
10 WSHC A1/110, 1757M.
11 WSHC 873/262. Lease, Sir John Hopkins to John Amor, 16th April 1795.
12 Mary Plummer (1632; WSHC P3/P/190); Thomas Bray (1639; WSHC P3/B/420); Elizabeth Fisher (1671; WSHC P1/F/141); Thomas Pope (1688; WSHC P3/P/465); Richard Garraway (1687; WSHC P3/G/327); John Mills

Most probate inventories describe furniture, sometimes in detail, although there are occasional frustrating inventories like that of John Rose (1720)[1], whose appraisers despaired of making a full listing, and merely recorded that 'all ye houssell goodes' were worth £50. There were others, however, who only had a 'bed' that is, a mattress, which must have lain on the floor. The widow Edith Mortimer (1633)[2] only had her bed. Robert Rogers (1687)[3] had 'in ye chamber one flocke beade', together with 'one cufferlede [coverlet] & a peare of blankets', altogether worth 17s. The only other furniture he had in his house was 'in ye hall one table bord'. Mary Tompkins (1681),[4] a poor widow, similarly had merely an 'ould flocke beed, 1 bollow [pillow], 1 blstter [bolster], one peare of ould blankets, one sheet', together worth 6s 6d. She had no other furniture at all, although it is possible she lived with her family; her 'wearing apparrell' had the relatively high value of £5, which suggests that she had once been better off. John Harper (1705)[5] merely had 'a bedd matt & cord, blanketts, rug', and 'one paire of sheets', together worth 15s. He also had '2 ordinary chaires' worth 1s, but no other furniture. James Baldveen (1628),[6] who identified himself as a husbandman in his will, but whose appraisers regarded him as a yeoman, had two bedsteads, but no other furniture.

In the sixteenth century, the 'great amendment of lodging' which William Harrison described in 1587, was still proceeding. Harrison could remember a time when 'our fathers, yea and we ourselves also, have lien full oft upon straw pallets, on rough mats covered only with a sheet, under coverlets made of dagswain or hap-harlots ... and a good round log under their heads instead of a bolster or pillow'. Pillows were 'thought meet only for women in childbed'.[7]

Most seventeenth-century inventories list beds and bedding, although the language used to describe them varies from the language that would be used today. The 'bed' was the mattress, which might be stuffed with flock (wool dust), or perhaps the more comfortable feathers. The bedstead was the frame on which the bed was placed. The two together formed the 'bed performed', that is, fully set up. The bed-tye (the mattress case) was occasionally mentioned separately; it might be made of 'ticking' (hard linen).

(1680/1; WSHC P3/M/324); John Pope (1711; WSHC P1/P/495).
1   WSHC P3/R/365.
2   WSHC P3/M/117.
3   WSHC P3/R/254.
4   WSHC P3/T/288.
5   WSHC P3/H/860.
6   P3/B/294.
7   Harrison, William. *The Description of England,* ed. Georges Edelen. Cornell University Press, 1968, p.201.

There were three main types of bedstead: the 'high' or 'standing' bedstead', the 'truckle' bedstead, and the four poster. The high bedstead was solidly built, and had room underneath for storage of the low or 'truckle' bedstead, used by servants or children. Only a few truckle bedsteads are mentioned in the inventories, and it is probable that most of the bedsteads listed were standing bedsteads, although many were not described as such. The elite might have a four poster or 'tester' bedstead – a standing bedstead with a tester (or canopy) above, supported either by four posts, or hung from the ceiling. The tester was used to hang curtains and valance to keep out the winter draughts.

Bedding included linen and canvas sheets (the canvas used under the mattress), coverlets, woollen blankets, rugs, pillows, and bolsters. Pillows and bolsters, like the 'bed', were stuffed with flock or feathers (Charles Sumers' bolster had both[1]). The 'pillowbear' was the case.

The sleeping arrangements of William Hayward the shepherd in 1609/10 were, perhaps, typical. He had in his chamber, 'two borden bedsteds, one flocke bede, three coverlets, one pare of blanckets, on bolster of fethars and one of flockes' together worth £1 6s 8d.[2] He also had '3 shetts one table cloth and a pellowe bere'. He and his wife probably occupied one of his bedsteads, his daughter Parnell the other. John Peart, the vicar, when he died in 1621, had a 'joyned bedstedd', that is, a better quality one, made using mortice and tenon joints rather than nails. He bequeathed it, with a flock bed and other bedding, and a variety of other goods to his son-in-law, Richard Davis.[3] This bedstead was probably the one kept in his 'chamber over the hall', valued at 30s. Peart also had three feather beds with two bedsteads in his 'beddchamber', worth £10. One of the bedsteads was probably occupied by Peart and his wife, the other had been occupied by his daughter before her marriage. The third bed probably lay on the floor, used by a servant. Richard Chesterman and his wife in 1611 had one bed between them worth 4s (we do not learn whether it was double).[4] They also had two bolsters, and ten sheets, valued at 8s.[5] Most decedents (apart from the inn-keepers) had only enough beds for the members of their household; there were none to spare. Despite her many adult offspring and grand-children, Elizabeth Pope in 1618 only had 'ye bed that nowe I lye upon', although it was well-furnished; her inventory includes 'in

1   WSHC P3/S/634.
2   WSHC P3/H/56.
3   WSHC P3/P/101.
4   WSHC P3/C/57.
5   Although the 'x' in the mss may have been mis-read.

bedding one feather bedde & two bolsters one pellowe one payre of blankets & three courlets', valued at £3.[1] She also had sheets made out of holland (a fine linen fabric), lockeram (a coarse loosely woven linen), and canvas (a coarse unbleached cloth made from hemp or flax, frequently used for supporting mattresses). George Brown (1619)[2] had two feather beds in his bed chamber, but also four 'old boxd bedsteeds' elsewhere, perhaps used by servants. He was a relatively wealthy yeoman.

The elite were able to afford the more comfortable tester bed, equipped with curtains to keep out the draughts inevitable in early modern houses. Most inventories do not use the word 'tester' to describe them, but their presence is evidenced by the presence of 'curtains' and 'valence'. Maud Truslow (1625) had these around her bed.[3] So did both Jean Pope (1712/13),[4] and the widow Edith Cruse (1753).[5] Walter Pope (1633)[6] had a 'standing bedsteed, with a tester over it', which he bequeathed to his son John. This was one of the two 'bedsteeds', together worth 13s 4d, recorded in his inventory. The second (which did not have a 'tester') was left to his son Walter. Walter senior's inventory also lists 'two flocke beds with their furniture' (worth £1 13s 4d), which must have been the mattresses used on these bedsteads. The only other inventory actually listing a 'tester bedsteed' was that of John Phelps als Bromham (1662).[7]

Pairs of curtains and valence are recorded in the inventories of several members of the Griffin family: Peter Griffin [8] had three pairs in 1689, Joseph Griffin, yeoman, one in 1719,[9] John Griffin, two in 1722,[10] and Jean Griffin, one in 1727/8.[11] Peter Griffin was one of the wealthiest yeomen farmers in the parish, with an inventory valued at just over £858. He kept his pairs of curtains and valences in three different chambers. There was a truckle bed under one of his bedsteads. He also had two 'livery bedsteeds' in his 'chamber over the parlour' (probably for his maids) and two more in his 'men's servants chamber'. That suggests that he had four living-in servants (although the truckle bed may have been used by a child). Other labourers no doubt lived out.

1 WSHC P3/P/78.
2 WSHC P3/B/179.
3 WSHC P3/T/86.
4 WSHC P3/P/644.
5 WSHC P3/C/935.
6 WSHC P3/P/197.
7 WSHC P1/B/416.
8 WSHC P3/G/413.
9 WSHC P3/G/465.
10 WSHC P3/G/485
11 WSHC P3/G/517

Inn-keepers, of course, needed to provide good beds for their customers. In 1707, there were five pairs 'of curtains & valens' at the village inn, the Catherine Wheel, which was kept by Walter Stretch.[1] Perhaps these were hung on the bed in which William Stukeley subsequently slept. Thomas Fry, who was keeping the inn at West Kennett when he died in 1709, similarly had four pairs for his customers' use.[2] Almost half a century later, in 1748/9, Thomas Hunter, owner of the White Lion, also had four pairs.[3] Lemuel Fowler (1670)[4] at the White Hart had nine bedsteads for his customers, although these are not described as 'testers' and had no 'curtains'. His customers evidently frequently shared rooms, if not beds; there were three beds in the 'chamber over the kitchen, three in the 'chamber over ye parlour', and two in the 'chamber over the brewhouse'. There was also one actually in the parlour. Guests sleeping there would not have had much privacy!

Most people had bedsteads. Table boards and seating were almost as common, although in the early seventeenth century a number of decedents had bedsteads but no tables or chairs. Richard Chesterman (1611),[5] whose 'bed', valued at 4s., has already been mentioned, had no other furniture whatsoever. Nor did the widow Edith Mortimer (c.1633)[6], whose bed was valued at £2 10s – rather more than Chesterman's. Suprisingly, the vicar, John Peart (1621),[7] also did not have seating, unless it is hidden under rubrics such as 'other necessaries'.

Most tables were boards sitting on trestles. Katherine Browne's[8] was described as a 'tablebord planke'. Table boards were usually long, but Joseph Griffin (1719)[9] had a 'round table board'. Most decedents owned at least one table board and trestles (or a frame), together with seating. Many owned more. John Jacob (1670),[10] who owned five bedsteads, also had in his parlour '2 table bords, tenn joyne stooles, two chayers, with some other goods'. In his hall there was another table board, although no seating. Jacob was a wealthy yeoman, whose inventory was valued at £438. His ten 'joyne stooles' suggest the number of family members and servants who might sit down for a meal

1   WSHC P1/S/709.
2   WSCH P3/F/266.
3   WSHC P3/H/1256.
4   WSHC P3/F/135.
5   WSHC P3/C/57.
6   WSHC P3/M/117.
7   WSHC P3/P/101.
8   WSHC P3/B/236.
9   WSHC P3/G/465.
10 WHSC P3/IJ/101.

together. He had six children, a wife, and a father who may have lived with him. He probably also had a servant. But he only had five bedsteads, suggesting that they were doubles, and shared.

Richard Brown, tailor (1695),[1] had a much smaller household; he and his wife had no children, although they may have had a servant. In his hall he had a 'tabell board and 2 jint stooles & a jint chaire'. Three people could sit down for dinner. But he also had 'in ye shope [workroom] a tabell board & tow chaires & a paire of sheres & a pressing ier & other thing'. This table board was probably used for work purposes. So were the two chairs in the same room; one, perhaps, was for an apprentice. Brown also had a desk in his chamber; it is not clear what that was used for.

Two other decedents had desks. One was used by John Peart, the vicar (1621),[2] perhaps to write his sermons and store his books. John Cue's 'desk box' was in his buttery chamber in 1687.[3] So were four 'joynt stooles', one of which was presumably used for sitting at the desk. Desks, incidentally, might be accompanied by ink pots, although only one is actually mentioned in the probate inventories. Many of Sir Richard Holford's letters, which have been heavily quoted from here, must have been written using the sand dish (used for blotting) and ink pot which his widow bequeathed to his son in 1723.[4]

There were a variety of other tables. Maud Truslow[5] had a 'drawing table bord', presumably one that was extendable, in her parlour. In the same room she also had a 'paire of tables'; in her inner lodgings there was a' little table', and the buttery held an 'old table bord with a frame'. Two innkeepers, Walter Stretch (1707)[6] and Thomas Fry (1709)[7] had several 'tables' each, presumably of better quality than mere trestles (which Stretch also had). A few others may also have had proper 'tables':[8] John Brown (1622),[9] Richard Parr, yeoman (1632),[10] Charles Sumers (1682).[11] Peter Griffin (1689)[12] had a side table as well

1 WSHC P1/B/646.
2 WSHC P3/P/101.
3 WSHC P3/C/515.
4 TNA PROB 11/590/280.
5 WSHC P3/T/86.
6 WSHC P1/S/709.
7 WSCH P3/F/266.
8 But sometimes it is apparent that furniture described as 'tables' in the inventories were actually table boards.
9 WSHC P3/B/218.
10 WSHC P3/P/184.
11 WSHC P3/S/634.
12 WSHC P3/G/413.

as a table board in his parlour. Anne Griffin, spinster (1738)[1] was possessed of a 'large oval table'. She and John Clements, the schoolmaster (1798),[2] both had dressing tables. Griffin had a looking glass on hers, but Clements' table was equipped with a 'swing glass' presumably like a modern dressing table.

Greater luxury was provided by table cloths and napkins, which were intended to be used to clean up after eating with the fingers. 'The table linninge bellonge to the house' recorded in the inventory of the innkeeper Thomas Fry (1691)[3] was valued at £1. His son, another Thomas (1709),[4] similarly had 'towells, napkins & table cloth' worth 10s. A few of the elite similarly had napkins and table cloths. Two of the table napkins owned by Maud Truslow (1625) were made of 'hollen', that is, Holland, a fine linen fabric already mentioned.

Table boards were usually accompanied by seating, but not always. Richard Cue (1659)[5] had a table board, but nothing to sit on (unless it was included under the rubric 'other lumber'). Of course, it is quite possible that such decedents used seats owned by others who perhaps lived with them.

The seats usually associated with table boards were forms[6] (without backs), benches (probably with backs), or stools. The best of these were probably the 'joint stools', made by a joiner using mortice and tenon. Thomas Jordan (1719)[7] had 'in ye hall a tabell board & stooles & chaires'; his appraisers valued his estate at just over £10. Richard Parr, yeoman (1632),[8] whose inventory was valued at just over £46, had 'one table board and frame & six ioyned stooles four chayres … & benches'. His seating provision probably indicates the size of his household. The mercer, Thomas Stevens (1673/4)[9], had 'one longtable & frame and forme & joine stools one cobberd … & settle'.

Chairs were not quite as common as benches, forms, and stools, although many had them. The innkeepers, as one might expect, had substantial numbers. Both Walter Stretch (1707/8)[10] and Thomas Fry (1709)[11] had eighteen chairs each in their inns. Stretch had twelve in his parlour, and six in his hall.

1　WSHC P3/G/584.
2　WSHC P3/C/1138.
3　WSHC P3/F/211.
4　WSCH P3/F/266.
5　WSHC P3/K/86.
6　Sometimes the trestles were described as forms.
7　WSHC P1/IJ/167.
8　WSHC P3/P/184.
9　WSHC P3/S/535.
10　WSHC P1/S/709.
11　WSCH P3/F/266.

He also had five 'joynt stooles' in the hall. Fry had no other seating. The vicar, John White (1712),[1] had '5 chaires & stooles and other small furniture' in his 'lodging chamber'. There were also eight 'leather chairs' and two 'tableboards' in his hall, and another four leather chairs in his kitchen. The leather chairs (which were not valued separately) suggest he was a wealthy man, and indeed his inventory was valued at £531 12s 0d. Cane was another material from which chairs were made; Anne Griffin (1738) had 'three kane chairs', valued at 6s. She also had 'six rush bottomed chaires', worth 3s. These were not as expensive as leather chairs; her inventory was valued at just over £53 – a tenth of White's. Greater comfort in seating was provided by the upholsterer's work; following his 1740 renovation of the manor, Richard Holford spent £19 15s 4d paying Gabriel Cruse, the upholsterer.[2]

Settles were another type of seating owned by a few decedents. They were benches with arms, storage underneath, and solid high backs to keep out the draughts usual in seventeenth-century houses. Some had winged ends. They could seat several people around the fire, and were very durable. We have already seen that one was owned by Thomas Stevens. Joseph Wallis (1680)[3] had a settle in his hall, where there were also two stools, two chairs, and a table board, valued with other goods at £1. He bequeathed the settle to his son Thomas. William Bray (1699)[4] also kept a settle in his hall, with similar furniture valued at £1 10s 0d. Thomas Hunter (1748/9), the innkeeper,[5] kept his in his 'best parlor' for his guests. The tailor Andrew Mills' 'seattell' (1669)[6] was worth relatively little; it was valued with his two books at 5s.

Close stools were more of a luxury. Three are recorded in the inventories; those of John Bromham als Phelps (c.1663),[7] Nathaniel Power (1670),[8] and Thomas Hunter (1748/9).[9] Visitors to Hunter's inn did not have to use an outside privy, although even he did not possess a water closet; they were rare in our period. Other luxuries included the looking glass that Peter Griffin (1689) had in one of his chambers, and the clock that stood at the head of his stairs.[10] Walter Stretch's clock and case (1707) stood in a more prominent position

1   WSHC P3/W/671.
2   WSHC 184/5. Gabriel Cruse's bill, 1740.
3   WSHC P1/W/349.
4   WSHC P3/B/986.
5   WSHC P3/H/1256.
6   WSHC P3/M/60.
7   WSHC P1/B/416.
8   WSHC P3/P/329.
9   WSHC P3/H/1256.
10 WSHC P3/G/413.

in the parlour of his inn.[1] Several clocks in the manor house, including a 'terret'[turret?] clock', had to be cleaned in 1790, at a cost of 17s.[2] But the poor had to set their internal clocks by sunrise, high noon, and sunset.[3]

The 'painted cloths' that could be hung on walls, both for decoration, and also to keep out draughts, were perhaps more affordable. These were only mentioned once in the probate records, when Katherine Brown (1622/3) gave the 'painted cloth that hangs by the wall' to her grand-daughter Katherine. It hung in the 'chamber over the hall'.[4] It was valued with two coffers and a box at a mere 5s. The absence of other mentions may be due to the fact that they were cheap enough to be hidden under terms such as 'other lumber' or 'things forgotten'.

In addition to beds, tables, and seats, many decedents also had coffers, cupboards, chests, and other storage furniture. Coffers might be described as 'little', 'large', or 'old'. They were used to store a variety of goods. Maud Truslow had four coffers 'with pewter of all sortes'.[5] Bridget Dyer had a 'brueing coffer' in her kitchen,[6] perhaps containing malt. Robert Clements (1797)[7] had a 'large coffer and glass'; was the glass stored in the coffer? Those possessing important documents such as deeds or apprenticeship indentures would probably have used coffers or chests to store them out of harm's way. But perhaps the commonest use was for the storage of linen and 'wearing apparel'. Margery Brown (1620)[8] had 'five coffers one presse and one side board' in which she probably stored her 'five paire of sheets with pillowbeers table & coatsh [?] and napkins'. Katherine Brown (1623) [9] had her 'greate coffer and all that is therein, one payre of sheetes, and all my wearing apparell', which she bequeathed to Katherine Mortimer. John Peart (1621) [10] had 'certaine linen in the coffers'. Katherine Brown's 'greate coffer' held a pair of sheets and her 'wearing apparrell'.[11]

1   WSHC P1/S/709.
2   WSHC 184/7. May & June 1791 account.
3   Wilson, *Forgotten Labour*, op cit, p.163.
4   WHC P3/B/218.
5   WSHC P3/T/86.
6   WSHC P3/D/76.
7   WSHC P3/C/1134.
8   WSHC P3/B/195.
9   WSHC P3/B/236.
10 WSHC P3/P/101.
11 WSHC P3/B/236.

Clothes

We have very little information on the clothes Avebury people wore, although it is probable that the labourers' clothes were made at home. In Clyffe Pipard, labourers 'wore an under-smock of light wool or linen, a loose shirt or smock, a leather jacket, breeches and hose, leather boots or shoes, and some kind of legging'.[1] Leather gloves and boots were indispensable, although leather became increasingly unaffordable towards the end of the eighteenth century. Labourers probably wore wool under these garments in the winter, and linen in the summer. In Avebury, clothing was similar, although our evidence is more limited. The appraisers of probate inventories usually used the term 'wearing apparel' as a catch all phrase, without describing clothing any further, and sometimes valuing it with the 'money in his purse'. Richard Pope (1682)[2] had 'his wearing apparel' valued at £5. Toby King (1682),[3] the blacksmith, had 'wearing apparell & mony in his purs' valued at £6. In 1682, Charles Sumers' 'wearing clothes', worth £1, were in his 'lodging chamber'.[4] Maud Truslow's clothes were valued at £10 in 1625.[5] Richard Jones, who succeeded Sir Adam Williamson as lord of Avebury manor in 1798, regularly appeared at church dressed in a scarlet coat, with a sword, in other words, in full-dress court attire.[6]

Very occasionally, clothes were bequeathed and described in wills. Joan Pope (1610)[7] left her daughter Ann Truman 'one gowne cloath which is at the weavers' (it must have been made of wool); also 'my best wearing gowne, two petticotes and halphe of my wearing linen'. The other half of her linen went to her daughter Alice. Elizabeth Pope (1618)[8] gave Alce Vurston 'my oulde medley gowne, my oulde peticote, my wastcooate, my beste hatte, & my beste hollande aprene'. 'All ye reste of my wearing apparell not given both lynnen & woollen' was to be divided equally between Joan Cue and Agnes Plummer. The total value of Elizabeth's clothes (both linen and woollen) was £2. Edith Pope (1624)[9] gave Helen Church 'a goune and a hatte'.[10] Joan Green

---

1 Wilson, *Forgotten Labour*, op cit, p.167-8.
2 WSHC P1/P/1006.
3 WSHC P3/K/106.
4 WSHC P3/S/634.
5 WSHC P3/T/86.
6 King, Bryan. 'Avebury: Archaeological Varia', *WAM* 14, 1874, p.232.
7 WSHC P3/P/33.
8 WSHC P3/P/78.
9 WSHC P3/P/126.
10 WSHC P3/P/126.

(1721/2)[1] gave her mother her 'best blacke scarfe & my best black hoode & my best blacke silke cote and my best hood & cloke', as well as £200. Edith Cruse, widow, (1753) thought that her young niece would like to have her 'best blacke scarfe & my best black hoode & my best blacke silke cote and my best hood & cloke'.[2] Only a few men mentioned items of clothing in their wills. Richard Bushell (1716)[3] bequeathed his 'best great coate,' to his brother in law, Richard Norris.[4] Richard Mortimer (1750)[5] mentioned 'my best suit and silver buckles'. William Spackman, yeoman (1763),[6] and John Clements the schoolmaster (1798)[7] both mentioned their silver buckles.

Fireside Utensils and Fuel

In contrast to wearing apparel, the goods around firesides were described by appraisers in great detail. Most decedents had fire places, although frequently, as already suggested, they did not have chimneys. The hearth was a focal point in every house. It was surrounded by fireside implements and cooking utensils. Those possessed by William Bray have already been described. Maud Truslow's 1625 inventory[8] lists a wide variety of fireside implements. She had in her parlour 'an iron plate to stand behind the fyre', that is, a fire back to confine the fire to its grate. The grate – that is, the framework of iron bars holding the fire in place - is not specifically mentioned in her inventory, but it is in many others. In her hall were 'one iron rack, i paire of iron racks, i paire of iron andirons, & one paire of iron dogges, iiii [ ] hangers i iron crook & vi spits'. In the 'chamber above the white house', which seems to have been used as a store room, were 'i paire of andirons, ii paire of dogges, ii pair of fire tonges, I fire shovell', and a 'fire pyke'. The iron racks, andirons, and dogs were used to support the logs in the fire. Tongs and pikes were used to stir the fire up; a few decedents, for example, Anne Griffin (1738),[9] used bellows for this purpose. The shovel was used to remove ash, or perhaps to shovel coal. Andirons had uprights from which hangers could be hung to support pots over the fire, or to support spits. Similar implements were listed in many inventories, although perhaps not so many of them. They are also recorded elsewhere. In 1740, for

1 WSHC P3/G/480.
2 WSHC P3/C/935.
3 WSHC P1/B/825.
4 WSHC P1/B/825.
5 WSHC P1/M/592.
6 WSHC P3/S/1401.
7 WSHC P3/C/1138.
8 WSHC P3/T/86.
9 WSHC P3/G/584.

example, Richard Holford purchased new 'tongs, shovel & poker' from John Wilkins, a whitesmith of Marlborough. Wilkins also supplied him with a stone grate, and new locks and keys.[1]

Fuel for the fire was provided by firewood, collected from the hedgerows and woods, and also by coal. In 1791, Richard Hickley had three stacks of faggots in his yard, together with two stacks of 'billet wood' (these were larger pieces of wood, perhaps three feet in length, and ten inches round).[2] His accounts show that he paid 5s in April 1794 'to carriage load of wood for Mrs Rennald' at the manor house.[3] Firewood is occasionally mentioned in inventories: Christopher Battington (1636) had 'timber & firewoode' valued at £3 10s.[4] In 1622, John Browne's 'wood for the fyre' was worth £1[5]. When Richard Truslow agreed with his mother Bridget to take over Beckhampton Farm in 1694, he also agreed to provide her with fuel.[6] He was to fetch her 'two good waggon loads of firewood to be drawne with five horses' every year. Given that the area was not well wooded, he was also to 'fetch from the coal pitt in or near Kingswood three quarters and halfe of good coale of the pitt'. Kingswood was over thirty miles distant, but it is likely that others also travelled to Kingswood to fetch coal, despite the fact that its transportation was expensive. In 1742, fifteen quarters of coal were purchased for Avebury Manor at 6s 6d per quarter, totalling £4 17s 6d.[7] William Philpot, in his 1786 will, instructed his executors to deliver 'a load of wood and half a load of coals' every year to several of his legatees[8]. When Richard Hickley, in 1793, took beer to Bristol to be shipped to the Williamsons in Jamaica, he used his waggon to bring back a load of coal.[9] Hickley's accounts record numerous occasions when he fetched coal.[10] It was also purchased at Hungerford from a Newbury merchant.[11] Coal, incidentally, implies chimneys, and the need for a sweep. Hickley paid nine shillings to have the manor house chimneys swept in February 1792. The house had a number of chimneys requiring attention[12]

1 WSHC 184/5. Wilkins account, 1740.
2 WSHC 184/4/1. List of stock, 1791.
3 WSHC 184/7.
4 WSHC P3/B/368.
5 WSHC P3/B/218.
6 WSHC 371/1, pt.3. Conveyance, 26th December 1694.
7 WSHC 184/5.
8 WSHC P3/P/1027.
9 WSHC 184/6. Richard Hickley to Mrs Williamson, 8th November 1793.
10 WSHC 184/7.
11 WSHC 184/6. Richard Hickley to Mrs Williamson, June 1794.
12 WSHC 184/7.

Hickley probably had to go to one of the local market towns to find a sweep. It is likely that other purchasers of coal in Avebury would have done the job themselves.

Coal was recorded in several probate inventories. In 1706, for example, George Arnold had 'three quarters of coale'[1]. In 1720, Thomas Jordan had 'in ye coale house a small parsell of coale' valued at 1s 6d. John Fowler, innkeeper at the Catherine Wheel, needed a reliable source of fuel to keep his customers warm; he had 'coals' worth £2 10s[2]. Margaret Hayward (c.1663) [3] and Peter Griffin (1689) [4] both had 'sea coles'; the description suggests that these may have been transported by sea. Griffin's were valued at £4. The use of coal gradually increased in our period; for every ton of coal used in the seventeenth century, fourteen tons were being used in the eighteenth century.[5]

Fires provided light in the long winter evenings for those who sat around the hearth on their settles or benches. Those who could afford it also used candles made either from rushes dipped into mutton fat, or by hemlock stems filled with hot tallow.[6] Candles were provided for the congregation at St. James's on dark evenings; there are still holes for them in the rood loft.[7] William Hayward (1609/10), the shepherd, had five 'candell stickes'.[8] Elizabeth Pope's single candlestick in 1618 was made of brass.[9] Richard Cripps (1670) had one made of pewter; he was a blacksmith, so may have made it himself.[10] Four pewter candlesticks are mentioned in the inventory of Toby King (1685), another blacksmith; he thought them sufficiently important to bequeath one pair to his daughter Margery. He also had iron candlesticks.[11] Peter Griffin (1689) had three pewter candlesticks.[12] Guests at Thomas Fry's inn at West Kennett (1691) would have gone to bed by the light of either brass or iron candlesticks.[13] His widow Margaret (1691/2) had a candlestick made of

1   WSHC P3/A/259.
2   WSHC P3/F/368.
3   WSHC P3/H/369.
4   WSHC P3/G/413.
5   Roberts, op cit, p.6.
6   Stedman, op cit, p.238.
7   WSHC D1/5/2/31.
8   WSHC P3/11/56.
9   WSHC P3/P/78.
10 WSHC P3/C/352.
11 WSHC P3/K/106.
12 WSHC P3/G/413.
13 WSHC P3/F/211.

'tinning'.[1] Thomas Hunter (1748/9)[2] made better provision for the guests at his inn: he had a 'lanthorn' worth 2s in his closet, and a 'lamp' in his kitchen. Many candles were needed to light the manor house: in 1741, Mr Holford paid Thomas Vincent, a chandler of Calne, the substantial sum of £2 4s 8d for them.[3] Almost half a century later, in 1785, Richard Hickley bought both candles and rush lights from (presumably) another Thomas Vincent. Vincent also supplied soap and turpentine.[4]

Kitchen Utensils

Goods in kitchens usually included kitchen utensils, which were also frequently found beside hearths in rooms such as the hall and the parlour. Maud Truslow, whose fire implements were discussed above, also possessed 'brasse pannes, iiii brasse potts, 2 skylletts, ii chaffen dishes, iii brasse kittles, i brasse furnish, iii paire of pothooks, [and] iii iron dripping pans', stored in her 'chamber over the whitehouse' [the dairy]. The cooking pot, according to Roberts, was 'the one basic and indispensable utensil', used for all sorts of cooking purposes, as well as for heating water.[5] It was hung over the fire with a hanger and crook. Pots made of brass, pewter, and iron were common. So were kettles, used for heating water, and frequently made of copper, although the poorest relied on iron. The wealthier, like Sir Adam Williamson in 1798, had tea kettles.[6] A few utensils were made of earthenware or 'treen' (wood); Walter Stretch (1707) still had some 'small vessel of wood and earth'. But pewter had mostly supplanted these materials in the previous century. Pothooks were used to suspend pots and kettles above the fire, either from andirons or from an iron bar above the fireplace. The skillet was also common; it was a three legged cooking pot with a long handle, which could be stood above the embers. Maud did not possess a porringer, but a few decedents did; this was a bowl made of pewter (or perhaps earthenware), perhaps with a cover and ear-shaped handles, used for porridge, soup, or broth. Food could be kept warm by using a chafing dish, placed on a brazier or 'chafer' containing hot ash or burning charcoal. It might be served up on pewter platters, and eaten with the fingers, without the aid of cutlery (except perhaps a knife). Hence the need, at least in elite houses, for napkins. Maud kept 'pewter of all sorts' in her maids' chamber. That probably included

1 WSHC P3/F/216.
2 WSHC P3/H/1256.
3 WSHC 184/5. Vincent's bill, 1741.
4 WSHC 184/5. Vincent's bill, 1785.
5 Roberts, op cit, p.43.
6 TNA PROB11/1315/187.

drinking vessels. The goods in Richard Dyer's 1649 inventory[1] included 'xiiii[li] & a halfe of other pewter, namely one flagon, one ale quart pott, one wine quart pott, two wyne pynt potts, & two chamber potts, praysed at viiid per li'. Dyer had been innkeeper at the White Hart;[2] he also had 'twenty pound of pewter dishes to sett meat to the table, praysed at ten pence the pound'. In earlier days platters and drinking vessels had been made of 'treen ware'; such goods do not appear in Avebury inventories, except perhaps as Elizabeth Pope's 'oulde treen ware' in 1618.[3] However, the barrels and keives which housewives used to store their drink continued to be described as 'treen ware'.

Food

We know little about the food that was prepared in Avebury's early modern kitchens. Perishable food for domestic consumption was not listed in the probate inventories which record other material goods. Inventories did, however, list food kept for sale, and also, as has been seen, mentioned implements used in food preparation. Some of the agricultural produce mentioned in Chapter 6 was almost certainly consumed in Avebury. Poor women regularly gleaned in Avebury's open fields after the harvest.[4] In 1699, the poor had a bonanza when the rector's tithe dispute with John Rose led him to refuse to cut the wheat Rose had left for him in a field. William Skeat tells us that 'there it stod soe long that the poore people cutt & fetcht it all away'.[5] We know that bread was the staple food for labourers,[6] although it is only mentioned once in the inventories. In 1778, William Herbert[7] left 40 shillings to be distributed amongst Avebury's poor 'in bread'. It is likely that, in the late eighteenth century, they had to purchase it from Avebury's baker, Thomas Strange.[8] As we have seen, Avebury yeomen and husbandmen produced much wheat and barley. Curiously no corn miller has yet been identified.

Barley was used to make malt, which was used for brewing drink. The usual drink was ale or beer, brewed from malt, and usually stored in barrels or kieves. Water was frequently contaminated. When Sir Richard Holford visited Avebury in 1698, however, he found the drink brewed by William Skeat 'sower

1 WSHC P1/D/95.
2 Raymond, Stuart A. 'The Inns of Avebury, c.1600-1800', *WAM*, 117, 2024, p.160.
3 WSHC P3/P/78.
4 GA D1954/E2/8.
5 WSHC 184/1, pt.1. Letter, William Skeat to Sir Richard Holford, 29th January 1699/1700.
6 Wilson, op cit, p.165.
7 WSHC P3/H/1431.
8 See chapter 7, p.314.

& unwholesome, therefore I drank very little being better please with whay, milk & water & the like'.[1] In the 1790s, Richard Hickley regularly brewed beer both for use at home, and to send to his master in Jamaica.[2] Tea and coffee did not become common until the mid-eighteenth century, although it was available in at least two of Avebury's inns. Two innkeepers, John Fowler (1745)[3] and Thomas Hunter (1749), both had tea kettles.[4] The one owned by Lady Holford in 1723 was made of silver.[5] The widow, Edith Cruse, also owned one in 1753.[6]

The importance of malt was emphasised by the fact that Joanna Truslow gave a bushel of malt to 'every household in Abery that have no plough', that is to every poor household, in her 1567/8 will. They could all use it to brew their own drink. She also gave a bushel to several local churches.[7] Richard Brown (c.1572) specifically mentioned the equipment for making malt in his will;[8] in addition to making his wife his residuary legatee, she was 'to have my mill and malt stonne except that she do mary'.

The activities of maltsters have also already been discussed.[9] However, both malting and brewing could be done at home. Several rooms set aside for brewing have already been mentioned. Toby King, the blacksmith (1685),[10] had 'in ye brewing roome one furnise and cover, grate frame & doore and the brisks that it hangs in'. He also had 'more of brewing vessell, one moushing tub, to littell cowls, two littell tubs & 4 ciuers'. The 'mashing tub' was used to mix barley with water to make mash, the first step in brewing. The 'cowls' were open tubs used for cooling the brew.

The innkeepers, of course, had plenty of drink in their cellars. When Walter Stretch, landlord of the original Catherine Wheel, died in 1709, he had 14½ hogsheads of beer in his two cellars, valued at £50 15s 0d. Forty years later (1749), Thomas Hunter[11] of the White Lion had a slightly wider range of drinks on offer. On the 'barrel horses' in his cellar there were 'five barrels of

1 WSHC 184/1, pt.1. Letter, Sir Richard Holford to William Skeat, undated [c.1698].
2 WSHC 184/6, passim.
3 WSHC P3/F/368.
4 WSHC P3/H/1256.
5 TNA PROB 11/590/280.
6 WSHC P3/C/935.
7 TNA PROB 11/51/51.
8 WSHC P1/1Reg/82B.
9 Above, p.321-2.
10 WSHC P3/K/106.
11 WSHC P3/H/1256.

small beer', and 'twelv hogsheads of strong beer', as well as 'eighteen bottles of cyder' and five empty barrels. The 'strong beer' alone was worth £60; the small beer was worth five guineas, and the cyder 13s 6d. Five years later (1745), John Fowler[1] of the Hare and Hounds could also offer ale, brandy, rum, and gin. It is probable that all the innkeepers brewed their own drink. When the licensee at Beckhampton House sold up in 1835, the goods for sale included casks, a mash tub, malt mill, hop strainer, and wort tubs – all items used in brewing.[2]

Hops are rarely mentioned in the brewing process in Avebury. However, Richard Holford did obtain hops from Faversham in 1741,[3] and Thomas Hunter had 30 pounds of hops ready to brew for his customers at the White Lion.[4] Raisins were also probably used for brewing: Richard Hickley purchased '12 pound raisins for the wine' in November 1793.[5]

Drink itself was rarely mentioned in the inventories of those who did not keep it for sale. However, barrels and kieves are frequently mentioned. Joseph Wallis (1680),[6] for example, had four barrels in his chamber. George Arnold's four barrels (1706)[7] were in his buttery with 'some other vessels of wood & some lumber'. A century earlier, Thomas Phelps als Bromham (1621/2)[8] had 'in the buttrie barrels kevers with other nessessaries' worth £1. In 1794, Richard Hickley complained that he had 'so many people to drink small beer all the summer, and in short winter too, as all the farmers finds the carters in beer winter and summer'.[9] Farmers evidently were expected to supply their workmen with all the small beer they wanted, especially at harvest.

Bread and ale was not, of course, enough. Meat was also desirable. John Brown of Westcott (1622)[10] had 'flesh meat' worth 30s. Margaret Hayward's appraisers (c.1664/5)[11] valued her twelve fitches of bacon 'with other meat'. Toby King, the blacksmith (1685),[12] had fifteen pewter dishes 'to hold meat'. Some mutton was eaten, given the importance of wool in Avebury's economy.

1 WSHC P3/F/368.
2 Wadsworth, Alan, ed. *The Farming Diaries of Thomas Pinniger, 1813-1837.* Wiltshire Record Society 74. 2021, p.lxxii-lxxiii.
3 WSHC 184/5.
4 WSHC P3/H/1256.
5 WSHC 184/7.
6 WSHC P1/W/349.
7 WSHC P3/A/259.
8 WSHC P3/P/93.
9 WSHC 184/6. Letter, Richard Hickley to Mrs Williamson, 30th November 1794.
10 WSHC P3/B/218.
11 WSHC P3/H/369.
12 WSHC P3/K/106.

In 1780, as has been seen, the butcher John Wiltshire regularly supplied Arthur Jones at the manor house with mutton.[1] The local mutton, however, was of poor quality. Beef appeared on the tables of the elite; Wiltshire's 1780 bill to Jones also included beef. William Skeat had salted beef in his cellar.[2] But cattle were usually kept for milk, rather than beef. Indeed, the manorial bailiff evidently had no beef cattle in December 1792, when he purchased 74 pounds of beef for £1 1s 7d.[3]

Rabbits and hares were probably found on many table boards. Rabbits, as we have seen, were originally bred for the lord of the manor, but no doubt others enjoyed them too. By the end of our period, many rabbits had escaped from their warrens, and become plentiful on the Downs.[4] The poor were probably adept at trapping them. Poaching was common. John Britton, the distinguished topographer, learned to poach in his late eighteenth century childhood at Kington St Michael, just a few miles from Avebury, and did not think that was unusual.[5] He put it down to 'the absence of all moral and legal authority in the parish'. It was, however, difficult to detect – and therefore rarely recorded. In 1719, John Hiscock, yeoman of Avebury stood bond with John Fishlock of Overton, who was accused of feloniously slaying a deer.[6] In 1767, William Reeves of Avebury was convicted of poaching in Wroughton Coppice.[7] He was caught in possession of a hare, and fined £5. In 1793, Richard Hickley accused Joseph Robbins of being 'a very great enemy to the game', and of being 'employed by the hunters and coursers to find hares for them, and if there is a hare in the parish he knows where to find it.' Robbins was given 'a good repremand', and told that 'the General' i.e. Adam Williamson would be informed.[8]

The venison from deer was similarly intended for the tables of the elite. Arthur Jones of Avebury Manor wrote several letters to Lord Bruce in the 1770s thanking him for the gift of venison.[9] It was less easy for poachers to escape detection, but it is likely that venison also occasionally reached their

1 See above, p.315
2 WSHC 184/1. Letter, a servant of Sir Richard Holford to William Skeat, December 1698.
3 WSHC 184/7.
4 Watts, op cit, p.112.
5 Britton, John. *The Autobiography of John Britton*. 1850, p.29.
6 WSHC A1/110, 1719M.
7 WSHC A1/260/1767.
8 WSHC 184/6. Richard Hickley to Mrs Williamson, 8th November 1793.
9 WSHC 9/35/178. Lord Bruce regularly sent gifts of venison to the neighbouring gentry; cf. Stedman, op cit, p.263.

tables. John Fishlock of Overton was not the only venison poacher in the vicinity.[1]

Pigs provided more legitimate meat for the poor. Attention has already been drawn to their ubiquity. Richard Cripps, the blacksmith (1670), had 'one flitch & a halfe of bacon' in the room above his shop. John Jacob's 'two flitches of bacon' were valued at 30s in 1670. John Cue (1687)[2] had a bacon rack amongst his possessions; he also had five 'hogs', that is, castrated boars raised for slaughter.[3] Jean Pope (1712/13), a wealthy widow,[4] had no fewer than 'thirteen sides of bacon' in her buttery. Walter Stretch (1707),[5] the innkeeper, had '8 flitches of bacon' waiting for his customers.

Other meat was also available in Avebury, although there is limited written evidence. Richard Holford's 'house bill' in October 1741 listed pork, bacon, mutton, beef, chicken, and pigeons, as well as butter, suet, and honey.[6] This was probably produce supplied by Peter Griffin, his tenant, as was the cream, cheese, milk, eggs, and other produce supplied to Stayner Holford in 1743.[7] Fish was also available. In 1729, Thomas Smith was constructing a fish pond at West Kennett.[8] Stukeley tells us that a megalith was used as a fish slab on market days.[9] Richard Hickley paid 'Hancock the fishmonger' £1 4s 8d in May 1794.[10] One wonders whether the poor fished surreptitiously in the Winterbourne and the Kennet, or stole from Smith's fish pond.

The dovecotes discussed above yielded a good supply of pigeons. They provided young, unfledged squabs, which were regarded as a delicacy for elite tables.[11] Pigeon pie was on the table in the parlour when Sir Richard Holford's servants were giving trouble in 1696.[12] Peter Griffin's 1721/2 proposal to rent Avebury farm from Lady Holford included the provision that the landlady was to 'reserve to herselfe yearly a dozen of pidgeons 6 fatt capons or 3 turkeys.[13] The

1   WSHC A1/110, 1719M.
2   WSHC P3/C/515.
3   The word was also used for yearling sheep unshorn.
4   WSHC P3/P/644.
5   WSHC P1/S/709.
6   WSHC 184/5. Richard Holford's house bill, 1741.
7   WSHC 184/6. Stayner Holford's bill from Peter Griffin, 1743.
8   WSHC 568/7. Lease, Thomas Smith to Robert Caswell, 3rd September 1729.
9   Gillings, et al. *Landscape,* op cit, p.291.
10   WSHC 184/7.
11   McCann, op cit, p.1.
12   WSHC 184/1, pt.1. Letter, William Skeat to Sir Richard Holford, c.23rd November 1698.
13   WSHC 184/1, pt.2. Peter Griffin's proposal, 9th Jan 1721/2.

vicar claimed tithe of 'pidgions, turkeys, geese, ducks'.[1] Sir Richard Holford denied his entitlement, but said he would give him some pigeons from the pigeon house anyway.[2] In 1743, Peter Griffin promised Stayner Holford to 'make a reserve of some pidgeons for you' on his next visit.[3] Half a century later, Richard Hickley was regularly selling pigeons – a 1794 statement shows that he sold no fewer than 55 between 21st April and 30th May, making a total of 14s 3d.[4]

Whether the poor enjoyed pigeon pie is not known, but the likelihood is that they did – poached, like the rabbits. Poultry were probably also important. They were not sufficiently valuable to be listed in inventories, but are likely to be included under the rubric, 'things forgotten'. Eggs were probably an important component of the diet of Avebury's husbandmen. We know that turkey and geese featured in the diet of the elite: the basket that William Skeat despatched to Sir Richard Holford's London residence in early 1700 included both.[5] It is less likely that husbandmen and labourers dined on them. It was only the elite who had access to a wide variety of food. Others had much less choice

Milk was probably drunk straight from the cow. But it also provided another important component of the diet: butter and cheese. Cheese, like bread, was particularly important for labourers. Avebury's dairying industry has already been discussed. A number of inventories record dairy produce, presumably for sale. George Brown (1619), for example, had 'cheese butter and baken' worth £2. William Bray (1699)[6] had four cheeses, valued with his bed and other furnIture at £2 10s 0d. Many inventories record cheese cowls and kivers (tubs for the whey), cheese presses and other cheese-making equipment; there were also many cheese racks for storage.

As has been seen, there were many gardens.[7] They were attached to the meanest hovels, and to the largest farm houses. There were also a number of orchards. A garden meant that both rich and poor could grow their own fruit and vegetables. The range of garden crops has already been discussed; they were probably more important to the poor than is apparent in the sources.

1 WSHC 184/1, pt.2. Letters, John White to Sir Richard Holford, 29th January 1696/7; H. Wall to Sir Richard Holford, 5th June 1698;
2 WSHC 184/1, pt.2. Letter, Sir Richard Holford to John White, 2nd April 1710.
3 WSHC 184/1, pt.2. Letter, Peter Griffin to Stayner Holford, 23rd April 1743.
4 WSHC 184/7.
5 WSHC 184/1, pt.1. William Skeat to Sir Richard Holford, 29th January 1699/1700.
6 WSHC P3/B/986.
7 See above p.268-9.

Members of the elite might also eat imported food. We have already seen that William Skeat occasionally sent baskets of fruit and other food from Avebury to his landlord in London. Those baskets were sometimes returned containing exotic foods such as the '6^{li} of raisons, 4^{li} of currents, 8^{li} of sugar & spice', that his landlord sent down to Avebury in January 1699/1700.[1]

Entertainment and Leisure

Leisure for the Holford family included frequent visits to Avebury, especially during the legal vacations. Sir Richard sometimes spent several weeks on his manor,[2] sometime just a few days.[3] Lady Holford might stay for longer. Both also visited their other manor at Westonbirt. Some of their vacation activities are recorded in both Holford's letters, and in his diary, and shine a light on social relations in the parish.

Sharing meals was an important part of the culture of the gentry and yeomanry, and indeed of the lower orders as well. When the manorial court met, it was the custom to entertain the homage to dinner. After harvest, the labourers expected a harvest supper, which in the 1790s was provided by Richard Hickley.[4] Almost a century earlier, Sir Richard Holford's diary[5] frequently mentions his dinner guests, and the places where he himself was entertained. Sir Richard was not impressed when the homage came to dinner in 1700. He records that 'Farmer Skeat invited all the jury & they brought as many more; there was victuall enough for them and all of them very cheerful but lamentable troublesome'. It is not clear whether he was referring to their uncouth behaviour at table, or to their inability (or perhaps their refusal) to make their presentments in the way he thought appropriate. Most of his other guests were of higher social status, although not all of them appreciated his hospitality. On 10th August 1711, John White, the vicar, 'told me I gave him a good dinner but run the spitt into his guts, and such like nonsensical reviling stuff and went away in a seeming passion'. Holford had told him off for rejecting the attempts of the Chancellor of the Diocese to reconcile him with his parishioners. Even so, White was again invited to dinner on 3rd October. He 'put a rude answer'! White's successor, John Mayo, who visited on

1 WSHC 184/1, pt.1. Letter, Sir Richard Holford to William Skeat, 29th January 1699/1700.
2 WSHC 184/1, pt.1. Letter, Sir Richard Holford to William Skeat, c.1698.
3 WSHC 184/1, pt.1. Letter, Sir Richard Holford to Archdeacon Yates, 14th July 1698.
4 WSHC 184/6. Letters, Richard Hickley to Mrs Williamson, 6th November 1792 & 27th September 1794.
5 WSHC 184/8.

17th August 1714, was perhaps a more congenial dinner guest.

Holford used invitations to dinner to discuss business with his tenants and others. On 27th January, 1711, for example, John Rose visited him in London; they 'had a great deal of discourse'. On the following 10th February, Farmer Skeat also dined with him in London; Holford 'prayed him to be kind and assisting to John Rose', who Holford hoped would succeed Skeat as his tenant. When Holford visited Avebury in August 1711, Skeat, his wife, and his mother, together with John Rose, the vicar John White, and Holford's three tenants at Beckhampton, the widows Rose and Ponting, and Frances Bradfield, all came to dine.[1]

Holford's diary also mentions many occasions when he and his wife were entertained. On 4th October 1711 he dined with Madam Percival at Clatford. There was 'great plenty & great decency' when he visited William Norris at Nonsuch on 19th August 1714. They were 'very genteely entertained by Mr. Nath Stevens at Chevenage' in the following month. He and his wife frequently patronised inns when they were travelling – The Bear at Reading, the Angel at Marlborough, the Tunns at Bath, the Red Lyon at Eaton Stoney, the George in Wells, are all mentioned in his diary.

Holford evidently enjoyed using his coach.[2] He and his wife took several 'turnes' across Lansdowne when they were staying in Bath in 1714. More locally, Lady Holford took Mrs Mayo for a drive across the Downs whilst their husbands were digesting a good dinner. They also enjoyed sight-seeing; at Malmesbury, they visited the Abbey, King Athelstan's monument, and 'what else was to be seene'. At Marlborough, they went to see the Mount.

Holford and many other gentry also enjoyed the chase. We have already encountered John Aubrey hunting deer with Col Penruddock in 1649, at the beginning of our period. At the end of our period, in 1799, it was said that Avebury Manor was 'situated in a fine sporting country, abounding with partridges and hares, and within a small distance of a pretty pack of harriers'.[3] There was a dog kennel at Avebury manor in 1695,[4] and at West Kennett in 1723.[5] When Sir John Hopkins leased an Avebury farm to John Amor in 1795, he reserved 'liberty of hunting, hawking, fishing and fowling' to himself.[6] Gamekeepers, as has been seen, were employed by the manorial

1 GA D1956/E2/8.
2 WSHC 184/8.
3 *Salisbury and Winchester Journal* 24th June 1799.
4 WSHC 184/4. Plan of the house, gardens and barton, 1695.
5 Somerset Heritage Centre. DD/PO/6. Lease, 3rd September 1723, Richard & Thomas Smith to Francis Popham.
6 WSHC 873/262. Lease, Sir John Hopkins to John Amor, 16th April 1795.

lords in the late eighteenth century. Dogs were kept for hunting, although documentation is limited. Walter Sloper, the attorney, gave William Skeat a greyhound c.1697, which Skeat promised to keep for his landlord.[1] In 1703, Skeat's son Emanuel was accused of keeping two greyhounds as hunting dogs, 'contra forma statut'.[2] The tightening of game laws to prevent inferiors hunting – even inferiors as prominent in the community as Skeat - was proceeding, as 'gentlemen adopted an attitude of proprietory exclusiveness towards the game they controlled'.[3] Skeat was unimpressed; he had been appointed as Sir Richard Holford's gamekeeper,[4] and was probably thereby emboldened to threaten Charles Tooker's son that if he 'came to hunt in your [Holford's] manour he would shoote his dogs, without any provocacon'.[5] When Tooker junior drove a brace of hares across his farm Skeat interfered with the sport by killing them himself, thus provoking a letter of complaint to his landlord. Skeat and other yeomen farmers probably objected to crops being trampled by hunters, although they were not averse to hunting themselves. Tooker (who was a Justice of the Peace) was 'informed he [Skeat] hath killed a brace of hares in a day with his greyhounds'.

Several other dogs appear in our records. Richard Truslow had a greyhound and a 'small curr dog' with him c.1603 when he tried to prevent the servants of Sir James Mervyn depasturing his sheep on West Down; he was accused of setting them on the sheep.[6] Reuben Horsell's 'little mongrel dog', was sketched by Stukeley[7]. In 1780 Mr Williams of Beckhampton House offered a reward to the finder of 'a red wire-hair'd terrier bitch, with head and ears like a fox', and answering to the name of Fury;[8] the dog was presumably kept for sport, but was evidently important to its owner. Dogs kept in a run gave early warning of anyone approaching, and there was a dog run at the manor.[9] There

1   WSHC 183/1, pt.2. Letter, Sir Richard Holford to Charles Tooker, 4th January 1697/8.
2   WSHC A1/110, 1703M.
3   Underdown, David. *Revel, Riot and Rebellion: Popular Politics and Culture in England 1603-1660*. Clarendon Press, 1985, p.22.
4   WSHC 184/1, pt.2. Sir Richard Holford to John Rose, 7th June 1710.
5   WSHC 184/1, pt.2. Letters, Charles Tooker to Sir Richard Holford, c.29th December 1697, and Sir Richard Holford to Charles Tooker, 4th January 1697/8.
6   STAC8/5/1. He also used dogs in a similar altercation c.1605; see TNA STAC8/281/25.
7   Piggott, Stuart. *William Stukeley: an eighteenth-century antiquary*. Thames & Hudson, 1985, p.63.
8   *Salisbury and Winchester Journal* 20 August 1781
9   Brian Edwards provided this information.

was also a dog basket in the servants' hall in 1788.[1] Richard Hickley paid the butcher 'for sheep's heads & meat for the dogs' in November 1791.[2] In 1794, he obtained two hounds to send to Mr Belford in Jamaica.[3] Dogs were also kept for practical purposes: the sheep dog was almost certainly an important companion for the shepherd, and greatly eased his labours, although none are specifically mentioned in our documentation.[4]

It is evident that there were also cats, as meat for cats was purchased in 1793. But we know no more about them.[5] It may be that birds of prey were also kept: John Aubrey records that James Long and Inigo Jones were 'wont to spend a week or two every autumn at Avebury in hawking', c.1655.[6]

In 1793, a number of gentlemen formed the Beckhampton Club, probably based at the Catherine Wheel, in order to shoot game together. One wonders whether this grew into the so-called 'Beckhampton Club', which met to determine nominations for Parliamentary elections.[7] Richard Hickley did not think much of their chances of shooting partridges, although he acknowledged that 'Adam Wiltshire [the gamekeeper] had tollerable luck for the first day: six brace of birds and one hare'.[8] But he was dubious about the activities of one Mr Northey, who claimed to have received a letter from 'the General' instructing his gamekeeper not to engage in shooting whilst the gentlemen of the Club were present. Hickley thought there was no such letter.[9] He was even more annoyed when the gamekeeper was subsequently accused of destroying game; he 'did not believe a word of the matter'.[10] The 'gentlemen' had also 'taken it into their heads that the farmers destroys it', and sought to agree with the farmers not to shoot until the harvest was over, provided that the game was preserved for them.[11] In fact, Hickley had conveniently forgotten that he had paid Wiltshire in previous years - £5 8s 3d in October 1791, £2 11s 6d in May 1792 - precisely 'for kiling

1   WSHC 271/6.
2   WSHC 184/7.
3   WSHC 184/6. Letters, Richard Hickley to Mrs Williamson, 30th July 1794 & 31st August 1794.
4   Gurney, Peter. *Shepherd Lore: the last years of traditional shepherding in Wiltshire.* Wiltshire Folk Life Society, 2010, p.22-30.
5   WSHC 184/6. Letter, Richard Hickley to Mrs Williamson, 31st March 1793.
6   Aubrey, John. *Monumenta Brittanica,* ed. John Fowles. Milborne Port: Dorset Publishing, 1980. Vol.1, p.20.
7   Waylen, James. *A history, Military and Municipal, of the ancient Borough of Devizes.* Longman Brown & Co., 1859, p.431.
8   WSHC 184/6. Letter, Richard Hickley to Mrs Williamson, 3rd September 1793.
9   WSHC 184/6. Letter, Richard Hickley to Mrs Williamson, c. September 1793.
10 WSHC 184/6. Letter, Richard Hickley to Mrs Williamson, 8th November 1793.
11 WSHC 184/6. Letter, Richard Hickley to Mrs Williamson, 31st August 1794.

game'.[1] In order to keep the farmers happy, an annual dinner at the Catherine Wheel[2] was begun in 1794. All but two of the leading farmers of the parish attended the first one. At the same time, Adam Wiltshire, the gamekeeper, was paid five guineas not to shoot game.

Members of the Beckhampton Club were described as 'shooters' by Richard Hickley.[3] We have no details of their guns, although it may be noted that Hickley himself paid a shilling for 'powder & shot' in January 1795.[4]

Earlier probate inventories record a number of guns. These were probably used in hunting, although they were also used for defensive purposes. In 1664, John Phelps als Bromham had a gun in his hall[5]. Nathaniel Power, the vicar, had two guns when he died in 1670[6]. Sir Richard Holford ordered William Skeat to keep a gun 'to defend his house and preserve his goods'.[7] When John Rose died in 1720, Thomas Alexander joked that Rose had so much wealth in his house that his family 'borrowed all ye guns in the village to keep guard'.[8] In 1749, Thomas Hunter had two guns worth ten shillings[9]. Guns, of course, were dangerous, as Henry Spencer discovered when he was accidentally shot and killed by William Ball in 1768.[10] They may have been used for military purposes during the Civil War.

Swords were another weapon which appear in a few of our records. John Shuter, who died in 1589, had 'his sworde and buckler', which 'he did keepe for his own use', and which he offered to his son Christopher.[11] The sword which Peter Griffin kept in his hall in 1689[12] may have been used during the Civil War, and probably kept handy during William of Orange's invasion in 1688. Sir Richard Holford probably had a sword; when his dispute with John White was at its height, William Skeat recommended that 'you must be sartain to bring a good soarde with you for ye parson is in a greate rage against you', and had

1 WSHC 184/7.
2 Named the Beckhampton Inn in this correspondence.
3 WSHC 184/6. Richard Hickley to Mrs Williamson, 9th September 1793.
4 WSHC 184/7.
5 WSHC P1/B/416.
6 WSHC P3/P/329.
7 WSHC 183/1, pt.2. Letter, Sir Richard Holford to Charles Tooker, 4th January 1697/8.
8 WSHC 184/1, pt.2. Letter, Thomas Alexander to Lady Holford, 12th December 1720.
9 WSHC P3/H/1256.
10 Hunnisett, R.F., ed. *Wiltshire Coroners' Bills, 1652-1794*. Wiltshire Record Society 36. 1980, no.585.
11 TNA PROB/11/61/207.
12 WSHC P3/G/413.

threatened 'deadly mischief'.[1]

It is likely that men frequently carried long walking staves or cudgels with them, perhaps for self-defence, but primarily to help control sheep or cattle. Few appear in the records. In altercations between the men of Sir James Mervyn and Richard Truslow on West Down, which occurred c.1603 and c.1605, all of those involved were carrying staves five or six feet long; some also carried daggers on their backs. Richard Parr had a stake which he 'took out of the hedge going thither'. Stephen Taylor, one of those charged with riotous behaviour, hoped that he could get away with telling the Court of Star Chamber that he sought to keep Mervyn's sheep off the Down by 'striking his staffe upon the ground'.[2]

No other military equipment is mentioned in the probate inventories, although adult males were obligated to bring their armour to musters when called. They were also expected to practise archery at the butts, which were regularly presented as being in need of repair in the late sixteenth and early seventeenth centuries.[3]

Little evidence survives regarding other sports, although we can be sure that the regular round of calendar customs was maintained. The festivals of the church were celebrated with eating, drinking, and sports. During Elizabeth's reign, the custom was for the parishioners to gather at Avebury Trusloe manor house on the Tuesday in Rogation Week, when the Truslows made 'great cheer'.[4] May games and dancing, which had been banned during the Interregnum, were re-introduced to Avebury after the Restoration. The maypole may have been re-erected close to the spot where dissenters met,[5] perhaps placed there in order to taunt them. Celebrations were also in order at other times. When Lord Howe gave 'the French a handsome drubbing' in 1794, the bells were rung, and the ringers given six shillings.[6]

Aubrey tells us that festivities attending sheep shearing in the early summer were kept up 'on the Downes in Wiltshire and Hampshire'.[7]

1 WSHC 184/1, pt.1. Letters, William Skeat to Sir Richard Holford, 23rd February 1698/9 & 12th May 1699.
2 TNA STAC8/5/1; STAC8/281/25.
3 WSHC 192/12A-M.
4 TNA E134/41Eliz/Hil8.
5 Gillings, Mark, Peterson, Rick, & Pollard, Joshua. 'The destruction of the Avebury monuments', in Cleal, Rosemary, & Pollard, Joshua, eds. *Monuments and material culture: Papers in honour of an Avebury Archaeologist: Isobel Smith*. Hobnob Press, 2004, p.158.
6 WSHC 184/6. Letter, Richard Hickley to Mrs Williamson, June 1794.
7 Cited by Sharpe, J.A. *Early Modern England: A Social History 1550-1760*. Edward Arnold, 1987, p.281.

Competitive sports were popular in other parts of early seventeenth-century Wiltshire.[1] On 7th September 1747, the *Bath journal* announced that Silbury Hill would be the venue for 'bull-baiting, backsword playing, dancing and other divertions' on 12th October; 'wrestling, a smock and ribbons run for, and foot-ball playing, eight of a side' would follow on 13th October. Over 6,000 people were said to have attended similar events eleven years previously.

More genteel sports were also played in Avebury. A cricket pitch was created behind Beckhampton House in the 1770s; the first match there was recorded in 1774, between teams from Devizes and Marlborough. The following year a team from Calne also played.[2]

A crowd estimated at 20,000 witnessed a different sort of entertainment on Beckhampton Down in 1798. The Wiltshire Yeomanry Cavalry were being reviewed by Lord Bruce. Ten regiments, made up of 'the principal gentleman and opulent farmers of the county', 'went through their various evolutions with a spirit and exertion that would have been creditable even to veterans'.[3] It was perhaps for this event that Richard Hickley paid £2 9s 6d for 'cloathing for Miles in the cavelry' in May 1798, and advanced him a further £1 4s 0d.[4]

Most of the leisure activities of poorer Aveburians are hidden from our view. But we do know that one 'luxury' they enjoyed was tobacco. Many Avebury residents smoked. Numerous tobacco pipe fragments of the seventeenth and eighteenth centuries have been excavated, many associated with the sites of stone breaking[5]. It seems likely that, whilst the stones were actually being burnt, labourers smoked. The pipes were mostly made in Marlborough, and presumably tobacco was obtained there too. Smoking was not confined to the poorer classes. The vicar, John Mayo, thanked Sir Richard Holford for 'the paper of tobacco' which he sent down from London in 1715.[6]

A very few decedents had books. There was a good library at Avebury manor when Lady Susanna Holford was residing there. She prepared a detailed schedule of books (which sadly does not survive) to be divided up between members of the family. Amongst them was a 'book of written receipts of physick and housewifery', given to her daughter in law Sarah. Susanna also mentioned various portraits of the family, at least one of which had been

1 Ingram, Martin. *Church Courts, Sex, and Marriage in England 1570-1640*. Cambridge University Press, 1990, p.102-3.
2 Parslew, Patricia. *Beckhampton: Time Present and Time Past*. Hobnob Press, 2000, p.40.
3 *Leeds Intelligencer* 25th June 1798.
4 WSHC 184/7.
5 Gillings, et al. *Landscape,*op cit, p.301-2.
6 WSHC 184/1, pt.2. Letter, John Mayo to Sir Richard Holford, 16th June 1715.

painted by Sir Godfrey Kneller.[1] In 1742, her husband's grandson Richard bequeathed his books and pictures, many of which Susanna had passed on to him, to his brother Stayner.[2] They included a portrait of Samuel Holford.[3] Richard's library was extensive, and was listed in Stayner Holford's law suit against Mrs Metcalfe. As already noted, he was 'reading law', and had a good collection of legal works such as the *Statutes at Large*, various law reports, and Swinburne's *Wills*. But his library also included works on a wide range of other subjects, for example, political philosophy (Hobbes' *Leviathan*), theology (Archbishop Tillotson's *Works*), history (Clarendon's *History of the Rebellion*), ballads (the *Beggars Opera*), and household management (*The Country House Wife*). It would be interesting to know if anyone other than their owner used this collection, which, fifty years later, probably formed the basis of Adam Williamson's library. He had a bookcase containing over 400 books, together with 'sundry magazines', in his 'little parlour', on the ground floor.[4] The books on its lower shelves suffered when the house was flooded in 1792[5]. Williamson also had a 'desk and bookcase' in his chamber.

Books were also owned by the clergy. John Peart,[6] the vicar, had a small theological library when he died. Its contents are described in the next chapter. Interestingly, he bequeathed specific books to various leading members of his congregation, obviously expecting his legatees to be able to understand them. His successor, Nathaniel Power (1670) had books valued at £3, but his appraisers gave no description of them.[7] Another successor, John White (1712), had 'books and other small things' worth £6 in his study.[8]

The bible, and the *Book of Common Prayer*, as one might expect, were amongst the few books specifically mentioned in laymen's wills and inventories. Toby King (1685), the blacksmith, gave each of his children a bible in his will.[9] His son John received 'a greate bible and a smaller bible and exedence & gramer and other bookes'.[10] King had no fewer than 'five bibls' in his possession, as well as 'maney other good books to read'. Thomas Bray (1657) similarly gave his

---

1 TNA PROB 11/590/280. It may be noted that he also painted the portrait of William Stukeley, who was a frequent visitor to Avebury.
2 TNA PROB/11/721/329.
3 TNA C11/818/16.
4 WSHC 271/6.
5 WSHC 184/6. Letter, Richard Hickley to Mrs Williamson, 4th September 1792.
6 WSHC P3/P/101.
7 WSHC P3/P/329.
8 WSHC P3/W/671.
9 WSHC P3/K/106.
10 WSHC P3/K/106.

kinsman, John Pope, 5s 'to buy him a bible'.[1] The widow Edith Cruse (1753) gave 'one bible [and] one common prayer book' to her nephew John Penney.[2] Richard Parr (1632) had a 'bible & other books' worth 10s.[3] Lady Holford in 1722 had a 'large common prayer book with silver clasps and plated with silver'.[4] It is likely that bibles and prayer books were also owned by other decedents whose appraisers recorded books in their inventories. In her study, Maud Truslow (1625) had 'a fewe old books'.[5] John Bromham als Phelps had 'some books' amongst other goods in his hall chamber in 1662.[6] Two books were amongst the possessions of Andrew Mills, taylor (1670).[7] George Arnold (1706) had 'one table board & frame & some few bookes' in his inner room.[8]

The only other book we know of in a layman's possession was by William Stukeley – probably his *Abury: a Temple of the British Druids*. According to Rev John Whitaker, who visited in 1772, it was owned by 'the schoolmaster', that is, John Clements.[9] One wonders what other books were in Clements' possession.

At the end of the eighteenth century (or perhaps the beginning of the nineteenth), Avebury's book lovers were encouraged by the establishment of a book club amongst them. This was organized by Charles Lucas, the young curate.[10]

Health

Illness was a perennial topic of discussion in the Holford letters. In eighteenth-century conditions, illnesses could be much more serious than they are today. We have already discussed the high mortality which resulted from the outbreak of the plague in the early eighteenth century.[11] Colds were a much more minor affliction, but are mentioned in the Holford letters on several occasions. In 1754, Henry Howson commented that 'I have not been well

1   WSHC P3/B/480.
2   WSHC P3/C/935.
3   WSHC P3/P/184.
4   TNA PROB 11/590/280.
5   WSHC P3/T/86.
6   WSHC P1/B/416.
7   WSHC P3/M/60.
8   WSHC P3/A/259
9   Nichols, John. *Illustrations of the literary history of the Eighteenth Century*, vol. IV. John Nichols & Son, 1822, p.856.
10 Moody, Robert. 'The Reverend Charles Lucas (1769-1854) of Avebury and Devizes – a forgotten novelist, miscellaneous writer and crusading clergyman', *WAM*, 104, 2011, p.227.
11 See above, p.52-4.

for near three weeks past, having had a very bad cold, attended with a fever, which has confined me'.[1] In January 1767, Stayner Holford had 'purposed waiting on' Edward Popham, JP, 'this day, but am out of order with a cold'. His cousin Robert Holford had 'an ugly cold', when he departed for the East Indies in 1742, but his father hoped that 'a change of air & exercise will do him good'.[2] Stayner Holford thought that 'decoction of camomile flowers & Roman wormwood', which his nephew took with him, would help; they had 'often cured me'. But remedies for disease were generally unreliable, and skill in dealing with injuries was frequently lacking.

We have already discussed the poor quality of professional health care available in Avebury in our period.[3] Accidents were probably common, and could prove fatal. John Shuter died after an amateur bone-setter tried to set his ribs.[4] One of his successors, William Skeat similarly suffered when a limb of a tree fell on him in January 1698. He wrote to Sir Richard Holford, noting that he had 'ben under ye surgents hands ..., & when I will be well God noues'.[5] He seems to have recovered, although twelve months later he wrote to his landlord, 'hopeing you are in good health but for my selfe & some of my family are at present much out of health'.[6] In 1709, one of the reasons Skeat gave for giving up his farm was that 'hee is groweing old & is infirme, and his wife very crazy, and not fit for soe much troble'.[7] Another injury occurred in 1731, when John Caswell 'broke his right hand, wrist & hurt his left sholder'; in consequence, he could only make his mark on a legal document.[8]

Lady Holford had also been ill at the beginning of 1697, when the Vicar, John White, wished 'the recovery of your good Lady'.[9] A year later, she was 'much better than at summer, but is weake and very tender'.[10] Skeat commiserated with the Holfords just before his accident; he was 'sory to here that my Lady has ben elle, but God be thanked you say shee is sum thing

1   WSHC 184/1, pt.1. Letter, Henry Howson to Stayner Holford, 21st March 1754.
2   WSHC 184/1, pt.2. Letter, Robert Holford to Stayner Holford, 3rd March 1742/3.
3   See above, p.324-5.
4   TNA STAC 8/269/32.
5   WSHC 184/1, pt. 1. Letter, William Skeat to Sir Richard Holford, 30th January 1698/9.
6   WSHC 184/1, pt. 1. Letter, William Skeat to Sir Richard Holford, 29th January 1699/1700.
7   WSHC 184/1, pt.2. Sir Richard Holford to 2nd June 1709.
8   WSHC 371/1, pt. 5.
9   WSHC 184/1, pt.1. Letter, John White to Sir Richard Holford, 29th January 1696/7.
10 WSHC 184/1, pt.2. Letter, Sir Richard Holford to Charles Tooker, 4th January 1697/8.

beter'.[1] She was again 'extreame ill' in early 1709, but 'now some what better, yet very weake'.[2] In early 1712, Holford noted that 'my poore wife is & hath been indisposed these six weeks past, & is now confined to her chamber'.[3] In early May 1712 she spent a further sixteen weeks in her chamber, and Sir Richard experienced 'the conversation of doctors, apothecaries and nurses'.[4] In June 1715, she was again in 'but a weak condition'.[5] We cannot tell the nature of Lady Holford's illnesses, nor the cause of the 'fites' which afflicted Mrs Bromham and were 'as bad as ever' in 1696.[6] 'Litel master's nose' was also giving trouble in 1698,[7] and Holford himself was not immune from illness; in June 1709 he had been 'indisposed for some dais', probably worrying about his wife's malady.[8] In the event, Lady Holford outlived her husband. We have already seen how he sought medical advice for a 'sore toe' in 1717.[9]

John White, the vicar, was another victim of ill health; Sir Richard Holford 'forebore to troble him dureing his illness', and waited until his health recovered before pursuing his dispute over tithes.[10] But by May 1712 White was 'dangerously ill', after what was probably a long illness; he was buried 22nd October 1712.

Arthur Jones was another sufferer; in December 1786, he 'felt an unpleasant sensation in my bowels', and 'was forced to be very attentive to what I eat and drink'.[11] Although he had the attention of Mr Devans, who was presumably a medical practitioner, he also sought the advice of his niece, Anne Williamson, and decided to try 'tincture of rhubarb' as a remedy. Apparently, it

1 WSHC 184/1, pt. 1. Letter, William Skeat to Sir Richard Holford, 9th December 1698.
2 WSHC 184/1, pt.2. Letter, Sir Richard Holford to Richard Chandler, 2nd June 1709.
3 WSHC 184/1, pt.2. Letter, Sir Richard Holford to John Brinsden, 24th January 1711/12.
4 WSHC 184/1, pt.2. Letter, Sir Richard Holford to John Brinsden, 21st May 1712.
5 WSHC 184/1, pt.2. Letter, John Mayo to Sir Richard Holford, 15th June 1715.
6 WSHC 184/1, pt.2. Letter, William Skeat to Sir Richard Holford, 4th January 1695/6.
7 WSHC 184/1, pt.1. Letter, William Skeat to Sir Richard Holford, c.23rd November 1698.
8 WSHC 184/1, pt.2. Letter, Sir Richard Holford to Richard Chandler, 2nd June 1709.
9 GA D1956/E2/8.
10 WSHC 184/1, pt.2. Letters, Sir Richard Holford to John Rose, 23rd November 1710; Sir Richard Holford to John Brinsden, 24th January 1711/12 & 21st May 1712.
11 WSHC 271/16. Letter, Arthur Jones to Ann Williamson, 8th December 1786.

had to be made with the best brandy, and his niece (who was then in London) was asked to send him some. Whatever the problem was, it probably killed him in the long term: he was buried 7th July 1789.

Men like Holford, White, and Jones could call on such medical advice as was available. It is unlikely that the labouring classes could do so: they were expected not to be sick. The Duke of Marlborough, as we have seen, expressed the opinion that 'the lower orders are never ill'.[1] That, obviously, was not true, and some employers did attempt to look after their workers in their illnesses. When William Harper, a shepherd who was valued by Richard Hickley, died 'of a mortification in his bowels' in 1793, Hickley consoled himself with the thought that he had been 'properly attended, and all the care taken of him that lay in my power'.[2] Similarly, when Joseph Brown, a long serving servant, lay dying of a 'stoppage of urine', Hickley summoned Mr Pinkney of Marlborough to attend him.[3]

The clergy were another potential source of advice. John Mayo, as we have seen, was the son-in-law of a Calne apothecary, and was called on to treat Sir Richard Holford's toe. The probability is that other clergy also had some medical expertise. They were more highly educated than their parishioners; the latter therefore expected them to be able to provide some medical assistance. That was, of course, but one small aspect of the duties that the clergy were expected to perform, and which we now review.

---

[1] Jones, Eric L. *Landed Estates and Rural Inequality in English History: from the mid-seventeenth century to the present.* Palgrave Macmillan, 2018, p.40.
[2] WSHC 184/6. Letter, Richard Hickley to Mrs Williamson, 4th June 1793.
[3] WSHC 184/6. Letter, Richard Hickley to Mrs Williamson, 1st February 1794.

9
RELIGION IN AVEBURY: CHURCH AND DISSENT

THE CHURCH IN our period was at the centre of village society; indeed, from a theological perspective, the parishioners were the church. Their building, St. James, stood (and still stands) at the centre of the village, next to the manor house.[1] It is by far the oldest building in the parish (other than the megaliths), and was described by Pevsner as 'archaeologically uncommonly interesting'. It has an Anglo-Saxon nave with two windows of that date. The aisles are twelfth century, as is the font in which babies have been baptised for most of the last millennium. It is carved with images of dragons, and of a bishop. Despite Avebury's subsequent puritan history, the church still retains its medieval rood loft, which dates from 1460. It was dismantled and successfully hidden behind lathe and plaster at the Reformation, but re-discovered in 1810, perhaps by the antiquarian curate, Charles Lucas.[2] It was re-installed c.1879.[3] The stalls are said to have been made out of Jacobean pews, which suggests that renovations were being made in the early seventeenth century. That conclusion is supported by the fact that the south porch, windows, and bells needed repair in 1613,[4] and that three of the five bells are dated 1619 and 1620.[5]

1 The following comments are based on Pevsner, Nikolaus. *Wiltshire*, ed. Bridget Cherry. The Buildings of England. 2nd ed. Yale University Press, 2002, p.101-2, on the early twentieth century inventory of church goods, WSHC D1/5/2/31, and on the description by British Listed Buildings https://britishlistedbuildings.co.uk
2 Moody, Robert. 'The Reverend Charles Lucas (1769-1854) of Avebury and Devizes – a forgotten novelist, miscellaneous writer and crusading clergyman', *WAM*, 104, 2011, p.225.
3 *Avebury St James: a Guide to the Church of St. James, Avebury, and the church St. Mary Magdalene, Winterbourne Monkton*. Avebury P.C.C., 1982, p.6. WSHC D1/5/2/31.
4 WSHC D1/42/28, f.35-71 & 61r-62r. I owe this reference to Steve Hobbs.
5 For the bells, see Walter, H.B. *The Church Bells of Wiltshire: their Inscriptions and History*. 1929, p.16.

Another can be dated to c.1649-50, when the churchwardens whose names are inscribed on it held office.[1] The fifth, cast by the celebrated bell maker Richard Phelps, a native of the parish, was hung in 1719. What happened to the four bells in the church in 1553 is not known; perhaps they were lost. The church still has a chalice and paten dated 1606, and another paten presented by William Dunch, lord of the manor, in 1636. The parish chest is dated 1634. It seems probable that the gallery taken down in 1879 was erected during the seventeenth or eighteenth century. Before the restoration of that year, the church had 345 sittings, including 104 in the gallery.[2]

St. James was the venue for the formal gatherings which met week by week for worship, and which celebrated the ritual year. It was also the place where notice was given of events such as the meetings of the manorial court, and of the vestry. When Parliamentary enclosure was proposed in 1791, John Ward, Adam Williamson's agent, came over from Marlborough, posted a notice concerning it on the church door, and attended services on three successive Sundays, so that he could explain what was proposed after services.[3]

The church calendar mirrored the agricultural year, celebrating birth, growth, death, and resurrection.[4] Church festivals were at the heart of the community's affirmation of its identity, and were intended, at least in part, to express its aspiration for neighbourly amity and cooperation. The Holford letters are full of exhortations to neighbourliness.[5] In Avebury, however, the rituals did not always achieve their desired effect. The Holford letters are also full of dismay at the contentiousness of the vicar and his demands for tithe. Puritanism was present in the parish even before the Civil War; afterwards, the personalities of a clergyman, a manorial lord, and his chief tenant, played important roles in fostering divisions, which were literally set in stone when a Presbyterian Meeting House was built in 1707.

Beliefs were usually formally expressed in the religious preambles of wills.[6] Whilst these clauses were frequently formulaic, and likely to express the beliefs of scribes rather than testators, the opinions of the latter sometimes

1   They were John Burchell and John Trusler (recte Truslow).
2   WSHC D1/61/29/8. See also King, Bryan. 'Avebury: Archaeological Varia', *WAM* 14, 1874, p.231; Nightingale, James. *The Church Plate of the County of Wilts.* 1891, p.134-5.
3   WSHC 184/6. Letter, Richard Hickley to Mrs Williamson, 22nd August 1791.
4   Underdown, David. *Revel, Riot, and Rebellion: Popular Politics and Culture in England, 1603-1660.* Clarendon Press, 1985, p.14.
5   WSHC 184/1.
6   Spufford, Margaret. *Contrasting communities: English Villagers in the Sixteenth and Seventeenth Centuries.* Cambridge University Press, 1974, p.334.

come through in strongly expressed more individualistic declarations. John Shuter (1588/9), for example, had 'a sure and a faithfull hope of a ioyfull resurrection thorough the merits of my onlie savyoure and Redeemer Jesus Criste'.[1] Richard Trewman (1616) had 'full assurance of my saluation by the onley miritte & passion of my alone saviour Christ Jesus'.[2] Bridget Dyer (1625) was assured by her faith 'that for his Son Jesus Christes sake my syns ar forgiven & my soule saved in the day of the Lord'.[3]

The possession of bibles offers another possible indication of intensity of belief, although they may also reflect social status. Those mentioned in Avebury probate records have already been discussed.[4] It is evident from probate records that ownership of bibles was increasing in early seventeenth century Wiltshire.[5] Bequests to the church, however, were declining. In 1563, Andrew Mortimer gave 8d each to his parish church, and to Salisbury Cathedral.[6] His goods were valued at only just over £30. Four years later, Joan Truslow left 6s 8d to Avebury church, 12d to the 'mother church' at Salisbury, 2s to the church at Winterbourne Monkton, and 'one bushell of malte' each to the parish churches of Yatesbury, Berwick Bassett, and East Kennett. She also established an annuity of 2s per annum for 'the poore folke of the almes howse in Marleborough for ever'.[7] Truslow was a wealthy testator, but the Cathedral, the parish church, and the Avebury poor continued to attract bequests such as these until the Civil War. There were too many to give a full list here. In 1603/4, Thomas Andrews left 5s for 'my parishe', and 4s for 'the viccar'.[8] In 1632, Richard Smith bequeathed 20s for the 'reparacons of my parish church of Avebury'. He gave another 20s for the parish poor.[9] John Goldsmith in 1639/40 extended his charity to St Pauls Cathedral (10s) and to the church in what was probably his home parish of Berwick Bassett (£1) as well as remembering both the church and the poor of Avebury.[10] The latter received £5, which was 'to be putt forth att interest to be given to eight of the poorest

---

1 TNA PROB 11/124/472.
2 WSHC P3/T/50.
3 WSHC P3/D/76.
4 See above, p.379-80.
5 Ingram, Martin. *Church Courts, Sex, and marriage in England 1570-1640*. Cambridge University Press, 1990, p.115. Ingram studied the probate records of Keevil.
6 WSHC P1/Reg/76B.
7 TNA PROB 11/51/51.
8 TNA PROB 11/103/328.
9 TNA PROB 11/163/542.
10 WSHC P1/G/142.

people yearelie on St Thomas day twelve pence a peece the five poundes to remaine as a stocke for ever'. William Dunch, the lord of Avebury manor, gave rather more, as befitted his status. In 1630, he bequeathed £10 to Avebury church, and £10 to Avebury poor.

After the Civil War, only two such charitable bequests were made before the end of the century. Christopher Spencer (1652)[1] and John Phelps (1662)[2] both gave £1 to the parish poor. In 1710, John White, the rector, bequeathed 2s 6d each to twenty poor families in Avebury, and to ten poor families in Manningford Bruce (his other incumbency).[3] But there were only five similar bequests in the rest of the eighteenth century. In 1718, Sir Richard Holford left £30 to be invested; the interest was to be used to provide the poor with 'good wholesome beef'.[4] This charity seems to have been lost by 1786.[5] Hannah Smith left five guineas to the poor in 1752.[6] So did her sister in law Elizabeth Smith in 1765; she included the poor of East Kennett in her bequest.[7] In 1779, William Herbert bequeathed £2 to purchase bread for the poor;[8] in 1798 Sir Adam Williamson bequeathed £10 for the same purpose.[9]

Dissent[10] undoubtedly had an impact on charitable bequests. Two Avebury testators remembered the local dissenting cause. John Pope made a loan of £20 in 1711,[11] and Richard Bailey gave an annuity of £2 per annum to support the dissenting minister in 1780.[12] Avebury's dissenters probably benefited from the charity established by Caleb Bailey of Berwick Bassett, which supported dissenting ministers.[13]

The most substantial charitable bequest was made by Lady Holford, whose 1723 legacy of £200 provided the funding to establish Avebury's charity school.[14] It may be that Sir Richard had intended her to make this bequest,

---

1 TNA PROB 11/222/58.
2 WSHC P1/B/416.
3 WSHC P3/W/671.
4 TNA PROB 11/564/122.
5 *Reports from Commissioners [concerning charities]*. HMSO, 1835. Vol.XXI, part II, p.1339.
6 TNA PROB 11/795/275.
7 WSHC 118/88. This will does not seem to have been proved.
8 WSHC P3/H/1431.
9 TNA PROB 11/1315/331.
10 The word 'nonconformist' did not come into use until the late eighteenth century, when Methodists hotly denied that they were dissenters.
11 WSHC P1/5Reg/31.
12 WSHC P3/B/1679.
13 See below, p.XXX
14 WSHC PROB 11/590/281.

since he left her the money to do it. He himself bequeathed £30 to Avebury's poor, to be invested by the minister and churchwardens; he also gave £20 to Sherston poor, and another £20 to Westonbirt poor.[1] Arthur Jones, the half-brother of Sir Richard's grandsons, made a small addition to this bequest when he gave £5 'for the countenancing and encouraging the school master and school' in 1784.[2] Lady Holford, incidentally, also bequeathed £10 to the parish of Bucknell (Oxfordshire) 'for the benefit of the poor of the place where I received my first being'.

The church at Avebury (probably the rectory was meant) was said to be worth £98 5s 2d annually in 1548, when it was in the proprietorship of the College at Fotheringhay (Northamptonshire).[3] In the medieval period, the College had impropriated most of the great tithes; at the Reformation, they were confiscated and sold off to local landowners. They were bought and sold like any other property: for example, in 1713, Charles Tucker and Thomas Fowle paid £300 for the tithes of West Kennett.[4] Their ownership was sometimes disputed; in 1585, John Truslow sued two of his tenants when they refused to pay impropriated tithes, arguing that they were due to the vicar.[5] Similarly, in 1670, Robert Baynton sued John Truslow and others for the tithes he claimed.[6] And in the late 1680s, Thomas Pontin was sued by John Griffin because he had paid his hay tithes to the vicar, John White, rather than to Griffin, the lay impropriator.[7] The verdicts in these cases are not known. However, it appears that only the great tithes of a few smallholdings were retained by the vicar, who was also able to claim the small tithes.[8] He claimed a pension of £4 from the rectorial tithes, which was confirmed in 1572, and had been increased to £12 by 1682.[9] Incidentally, the Rectory lands also paid 40s per annum to the vicar of Winterbourne Monkton.

When John Forsyth, the vicar, was plundered by Royalist soldiers in 1643, his tithe and Easter books were lost, so that he had no written record

1 TNA PROB 11/564/122.
2 TNA PROB11/1181/174.
3 Jope, E.M. 'The Saxon and Medieval Pottery from Alexander Keiller's Excavations at Avebury', *WAM*, 92, 1999, p.64.
4 WSHC 1366/5.
5 WANHS Wiltshire Genealogy v.A-A, p.84.
6 WANHS Wiltshire Genealogy, v.A-A, p.127.
7 TNA E134/3Jas2/East17; E134/2and3Jas2/Hil2.
8 Hobbs, Steven, ed. *Wiltshire glebe terriers 1588-1827*. Wiltshire Record Society 56. 2003, p.17-18.
9 TNA LR2/191, f.141;. E178/2406; *VCH Wilts.*, vol.12, p.102; Hobbs, op cit, p.17.

of his own dues. He had earlier brought a case against William Dunch in the Court of Arches concerning his Beckhampton tithes, but we have no details of the outcome.[1] In his Chancery bill against his debtors, he stated that the vicarage was worth £40 per annum.[2] Against that, when Forsyth applied for an augmentation to his benefice in the 1630s, he claimed that it was worth no more than £20 per annum.[3] The truth was probably somewhere in between, although in 1535 it had been valued at a mere £9 0s 8d by the surveyors of the *Valor Ecclesiasticus*. We learn from John White's presentment of the dissenting minister in 1698 that Easter offerings were due to the vicar.[4] In 1700, it was stated that the custom of the parish was to pay an Easter offering of 2d per person, plus a tithe of 1d for every garden.[5] Vicars also claimed tithe on two 'ell ridges' of land next to the church – a claim which led to considerable dispute between manorial lords and vicars, as we will see. Some vicars let out their tithes, so that they did not have the bother of collecting them; in 1711, John Rose, when his landlord was discussing John White's various claims to tithe, pointed out that he had once rented White's tithes.[6]

In 1707, Cornelius Yeate, the Archdeacon of Wiltshire, examined Richard Smith (the rector's brother in law) and James Pope as to the value of the vicarage; they certified that it was worth £48 at the most, and that it would probably not be let for that amount (although it had not been let in their memory).[7] Shortly after, the vicarage was valued at £50.[8] It was described as a 'poore feeble vicaridge' by John Brinsden, a neighbouring incumbent (and perhaps curate),[9] when he was defending the vicar's claim to tithe on the two 'ell ridges'. He probably exaggerated its poverty. Vicars found ways of augmenting their income: John White, for example, owned his own small estate, as well as being the pluralist incumbent of Manningford Bruce. In the late eighteenth century the Mayos were a dynasty of schoolmasters, and managed to increase their income by annexing the neighbouring parish of Winterbourne Monkton.

Avebury was merely a perpetual vicarage; its great tithes had been appropriated, and the living was not particularly attractive to ambitious clergy.

1   TNA E134/9and10Chas1/Hil1. Evidence of Richard Long.
2   TNA C2/Chas1/A9/39.
3   WANHS mss 665, f.204.
4   WSHC D1/54/14.
5   TNA C10/534/43; WSHC 1569/5.
6   WSHC 184/8.
7   WSHC D1/3/5/1.
8   WSHC D1/5/5/3.
9   WSHC 184/1, pt.2. Sir Richard Holford to John Brinsden, 22nd November 1711.

The Rectory had been granted to Cirencester Abbey in 1139.[1] In 1535, its lands were let to Thomas Truslow, for a rent of £41 per annum; the vicar of Avebury paid 6s to take the view of frankpledge.[2] The manor of Avebury, however, had been owned by the Priory of Avebury (and subsequently by Fotheringhay College),[3] a situation which led to much dispute over tithes between the two ecclesiastical institutions. There was also a free chapel at Beckhampton, which had its own tithes, and was dissolved c.1549. In the 1535 *Valor Ecclesiasticus*, when the priest was John Person, it was valued at £4 18s per annum (probably under-valued), although the priest had to pay 8s to Malmesbury Abbey, and 2s to the vicar of Avebury. It was presumably dissolved because it was regarded as a chantry, that is, its purpose was to pray for the dead in purgatory. Its estate provided a minor source of income for John Warner, the last priest, who was Regius Professor of Medicine at Oxford, and who probably never visited. At the dissolution, he was granted the estate. In practice it had probably served as a chapel of ease for the inhabitants of Beckhampton, who henceforth had to walk to Avebury to attend church. In the seventeenth century the inhabitants of Stanmore were said to still bury their dead in the graveyard of the ruined chapel[4].

The Reformation was an important event in Avebury history. The effect of the dissolution on landholding,[5] and on tithes,[6] has already been discussed. Edward VI's commissioners seized a chalice, a small quantity of plate, and three bells (or perhaps four), in 1553.[7] We have already noted that the rood loft was preserved from destruction by being hidden under lathe and plaster. The fact that it was not discovered by the authorities during Elizabeth's reign argues for the strength of support for the old order during the Reformation: many people must have known where it was. Support for the old religion was not immediately diminished by protestant preaching: Aveburians heard no sermons in 1553.[8] The altar was replaced by a 'communion table', although that was so substantial a fixture by 1621 that the vicar, John Peart, wished to be buried under it.[9]

1   *VCH Wilts.*, vol.12, p.100.
2   *Valor Ecclesiasticus*, vol.2. 1814, p.466.
3   *VCH Wilts.*, vol.3, p.392.
4   *VCH Wilts.*, vol.12, p.102.
5   See above, p.209-10.
6   See above, p.225-6.
7   Carrington, F.A. 'Church goods', *WAM*, 1, 1854, p.93; Walcott, Mackenzie E.C. 'Inventories of church goods and chantries of Wilts', *WAM*, 12, 1870, p.366.
8   *VCH Wilts.*, vol.3, p.30.
9   WSHC P3/P/101.

After the Reformation, the Crown became the patron of the living, although John and Joan Truslow made the presentation in 1561. The late sixteenth and early seventeenth century clergy are mostly mere names; we know little about them.[1] Richard Porte, who held a Cambridge Master's degree, and an Oxford B.D., was instituted at Avebury in 1530; he probably resigned when he became rector of Ashton Keynes, where he served from 1543 until 1557.[2] Robert Stevenson, vicar in 1545,[3] was deprived in 1554,[4] probably for his marriage; he was instituted as rector of Wotton Rivers the following year.[5] Edwardian clergy who married were frequently deprived under Queen Mary, but allowed to continue their ministrations elsewhere. Stevenson's successor at Avebury, Thomas Cockes, who had previously served as vicar of Wilcot, died in 1557, and was succeeded by William Wotton, who had been a curate at Stanton St Bernard. However, we hear no more about him. Instead, we read that Robert Stevenson, who had supposedly been deprived under Mary, resigned as vicar in 1561. It is probable that, on the accession of Elizabeth, his deprivation was overturned.

The next two vicars, Anthony Webb, who was instituted in 1561, and John Barker, instituted in 1584,[6] are mere names. Webb witnessed the wills of Andrew Mortimer in 1563,[7] and of Joan Truslow in 1567/8,[8] but otherwise no record of him can be found. Barker had probably graduated from Christ Church, Oxford, as a Master of Arts in 1575.[9]

We know rather more about John Peart. He was presented in 1587, when he was aged c.29,[10] and his attendance at several visitations was recorded.[11]

1 They are listed by the Clergy of the Church of England Database https://theclergydatabase.org.uk, where details of sources are given.
2 His tenure predates the Clergy database, but his name is identified in the *Valor Ecclesiasticus*, vol.2. 1814, p.133. See also *Alumni Oxoniensis* and *Alumni Cantabrigienses*.
3 He paid 8s towards the 'benevolence' of that year; cf. Ramsay, G.D., ed. *Two sixteenth century taxation lists, 1545 and 1676*. WANHS Record series 10. 1954, p.23. He made a presentment in the early 1550s; cf. WSHC D1/43/1, f.144.
4 WSHC D1/2/16.
5 WSHC D1/2/16. Over 37 Wiltshire clergy were deprived in 1554; cf. *VCH Wilts.*, vol.3, p.31.
6 For Barker's presentation, see TNA C66/1248, m.42.
7 WSHC P1/Reg/76B.
8 TNA PROB 11/51/51.
9 *Alumni Oxonienses*.
10 TNA C66/1295, m.35. He was said to be aged 40 in 1598; cf. WSHC D1/42/16, f.189r-191v. I owe this reference to Steve Hobbs.
11 Clergy of the Church of England database https://theclergydatabase.org.uk/

He took seriously the responsibility of caring for his parishioners, acting as bondsman when two of them sought marriage licences.[1] He was also a witness in a defamation case in 1598.[2] Probate records reveal his involvement at times of bereavement: he witnessed both of John Shuter's wills (Shuter was blind, so Peart had to read one to him)[3], was named as overseer (or supervisor) in four[4], valued two probate inventories,[5] and acted as bondsman in an administration bond.[6] He also took seriously his need to be informed as a preacher. His name does not appear amongst the alumni of either university, but his 1621 will[7] does tell us that he possessed some interesting books, including works by men such as Martin Luther, Bullenger, Peter Martyr, and Erasmus. He evidently read the theology of the day, even if he had not studied at Oxbridge. His copy of Martyr's *Common places* was bequeathed to John Nichols, 'preacher'.[8] A number of his parishioners received his other books, suggesting that there was an appetite for theology amongst parishioners.

Unfortunately, little is known about Peart's family. His executor was Mary Peart, a 'kinswoman', and he bequeathed some livestock to his son in law, Richard Davis. His wife had presumably pre-deceased him, and he only had one daughter. He also had a sister in law, Elizabeth Patrick, but other relatives have not been traced. His probate inventory was valued at just under £48,[9] including books valued at 30s, and a desk, presumably where he prepared his sermons. His 'wearing apparell' was valued at £5, indicating that he was comparatively well dressed. He also possessed 3 'kine', a horse, 'hoggs & stores' (ie.pigs), poultry, bees, a hay rick, wheat, and grain, and probably farmed his glebe himself.

Peart was succeeded as vicar by John Forsyth, a Scot, who was presented by the Crown, and instituted on 3rd October 1621, by the Archbishop of

1 William Bath in 1619, and Henry Player and Margaret Hayward in 1619/20; cf. Nevill, Edmund, ed. 'Marriage licences of Salisbury', *Genealogist*, new series 24, 1908, p.95.
2 WSHC D1/42/16, f.189r-191v. I owe this reference to Steve Hobbs.
3 TNA PROB11/124/472 & PROB11/78/167. For the reading of the will, see TNA C21/S32/14. The two wills are discussed above, p.136-8.
4 The wills of Thomas Pope, WSHC P3/1Reg/95; William Griffin, TNA PROB11/108/10; Richard Trewman, WSHC P3/T/50; Elizabeth Pope, WSHC P3/P/78.
5 The inventories of Richard Trewman and Elizabeth Pope; see previous note.
6 For Alice, widow of Andrew Mills; WSHC P3/M/60.
7 P3/P/101;
8 Perhaps the rector of Long Ashton.
9 The appraisers made an error in the addition.

Canterbury (during a vacancy in the Salisbury see).[1] It seems likely that he was also rector of Sedgehill Chapel, in Berwick St. Leonard, to which he was instituted 26th July 1622. He witnessed the will of Frysy Baldveen, widow, in 1630/31.[2] He married Elizabeth Nicholas, the sister of a judge; she brought him an estate valued at £20 per annum, in addition to his vicarage. He also derived an income from money-lending; Chancery records reveal that in the mid-1640s, following the turmoil of the Civil War, he sued a number of debtors for payment.[3] The couple had three children: Thomas, Nicholas and Robert, as well as a step son, Peter Brewer (his wife had been previously married).[4] Peter was apprenticed to Marmaduke Burde, an apothecary in Devizes, in 1632. Forsyth was still in Avebury in 1643, when Devizes was garrisoned for the King. The vicar was a Parliamentary supporter, whose eldest son was a soldier in the Parliamentary army. Consequently, he and his family suffered severely at the hands of the cavaliers. His house was plundered, he lost goods valued at over £400, and he spent ten months imprisoned at Oxford before being exchanged for a royalist supporter.[5] His wife died as a result of the rough handling she received from the soldiers, thus depriving her husband of the income from her estate (which she held for life only). It may well be that he too died soon after he returned from prison.

There is no further evidence for a vicar in Avebury until Nathaniel Power was instituted on 8th September 1660 – one of the earliest known post-restoration institutions[6]. His son Nicholas's memorial in the Chancel records his death on 27th April 1660, and describes Nathaniel as 'minister of Avebury'.[7] One wonders if the stone mason made this inscription before Nathaniel was instituted. If so, that suggests he was one of those ministers installed under the Interregnum regime who sought ordination and institution as soon as he could after the Restoration. The parish was probably much influenced by Sir

1   WANHS mss 665, f.203.
2   WHSC P1/B/230.
3   TNA C2/Chas1/A9/39.
4   Kite, Edward. 'Judge Nicholas, his parentage and birthplace', *Wiltshire Notes & Queries*, 3, 1899, p.510. She also had a daughter by her previous husband named Mary, but it is not clear whether she was alive when she re-married
5   TNA C2/Chas1/A9/39. See also Raymond, Stuart A. 'A Plundered Minister', *Wiltshire Recorder: the Annual Newsletter of the Wiltshire Record Society*, 23, 2024, 3-4.
6   According to the Clergy of the Church of England database https://theclergydatabase.org.uk/, it is recorded in a return to the First Fruits office, rather than in the Bishop's register.
7   Hearne, Thomas, ed. *Remarks and Collections of Thomas Hearne*, vol.10, ed. H.E.Salter. Oxford Historical Society, 67. 1915, p.187.

Edward Bayntun, a prominent Presbyterian, who had commanded Wiltshire's Parliamentary forces at the beginning of the Civil War, and who lived in Avebury after his houses at Bromham and Bremhill had been destroyed by Royalist forces.[1] It may be that Presbyterianism took root in the parish during this period.

Nicholas was Nathaniel Power's only son by his first wife. By 1663 he was a widower, and married again. His second wife was Mary Aland of Langley Burrell.[2] Nathaniel's name, like that of John Peart, appears in his parishioners' probate records. In 1661 he took the oath of Margaret Hayward as executor of her husband's estate.[3] He valued the estate of Richard Davis,[4] and witnessed Richard Bray's will.[5] His own 1670 inventory reveals ownership of books valued at £3 – double the value of John Peart's books, but unfortunately not identified. Like Peart, he also had livestock and arable crops: four pigs, two cows, a horse, ricks of peas and hay, and three quarters of wheat, as well as an acre of wheat still in the ground. He too evidently farmed his glebe. The inventory also includes evidence of another source of income: his 'lammas tithe' from Mr Robert Baynton was worth £6. When Nathaniel died, he left no will, and his widow Mary administered his estate. His son, Nathaniel, baptised 6th April 1668, became an orphan when he was barely two years old.

John White was probably the son of Edward White of Beaminster, Dorset, and was born c.1644.[6] If the identification is correct, he was educated at Netherbury School in Dorset, and matriculated at Cambridge in 1668. He took his bachelor's degree in 1668/9, and his master's in 1674. He was instituted as vicar of Avebury on 10th January 1670/71. He was to serve his benefice for over forty years, until his death in October 1712. He was licenced to preach throughout the diocese in 1677; from 1679, as has been seen, he also held Manningford Bruce in plurality. In addition to the rectorial income, he also had a private estate. In 1677, Robert Baynton granted him a copyhold

---

1 www.historyofparliamentonline.org/volume/1604-1629/member/bayntun-sir-edward-1593-1657
2 Nevill, Edmund, ed. 'Marriage licences of Salisbury', *Genealogist* NS 31, 1915, p.267. Assuming, that is, that the marriage licence was used.
3 WSHC P3/H/339.
4 WSHC P3/D/130.
5 WSHC P3/B/573.
6 *ACAD: A Cambridge Alumni Database* https://venn.lib.cam.ac.uk. His memorial inscription gives his age as 70, implying he was born in 1642; cf. Phillipps, Thomas. *Monumental inscriptions of Wiltshire,* ed. Peter Sherlock. Wiltshire Record Society, 53. 2000, p.209.

messuage in the manor of Avebury Trusloe.[1] This became the subject of a dispute with a new owner, Peter Griffin (a leading dissenter), in 1682, but White succeeded in maintaining his right to the copyhold, which included a close called Juggins, in Westbrook.[2] In 1704, White purchased a portion of the manor of Avebury Trusloe, which presumably included his copyhold, from John Griffin.[3] In 1682, his father in law arranged for him to take over as mortgagee of a copyhold yardland called Chestermans, plus other property called Higdens. The mortgage may have been part of his wife's dowry, although that is not stated in the indenture; it was worth £117.[4] He was also entitled to a pension of £10 per annum from other lands in Westbrook.[5] In 1707 he invested £300 to obtain an annuity of £31 per annum from lands in Barbor's Court, Fostbury, and Higdens, in West Kennett, on mortgage.[6] Two years later, however, the mortgage was paid off.[7] His estate was sufficient to enable him to leave £200 to all his children except William, who inherited his freehold estate. When he died the value of his personal estate was over £530. He had two cows, two yearlings, and a quantity of un-threshed wheat in his barn, but the probability is that, unlike his predecessors, he let most of his glebe. His inventory records 'in money due to the deceased', £400. He also had £50 'in desperate debts, if recoverable'.[8] He evidently lent money to many people; for example, Richard Cue owed him £5 when he died in 1678.[9] In the early nineteenth century the estate still in the hands of his heirs was sufficiently large to be the subject of a law suit between the descendants of his two daughters[10].

John White married Mary, the daughter of Richard Smith of Beckhampton; his father in law presented him to the rectory of Manningford

1 TNA C5/577/76.
2 WANHS Genealogy v.A-A, f.132.
3 According to *VCH Wilts.*, vol.12., p.93. But it may be that White actually purchased the property from Sir Richard Holford, who purchased Griffin's estate (including the property rented by White) in 1703; cf.184/4/1.
4 WSHC 435/24/1/4.
5 WANHS Genealogy v.A-A, f.132.
6 WSHC 568/4. Mortgage by lease & release, 2nd/3rd December 1707, Richard Grinfeild & Thomas Grinfeild to John White.
7 WSHC 568/4. Lease for a year, Thomas Grinfeild & John White to Richard Grinfeild, 23rd December 1709.
8 WSHC P3/W/671.
9 TNA C6/98/30.
10 WSHC 4270/1. These papers give details of the family's pedigree noted below, although these have been checked where possible against Avebury parish register.

Bruce in 1679,[1] and signed the Avebury terrier of 1682 as churchwarden.[2] In 1677, soon after his marriage – and before he became vicar - he was granted a copyhold tenement in the manor of Avebury Trusloe. One wonders if that was also part of Mary's dowry.[3] His eldest son, John, was baptised 14th August 1675. When he was 15 he was sent to Oxford, where he matriculated at Queens College in April 1691, and gained his B.A. from Merton College in February 1694/5. Evidently he was destined for the church, but he was buried in his college chapel on 20th May, 1696[4].

There were four other sons: Richard, Thomas, William, and Charles, whose baptisms have not been traced. Richard followed his brother to the grave at the age of 19 in 1697.[5] His death occasioned Sir Richard Holford to write to the vicar: 'I think it becomes me as a neighbour & a Christian to condole with you upon the death of your son' (although the remainder of his letter was concerned with the Chancery case between the two men).[6] Thomas had two boys by the time of his father's death in 1712 – Thomas and John – both of whom died childless. William acted as his father's executor, and inherited his property. By 1736 he was living at Easton.[7] He sold his father's freehold in Avebury Trusloe to Robert Rose, who sold it again in 1755[8]. But like his nephews he remained childless. Charles is not mentioned in his father's will, so probably pre-deceased him. In 1707 he was apprenticed to a London apothecary.[9]

White also had three daughters: Ann, Elizabeth, and Frances. They were all unmarried at their father's death, but legacies of £200 each enabled two of them to marry soon afterwards: Ann married her first cousin, James White of Rowde, on 16th July 1713; Elizabeth married John Griffin on 6th January 1713/14.

1 VCH Wilts., 10, 1975, p.117; Clergy of the Church of England database www.theclergydatabase.org.uk.
2 Hobbs, Steven, ed. *Wiltshire glebe terriers 1588-1827*. Wiltshire Record Society 56. 2003, p.18. Smith is frequently referred to by White as 'Father Smith' in White's letters; cf. WSHC 184/1. See also 184/1, pt.2. Necessary Remarks on the Dispute depending on tithes.
3 TNA C5/577/76.
4 *Alumni Oxonienses*.
5 Phillipps, Thomas, Sir. *Monumental Inscriptions of Wiltshire*, ed. Peter Sherlock. Wiltshire Record Society, 53. 2000, p.209.
6 WSHC 184/1, pt.2. Letter, Sir Richard Holford to John White, 29th April 1697.
7 WSHC 488/1. Lease and release, 20/21 August 1736.
8 *VCH Wilts.*, vol.12., p.93.
9 Webb, Cliff. *London Livery Company Apprenticeship registers, v.42: Society of Apothecaries, 1670-1800, with Masons Company, 1619-1639*. Society of Genealogists Enterprises, 2006, p.87.

White's ministry, despite its length, was not a happy one. He was one of those 'underpaid and over-taxed parochial clergy, who felt isolated and in need of protection against competition from dissenters',[1] and was upset when the Toleration Act 1689 legalised dissenting worship. We have already seen that White regarded William Skeat, the farmer of Avebury Great Farm, as his chief enemy. One of the first things Sir Richard Holford did when he purchased the manor of Avebury was to write to the vicar, bemoaning 'the heats increased & blowne into a flame, & a mutuall inclination to neighborly squabbles'. Holford's letter did not achieve his end; in 1697, White set out his bill of complaint against nine parishioners who had failed to pay what he thought were his dues.[2] Several of the defendants were dissenters. Skeat's comment was that, 'if hee winn this sute, hee will grow so corrageous that hee will almost think himselfe the next man unto a king, that unless it bee as it were in prison & slavery none can live by him'.[3] Holford's over-bearing manner probably did not help; his demand for deference after the parishioners won the 1711 suit against the vicar elicited White's remark that his host 'gave him a good dinner, but run the spitt into his gutts'.[4] The vicar was not prepared to be subservient to the manorial lord.

Despite the negative attitude of Holford and his neighbours, White did have his supporters; when, in 1711, Holford launched another suit against White, John Brinsden, the vicar of Winterbourne Monkton, wrote what can only be described as a searing attack on Holford's behaviour.[5] Holford vigorously defended his actions, arguing that White's demands might result in the payment of '£40 per annum more than rightfully due'.[6] In the correspondence which followed he obliquely reminded Brinsden of his youthful indiscretion in fathering a bastard child.[7]

It may be suspected that Holford supported the Whig cause, although there is no direct evidence. He told White that Bishop Burnet had several times mentioned 'his dislike as well of the rude & unmannerly behaviour towards you, as of your haughty & passionate behaviour towards them, & of

1 Jones, J.R. *Country and court: England 1658-1714.* Edward Arnold, 1978. p.322.
2 WSHC 1569/5.
3 WSHC 184/1, pt.1. Letter, William Skeat to Sir Richard Holford, 19th February 1699/1700.
4 WSHC 184/8.
5 WSHC 184/1, pt.1. Letter, John Brinsden to Sir Richard Holford, 13th November 1711; 1 January 1711/12.
6 WSHC 184/1, pt.2. Letter, Sir Richard Holford to John Brinsden, 24th January 1711/12.
7 WSHC 184/1, pt.2. Letter, Sir Richard Holford to John Brinsden, 21st May 1712.

your bad example'.[1] Part of the problem was Skeat's leading role in Avebury's dissenting cause. Holford opposed dissent. Nevertheless, he did not see it as his role to do much about it (although he did reject a Quaker who wished to succeed Skeat as tenant). Nor did he see his support for the Church of England to be contradicted by his determination not to pay any more tithe to the vicar than he rightfully owed. Tithe, to Holford, was an important issue.[2] Most of Avebury's post-Reformation tithes, as already noted, were in the possession of laymen, but White was still entitled to tithe on two 'ell ridges' of land beside the church. It had been the subject of a modus of £3 since time immemorial, although records had been lost when the Civil War vicar, Forsyth, was plundered in 1643. White also claimed an additional £1 for the small tithes on a range of goods such as the produce of orchards and gardens, the agistment of cattle, pigeons, eggs, calves, milk, etc.[3] Holford had consulted White concerning tithes before buying the manor, and been assured that the vicar was content with what was then the current arrangement.[4] White, however, appeared to change his mind, and seemed to be demanding far more than he was currently receiving, but refused to specify what he was demanding. In February 1689, Skeat thought that 'Mr White will take his tith in cind. Of what to pay him I can't tell'.[5] A few years later, in 1696, White expressed his intention 'to take the tithes that are due to me upon your farm in kind', because he thought 'Skeate falsifyes his word & wil not perform any bargain that he makes with me'.[6]

The modus may or may not have reflected the true value of the tithes if taken in kind. But landowners wished for certainty about such matters, and Holford determined to obtain it. Ignoring the fact that the vicar was entitled to take tithes in kind, and taking into account the fact that he was also thought to be treating other parishioners unreasonably, Holford demanded that White should place his demands in writing. 'Hee had often & in a very disdainefull & haughty manner refused to let mee know his dues'.[7] White's father in law,

1 WSHC 184/1, pt.2. Letter, Sir Richard Holford to John White, 11th January 1695/6.
2 For another account of the Avebury tithe dispute, see Spaeth, op cit, p.134-41.
3 WSHC 184/1, pt.2. Holford's copy of White's 'account of tithes', written on letter, Humfry Wall to Sir Richard Holford, 5th June 1698.
4 TNA C5/166/23.
5 WSHC 184/1, pt.1. Letter, William Skeat to Sir Richard Holford, 23rd February 1698/9.
6 WSHC 184/1, pt.1. Letter, John White to Sir Richard Holford, 4th April 1696.
7 WSHC 184/1, pt.2. Letter, Sir Richard Holford to Cornelius Yeate, 8th March 1697/8.

Richard Smith,[1] and Cornelius Yeate, the Archdeacon, both attempted to arbitrate. Yeate promised Holford that if White refused 'to give a full answer to your reasonable demands', he would 'represent [White's] obstinacy to my Lord Bishop of Sarum'.[2] Eventually, however, Holford felt it necessary to sue White in the Court of Chancery.[3] Holford, as a Master of the Court, was well-placed to sue, and forced White to a settlement.

At the same time, a number of others were also in dispute with White. William Smith of Calne advised Holford that, after several meetings, and despite John Brinsden's support for White, the disputants had finally come to an agreement, whereby they 'made an article with the contents of each man's dues, what itt is, & what to pay & when, and hath covenanted for all the ell ridges at Backhampton at the old rate dureing Mr White's continuance of being vicar of Avebury, & further wee have caused him to seal unto us a bond of £100 to perform as above'.[4] Both parties were to pay their own costs. Smith advised Holford that White 'pretendeth much reformation touching peace'.

When Holford's suit was settled, White had to pay costs of £40 – equivalent to a year's income from his vicarage.[5] Holford attempted to sugar the pill by giving White's children £16 13s 3d between them, as a demonstration 'of my friendship', and in an attempt to revive a neighbourly relationship.[6] However, White's behaviour, at least in Holford's view, did not, improve. Despite the order for costs, Holford complained that the amount White paid to him amounted to 'not halfe what I might fairely expect'.[7] And in 1708 he did take his tithes in kind.[8] Holford was 'somewhat allarmed' at the prospect that he would continue to do so: he wanted certainty.[9] John Brinsden, who Holford subsequently asked to arbitrate, scornfully answered this point by observing that it was 'no more than is done at some time or other in most

1 WSHC 184/4, pt.2. See, for example, the opinion' he gave on 27th June 1696.
2 That is, Bishop Burnet. WSHC 184/1, pt.2. Letter, Cornelius Yeate to Sir Richard Holford, 28th February 1699/1700.
3 TNA C5/166/23; WSHC 184/1 &184/4, pt.1
4 WSHC 184/1, pt.1. Letters, William Smith to Sir Richard Holford, 28th January 1700/1 & 11th February 1700/01.
5 WSHC 184/1, pt.2. Letter, Stayner Holford to Peter Holford, 2nd December 1756.
6 WSHC 184/4, pt.2. Memorandum between Sir Richard Holford and John White, 2nd October 1701.
7 WSHC 184/1, pt.2. Letter, Sir Richard Holford to John White, 22nd July 1708.
8 WSHC 184/1, pt.2. Letter, Sir Richard Holford to John White, 30th October 1708.
9 WSHC 184/1, pt.2. Letter, Sir Richard Holford to John Brinsden, 22nd November 1711.

parishes in the Kingdom by clergy and impropriators, and is done in the parish of Avebury by the impropriators, and yet no man thereby alarmed'.[1]

By 1711, Holford was contemplating another Chancery suit against White, demanding again that the vicar spell out his demands. He went to deliver a *sub pena* (a summons to answer in Court) personally to White, but withdrew it when White, 'upon sight thereof hee made most grevious complaints that by indisposition and prayed for God sake & for Christ's sake that I would then forbeare to serve him with it. Whereupon in charitable compassion, I told him I [Holford] would then forbeare'. Holford then invited John Brinsden, the vicar of neighbouring Winterbourne Monkton to arbitrate. But he insisted that White must provide an answer to his complaints, and compile a true terrier.[2]

In fact, two terriers had been made by White, one in 1682, soon after he became vicar,[3] another in 1705, which has disappeared.[4] He had refused to disclose the existence of the latter to Holford. It is not clear whether Holford checked for terriers in the Diocesan registry; he thought that they ought to be kept in the parish chest for ease of access.[5] The 1682 terrier replaced a terrier (now lost) made during the episcopate of Seth Ward (1662-7)[6]. After the initial Chancery case, William Smith thought that 'Mr White is contented to make a new terrier betwixt this & Easter,[7] according to the right coustom of the place, with the approbation of the majoryty of the parish, & will give bond soe to doe, by entering the contents in an article, but Mr Brunson he entered into this cavitt to know who should be the absolute judge, in sort of a battering way, to which I gave this answer, that when the new terrier was made, that if in case that Mr White should insist upon any thing that the majoryty should oppose, that then & in that case, for expedition & confirmation of the same,

1   WSHC 184/1, pt.2. Letter, John Brinsden to Sir Richard Holford, 1st January 1711/12.
2   WSHC 184/1, pt.2. Letter, Sir Richard Holford to John Brinsden, 1st November 1711.
3   Hobbs, op cit, p.17-18.
4   WSHC 184/1, pt.2. Letter, John Brinsden to Sir Richard Holford 13th November 1711.
5   WSHC 184/1, pt.2. Sir Richard Holford to John Brinsden, 21st May 1712.
6   WSHC 148/ pt.2. John Brinsden to Sir Richard Holford, 13th November, 1711. This terrier does not appear in Hobbs, *Wiltshire Glebe Terriers 1588-1827*. Wiltshire Record Society 56. 2003.
7   No new terrier was ever made, although Stayner Holford thought one might have been made in 1705; cf.184/2, 'More Necessary Remarks'. If it was made, it was never deposited in the Bishops' Registry; cf. Hobbs, Steven, ed. *Wiltshire glebe terriers*.

Mr White should goe before a magistrate, if to goe as hee would say, & there to attest the same upon oath, soe that if wee cannot make it all goe well as wee would, wee would make it as well as wee can'.[1] Smith's hope was not to be realised; a new terrier was never made, as far as can be traced.

When White purchased John Griffin's estate in 1704 he threatened two poor cottagers with eviction from their houses unless they took out leases and paid entry fines of £10 each. Christopher Page and John Jerome wrote to Sir Richard Holford, asking for his assistance against White's demands.[2]

Disputes between clergy and parishioners were common in our period; Spaeth has calculated that they affected two in three parishes during White's lifetime.[3] Some were relatively minor incidents in the life of the parish; in others the incumbent quarrelled repeatedly with his congregation. White was one of the most litigious clergymen in Wiltshire;[4] he seems to have had a quarrelsome and litigious nature, which poisoned religious life in his parish, damaged his own authority, and threatened the authority of the church.

White's demands for tithes did not encourage good relationships with his parishioners. Nor did his lax performance of his duties, or his hatred of dissent. His name is almost totally absent from the probate records of his parishioners. He witnessed the administration bond of Jane Pope, as administrator of her husband James Pope's estate, in 1680. And he witnessed Richard Pope's will five years later. That is all. It seems probable that the vicar's dislike of his parishioners meant that the dissenting cause in Avebury thrived. One wonders whether his supposedly sour disposition had anything to do with the death of two or three of his sons in their early manhood.

On White's death in 1712, Holford thought that John Brinsden, who had been doing White's 'duty', might succeed him.[5] In the event, White's incumbency was followed by the Mayo dynasty, four members of which served the parish in succession until 1823. The Mayos were a local family, descended from John (I) Mayo of Devizes.[6] Other descendants continued to reside in

---

1 WSHC 184/1, pt.1. Letter, William Smith to Sir Richard Holford, 28th January 1700/01.
2 WSHC 184/1, pt.1 Letter, 18th April 1707.
3 Spaeth, Donald A. *The Church in an Age of Danger: Parsons and Parishioners, 1660-1740*. Cambridge University Press, 2000, p.22, 133 & 141.
4 Spaeth, op cit, p.144.
5 WSHC 184/1, pt.2. John Brinsden to Sir Richard Holford, 21st May 1712.
6 Except where otherwise stated, the following information about the Mayo family is taken from Mayo, Charles Herbert. *A genealogical account of the Mayo and Elton families of the counties of Wilts and Hereford*. Chiswick Press, 1882.

Devizes; John and James Mayo, linen drapers, were insured for £3000 in 1779.[1] John (I)'s eldest son, John (II), was baptised in 1673, and studied at Hart Hall, Oxford. He was ordained deacon in 1704, and priest in 1705, serving curacies at All Cannings and Blackland, before being instituted as vicar of Avebury in 1712. Despite being vicar of Avebury, he was still serving as a curate elsewhere in the mid-1730s, and receiving £16 per annum for doing so.[2] He also had an income of about £100 per annum from an apothecary's shop, presumably in Calne.[3] His wife, Mary Hayward of Calne, was the daughter of a medical man, Dr. William Hayward,[4] and may have inherited the shop from her father. Their four children, John (III), James, Elizabeth, and Benjamin, were all baptised in Calne, and John (II)'s will indicates that he had a house there, which he left to his second son, James. He also had property at 'Colstone' (presumably Calstone Wellington) which was the inheritance of his eldest son John. In 1727/8 he took a three-life lease of several acres at Blackland from George Duckett.[5]

John (II) Mayo's residence in Calne did not escape the Bishop's notice. In c.1736, his parishioners petitioned the bishop,[6] complaining that his non-residence, and his duties elsewhere on a Sunday, meant that they only had one service on the Sabbath, not the two which his predecessors had always provided. John Loveday reported in 1729 that they sometimes had no services for a fortnight, especially when Mayo was ill (as he frequently was).[7] Consequently, the petitioners reported that some went to the alehouse, some 'to play', and some to hear the dissenting minister. In addition, the parishioners complained that 'wee often have been put to the expence of time or money in sending after him to baptise or visit the sick, celebrate the Lord's supper, and bury the dead'.

The response of the bishop to this petition can be inferred from the fact that, within a year or two, John (II) had appointed a curate (see below). The bishop had probably insisted that he did so. His son's later observation that he had spent some twenty years of his youth in constant residence at Avebury

1 Haycock, Lorna. *In the newest manner: the economy and society of Devizes, Wiltshire, 1760-1820.* University of Portsmouth Ph.D., 2001, p.341.
2 WSHC D1/47/3.
   WSHC 212B/1274. LEASE, 12TH MARCH 1727/8
3 WSHC D1/47/3.
4 Marsh, op cit, p.214.
5 WSHC 212B/1274. Lease, 12th March 1727/8.
6 WSHC D1/47/3.
7 Hearne, Thomas, ed. *Remarks and Collections of Thomas Hearne,* vol.10, ed. H.E.Salter. Oxford Historical Society, 67. 1915, p.187.

does not quite tally with the parishioners' observations.[1]

John (II) resigned his incumbency in 1747, and died in 1752. Benjamin, his youngest son, was intended for the church. He graduated from Queens College, Oxford, but became an apothecary in Calne, and died unmarried in 1750. The other two sons, however, followed their father into the church. John (II) purchased the presentation of Beechingstoke and presented his eldest son, John (III), to it in 1737.[2] In 1762, he became vicar of Wilcot.[3] The other son succeeded his father in Avebury.

James (I) Mayo was educated at Bentley's School in Calne, where he was able to learn Latin.[4] He took his Oxford B.A. degree in 1738, was ordained deacon in 1739, and priest in 1743. He became his father's curate,[5] succeeded him as vicar in 1747,[6] and became vicar of the united parish of Avebury and Winterbourne Monkton when the two merged in 1767.[7] The merger cost the vicar nearly £100, but presumably increased his revenue.[8] He inherited his father's house in Calne. He also purchased property at Quemerford. In 1756, conscious of the limited resources of his benefice, he sought unsuccessfully to resurrect White's dispute with the Holford family over tithes.[9] His refusal to acknowledge the deference which the Holford's expected from the clergy led to him being described as an 'intolerably troublesome' priest.[10] In the following year, however, he succeeded in augmenting his income by becoming usher of his old school, and teaching Greek, Latin, and English. He became headmaster in the following year[11], and was residing there in 1783. When he said that he had been living in Calne for 'some years past', the phrase perhaps hid the fact

1 Ransome, Mary, ed. *Wiltshire Returns to the Bishop's Visitation Queries 1783*. Wiltshire Record Society 27. 1972, p.29.
2 Hobbs, Steve, ed. *Gleanings from Wiltshire parish registers*. Wiltshire Record Society 63. 2010, p.16.
3 Marsh, A.E.W. *History of the Borough and Town of Calne*. Calne: Robert S. Heath, 1903, p.215. Carlisle, Nicholas. *Concise Description of the Endowed Grammar Schools in England and Wales*. Baldwin, Cradock & Joy, 1818. Vol.2, p.742.
4 Marsh, op cit, p.214. For Latin, see *VCH Wilts.*, vol.17, p.111.
5 WSHC D1/14/11/6.
6 In the 1783 replies to bishop's queries, he claimed to have been instituted in 1746, but as his father only resigned in 1747 he was clearly in error; cf. Ransome, op cit, p.30.
7 During the Interregnum, Winterbourne Monkton had been merged with Berwick Bassett; cf. *VCH Wilts.*, vol. 3, p.43.
8 Ransome, op cit, p.26.
9 WSHC 184/2. Letters between James Mayo & Stayner Holford, August 1756.
10 WSHC 184/2. Peter Holford to Stayner Holford, 11th December, 1756.
11 Marsh, op cit, p.214.

that he had been living there for two or three decades. However, he claimed that he had been 'under an absolute necessity of accepting and of submitting to the laborious employment of school teaching, in order to support his numerous family. His two wives gave him no fewer than nineteen children! Most were baptised in Calne. Mary Blanchard bore ten of them, but died in 1767. He married Ann Rose in 1769, who bore a further nine. In the year that Mary died, he was instituted to the rectory of Ditteridge, where he appointed a curate,[1] whilst retaining Avebury. That would have helped him to support the rapidly increasing number of his children, although he was evidently still worried about the future for them: his 'present income being scarce adequate for the most economical disbursements', he was unable to make provision for them, and begged his bishop 'to look hereafter with a charitable and compassionate eye' on them, 'when it shall please God to remove me'. He died in 'distressed circumstances' in 1789, leaving fifteen children, some very young.[2]

Only one of James's sons followed him into the church: his namesake James. James II graduated from Oxford in 1777, immediately entering deacon's orders, and very briefly served his father as curate (being so described in the banns register) before becoming second master of the Grammar School at Wimborne Minster in the same year. Ten years later he became head master, and held the post until his death. In 1779 he took priest's orders, and was immediately instituted to the rectory of Blackland (where he probably still held his grandfather's lease). He also served two curacies. In 1780 he was licenced as curate at Chalbury (close to Wimborne). In 1787 he became curate at Huish, which is not far from Avebury, and where his cousin, Charles, was rector.

When James (I) Mayo died, it is probable that the care of his younger children devolved upon James II. Consequently, Arthur Jones was asked to use his influence with Lord Ailesbury to secure James's succession to his father's incumbency.[3] That was 'very contrary to my uncle's inclinations', according to Mrs Williamson, presumably because of the pluralism and non-residence that would be involved. Nevertheless the family's financial difficulties persuaded him to do so, and he persuaded Lord Ailesbury to use his influence with the Lord Chancellor to secure the nomination. He hoped that gratitude would compel the new vicar not to show 'the least disposition to call in question the ancient modus'. The £4 modus that Sir Richard Holford had been willing to

1 Ibid, p.88.
2 WSHC 271/3.
3 WSHC 271/3.

pay to John White when he was lord of the manor was still appearing in the bailiff's accounts in the early 1790s.[1]

At the same time as he became Avebury's vicar, James purchased the advowson of Blackland.[2] He never resided at Avebury (and probably not at Blackland either); as we will see, he employed stipendiary curates to undertake his vicarial duties. His affairs were managed by an agent, John Flower, who in 1803 reported that he had collected a total of £141 15s 4d, presumably from tithes, rents of glebe, etc. After various deductions, Mayo received £88 12s 6d.[3] He did not benefit from enclosure in the 1790s, unlike other incumbents; as already noted, most of the great tithes were in the possession of lay impropriators rather than the vicar, and the tithe of two ell ridges which had previously been the subject of dispute were not exchanged for land by the Commissioners: Richard Hickley objected when it was proposed to allocate land to the vicar in order to commute the tithe.[4]

James (II) Mayo married a girl from Wimborne, and was buried at Tarrant Keyneston in 1822. At Avebury (and at both Blackland and Wimborne), he was succeeded by yet another Mayo, his son James III.

As far as we know, for most of the seventeenth century vicars resided. We have already noted, however, that in the eighteenth century, the Mayo family spent much of their time in Calne, riding over each Sunday to 'do duty'. James (I) Mayo's excuse for this was the need for additional income to support his family. He claimed that previous bishops had allowed this 'indulgence', and that they recognised his straitened financial position. His response to Bishop Barrington's visitation queries[5] attempted to make it clear that the parish was not being neglected in consequence of non-residence.

One response of bishops to clergy non-residence was to insist on the appointment of curates. As has been seen, curates (sometimes the sons of the vicar) were occasionally appointed for limited periods. That changed when James (II) Mayo became vicar in 1789; his residence in Wimborne Minster required him to appoint curates who could take full responsibility for the parish.

There is no direct record of curates (the word is used here in its modern sense, rather than the older usage referring to clergy in general) at Avebury

1 WSHC 184/7.
2 'Blackland', in *VCH Wilts.*, 17. www.british-history.ac.uk/vch/wilts/vol17/pp17-27.
3 WSHC 727/3/4.
4 WSHC 184/6. Letter, Richard Hickley to Mrs Williamson, 31st March 1793.
5 Ransome, op cit, p.26-30.

before the Mayo dynasty, although John Nicholls, clerk, who witnessed George Mortimer's will in 1613,[1] and was described as a preacher in John Peart's 1621 will,[2] may have been one. Some of the clergy who took affidavits for burial in woollen during John White's incumbency (see below) probably also served as curates. The name of John Brinsden, vicar of Winterbourne Monkton, is frequently mentioned in our records. His living was very poor (it was subsequently merged with Avebury), and it is quite likely that White employed him as curate. The Mayo dynasty employed several curates. John Collinson was curate in 1739, when he signed the order in the vestry book dismissing one schoolmaster and appointing another.[3] He had been ordained by the Bishop of Gloucester at Westminster on 14th April 1739, so this was his first curacy. He had probably moved on by 1743, when the vicar's son became Avebury's curate.[4] Collinson claimed to have studied at Queens College, Oxford, although is not mentioned in the University's list of alumni. He became vicar of Rowde in 1762; his career in the intervening years has not been traced.

Between 1760 and 1772, John Bromwick, curate of East Kennett, occasionally signed the Avebury marriage register as 'minister', and may conceivably have served as curate in Avebury as well. John Buchanan signed his name in the register as 'curate' when he conducted the marriage of George Griffin and Hannah Ely. He cannot otherwise be traced. In 1777, James Mayo (probably briefly) served his father as curate; the only evidence for this is the fact that he called banns on one occasion.

During the incumbency of James (II) Mayo, curates were employed more regularly. In 1789 David Williams conducted three marriages, and called a number of banns, signing himself alternately as minister and as curate.[5] He was probably also the vicar of Great Bedwyn. He was followed by Richard Purdy (vicar of Broad Hinton) in 1789-90, Thomas Henry Hume (who succeeded Purdy at Broad Hinton), in 1790, John Evans in 1790-91, William Turton (curate of Wanborough) in 1791-2, and William Chester in 1792, just after his ordination as deacon at St George's, Hanover Square. All of them conducted marriages and several called banns, although Turton is said to have 'omitted' to make entries in the banns register. William Chester, who came from a

1 TNA PROB11/122/637.
2 WSHC P3/P/101.
3 WSHC D1/41/4/48.
4 WSHC D1/14/11/6.
5 Another David Williams, perhaps related to this curate, became stipendiary curate in 1816. It is possible that Sarah Ann Williams, who married Charles Lucas in 1803, was a relation.

Cheltenham clerical family, graduated BA from Worcester College, Oxford, in 1790, aged 19.[1] He was just under age for ordination, but John Ward (the Lord of the manor's attorney) prevailed on Lord Ailesbury to speak to the bishop about the matter, so that Chester could fill the vacant curacy.[2] He did not, however, remain in post for very long; by September 1792 he and his wife (from Marlborough) had emigrated to Jamaica, and were being recommended to the Williamsons.[3] He was, however, unable to obtain ordination as a priest, perhaps because there was no bishop in the West Indies.

Chester was succeeded by Charles Lucas, who served as stipendiary curate from c.1790 until 1816.[4] He had been educated by a dissenting schoolmaster at Devizes, at the Grammar School in Salisbury under Rev John Skinner, at Harrow School, and finally at Oriel College, Oxford, where he matriculated in 1786. By 1793 he had a master's degree.[5] In 1795 he was admitted to the freedom of the City of London, as a draper.[6] He inherited £2000 from his father, which he probably used to purchase land in Devizes, and was not totally reliant on his stipend. Nevertheless, he was a conscientious curate, firstly at Huish (where the Avebury vicar had served as curate before him), and then at Avebury, where he had sole charge of the parish since his vicar was non-resident. Lucas's name is regularly mentioned in the marriage and banns register; Mayo's name does not appear in them during Lucas's curacy, although Evans and Hume did conduct the occasional marriage, presumably when Lucas was unavailable. Lucas was indefatigable in encouraging the straw plaiting school and cleaning up the cottages of the poor just after the end of our period.[7] Nor did he neglect his better-off parishioners: he ran a book club for them.

1 *Alumni Oxonienses*.
2 WSHC 184/6. Letter, John Ward to Adam Williamson, 22nd March 1792.
3 WSHC 184/6. Letters, John Ward to Adam Williamson, 20th September 1792 & 1st January 1793.
4 For his biography, and much of the following paragraph, see *Oxford Dictionary of National Biography* www.oxforddnb.com; Moody, Robert. 'The Reverend Charles Lucas (1769-1854) of Avebury and Devizes – a forgotten novelist, miscellaneous writer and crusading clergyman', *WAM*, 104, 2011, p.221-36; Waylen, James. *A History, Military and Municipal, of the ancient Borough of Devizes*. Longman Brown & Co., 1859, p.563-4.
5 This is not recorded in *Alumni Oxonienses* (which is not always accurate), but see https://theclergydatabase.org.uk, & Moody, op cit, p.222.
6 LMA COL/CHD/FR/02.
7 Bernard, Thomas. 'Extract of an account of the introduction of straw platt at Avebury', *The Reports of the Society for Bettering the Conditions and increasing the Comforts of the Poor*, 4, 1802-5, p.96.

In 1814, Lucas was said to be the stipendiary curate, with a stipend of £50, plus surplice fees, the use of 6 acres of the glebe, the feed of two churchyards, and the vicarage house, where he resided.[1] He was first listed on the Avebury land tax assessments in 1795, when his property (presumably the glebe) was valued at £13 per annum.[2] He paid hair powder tax in 1796:[3] the use of hair powder clearly indicates his high social status. Amongst his duties was making the return for the 1801 census.[4] He seems to have been the first clergyman at Avebury to take an active interest in antiquarian matters, and wrote a poetic 'descriptive account' of the Avebury monument[5]. He also wrote a political tract, and several novels, which were intended as propaganda in the anti-Jacobin cause: in that, he was at one with Richard Hickley, the manorial bailiff and sometime churchwarden.

Lucas married Sarah Ann Williams, the daughter of the perpetual curate of Heytesbury, in 1803. She may have been related to the 1789 curate of that name, and also to David Williams, who succeeded Lucas in Avebury when he moved to become curate at Devizes in 1816.[6]

The major duty of the vicar was to lead worship. John White was licenced as a preacher throughout the diocese. His congregation expected to hear sermons. When Sir Richard Holford visited Avebury in 1696, he was displeased when White failed to preach.[7] White pointed out that, at other times 'when I was not at home I procured other ministers to your great content'. John Rose, during White's final illness, shared Holford's concern. Rose pointed out that White was 'not able to preach', and commented that 'ye shepherd is wiling to have his rest, but cares not if ye flock go astray'; he asked Sir Richard Holford (his landlord) to 'desire him to get a supply'.[8] Rose's concerns were probably misplaced; we do learn of several clergy who stood in for White. Mr. Jackson, probably the vicar of Aldbourne, preached on 7th August 1711.[9] A

1   From the Clergy of the Church of England database https://theclergydatabase.org.uk/, citing WSHC D1/8/1/1.
2   WSHC A1/345/18A.
3   WSHC A1/395.
4   Marriage register 1754-1803; note under entry 72.
5   Lucas, Charles. *A descriptive Account in blank verse of the Old Serpentine Temple of the Druids at Avebury in North Wiltshire*. 2nd ed. 1801. See also 'Avebury: Focus on 18th century vandalism', *The Heritage Journal*. https://heritageaction.wordpress.com/2010/04/19/avebury-focus-on-18th-century-vandalism/
6   Clergy of the Church of England database https://theclergydatabase.org.uk
7   WSHC 184/1, pt.1. Letter, John White to Sir Richard Holford, c.10th October 1696.
8   WSHC 184/1, pt.2. John Rose to Sir Richard Holford, 23rd February 1711/12.
9   WSHC 184/8.

few months later, John Brinsden rode over from neighbouring Winterbourne Monkton 'to officiate for him', and 'preached ... a very good sermon'.[1]

Services continued to be conducted in much the same way throughout our period. In 1783, Rev. James Mayo regularly rode over from Calne to conduct 'divine service' from the *Book of Common Prayer*, alternately at Avebury and Winterbourne Monkton. When he had been curate to his father in the 1740s, he had revived the old practice of reading the homilies which encapsulated the 'pure doctrine of the Gospel', in order to counter Methodist allegations that the Anglican clergy had departed from those doctrines. Prayers and homilies were also read on week days after the three principal festivals, and on some other holy days.[2] The Holy Sacrament was administered at Christmas, Easter, Whitsuntide, and Michaelmas.[3] In 1783, there were generally about forty communicants. In Winterbourne Monkton, Mayo thought that some parishioners were 'deterred from communicating under a notion that they thereby bind themselves to lead a better and more Christian life than they are otherwise obliged to do, under a heavier and more severe punishment hereafter'.[4] It is probable that the same applied in Avebury.

The clergy also had responsibility for baptising children, and for conducting marriages and funerals. The refusal of John White to baptise babies, and to bury the dead (especially dissenters), were major causes of complaint against him when he came before the Consistory Court in 1711.[5] He was not the only vicar to attract criticism in such matters. The importance of these rituals provided another reason why parishioners c.1736 objected to John (II) Mayo's residence in Calne: it meant that someone had to go to Calne to fetch him whenever there was a birth or death.[6] Marriages, of course, required banns to be called, and hence more notice. Between 1754 and 1788, and probably earlier, the vicar was usually the celebrant at marriages; they were regularly witnessed by John Horsell and Samuel Fowler, successive parish clerk, and occasionally by churchwardens.

We do not know whether baptisms were usually conducted by the vicar, although it seems likely that any clergy who happened to be in the vicinity

---

1 WSHC 184/1, pt.2. Letter, John Brinsden to Sir Richard Holford, 13th November 1711; 184/8.
2 The *Book of Common Prayer* listed 30 feast and holy days on which services were to be read; see Spaeth, op cit, p.188 (note 67).
3 Ransome, op cit, p.27.
4 Ransome, op cit, p.238.
5 See below, p.426-8.
6 WSHC D1/47/3.

might be called upon. We have slightly more information on funerals.[1] Clergy had to take oaths certifying burial in woollen, and to record them in the parish register. During his incumbency (1661-1712) John White never heard these oaths.[2] That was done by other local clergy, notably John Brinsden from neighbouring Winterbourne Monkton. It is probable that they officiated at the funerals as well. It may be that Thomas Johnson, rector of Yatesbury, took the funeral of John Burshall in 1672; that may be what Burshall intended when he bequeathed him ten shillings in his will.[3] Henry Hindley, Johnson's successor in Yatesbury, occasionally came over in the 1690s. So did Benjamin Smith, rector of Overton. William Spencer, curate at East Kennett, and Latimer Crosse, his successor, both administered the oath. John Jennings, curate of the chapel at Cherhill, did so once in 1683, but not after he became Rector of Blackland. One wonders whether any of these men served John White as curate. Lewis Morse, rector of Preshute, who was licenced to preach throughout the Diocese, perhaps came to preach the funeral sermon for Sarah Ley in 1698. Justices of the Peace, such as Charles Tooker, also sometimes heard the affidavit oath being taken. After John White's death in 1712, affidavits concerning burial in woollen ceased to be recorded in the parish register.

Most people were buried in the churchyard. Many testators requested that in their wills, for example, Richard Brown in 1572,[4] and John Parsons in 1577.[5] John Goldsmith in 1639/40 qualified that request by asking for burial 'neare unto the place where my wife was buryed before'.[6] Similarly, in 1728, Frances Truslow wished to be buried beside her son Thomas.[7] Some sought a more prestigious burial. When Richard Spenser made his will in 1561, he asked for burial 'in the churche or churche yards of Aberye'.[8] So did William Griffin in 1605/6,[9] and Richard Trewman in 1616.[10]

Burial in church was reserved for the parochial elite. Henry Howson, gent., had evidently been buried in a vault within the church, since, in 1787, his widow, Sarah Dyke Howson, wished to be 'interr'd in the parish church of Avebury in the vault or grave with my late dear husband'. Burial in the chancel

1 For funeral procedure, see Spaeth, op cit, p.199.
2 Parish register.
3 WSHC P3/B/619.
4 WSHC P1/1Reg/82B.
5 WSHC P3/1Reg/21A.
6 WSHC P1/G/142.
7 WSHC P3/T/517.
8 WSHC P1/2Reg/110A.
9 TNA PROB 11/108/10.
10 WSHC P3/T/50.

was even more prestigious. Two manorial ladies, Joan Truslow (1567/8),[1] of Avebury Trusloe manor, and Lady Susanna Holford (1723),[2] of Avebury manor, both wished to be buried there. So, in 1621, did John Peart, the vicar, who specified that he was to be 'decently buryed in the chancel under the communion table of Avebury'.[3]

Funerals could be important community events. In his journal, Sir Richard Holford described the 'wake' following the burial of John Pope on 1st April 1711. He described Pope as 'a very quiet, honest, laborious, industrious man, & a very inoffensive neighbour, & often frequented the parish church'. Nevertheless, he was a dissenter, so John White refused to conduct his funeral service. Nevertheless, at least sixty people turned out to follow the corpse, and to attend the wake, where there was an abundance of 'cakes, wine & good drink'.[4] That contrasted with the numbers attending the funeral of Joseph Brown, an aged servant of the manor, in 1794. According to Richard Hickley, he was buried 'in a very decent manner, my self & wife, John Clements & his wife, the gardener & Mrs. Mitchel, Stephen Crook & Ruth were the mourners'. No cake or ale![5]

Clergy might also be asked to conduct memorial services where funerals took place elsewhere. In 1752, Hannah Smith made elaborate provisions to be buried in her father's vault at Great Amwell, Hertfordshire, but gave the 'minister of the parish of Avebury' two guineas 'for preaching a funeral sermon the Sunday after my funeral'.[6]

Another duty of the Vicar was to catechise the children. Humphry Robinson in 1711 deposed that John White had asked his congregation if there were any children ready to be catechised, but none had come forward. In the same case, Robert Phelps deposed that children had been catechised prior to a visit by Bishop Burnet to confirm them, but otherwise White had not catechised.[7] His successor, John (II) Mayo regularly did so, encouraging them to 'learn & say their catechism publickly in the church'[8]. In 1716, he sent a statement to Sir Richard Holford, showing that he had spent 8s 5d for this purpose, 'on your account', in the previous year. Presumably he regularly gave prizes of a penny or two to the children, which were paid

1 TNA PROB 11/51/51.
2 WSHC TNA PROB11/590/280.
3 WSHC P3/P/101.
4 GA D1956/E2/8.
5 WSHC 184/6. Letter, Richard Hickley to Mrs Williamson, 1st February 1794.
6 TNA PROB 11/795/275.
7 WSHC D1/42/68.
8 WSHC 184/1, pt.2. Letter, John Mayo to Richard Holford, 16th June 1715.

for by the manorial lord. It seems that Farmer Rose also offered to support the work. It was perhaps to thank him for his catechising work that Lady Holford left Mayo £5 in her 1722 will.[1] His work was being continued in 1783 by his grandson, Rev. James Mayo. He had been 'obliged to content myself with instructing children only', as servants could not be persuaded to attend. Catechising took place on Sunday afternoons in the summer, after 'the second lesson' (presumably evening prayer, which was frequently said in the afternoons).

Vicars were also expected to attend the visitations of bishops and archdeacons (with their churchwardens). Sometimes they were asked to preach at these events. And they had to pay procurations and synodals.[2] In 1754, James (I) Mayo was summoned to attend at St Peter's, Marlborough, in order to choose proctors for Convocation.[3] Mention has already been made of the fact that clergy were often sought out to deal with probate matters. The fact that they were literate also meant that their services were sometimes sought as scribes. Richard Long, the vicar of neighbouring Winterbourne Monkton (and perhaps a relation of Kingsmill Long, one of the trustees of the manorial estate) was asked to audit the accounts of the manorial bailiff in the early 1630s. A century later, John Rose, tenant of Avebury Great Farm, was illiterate, but needed to conduct a regular correspondence with his landlord, Stayner Holford. He therefore recruited James (I) Mayo, the vicar, as his amanuensis. The latter was 'awaked & surprised ... out of a very sound sleep' at 5 a.m. one morning, to be informed 'that I am always to have the honour of being his scribe in writing to you'.[4] It is possible that a previous vicar had provided a similar service to John Brown, another substantial farmer of the earlier eighteenth century, who was also illiterate.[5] Brown's illiteracy posed a serious problem for his administrator in 1732, since his failure to keep records hindered the preparation of an adequate inventory.

Another task of the clergy was to promote charity. They were regularly required, during Sunday services, to read 'briefs' appealing for donations to some charitable object. For Avebury, most such briefs have been lost. We do, however, have a list of contributors to the fund for re-building St Paul's Cathedral after the great Fire of London.[6] Contributions were collected by

1 TNA PROB 11/590/280.
2 WSHC D3/2.
3 WSHC D2/3/2.
4 WSHC 184/1, pt.2. Letter, James Mayo to Stayner Holford, 27th April 1746.
5 TNA C11/363/65.
6 LMA 25565/24, f.18-19.

John White, the vicar, and his churchwardens in 1678. A total of 13s 6d was raised from 27 individuals, who mostly gave just a few pence each.

More formally, clergy were frequently expected to act as trustees to local charities. Avebury was no exception to this rule. We have already seen that when Lady Holford bequeathed £200 to establish a school for the poor, she named the vicar and parish officers as trustees.[1] It is likely that the vicar regularly visited the school; the former schoolmaster, John Clements, was described as 'a great advocate for the parson' in 1792.[2]

Another task which incumbents sometimes undertook was to support neighbouring clergy. In 1662, Nathaniel Power was asked, with other incumbents, to sign a testimonial certifying that the curate of Alderton, Christopher Simons, was 'of a Godly conversation & orthodox in doctrine and conformable to the discipline of ye church of England'.[3] Simons (or Simmons) had been ordained both deacon and priest in 1660 – one of the earliest ordinations after the Restoration - and was instituted as vicar of Seagry in 1666. Similarly, clergymen from Calne, Woodborough, and Winterbourne Monkton all signed letters testimonial for James (I) Mayo when he was seeking ordination as a priest.[4]

Clergy might also, on occasion, be expected to undertake duties on behalf of their bishop. In 1733, for example, John (II) Mayo was asked to join other commissioners to report on a proposal to amalgamate the livings of Cherhill and Calne.[5] The secular courts might also call on the clergy for assistance; the Archdeacon, Cornelius Yeate, was commissioned to hear witnesses at Marlborough in an Exchequer case between two Avebury men, Peter Griffin and Thomas Pontin, in 1688.[6] Another duty was to defend the rights of the vicarage and church. We have already seen how John White and his successors defended their right to tithe; James (I) Mayo was also called on to prevent the use of the churchyard as a drove way for cattle.[7]

The role of the clergy in leading worship was supported by the parish clerk. After the Reformation, it became his responsibility to lead both responses to Cranmer's prayers, and any singing. He was expected to be literate, and in some parishes took responsibility for compiling the parish register. In Avebury,

1 TNA PROB 11/590/280. See above, p.171-3.
2 WSHC 184/6. Letter, Richard Hickley to Mrs Williamson, 4th December 1792.
3 WSHC D1/14/1/1a, f.121.
4 WSHC D1/14/1/11/6. For some other testimonials for James Mayo, see WSHC D5/5/1/3.
5 WSHC D1/41/4/56/3.
6 TNA E134/3Jas2/East17.
7 WSHC 184/1, pt.1. Letters between John Mayo and John Scane, 11 & 12 February 1756.

unfortunately, we know little of what his other duties were, although we do learn that the parish clerk in 1662 was 'very serviceable and able'. In 1739 he was expected to give notice to all concerned that the parish schoolmaster had been dismissed,[1] so it may be that he acted as clerk and general factotum to the vestry. In 1811, Edward Chivers, the newly appointed parish clerk, promised 'to conduct myself soberly, honestly, and in the fear of God, particularly to take care to avoid falling into that evil habit destructive to worldly prosperity, reputation and morality, frequenting public houses'.[2] Parish clerks were paid; in 1793, Richard Hickley, the churchwarden, was due to pay 'Fowler' half a crown (2s 6d) at Easter 1794.[3]

Very few Avebury parish clerks in our period can be named, although that may be because they stayed in post for long periods. Richard Bray, parish clerk c.1640, was given £1 in the will of John Goldsmith[4]. John Harper was the parish clerk when he stood bond with Ruth Pope in 1681.[5] Reuben Horsell, Stukeley's 'lover of antiquities', served as parish clerk when Stukeley was visiting in c.1719-24[6]. In 1711, he had been involved as parish clerk in the dispute over the burial of Richard Bailey, the Presbyterian; he was sent to inform the mourners that White refused to conduct the funeral service, and also carried out his instruction to lock up the *Book of Common Prayer* so that no-one else could use it.[7] Reuben was succeeded by his son Reuben,[8] who stood bond when George Webb senior, of East Kennett, sought a marriage licence to marry the Avebury widow, Susan Minty, in April 1750.[9] Reuben II was probably succeeded in his turn by his brother John.[10] Before he took on that role, John had been called upon to ring the bell for the funeral of Richard Holford, and to find ten men to 'beare his

1 WSHC D1/41/4/48.
2 Parish Register.
3 WSHC 184/6. Richard Hickley to Mrs Williamson, 1st April 1794. The payment is recorded in WSHC 184/7.
4 WSHC P1/4/142.
5 WSHC P3/T/288.
6 Stukeley, William. *Abury: a Temple of the British Druids ... .* 1743, p.22.
7 See below, p.428. WSHC D1/42/68.
8 Markham, Sarah. *John Loveday of Caversham, 1711-1789: the Life and Tours of an Eighteenth-Century Onlooker.* Michael Russell, 1984, p.41.
9 Sarum Marriage Licence Bonds www.findmypast.co.uk/articles/world-records/full-list-of-united-kingdom-records/life-events-bmds/sarum-marriage-licence-bonds
10 According to Rev John Whitaker, writing in 1772, Reuben Horsell's successor as parish clerk was 'John ', presumably Reuben Horsell's son. See Nichols, John, ed. *Illustrations of the literary history of the eighteenth century. Vol.IV.* John Nichols & Son, 1822, p.855

corps to ye church' in 1742. He had 5s for the bell ringing, and 1s for the ten men.[1] Subsequently, he was frequently called upon to sign the printed marriage register after it had been introduced by the 1754 Marriage Act. When he died in 1765, his widow Mary regularly witnessed the register until 1769. Bartholomew Horsell, who was probably John's nephew, also acted occasionally as a witness between 1755 and 1786, perhaps aspiring to succeed his uncle. He was illiterate, which may have excluded him from consideration for the post. Samuel Fowler also began to regularly sign in 1765; on his death in 1798 the parish register notes that he had served as parish clerk for 27 years. He was succeeded by his son William,[2] who regularly signed the marriage register after his father's death, and who was buried in 1810 aged 35.

The Clerk's singing in church was complemented (if that is the right word!) by a choir, at least in the late eighteenth century. The churchwarden paid the 'singers' two crowns (10s) for their efforts over the previous two years in 1794.[3]

Churchwardens were chosen at the Easter meeting of the vestry, and sworn in at visitations (Bishops' visitations were usually held at St Mary's, Devizes).[4] Two churchwardens were usually appointed, but one was supposedly nominated by the vicar in accordance with the 1604 Canons.[5] In Avebury, that probably did not always happen; as we shall see, in 1691 two of the churchwardens were dissenters. Churchwardens mostly served for one or two terms, but a few were in post for many years: John Scane, the manorial bailiff, served for eight years between 1757 and 1782;[6] Richard Hickley, his successor as bailiff, served for most of the 1780s and 1790s, if not longer.[7] Churchwardens had sidesmen to assist them, but only a handful of their names have come down to us: John Burchell served in 1662 and signed the churchwardens' presentment.[8] So did James Pope and Walter Stretch in 1701.[9]

1 WSHC 184/4. Horsell's invoice, 1742.
2 Hobbs, Steve, ed. *Gleanings from Wiltshire parish registers*. Wiltshire Record Society 63. 2010, p.13.
3 WSHC 184/6. Letter, Richard Hickley to Mrs Williamson, 1st April 1794. A similar payment is recorded in his accounts for January 1795; cf. WSHC 184/7.
4 WSHC D1/50/1. The same probably applied to archdeacons' visitations.
5 Ransome, op cit, p.29.
6 WSHC D3/15/15-18.
7 WSHC D3/15/19-21.
8 Grout, Diana, & Grist, Mervyn, eds. *Churchwardens presentments, 1662, for 73 parishes between Bradford on Avon and Devizes*, vol.2. Wiltshire Family History Society, 2014, p.5, transcribing WSHC D1/54/1/2.
9 WSHC D1/54/17/3/69.

It has already been pointed out that the church in our period was much more involved in government than is the case today, and we have already discussed some aspects of the roles of churchwardens and other parish officers in what we would now call secular government. That role was emphasised in the early 1790s, when the royal arms of George III were erected in the church. The initials of the two churchwardens in office at the time – RH and WJ - are at the foot of the painting, enabling us to identify Richard Hickley and William Jefferies, who held office together from 1792 until 1794.[1] But the major duty of the churchwardens, then as now, was to keep the church in good repair, and to report any defects to the Archdeacon or Bishop. There was 'no carpet to lay upon the communion table' in the early 1550s.[2] In 1593, they reported that 'the last winde' had damaged the church windows.[3] John Pope, churchwarden in 1589-91, was presented by his successors for 'breckinge upe the belfre dore' – and presumably not replacing it adequately[4]. It was the responsibility of the owner of the rectorial tithes to maintain the chancel, and in 1595/6 the lord of the manor, Mr Dunch, was presented because 'ye chancel ... be in decay'.[5] In 1596, 'the bounds of the churchyard [were] in decaie'.[6] A couple of years later, Richard Bartlett was in trouble 'for not repayring the church';[7] he had presumably not contributed to some communal effort. In 1614, the vicar presented that a pulpit cloth was needed.[8] In 1619, the tower was said to be 'in default'.[9] James Pope, churchwarden in 1621, reported that 'the church bounds are lately repayred', so that cattle could be kept out, and 'that the glasse windows are now sufficiently repaired'.[10] 'Certayne defects in their parish ornaments' were presented in 1622.[11] In 1630, John Griffin was accused of 'spoiling of the churchway ioyning to Brunsdens Barne'.[12] In 1639, Richard Chesterman bequeathed ten shillings 'towards the making of an arche in place of the pillare next to the south doore of the church of Aveburie'.[13]

1   WSHC D3/15/20.
2   WSHC D1/43/1, f/144.
3   WSHC D3/7/1. f.35.
4   WSHC D3/7/1, f.89.
5   WSHC D3/7/1, f.135.
6   WSHC D3/7/1, f.151.
7   WSHC D1/39/2/4.
8   WSHC D1/39/2/7, f.56v
9   WSHC D3/4/5, f.47.
10 WSHC D3/4/5, f.110.
11 WSHC D3/4/6, f.2.
12 WSHC D3/4/6, f.98.
13 WSHC P3/C/239.

After the Restoration, in 1662, the churchwardens presented that, after the depredations suffered during the Interregnum, they needed a surplice, the *Apology* of Bishop Jewell, and two books of homilies, and that the bounds of the church were 'imperfect'.[1] The 'walls and windows of our church' were in default, but under repair, in 1698.[2] At the Archdeacon's visitation of 1707, the churchwardens presented 'the leds of the Tower in default'.[3] The 1717 presentment of 'the church leds' probably refers to the same problem.[4] In 1719, a new bell founded by Richard Phelps was installed. The bell named the two current churchwardens and the vicar, as well as the founder.[5] Richard Hickley, as churchwarden in 1794, had to deal with water damage; he thought 'the copper on the church will now do very well, as I don't find little or no rain come through since the man has attened it'.[6]

The parish, like most others, possessed a copy of Fox's *Book of Martyrs*, given by either Thomas or William Bray. This was evidently well thumbed, as in 1705 it was sent for re-binding to Mr Buckridge of Warminster. At the Archdeacon's visitation it was reported that it 'is not yet returned for want of paying ye binding', and the court ordered payment[7]. One wonders whether the cost of rebinding attracted controversy in the parish, and whether the churchwardens at this time (Richard Greene and Humphry Robinson) needed to secure themselves from complaints by securing a court order before making payment. Rates could be controversial, and not all were prepared to pay. Thomas Pope was presented in 1621/2 'for not paying a rate'.[8]

We do not have much information on the regular day to day happenings in the parish. All that can be said is that, as has been seen, services were usually regularly conducted, baptisms carried out, marriages conducted in the church porch, and parishioners buried in the churchyard. In 1639 Thomas Bray bequeathed £3 to purchase a 'book of matins', presumably a copy of the *Book of Common Prayer*, to be used in church.[9] Bells were rung for services, to celebrate important national events, and to call locals to funerals. Marjorie

---

1 Grout & Grist, op cit, p.5.
2 WSHC D1/54/16/3.
3 WSHC D3/12/15.
4 WSHC D3/12/21.
5 Mayo, Charles Herbert. *A genealogical account of the Mayo and Elton families of the counties of Wilts and Hereford*. Chiswick Press, 1882, p.155.
6 WSHC 186/4. Letter, Richard Hickley to Mrs Williamson, 30th July 1794.
7 WSHC D3/12/13.
8 WSHC D3/4/5, f.80v.
9 WSHC P3/B/420.

Brown bequeathed twelve shillings to the ringers at her funeral in 1620.[1] When Sir Richard Holford arrived from London to visit his manor on 1st August 1711, Lady Drake gave the ringers five shillings,[2] presumably because they rang the bells to celebrate his coming. We have already seen that social celebrations took place at festival times such as Rogation.[3] It may be that some of these events helped to raise money to pay the parish clerk, as the 'clark's ale' did in neighbouring Winterbourne Monkton in the early 1770s.[4]

At least some of the pews in the church were privately owned, and could be bought and sold. When Sir Richard Holford in 1702 offered to purchase John Griffin's property at Eastbrook and Westbrook, he offered an additional £16 if Griffin's seat in the church was included.[5] In 1710, and again in the 1730s, when the Free Chapel lands and other farms at Beckhampton were sold, the pews assigned to them were sold with the property[6]. In 1752, the vicar and churchwardens authorised Stayner Holford to erect a new pew for his servants in the south aisle, 'the consent of all who sit in the said part having been first obtained'.[7]

The church did endeavour to enforce attendance at church. In 1589 'a gentlewoman dwelling at Kennett' was presented 'for not coming to the church'.[8] Thomas Pope and his wife were accused of not receiving communion at Easter in 1593.[9] In 1624, John Pope, was presented 'for not frequenting his parish church'.[10] In 1634, it was Christopher Pope who was prosecuted 'for not coming to church'.[11] James Pope served as churchwarden in 1621 and 1634, but on the latter occasion was presented by the vicar for negligence.[12] The Popes were probably related. Thomas Martin was prosecuted on the same day as Christopher Pope for 'not receaving the communion at Easter'. That was also the accusation made against Thomas Mortimer and his wife in 1634.[13] A few years earlier, in 1619, Mary Lawrence had been presented 'for not coming

1 WSHC P3/B/195.
2 GA D1956/E2/8.
3 See above. p.377.
4 WSHC D1/42/161, f.48v.
5 WSHC 184/4, pt.1. Sale Particulars, 1702.
6 WANHS Genealogy v.A-A, f.144; WSHC 371/1, pt.4 & 5.
7 WSHC 184/8.
8 WSHC D3/7/1, f.6v.
9 WSHC D3/7/1, f.97v.
10 WSHC D3/4/6, f.28; D1/39/2/12,f.24v.
11 WSHC D1/39/2/12. f.24v.
12 WSHC D1/39/2/12, f.10v.
13 WSHC D1/39/2/12, f.18v.

to the church'.[1] Richard Davis's occasional absences in 1626 were explained by the fact that 'sometymes when market daies have fallen on hollidaies he have gon to the market to buy his provision'.[2]

There is no direct evidence of the reasons for most of these absences. Few pre-Civil War separatists have been identified in Wiltshire,[3] although it may be noted that the names of Pope and Mortimer were associated with dissent after the Restoration (see below). Puritanism can probably be discounted as a motive, since the vicar, John Forsyth, had puritan sympathies himself. So did the Dunch family, lords of the manor. Walter Dunch married a daughter of James Pilkington, Bishop of Durham, a Marian exile and ardent protestant.[4] The phraseology of Walter Dunch's will is sufficiently unusual to suggest his sympathies: he bequeathed 'my sowle to Almight God beseeching him to strengthen my faithe and to guyde me with his holye spirite unto the end and in the end trusting to inherite everlasting lyfe by the onely meritts and passion of my Lorde and Savyor Jesus'.[5] There can be no doubt about his daughter Deborah's sympathies. She married Henry Moody of Garsdon (Wilts) in 1604. He died in 1629. Her faith led her to emigrate to North America in 1636.[6] She settled in Massachusetts. However, her stance on infant baptism was not accepted by her congregation, so she moved on to found a village – Gravesend – on Long Island.[7] The extent to which the Dunch's influenced puritanism in Avebury is not clear, given that they were not always resident.

During the Civil War, Puritanism flourished in the area. It was probably propagated in the 1630s and early 1640s by John Forsyth, the vicar, who, as has been seen, was a Parliamentary supporter. As a Scot, he would have been familiar with Scottish Presbyterianism. It may be that some Avebury folk were encouraged to go 'gadding' to sermons at Calne, where there was a sizeable 'Godly' congregation.[8] We have already seen that Sir Edward Bayntun, a leading lay advocate of Presbyterianism, actually resided in Avebury for most of the 1650s. It is worth repeating that the Bayntun family also owned property in Bromham and Bremhill – which, with Avebury, were the three parishes in

1 WSHC D3/4/5, f.46v.
2 WSHC D3/4/6, f.47.
3 Ingram, Martin. *Church Courts, Sex, and marriage in England 1570-1640.* Cambridge University Press, 1990, p.91.
4 *Oxford Dictionary of National Biography*
5 TNA PROB11/84/49.
6 WANHS Wiltshire Genealogy v.A-A, f.108.
7 *Oxford Dictionary of National Biography* www.oxforddnb.com. See also WANHS Wiltshire Genealogy v.A-A, p.108.
8 Ingram, op cit, p.94-5.

the Deanery of Avebury with the highest numbers of dissenters in 1676.[1] In 1662, the churchwardens presented that there were no 'sectaries' in the parish. Their definition of 'sectary' was probably different from that of the authorities! Persecution of dissent was never popular in Avebury, even at this early date.[2] Nevertheless, John Jacob was presented at Quarter Sessions 'for not comeing to his parish church' on 3rd December 1664. His accuser was the constable of the Hundred, Richard Phelps.[3] Jacob and another parishioner had already been cited to appear in the Consistory Court in the previous September.[4] Although the vicar, John White, attributed the establishment of a 'hellish conventicle' to William Skeat, the leading farmer in the parish, he only arrived c.1695, and was certainly not the first dissenter in the parish.

Some local ministers were devoted to the puritan cause. That included John Forsyth, the Civil War vicar, who probably escaped ejection in 1662 only because he died too early. It is not surprising that when the 1662 Act of Uniformity required all ministers to declare their consent to the contents of the *Book of Common Prayer*, substantial numbers felt unable to do so, and were removed by the authorities, despite the extensive support they had amongst their congregations. Many of the latter followed their ministers into dissent. When William Hughes, the vicar of St Mary's, Marlborough, was ejected from his living in 1662, he 'gathered' his church.[5] Fourteen years later, in 1676, perhaps a tenth of the population of Marlborough were dissenters.[6] Similarly, Thomas Jones, ejected from Calne, founded the Presbyterian church in that

---

1 Turner, G. Lyon. *Original records of Early Nonconformity under Persecution and Indulgence*. T.Fisher Unwin, 1911, vol.1, p.132. There were 25 in Avebury, 78 in Bremhill, and 50 in Bromham. According to the episcopal returns of 1669 (Turner, op cit, vol.3, p.812), there were between 200 and 300 dissenters in Winterbourne Monkton. That figure is very dubious, especially since in 1676 there were only 81 inhabitants there!
2 For the rapid decline of presentments for dissent after the Restoration, see Spaeth, op cit, p.66-7.
3 WSHC A1/110, 1665 M, f.137.
4 WSHC D1/41/1/41, pt.1.
5 Stribling, S.B. *History of the Wilts & East Somerset Congregational Union ... 1797-1897*. Centenary Meeting, 1897, p.18-19; Gunn, H.Mayo. *A Memorial of the Nonconforming Clergy of Wilts and East Somerset in 1662*. Jackson, Walford and Hodder, 1862, p.22.
6 Dunscombe, Hilary. *Avebury: a Five Mile Chapel*. 3rd ed. by Herbert Jones. www.oodwoc.co.uk/ph_Avebury_history2.htm. See also Stedman, A.R. *Marlborough and the Upper Kennet country*. [Marlborough College?], 1960, p.201, Gunn, op cit, p.22, & Stribling, op cit, p.18-19.

town.[1] The 1662 act only marked the beginning of persecution. It was followed by the Conventicle Act of 1664, prohibiting gatherings of more than five people for dissenting worship, and by the Five Mile Act, 1665, which banned dissenting minsters from residence within five miles of any corporate town[2]. Avebury experienced the consequences of that act. It was just over five miles from several corporate towns – Marlborough, Calne, Chippenham, Devizes, Wootton Bassett, Pewsey. It therefore attracted a number of ejected ministers.[3] Dr Thomas Rashley, ejected from Salisbury Cathedral, re-located to Avebury,[4] although he was subsequently said to be living in Lydiard Millicent, and was described as 'itinerant'.[5] He was a graduate of Cambridge University, and had served as a minister in New England, but had never been episcopally ordained.[6] In 1669, John Baker, who had been expelled from Chiseldon in 1663,[7] lived in the house of John Goddard (an excommunicate), in Winterbourne Monkton, where he was active in preaching.[8] Together with Thomas Mills of Calne, he opened a chapel at Avebury in 1670.[9] Baker was described as a 'man of very warm affections' by Calamy.[10] After the Declaration of Indulgence,

1 *VCH Wilts.*, vol.3, p.104 & 106.
2 This point is made by Edwards, Brian. 'Changing Avebury', *The Regional Historian*, 12, 2004, p.3. See also Gillings, Mark, Pollard, Joshua, Wheatley, David, & Peterson, Rick. *Landscape of the Megaliths: excavations and fieldwork on the Avebury monuments 1997-2003*. Oxbow Books, 2008, p343-5.
3 For a brief history of the cause, see Dunscombe, Hilary. *Avebury: a Five Mile Chapel.* 3rd ed. by Herbert Jones. www.oodwoc.co.uk/ph_Avebury_history2.htm.
4 Calamy, Edmund. *The Nonconformists Memorial.* Rev. ed.Button & Son, 1802, vol.3, p.373; WANHS mss 665, f.203; Matthews, A.G. *Calamy Revised*, Clarendon Press, 1934, p.403.
5 Gordon, Alexander. *Freedom after Ejection: a review (1690-92) of Presbyterian and Congregational Nonconformity in England and Wales.* Manchester University Press, 1917, p.124.
6 ACAD: A Cambridge Alumni Database https://venn.lib.cam.ac.uk.
7 Clergy of the Church of England database https://theclergydatabase.org.uk/; Matthews, op cit, p.23.
8 Turner, G.Lyon. *Original records of Early Nonconformity under Persecution and Indulgence.* T.Fisher Unwin, 1911, vol.2, p.1058. He is unlikely to be identical with the John Baker, whom Turner says was ejected from Curry Mallet (Somerset); cf. Turner, op cit, vol.2, p.1089, 1095, 1104, 1106, 1112, 1115, & 1116.
9 Turner, op cit, vol.1, p.109; vol, 2, p.1058. Turner says Mills was from Curry Mallet (Somerset). He may perhaps not have possessed Anglican orders, and been ejected in 1660; the Clergy of the Church of England database https://theclergydatabase.org.uk/ reports the institution of a new rector there in that year. See also Stribling, op cit, p.23, & Matthews, op cit, p.350.
10 Calamy, Edmund. *The Nonconformists Memorial.* Rev. ed.Button & Son, 1802,

1672, he moved to London, and was licenced to preach at Whitecross Street, Cripplegate.[1] Noah Webb, another ejected minister, is said to have travelled up from Upton Grey (Hampshire) every week for nine months in the 1670s to preach at Avebury.[2] One wonders whether he was the Noah Webb of Draycot Foliat from whom John Phelps of Avebury purchased Draycot Farm[3]. One wonders also whether he was related to Nathaniel Webb, who was ejected from neighbouring Yatesbury, and returned to live in Bromham, his native parish, where the Presbyterian Baynton family supported the dissenter's meeting house he licenced in 1672.[4] Calamy says that Nathaniel occasionally preached at 'other places as opportunity offered'. That included Calne, where he attracted congregations numbering several hundred[5] and probably also included Avebury. In 1695, according to John White, a 'Mr. Roussell of Cadnam' was a preacher at dissenters' meetings.[6] John Phelps, incidentally, took the oath against transubstantiation as a dissenting preacher c.1701.[7]

Dissenters were regularly meeting at Avebury in the 1660s. There were usually thirty or thirty-two In 1669.[8] In 1676, John White, the vicar, thought there were twenty-five.[9] That figure may be compared with the 181

vol.1, p.361.
[1] Turner, op cit, vol.2, p.972. See also Surman Index https://surman.english.qmul.ac.uk
[2] Calamy, Edmund. *The Nonconformists Memorial.* Rev. ed.Button & Son, 1802, Vol.2, p.284. According to Calamy, he was ejected from Chieveley (Berkshire). There is no record in the Clergy of the Church of England database https://theclergydatabase.org.uk/, probably because he had not been episcopally ordained or instituted. Chieveley had been sequestered by the Parliamentary authorities. See also *VCH Wilts* 12, p.103. It is possible that he preached at Aldbourne rather than Avebury; that is stated by Schomberg, Arthur. 'Wiltshire Nonconformists', *Wiltshire Notes & Queries* 8, 1914-16, p.367, and by Matthews, op cit,p.516.
[3] *VCH Wilts.*, vol.9. 1970. www.british-history.ac.uk/vch/wilts/vol9/pp43-49. See also
WSHC 212B/1790.
[4] Turner, op cit, vol.1, p.254, & vol.2, p.1058 & 1060. Waylen, James. *A history, Military and Municipal, of the ancient Borough of Devizes*. Longman Brown & Co., 1859, p.332-3. *VCH Wilts.*, vol.17, p.109.
[5] Gunn, H.Mayo. *A Memorial of the Nonconforming Clergy of Wilts and East Somerset in 1662*. Jackson, Walford and Hodder, 1862, p.23.
[6] WSHC 184/1. Letter, John White to Sir Richard Holford, 25th January 1695/6.'Cadnam' is probably Cadenham, in Bremhill parish.
[7] WSHC A1/239.
[8] Turner, op cit, vol.1, p.109.
[9] Turner, op cit, vol.3, p.812.

conformists said to attend the Church of England.[1] In 1669, meetings were held at the houses of Peter Griffin and Richard Morris, in the centre of the henge; attendees were described as being 'of several sorts'.[2] In 1682, Peter Griffin, John Cue, Samuel Morris, Richard Morris, and their wives, were all presented at Quarter Sessions because they 'did not repayre to theire owne parish church att Avebury ... to heare divine service or sermon att any tyme within the space of six months last past'.[3]

One of the members of the Hundred Jury which made this presentment was Thomas Mortimer of Avebury. According to his fellow jurors, he had 'himselfe related theyr [Avebury's dissenters] several delinquencyes to some of us out of court', but had refused to present them. His failure to control his tongue resulted in Mortimer being presented for neglect of his duty.[4]

When Sir Richard Holford purchased Avebury manor in 1695, he was disturbed by 'the impertinent differences betweene you [John White, the vicar] and some of the neighbours', which he thought helped to explain the increasing 'separation in the publick worship of God, & participation of the holy and blessed communion of our Lord's supper'.[5] Holford may not have been fully aware of the origins of Avebury dissent, but he was right in thinking that continuing disputes over tithe would encourage its growth. It did. But it did not help Holford's cause that his tenant, William Skeat, himself also a relative newcomer to the parish, was seen by White as one of the dissenters' leading protagonists. It bears repeating that White described Skeat as 'my profest enemy, as appeares sufficiently by his setting up a hellish, factious, scandalous, & schismatical conventicle in opposition to me, & by his exposinge me in all company where he comes, thinking therby to take away my good nam[e]'.[6] He regretted that 'some good lawes are repealed which kept such rude abusive fellowes in order' presumably referring to the 1689 Toleration Act, but reiterated that 'there is still law enough in force to punish them that let their tongues run at what rate they please to wound their

---

1 Whiteman, Ann, ed. *The Compton Census of 1676: a Critical Edition*. Records of Social and Economic History new series 10. Oxford University Press, for the British Academy, 1986, p.129; WSHC D1/27/1/4/66 & 68.
2 Turner, op cit, vol.1, p.109 & 812.
3 WSHC A1/110, 1682M, f.90.
4 WSHC A1/110, 1682M, f.90v.
5 WSHC 184/1, pt.2. Letter, Sir Richard Holford to John White, 11th January 1695/6.
6 WSHC 184/1, pt.1. Letter, John White to Sir Richard Holford, undated; c.25th January 1695.

neighbours' reputation'.[1] Holford, however, thought that the 'great strife & contentions' between White and Skeat arose, 'more out of humour and passion than any substantiall cause'.[2]

The dispute undoubtedly helped the dissenting cause. It is a mistake, however, to think of a sharp division between those who attended the established church and those who were dissenters. Although the clergy and some separatists saw a stark separation between the two, most parishioners merely saw various shades of grey. The leading dissenter, Thomas Robinson, nevertheless claimed that he regularly 'frequented his parish church of Avebury on Sundays'.[3] A number of post-restoration dissenters in Avebury even served as churchwardens, although refusing to present dissenting activities. Thomas Mortimer, the juryman presented for refusing to present dissenters at Quarter Sessions, served as churchwarden in 1674.[4] Other churchwardens were also sympathetic. John Cue went on from his presentment to be churchwarden in 1683-4[5] and 1698-9.[6] John Pope, the dissenter who White had refused to bury in 1711, nevertheless 'often frequented the parish church'.[7] During the 1681 Archdeaconry visitation, John White, the vicar, presented John Phelps, with his wife Anne, 'for not coming to church to hear divine service read, and for not receiving the sacrament'[8]. Phelps became churchwarden in 1689. Two years later, in 1691, White's 'profest enemy', William Skeat, began a two-year term as churchwarden.[9] For his first year, he served with Joseph Hayward, another dissenter. When the two made their presentment at the Archdeacon's visitation in 1689, they reported that they 'did not at present know any person or thinge in our church or parish presentable',[10] despite the steam which almost visibly rises from some of the vicar's letters to Sir Richard Holford. The previous year, White had provided an 'information' against John Phelps, William Skeat, John Rose, and John Pontin to Quarter Sessions.[11] The cause is not stated, but it was probably to do with their dissent. White cannot have been pleased when, in

1   WSHC 184/1, pt.1. Letter, John White to Sir Richard Holford, 7th January 1702/3.
2   WSHC 184/1, pt.2. Letter, Sir Richard Holford to John White, 22nd July 1708.
3   WSHC D1/42/68.
4   WSHC D1/54/6/3.
5   WSHC 54/10/3.
6   WSHC D1/54/16/3.
7   GA D1956/E2/8.
8   WSHC D3/12/2.
9   WSHC D3/12/5; D3/15/3.
10 WSHC D3/12/5
11 WSHC A1/165/3, f.40v.

1683, one of his sermons was described as 'ribble rabble' by a member of his congregation. Thomas Etwall asked John Mills, his host at dinner after the morning service, 'what benefit he could reap by being at church' and declared that he 'did not beleeve one word [of the sermon] to be true'.[1] John Sparks, who was also present, was so offended by Etwall's words that he complained to a Justice of the Peace, who placed an 'information' before Quarter Sessions. It is surprising that White did not make more use of his ability to present his parishioners at ecclesiastical visitation.

The rector's attitudes towards his parishioners did not help his cause: he was determined to enforce his rights to tithe, and upset many by doing so. In 1695, he threatened to sue Farmer Skeat, and had already sued John Mills over a bond for £20.[2] In 1697, he brought an Exchequer bill against nine Beckhampton men for withholding their tithes.[3] He was accused of 'singling out the poorest of your orators who are least able to defend themselves', 'on purpose to plague them'. Joseph Hayward, who was one of those who felt oppressed by the vicar's demands, knew that White had 'a very passionate temper', and had therefore been 'the more solicitous to prevent [him] taking any advantage'. Nevertheless, White sued him in the Court of Exchequer (rather than following the less costly procedure of taking him before two Justices of the Peace),[4] causing him to incur a debt of £6 in legal fees, plus other expenditure, and almost forcing him to go 'on the parish'. Sir Richard Holford commented to Cornelius Yeate, the Archdeacon, 'that there is little justice & less charity in the prosecution',[5] and noted 'poor Hayward ruined' as one of the topics he deliberately did not mention in a letter to White over a decade later.[6] In response to White's provocation, six poor cottagers (assisted by local gentlemen) brought a case against him in Chancery, as the Hayward

---

1 WSHC A1/110, 1683M, f.150. One wonders if this was the former vicar of Bishops Cannings; cf. https://theclergydatabase.org.uk/. He had been appointed vicar under the authority of the Parliamentary Committee for Plundered Ministers in 1651, but had been allowed to retain his position after the Restoration. However, he had ceased to be vicar c.1680.
2 WSHC 184/1, pt.1. Letter, John White to Sir Richard Holford, 1695. Mills had counter-sued; see TNA C5/274/72.
3 Spaeth, op cit, p.136.
4 This procedure had recently been introduced by Act of Parliament; see Spaeth, op cit, p.79-80.
5 WSHC 184/1, pt.2. Letter, Sir Richard Holford to Cornelius Yeate, 8th March 1697/8. See also 184/1, pt.2. Letter, Sir Richard Holford to Richard Smith, 9th November 1697.
6 WSHC 184/1, pt.2. Letter, Sir Richard Holford to John White, 4th October 1711.

case seemed to threaten them all.[1] John Rose's wife had already endeavoured to prevent White's sixteen year old son from taking more than the vicar's due, but had been accused of 'battery', and found guilty, despite the fact that she had merely attempted to re-take wheat which the vicar had no right to. Sir Richard Holford commented that White's 'usage of Mills, Hayward & others of his paoor neighbors made me endeavour not to lye at his Mercy, nor subject myself to his humor'.[2] As we have seen, he sued White in Chancery, and forced him to a settlement concerning his own tithe.

Tithe issues, however, re-surfaced in 1710, when White brought cases against Richard Caswell, a member of the Phelps family, and Mr Pontin, in the Consistory Court. Caswell complained to Sir Richard Holford that White was 'prosecuting of him with great severity', and asked him for support.[3] In the event, Caswell was excommunicated for non-payment.[4] In the midst of the proceedings, Holford purchased the estate leased by Caswell at Beckhampton,[5] and complained that White was seeking from his tenant 'a great deal more for his tythes than was his due, or was ever paid or taken for that farme'.[6] That opinion was occasioned by White's demands on Holford's new estate, but was no doubt informed by the litigation against Caswell and Pontin. Holford himself withheld litigation due to White's illness.

Caswell and Pontin, however, countered White's accusations in the Consistory Court by bringing accusations against him. According to Holford's 1711 diary, they accused him of 'not burying the dead, not catechizeing the children, not christening, & not visiteing the sick'.[7] Evidence for the first accusation is detailed below. This was perhaps the only occasion on which the Consistory Court actually sat in Avebury.[8] One wonders whether Holford used his influence with the Bishop to persuade the Chancellor, Dr. Loggan, to visit the parish. That would have made it much easier to ensure that witnesses attended the court. Loggan found in favour of the plaintiffs, and awarded them costs, declaring that 'if complaint thereof made to him [again] hee would compell him thereto'. He also granted Caswell absolution for his

1 TNA C10/534/43.
2 WSHC 184/1, pt.1. Letter, Sir Richard Holford to Mr. Smith, 22nd February 1700.
3 WSHC 184/8.
4 WSHC D1/39/1/67, f.139-69, passim.
5 WSHC 184/1, pt.2. Letter, Sir Richard Holford to John White, 4th October 1711.
6 WSHC 184/1, pt.2. Sir Richard Holford to John Brinsden, 21st May 1712.
7 WSHC 184/8. See also the Act Book, D1/39/1/67, f.168 & 168v, and Spaeth, op cit, p.150-51.
8 WSHC D1/39/1/67, f.168.

excommunication. Loggan spent three days at Avebury hearing the case.[1] But not even the Chancellor of the Diocese could bring peace. Caswell agreed to pay 11s 4d for his tithes,[2] but the vicar was bitter about Loggan's judgement, and passionately denied to Holford 'that the Chancellor had dealt wonderfully kind towards him & his adversaries in reconciling them'.[3] But White was a sick man, 'it being as much as he can do to go from his bed to the fire and back againe'.[4] He never recovered, dying late the following year.

Dissent strengthened in early eighteenth-century Avebury. Skeat, of course, gave it the support of the parish's leading farmer. John Griffin, who may have served as churchwarden in 1700-1701[5], was another prominent dissenter and local landowner. John and Richard Fowler, innkeepers at West Kennett and Beckhampton respectively, also gave their support[6]. Influential support was provided by Caleb Bailey, whose dissenting charity is discussed below. At the end of the seventeenth century, it may be that the dissenters were able to afford their own minister. Jonathan Rashley was paid £6 per annum from the Presbyterian's national 'Common Fund' for preaching at Avebury between 1692 and 1699.[7] He also taught school in Avebury; at least, that was one of the charges against him made by John White, the vicar, who presented him at visitation in 1698.[8] Rashley was probably the son of Dr Thomas Rashley, one of the ejected ministers mentioned above.[9] According to White, Rashley preached and kept a 'conventicle' without 'being qualified by law' (that is, probably, not having taken the oaths required of dissenting ministers under the Toleration Act). He kept his school without a licence, and, perhaps worst of all from White's point of view, he refused to pay the vicar's Easter dues. The mention of such dues suggests that he was residing in Avebury.

The dissenters probably gained members as a result of the contentiousness of John White, the vicar, who evidently hated dissent. In 1698, he refused to bury a parishioner who was presumably a dissenter: William Skeat reported

1 WSHC 184/8.
2 WSHC D1/42/67.
3 WSHC 184/8.
4 WSHC 184/1, pt.2. John Brinsden to Sir Richard Holford, 13th November, 1711.
5 Waylen, James. *A History, Military and Municipal, of the Town ... of Marlborough ...*. John Russell Smith, 1854, p.436.
6 Gillings, Mark, Pollard, Joshua, Wheatley, David, & Peterson, Rick, eds. *Landscape of the Megaliths: excavation and fieldwork on the Avebury Monuments, 1997-2003*. Oxbow Books, 2008, p.347.
7 Gordon, op cit, p.337.
8 WSHC D1/54/14.
9 Matthews, op cit, p.403; Gordon, op cit, p.337.

to his landlord that 'wee have had a naibor which have lost his wife ye 14 day of this instant Febary & went to ye parson to bery her, & hee refuesed to doe it, & would not let her have christen burrell, nor would not let ye bell ring for her'.[1] White's refusal to bury dissenters became notorious, and led to him being sued in the Consistory Court in 1711. We do not know whether he refused to conduct any other funerals before 1708, but in that year Ruth Mills similarly suffered; the vicar described her as 'formerly a lewd woman', but may have had a grudge against her.[2] Two years later, Richard Bailey, one of the founders of the Meeting House, died. That brought out White's hatred of dissent; he refused to conduct Bailey's funeral service because he was a Presbyterian. Indeed, he instructed Reuben Horsell, the parish clerk, to lock up the parish's copy of the *Book of Common Prayer*, so that John Brinsden, vicar of neighbouring Winterbourne Monkton, who was present, could not conduct a service either.[3] After Bailey's burial, the vicar told Richard Phelps that he would 'bury no more of the Presbyterians, nor suffer any body else to bury them'.[4] Walter Alexander suffered in the same way in February 1710/11. Parishioners tolled the bell for him, but White derived malicious amusement from the fact that they buried Alexander facing west, rather than east.[5] We have already seen that Sir Richard Holford attended a wake for John Pope, who was buried in April 1711 without a funeral service.[6] That may have been the catalyst which led Holford to encourage the suit against White in the Consistory Court, and which persuaded Humphry Robinson (Pope's father in law, and a prominent dissenter) to give evidence against White.[7] White, as has been seen, was rebuked for his neglect by the diocesan Chancellor, but the seriousness with which the issue was considered is reflected in Sir Richard Holford's subsequent letters to John Brinsden in November 1711[8] and May 1712.[9] White was also accused of neglecting to catechise the children, or to read prayers on holy days. It is not surprising that White's attitude offended his parishioners, and probably encouraged the growth of dissent.

1 WSHC 184/1, pt.1. Letter, William Skeat to Sir Richard Holford, 26th February 1697/8.
2 WSHC D1/42/68. Many years earlier, in 1695, Ruth had sued the vicar in Chancery; see TNA C174/72.
3 WSHC D1/42/68. See also Spaeth, op cit, p.201.
4 WSHC D1/42/68.
5 Spaeth, op cit, p.201.
6 GA D1956/E2/8. See above, p.411.
7 Although he did not mention Pope in his deposition.
8 WSHC 184/1, pt.2.
9 WSHC 184/1, pt.2. Letter, 21st May 1712.

That growth resulted in the building of a meeting house, despite the opposition of the vicar, and of the lord of the manor. In March 1706/7, White thought that stone taken from Sir Richard Holford's lands by Skeat might be 'employed in the building of a conventicle house'. Holford responded that 'you apprehend my stones may be employed to the building of a conventicle house for hippocrits, which I must & will oppose'. He did not, however, think that his opposition would 'signifie much to these people',[1] not, presumably, even to his tenant, William Skeat, who may have supplied the stone. Holford was opposed to 'schism', but he does not seem to have regarded it as his business to interfere except when his own property was to be used.

We do not know whether the Meeting House was in fact built with Holford's stones. It must have been almost finished by the date of his letter. 'A new erected house lately built on part of the garden ground of and belonging to a tenement of Samuel Morris at Westbrook (presumably a purpose built chapel) was licenced for Presbyterian worship on 31st March 1707.[2] It was described as a 'meeting house for protestant dissenters' in a 1724 deed.[3] It has been suggested that Silbury House (sometimes known as Norris's Farmhouse), on the other side of the road, was built c.1711 to serve as a manse for the dissenting minister.[4] Both were built within the stone circle, close to the Catherine Wheel and the Cove. Some have attempted to argue that they were deliberately sited within a pagan monument. That is unlikely; rather, they were built in that position merely because Morris happened to own the land.

For the eighteenth century, we only have the names of a handful of dissenting ministers. We know that the minister in 1753 was judged to be 'an honest sensible man' by Arthur Jones, but his name is not known.[5] It is likely that the chapel was occasionally served by lay preachers. A minister cost money, and dissenting preachers depended entirely on their congregations for financial support. They were not well paid; in 1736, the minister received half of the income that the vicar received, despite preaching twice on the Sabbath when the vicar only preached once.[6] Dissenting ministers relied on 'the crumbs which fall from the rich man's table', as James (I) Mayo, the vicar, scathingly put

1   WSHC 184/1, pt.1. Letter, Sir Richard Holford to John White, 6th March 1706/7.
2   Chandler, J.H., ed. *Wiltshire Dissenters' Meeting House Certificates and Registrations, 1689-1852*. Wiltshire Record Society 40. 1985, p.14.
3   WSHC 529/185.
4   *Appraisal of Buildings on the Avebury Estate, part 1. Conservation Plan*, for the National Trust. Ferguson Mann Architects, 1999. Unpublished report held by WBR. By 1794 it was in the ownership of James Hiscock.
5   WSHC 184/3. Memoranda by Nicholas Jones, 4th October 1756.
6   WSHC D1/47/3.

it in 1756.[1] That fact was acknowledged by Caleb Bailey when he established his charity. Bailey himself, lord of the manor of nearby Berwick Bassett, took the oath of allegiance in 1701 as a dissenting preacher, presumably so that he could ride over to Avebury to conduct the occasional service.[2] In 1715, the dissenting minister, John Bale, preached to a congregation numbering 130.[3] Bale served as minister at Avebury, probably until 1728, when he moved to Beckington (Somerset).[4] Joshua Griffith replaced him; he had previously served at Tewkesbury (Gloucestershire). [5]

By c.1700, several local dynasties were woven into the fabric of Avebury dissent.[6] The survival of dissent in Avebury depended on the support of these faithful families, rather than on outstanding preachers.[7] Sadly, we have no list of members or attendees at the dissenting chapel. We do, however, have a register of dissenters' children born between 1696 and 1712. This was entered into the parish register by the hostile vicar, John White, between 1696 and 1712, so that the duty on births, marriages and deaths imposed during those years could be collected. The names of 37 children (from perhaps 21 families) were entered. In the same period, 133 Anglicans were baptised. The duty was abolished in 1705, but entries continued for some years, enabling us to identify many of Avebury's dissenters. Dissent was transmitted through families.[8] Some surnames from White's list recur in a dissenting context throughout the eighteenth century. Many of them are also found in the meeting house certificates: signatories in 1707 included John Griffin, Richard Morris, Edward Cue, Richard Bailey, and Thomas Cue.[9] Sixteen years later, in 1723, another certificate was signed by Joseph Hayward, Thomas Griffin, George Arnold, Edward Cue, Thomas Robinson and Samuel Morris, for the 'house called the meeting house'.[10] This chapel was described as 'Independent', but it is likely that it was the same building

1   WSHC 184/2. Letter, James Mayo to Staynor Holford, 19th August 1756.
2   WSHC A1/110, 1701M.
3   *VCH Wilts*, 3, p.107 (note 84). Surman Index Online https://surman.english.qmul.ac.uk. The Surman index records that Bale was at Avebury from 1717 until 1728, despite the record in John Evans' list as cited by the *V.C.H.*
4   Dissenting Academies Online https://dissacad.english.qmul.ac.uk
5   Surman, op cit.
6   Horn, Pamela. *The Real Lark Rise to Candleford: Life in the Victorian Countryside.* Amberley Publishing, 2012, p.162.
7   *VCH Wilts.*, vol.3, p.120.
8   Spufford, Margaret. *Contrasting communities: English Villagers in the Sixteenth and Seventeenth Centuries.* Cambridge University Press, 1974, p.280 & 294.
9   Chandler, op cit, p.14.
10 Chandler, op cit, p.20.

that had previously been licenced as 'Presbyterian'; some of those who signed in 1723 had previously signed in 1707. The 1720 will of John Pope[1] provided for £20 to be lent 'towards the keeping of the Meeting House in Abery in repeare' for a term of fifteen years.

Little is known of the dissenting cause for the ensuing half century. The non-residence of the Mayo dynasty tended to increase chapel congregations: John Loveday noted in 1729 that 'Mayo lives at Calne: Presbyterians increase here'.[2] The parishioners complained c.1736 that the lack of two services on a Sunday meant that some went to hear the dissenters' minister.[3]

Mention has already been made that Richard Bailey (the son of the Richard Bailey who signed the 1707 certificate), when he died in 1783, left a bequest of two guineas per annum to the minister of the meeting house as long as it continued.[4] At that time, the chapel was served by one Davis, who lived in Marlborough.

Licences were again obtained in 1785 and 1790, this time for 'the dwelling house of Mr Richard Thring'.[5] Thring was a descendant of Richard Bailey senior, so, unless the cause had split (which seems unlikely), these licences actually referred to the chapel.[6]

The Presbyterians in Avebury were probably the only dissenters in the parish until the late eighteenth century, when Methodism threatened to make inroads. The vicar, James Mayo, reported in 1783 that there was an 'unlicensed house' where the Calvinistic Methodist Cornelius Winter occasionally preached.[7] Winter, with the supposed support of Lady Huntingdon, seems to have taken over a former Presbyterian meeting house in Marlborough, and ran a dissenting academy, generally with no more than three or four students at a time.[8] Two of his students, John and William Griffin, may perhaps have been connected with the Avebury family of that name.[9] It is likely that some of his students came with Winter to preach at Avebury. Such occasions were described by William Jay:

1 WSHC P1/P/495.
2 Markham, op cit, p.42.
3 WSHC D1/47/3.
4 WSHC P3/B/1679.
5 In 1790 it was referred to as being owned jointly by Richard Thring and Robert Nalder, who were probably acting as trustees.
6 Chandler, op cit, p.35 & 38.
7 Ransome, op cit, p.27.
8 Ransome, op cit, p.155. See also Stribling, op cit, p.21.
9 Dissenting Academies Online https://dissacad.english.qmul.ac.uk/index.php. But see below.

'There are few things in my life that I can remember with so much melting pleasure, as my going with him – walking by the side of his little horse, and occasionally riding – on a fine summer's evening, into a neighbouring village, and returning again the same night, or very early in the morning. In these instances I was required to take sometimes a part, and sometimes the whole of the service; but it was a privilege rather than a task to do anything before him … . He engaged his students to preach very early after they were with him. This arose partly from the state of the neighbourhood, which wanted help. Souls were perishing for lack of knowledge'.

Winter also 'imagined the sooner the young men began the more facility and confidence they would acquire'.[1] His 'unlicensed house' at Avebury served as a training ground for Calvinistic Methodist ministers.

The vicar, James Mayo, accused Winter of preaching anti-nomianism, that is, the doctrine that one might be 'saved without works', which he thought 'the great enemy of souls'. The number of Winter's adherents in both Marlborough and Avebury was, however, decreasing. The vicar thought that only two or three families, 'one of the rank of farmer, the other poor', frequented Winter's meetings.[2] Mayo hoped that, at least in Avebury, this was due to his attempt at 'living rather than preaching against them', 'taking diligent heed in all things that the ministry be not blamed', and reading the homilies that Methodists complained were not being read. Nevertheless, Mayo did, as we have seen, lay himself open to the charge of non-residence. Winter himself thought that the Marlborough district was 'a high church area, and full of prejudice against Methodism'.[3] He was evidently not wrong!

When Winter moved to Painswick in 1788, one of his (probable) students, William Griffin, became minister at Avebury.[4] The Surman Index claims that he had worked as an agricultural labourer, and was 'uneducated', except perhaps by Winter. It is possible that he was related to Avebury's Griffin family, although he is said to have been born near Lechlade. Avebury Methodists were still meeting in 1804 Avebury,[5] although no meeting house certificate is recorded.[6]

1 Jay, William. *The Works of the Rev. William Jay, of Argyle Chapel, Bath. Vol.III.* Harper & Brothers, 1849, p.63-4. See also Stribling, op cit, p.20-21.
2 Ransome, op cit, p.27.
3 Jay, William. *Memoirs of the life and character of the late Rev. Cornelius Winter*. New York, Samuel Witing & Co., 1811, p.130.
4 Surman Index Online, op cit.
5 WANHS MSS 1290, f.40.
6 There is no mention of Avebury Methodism in Chandler, J.H., ed. *Wiltshire Dissenters' Meeting House Certificates and Registrations, 1689-1852.* Wiltshire

During William Griffin's pastorate in Avebury, he is said to have kept school, presumably for nonconformist's children (perhaps including Presbyterians as well as Methodists?). They were excluded from the charity school established under Lady Holford's will,[1] so his services were badly needed. One wonders whether any dissenter's children were actually prevented from attending the school established under Susanna Holford's will. She had limited provision to 'children whose parents often frequent the church'.[2]

By contrast, Caleb Bailey's will of 1750[3] left a substantial sum of money 'to give to persons who shall preach or study to be fit to preach to congregations of the Presbyterian, Baptist, or Independent denominations'.[4] Bailey had been lord of the manor of Berwick Bassett, and very active in the local land market. He had served as a Justice of the Peace,[5] and had once been nominated to serve as sheriff of the county (although he did not serve).[6] He was also the author of a *Life of Jesus*,[7] and, as already noted, took the oath as a dissenting preacher in 1701.[8] His will, and therefore his charity, was challenged by his cousin Edward Bailey, but whether that was due to Edward's opposition to dissent, or simply because Edward was Caleb's heir at law if the will was void, is not clear.[9]

Bailey named a number of trustees in his will. Several of them, together with their successors, had Avebury connections. John Nalder of West Kennett, together with his brother Thomas of Winterbourne Monkton, were amongst them. Richard Bailey, who paid land tax on John Nalder's farm in Avebury, was another.[10] James Thring of Wilton, who married Richard Bailey's sister

Record Society, 40. 1984.
1 See above, p.171.
2 WSHC 184/8.
3 TNA PROB11/782, f.93. Caleb had no childen.
4 For an account of this charity, see Reeves, K.M. 'The Caleb Bailey Charity', *Baptist Quarterly* 26(2), 1975, p.62-7.
5 Law, Alexander. 'Caleb Bailey, the demolisher', *WANHM* 64, 1969, p.104. One wonders if he was related to Thomas Bailey, rector of Mildenhall, who was a prominent Fifth Monarchist, and a commissioner for ejecting royalist clergy during the Interregnum; cf. Hobbs, Steve, ed. *Gleanings from Wiltshire Parish Registers*. Wiltshire Record Society 63. 2010, p.180; Gunn, H.Mayo. *A Memorial of the Nonconforming Clergy of Wilts and East Somerset in 1662*. Jackson, Walford and Hodder, 1862, p.22.
6 In 1720, cf. Jackson, J.E. 'Sheriffs of Wiltshire', *WAM*, 3(8), 1856-7, p.226
7 He took the oath in support of the articles of religion required of dissenting preachers in 1701; cf. A1/239.
8 WSHC A1/110, 1701M.
9 TNA C11/2124/5.
10 WSHC 184/3. Land tax assessment 1866; A1/345/18A. Land tax assessment 1781.

Elizabeth, was also named. The money raised from Caleb's personal estate was invested in lands in North Bradley, and probably in Avebury as well.[1] Thomas Nalder died in 1756, but his brother made sure that the charity benefited the cause in Avebury. John Nalder kept in his own hands £400 invested in 3% government stock; the interest was always used to support the 'minister oficiating at Averbury'.[2] When James Thring and Richard Bailey both died, John Thring, James's son, and Richard's nephew, acted as executor for both of them, and inherited both of their trusteeships, together with his uncle's property at Avebury and Ogbourne St George.[3] His new trusteeship prompted him to carry out an investigation into the charity's mal-administration, which has been studied in detail by Reeves.[4] His inheritance meant that he was able to play a leading role in Avebury dissent. His 'dwelling house' in Avebury was licenced for dissenting worship in 1785, and again in 1790 (when it was described as the property of Richard Thring and John Nalder).[5] Both licences described the cause as 'Independent', but, in view of the fact that the property licenced was described as a 'dwelling house', rather than a 'chapel', one wonders whether he was providing a meeting place for Winter's Methodists. Be that as it may, it was probably Caleb Bailey's bequest which caused James Mayo, the rector, to observe in 1783, that the Independents 'would have dwindled and sunk to nothing long before this time had it not been for the unseasonable encouragement and support unfortunately given to them some tyme ago by that arch-miser'.[6]

There were no Quakers in Avebury. One who would have been 'a very able and very fit & well quallified tennant' of Avebury Farm was rejected as such by Sir Richard Holford because he 'would have given great distaste to Mr White, & given him a handle to bee troublesome'.[7] One wonders if this was John Withers of Nursteed, Bishops Cannings, who was probably a member of the Devizes Meeting, and was described as a yeoman in his 1719 will.[8]

1   We only have accounts covering North Bradley in WSHC 1281, but various deeds relating to lands in Avebury were signed by three of the trustees, and probably related to the charity.
2   WSHC 1281/7.
3   WSHC P3/B/1679.
4   Reeves, op cit; WSHC 1281.
5   Chandler, J.H., ed. *Wiltshire Dissenters' Meeting House Certificates and Registrations, 1689-1852*. Wiltshire Record Society, 40. 1985, p.35 & 38.
6   Ransome, op cit, p.27.
7   WSHC 184/1, pt.2. Letters, Sir Richard Holford to Richard Chandler, 2nd & 15th June 1709.
8   WSHC P24/865. See also https://qfhs.co.uk/public_html/wills/az/wtext/

Another Quaker, Thomas Neate, made his affirmation in the Archdeaconry court in 1752, when he was named as one of the executors of Robert Caswell of Yatesbury's will; Caswell had formerly served as an Avebury churchwarden. Thomas Nalder, the prominent dissenter, was another of his executors.[1] There were Quakers in neighbouring Winterbourne Monkton in 1669, but no more is heard of them.[2]

It has been suggested that dissent was linked to stone-breaking[3], but this is dubious. The argument is based on the animosity between Anglicans and dissenters. But it ignores the fact that the leading exponent of Anglicanism, John White, was himself guilty of stone destruction. Sir Richard Holford recorded that White himself 'wrongfully broke & carried away a great stone which I would not have parted with for 5^{li} in the place where hee broke it'.[4] It is also worth noting that Caleb Bailey, reputedly one of the leading stone breakers, and also a leading dissenter and substantial landowner, seems to have displayed 'real penitence' for his destructive role[5]. He would not have done so if he had been motivated by religious considerations. As for Thomas Robinson, he was said to have promised Stukeley that he would spare the megaliths still standing in his fields.[6] For him, it had proved to be an expensive way of obtaining stone; he complained that breaking up two of the stones had cost him £8. That was hardly a religious argument. Anglicans and dissenters were equally guilty of stone breaking, and dissenters would not have apologised for actions stemming from their religion. It must be concluded that dissenting religious principles had little relevance to stone-breaking – except, that is, in so far as pieces of the megaliths were used in the building of the dissenters' chapel.[7]

It may, however, be true that Stukeley's disdain for the lower orders caused him to implicate supporters of the dissenting cause in stone-breaking,

---

withers_005.html. Thomas Withers of Bishops Cannings, who was imprisoned as a Quaker for 6 years in 1656, was probably a relation; cf. *VCH Wilts.*, vol.3, p.104 & 116.

1   WSHC P3/C/916.
2   Turner, op cit, vol.1, p.109.
3   Gillings, Mark, Pollard, Joshua, Wheatley, David, & Peterson, Rick. *Landscape of the Megaliths: Excavations and Fieldwork on the Avebury Monuments 1997-2003.* Oxbow Books, 2008, p.343-7. Gillings, Mark, Peterson, Rick, & Pollard, Joshua. 'The destruction of the Avebury monuments', in Cleal, Rosemary, & Pollard, Joshua, eds. *Monuments and material culture: Papers in honour of an Avebury Archaeologist: Isobel Smith.* Hobnob Press, 2004, p.152-60.
4   WSHC 184/1, pt.2. Holford to John Rose, 23rd November 1710.
5   Law, Alexander. 'Caleb Bailey, the Demolisher', *WANHS* 64, 1969, p.102.
6   Gillings, et al, 'Destruction', op cit, p.153.
7   www.minervaconservation.com/projects/avebury.html

rather than to blame gentry like Sir Richard Holford and Ralph Stawell – who also bore some responsibility for the destruction of the monuments. But the fact that the men he accused were dissenters was probably fortuitous. Their dissent is not even mentioned. Nor is the sarsen in the walls of the dissenting chapel. Likewise, Caleb Bailey, the stone-breaking leading gentry supporter of the dissenting cause escaped Stukeley's pen. If Stukeley had thought that dissent had something to do with stone-breaking, he would surely have said so. For Stukeley, blame was to be attached to the lower orders, not to his social equals and superiors.

By contrast to dissent, Roman Catholicism was almost absent from seventeenth and eighteenth century Avebury, as far as can be judged. That is despite the evident support for the old religion in Elizabeth's reign, as demonstrated by the survival of the rood loft.[1] In 1600 William Baldwin of Avebury was fined forty shillings for recusancy (refusal to attend church), and the tithingman was ordered to conduct him to gaol.[2] In 1624 a servant of William Dunch was presented for 'being absent from church by the space of three months'.[3] His name was John Eyreshman, which suggests he was Irish, and hence perhaps Catholic. In 1636, the Hundred constables presented that 'wee have noe recusant within or hundred as wee know of'.[4]

The only other possible opposition to the established church we know of in Avebury relates to an incident that occurred in 1718. Edward Biss, the rector of Portbury in Somerset, perhaps an Oxford acquaintance of John (II) Mayo, was convicted at Salisbury Assizes of saying at Avebury that James, the Old Pretender, was 'my master and my king, the rightful king', suggesting that he may have been a non-juror. Thomas Hearne, who also knew him at Oxford, expressed the opinion that he was mad.[5]

There were also traces of older religions. Aubrey 'described the common people as living in a world more or less imbued with supernatural beliefs'.[6] Fairies were supposed to have led a certain rustic 'a dance to the Devizes' over

---

1   See above, p.384.
2   WSHC A1/150/2, f.27. It is possible, of course, that he did not attend for some other reason.
3   WSHC A1/110, 1624M, f.153.
4   WSHC A1/110, 1636M, f.236. The statement was repeated in 1642; cf. A1/110, 1642M, f.150.
5   Hearne, Thomas. *Remarks and collections of Thomas Hearne*, vol.6. Oxford Historical Society, 1902, p.258-60.
6   Sharpe, J.A. *Early Modern England: A Social History 1550-1760*. Edward Arnold, 1987, p.308.

the Beckhampton downs when he was carrying corn on Hackpen.[1] The local tradition that the stone circle was once a place of worship was recorded by Thomas Twining in 1723.[2] When Edward Drax excavated Silbury in 1776, he reported that 'lights' had reputedly been seen on a nearby barrow[3]. Stukeley recorded that the country people celebrated Palm Sunday by meeting at the top of Silbury Hill, 'when they make merry with cakes, figs, sugar and water fetch'd from the Swallow Head'. He assumed that this gathering could be traced back to the burial of 'the great King', reputedly discovered when Mr Holford ordered the planting of trees on the hill's summit in 1723.[4] Over a century later, in 1858, William Long reported that this custom was still being observed.[5] Meaden traces this celebration back to an ancient fertility rite to celebrate spring, which had been adapted by the church for its own purposes.[6] Other traces of ancient religion can also be found. The Norman font at neighbouring Winterbourne Monkton, for example, bears a carving of a fertility goddess.[7] What is one to make of the dragon on the font at Avebury?

1 Waylen, James. *A History, Military and Municipal, of the Ancient Borough of Devizes*. Longman Brown & Co., 1859, p.127-8.
2 Twining, Thomas. *Avebury in Wiltshire*. Jos Downing, 1723, p.7.
3 Edwards, Brian. 'Silbury Hill: Edward Drax and the excavations of 1776', *WAM*, 103, 2010, p.259.
4 Stukeley, William. *Abury: a temple of the British Druids* ... . 1743, p.41 & 48. Lukis, W.C., ed. *The Family Memoirs of the Rev. William Stukeley, M.D., ... vol.III*. Surtees Society 80, 1885, p.245 & 275.
5 Long, W. 'Abury', *WAM*, 4, 1880, p.340.
6 Meaden, Terence. *The Secrets of the Avebury Stones: Britain's Greatest Megalithic Temple*. Souvenir Press, 1999, p.122.
7 Meaden, op cit, p.116.

SUBJECT INDEX

Absentees, 210, 220, 228
Accidents, 40, 381
Act of Uniformity, 1662, 420
Administration Bonds, 56, 78, 86, 152, 155, 163, 318, 321, 392, 401, 414
Agricultural Labourers. *See* Labourers
Ale, 317, 320, 341, 366, 368, 411
Ale Houses, 302, 402
Ale Sellers, Unlicensed, 317
Alms House, 386
Amercements, 73, 142
Annuities, 57, 93, 94, 97, 98, 106, 109, 119, 142, 163
Anvils, 310
Apothecaries, 279, 311, 324, 325, 383, 393, 396, 402, 403
Apples, 268, 269, 270
Apprenticeship, 54, 66, 67, 68, 70, 74, 78, 80, 85, 93, 97, 115, 140, 154, 156, 162, 277, 278, 279, 280, 304, 318, 324, 360
Apprenticeship, Pauper, 181, 182, 280, 281
Apricots, 269, 270
Arable, 14, 20, 22, 101, 106, 108, 110, 114, 121, 124, 132, 166, 224, 228, 239, 251, 253, 254, 255, 256, 258, 274, 275
Archaeological Finds, 11, 12
Archbishop, 392
Archdeaconry Court, 170, 435
Archdeacons, 200, 389, 399, 413, 416, 425
Archery, 377
Armies, 17, 18, 30, 31, 311
Armourers, 279
Army, 165
Assault, 67, 72, 74, 139, 194, 195, 196, 197, 426
Assizes, 77, 123, 131, 194, 197, 212
Attics, 340, 344, 350, 351
Attorneys, 33, 93, 97, 111, 146, 223, 246, 298, 326, 374, 407

Bacon, 264, 266, 286, 294, 340, 368, 370

Badgers. *See* Chapmen
Bailiffs, 87, 117, 142, 169, 170, 189, 224, 225, 226, 228, 231, 236, 241, 277, 288, 289, 295, 296, 297, 341, 347, 348, 349, 369, 405, 412, 415
Bakers, 314, 366
Bankruptcy, 63, 94, 99, 133, 134, 236, 256, 262, 284, 289, 323
Baptisms, 52
Barley, 79, 111, 120, 194, 258, 259, 261, 292, 308, 321, 366, 367
Barns, 6, 15, 186, 295, 301, 303, 333, 335, 337, 338, 340, 341, 342, 348, 395
Barrels, 304, 305, 321, 339, 366, 367, 368
Barristers. *See* Lawyers
Bastards, 60, 75, 119, 142, 156, 163, 164, 181, 182, 183, 202, 203, 283, 287, 397
Bastardy Bonds, 67
Bath Chronicle, 12, 41
Battles & Skirmishes, 18, 30
Beans, 268, 269, 270
Beckhampton Club, 300, 375, 376
Beds & Bedding, 74, 285, 286, 338, 339, 340, 353, 354, 355, 356, 360, 364, 371
Beef, 263, 294, 314, 315, 369, 370, 387
Beer, 20, 33, 286, 294, 305, 321, 341, 363, 366, 367, 368
Bees, 120, 267, 268, 310, 392
Beggars. *See* Vagrants & Vagrancy
Beliefs, 385, 386, 436
Bell Founders, 55, 115, 278
Bell Ringers, 234, 377, 415, 418, 428
Bells, 115, 124, 131, 171, 377, 384, 385, 390, 417, 428
Bibles, 74, 311, 379, 380, 386
Bird Scaring, 60
Blacksmiths, 70, 73, 89, 124, 155, 229, 235, 244, 245, 246, 259, 264, 266, 267, 274, 309, 310, 311, 312, 339, 340, 341, 361, 364, 367, 368, 370, 379

Bonds, 233, 243, 244, 246, 302, 310, 311, 313, 317, 399, 400, 425
Bones, Medicinal Properties, 7
Book Club, 380, 407
Book of Common Prayer, 74, *379, 380, 409, 414, 417, 420, 428*
Books, 311, 357, 359, 378, 379, 380, 392, 394
Books, Theological, 79, 160, 379, 392
Boundaries, 188
Box, 307
Bread, 170, 173, 175, 178, 199, 294, 314, 339, 340, 366, 368, 371, 387
Brewhouses, 307, 320, 341, 345, 347, 350, 351
Brick, 332, 334, 335, 342, 350, 351
Brick Kiln, 335
Bricklayers, 71, 306
Brickmakers, 335
Burials, 52, 53, 54
Butchers, 156, 167, 301, 314, 315
Butlers, 282, 285, 300
Butter, 66, 263, 264, 265, 339, 370, 371
Butteries, 310, 336, 337, 338, 339, 341, 344, 345, 349, 351, 357, 368, 370
Butts, 189, 377

Cabbages, 268, 269, 270
Caleb Bailey's Charity, 57, 59, 72, 116, 151, 218, 224, 226, 228, 427, 430, 433, 434
Cambridge University, 391, 394
Candles & Candlesticks, 66, 85, 323, 364, 365
Carpenters, 69, 70, 71, 109, 126, 127, 128, 130, 140, 153, 221, 229, 262, 279, 280, 287, 293, 301, 302, 303, 304, 305, 306, 321, 323, 338, 340, 351
Carriers, 29, 32, 33, 34, 35, 39, 311
Cart Houses, 302, 304, 308, 342, 349
Carters, 291, 292, 368
Casual Labour, 290, 292, 293, 295
Catechising, 411, 412, 426, 428
Cats, 375
Cattle, 22, 24, 31, 38, 39, 81, 83, 106, 118, 119, 120, 122, 123, 135, 136, 188, 214, 231, 238, 239, 240, 249, 263, 264, 265, 276, 301, 311, 312, 338, 340, 348, 369, 377, 392, 394, 395, 398, 413, 416
Cattle Market, 28
Cavaliers. *See* Royalists

Cellars, 20
Census, 1801, 51, 52, 276, 408
Chairs, 317, 338, 353, 357, 358, 359
Chambers, 285, 302, 337, 338, 339, 340, 344, 345, 346, 347, 350, 351, 353, 354, 355, 356, 357, 359, 360, 361, 362, 365, 366, 368, 379, 380, 382
Chancellor, DIocesan. *See* Diocesan Chancellor
Chancery, Court of, 17, 63, 78, 84, 86, 91, 93, 94, 95, 118, 131, 134, 137, 144, 157, 158, 160, 166, 197, 218, 236, 244, 247, 267, 270, 309, 324, 326, 389, 393, 396, 399, 400, 425, 426
Chantries, 390
Chapmen, 85, 134, 322, 323
Charitable Bequests, 57, 171, 218, 245, 327, 386, 387, 413, 433
Charity Commissioners, 173
Charity School. *See* Holford Charity
Cheese, 18, 33, 195, 233, 235, 263, 264, 265, 266, 286, 334, 339, 340, 341, 370, 371
Cheese Presses, 321, 341, 371
Cherries, 269, 270
Chicken. *See* Poultry
Children, Poor. *See* Poor Children
Children's Employment, 276, 278, 293, 316, 357
Chimneys, 336, 345, 346, 362, 363
Church, 384, 386, 387, 388, 401, 413, 416, 418, 420, 437
Church Calendar, 377, 385
Church Rates, 169, 170, 417
Churchwardens, 56, 62, 63, 72, 78, 81, 84, 85, 87, 88, 90, 101, 104, 105, 108, 109, 110, 111, 113, 115, 117, 121, 122, 124, 126, 128, 131, 132, 134, 135, 139, 140, 141, 142, 143, 145, 151, 158, 161, 162, 163, 168, 169, 170, 171, 181, 202, 203, 280, 329, 334, 388, 396, 408, 414, 415, 416, 417, 418, 420, 424, 427, 435
Civil War, 17, 30, 33, 76, 148, 190, 198, 278, 311, 376, 385, 386, 393, 394, 398, 419, 420
Clergy, 324, 379, 383, 389, 391, 397, 400, 401, 403, 404, 405, 406, 408, 409, 410, 411, 412, 413, 424, 433
Clergy, Dissenting. *See* Ministers, Dissenting, *See* Ministers, Dissenting

SUBJECT INDEX 441

Clothes. *See* Wearing Apparell
Clothiers, 175, 227, 315, 316
Clover, 251, 258, 261, 262, 301
Club Movement, 18
Coach Guards, 295
Coach Houses, 348, 350, 351
Coach Passengers, 320
Coaches, 3, 4, 10, 12, 15, 22, 28, 29, 32, 35, 36, 38, 39, 40, 284, 321, 373
Coachmen, 16, 32, 34, 40, 197, 284, 311
Coal, 33, 36, 310, 341, 362, 363, 364
Cob, 332, 336
Coffee, 367
Coffers, 283, 339, 360
Coffins, 304, 325
Collar Makers, 280, 312, 313
Common Fields. *See* Open Fields
Commons, 42, 83, 84, 101, 106, 110, 114, 135, 150, 188
Communion, 121, 193, 409, 418, 423
Compton Census, 51
Consistory Court, 74, 121, 127, 128, 169, 202, 284, 323, 409, 420, 426, 428
Constables, High. *See* High Constables
Constables, Parish, 18, 87, 115, 125, 154, 168, 169, 170, 175, 177, 188, 193, 198, 199, 200, 322
Coopers, 304, 305
Copyholds, 58, 101, 112, 113, 119, 135, 137, 150, 155, 185, 202, 215, 216, 219, 230, 236, 237, 249, 322, 394, 395, 396
Cordwainers. *See* Shoemakers
Corn, 83, 122, 156
Corn Chandlers, 69
Cottages & Cottagers, 58, 59, 68, 69, 72, 73, 85, 101, 102, 107, 110, 122, 123, 133, 153, 164, 172, 178, 186, 220, 230, 238, 239, 242, 295, 307, 308, 318, 328, 334, 336, 344, 401, 407
Cotton, 70, 174, 319
Court Books, Hundred, 188
Court of Arches, 389
Court Rolls, Manorial, 169, 185
Cow Stalls, 265, 301
Cows. *See* Cattle
Credit, 54, 243, 244
Creditors, 18, 39, 84, 117, 133, 152, 163
Crime, 40, 41
Crown, 19, 77, 160, 209, 210, 211, 213, 225, 237

Curates, 86, 108, 241, 380, 384, 389, 391, 402, 403, 404, 405, 406, 407, 408, 409, 410, 413

Daggers, 377
Dairies, 307, 340, 341, 345, 347, 349, 365
Dairymen, 291, 292
Dancing, 377, 378
Dearth. *See* Famine
Death Rates, 52
Debts, 70, 76, 83, 118, 132, 149, 152, 159, 161, 163, 167, 172, 211, 214, 215, 243, 245, 246, 247, 302, 318, 323, 328, 393
Debts, Desperate, 243, 244, 245, 310, 313, 395
Declaration of Indulgence, 1672, 421
Deer, 271, 369, 373
Demography, 51, 52, 53, 54
Dinner Guests, 372, 373, 376, 397, 425
Diocesan Chancellor, 372, 426, 427, 428
Diseases, 32, 52, 53, 54, 97, 165, 166, *325*, 380, 381, 382, 383
Dissenters, 10, 13, 19, 51, 52, 54, 57, 58, 61, 63, 83, 85, 86, 101, 102, 103, 104, 105, 119, 120, 123, 129, 138, 139, 153, 173, 218, 228, 247, 311, 377, 387, 395, 398, 401, 411, 419, 420, 422, 423, 424, 427, 428, 430, 431, 433, 435, 436
Dissenters' Children, Register of, 57, 85, 103, 127, 430
Dissolution, 211, 236, 390
Dogs, 33, 373, 374, 375
Dovecotes, 212, 271, 343, 349, 370
Downlands, 14, 15, 16, 17, 20, 22, 24, 26, 28, 31, 32, 40, 41, 42, 81, 108, 178, 231, 232, 250, 251, 252, 253, 256, 259, 263
Drinking, 188
Drought, 251
Drovers, 27, 28, 38, 39, 311, 320
Drowners, 22, 292
Dung, 250, 256, 257, 258, 266, 270, 290, 292, 293
Dyers, 316

East India Company, 95
Easter Offerings, 86, 389
Ecclesiastical Courts, 200, 201, 203
Eggs, 267, 370, 371, 398
Elections, Parliamentary, 56, 67, 68, 128, 150, 308, 375

Elopement, 166
Enclosure, 7, 19, 20, 23, 38, 66, 72, 107, 108, 114, 153, 174, 204, 209, 221, 222, 223, 224, 225, 275, 294, 299, 385, 405
Enclosure Commissioners, 23, 224, 225, 299, 405
Eviction, 84, 177, 208, 235, 239, 251
Excavations, 5, 8, 24
Exchequer, Court of, 77, 82, 86, 112, 118, 120, 141, 197, 206, 212, 237, 425
Excise Officer, 207, 221
Excommunication, 421, 426, 427

Fairs, 16, 17, 28, 53
Famine, 52, 251
Farm Servants, 284, 289
Farriers, 311
Fences, 256, 257
Fertility, 253, 255, 256, 257, 258
Fire Places, 338, 339, 362, 365
Fires, 89, 150, 152, 186, 333, 334, 342, 344
Fireside Implements, 362, 363
Firewood, 294, 333, 341, 363
Fish, 271, 272
Fish Ponds, 370
Fish Slabs, 301, 370
Fishmongers, 279, 317, 370
Five Mile Act, 1665, 421
Flint, 335
Floods, 20, 21, 23, 29, 63, 251, 379
Fonts, 384, 437
Food, 278, 283, 294, 337, 338, 340, 366, 371, 372
Footmen, 29, 284
Fowls. *See* Poultry
Freeholders' Books, 57, 58, 67, 69, 73, 89, 103, 105, 109, 113, 117, 125, 128, 134, 146, 153
Fruit, 234, 235, 268, 269, 270, 286, 371, 372
Fullers, 281, 316
Funeral Director, 89
Funerals, 285, 409, 410, 411, 414, 417, 418
Funerals, Dissenters, 57, 414, 426, 428
Furniture, 147, 155, 330, 332, 352, 353, 355, 356, 359, 360

Gallery, 385
Gamekeepers, 69, 84, 106, 285, 296, 299, 300, 318, 373, 374, 375, 376

Gardeners, 268, 269, 270, 285, 295, 296
Gardens, 9, 20, 24, 25, 26, 230, 234, 235, 238, 239, 262, 268, 301, 302, 304, 307, 336, 337, 346, 349, 371, 389
Geese, 267, 371
Gentry, 71, 132, 135, 140, 141, 161, 164, 168, 190, 191, 201, 203, 208, 210, 218, 219, 329, 351, 372, 373, 436
Gibbet, 196
Glasshouses, 303
Glaziers, 58, 88, 234, 300, 307, 308
Gleaning, 197, 366
Glebe, 229, 392, 394, 395, 405, 408
Glebe Terrier, 143, 219, 374, 396, 400, 401
Grass, 15, 20, 22, 31, 233, 251, 260, 261, 262, 263, 265, 273, 275
Greenhouses, 268
Grocers, 66, 80, 144, 279, 323
Grocers Company, 278
Gunmakers, 279
Guns, 376

Haberdashers, 89
Hair Powder Tax, 153, 408
Halls, 335, 337, 338, 339, 345, 348, 350, 351, 353, 354, 356, 357, 358, 359, 360, 362, 365, 375, 376, 380
Hares, 315, 369, 373, 374, 375
Harrows, 310, 342
Harvest, 65, 236, 250, 251, 259, 261, 264, 266, 292, 293, 342, 366, 368, 372
Harvest Work, 230, 237, 296
Hatchments, 77
Hawking, 373, 375
Hay, 21, 22, 212, 233, 240, 251, 258, 259, 260, 261, 273, 274, 275, 292, 301, 308, 309, 343, 388, 392, 394
Haywards, 188
Health, 94, 97, 242, 269, 289, 380, 381, 382, 383, 427
Hearth Tax, 51, 82, 102, 111, 112, 114, 123, 143, 148, 162, 206, 337, 347
Hedges, 26, 185, 189, 195, 224, 234, 257
Hemp, 260
Heraldic Arms, 77, 110, 157
Heriots, 237
High Constables, 56, 57, 59, 69, 73, 78, 90, 101, 104, 108, 111, 134, 142, 143, 162, 169, 175, 182, 189, 190, 191, 192, 193, 198, 230, 241, 283, 323

SUBJECT INDEX 443

Highway Rates, 184
Highway Surveyors, 63, 168, 170, 175, 184, 192
Highwaymen, 195, 196
Hiring Fairs, 283
Hives. *See* Bees
Holford Charity, 88, 97, 171, 172, 173, 179, 277, 327, 328, 334, 387, 433
Homage, 81, 154, 237, 372
Homilies, 409, 417, 432
Honey, 370
Hops, 270, 322, 368
Horses, 11, 16, 29, 35, 38, 40, 83, 97, 110, 114, 122, 123, 136, 186, 199, 231, 233, 234, 240, 262, 272, 273, 274, 295, 297, 310, 311, 312, 313, 320, 338, 343, 349, 363, 392, 394, 432
House of Commons, 146
House of Lords, 91
Housekeepers, 283, 285, 286
Houses, 5, 10, 12, 13, 15, 16, 24, 27, 28, 37, 42, 181, 186, 188, 191, 206, 283, 301, 302, 311, 318, 329, 330, 331, 332, 333, 334, 335, 336, 337, 338, 339, 340, 344, 348, 349, 350, 351, 352, 355, 359, 371, 394
Houses of Correction, 282
Houses, Pauper, 174, 179, 303, 336
Huguenots, 95
Hundred Constables. *See* High Constables
Hundred Courts, 62, 69, 73, 108, 129, 168, 169, 188, 189, 190, 192
Hunting, 300, 373, 374, 376
Hurdles, 255, 256, 289, 290, 300, 308, 309, 341

Illegitimacy. *See* Bastards
Illnesses. *See* Diseases
Injuries, 62, 137, 139, 324, 381
Inmates, 185, 186
Innkeepers, 8, 67, 68, 88, 151, 152, 259, 274, 319, 320, 322, 323, 341, 343, 357, 358, 359, 364, 366, 367, 368, 370, 427
Inns, 9, 13, 27, 30, 37, 38, 39, 89, 92, 146, 150, 151, 152, 320, 331, 351, 358, 367, 373
Inquisitions Post Mortem, 75, 77, 141
Insurance, 314, 334, 402
Interest, 64, 79, 132, 172, 206, 245, 246, 311, 386, 387, 434

Interregnum, 148, 149, 184, 215, 393, 417

Jurors, 56, 58, 61, 62, 67, 70, 73, 77, 78, 81, 90, 101, 102, 103, 105, 107, 108, 110, 111, 114, 117, 124, 125, 128, 129, 134, 137, 139, 143, 146, 150, 151, 159, 160, 163, 169, 182, 189, 190, 191, 192, 193, 194, 282, 423, 424
Justices of the Peace, 7, 169, 180, 182, 189, 190, 191, 193, 194, 197, 203, 281, 283, 287, 300, 374, 401, 410, 425, 433

Kennett & Avon Canal, 41, 42
Kings Bench, 137
Kitchen Utensils, 338, 365, 366
Kitchens, 321, 337, 338, 339, 341, 344, 345, 347, 349, 351, 359, 360, 365
Knight Service, 77, 160

Labourers, 55, 67, 69, 85, 100, 105, 109, 126, 130, 154, 169, 181, 182, 195, 200, 235, 242, 283, 288, 289, 290, 291, 292, 293, 294, 295, 296, 306, 315, 334, 336, 355, 361, 366, 371, 372, 378, 432, *See also* Casual Labour
Land Tax, 56, 58, 63, 65, 68, 71, 72, 73, 74, 84, 88, 89, 99, 100, 104, 106, 107, 109, 119, 120, 125, 129, 130, 133, 134, 152, 153, 205, 207, 208, 220, 226, 227, 228, 229, 230, 234, 239, 240, 241, 242, 248, 308, 322, 408, 433
Land Tax Assessors, 56, 66, 73, 87, 90, 104, 107, 108, 221
Landowners, 203, 208, 209, 210, 220, 221, 223, 225, 226, 228, 229, 239, 246, 248, 257, 272, 301, 388, 398
Lawyers, 75, 90, 91, 94, 95, 96, 100, 145, 146, 217, 248, 325, *See also* Attorneys
Leases, 208, 210, 211, 217, 219, 225, 229, 231, 232, 233, 234, 235, 236, 237, 238, 239, 240, 241, 249, 253, 254, 257, 258, 270, 283, 310, 314, 317, 336, 337, 347, 352, 402, 404
Leisure, 372, 378
Licencing, 188, 203
Lime Burners, 306
Literacy & Illiteracy, 64, 73, 74, 103, 130, 131, 133, 173, 277, 412, 413, 415
London Evening Post, 28
London Gazette, 116, 134

Lord Chancellor, 404

Machinery, 316
Maids, 120, 265, 284, 285, 286, 287, 288, 289, 345
Malt, 259, 260, 294, 321, 322, 338, 339, 343, 344, 345, 360, 366, 367, 386
Malt Houses, 28, 103, 104, 166, 320, 321, 343, 349
Malt Mills, 321, 367, 368
Maltsters, 58, 71, 89, 102, 103, 151, 166, 321, 322, 343, 367
Manorial Courts, 81, 101, 121, 168, 169, 184, 185, 186, 187, 188, 192
Manors, 55, 69, 75, 76, 82, 83, 92, 93, 94, 96, 97, 100, 114, 115, 134, 140, 147, 148, 149, 157, 158, 159, 161, 165, 169, 209, 210, 211, 212, 213, 214, 215, 216, 217, 219, 220, 225, 227, 228, 230, 231, 236, 237, 238, 239, 247, 248, 249
Manse, Nonconformist, 343, 429
Markets, 10, 17, 18, 28, 31, 34, 39, 41, 196, 199, 261, 292, 301, 330, 364, 370, 419, 433
Marriage Act, 1753, 52, 106
Marriage Register, 67, 100, 173, 289, 319, 406, 415
Marriages, 52, 54, 406, 409, 417, 430
Masons, 69, 70, 71, 234, 235, 300, 305, 306, 307
Masters in Chancery, 91, 94
Maypole, 377
Meadows, 20
Medics, 213, 246, 323, 324, 325
Meeting House Licences, 57, 86, 102, 127
Members of Parliament, 75, 76, 92, 148, 156, 227
Methodism, 431, 432
Militia, 122, 198, 199, 285, 378
Milk, 263, 264, 265
Millers, 366
Ministers, Dissenting, 54, 57, 171, 173, 387, 389, 402, 420, 421, 422, 427, 429, 430, 431
Mobility, 53
Moles, 125, 259
Money, 243, 244
Money Lenders. *See* Creditors
Mortality, 53, 54

Mortgages, 58, 62, 68, 80, 103, 105, 113, 130, 143, 145, 146, 150, 151, 159, 161, 163, 246, 247, 248, 294, 302, 311, 323, 395
Murder, 169
Musters, 198, 199

Mutton, 254, 275, 314, 315, 368, 369, 370
Napoleonic Wars, 199, 200
National Trust, 13, 21, 271, 342, 343
Needlework, 277
Non-Jurors, 436
Non-Residence of Vicar, 51, 402, 404, 405, 431, 432

Oats, 258, 259, 260, 308, 341
Onions, 268, 269
Open Fields, 19, 20, 22, 23, 60, 86, 114, 124, 133, 166, 221, 251, 252, 256, 258, 264, 366
Orchards, 258, 268, 270, 337, 345, 348, 349, 371, 398
Ovens, 314, 338, 339, 345, 349
Overseers of the Poor, 60, 72, 74, 75, 84, 86, 87, 105, 126, 132, 134, 141, 153, 168, 169, 170, 171, 174, 176, 177, 179, 180, 181, 182, 183, 199, 203, 280, 281, 309, 319
Owner Occupation, 221, 228
Oxen, 263, 264, 273, 274, 275, 291, 311, 331, *See Also* Cattle
Oxford University, 94, 96, 277, 390, 391, 396, 402, 403, 404, 406, 407, 436

Pack-horses, 29, 32
Painters, 279, 307
Pantries, 340, 347, 351
Parish Accounts, 170
Parish Chest, 171, 177, 180
Parish Clerks, 7, 9, 42, 65, 79, 98, 99, 100, 313, 317, 409, 413, 414, 415, 418, 428
Parish Register, 52, 53, 54
Parliamentarians, 17, 18, 19, 24, 31, 33, 393, 394, 419
Parliamentary Elections. *See* Elections, Parliamentary
Parlours, 338, 339, 344, 345, 346, 348, 350, 351, 355, 356, 357, 358, 360, 362, 365, 370, 379

SUBJECT INDEX

Pasture, 77, 101, 106, 110, 122, 133, 150, 152, 188, 213, 214, 217, 218, 219, 221, 230, 231, 239, 252, 253, 263, 312, 336
Paten, 76
Patrons, 391
Paupers, 55, 156, 173, 174, 175, 177, 178, 179
Pedlars. *See* Chapmen
Pennings, 256, 257, 290
Petition, 51, 71, 146
Pews, 384, 418
Pewter, 338, 339, 360, 364, 365, 366, 368
Pigeon Houses. *See* Dovecotes
Pigeons, 267, 271, 272, 370, 371, 398
Pigs, 83, 122, 186, 189, 249, 264, 266, 301, 310, 315, 341, 370, 392, 394
Plague, 52, 53, 54, 175, 322, 325, 380
Ploughmen, 291, 292, 293
Ploughs & Ploughing, 72, 117, 253, 273, 274, 275, 293, 310, 342
Plumbers, 88, 308
Plundering, 17, 18, 244
Poaching, 126, 194, 195, 369, 370, 371
Ponds, 24
Poor, 60, 67, 74, 79, 88, 99, 142, 170, 172, 173, 174, 175, 177, 178, 179, 181, 197, 199, 208, 242, 246, 276, 282, 294, 295, 316, 328, 329, 330, 336, 337, 351, 360, 366, 367, 369, 370, 371, 386, 387, 388, 401, 406, 407, 425, 432
Poor Children, 171, 172, 173, 276, 277, 327, 413
Poor Rates, 134, 170, 174, 175, 202, 205, 225, 316
Poor Relief, 14, 86, 87, 170, 173, 174, 175, 179, 180, 181, 183, 242, 295, 313, 314
Population. *See* Demography
Portraits, 146, 147, 378, 379
Postal service, 33, 34
Potatoes, 262, 268, 269
Poultry, 195, 267, 315, 370, 371, 392
Pound, Common, 186, 187, 189, 190
Presbyterian's Common Fund, 427
Presbyterians, 394, 419, 420
Presentments, 169, 170, 175, 181, 182, 185, 186, 188, 189, 190, 191, 192, 193, 195, 198, 200, 202, 203, 389, 415, 417, 418, 420, 423, 424, 427, 436
Probate, 54, 74, 82, 99, 117, 151, 201, 202, 315, 316, 360, 386, 392, 394, 401, 412

Probate Inventories, 63, 66, 78, 99, 102, 104, 111, 112, 113, 117, 120, 122, 125, 128, 131, 141, 151, 152, 155, 159, 160, 161, 162, 201, 243, 244, 245, 249, 254, 255, 259, 260, 261, 262, 263, 264, 265, 266, 267, 268, 301, 309, 310, 311, 313, 317, 321, 329, 337, 338, 339, 340, 342, 345, 351, 352, 353, 354, 355, 356, 357, 358, 359, 361, 362, 364, 366, 371, 376, 377, 392, 394, 395, 412
Puritanism, 76, 121, 149, 385, 419

Quakers, 232, 398, 434, 435
Quarter Sessions, 34, 35, 57, 58, 60, 61, 62, 67, 69, 73, 74, 79, 82, 83, 90, 101, 102, 103, 105, 107, 108, 109, 110, 111, 113, 114, 115, 117, 119, 125, 129, 131, 134, 137, 139, 140, 142, 143, 160, 162, 169, 175, 177, 182, 184, 189, 190, 191, 192, 193, 194, 195, 196, 197, 198, 278, 282, 287, 420, 423, 424, 425

Rabbit Warrens, 300, 369
Rabbits, 271, 315, 369
Railways, 275
Rape, 260
Rates, 174, *See also* Church Rates, Poor Rates, Highway Rates
Rats, 259, 293
Reading, 172, 173, 277
Recognizances, 60, 72, 139, 176, 177, 193, 195, 196, 287
Religion, Prehistoric, 436, 437
Religious Preambles, 385, 386
Rent, 56, 60, 61, 62, 73, 80, 84, 85, 94, 102, 105, 106, 110, 113, 131, 140, 141, 147, 148, 150, 154, 156, 157, 159, 164, 215, 216, 218, 225, 227, 230, 231, 232, 233, 234, 235, 236, 237, 238, 239, 242, 248, 250, 253, 257, 291, 314, 333, 336, 390
Ricks, 259, 260, 261, 308, 309, 349, 394
Rioting, 194, 197, 199, 283, 284, 308, 316, 377
Roads, 9, 10, 12, 14, 16, 22, 23, 27, 28, 29, 30, 31, 32, 33, 34, 35, 36, 37, 38, 39, 40, 41, 42, 178, 185, 189, 191, 192, 204, 299, 303, 320, 322, *See* also Turnpike
Rogation, 377, 418
Roman Catholicism, 436
Rood Loft, 364, 384, 390, 436

Rother Beast. *See* Cattle
Royal & Sun Alliance, 334
Royal Arms, 171, 416
Royal Mail, 38, 41
Royal Mint, 75
Royalists, 17, 18, 19, 30, 33, 76, 148, 149, 388, 393, 394
Rye, 259, 260

Sack Weaver, 181
Saddler, 279, 312, 313, 340
Sarsen, 330, 331, 332, 336, 343, 344, 351
Saw-pits, 302
Schools & Schoolmasters, 55, 64, 65, 66, 67, 71, 97, 171, 172, 173, 246, 276, 277, 327, 387, 388, 389, 403, 404, 407, 414, 427, 433
Sermons, 340, 357, 390, 392, 408, 409, 419, 425
Servants, 65, 67, 79, 126, 134, 139, 147, 182, 199, 269, 270, 272, 277, 282, 283, 284, 285, 286, 287, 288, 289, 292, 294, 295, 300, 315, 320, 325, 340, 346, 354, 355, 356, 357, 370, 374, 375, 383, 411, 412, 418, 436, *See* Also Maids
Settlement, 86, 175, 177, 179, 180, 181, 281, 295
Settlement Certificates, 86, 177, 180
Settlement Examinations, 75, 179, 180, 181, 281, 282
Settlement, Family, 111, 134, 144, 148, 159
Shearers, 290, 292
Sheep, 3, 14, 15, 20, 21, 22, 24, 27, 28, 31, 32, 83, 110, 114, 118, 120, 121, 122, 123, 124, 131, 133, 136, 188, 189, 196, 212, 214, 223, 230, 231, 240, 249, 250, 251, 252, 253, 254, 255, 256, 257, 258, 259, 260, 261, 262, 263, 274, 275, 284, 288, 290, 291, 301, 310, 315, 338, 341, 374, 375, 377
Sheep Bells, 256
Sheep Cotes. *See* Pennings
Sheep Folds, 20, 22, 251, 255
Sheep Shearing, 377
Shepherds, 60, 99, 120, 255, 256, 288, 290, 291, 292, 316, 338, 354, 364, 375, 383
Sheriffs, 76, 190, 191, 227
Shoemakers, 99, 103, 154, 278, 301, 313, 314, 318, 340
Shooting, 375, 376

Shopkeepers, 66, 85, 129
Shops, 301, 302, 309, 311, 312, 313, 317, 323, 325, 340, 342, 351, 370, 402
Sidesmen, 124, 415
Slander, 202
Slavery, 282
Smallpox, 52, 53, 166
Snow, 40, 179
Soap, 329, 365
Soldiers, 163, 165, 198, 199, 200, 388, 393
Spanish Fleet, Capture of, 92
Spinners, 315
Spinning, 174, 178
Spinning Machines, 175, 178, 199
Spinning Turns, 316, 338
Spinsters, 178, 316
Sports, 377, 378
Stables, 293, 302, 304, 306, 307, 333, 336, 337, 343, 348, 351
Star Chamber, 197, 212, 377
Statute Labour, 184, 192
Staves, 377
Stay Makers, 71
Stewards, 232, 325
Stocks, 188, 189, 190
Stones, Megalithic, 3, 4, 5, 6, 7, 8, 9, 10, 11, 12, 13, 15, 26, 27, 42, 99, 108, 437
Destruction, 9, 10, 55, 106, 128, 130, 146, 150, 153, 296, 302, 310, 330, 331, 378, 435
Straw, 233, 257, 258, 273, 330, 331, 332, 333, 349
Straw Plaiting, 178, 179, 276, 317, 329, 407
Studies, 340, 345, 350, 379, 380
Subsidy, 75, 76, 81, 110, 111, 120, 121, 135, 138, 140, 141, 143, 157, 158, 159, 162, 248, 249
Surgeons. *See* Medics
Surveyors, 65
Surveys, 24, 28, 110, 121, 184, 221, 230, 268, 285, 298, 300, 337, 345
Swords, 376

Tables, 283, 303, 317, 338, 353, 356, 357, 358, 359, 360, 372, 380, 429
Tailors, 70, 279, 280, 315, 317, 318, 323, 324, 357, 359
Tallow Chandlers, 279
Tanners, 313
Tea, 367

SUBJECT INDEX

Tenants, 55, 58, 61, 62, 77, 79, 82, 83, 85, 87, 94, 101, 109, 110, 112, 116, 121, 123, 124, 130, 131, 132, 133, 135, 138, 139, 141, 143, 149, 153, 158, 162, 168, 177, 185, 186, 188, 191, 203, 205, 206, 208, 209, 218, 219, 220, 221, 226, 227, 229, 230, 231, 232, 233, 234, 235, 236, 239, 240, 241, 242, 243, 250, 252, 253, 254, 256, 257, 260, 277, 286, 294, 296, 297, 300, 303, 308, 309, 314, 318, 332, 333, 334, 337, 341, 347, 348, 349, 350, 370, 373, 385, 388, 398, 412, 423, 426, 429
Tenants in Chief, 77
Tenants, Sub-, 58, 101, 141, 163, 233, 257
Thatch, 25, 261, 290, 308, 309, 332, 333, 334, 336, 342, 344, 351
Thatchers, 276, 300, 308, 309, 332
Theft, 55, 79, 194, 195, 196, 251
Tilers, 298, 333
Tiles, 309, 333, 343
Timber, 25, 27, 301, 330, 334, 335, 340, 363
Timber-Frames, 302, 332, 334, 342
Tithes, 58, 65, 69, 82, 83, 86, 107, 113, 118, 123, 127, 130, 131, 139, 150, 153, 158, 159, 161, 162, 194, 197, 209, 213, 214, 225, 226, 231, 260, 263, 267, 271, 284, 285, 297, 382, 385, 388, 389, 390, 398, 399, 400, 401, 403, 405, 416, 425, 426, 427
Tithingmen, 57, 61, 63, 69, 72, 73, 81, 82, 84, 90, 105, 108, 111, 113, 121, 131, 143, 151, 160, 168, 169, 182, 188, 189, 190, 193
Tithings, 27, 168, 169, 188, 190, 198, 205
Tobacco, 85, 323, 378
Toilets, 303, 346, 350, 359
Toleration Act, 1689, 397, 423, 427
Toll Collectors, 319, 320
Toll Houses, 37, 203, 204, 304, 319, 320
Topography, 14
Tradesmen, 276, 277, 278, 296, 300, 301, 311
Trees, 6, 11, 25, 26, 27, 186, 251, 268, 270, 293, 346, 437
Turkeys, 267, 370, 371
Turners, 279, 301
Turnips, 55, 195, 251, 252, 261, 262
Turnpike, 14, 27, 28, 29, 30, 32, 35, 36, 37, 38, 39, 40, 41, 146, 151, 184, 203

Turnpike Keepers, 154
Turnpike Trustees, 11, 27, 31, 37, 66, 89, 108, 153, 175, 203, 204, 303
Tylers, 85, 234

Vagrants & Vagrancy, 14, 174, 175, 176, 177, 179
Vegetables, 268, 269, 371
Venison, 369, 370
Vermin, 259
Vestry, 170, 171, 172, 173, 174, 184, 298, 327, 329, 385, 406, 414, 415
Vestry Book, 171
Vestry Clerk, 64, 103, 170, 172
Vetches, 258, 261, 262, 342
Vicarage, 350, 389, 393, 399, 408, 413
Vines, 269
Vintners, 278
Visitation, Heraldic, 90, 135, 141, 157, 160
Visitations, Ecclesiastical, 158, 200, 201, 391, 412, 415, 424
Voting, Right to, 56, 58, 67, 68, 103, 109, 128, 150, 156, 191, 308

Wages, 180, 193, 282, 285, 289, 293, 294, 295, 299
Wardship, 76, 160
Water, 330, 350, 365, 366
Water Closets. *See* Toilets
Water Cress, 269
Water Meadows, 14, 21, 22, 23, 258, 260, 261, 292, 307
Wealth Distribution, 248, 249
Wearing Apparel, 178, 179, 195, 200, 278, 353, 360, 361, 362, 392
Weather, 16, 40, 236, 250, 251, 254, 256, 259, 261, 262, 293, 332, 333
Weavers, 276, 279, 281, 315, 316, 317, 361
Weavers, Sack, 295
Wells, 24, 301, 304
Wheat, 120, 122, 155, 233, 250, 251, 253, 258, 259, 261, 274, 292, 293, 301, 308, 332, 341, 366, 392, 394, 395, 426
Wheelwrights, 70, 126, 279, 280, 301, 303, 304, 305, 321
Whigs, 397
Whipping, 175, 176, 183, 195
White Houses. *See* Dairies
Whitewash, 349

Wills, 66, 71, 79, 86, 88, 104, 120, 136, 141, 201, 245, 278, 287, 288, 361, 362, 379, 385, 391, 392, 410, 433
Wiltshire Yeomanry Cavalry, 200, 378
Window Tax, 58, 66, 84, 109, 349, 352
Windows, 308, 344, 349, 351, 352
Windows, Church, 384, 416, 417
Women's Employment, 276, 283, 292, 316, 366
Women's Work, 292

Wood, 25, 204, 234, 301, 335, 363, 365, 368
Woodhouses, 301, 333, 351
Wool, 250, 251, 254, 255, 267, 310, 315, 361, 368
Woollen Industry, 315, 316
Workhouses, 178
Worship, 385, 397, 408, 409, 413, 421, 423, 429, 434, 437
Writing, 172, 173, 277, 327, 398, 412

PLACE INDEX

Yellow Fever, 165
Yeomen, 56, 69, 72, 81, 87, 102, 103, 110, 114, 119, 122, 124, 139, 140, 149, 154, 155, 161, 208, 210
Aldbourne, 51, 212, 271, 315, 408, 422
Alderton, 413
Alexander Keiller Museum, 343, 348
All Cannings, 14, 61, 402
Alton Priors, 28
Amwell Magna (Herts), 147
Ashton Keynes, 391
Avebury Down, 256
Avebury Great Farm, 77, 80, 83, 94, 102, 131, 133, 138, 142, 143, 168, 208, 214, 218, 230, 231, 232, 234, 248, 250, 252, 253, 254, 256, 257, 263, 265, 267, 270, 273, 286, 290, 291, 294, 297, 300, 312, 332, 334, 341, 347, 397, 412
Avebury Tithing, 73, 168, 198, 205, 220, 222, 248, 337
Avebury Trusloe, 17, 26, 27, 76, 82, 83, 114, 115, 117, 136, 137, 150, 157, 161, 184, 185, 186, 209, 211, 212, 214, 215, 216, 227, 236, 237, 239, 247, 249, 254, 258, 289, 296, 297, 340, 344, 351, 352, 377, 395, 396, 411
Axford, 119

Back Street Tithing, 169
Bannings, 336, 350, 351
Bar Close, 20, 23, 26, 257
Barbor's Court, 140, 395
Barbury, 230
Barnard's Inn, 78, 80, 143, 146

Bath (Som), 7, 28, 32, 33, 35, 36, 38, 39, 97, 116, 165, 179, 246, 311, 314, 321, 325, 334
The Tunns, 373
Bath Road, 3, 4, 16, 30, 35, 42, 146, 177, 184, 272, 319, 320
Beaminster (Dor), 394
Bear Inn, 27, 38, 39, 41, 320
Beckhampton, 6, 8, 9, 10, 14, 16, 17, 18, 20, 26, 27, 28, 30, 31, 33, 35, 37, 38, 39, 40, 41, 42, 51, 61, 68, 69, 77, 79, 80, 81, 82, 92, 96, 98, 100, 107, 110, 112, 113, 114, 123, 124, 128, 130, 131, 133, 141, 142, 146, 151, 158, 159, 161, 162, 163, 164, 168, 175, 176, 182, 184, 185, 186, 188, 193, 195, 196, 199, 200, 203, 204, 205, 209, 212, 213, 214, 216, 217, 218, 220, 221, 225, 226, 227, 228, 229, 231, 238, 240, 241, 242, 248, 249, 253, 257, 283, 284, 287, 295, 300, 301, 303, 304, 307, 309, 312, 313, 320, 333, 336, 337, 344, 352, 373, 389, 390, 395, 399, 418, 425, 426, 427, 437
Beckhampton Chapel, 61, 76, 82, 158, 159, 161, 162, 209
Beckhampton Common, 238
Beckhampton Down, 378
Beckhampton Farm, 216, 298, 363
Beckhampton House, 152, 240, 336, 351, 368, 374, 378
Beckhampton Tithing, 190, 198, 205, 248
Bedminster (Som), 176, 282
Beechingstoke, 204, 403
Bell Close, 219
Bengal, 165

PLACE INDEX 449

Berwick Bassett, 7, 16, 37, 57, 64, 75, 78, 79, 104, 106, 107, 118, 119, 144, 154, 192, 197, 218, 278, 300, 326, 386, 387, 403, 430, 433
Berwick St. Leonard, 393
Beverley (Yks), 156, 157, 314
Bishops Cannings, 14, 34, 61, 62, 64, 103, 114, 130, 140, 180, 299, 425, 434
Bishopsgate, 92, 93, 100
Blackland, 116, 196, 402, 404, 405, 410
Blenheim (Oxon), 220
Blowhorn Street, 290
Bradford on Avon, 199, 281, 316, 324
Bratton, 29
Bray Street, 35, 344, 350
Brays Farm, 63, 133
Bremhill, 19, 26, 133, 138, 183, 394, 419, 420, 422
Brinkworth, 199, 202, 260
Bristol, 28, 31, 33, 34, 35, 36, 38, 39, 70, 144, 177, 210, 363
Broad Close, 219
Broad Hinton, 104, 109, 406
Broad Town, 172, 268, 296
Broadmead, 230
Bromham, 19, 27, 209, 213, 215, 218, 394, 419, 420, 422
Brow Cottage, 351
Brunsdens, 23, 27, 102, 103, 106, 109, 205, 216, 218, 219, 232, 253, 303, 304, 306, 308, 310, 335
Bucknell (Oxon), 388
Burbage, 224
Burderop, 115
Bushton, 111
Butler's Cottage, 344

Cadenham, 422
Calne, 17, 35, 36, 52, 53, 71, 106, 114, 116, 118, 120, 123, 136, 164, 173, 191, 195, 197, 204, 219, 234, 265, 272, 273, 277, 278, 286, 306, 312, 315, 325, 365, 378, 399, 402, 403, 404, 405, 409, 413, 419, 420, 421, 422, 431
Calstone Wellington, 14, 18, 64, 309, 402
Cambridge, 421
Canada, 200
Cannings Hundred, 18
Carpenter's Cottage, 24, 302, 334
Catcomb, 25, 230

Catcomb Tithing, 169, 188
Catherine Wheel, 4, 8, 9, 13, 27, 30, 37, 38, 39, 55, 88, 132, 150, 151, 201, 204, 218, 219, 222, 230, 241, 262, 320, 322, 333, 352, 356, 364, 367, 375, 376, 429
Catherine Wheel (Bishopsgate), 92, 93, 100
Chancery Lane, 54, 90, 96
Chantry Farm, 213
Chapel Corner, 344
Chapel Field, 8
Chapel, Dissenters. *See* Meeting House
Charlton, 115
Chavenage (Glos), 373
Cheltenham (Glos), 407
Cherhill, 14, 17, 29, 30, 36, 37, 38, 40, 61, 179, 196, 204, 209, 219, 220, 298, 410, 413
Cherhill Hill, 35, 40, 204
Cherry Court, 234, 301, 309
Chestermans, 124, 125, 143, 213, 227, 240, 395
Chieveley (Berks), 422
Chilton, 161
Chippenham, 31, 32, 39, 196, 201, 240, 247, 316, 421
Chirton, 56
Chiseldon, 109, 110, 115, 116, 124, 299, 421
Christian Malford, 36, 56
Church, 286, 288, 327, 331, 350, 384, 385, 386, 389, 390, 398, 410, 411, 415, 416, 417, 418, 419, 420, 423, 424, 425, 433, 436
Church Close, 239
Churchway, 185
Churchyard, 318, 332, 344, 410, 413, 416, 417
Cirencester (Glos), 157, 158, 390
Cirencester Abbey, 209, 211, 236
Clatford, 196, 373
Cleeve, 104, 109
Clifton (Beds), 147
Clyffe Pypard, 68, 105, 111, 171, 213, 247
Coate, 34, 293
Coles Bargain, 220, 228
Colnbrook (Bucks), 176
Compton Bassett, 71, 135, 136, 299, 335
Cornwall, 12
Corsham, 89, 247, 334
Cothelstone (Som), 148, 149, 214

Courtray (Belgium), 96
Cove, The, 4, 13, 429
Cowdown, 188
Cricklade, 283
Cripplegate. Whitecross Street, 422
Curry Mallet (Som), 421

Devizes, 14, 17, 18, 29, 31, 32, 33, 34, 35, 39, 41, 52, 53, 54, 56, 64, 78, 126, 140, 176, 179, 191, 195, 196, 198, 199, 200, 201, 204, 221, 227, 246, 281, 282, 283, 298, 309, 316, 322, 324, 327, 375, 378, 393, 401, 402, 407, 408, 415, 421, 434, 436
Black Bear, 39
Devon, North, 338
Ditteridge, 404
Dorset, 215
Draycot Cerne, 4
Draycot Foliat, 85, 107, 109, 110, 114, 115, 116, 422
Drayton Farm, 116
Dunwich (Suff), 75

East Down, 20, 263
East Greenwich, 160
East Ilsley, 28
East Indies, 381
East Kennett, 5, 7, 14, 59, 60, 72, 73, 75, 81, 96, 105, 107, 109, 153, 154, 155, 168, 178, 188, 190, 191, 193, 198, 204, 205, 216, 220, 248, 386, 387, 406, 410, 414
East Kennett Tithing, 190
East Overton, 291
Eastbrook, 24, 27, 58, 85, 88, 89, 102, 105, 111, 113, 114, 150, 151, 155, 219, 225, 247, 304, 312, 418
Eastbrook Tithing, 169, 188
Easton, 396
Eastwell, 219
Eaton Stoney (Som), 373
Edington, 90
Essex, 146
Exford (Som), 75

Falmouth (Cornwall), 34
Fifield, 81
Figheldean, 72
Fish Street, London, 146
Fisherton Gaol, 41, 195, 323

Fitzhead (Som), 149
Flanders, 96
Flying Waggon, 241, 319, 320
Folly Hill, 38
Folly Hill Field, 224
Folly Inn, 27, 320
Fostbury, 395
Fotheringhay (Northants), 135, 209, 231, 346, 388, 390
Fowlers, 119
France, 169, 205
Free Chapel. *See* Beckhampton Chapel
French Way, 41
Freshford (Som), 33
Froxfield, 91, 298
Furze Down, 20
Fyfield, 30, 36, 330, 335

Galteemore, 10, 216, 226
Garsdon, 419
Gloucestershire, 199, 215
Goddard's Farm, 61, 212, 237
Goddards, 308
Gravesend (New England), 419
Gray's Inn, 75, 95, 142
Great Amwell (Herts), 32, 411
Great Barn, 6, 9, 13, 32, 342
Great Bedwyn, 153, 406
Green Street, 13, 27, 29, 31, 36, 39, 129, 302, 312, 333, 343
Gretna Green, 166
Griffin's Close, 214
Griffin's Farm, 158, 216, 246
Gutton Lane, 148

Hackpen, 20, 27, 29, 42, 122, 214, 252, 437
Hackpen Field, 239
Hampshire, 377
Hampton Road (Glos), 125
Hanover Square, 166, 406
Hare & Hounds, 9, 27, 30, 37, 38, 100, 203, 221, 319, 320, 368
Harrow (Mx), 407
Hartley Wespall (Hants), 149
Heddington, 133, 299
Heytesbury, 327, 408
Higdens, 83, 125, 130, 131, 209, 213, 227, 234, 240, 241, 395
High Street, 58, 77, 336, 344, 351
Highway, 120

PLACE INDEX

Highworth, 73
Hilmarton, 25, 77, 80, 112, 169, 230
Hinton, 133
Hitchcock's Farm, 24
Holborn, 95
Holford (Cheshire), 90
Hollis Cottage, 351
Home Close, 219
Horton, 339
Horton Down, 256
Houndsplot Field, 214, 226, 228
Huish, 177, 182, 404, 407
Hungerford, 18, 33, 77, 80, 132, 148, 161, 165, 305, 363
Hythe, 200

Imber, 90
Inner Temple, 137, 326
Ireland, 177

Jamaica, 34, 87, 163, 165, 166, 210, 228, 265, 269, 271, 282, 285, 297, 299, 305, 314, 341, 363, 367, 375, 407
Jasmine Cottage, 351
Juggins, 395

Keevil, 180, 386
Kellaways, 135, 137, 138
Kennet & Avon Canal, 175
Kennet, River, 370
Kennett Avenue, 8, 10, 16, 28, 219, 221, 331
Kennett Fields, 106, 107, 222
Kennett Tithing, 189, 190, 248
Kennett, River, 14, 23, 29
Kingswood (Glos), 363
Kingswood (Gloucestershire), 12
Kington St Michael, 35, 324, 369
Knoyle Down, 212

Lacock, 17, 65, 210
Langley Burrell, 394
Lechlade (Glos), 432
Leigh Delamere, 75
Lincoln's Inn, 3, 90, 91, 92, 94, 95, 96, 97, 100
Lincoln's Inn Fields, 97
Little Acre, 344
Little Avebury Farm, 215
Little Bedwyn, 261
Little Wittenham (Berks), 75

Littlecote, 272
Lockeridge, 140, 141, 150
London, 14, 15, 28, 31, 32, 33, 34, 35, 42, 54, 80, 95, 96, 110, 115, 144, 146, 148, 179, 220, 227, 233, 244, 247, 248, 267, 270, 276, 278, 279, 301, 311, 317, 326, 347, 372, 378, 383, 396, 407, 418
Long Ashton (Som), 392
Long Close, 218
Long Island (New England), 419
Lower Cow Leaze, 219
Lydiard Millicent, 421
Lydiard Tregoze, 21, 109
Lyneham, 307

Maidenhead (Berks), 16
Malmesbury, 76, 287, 316
The Abbey, 373, 390
Manningford, 85
Manningford Bruce, 56, 143, 387, 389, 394, 396
Manor Farm House, 24
Manor House, 12, 17, 20, 24, 26, 27, 94, 98, 148, 149, 166, 210, 214, 231, 233, 235, 238, 285, 307, 308, 309, 315, 321, 331, 334, 335, 337, 344, 345, 346, 347, 348, 350, 352, 360, 363, 365, 369, 377, 384
Manton, 120
Marden, 71
Marlborough, 7, 10, 17, 18, 21, 23, 28, 29, 30, 31, 32, 33, 34, 35, 36, 37, 39, 51, 52, 53, 54, 60, 70, 77, 80, 101, 103, 116, 133, 147, 150, 156, 158, 163, 175, 177, 179, 180, 181, 183, 191, 199, 201, 203, 219, 223, 246, 261, 265, 277, 283, 290, 295, 298, 305, 311, 319, 322, 324, 325, 326, 330, 333, 363, 378, 383, 385, 386, 407, 412, 413, 420, 421, 431, 432
Black Swan, 38
Castle Inn, 38
Duke's Arms, 38
Half Moon, 33
Post House, 33
The Angel, 373
The Mount, 373
Marlborough Downs, 14, 16, 17, 51
Massachusetts, 419
Meeting House, 10, 13, 14, 27, 61, 105, 106, 108, 127, 130, 228, 331, 351, 385, 422, 428, 429, 431

Melksham, 75, 180, 281, 316
Mendip Hills, 12
Middle Temple, 326
Middlesex, 91, 176
Mildenhall, 70, 103, 109, 299, 433
Miles, 378
Mill Field, 6, 31
Milton (Oxon), 80
Mitcham (Surrey), 220
Monmouthshire, 227
Monument Yard (London), 146
Mortimer's Tenement, 214
Myddle (Shropshire), 263

Nether Street Tithing, 169
Netherbury (Dor), 394
New England, 54, 421
New Woodstock (Oxon), 92
Newbury (Berks), 247, 363
Newnham (Glos), 227
Nonsuch, 191, 218, 299, 335, 373
North Bradley, 434
North Field, 19, 230
Northehey, 230
Nursteed, 434

Ogbourne, 30
Ogbourne Maizey, 71
Ogbourne St Andrew, 138, 230, 299
Ogbourne St George, 58, 59, 322, 434
Old Bakery, 332, 334
Old Eagle, 29
Old Orchard, 234
Overton, 14, 60, 111, 140, 141, 144, 149, 154, 177, 193, 202, 369, 370, 410
Oxford, 17, 18, 31, 79, 198, 393, 436
Oxford University, 213

Painswick (Glos), 432
Parsonage Barn, 214
Parsonage Barton, 271
Parsonage Close, 105
Parsonage Down, 212
Parsonage Farm, 82
Parsonage House, 10, 286, 344
Pearce's Cottage, 338
Penn, 77
Perry's Cottage, 313, 340
Pewsey, 42, 88, 421
Pickedstone Piece, 121

Pickwick, 35
Plough Way, 27
Pool Court (Worcs), 247
Pophams, 215, 218, 219, 232, 298, 303
Port Bridge, 189
Portbury (Som), 436
Porton, 133
Portsea (Hants), 88, 93, 98, 100
Portsmouth (Hants), 34, 93
Portugal, 163
Potterne, 71, 219, 220, 322
Potterne Hundred, 18
Preshute, 72, 86, 120, 149, 177, 410
Preston Candover (Hants), 214
Purton, 63

Quemerford, 403

Ramsbury, 138, 272
Ratland Field, 106, 226
Reading (Berks), 23, 38, 220
The Bear, 3, 373
Rectory, 157, 158, 159, 162, 197, 209, 211, 212, 215, 314, 388, 390
Red Lion, 334
Ridgeway, 14, 20, 28, 36, 39
Rockbourne (Hants), 76
Rockley, 138
Rose Cottage, 334, 339, 344
Roundway, 281
Roundway Down, 18, 30
Rowde, 396, 406
Rowden, 31, 140
Rowses, 77, 79, 136, 137, 209, 213, 228, 248

Salisbury, 169, 197, 201, 407, 436
Salisbury Cathedral, 79, 120, 386, 421
Sandy Lane, 28, 37
Seagry, 133, 413
Sedgehill Chapel, 393
Seend, 281, 292
Selkley Hundred, 51, 69, 70, 73, 78, 82, 90, 111, 113, 114, 117, 123, 126, 140, 141, 143, 160, 162, 168, 169, 175, 182, 188, 190, 192, 198
Semington, 180
Sevington, 75
Shalbourne, 80
Sheldon, 27
Shepherds Shore, 16, 29, 30, 35, 37, 40

PLACE INDEX

Shepton Mallet (Som), 40
Sherston, 96, 388
Shippon(Oxon), 96
Shipton (Oxon), 80
Silbury, 4, 11, 12, 16, 21, 22, 23, 25, 29, 38, 192, 204, 378
Silbury Hill, 298, 303, 437
Silbury House, 336, 343, 351, 429
Silbury Meadow, 6, 224
Siston (Glos), 92, 96
Smithfield, 28, 54
Somerset, 191, 215
South Broom, 132, 138
South Down, 214
South Field, 19
South Meadow, 20, 23
South Street, 72, 172
Southover (Som), 96
Southwick (Hants),, 76
Spain, 205
Spanish Town (Jamaica), 165
Spye Park, 19
St Domingue, 165, 282
St Dunstan's in the West, 90, 91, 92, 94, 96
St Magnus the Martyr, 146
St Martins in the Field, 76
St Olave's Hart Street, 95
St Paul's Cathedral, 79, 101, 113, 115, 122, 123, 144, 162, 386
St Stephen Walbrook, 146
Standley, 26
Stanmer, 213
Stanmore, 158, 390
Stanton St Bernard, 391
Steeple Ashton, 316
Stockley, 114
Stonehenge, 15
Strand (London), 97
Sutton (Sur), 93
Sutton Draycott, 36
Swallow Head, 22, 23, 437
Swindon, 15

Tan Hill, 16, 17, 53, 54, 256
Tarrant Keyneston (Dor), 405
Taunton (Som), 19, 148
Teffont Evias, 158
Tenantry Field, 20
Tewkesbury (Glos), 430
Thames, River, 23

Thornhill, 27, 252
Tidenham (Glos), 247
Totterdown, 335
Trowbridge, 68, 199, 280, 281, 292, 316, 325
Truslow's Farm, 61, 96, 163, 214, 216, 351
Tytherton, 133

Upavon, 72
Upham, 212
Upper Cow Leaze, 219
Upton Grey (Hants), 422
Urchfont, 153
Ushant, 199

Vine Cottage, 72

Waden Hill, 16, 20, 214, 224, 331
Waggon & Horses, 27, 38, 320
Wales, 36
Wall Ditch, 3, 13, 186, 187, 211, 214, 221, 222
Wanborough, 406
Wansdyke, 14, 17, 28
Wanting (Berks), 144
Warminster, 323, 417
Warwicks, 77, 79, 80, 81, 120, 121, 141, 197, 209, 219, 220, 298
Weedon Field, 204, 320
Wells (Som), 36, 96
The George, 373
West Down, 14, 20, 122, 197, 212, 214, 252, 256, 257, 290, 291, 295, 374, 377
West Field, 19, 230, 239, 252
West Indies, 407
West Kennett, 8, 10, 14, 16, 20, 24, 26, 27, 28, 32, 37, 51, 58, 59, 60, 63, 80, 105, 106, 107, 124, 140, 142, 143, 145, 146, 147, 153, 168, 180, 184, 185, 188, 190, 192, 196, 198, 199, 204, 205, 209, 213, 214, 216, 219, 220, 221, 223, 225, 226, 228, 229, 231, 238, 241, 245, 247, 248, 253, 258, 271, 272, 287, 291, 303, 311, 312, 320, 321, 324, 326, 329, 331, 333, 335, 336, 342, 343, 349, 351, 352, 356, 364, 370, 373, 388, 395, 427, 433
West Kennett Barrow, 11, 146
West Kennett House, 351
West Kennett Tithing, 190, 198, 205
West Lavington, 138, 228

West Overton, 21, 36, 268, 324
Westbrook, 14, 24, 27, 35, 77, 81, 82, 121, 143, 302, 395, 418, 429
Westbrook Tithing, 169, 188
Westbury, 175
Westcott, 368
Westonbirt (Glos), 36, 91, 92, 94, 96, 97, 98, 199, 217, 234, 334, 347, 372, 388
White Hart, 27, 28, 229, 245, 320, 356, 366
White Lion, 308, 320, 351, 356, 367, 368
Whitechapel, 115, 278
Whitley, 180
Wilcot, 28, 146, 391, 403
Willems, 199
Wilton, 59, 229, 433
Wiltshire, North, 292
Wimborne Minster (Dor), 229, 404, 405
Windmill Hill, 11, 14
Winterbourne Bassett, 196, 209
Winterbourne Dauntsey, 135, 227
Winterbourne Gunner, 136, 138
Winterbourne Monkton, 7, 14, 60, 64, 74, 104, 109, 112, 119, 123, 159, 173, 177, 182, 183, 214, 225, 304, 326, 330, 386, 388, 389, 397, 400, 403, 406, 409, 410, 412, 413, 418, 420, 421, 428, 433, 435, 437
Winterbourne, River, 7, 10, 14, 20, 21, 22, 23, 25, 27, 36, 191, 332, 370
Wiveliscombe (Som), 149
Wolcot (Som), 154
Woodborough, 112, 232, 313, 413
Wootton Bassett, 99, 138, 247, 283, 302, 322, 331, 421
Wootton Rivers, 183
Worcester (Worcs), 77, 79
Wotton Rivers, 391
Wroughton, 28, 59, 161
Wroughton Coppice, 126, 369

Yatesbury, 14, 28, 63, 75, 126, 135, 136, 154, 156, 386, 410, 422, 435
Yelden (Beds), 132

NAME INDEX

Ailesbury
    Lord, 298, 404, 407
Ailesbury, Earl of, 42
Aland
    Mary, 394
Alexander
    Ann, 64, 69
    Grace, 194
    Richard, 55, 178, 195, 279, 305
    Thomas, 131, 299
    Walter, 188, 428
    William, 64, 279, 299, 327
Allaway
    Martha, 68
Allen
    Anthony, 24, 190
Allen Family, 258
Allsop
    Christopher, 325
Amor
    Henry, 56
    John, 56, 225, 239, 253, 258, 352, 373
    Richard, 57, 169, 188, 189
    William, 56
Amor Family, 56, 57
    Andrew
    Thomas, 193
Andrews
    Thomas, 141, 268, 386
Angell
    John, 292
Anne, Queen, 3, 4
Anstie
    John, 316
Archard
    Henry, 309
Arnall
    Elizabeth, 155
Arnold
    Edith, 118
    George, 245, 280, 312, 341, 364, 368, 380, 430
Ashe
    John, 33

NAME INDEX

Askew
    Ann, 78
    Anthony, 95
    Elizabeth, 95
Aubrey
    John, 4, 5, 8, 9, 12, 22, 28, 326, 330, 332, 373, 375, 377
Austin, 284
Axford
    Christopher, 193, 194
    Elizabeth, 56
Ayloffe
    Mr, 331

Bailey, 296
    Betty, 182
    Caleb, 7, 57, 58, 59, 60, 73, 86, 103, 104, 105, 108, 151, 156, 166, 218, 258, 291, 318, 321, 387, 427, 430, 433, 434, 435, 436
    Daniel, 281
    Edward, 57, 144, 433
    Elizabeth, 57, 59, 144, 434
    Giles, 104
    John Oriel, 106
    John Orrell, 315
    Jonathan, 24
    Martha, 182
    Moses, 57
    Mr, 33
    Penelope, 183
    Richard, 57, 58, 59, 66, 72, 107, 218, 307, 322, 387, 414, 428, 430, 431, 433, 434
    Ruth, 57, 58, 71
    Sarah, 106, 183, 315
    Thomas, 433
    William, 291
Bailey Family, 57, 59
Baker
    John, 421
Balden
    John, 121, 196, 202
Baldveen
    Frissy, 112, 141
    Frysy, 393
    James, 79, 353
Baldwin
    John, 323
    William, 436

Bale
    John, 430
Ball
    Elizabeth, 181
    Isaac, 67, 72, 195
    William, 300, 318, 376
Bankard
    John, 281
Banning
    John, 216, 350
Barclay
    John, 76
Barker
    John, 391
Barnes Family, 56
Bartlett
    James, 115
    Katherine, 142
    Richard, 416
Baskerville
    Francis, 62
    John, 149, 231
    Mary, 62
    Thomas, 120, 197
Batchelur
    Francis, 312
Bath
    William, 392
Battington
    Christopher, 112, 254, 258, 260, 264, 267, 274, 343, 363
Baynton
    Edward, 19
    Edward, Sir, 76, 81, 82, 112, 184, 190, 198, 215, 216, 247, 394, 419
    Mary, 249
    Robert, 113, 114, 122, 150, 162, 215, 216, 297, 388, 394
Baynton Family, 209, 419
Beake
    John, 218, 238, 253, 256, 258, 333, 352
Beauchamp family, 209
Beaven Family, 177, 242, 314
Belford
    Jemima, 166
    Mr, 375
Benger
    Anne, 140, 209
Bennet
    Francis, 297

Bennett
 John, 232
 Thomas, 197
Beverstone, 203
Biss
 Edward, 436
Blake
 John, 199
Blanchard
 Mary, 404
Bodham
 Thomas, 292
Bodwell
 Harry, 318
Bradfield
 Elizabeth, 336
 Frances, 373
 John, 216, 336
Bradney
 Richard, 197, 284, 286
Bray
 Ann, 193, 194
 John, 278
 Katherine, 340
 Richard, 79, 317, 394, 414
 Thomas, *111*, 280, 352, 379, 417
 William, 118, 188, 194, 260, 339, 341, 342, 359, 362, 371, 417
Brewer
 Peter, 324, 393
 William, 168
Briant
 Hannah, 182
Bridgeman
 John, 134, 291, 293
Brinsden
 John, 7, 119, 182, 183, 326, 330, 389, 397, 399, 400, 401, 406, 409, 410, 428
Britton
 John, 35, 369
Brokenbrow
 Mary, 64, 68
Bromham
 Mrs, 382
 Nicholas, 110, 230, 337
 Richard, 110
Bromham als Phelps. *See* Phelps
 John, 335, 341, 342, 359, 380
Bromwich
 Thomas, 279

Bromwick
 John, 406
Brookes
 John, 40, 195
Brown, 179
 Catherine, 288
 George, 72, 105, 106, 109, 160, 237, 267, 273, 288, 338, 355, 371
 John, 84, 100, 151, 196, 218, 219, 226, 228, 232, 238, 239, 247, 253, 277, 279, 282, 283, 303, 305, 357, 368, 412
 Joseph, 67, 325, 383, 411
 Katherine, 141, 160, 360
 Margery, 160, 267, 360
 Marjorie, 418
 Martha, 72, 106, 109
 Richard, 237, 268, 287, 317, 357, 367, 410
 Susanna, 283
 Thomas, 190, 209
Browning
 John, 127
 Martha, 127
 Stephen, 220, 221, 302
Bruce
 Lady, 200
 Lord, 369, 378
Brunsden, 324
 John, 237
Bryant
 John, 112
 Mary, 112
Buchanan
 John, 406
Buckridge
 Mr, 417
Bull
 John, 116
Bullenger, 392
Bunts
 Elizabeth, 183
Burchell
 John, 385, 415
Burde
 Marmaduke, 324, 393
Burgeman
 Thomas, 186
Burnet
 Bishop, 397, 399, 411

NAME INDEX

Burress
  Mary, 74
Burris
  Thomas, 180
Burroughs
  Ann, 59
  Betty, 60
Burrows
  Thomas, 168, 280
Burry
  Adam, 59, 60, 291, 293
  Alice, 59
  Anne, 59
  Elizabeth, 59, 336
  Frances, 59
  Martha, 60
  Mary, 59
  Susan, 60
  Susanna, 59, 336
  Temperance, 60, 174
  Thomas, 60
  William, 59, 60, 336
Burry Family, 59, 60
Burshall
  John, 410
Bushell
  Lucy, 201
  Richard, 362
Butler
  Mary, 154
Button
  Ruth, 76
  William, 158, 209, 212
  William, Sir, 76, 182
Button Family, 212

Cannington
  Daniel, 282
  Maria, 282
Cary
  Edward, 213
  James, 24, 308
  John, 176, 281, 301
  Richard, 279
  Thomas, 308
Cary Family, 194, 352
Caswell
  Edmund, 62, 64
  Elizabeth, 62, 63, 64, 133
  Hester, 61
  John, 61, 62, 64, 174, 205, 242, 243, 304, 307, 308, 324
  Joseph, 229, 310
  Mary, 61, 62, 63
  Michael, 62, 64
  Richard, 61, 62, 64, 118, 216, 242, 243, 253, 257, 284, 352, 426, 427
  Robert, 61, 63, 64, 238, 253, 349, 435
  Thomas, 62, 64
  William, 62, 63, 133, 168, 190, 192, 241
Caswell Family, 60, 64, 128
Caswell Family (pedigree) viii, ix
Chamberlain
  Stayner, 105, 146, 333, 350
  Thermuthis, 146
Chandler
  John, 55, 195
  Richard, 33, 232
Chapman
  Ann, 68
  Joseph, 68
  Phoebe, 68
  William, 68, 312, 313
Charles I, 148, 176
Charles II, 4, 19
Cheevers
  Mary, 80
Chester
  William, 406
Chesterman
  John, 213
  Margaret, 286
  Richard, 202, 354, 356, 416
Chivers
  Edward, 414
  Frances, 321
  Gabriel, 308, 332
  John, 156
  Joseph, 308
  Martha, 174
  Robert, 180
Chiverson
  Mary, 156
Church
  Alice, 177
  Helen, 361
Churchill. *See* Marlborough, Duke & Duchess of
Clarke
  Thomas, 79, 194

Clements
    Ann, 66, 67, 68, 313, 327
    Hannah, 68
    John, 64, 65, 67, 68, 71, 88, 99, 130, 170, 172, 221, 229, 239, 298, 299, 300, 307, 319, 323, 327, 358, 362, 380, 411, 413
    Joseph, 64, 65, 67, 68, 229
    Leah, 69, 344
    Martha, 68
    Mary, 64, 67
    Patience, 68
    Robert, 65, 66, 69, 88, 106, 109, 130, 299, 300, 307, 323, 344, 360
    Ruth, 68
    Sarah, 64, 196, 229
    Stephen, 69
    William, 64, 68, 152, 229, 279
Clements Family, 64, 69
Clements Family (pedigree) viii, ix
Cleverly
    John, 322
Clifford
    Richard, 237
Cockes
    Thomas, 391
Coffe
    Robert, 202
Colby
    John, 230
Coleman
    Charles, 40, 195
Colley
    Captain, 122, 198
Collins
    Dinah, 126
Collinson
    John, 406
Colt Hoare
    Richard, Sir, 7
Compton
    Susanna, 71
Cooke
    Anne, 114
Coombes
    John, 73
Cooper
    John, Sir, 76
    Margaret, 76
    Nathan, 118

Coxhead
    Thomas, 282, 285
Crawford
    Earl, 18
Crewe
    Sarah, 91
Cripps
    Jane, 144
    Richard, 82, 162, 245, 259, 266, 267, 274, 310, 311, 312, 340, 364, 370
    Thomas, 144, 192
Crook
    Ambrose, 70, 280, 302, 303
    Ann, 71, 72
    Barnabus, 72
    George, 303, 312
    John, 70, 185
    Philip, 66, 70, 71, 72, 221, 305, 306
    Rachel, 71, 72, 322
    Richard, 71, 72
    Robert, 70
    Samuel, 306
    Stephen, 23, 70, 71, 229, 280, 293, 303, 304, 305, 411
    Susanna, 71
    William, 66, 69, 70, 71, 72, 106, 109, 133, 174, 202, 223, 224, 226, 228, 239, 302, 305, 306
Crook Family, 69, 70, 71, 73
Crosse
    Latimer, 410
Cruse
    Edith, 74, 282, 355, 362, 367, 380
    Gabriel, 359
    John, 66, 73, 74, 243, 309
    Mary, 73
    Penney, 74
Cruse Family, 73, 74
Cue
    Ann, 102
    Edward, 291, 430
    James, 174, 303, 336
    Joan, 118, 277, 361
    John, 16, 67, 82, 102, 113, 155, 219, 245, 285, 302, 314, 357, 370, 423, 424
    Martha, 316
    Mary, 67, 117
    Richard, 79, 82, 102, 117, 141, 252, 264, 277, 321, 358, 395
    Thomas, 430

NAME INDEX

Walter, 118
Curr
    John, 196, 301
Currier
    Henry, 74
    Jane, 66, 74, 75, 281
    John, 66, 74, 75, 281
    Katherine, 74, 79
    Sarah, 74
Currier Family, 74, 75
Curry
    Sarah, 285
Cuss. *See* Cruse

Dangerfeld
    Robert, 278
Dangerfield
    Ann, 100
Davis, 431
    Joan, 102
    Richard, 82, 237, 354, 392, 394, 419
    T, 348
    Thomas, 237, 305
    William, 77
Day
    Elizabeth, 154
Dean
    Stephen, 38, 295
Deavin
    Joseph, 72
    Sarah, 133, 239
Defoe
    Daniel, 15, 255, 259, 274
Dell
    Mary, 319
    Stephen, 319
Devans
    Mr, 382
Dew
    John, 73
Dismore
    Alexander, 305
Dixon
    Rachel, 65, 69, 229
    Thomas, 65, 199, 318
    William, 65
Dobson
    John, 68, 106
Dolman
    John, 309

Dorchester
    Roger, 139
Dore
    John, 224, 334
Dore family, 224
Douggan
    Mr, 178
Dowdeswell
    Elizabeth, 247
Drake
    Lady, 418
Drax
    Edward, 12, 437
Duck
    Sarah, 79, 111, 194
    Stephen, 289
Duckett
    George, 402
Dunch
    Anne, 76
    Deborah, 75, 76, 159, 301, 419
    Margaret, 76, 249
    Mary, 76
    Mr, 337
    Ruth, 76
    Walter, 75, 272, 419
    William, 17, 22, 75, 76, 77, 121, 141, 161, 210, 211, 212, 213, 214, 219, 231, 247, 285, 288, 296, 297, 341, 346, 385, 387, 389, 416, 436
Dunch Family, 75, 76, 210, 211, 217, 219, 419
Dyer
    Bridget, 141, 280, 339, 360, 386
    Christopher, 280
    Richard, 366
Dyke
    Mary, 112
    Mr, 240
    Thomas Webb, 224, 227
Dymer
    Anne, 202

Eacott
    Thomas, 308
Ealy
    Mary, 177
    William, 177
Eatall
    Joseph, *111*

Ruth, 123
Eatwell
　John, 304
Edmunds
　Leonard, 182, 287
　William, 218, 241
Edward VI, 390
Edwards
　John, 95
　Nicholas, 177
Ely
　Hannah, 406
Emly
　Walter, 24
Emot
　John, 196
Erasmus, 392
Etwall
　Thomas, 425
Evans
　John, 406, 407
Evens
　Arise, 176
Exall
　James, 171, 172, 173
　Thomas, 327
Eyles
　Mary, 308
Eyreshman
　John, 436

Fisher
　Elizabeth, 352
Fishlock
　John, 369, 370
Flower
　John, 405
Forsyth
　John, 17, 161, 198, 214, 244, 324, 388, 389, 392, 393, 419, 420
　Nicholas, 393
　Robert, 393
　Thomas, 393
Foster
　John, 297
Fowle
　Thomas, 388
Fowler
　James, 304
　John, 11, 66, 151, 364, 367, 368, 427

　Lemuel, 259, 274, 341, 356
　Mary, 293
　Richard, 9, 304, 427
　Samuel, 66, 229, 280, 287, 303, 304, 305, 351, 409, 414, 415
　Thomas, 24
　William, 67, 221, 319, 415
Fox
　Widow, 97
Franklin
　John, 41
　Richard, 248
Freke
　Edward, 183
Fribbens
　John, 317
Fry
　Daniel, 24
　Margaret, 364
　Thomas, 86, 145, 245, 280, 356, 357, 358, 364
　William, 281
Fulmer
　Margaret, 182, 287
Furnil
　Sarah, 103

Gale
　Mary, 286
　Sarah, 195, 286
　Thomas, 286
Gammon
　Sarah, 153
Garraway
　Richard, 352
Garroway
　Richard, 125, 193, 244
George III, 171, 416
Gibbons
　Charles, 190
Giddance
　Charles, 67, 182
Gilbert
　John, 188
　Thomas, 182, 188, 202
Gilmour
　Walter, 29
Gilpin
　Parson, 15
Glasier & Co, 39

NAME INDEX

Goatley
　Edmund, 256
Goddard
　Edmund, 212
　John, 421
　Mary, 219
　Richard, 237
　Thomas, 212, 318
Godman
　Henry, 230
Godwin, 314
　Isaac, 196
　Susan, 288
Goldsmith
　Ann, 78
　Benjamin, 78, 80, 278
　Deborah, 78, 80
　Eleanor, 80
　Elizabeth, 78
　George, 78, 80, 114
　Henry, 78, 79, 80, 143, 146
　John, 77, 78, 79, 80, 112, 121, 137, 161, 197, 231, 246, 288, 386, 410, 414
　Joseph, 78, 79
　Mary, 78, 80
　Thomas, 78, 79, 80, 114, 194, 231, 248
Goldsmith Family, 77, 80, 228
Goodcheap
　John, 183
Goodship
　Sarah, 308
Gooff
　Sarah, 74
　William, 74
Goring
　Lord, 30
Gough
　Robert, 188
Goulding
　Anne, 247
Grant
　John Griffin, 39, 280
　Mr, 252
　Walter, 105
Gray
　H. St George, 8
Green
　Farmer, 6, 10
　Isaac, 168
　Joan, 361
　Marian, 142
　Mr, 34
　Richard, 142, 241, 417
　Rose, 203
Greenway
　Richard, 185, 188
Griffin
　Ann, 85
　Anne, 83, 316, 358, 359, 362
　Edith, 256
　Elizabeth, 85
　Farmer, 6, 10
　George, 406
　Hannah, 240
　Henry, 278
　John, 31, 74, 81, 82, 83, 99, 102, 113, 118, 119, 139, 150, 151, 196, 198, 208, 216, 224, 228, 239, 244, 245, 278, 323, 326, 340, 350, 355, 388, 395, 396, 401, 416, 418, 427, 430, 431
　Joseph, 82, 83, 118, 151, 166, 189, 195, 332, 341, 355, 356
　Mr, 72, 240
　Peter, 20, 30, 34, 81, 82, 83, 84, 85, 94, 113, 114, 122, 123, 151, 168, 187, 188, 203, 215, 234, 235, 237, 245, 246, 251, 257, 259, 260, 263, 265, 266, 270, 273, 277, 285, 286, 294, 300, 340, 341, 352, 355, 357, 359, 364, 370, 371, 376, 395, 413, 423
　Rebecca, 83
　Sarah, 83, 240
　Susan, 185
　Susanna, 101
　Thomas, 80, 81, 86, 104, 118, 135, 166, 229, 239, 317, 321, 339, 430
　Timothy, 81
　William, 81, 83, 158, 173, 410, 431, 432, 433
Griffin Family, 42, 80, 85, 135, 210
Griffith
　Joshua, 430
Grinfield
　Thomas, 247
Grubbe
　Henry, 219
　Mr, 106
　Phoebe, 63, 220
　Thomas, 220
　Walter, 37, 145, 219, 238

William, 220
Grubbe Family, 107, 154, 204, 219, 331, 343
Gully
  Benjamin, 177
  H.
  T., 270

Hacker
  Betty, 285
Hall
  Joanna, 168
Hamor
  Thomas, 278
Hancock
  Joan, 60
  Thomas, 188
Harding
  John, 141
  Richard, 141, 145, 273, 321, 336
Harper
  John, 186, 353, 414
  William, 291, 317, 383
Harrison
  Ann, 164
  Anne, 162
  William, 353
Harvey
  William, 157
Hatchet
  Thomas, 309, 334
Hatchett
  Mr, 226
  Thomas, 241
Hatherall
  John, 203
Hawes
  Francis, 220
Hawkes
  Mr, 298
Hawkins
  Sarah, 287
Haworth
  John, 188
Haynes
  B, 299
Hayward, 425
  Benjamin, 85
  Elizabeth, 85, 86
  Henry, 85, 86
  John, 82, 85, 111, 122, 264, 338
  Joseph, 85, 86, 177, 267, 270, 274, 314, 323, 424, 425, 426, 430
  Margaret, 82, 258, 364, 368, 392, 394
  Mary, 86, 87, 325, 402
  Parnell, 354
  Sarah, 321
  William, 87, 159, 255, 290, 316, 338, 354, 364, 402
Hayward Family, 85, 87
Head
  Daniel, 195
Hearne
  Thomas, 436
Heath
  Joanna, 55
  Robert, 55, 195
  William, 247, 302
Hedges
  John, 196
Henshaw Family, 140, 141
Henslow
  Catherine, 213
  Ralph, 213
  Thomas, 213
Herbert
  William, 66, 67, 366, 387
Herne
  Joseph, 322
Hertford
  Earl of, 140
Hickes
  Sarah, 3, 90
Hickley
  Mary, 88, 288
  Richard, 12, 16, 20, 23, 24, 25, 31, 32, 33, 34, 39, 42, 65, 66, 87, 88, 108, 165, 166, 169, 170, 174, 175, 177, 178, 184, 188, 196, 199, 200, 204, 205, 206, 223, 224, 226, 236, 241, 242, 250, 251, 252, 254, 256, 258, 260, 261, 262, 264, 266, 267, 269, 271, 272, 274, 275, 277, 285, 288, 289, 290, 291, 292, 293, 294, 296, 297, 299, 303, 305, 308, 311, 312, 313, 314, 316, 318, 321, 322, 325, 329, 332, 334, 348, 363, 364, 365, 367, 368, 369, 370, 371, 372, 375, 376, 378, 383, 405, 408, 411, 414, 415, 416, 417
Hickley Family, 87, 88
Highway
  John, 306

NAME INDEX

Hillier, 195
   Ann, 126
   Frances, 164, 280
   George, 107
   James, 305
   Rebecca, 73
   Thomas, 304, 305
   William, 66
Hindley
   Henry, 410
Hinton
   William, 40
Hiscock
   John, 186, 252, 369
   Sarah, 284
Hitchcock
   Alice, 88
   Daniel, 252
   Henry, 322
   James, 68, 88, 89, 134, 152, 230, 352
   Mary, 88, 152, 287
Hitchcock Family, 88, 90
Hitchins
   John, 284, 285
Holbrook
   John, 318
Holford
   Ann, 93, 94
   Elizabeth, 92, 95
   Peter, 23, 95, 98, 199, 223, 224, 226, 240
   Richard, 24, 32, 92, 93, 94, 95, 96, 97, 99, 100, 172, 234, 268, 284, 288, 293, 299, 300, 305, 306, 309, 314, 318, 348, 352, 359, 363, 365, 368, 370, 379
   Richard, Sir, 3, 5, 6, 11, 16, 24, 25, 29, 32, 33, 35, 36, 41, 53, 54, 61, 62, 69, 86, 90, 91, 92, 93, 95, 96, 97, 98, 102, 119, 123, 128, 131, 138, 139, 143, 150, 163, 170, 184, 187, 191, 197, 199, 205, 206, 208, 210, 213, 215, 216, 217, 218, 220, 226, 231, 232, 234, 239, 242, 246, 250, 253, 257, 260, 265, 267, 268, 270, 271, 272, 277, 279, 284, 286, 292, 293, 295, 298, 300, 301, 306, 307, 309, 325, 326, 333, 335, 341, 347, 348, 357, 366, 370, 371, 372, 373, 374, 376, 378, 381, 382, 383, 387, 396, 397, 398, 400, 401, 404, 408, 411, 418, 423, 424, 425, 426, 428, 429, 434, 435, 436
   Robert, 7, 11, 30, 42, 85, 93, 94, 95, 96, 97, 98, 163, 164, 172, 217, 235, 238, 295, 381
   Robert Stayner, 98
   Samuel, 20, 62, 96, 97, 252, 258, 270, 284, 286, 348, 379, 437
   Sarah, 91, 95, 97
   Sarah Crue, 91
   Stayner, 30, 32, 34, 60, 65, 66, 72, 84, 88, 93, 94, 95, 97, 98, 100, 105, 133, 134, 168, 171, 191, 199, 203, 205, 206, 210, 221, 222, 228, 235, 236, 252, 255, 257, 258, 267, 284, 288, 291, 293, 296, 297, 306, 307, 308, 311, 335, 344, 347, 349, 352, 370, 371, 379, 381, 412, 418
   Susanna, 96
   Susanna, Lady, 3, 53, 64, 83, 92, 95, 96, 97, 164, 171, 173, 234, 246, 277, 327, 367, 370, 372, 373, 378, 380, 382, 387, 388, 411, 412, 413, 433
   Susannah, Lady, 245
   Trotman, 96
Holford Family, 72, 90, 94, 98, 100, 210, 301, 372, 380, 403
Holford Family (pedigree) x, xi
Hollery
   William, 64
Holmes
   John, 203
Hooper
   John, 186
Hopkins
   Anne, 111
   John, 111
   John, Sir, 56, 239, 352, 373
   Mary, 107
   Thomas, 116
   William, 227
Hopton
   Lord, 30
Horsell
   Ann, 100
   Bartholomew, 99, 100, 415
   Elizabeth, 100
   Esther, 99
   Henry, 99, 100, 307
   Jacob, 200
   John, 99, 100, 313, 318, 409, 414, 415
   Mary, 100, 392, 415
   Nathan, 221, 291, 293

Nathaniel, 99, 100
Reuben, 7, 9, 10, 42, 98, 99, 100, 313, 374, 414, 428
Susanna, 100
William, 100
Horsell Family, 98, 99, 100
Horton
John, 123
Howard
Mr, 133
Thomas, Colenel, 17
Howe
Lord, 199, 377
Howson
Henry, 14, 71, 88, 176, 205, 221, 410
Sarah Dyke, 66, 227, 246, 410
Hughes
William, 420
Hulbert
John, 188
Hume
Thomas Henry, 406, 407
Hungerford
Lord, 169
Hunt
William, 220
Hunter
Joan, 344
John, 89, 307
Thomas, 60, 66, 88, 104, 269, 307, 318, 343, 344, 351, 356, 359, 365, 367, 368, 376
Huntingdon
Lady, 431
Hunton
Philip, 171, 327
Hutchinson
Daniel, 279

Illingworth
Miles, 282
Irishman
John, 285

Jackson
Mr, 408
Jacob
John, 82, 111, 115, 255, 264, 273, 338, 356, 370, 420

James
Benjamin, 164, 201
Mary, 201
James II, 31
James, Duke of Monmouth, 4, 31
James, Duke of York, 4
Jay
William, 431
Jefferies
William, 416
Jefferys, 179
Mr, 41
Sarah, 239, 240
William, 240
Jennings
Edmund, 296
John, 212, 410
Jenny A., 165, 334
Jerome
John, 208, 239, 401
Jewell
Bishop, 417
Johnson
Joseph, 318
Mr, 34
Thomas, 410
Jones
Ann, 97, 98, 101, 288
Arthur, 11, 24, 34, 39, 41, 67, 71, 87, 88, 93, 94, 98, 100, 101, 165, 181, 184, 199, 223, 226, 236, 268, 277, 285, 288, 292, 295, 297, 298, 299, 300, 303, 306, 308, 315, 325, 327, 344, 349, 369, 382, 383, 388, 404, 429
Evan, 93, 98, 100
Inigo, 375
Nicholas, 93, 100
Richard, 101, 166
Thomas, 93, 100, 101, 420
Umverie, 176
William, 176
Jones Family, 100, 101
Jordan
John, 306, 309
Thomas, 86, 99, 309, 339, 358, 364
Judd
John, 88, 288
Mary, 88

NAME INDEX

Keiller
　Alexander, 11, 13, 24, 312
Kew. See Cue
Killing
　Christian, 183
Kimber
　Mr, 33
King
　Betty, 240
　John, 379
　Margery, 364
　Toby, 82, 113, 274, 311, 339, 341, 361, 364, 367, 368, 379
Kneller
　Godfrey, Sir, 379

Ladd
　John, 347
Lambert
　Anne, 76
　Thomas, 76, 211
Lambourn
　Simon, 294
Lanfear
　Ambrose, 238
Lavington
　Hugh, 25
　Robert, 228, 229
　Thomas, 189
Lawrence
　Christian, 182
　Mary, 418
Laynes
　Ann, 135, 136
Lewis
　Charles, 108
　James, 70, 89, 246, 304, 311, 323, 325
　Richard, 247
Ley
　Sarah, 410
Liddall
　Robert, 171
Little
　William, 68
Loggan
　Dr., 426, 427
Long
　Edward, 252
　George, 214
　James, 4, 375

James, Sir, 31
　John, 168
　Kingsmill, 76, 211, 214, 286, 288, 412
　Richard, 412
　Walter, 306
　William, 8, 11, 437
Loveday
　John, 9, 29, 402, 431
Lovelock
　John, 296, 300
Lucas
　Charles, 7, 229, 241, 380, 384, 406, 407, 408
Luther
　Martin, 160, 392

Maccabee
　Thomas, 195, 293
Mackerell
　Elizabeth, 86
Madox
　Bridget, 247
Marlborough, Duke of, 204, 220, 224, 226, 227, 240, 289, 294, 383
Marlborough. Duchess of
　Sarah, 220
Martin
　Thomas, 418
Martyn
　Hannah, 147, 328
　Mrs, 228
　Samuel, 58, 65, 66, 69, 147, 172, 298, 313, 318, 322, 327, 328, 333, 350
Martyr
　Peter, 392
Mary, Queen, 391
Mason
　Mary, 88
Mathews
　Richard, 202
Mathews als Andrews
　Margaret, 201
Mauckes
　Elizabeth, 78, 80
May
　James, 304
Mayne
　William, 202
Mayo
　Benjamin, 402, 403

Charles, 204
Elizabeth, 402
James, 41, 107, 152, 153, 173, 204, 221, 224, 229, 235, 328, 402, 403, 404, 405, 406, 409, 412, 413, 429, 431, 432, 434
John, 53, 86, 97, 134, 171, 172, 324, 325, 372, 378, 383, 401, 402, 403, 409, 411, 413, 436
Mary, 325, 404
Mrs, 373
Mayo Family, 389, 401, 405, 406
Mazey
Edward, 239
Merewether
John, 246, 247
Merryman
Joseph, 247
Mervyn
Deborah, 76
James, Sir, 76, 159, 175, 190, 197, 198, 210, 211, 212, 284, 295, 346, 374, 377
Metcalfe
Ann, 93
Mrs, 94, 379
Michael
Elizabeth, 138
Mighell
Joseph, 204, 275
Miles
James, 237
Mills
Alice, 392
Andrew, 117, 182, 187, 188, 244, 283, 284, 317, 359, 380, 392
James, 82
John, 117, 125, 162, 252, 264, 268, 282, 337, 352, 425, 426
Mary, 287
Mr, 229, 242
Richard, 287
Ruth, 428
Sarah, 82
Thomas, 421
William, 86
Milsom
Susan, 60
Minty
Susan, 312, 414
Mitchell
Mrs, 285, 411

Moody
Deborah, 75, 419
Henry, Sir, 75, 419
Moor
Nanny, 67, 278
Moore
Joseph, 239
Mary, 116
More
Richard, 168
Morganwg
Iolo, 38
Morris
Joan, 102
Lydia, 103
Richard, 101, 102, 103, 185, 423, 430
Robert, 278
Samuel, 58, 101, 102, 103, 105, 170, 247, 278, 302, 314, 321, 423, 429, 430
Sarah, 103, 104
Temperance, 60
William, 21
Morris Family, 101, 103, 104
Morse
Lewis, 410
Mortimer
Andrew, 386, 391
Ann, 78, 194
Deborah, 78, 80
Edith, 137, 141, 160, 353, 356
George, 80, 99, 248, 253, 406
John, 186, 198, 237
Katherine, 360
Mary, 112
Mathew, 168, 192
Richard, 18, 66, 253, 362
Thomas, 79, 82, 113, 114, 198, 291, 418, 423, 424
Mortimer Family, 419
Munday
Richard, 297
Mundy
William, 228, 239

Nalder, 179
Ann, 72, 109
Elizabeth, 107
John, 104, 105, 106, 107, 109, 116, 130, 180, 190, 195, 204, 218, 219, 229, 241, 245, 247, 253, 286, 287, 294, 300, 302,

NAME INDEX

331, 433, 434
Martha, 104, 109
Mary, 106, 109
Mr, 10, 58, 72, 153, 241
Robert, 66, 104, 106, 108, 109, 189, 205, 224, 226, 228, 229, 239
Sarah, 104, 106, 224, 229, 315
Thomas, 63, 72, 104, 106, 107, 109, 219, 229, 241, 433, 434, 435
Nalder Family, 104, 107, 109
Nalder Family (pedigree) x, xi
Narborne
Mary, 122
Nash
Elizabeth, 107
Thomas, 243
Neat
Ann, 109
Mary, 126
Neate
Thomas, 63, 435
Nevil
Anne, 59
Nicholas
Elizabeth, 393
Nicholls
John, 406
Jonathan, 307
Nichols
John, 392
Norden
John, 298
Norman
Roger, 278
Norris, 335
James, 67, 154
John, 109, 221, 222, 223
Mr, 33, 84, 199, 222, 297
Nicholas, 295
Richard, 362
William, 23, 26, 27, 166, 191, 215, 216, 218, 219, 224, 225, 226, 238, 295, 298, 299, 303, 304, 306, 309, 335, 373
Norris Family, 80, 216, 218, 226
Northey
Mr, 375
Northumberland, Duke of, 38
Norton
Daniel, Sir, 76

Nurdan
William, 71
Nurden
John, 73
Nutt
Thomas, 307

Odey
James, 323
Odyon
Francis, 317
Orchard
Ann, 85
Henry, 85
Overton
John, 298, 309, 347

Page
Christopher, 208, 239, 401
Paget
Anne, 130
Paine
Tom, 178
Painter
Robert, 199
Paradise
James, 230
Parker
Constance, 237
John, 34
Parnell
John, 159
Maud, 159
Parr
Richard, 79, 141, 297, 339, 342, 357, 358, 377, 380
Parsons
John, 410
Patrick
Elizabeth, 392
Payne
Mary, 133
Richard, 202
Peart
John, 79, 136, 141, 160, 264, 267, 273, 354, 356, 357, 360, 379, 390, 391, 394, 406, 411
Mary, 392
Pembroke
Earl of, 21

Penney
  Grace, 283
Penney Family, 74
Penruddock
  Col, 373
  John, 4
Pepys
  Samuel, 4, 32
Percival
  Madam, 373
Perkyns
  Mr, 244
Perry
  Sarah, 315
Person
  John, 390
Phelps, 426, *See* also Bromham
  Ann, 81, 111, 112
  Anne, 114, 424
  Catherine, 112
  Eleanor, 115
  Elizabeth, 112, 196, 318
  Honour, 115
  John, 79, 82, 85, 110, 111, 112, 113, 114, 115, 116, 194, 237, 245, 255, 292, 301, 315, 321, 355, 376, 387, 422, 424
  Margerie, 112
  Mary, 85, 112, 115, 116, 196
  Richard, 80, 82, 107, 110, 111, 112, 114, 115, 116, 133, 159, 188, 216, 278, 385, 417, 420, 428
  Robert, 112, 114, 182, 323, 411
  Sarah, 111, 112
  Thomas, 110, *113*, 267, 289, 338, 368
  Timothy, 110, 111, 112, 114
  William, 18
Phelps Family, 80, 110, 111, 112, 114, 115, 116, 119, 210
Phillips/Phillipps
  John, 285, 300
  Thomas, 199
Philpot
  Mary, 76
  William, 66, 188, 193, 195, 200, 217, 227, 238, 239, 240, 363
Pickett
  Ann, 126
Piddle
  George, 182, 287

Pierce
  Elizabeth, 282
Pike
  Edmund, 135, 136
Pilkington
  Deborah, 75
  James, Bishop of Durham, 75, 419
Pincks
  James, 281
Pinfold
  Mary, 132
Pinkney
  Mr, 325, 383
Pinnell
  Nicholas, 202
Pinniger
  Thomas, 261, 305
Player
  Henry, 392
Plomer
  Elizabeth, 186
  Hannah, 146
  John, 186
  Margery, 186
  Richard, 230
  Robert, 147
  William, 146
Plummer
  Agnes, 361
  John, 255, 291
  Mary, 352
  William, 111, 278
Pontin
  Charity, 119, 120
  Edith, 216, 238
  Frances, 119, 120
  Jane, 138
  John, 26, 185, 196, 237, 290, 337, 424
  Mary, 119, 202, 238
  Mr, 426
  Thomas, 82, 113, 117, 118, 119, 120, 127, 144, 197, 244, 277, 314, 388, 413, 426
Pontin Family, 117, 118, 119, 120
Poore Family, 155
Pope
  Alexander, 282
  Alice, 120, 121, 361
  Ann, 124, 202

NAME INDEX

Christopher, 182, 237, 244, 287, 310, 418
Constance, 121
Daniel, 123, 124
Edith, 141, 237, 255, 361
Elizabeth, 120, 122, 123, 124, 125, 126, 338, 354, 361, 364, 366
Farmer, 253
Frances, 117, 123
Freezy, 79, 288
Hester, 61, 62
Isobel, 121
James, 40, 82, 120, 121, 122, 123, 124, 125, 126, 188, 193, 220, 221, 256, 261, 296, 339, 389, 401, 415, 416, 418
Jane, 122, 123, 124, 125, 126, 352
Jean, 266, 355, 370
Joan, 121, 182, 361
John, 61, 62, 86, 117, 120, 121, 123, 124, 125, 127, 155, 161, 192, 197, 202, 225, 230, 352, 380, 387, 411, 416, 418, 424, 428, 431
Mary, 123, 125, 126
Maud, 121
Nicholas, 123, 124, 186, 217
Richard, 121, 122, 123, 244, 401
Ruth, 127, 155, 414
Susanna, 123, 277
Thomas, 77, 82, 120, 121, 123, 170, 186, 219, 244, 288, 290, 291, 321, 352, 417, 418
Walter, 122, 123, 216, 217, 355
Pope Family, 120, 121, 122, 123, 125, 126, 419
Pope Family (pedigree) xii, xiii
Popham
Alexander, 112, 272
Edward, 381
Francis, 238, 349
George, 215, 326
Porte
Richard, 391
Porter
James, 39
Pottow
Jane, 73
Powell
Mary, 285
Stephen, 40, 195

Power
Mary, 394
Nathaniel, 111, 266, 273, 351, 359, 376, 379, 393, 394, 413
Nicholas, 393
Priestly
Joseph, Dr, 108
Prince of Wales, 31
Purdy
Richard, 406
Raniot
Monsieur, 325
Rashley
Jonathan, 171, 427
Thomas, 421, 427
Read
Ann, 93
Reazey
Edmund, 313
Reeves
Ann, 126
Elizabeth, 195
Joan, 202
Mary, 126
Robert, 126
William, 126, 369
Reeves Family, 126
Rennald
Mary, 241
Mrs, 228
Rennald Family, 166, 265
Rennell
Lord, 272
Richard Pope, 361
Richards
Robert, 185
Richardson
Richard, 221
William, 270, 296
Riddle
George, 337
Rider
Mr, 240
Rivers
William, 193
Robbins
Joseph, 369
Roberts
Mr, 133

Robertson
    Archibald, 16
Robins
    Edward, 168
Robinson
    Elizabeth, 127
    George, 127
    Humphry, 69, 70, 119, 126, 127, 128, 153, 197, 262, 266, 278, 301, 302, 306, 321, 335, 338, 340, 411, 417, 428
    John, 69, 103, 105, 129, 221, 247, 302, 323
    Martha, 119, 127, 197
    Mary, 103, 127, 129, 153
    Ruth, 120
    Thomas, 5, 6, 8, 58, 103, 127, 128, 129, 247, 302, 305, 309, 331, 333, 335, 344, 424, 430, 435
Robinson Family, 42, 126, 127, 128, 129, 130, 333
Robinson Family (pedigree) xiii, xiv
Rogers
    Alice, 88
    Robert, 278, 353
    Sarah, 229
    Thomas, 88, 89, 245, 280, 308, 318, 323
Romayne
    Elizabeth, 186
Romsey
    John, 291
Rose
    Ann, 404
    Elizabeth, 63, 133
    Jane, 132, 133, 151, 246, 298
    John, 25, 56, 63, 83, 94, 99, 102, 105, 123, 126, 130, 131, 132, 133, 134, 138, 140, 151, 168, 180, 191, 194, 205, 206, 220, 221, 234, 236, 249, 254, 256, 257, 258, 262, 263, 265, 266, 272, 273, 274, 277, 283, 284, 289, 291, 295, 300, 312, 322, 334, 347, 348, 353, 366, 373, 376, 389, 408, 412, 424, 426
    Joseph, 132, 194, 279
    Mary, 123, 132, 133, 216
    Rebecca, 132, 151
    Robert, 116, 131, 132, 133, 168, 222, 239, 396
    Simon, 312
    Sisily, 312
    William, 132

Rose Family, 130, 132, 133, 134
Rosewell
    John, 169, 189, 192
Rouse
    John, 193
Roussell
    Mr, 422
Rowe
    Charles, 308
Rumsey
    John, 67
Russ
    John, 241
Russell
    Jonathan, 229, 239
Rychards
    Robert, 159
Ryves
    Anne, 148

Sadler
    John, 161
    Thomas, 307
St John
    Oliver, 159, 160
St John Family, 21
Sanders
    John, 3, 5
Sartain
    Thomas, 27
Savage
    John, 116, 219
    Mr, 133
    Richard, 216
Scane
    Elizabeth, 288
    John, 236, 288, 297, 415
Scoles
    Edward, 144
    Mary, 144
Scotford
    Thomas, 280
Scott
    George, 75
    Sarah, 75
Seager
    Ann, 287
Sharington
    William, 230, 337, 345
    William, Sir, 75, 209, 210

NAME INDEX

Shepherd
 Alexander, 279
 Joseph, 319
Shilton
 Katherine, 69
Shipway
 John, 306, 307
Shuter
 Ann, 135
 Bridget, 136, 138
 Christopher, 135, 136, 137, 138, 376
 Constance, 135
 John, 77, 134, 135, 136, 137, 138, 157, 202, 213, 230, 231, 248, 324, 326, 344, 346, 376, 381, 386
 Philip, 135, 136, 138
 Richard, 135, 136, 137, 138, 213
Shuter Family, 134, 136, 137, 138
Sidfall
 Richard, 188
Simms
 Jane, 75, 281
 Sarah, 75, 281
Simons
 Christopher, 413
Simpkins
 Charles, 223, 224, 226, 227
 Mr, 56
Simpkins Family, 239
Sims
 John, 280
Skeat
 Emanuel, 138, 374
 Jane, 132, 138
 John, 138, 279
 William, 16, 22, 25, 31, 35, 113, 131, 138, 139, 144, 149, 170, 184, 192, 193, 195, 205, 208, 210, 232, 233, 234, 236, 254, 257, 260, 267, 270, 272, 279, 286, 298, 300, 311, 324, 326, 347, 348, 366, 369, 371, 372, 373, 374, 376, 381, 397, 398, 420, 423, 424, 425, 427, 429
Skeat Family, 138, 140
Skinner
 John, 407
Skuse
 Edith, 121, 244
 John, 121
 Maud, 121

Slag
 Ann, 124
Slaitch
 Mary, 279
Slie
 Thomas, 288
Sloper
 Walter, 326, 374
Smith
 Alice, 142, 143
 Andrew, 230
 Anne, 140, 213
 Benjamin, 144, 410
 Bryant, 321
 Catherine, 145
 Charles, 145
 Chrysostom, 145
 Dorothy, 142
 Elizabeth, 144, 145, 147, 387
 Francis, 142, 143
 Hamilton, 145
 Hannah, 32, 66, 67, 146, 147, 152, 387, 411
 Henry, 144, 145, 304
 Honor, 144
 James, 66
 Jane, 144, 145
 Joan, 144
 John, 142, 144, 183, 189, 230, 239
 Katherine, 142
 Lucy, 142, 143
 Marian, 142
 Mary, 142, 143, 144, 145, 148, 395
 Mr, 22, 206, 331, 347
 Mrs, 148
 Rachel, 72
 Rebecca, 142, 152
 Richard, 58, 59, 123, 124, 130, 140, 141, 142, 143, 144, 145, 185, 188, 192, 196, 213, 222, 231, 238, 247, 256, 288, 326, 336, 386, 389, 395, 399
 Stawell, 144, 146
 Thermuthis, 146
 Thomas, 26, 29, 63, 80, 83, 140, 141, 142, 143, 144, 145, 146, 147, 161, 184, 186, 209, 213, 222, 225, 231, 238, 248, 253, 272, 281, 288, 291, 297, 312, 326, 337, 349, 350, 370
 Uncle, 131
 William, 34, 138, 142, 272, 399, 400

Smith Family, 140, 142, 143, 144, 145, 146, 147, 148, 238
Smith Family (pedigree) xiv, xv, xvi, xvii
Smyth
    Alice, 202
Southey
    Robert, 321
Spackman
    William, 143, 145, 207, 238, 279, 320, 362
Sparks
    John, 425
Spencer
    Ambrose, 182
    Christopher, 182, 283, 387
    Elizabeth, 278
    Henry, 376
    John, 237
    Robert, 290
    Sarah, 287
    William, 410
Spenser
    Richard, 410
Sprules
    Joseph, 69
Stawell
    George, 148, 149
    John, Lord, 3, 138, 148, 149, 205, 215, 232, 233, 297, 342
    John, Sir, 6, 17, 18, 19, 22, 76, 80, 148, 191, 198, 214, 231, 233, 252, 272
    Ralph, Lord, 9, 148, 149, 162, 231, 249, 337, 436
Stawell Family, 210, 217
Stayner
    Elizabeth, 92
    Richard, Vice-Admiral, 92
Stephens
    Joan, 144
    Mary, 82, 150
    Sarah, 319
Stevens
    John, 244
    Nathaniel, 373
    Stephen, 16
    Thomas, 358, 359
    William, 257
Stevenson
    Robert, 391

Stiles
    William, 182
Stott
    Walter, 247
Stourton
    Lord, 212
Strange
    John, 71, 107, 229, 247, 302, 322
    Mr, 242
    Thomas, 314, 366
Stretch
    Alice, 149
    Christopher, 149
    George, 68, 84, 132, 150, 151, 152, 218, 247, 262
    Mary, 88, 123, 132, 134, 150, 151, 152
    Rebecca, 132, 151, 152
    Walter, 8, 128, 149, 150, 266, 356, 357, 358, 359, 365, 367, 370, 415
Stretch Family, 149, 151, 152
Stroud, 290, 308
    Ann, 68
Strugnell
    James, 229
Stuart
    James, the Old Pretender, 436
Stukeley
    William, 4, 5, 6, 7, 8, 9, 10, 11, 13, 23, 26, 27, 30, 35, 37, 42, 99, 128, 145, 146, 150, 296, 301, 302, 324, 327, 330, 331, 332, 356, 370, 374, 379, 380, 414, 435, 436, 437
Styles
    Elizabeth, 117
Sumers
    Charles, 354, 357, 361
Summers
    Charles, 264
Sutton
    James, 20, 23, 204, 221, 223, 224, 227, 240, 298
    Prince, 227
    Richard, 198
Swayne
    Ellis, 211, 297
    Mary, 76
Sweetapple
    Lettice, 268
Symes
    John, 71

NAME INDEX

Mary, 81
Richard, 185
Susanna, 71
Symonds
   Richard, 330

Talbot
   John, 65
Tanner, 179
   Daniel, 153
   John, 153
   Mr, 10, 107, 204
   Sarah, 153
   William, 153, 204, 220, 228, 229
Tanner Family, 153
Tarrant
   Thomas, 279
Taylor
   Edward, 66
   James, 16
   John, 297
   Stephen, 377
   Thomas
   William, 268, 296
Thring
   Elizabeth, 434
   James, 59, 218, 433, 434
   John, 434
   Richard, 59, 108, 224, 226, 228, 431, 434
Tilly
   Elizabeth, 154
   John, 67, 153, 154, 176, 238, 278, 319, . 320
   Mary, 67, 127, 153, 154
   Richard, 154
   Sarah, 320
   Thomas, 154, 314
Tilly Family, 153, 154, 220
Tomkins
   Cue, 155
   Elizabeth, 85, 124, 155, 156
   John, 113, 117, 154, 155, 186, 188
   Mary, 73, 85, 129, 155, 156, 316, 353
   Richard, 86, 117, 155, 156, 218
   Ruth, 155
Tomkins Family, 154, 156
Tompkins. *See* Tomkins
Tooker
   Charles, 7, 61, 81, 96, 123, 163, 191,
193, 194, 195, 197, 206, 212, 213, 216, 217, 225, 246, 257, 277, 352, 374, 410
   Eleanor, 160
   Thomas, 160
Toope
   Dr, 7, 324
Townsend, 324
Trewman
   Richard, 79, 244, 264, 310, 386, 410
Trotman
   Samuel, 92, 95
   Susanna, 3, 92, 217
Trotman Family, 92
Trugge
   Joanna, 157
Truman
   Ann, 361
Truslove
   Edward, 156
   John, 156
Truslow
   Alse, 157
   Ann, 160
   Bridget, 85, 161, 162, 163, 164, 212, 246, 277, 363
   Edward, 157
   Eleanor, 157, 160
   Elizabeth, 157
   Frances, 164, 238, 336, 337, 352, 410
   Giles, 160
   Henry, 164
   James, 160
   Jane, 164
   Joan, 211, 212, 271, 283, 296, 386, 391, 411
   Joanna, 157, 158, 343, 344, 367
   John, 10, 26, 77, 128, 141, 155, 157, 158, 159, 160, 161, 162, 163, 164, 194, 211, 213, 221, 237, 249, 268, 280, 302, 314, 336, 337, 385, 388, 391
   Maud, 160, 244, 269, 345, 355, 357, 358, 360, 361, 362, 365, 380
   Richard, 96, 110, 123, 155, 158, 159, 160, 161, 162, 163, 164, 188, 197, 211, 212, 216, 246, 284, 290, 301, 337, 363, 374, 377
   Thomas, 135, 142, 156, 157, 160, 164, 256, 314, 345, 390, 410
   Walter, 160, 162, 163, 201, 279

Truslow Family, 156, 157, 158, 159, 161, 162, 163, 164, 210, 211, 250, 263, 290, 377
Truslow Family (pedigree) xviii, xix
Tucker
　Charles, 388
Turke
　John, 115
　Mary, 115
Turton
　Turton, 406
Twining
　Thomas, 5, 330, 437
Tythener
　Constance, 135, 136

Underwood
　Charles, 291, 314
　Jane, 176
　Mary, 176
　William, 314

Vandeput
　Peter, Sir, 95
　Sarah, 95
Vincent
　Thomas, 365
Vivash, 314
Voysey
　Robert, 196
Vurston
　Alice, 361
Wait
　Edward, 309
　Thomas, 200
Wall
　Humphry, 33, 96, 246, 247, 326
Wallis
　Elizabeth, 58, 59, 247
　Joseph, 82, 102, 113, 313, 340, 359, 368
　Ruth, 58
　Thomas, 359
Want
　Daniel, 33
Ward
　John, 41, 223, 224, 298, 385, 407
　Seth, Bishop, 400
　Thomas, 298
Wardour
　Chideock, 158

Warner
　John, 213, 390
Warwick, Earls of, 209
Wasty
　Mary, 125
Weare
　William, 297
Weaver
　John, 34, 293
Webb
　Anthony, 391
　George, 310, 311, 312, 414
　Nathaniel, 422
　Noah, 422
　Thomas, 255, 291
　William, 312
West
　Ann, 180
　Edward, 180, 295
　Martha, 180
　Mr, 246
　William, 180
Weston
　Robert, 188
Wheeler
　Isaac, 280
Whitaker
　John, 37, 380
　Rev, 129, 327
Whitborne
　Roger, 301
White
　Ann, 396
　Charles, 279, 396
　Edward, 394
　Elizabeth, 396
　Frances, 396
　James, 396
　John, 7, 33, 57, 58, 74, 85, 86, 87, 91, 103, 112, 118, 123, 127, 128, 130, 131, 139, 144, 150, 194, 197, 215, 217, 232, 233, 239, 244, 245, 257, 267, 270, 272, 283, 284, 285, 321, 326, 340, 341, 359, 372, 373, 376, 379, 381, 382, 383, 387, 388, 389, 394, 395, 396, 397, 398, 399, 401, 405, 406, 408, 409, 410, 411, 413, 420, 422, 423, 424, 425, 426, 427, 428, 430, 435
　Jonathan, 71, 322
　Mary, 144, 196, 314, 395, 396

NAME INDEX

Rachel, 71
Richard, 396
Thomas, 396
William, 103, 133, 185, 188, 215, 395, 396
Whithorn
   Roger, 237, 283
Wild
   Samuel, 305
Wilkins
   John, 363
   Mr, 326
   William, 304
Willetts
   Henry, 325
William III, 31, 376
Williams
   Alfred, 15
   David, 406, 408
   Mr, 374
   Sarah Ann, 406, 408
Williamson
   Adam, Sir, 23, 25, 34, 41, 66, 87, 89, 101, 165, 166, 170, 204, 208, 210, 223, 224, 226, 228, 241, 250, 269, 273, 282, 285, 296, 297, 298, 299, 300, 306, 309, 314, 322, 334, 341, 349, 363, 365, 369, 379, 385, 387
   Anne, 11, 20, 25, 88, 101, 165, 174, 184, 199, 206, 224, 242, 265, 271, 294, 314, 382, 404
Williamson Family, 165, 166, 407
Willis
   John, 274
Wilmot
   Lord, 18
Wilson
   Robert, Sir, 166
Wiltshire
   Aaron, 167
   Adam, 300, 375, 376
   Elizabeth, 181
   John, 66, 166, 167, 258, 315, 320, 321, 369
   Joseph, 166
   Lucy, 166
   Michael, 229, 320
   Sarah, 166
   Thomas, 180
Wiltshire Family, 166, 167
Winter
   Cornelius, 431, 432
Withers
   John, 434
   Thomas, 434
Witt
   Francis, 321
Wood
   John, 296
Woodcock
   John, 323
Woodford
   Charles, 279
Woodman
   Elizabeth, 196
   Robert, 99, 258, 318
Woodrose
   Henry, 135
Worlidge
   John, 22
Wotton
   William, 391
Wyatt
   Joan, 283
Wylde
   Jane, 132
   Thomas, 132

Yeate
   Cornelius, 33, 389, 399, 413, 425
York
   Duke of, 199
Young
   Arthur, 15
   William, 291

www.ingramcontent.com/pod-product-compliance
Ingram Content Group UK Ltd.
Pitfield, Milton Keynes, MK11 3LW, UK
UKHW020208240325
456636UK00004B/10